THE AUTHOR.

UTTERMOST PART
OF THE EARTH

Indians of Tierra del Fuego

by E. Lucas Bridges

Introduction by A. F. Tschiffely

DOVER PUBLICATIONS, INC.
New York

" And ye shall be witnesses unto me
both in Jerusalem . . . and unto
the uttermost part of the earth "

Acts I, *verse* 8

TO

MY DEAR WIFE

" And o'er the hills, and far away
Beyond their utmost purple rim,
Beyond the night, across the day,
Through all the world she followed him "

TENNYSON

This Dover edition, first published in 1988, is an unabridged republication of the work first published by E. P. Dutton and Company, Inc., New York, 1949, under the title *Uttermost Part of the Earth*. To conserve space, in this edition the maps formerly on the endpapers and on a foldout leaf following page 142 now appear following page 19. Two other maps, formerly on foldout leaves facing page 274 and page 510, have been reprinted on regular pages, still facing pages 274 and 510, respectively.

Manufactured in the United States of America
Dover Publications, Inc.
31 East 2nd Street
Mineola, N.Y. 11501

Library of Congress Cataloging-in-Publication Data

Bridges, E. Lucas, 1874–1949.
    Uttermost part of the earth : Indians of Tierra del Fuego / by E. Lucas Bridges ; introduction by A. F. Tschiffely.
        p.   cm.
    Reprint. Originally published: New York : Dutton, 1949.
    Includes index.
    ISBN 0-486-25751-7
    1. Fuegians. 2. Bridges, E. Lucas, 1874–1949. 3. Ranchers—Tierra del Fuego (Argentina and Chile)—Biography. 4. Tierra del Fuego (Argentina and Chile)—Description and travel. I. Title.
F2986.B75 1988
982'.76061'0924—dc19
[B]   88-10257
                                                                          CIP

INTRODUCTION

By A. F. TSCHIFFELY

MANY YEARS AGO, WHILST LIVING IN THE ARGENTINE, OCCASIONALLY I heard stories about a certain *Inglés* who was a kind of "White Chief" among the Fuegian Indians, besides being looked upon by many as the uncrowned king of Patagonia. When, after having travelled through many parts of South and Central America and Mexico, I decided to visit Patagonia and Tierra del Fuego, my determination was to run this almost legendary *Indio Blanco* to earth.

In Tierra del Fuego I was informed that this will-o'-the-wisp was in a remote valley among the Andes in Southern Chile. There and then I made up my mind to continue my man-hunt. Some weeks later, after having traversed imposing mountain regions of singular beauty, I arrived at a ranch situated in a vast valley. A tall, weather-beaten figure came out of a door to greet me. . . . This was my man.

As I shook his powerful hand a smile played over his face, and under bushy eyebrows keen eyes sparkled. Presently the two of us were seated in comfortable Morris chairs in the living-room, and I observed that shelves were filled with excellent books. Their covers bore unmistakable testimony of having been handled frequently; they were not merely there as decorations or wall-paper. Mr. Bridges' wooden house was neat and its interior cosy, and had it not been for the scenery beyond the windows, I might have thought myself in some modest English or American country home.

For the next two or three days, during hours of leisure, my good host and I swapped yarns about the wilds; but as I had come to listen and learn, I made him do most of the talking. In his introductory note to this book he refers to the efforts I made to squeeze out of him a promise to write his memoirs, but Don Lucas was too tough a nut to crack in so short a time. As he explains, it was only during our next meeting in London that he finally capitulated. Shortly after, he left England to return to his distant home among the southern Andes.

Unfortunately, owing to a badly strained heart, caused by many years of tremendous physical exertion, Don Lucas had to give up his pioneering activities, and now lives in a flat in one of the Buenos Aires skyscrapers. *No hay mal de que bien no venga* (There is no ill out of which some good does not come), an old Spanish saying assures us; and this has certainly proved to be true in the case of my friend. Though obliged to take things very easy, he refused to remain idle, and accordingly set to work, with admirable zeal and energy, to compile the material for this book.

During a recent long visit to the Argentine I saw a great deal of Don Lucas, and had the privilege of being allowed to read his original manuscript.

I am confident that critics and readers alike will agree with me that this is a unique and valuable work. Apart from its ethnographical and other information, it contains more real romance than a hundred novels. This is history; an authentic unadulterated document about the Indian tribes, which, alas, have practically vanished. No writer, including Darwin, Captain FitzRoy and others, not to mention some of our modern "explorers," has really known the Fuegian Indians, let alone lived among them for many years and mastered their intricate languages, as has the writer of this book. But for Don Lucas, these practically unknown natives, legends and folklore, and much other interesting material, would have been irretrievably lost.

Don Lucas, I not only thank you for having so bravely stuck to the slow and tedious task of compiling and writing these memoirs, I also congratulate you for having enriched our bookshelves with a volume to which many will bow.

So to my dear friend and to the reader, many safe and pleasant trails!

A. F. TSCHIFFELY.

Chelsea, London.

FOREWORD

In the preface of a book which bears the modest title "of no impor-tance," Rom Landau makes a sound comment on the difficulties which beset those who attempt to write autobiographies.

> " Most of us cherish imaginary romantic notions about ourselves and only rarely succeed in breaking through the crust of self-deception. . . . In books of an auto-biographical background an occasional word of self-criticism is usually outweighed by pages of self-praise, however cunningly disguised."

The truth contained in these concise remarks has greatly delayed the production of my memoirs.

I have honestly tried to repress all " romantic notions " about myself, but doubt very much if I have succeeded. In all other respects, however, this is a true and unembellished account of my life in Tierra del Fuego.

Many of the details in the early part of the story are taken from my father's diary. As to the rest, when at a loss on some point I have written to Tierra del Fuego where my surviving brother and sisters still live, and when they have been unable to answer to my entire satisfaction I have invariably dropped the subject rather than take refuge in imagination or faulty recollection.

Besides my wife, my daughter and other members of the family, my thanks are due to Mr. Ian Bell and Mrs. W. H. Mulville for helpful suggestions regarding composition ; to Mr. A. A. Cameron, Col. Charles Wellington Furlong and the Director of the Librería Nacional del Colegio of Buenos Aires for generous permission to reproduce photographs ; to Dr. Armando Braun Menendez and Mr. W. S. Barclay for photographs and good counsel : and last, but not least, to Mr. Lawrence Smith for useful advice and especially for assistance in arranging the chapters.

Though I am deeply indebted to so many good friends, the reader should be equally thankful to one—Mr. A. F. Tschiffely, the author and traveller, who is well known for his great feat in riding from Buenos Aires to Washington without losing either of his horses.

In 1938, during a short visit which he paid to my nest amongst the mountains of Southern Chile, he tried his hardest to extract a promise from me that I would write these memoirs. About a year later, at a lunch which he gave in the Savage Club, London, having found out my great weakness, he proceeded to administer an overdose of flattery, and then, seizing his advantage, before I could recover he forced me into promising that this book should be written; so here it is.

When I had finished it, he read the MS. and made many valuable suggestions to bring my unwieldy mass of material into a reasonable compass.

If we are thanking this man for shortening my lengthy story, the blame for its ever having been written rests largely on his shoulders.

．　　　．　　　．　　　．

A year later, in 1946, my MS. found its way to London, and the well-known publishers whose name it now carries took a great interest in my story. They found, however, that it lacked cohesion and, like the country of its origin, was criss-crossed by precipitous gullies interspersed with tangled thickets and bogs.

One of their literary advisers, Mr. Clifford Witting, also liked the story, but considered that the gullies should be bridged and a clear track blazed through the thickets which even a stranger could follow.

So anxious was I that the historical value of my story should not be damaged, and that the book should remain in its entirety my own story told in my own way, that I only consented to the revision on condition that, should I be called away before it was finished, the remainder should be printed as I had written it. I am glad to say, however, that I have been able to see the revision through to the very end, and believe that the book as it now stands is a better book, more readable and more easily followed by those who have no knowledge of the people and country of which it tells.

Many hundreds of questions were fired at me by air mail, and I was glad that I had not attempted any romancing, for in that case I should have inevitably been caught out. With my answers Mr. Witting has been able to bridge the gullies and clear a path through the maze, and I feel convinced that many who follow this long trail to the end would like to join me in thanking him warmly for his good work.

E. Lucas Bridges.

Buenos Aires,
August, 1947.

CONTENTS

9

PART II

HARBERTON

1887–1899

PART III

THE ROAD TO NAJMISHK

1900–1902

PART IV

A HUT IN ONA-LAND

1902–1907

PART V

THE ESTANCIA VIAMONTE

1907–1910

CONTENTS

ILLUSTRATIONS

17

All the illustrations from " Los Onas " by the late Carlos R. Gallardo appear by courtesy of the Director, Librería Nacional del Colegio, Buenos Aires

MAPS

TIERRA DEL FUEGO

PATAGONIA

R. GALLEGOS

RIO GALLEGOS

CHILE

MAGELLAN STRAITS

CAPE PILLAR

DESOLATION ISLAND

RIESCO ISLAND

PUNTA ARENAS

GENTE GRANDE BAY

BRUNSWICK PENINSULA

PORVENIR

USELESS BAY

PORT FAMINE

SANTA INÉS ISLAND

CATHOLIC MISSION

DAWSON ISLAND

CLARENCE ISLAND

MERCURY SOUND

ADMIRALTY SOUND

SEAGULL CHANNEL

COCKBURN CHANNEL

SNIPE ROCKS

DARWIN

BRECKNOCK PENINSULA

LONDON ISLAND

SIDNEY ISLAND

DESOLATION BAY

NORTH-WEST ARM

GORDON ISLAND

LONDONDERRY ISLAND

NEW YEARS SOUND

SOUTH-WEST ARM

HOSTE ISLA

ROUS PENINSULA

PACIFIC

OCEAN

0 10 20 30 40 50 60 70 80 90 100 125 150 175 200
MILES

0 20 40 60 80 100 140 160 180 200
KILOMETRES

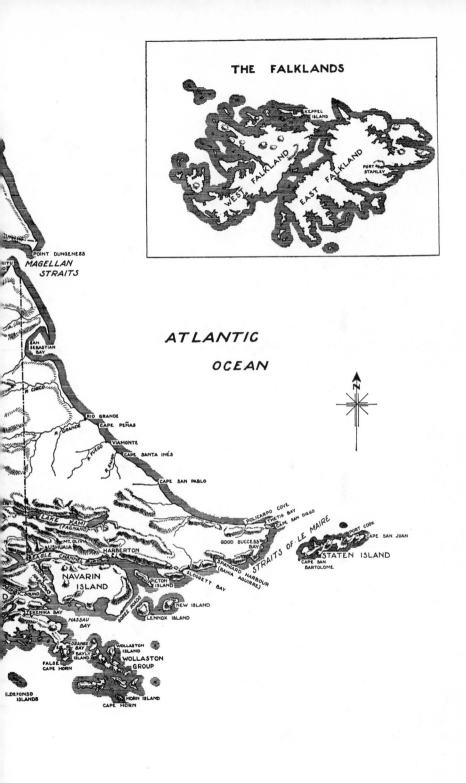

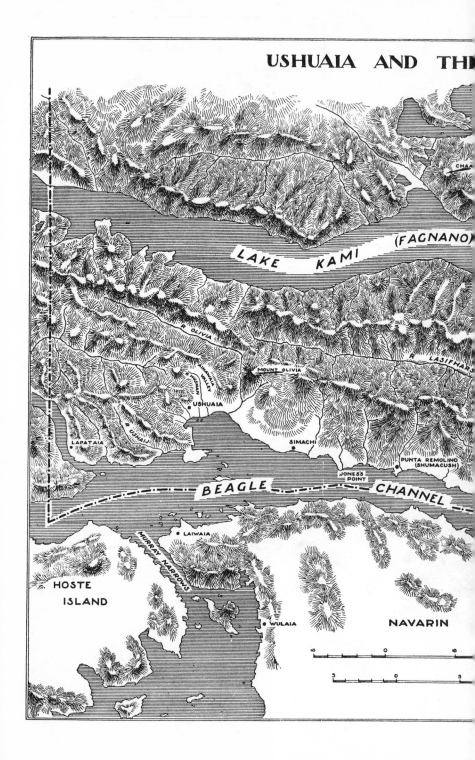

LAKE KAMI (FAGNANO)

CHAA

R. OLIVIA

R. LASIFHAR

R. HAMBRE

ARMANDO VALLEY

MOUNT OLIVIA

USHUAIA

R. USHAIA

LAPATAIA

SIMACHI

PUNTA REMOLINO
(SHUMACUSH)

JONE'S'S
POINT

BEAGLE CHANNEL

LAIWAIA

MURRAY NARROWS

HOSTE
ISLAND

WULAIA

NAVARIN

BEAGLE CHANNEL

N

NO-KAKE
MOUNTAIN

MOUNT CORNU

K-WHEIPENOHRRH

R. VAREA

R. EASTERN

BROWN
MOUNTAIN

FLAT TOP
MOUNTAIN

HARBERTON
MOUNTAIN

NO TOP
MOUNTAIN

PORT ADMIRAL BROWN
(UKUMAIA)

HARBERTON

CAMBACERES

GABLE
ISLAND

HAKENYESHKA
ISLAND

LAPA-YUSHA

SNIPE ISLAND

MOAT
BAY

MOUNT
MISERY

GARDEN ISLAND
BANNER COVE

ISLAND

PICTON
ISLAND

20   30   40
                              KM

10   15   20
                   MILES

PUERTO TORO
(AFLURUWAIA)

PROLOGUE

1871

I

LATE IN THE AFTERNOON OF WEDNESDAY, THE 27TH SEPTEMBER, 1871, THE *Allen Gardiner*, a topsail schooner of eighty-eight tons register, anchored in Banner Cove on the north coast of Picton Island, near the eastern end of the Beagle Channel, Tierra del Fuego—Fireland.

It was a landlocked harbour, for Garden Island, with its two wooded hills joined by a low, grassy isthmus, lay across the entrance to the cove; so, with the voyage from the Falkland Islands to Ushuaia nearly over, the crew had gone below for a well-earned rest. Two of the ship's three passengers, a man and a woman, came from the cabin and stood in silence side by side on the otherwise deserted deck.

They were about twenty-eight years of age. The woman was fair, with blue-grey eyes, of moderate build, and her height was barely five feet three. After weeks of sea-sickness she had lost the healthy colour acquired as a girl in the orchards of Devonshire, yet, in spite of her pallor, there was a glow on her face that neither suffering nor age would ever extinguish.

The man to whose arm she clung—for she was too weak to stand without support—was four inches taller than she, lean, upright and square-shouldered. In every line of his figure there was evidence of staunchness and reliability. His face was thin, clear-complexioned and dominated by dark, kindly eyes. His hair was jet black, his beard and moustache sparse enough to reveal a resolute mouth. When he spoke, his voice was eager, and even his smallest movement was dynamic. On such a man a woman might safely lean.

Below in their cabin slept the ship's third passenger: their daughter Mary, who was nine months old.

At that hour of dusk the land seemed to draw near to the anchored vessel, and the surrounding hills, covered with dark, evergreen forests, closed round the ship and were reflected in the still waters, which looked as solid as some metallic mirror. The overcast sky held the threat of snow, and the silence seemed uncanny after the noise and turmoil of the previous weeks.

After standing for some time drinking in the wonder of the scene, the woman looked up at her companion and said gently:

"Dearest, you have brought me to this country, and here I must remain, for I can never, never face that ocean voyage again."

2

It was from England that he had brought her. They had met two years before, in 1869, at a meeting of school-teachers in Bristol. He had told her how, as a boy of thirteen, he had gone with a party of missionaries to the Falkland Islands, from which, during his twelve years sojourn in those distant parts, he had paid many visits to Tierra del Fuego. In that and later conversations he had told her about the Yahgans, the canoe Indians of Tierra del Fuego, the southernmost inhabitants of the world. He had told her of the unkind climate, of the long, dreary winter nights, of the solitude, when one was completely cut off from the outside world, with league after league of impassable country separating one from the nearest settlement of civilized man, which was nothing more friendly than the Chilean convict station at Punta Arenas, on the north shore of the Magellan Straits. In this wild and desolate region, he had told her, there were neither doctors nor police nor government of any kind; and, instead of kindly neighbours, one was surrounded by, and utterly at the mercy of, lawless tribes without discipline or religion.

Such was the country where he proposed to settle and where, in the not-far-distant future, they were destined to throw off all help from the outside world and, alone and unassisted, wrest a livelihood from that stern land. It was a hard life that he had invited her to share with him, and she, small and gentle, with the dignity of a queen and the spirit of a Florence Nightingale, without hesitation had accepted his proposal.

They had been married five weeks after that first unforgettable meeting in Bristol, and two days later had embarked on the S.S. *Onega*, bound for the other end of the world.

Three weeks after leaving England they had anchored in the beautiful harbour of Rio de Janeiro, where they had been transhipped to the *Arno*, a large paddle-boat. The weather had been very bad, but in five days they had reached Montevideo, where they had been fortunate in finding another ship, the barque *Normanby*, for the twelve-day trip to Port Stanley, the capital of the Falkland Islands. The young wife had stayed in the Falklands for twenty-two months, while her husband had made frequent trips to Tierra del Fuego. In Stanley, Mary, their first child, had been born.

On the 17th August, 1871, they had set out on the last few hundred miles of the long journey from England to the place that was to become their home—Ushuaia. The voyage from the Falklands to Tierra del Fuego was always one to be dreaded, but this trip had been worse than most. It had taken the *Allen Gardiner* forty-one days in the face of a succession of storms, or, rather, one exceptional gale with occasional short lulls when it had paused to gather strength for renewed attacks. On the morning of the ninth day at sea they had sighted Cape San Diego, the easternmost point of the main island of Tierra del Fuego. It was then that their real troubles had begun. Twice their little vessel had beaten through the Straits of Le Maire, and twice she had been driven back by stress of weather. The gales that sweep the seas round Cape Horn have an evil reputation; and few in such cicumstances have passed through the Straits of Le Maire four times in one month. It is difficult to describe the mountainous waves made steeper by the world-famous " tide-rip " in those Straits, or the nights hove to and battened down, when water pounds on the deck or swills about in the bilge, and the creaking of timbers and spars is accompanied by the roar of the gale in the rigging, and the occasional machine-gun rattle of the storm-sails when, instead of filling, they shake in the wind.

Some conception of these seas can be gathered from the journal of George Anson, Commander-in-Chief of a squadron of His Majesty's ships, who led an expedition to the South Seas in 1741. On the 7th March of that year he wrote :

> " From the storm which came on before we had well got clear of Straits Le Maire, we had a continual succession of such tempestuous weather as surprised the oldest and most experienced mariners on board, and obliged them to confess that what they had hitherto called storms were inconsiderable gales compared with the violence of these winds, which raised such short and at the same time mountainous waves, as greatly surpassed in danger all seas known in any other part of the globe, and it was not without great reason that this unusual appearance filled us with continual terror; for had one of these waves broken fairly over us it must in all probability have sent us to the bottom."

Anson witnessed this storm from the deck of a 1,000-ton vessel. The *Allen Gardiner*, a tiny ship of eighty-eight tons, had ridden out a similar storm and had come through the same turmoil of wind and water. On one occasion the precious baby had been bruised, blackened and greatly frightened, when a violent jerk of the vessel had flung her from her cot into the cabin grate.

Eventually the *Allen Gardiner* had gained the comparative shelter of Good Success Bay, where she had lain with both anchors down for two days and nights. At length, tempted by a fair breeze, she had put to sea again; but the breeze had failed and the little schooner had drifted at the mercy of the waves and tide over fifty miles eastwards. Fortunately, she had cleared the rocks of Cape San Juan on the extreme end of Staten Island, where a northerly breeze had come to their rescue, and they had sailed westward along the outer southern coast of that rugged land till they had passed some twelve miles to the south of Cape San Bartolome; then on past Spaniard Harbour, now known as Bahia Aguirre, and Sloggett Bay, where, with improving weather and the shelter of New Island and Lennox Island, the ocean swell had greatly diminished, until, closing in on Picton, they had found tranquillity at last.

Thus, three years before I was born, did my father and mother, Thomas and Mary Bridges, with Mary, my sister, come to Tierra del Fuego.

PART I

USHUAIA
1826–1887

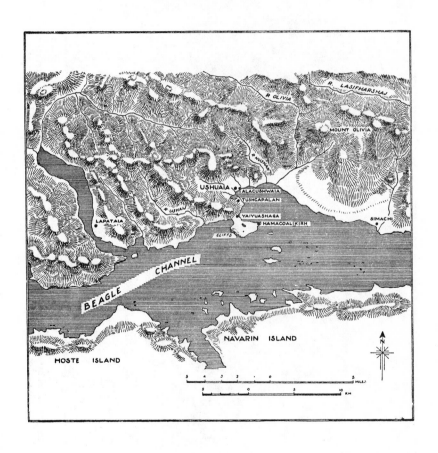

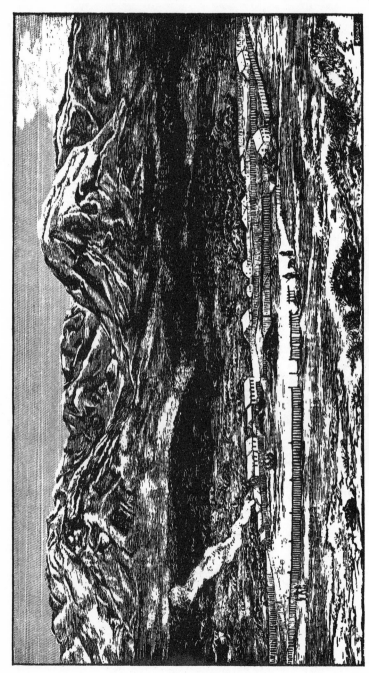

THE CHRISTIAN VILLAGE OF USHUAIA, TIERRA DEL FUEGO

From a photograph taken by an officer of the gunboat *Romanche* during the French expedition referred to in chapter 10. The harbour, which cannot be seen in the picture, lay between the settlement and the mountains in the background.

CHAPTER ONE

H.M.S. Beagle *Visits Tierra del Fuego. Jimmy Button, York Minster and Fuegia Basket Enjoy a Trip to England. Richard Mathews is Landed at Wulaia, Fails in his Task and is Taken Off by the* Beagle. *Some Observations Concerning Cannibalism.*

I

In the year 1826, eighty-five years after Anson's voyage to Tierra del Fuego, His Britannic Majesty's ship *Beagle*, of 200 tons burden, under the command of Captain (later Vice-Admiral) Robert FitzRoy, was sent by the Admiralty with three other vessels to make a study of the Southern Ocean, and especially to chart the intricate, little-known coasts of southern South America.

During the next four years that expedition did magnificent work, and many of the channels they discovered bear to this day the names of members of the ships' crews, or of British national heroes.

On one occasion during those years the *Beagle* dropped anchor in an open bay off the south-east coast of Tierra del Fuego, where a considerable headland and an island about six miles across gave them shelter from the prevailing wind. This island they named "Lennox," and the place of their anchorage "Goree Roads." Four boats were sent off to the northward to explore what appeared to be a bay running into a nest of mountains that lay to the west.

Several days passed, and Captain FitzRoy was growing anxious, when the boats appeared coming in from the south-west. What they had thought was a bay had turned out to be a beautiful channel, varying in width from about two to five miles and running parallel with the Magellan Straits through the mountain ranges from east to west. After following this channel westward for some forty miles they had become convinced, on account of the currents, that it ran right through the glacier-clad mountains that appeared to block it completely some thirty miles farther on. They had been about to turn back when they had spied a deep, narrow gorge, through which they could slip out into the Southern Ocean and so back through Nassau Bay to their ship in Goree Roads. The channel they had discovered they named "Beagle Channel," and the passage by which they had left it, "Murray Narrows," after Lieutenant Murray, who was in charge of the boating expedition. The island they had circumnavigated they called "Navarin Island." They had seen numbers of natives in their bark canoes, and had fired their guns when they believed they were about to be attacked.

The *Beagle* carried on with work in other parts, but before leaving for England found herself again in Fuegian waters, this time farther west.

Members of the crew were sent in a whale-boat on a short exploring trip, and somehow lost their boat, returning on a kind of raft. For this loss they blamed the natives. There is reason to doubt their story, but FitzRoy seems to have believed it and, it may be, was glad of an excuse (for their own good) of taking on board, as hostages, four young Yahgans who happened to be alongside.

The boat was not returned, and this good man took these young natives to England with the commendable intention of making a beginning towards raising them, and through them their people, to a better and happier way of life.

It seems to be the custom, in most parts of the world where white men have to christen natives, to choose for them the most fantastic names. The most intelligent of this party was named "Boat Memory." The others were a strongly-built, powerful, but surly man of about twenty, who was called "York Minster," after a rugged islet near Cape Horn, a short, smiling girl of nine, "Fuegia Basket," and a lad some five years her senior, "Jimmy Button." The last, it was stated, had been purchased from his parents in exchange for a button—a ridiculous story, as no native would have sold his child in exchange for H.M.S. *Beagle* with all it had on board.

When they reached England, Boat Memory went to the naval hospital at Plymouth, where he died of smallpox. The others were vaccinated and lodged at FitzRoy's expense in the house of a clergyman, the Reverend William Wilson, at Walthamstow, near London. They were sent to school, where they were instructed in useful arts such as carpentry and gardening. The two younger Fuegians showed some aptitude, taking kindly to this new life, but York Minster remained aloof and sullen.

Some nine months after their arrival, FitzRoy, with his three protégés, was summoned to appear before King William IV at St. James's Palace. The rumour had been spread that these children belonged to a race of cannibals, and details of horrible orgies to which they were addicted were recounted in England. The Fuegians lived, it was said, practically naked in their wretched bark canoes, eating seal, birds and fish, when not eating one another. However, these three were now to become Christians, under the careful tuition of the Reverend W. Wilson, and it was hoped that in due time they would carry the Gospel and some of the comforts of civilization back to their savage countrymen. Now, clean and clad in their best, they were led into the royal presence in Their Majesties' private apartments, and no doubt behaved quite naturally. Queen Adelaide soon joined the party, and the natives, especially little Fuegia Basket, found favour with both King and Queen. The King asked many questions, and was greatly interested in what FitzRoy told him of the natives and their country. Before they left, the Queen placed her own little lace cap on Fuegia Basket's head, whilst the King put one of his rings on her finger, at the same time giving her a sum of money for her trousseau. One wonders how many ladies of high degree, who had schemed and striven to get presented at Court, envied that little Fuegian girl the honour that was hers. Two years after these young people had been induced to embark on H.M.S. *Beagle* in the Fuegian channel, we find them leaving England on the same vessel, bound for their native land, with their kindly benefactor, FitzRoy, again in command. The good folk of Walthamstow, where they had spent over a year, made a collection for them and they had acquired a considerable quantity of clothing, tools, utensils, provisions, garden seeds, and even books, plates and dishes. On board went several distinguished passengers, amongst them Charles Darwin, the naturalist. Also, recommended by the Reverend W. Wilson, in whose house the Fuegians had lodged, went a young catechist, Mr. Richard Mathews. He was sent by the Church Missionary Society to continue the instruction of the Fuegians on the voyage out, and it was hoped that he would remain in Tierra del Fuego and with their help influence for good others of the tribe. As it was over a year before the vessel reached her destination, for she had hydrographic study to delay her voyage, the catechist had ample opportunity to carry on his work before arriving in Fuegian waters.

The *Beagle* anchored again in Goree Roads, and FitzRoy, Darwin, Mathews and the young Fuegians set off with three whale-boats and the pinnace laden with the goods they had brought from England. They entered the Beagle Channel and followed it till, reaching the Murray Narrows, they passed through them to Wulaia, on the west coast of Navarin Island.

The cargo was discharged in that sheltered cove. Land was dug and sown for a vegetable garden, and three huts were built; one for Mathews, one for Jimmy Button and the third for York Minster and Fuegia Basket, who were married soon after they landed. No doubt the wedding ceremony performed by the good Mathews was most original.

Hundreds of Yahgans arrived in their canoes from all directions and watched with curiosity the strange actions of these white men. FitzRoy and his companions had expected an interesting meeting between these natives and the three who had been absent so long. They were disappointed; there was no sign of pleasure or surprise, but rather a cool indifference. Many of the Indians, having satisfied their curiosity, retired.

After doing everything in his power for the comfort of Mathews and his three acolytes, FitzRoy left them to their fate and started back to the *Beagle*. Soon, however, he grew anxious about the lone Mathews and decided to return to Wulaia to see how he fared. His anxiety turned to dread when he saw various articles of clothing adorning natives in the canoes he passed on the way. On arrival at Wulaia, he found Mathews alive, but almost beside himself. Since the boats had left, the Indians had given him no rest, night or day, from their begging. When he had refused their demands, they had threatened him fiercely, making hideous faces at him, pelting him with pebbles, pulling his beard and snatching the things they coveted, in spite of the protests of his three pupils, Fuegia Basket, York Minster and Jimmy Button. All that Mathews now craved was to be taken away, for he felt that if left he would certainly be killed and eaten by these savages. The goods were divided among the three converts, and thus ended the first attempt to improve the conditions of the canoe Indians of Tierra del Fuego.

Fifteen months later, before finally leaving for England, FitzRoy returned with the *Beagle* and anchored in Wulaia. The place was deserted, but that evening a number of canoes crowded with natives appeared. One wild-looking savage, naked but for the bit of hide round his loins, with long, unkempt hair, gave them a military salute. It was Jimmy Button. After over three years of intensive training amongst the best of civilized men, he had returned to his natural state.

Despite his filthy appearance, Button was soon on board, cleaned up and dressed as a sailor, and was then taken to lunch with FitzRoy and his officers. It was noticed that his conduct in the use of knife, fork and spoon left nothing to be desired. He told FitzRoy how York Minster had built an exceptionally large canoe, the purpose of which was only explained when one night, assisted by the faithful Fuegia Basket, he had loaded it with all that was left of their combined possessions and had slipped away with his wife, leaving Button with only the scanty clothes in which he slept.

What FitzRoy had seen before and what he heard now from Jimmy Button was enough to convince him that it was useless to attempt to civilize these people. If he could have looked twenty-five years into the future and seen his guest instigating the massacre of trusting, unarmed missionaries engaged in their Sunday service at that same spot, this conviction would have been still further confirmed. It is, nevertheless, pleasant to record that Button presented FitzRoy, who had been such a friend to him, with his bow, arrows, and a spear, giving his other two best friends on the *Beagle* an otter skin each.

Lunch concluded, Jimmy left the vessel, which then weighed anchor. As she sailed away, it was noticed that Jimmy had made a huge smoke on the beach where he had landed. This they took as a signal of farewell.

2

Of the three years these young Yahgans lived amongst English people, half was spent on board the *Beagle* with FitzRoy. During this time they convinced him and others that the Fuegian Indians were cannibals. Even that searcher after truth, Charles Darwin, who was closely associated with the trio during the twelve months' voyage of the *Beagle*, accepted their testimony.

We who later passed many years of our lives in daily contact with these people can find only one explanation for this shocking mistake. We suppose that, when questioned, York Minster, or Jimmy Button, would not trouble in the least to answer truthfully, but would merely give the reply that he felt was expected or desired. In the early days their limited knowledge of English would not allow them to explain at any length, and, as we know, it is much easier to answer " yes " than " no." So the statements with which these young men and little Fuegia Basket have been credited were, in fact, no more than agreement with suggestions made by their questioners.

We can imagine their reactions when asked what was, to them, a ridiculous question, such as :

" Do you kill and eat men? "

They would at first be puzzled, but when the enquiry was repeated and they grasped its meaning and realized the answer that was expected, they would naturally agree. The interrogator would follow this with :

" What people do you eat? "

No answer.

" Do you eat bad people? "

" Yes."

" When there are no bad people, what then? "

No answer.

" Do you eat your old women? "

" Yes."

Once this game was started and their knowledge of English increased, these irresponsible youngsters, encouraged by having their evidence so readily accepted and noted down as fact, would naturally start inventing on their own. We are told that they described, with much detail, how the Fuegians ate their enemies killed in battle and, when there were no such victims, devoured their old women. When asked if they ate dogs when hungry, they said they did not, as dogs were useful for catching otter, whereas the old women were of no use at all. These unfortunates, they said, were held in the thick smoke till they choked to death. The meat, they stated, was very good.

This delectable fiction once firmly established, any subsequent attempt at denial would not have been believed, but would have been attributed to a growing unwillingness to confess the horrors in which they had formerly indulged. Accordingly, these young story-tellers allowed their imaginations full rein and vied with each other in the recounting of still more fantastic tales, emboldened by the admiration of the other two.

The belief that the Fuegians were cannibals was not the only mistake Charles Darwin made about them. Listening to their speech, he got the impression that they were repeating the same phrases over and over again, and therefore came to the conclusion that something like one hundred words would cover the whole language. We who learned as children to speak Yahgan know that, within its own limitations, it is infinitely richer and more expressive than English or Spanish. My father's *Yahgan* (or Yamana)-*English Dictionary*, to which I shall refer later, contains no fewer than 32,000 words and inflections, the number of which might have been greatly increased without departing from correct speech.[1]

[1] The Yahgans had, at the very least, five names for " snow." For " beach " they had even more, depending on a variety of factors : the position of the beach in relation

Darwin, when he saw the poverty and filth of these people, considered that, if he had not actually found the missing link for which he sought, these Fuegians were not far removed from it. Yet they had many social customs that were strictly observed, and though lying and stealing were usual, to call a man a liar, thief or murderer was a deadly insult.

Since Darwin and FitzRoy adopted the theory that these natives were cannibals, others have found proof to support it. For instance, one of them might discover a deserted village with signs of a huge fire having been made there, and in the long-extinguished embers find charred human bones, some possibly showing signs of having been gnawed. What better proof could be needed that the natives were cannibals? And yet the explanation may be simple. An Indian might have died in winter when the land was frozen like rock. In such circumstances his friends would have no adequate tools with which to dig a grave, and Yaghans, who lived on fish, would certainly not sink a body in the sea. They would make a great heap of firewood and burn the body with the wigwam where the death had taken place. They would then leave the spot and avoid it as long as possible, not for fear of ghosts, but because it recalled the sad event. Foxes might be responsible for gnawing the bones.

Relatives and friends hated to be reminded in any way of one who had died, so, on arriving at an encampment after a long absence, one had to be careful not to ask by name for anyone who was not present, in case he had died and the relatives be grievously offended.

My father tells in his journal that in periods of famine, when prolonged bad weather made fishing impossible, they ate thongs and the hide moccasins the men sometimes used in winter, but never had any of them proposed eating a human being. They would sternly rebuke anyone who, when pressed by hunger, ate a vulture, however fat and nicely roasted, on the score that it might, at some time, have fed on a corpse. They were indignant, as I myself can testify, when others tried to induce

to that of the speaker, the direction in which it faced, whether the speaker had land or water between it and himself—and so on. Words varied with the situation of the speaker. A word used in a canoe might differ from that used to describe the same thing when the speaker was on dry land. Further variations were brought in by the compass direction of the hearer and whether he, too, was ashore or afloat. For family connections sometimes so distant that, in English, they would need a sentence to explain, the Yahgans had as many as fifty different words, each descriptive of a particular, and often involved, relationship. Among the variations of the verb "to bite" was a single word that meant "coming unexpectedly on a hard substance when eating something soft"—*e.g.*, a pearl in a mussel.

them to join in what was, to them, such a revolting repast. For the same reason, they refused to eat fox, although it was later proved that another tribe—the Ona, or foot Indians—considered a fat fox a luxury.

It is interesting to note how many names have arisen through mistakes and even become permanent by finding their way into Admiralty charts. Early historians tell us of a place called Yaapooh, and speak of the people of that country. No such place or people existed, and this word is simply a corruption of the Yaghan name for otter, *iapooh*. No doubt FitzRoy, pointing towards a distant shore, asked what it was called. The Yahgan's keen eyes would spy an otter, and he would answer with the word, "Iapooh."

In all the charts of this country—both Spanish and English—a certain sound in Hoste Island bears the name Tekenika. The Indians had no such name for that or any other place, but the word in the Yahgan tongue means "difficult or awkward to see or understand." No doubt the bay was pointed out to a native, who, when asked the name of it, answered, "Teke uneka," implying, "I don't understand what you mean," and down went the name "Tekenika." Many instances of this kind could be cited, but these will suffice.

CHAPTER TWO

The Disastrous Expedition of Captain Allen Gardiner. My Father Goes to Keppel Island at the Age of Thirteen. The Massacre at Wulaia. My Father Takes Charge of the Mission on Keppel Island until the Arrival of the New Superintendent, the Reverend Whait H. Stirling. My Father and Mr. Stirling Pay their First Visit to Fireland. The Settlement at Laiwaia. It is Decided to Start a Settlement at Ushuaia. Mr. Stirling Lives at Ushuaia Alone for Six Months, then Returns to England. My Parents Arrive in the Falklands. My Sister Mary is Born.

I

CAPTAIN ALLEN GARDINER, R.N., HAD COME IN CONTACT WITH MANY uncivilized tribes during his voyages to distant parts of the Empire. He was tough, athletic and a popular figure in the Royal Navy; but the loss of his wife in 1834, when he was forty years of age, caused him to retire from the Navy and dedicate himself to the preaching of the Gospel among the heathen.

His deeds have shown that he was a man who might have walked cheerfully to the stake, so unshakable was his faith, yet in spite of, or perhaps because of, his high thinking and accomplishments, he seems to have lacked the sound common sense that is frequently the perquisite of less gifted mortals. In search of a field for his labours he tried Zulu-land, New Guinea, and later Bolivia, Chile and Patagonia, till his attention was finally drawn to Tierra del Fuego.

Gardiner was instrumental in founding the Patagonian Missionary Society, but they were incredibly poor, and he was impatient to get to work. In January, 1848, Gardiner, accompanied by four sailors, left England on the barque *Clymene,* which was bound for Lima with coal. The captain had agreed to put this party ashore in Tierra del Fuego with their whale-boat, their dinghy and six months' rations, which was all they could afford to take with them. Gardiner doubtless hoped to make contact with Jimmy Button's party, but an ocean-going merchant vessel could not be expected to go in as far as Wulaia, so he was landed at Banner Cove, Picton Island. The plan was foredoomed to fail. Winter was at hand, the antagonism of the Fuegians was a foregone conclusion, and a furious storm made it impossible for the landing-party even to pitch their tents. Reluctantly, Gardiner decided at the last moment to re-embark and return to England.

He was disappointed, but not defeated. In September, 1850, we find him on the *Ocean Queen*, again heading south. This time he brought two metal boats, both decked and twenty-four feet long, with sails and oars, each having its small dinghy. His companions were a Dr. Richard Williams, a young catechist named John Maidmant, Joseph Erwin, who was a carpenter, and three stalwart Cornish fishermen.

As before, they were landed at Banner Cove, though they still hoped to make contact with Jimmy Button. When last seen alive they were standing bareheaded, singing hymns on the decks of their little vessels, as the *Ocean Queen* disappeared round the nearby headland at the entrance to the harbour.

The rest of this pitiful yet glorious story was gathered from the saturated letters and diaries found nearly a year later scattered around the decomposing bodies of those devoted men. It has been published in different languages, but the brief, unbiased version by Dr. Armando Braun Menendez is the best I have read, and from it I have borrowed freely. It is called *Pequeña Historia Fueguina*.

When the vessel that had been their home for three months was lost to view, Gardiner and his companions started going over their supplies. At once an incredible and truly disastrous oversight was revealed. Their reserve supply of ammunition, on which they would have to rely for fresh meat, and, if the worst came to the worst, which constituted their only means of defence against the Indians, had been left behind on the *Ocean Queen*. There was no alternative but to find food where they could and pray that the need for defence would not arise.

Disillusionment followed swiftly. The party made no contact with Jimmy Button, and the Fuegians whom they met soon became unbearable. Gathering in ever-increasing numbers, they grew more and more menacing in their behaviour, and demanded or seized whatever took their fancy. Soon it became too dangerous for the party to camp on land. They withdrew to the boats and lay some distance off shore. The excited natives began to load their canoes with large stones—a type of missile that they were expert at throwing or slinging with great force. Allen Gardiner gave the order to move off. Oars were manned and the two boats made for the open sea, with the Indian canoes in hot pursuit.

The boats were too heavy to pull with oars alone, and the light canoes rapidly began to overtake them. Then, when capture and death seemed imminent, a suddenly freshening breeze enabled the boats to hoist sail and leave their angry pursuers far behind.

Now they were fugitives, and, looking for some place to hide, they reached a secluded nook they called Bloomfield Harbour,[1] some fifteen miles north-west of Banner Cove. The Indians watched their every movement, and they soon had to put to sea again and spend their time dodging the very people whom they had come so far to save. On one occasion, caught in a gale, they were beating about or hove-to for two days, and lost both their dinghies; their provisions, too, were badly damaged by sea-water.

On the dark, flat face of a large rock at the entrance to Banner Cove they painted in white the following legend, which, to my knowledge, was renewed from time to time for over fifty years:

DIG BELOW

GO TO SPANIARD HARBOUR

MARCH

1851

At the foot of the rock Gardiner left a bottle containing some letters and a message urging the rescue party to hasten to their aid.

Spaniard Harbour was well chosen, for so desolate is that country and so exposed the coast that it was seldom visited by either canoe or foot Indians.

The prevailing winds here are from the south-west, which might have persuaded them to make for the Falkland Islands, for they certainly had compasses and Gardiner must have been an expert navigator. That they did not attempt this we can only attribute to the fact that they expected a relief vessel within six months. But before the end of that time all were ill and starving.

An exceptionally severe winter set in, and the men were in no condition to meet it. One of their boats was washed ashore in Spaniard Harbour and damaged beyond repair. Scurvy broke out amongst them. Most of their remaining provisions, which they had hidden in a cave, were completely ruined by an abnormally high tide caused by a violent storm. The rest of the food must have been finished, in spite of the strictest rationing, in July. Then, with the exception of a fox they trapped, they had to live on the few fish or sea-birds they found washed ashore, together with some shell-fish and seaweed.

Dr. Williams, Erwin and the three Cornish fishermen were in a cave,

---

[1] This place now bears the name of Cambaceres.

while Gardiner and the catechist, Maidmant, were living not far away in one of the boats. In June, John Badcock, one of the fishermen, passed away, and as June and July went by others followed, yet still a wonderful peace remained with the survivors. By August only two were left alive—Dr. Williams and Allen Gardiner. Both were too weak to crawl the short distance between the cave and the boat.

Dr. Williams must have died about the 26th August. In his last letter he wrote that he would not change his situation with anyone on earth, and ended by saying, " I am happy beyond words."

Gardiner, the last to succumb, tried in vain to crawl to the cave to see if any there were left alive. He found the effort too much for him and returned to the boat, but had evidently not the strength to drag himself on board, for his body was found lying in the shingle alongside it. His last words were written on the 5th September, and show that he was not only resigned to his fate, but was also in a condition of ecstasy. He recorded that during the previous four days he had taken no nourishment, yet felt neither hunger nor thirst.

He left clear suggestions in writing as to how the work he had attempted could be carried forward. These plans were followed as closely as possible through trials and disasters to a successful conclusion. Though I am well aware that, within less than a century, the Fuegians as a race have become almost extinct, I deliberately use the word " successful."

2

When the news of Gardiner's fate reached England, it was not surprising that the newspapers raised a general outcry against this useless sacrifice of valuable lives in the thankless task of trying to reclaim these most distant and degraded savages.

The Rev. George Pakenham Despard, B.A., Pastor of Lenton, Nottinghamshire, was at that time honorary secretary of the Society founded by Gardiner. Besides his own children—three daughters and a son—he had adopted two other boys. One of these was my father, Thomas Bridges.

Mr. Despard combined with the kindest of hearts a character of exceptional energy and resolution. To such a man, the object being worthy, difficulty and opposition serve only as incentives to further endeavour, and his answer to this clamour was, " With God's help the Mission shall continue." Knowing that God has a tendency to help those who help themselves, he threw the full weight of his personality, influence and private means into the task.

The plan outlined by Captain Allen Gardiner during his last hours was to establish a settlement on an island of the Falkland group and purchase a vessel suitable for making the voyage to Tierra del Fuego. Further attempts to make contact with the Fuegians—particularly Jimmy Button, York Minster and Fuegia Basket, whom Admiral FitzRoy had taken to England nearly twenty years earlier—could then be made. If the confidence of the natives could be gained, Gardiner believed, some of the younger people might be induced to cross to the Falklands. They would not be detained there against their will, but would be permitted to return to their homes as soon as they wished. Their reports of the kind treatment they had received in the Falklands might persuade their friends to follow in their footsteps; and so might be built up a firm friendship between the Fuegians and the missionaries in the Falklands. Gardiner further suggested that the native language should be acquired by the white men with all speed; and, as soon as it was considered safe, a mission established in Tierra del Fuego.

The Rev. G. P. Despard wasted no time in translating Gardiner's ideas into actions. The Society obtained a grant of Keppel Island, one of the northern islands of the Falkland group, with an area of some 5,000 acres. They purchased a smart topsail schooner of eighty-eight tons register, gave it the name *Allen Gardiner* and placed it under the command of Captain Parker Snow, a tough sea-dog, who was instructed to select a crew.

In October, 1854, the *Allen Gardiner*, well found in all respects, with a house ready framed and other building materials, tools and quantities of biscuits and gifts for the natives, left Bristol, bearing with her the prayers and good wishes of Mr. Despard and the Society for which—as Allen Gardiner had done before him—he laboured with so much zeal.

In three months they reached the Falklands. A settlement was made on Keppel Island, gardens planted, and a year after the vessel had left England an attempt was made to carry out the next part of Allen Gardiner's plan.

The little schooner sailed to Tierra del Fuego and anchored in Wulaia. A number of canoes soon appeared, putting off from different creeks as the vessel was seen approaching. And standing in the bow of the foremost was the man they were most anxious to meet—Jimmy Button. No vestige remained of his four years with Englishmen, except that his vigorous shouts could be recognized as English. Though with long, dishevelled hair and practically naked, he seems to have retained a certain modesty acquired over twenty years earlier, for on seeing the captain's wife on board he at once asked for a pair of trousers, which he hastened to don, and then, naturally, asked for braces. Captain Snow talked long with Jimmy, pressing him to take a trip to Keppel Island on the *Allen Gardiner*. This offer was firmly refused, possibly because of Jimmy's wives and family, though they would probably all have been welcome, for fish, penguin and seal were superabundant in the Falklands and there would have been no difficulty about provisions. Jimmy did his utmost, however, to prevail on some of his countrymen to make the venture, but all in vain, and the vessel returned after this feeble effort to Keppel Island.

3

As no second attempt to get in touch with the Fuegians was made, the committee in England rightly felt that time was being wasted, and the vessel was recalled. It was plain that if useful work was to be done, a resolute, indomitable leader must be found, and the Rev. G. P. Despard volunteered to take charge of the next venture. No time was lost, and in 1856 he left England on the *Allen Gardiner*. With him went his wife and family, including my father, who was, at that time, a lad of thirteen.

Under the inspiring leadership of Mr. Despard, the second expedition of the *Allen Gardiner* met with far greater success than the first. It was not long before the Yahgans responded to overtures of friendship, and soon some of them were induced to venture with these white people on their return to Keppel Island. After four years of this kindly intercourse several of the natives had picked up some English and a few of the whites had acquired a smattering of the Yahgan tongue. My father, with the advantages of youth, enthusiasm and a quick ear, soon became more proficient than the rest, and was frequently called upon to act as interpreter by one side or the other.

Thus were the preliminary stages of Allen Gardiner's plan put into effect. There remained its culmination : the setting up of a mission in Tierra del Fuego. In October 1859, when amicable relations were believed to have been firmly established with the Yahgans, it was decided that the time for the enterprise had come. The *Allen Gardiner* was loaded with all necessary stores and equipment. The party included Captain Fell, who had taken the place of Captain Parker Snow on the vessel's second voyage

from Bristol, and Garland Philips, a catechist. Neither Mr. Despard nor my father was of the party. My father was greatly disappointed, but it was decided that it would be better for him to remain and continue his studies at Keppel Island. Also on the ship were three Yahgan families on their way back to Tierra del Fuego after ten months at the Keppel settlement. One of the men bore the name Schwaiamugunjiz. When he had been baptized in Keppel this had been shortened to Schwey-muggins, which, in its turn, had been corrupted into Squire Muggins.

The *Allen Gardiner* set sail. The months went by without news of her, and those who had stayed behind in Keppel fell prey to an ever-increasing anxiety. When five months had elapsed, Mr. Despard, fearing that the worst had happened, decided to go off in search of her. In a small cutter he sailed for Port Stanley, seventy miles away, in the hope that they had received information there about the missing vessel. But they could tell him nothing. While he was considering his next step, the schooner *Nancy*, under Captain Smiley, arrived in Port Stanley and was engaged at once to sail in quest of the *Allen Gardiner*.

They found her anchored at Wulaia, completely dismantled. Every article that the natives could possibly remove had been taken away. Only the hull and bare poles remained. On board they found the party's sole survivor, Alfred Cole, the ship's cook. He was half crazy after what he had been through, almost as naked as the Yahgans, and, from exposure and unaccustomed food, covered with boils.

This is the story he told :

The *Allen Gardiner*, after an uneventful voyage, had kept to the south of Navarin Island, beating through Nassau Bay, and had dropped anchor in Wulaia. They had scarcely lowered their sails when canoes swarmed round them with so much noise and excitement that they were not certain whether they were welcome or the opposite. When the Indian passengers from Keppel Island were doing up their bundles preparatory to leaving the vessel, one of the sailors complained to Captain Fell that several articles belonging to the crew had been stolen. Captain Fell gave orders for the bundles to be searched. This so enraged Squire Muggins that he sprang at the captain and grasped his throat with the evident intention of strangling him. Fell, however, was no weakling, and flung the angry young man far from him. When the bundles were examined, the missing property was found in them and returned to its rightful owners, to the further displeasure, it is to be imagined, of Squire Muggins and his friends.

In spite of this inauspicious start for the Tierra del Fuego Mission, the white men landed their materials and proceeded to erect a little building. They also started to put up a fence with wood from the nearby forest. While this work was in progress the natives caused much annoyance with their incessant begging and ill manners, and their reluctance to leave the side of the vessel, even at night. Jimmy Button, in particular, was a great nuisance with his constant and insatiable demands, and became very bad-tempered when they were not complied with. He had been too spoilt on previous visits of the Mission.

After a week of mist and rain, and despite the difficulties they had encountered, the missionaries and ship's crew had constructed enough of the new building to hold their first church service in Tierra del Fuego. On Sunday, the 6th November, 1859, a day of perfect weather, they landed from the *Allen Gardiner* in the long-boat, armed only with the Bible. With them went the entire crew, with the exception of Alfred Cole, the cook, who remained on board.

The catechist, Garland Philips, led the party into the little hut and three hundred natives—men, women and children—crowded round. The service began with a hymn.

From the deck of the schooner Cole watched the proceedings. He saw the party enter the building, heard the first lines of the hymn, then, helpless and terrified, witnessed what followed.

Some of the natives ran to the long-boat, carried off all the oars to a nearby wigwam and set the boat adrift. In the hut the hymn ceased abruptly, to be followed by a terrific hubbub. The natives had fallen on the party with clubs, stones and spears. Garland Philips and a Swedish sailor named Agusto fought their way out of the hut and reached the sea under a hail of stones. Philips waded out to the drifting long-boat and, waist-deep in water, was just scrambling into it when a stone flung by Tommy Button, Jimmy's brother, hit him on the temple. He fell back unconscious into the sea and was drowned. Agusto met with a similar fate, and ashore the rest of the little party were stoned, clubbed or speared to death.

The *Allen Gardiner* was armed with two small cannons for signalling or defence, but Cole was too frightened to use them, or even the small arms that were on board. Panic-stricken, he jumped into the dinghy and rowed to the opposite shore of the harbour. The Yahgans gave chase in their canoes, and were overhauling him when he jumped ashore and darted into the woods. The Indians took the dinghy in tow and returned to the vessel, which they proceeded most thoroughly to loot.

For many days poor Cole led a fearful existence, lying hidden in the woods by day and creeping out to the beaches when night fell, in search of mussels and limpets. But capture was inevitable. One day some natives caught sight of him, chased him and took him prisoner. They stripped him of all his clothes except his belt and a ring on his finger, and plucked out his beard, moustache and eyebrows, leaving him only with the hair on his head. This treatment was not necessarily prompted by cruelty, for it was in accordance with their own custom.

Cole did not share the ghastly fate of the remainder of the ship's company. His life was spared, and he lived with the Indians for three months before he was rescued by the *Nancy*.

The Yahgans, now in great fear of reprisals, gave the *Nancy* a more friendly reception than they had given the *Allen Gardiner* and did all they could to make amends. Even the renegade Jimmy Button worked hard to keep the *Nancy* supplied with fuel and water during her stay at Wulaia, a stay that was prolonged by the necessity to make the *Allen Gardiner* again seaworthy.

Captain Smiley and his crew worked wonders with the derelict schooner. They got her sufficiently rigged to be sailed back from Wulaia to the Falkland Islands—a voyage that was facilitated by the prevailing winds.

Before the two ships set sail, that cunning fellow, Jimmy Button, went to Captain Smiley and asked to be taken to Keppel Island—a trip that, up to then, he had persistently refused to make. Smiley immediately agreed, for there would thus be another person besides Alfred Cole to bear witness before the Justice in Port Stanley as to what had occurred at Wulaia on that fatal Sunday.

But Jimmy Button's evidence at the enquiry was not in agreement with the story recounted by Cole. Button disclaimed all responsibility and tried to lay the blame on the Ona tribe, who inhabited the main island. Why the Ona had left their own territory, crossed the Beagle Channel and traversed many miles of Navarin Island to murder the missionaries at Wulaia, Jimmy Button did not see fit to explain.

The authorities preferred to believe Alfred Cole. A punitive expedition to teach the Fuegians a sharp lesson was considered, but the missionaries showed that if there were to be such an act of vengeance, it would be impossible to follow it with the gospel of forgiveness which they still proposed to carry to these people.

It was subsequently established beyond all reasonable doubt that Jimmy Button had been the chief instigator of the massacre. This treacherous attack on those who had befriended him was probably prompted by a combination of resentment and jealousy: resentment because he had not been given all he demanded, and jealousy because other natives were being granted benefits that he alone had previously enjoyed. Yet even had his leadership been lacking, the missionaries and the crew of the *Allen Gardiner* might still have met the same tragic end. The unguarded schooner and the defenceless party ashore offered too tempting an opportunity to be resisted by such undisciplined children of Nature as the Fuegian Indians.

The affair just related was indeed a blow for the little group who had remained at Keppel Island. They mourned the loss of their eight friends and fellow-workers. It seemed to them incredible that those natives who had received such kindness at their hands, and appeared to be responding to their Christian teaching, should have turned and murdered their benefactors. It looked as though no spark of gratitude or decent feeling which might, they had hoped, have developed some day into a flame, existed in these benighted people. Even their indefatigable leader Despard, who had justly begun to feel that real progress was being made, was disillusioned. The fate of Captain Allen Gardiner followed by this still more startling tragedy weighed on his spirits; for a leader, however free from blame, feels responsible for the safety of each one of his followers.

Finally, after much serious and anxious thought, he decided to abandon further attempts to establish a mission in Tierra del Fuego. Before acting on this decision, he wrote to the headquarters in England of the Patagonian Missionary Society for instructions. In those days it took a long time for a reply to be received, and it was over two years before confirmation of his suggestion reached him from the homeland. Shortly afterwards, accompanied by his family and nearly all those who had come out with him from England, he set sail from Keppel Island in the *Allen Gardiner*, which by that time was badly in need of overhaul and repair.

4

Among those who waved the little schooner good-bye was Thomas Bridges, my father. Mr. Despard had offered him the choice of returning home or of remaining on Keppel Island; and he had elected to stay behind. To a life of comfort and safety with his foster-parents, he preferred to follow the bleak and lonely path that led not back to England, but on to Tierra del Fuego. Richard Mathews had failed and fled, Allen Gardiner had died of starvation, Garland Philips had been struck down and perished in the sea, George Pakenham Despard had given up in despair. One man alone remained to carry on the great work, and that man was Thomas Bridges.

And so, at the age of eighteen, he was left in charge of the settlement on Keppel. He had already lived there for over five years, but among agreeable companions. Now he was almost alone—and it was to be another year before the *Allen Gardiner* returned from England with a new superintendent to relieve him, for a time, of the onerous duties that he had so willingly undertaken.

To realize his ambition of winning over the Fuegians to the Gospel, he knew that he must first acquire a thorough mastery of their language. During that lonely year on Keppel he went far towards his goal. Among the few Yahgans who were left behind when the *Allen Gardiner* had made that last calamitous voyage to Wulaia were a married couple, Okoko, who had been baptized by the name of George, and his wife, Gamela. They were both intelligent, and lent themselves willingly as tutors. My father worked, and practically lived, with them, listening to their continuous chatter, for they were a talkative and laughter-loving pair. In this way he was able to unravel the mysteries of their intricate yet beautiful grammar. With the help of Ellis's phonetic system he began to compile a dictionary—a monumental work that was to occupy him for many years and was to have, before it found its resting-place in the British Museum, a queer and fantastic history that is told later in these pages.

The new superintendent was the Rev. Whait H. Stirling, who had been the Society's honorary secretary in England since the departure from there of Mr. Despard, and had volunteered to take over the post the other had relinquished in the Falklands. When he reached Keppel Island he was surprised to find that Thomas Bridges had practically mastered the native language and was already conversant with its intricate grammar.

With this proficient interpreter to accompany him, Mr. Stirling made his first trip to the Fuegian channels. It was also my father's first visit there, and took place towards the end of 1863. Since the massacre at Wulaia the natives had lived in constant dread of reprisals, and it was with evident trepidation that they approached the vessel. Mr. Stirling speaks in his letters of their obvious astonishment, as they slowly drew near in their canoes, to be hailed in their own tongue by a white man.

When they found that here was a man who could talk with them and understand their replies, their fears were soon dissipated. My father visited the various native settlements alone in the ship's dinghy, not because of any fear on Mr. Stirling's part, but to encourage sociability and avoid ostentation.

During the time of isolation since the massacre some terrible epidemic had visited these people, and there was a noticeable decrease in their numbers. Jimmy Button still lived and, by that time, had three sons. In the next four years over fifty Yahgans made the trip to Keppel Island, while my father paid frequent visits to their country. In 1866 Mr. Stirling took four Yahgan lads to England (not in the *Allen Gardiner*). Their ages varied from thirteen to eighteen and their names were Urupa, Sisoi, Jack and Threeboy. This last was a son of Jimmy Button. It seems that when Jimmy had been asked his name, he had thought the question related to the size of his family, and had answered, " Three boy." The name had stuck.

Late in the year 1867, with sympathetic encouragement and assistance, a small number of natives settled as farmers on Navarin Island. The spot chosen was Laiwaia, near the entrance to the Murray Narrows, which divide Navarin from Hoste Island and are an outlet from the Beagle Channel to the Southern Ocean. With materials for the new settlement on board, the *Allen Gardiner* anchored in Laiwaia's sheltered cove. On the 11th January, 1868, Mr. Stirling wrote on board a long letter to his children. From this we learn that my father was on shore with the Yahgans, building a log-house with four rooms in it and a bark roof, and fencing across an isthmus to enclose the goats that had been given to the natives at Keppel. The work was concluded, gardens were made and the goats landed. Then the new little settlement was handed over to George Okoko, Jack and two others, whose names were Pinoi and Lukka.

Meanwhile the coast of the Beagle Channel and the adjacent islands had been explored with a view to a white settlement in the country. For this there were certain essential requirements. It must be a place where a large number of small farmers could live and prosper, with decent gardens and a few cows and goats each. It must have a roomy harbour, easy of access for a fair-sized vessel. And it must be near the very heart of the Yahgan country and easy to reach from all sides by the

The North-West Arm of the Beagle Channel, west from Yendagaia.

Another part of the North-West Arm, also looking northward.

Both photos by courtesy of Col. Charles Wellington Furlong.

My father at the age of twenty-five.

natives. The sheltered, picturesque little harbour of Laiwaia, with its many nearby islets, was bad to enter or leave in certain conditions of tide or wind, even for the *Allen Gardiner*. Gable Island and the country on the main island to the east of it would have been ideal but for the fact that they were too far from the centre of Yahga-land. Wulaia was off the Beagle Channel, which was the main canoe route, and offered rather too little room for a considerable settlement of agriculturalists.

The final choice was Ushuaia. It had an ample, sheltered harbour and an expanse of open country fit for cultivation. It was easy of access from east and west along the Beagle Channel and it was near the Murray Narrows, the entrance to the Channel from the outer coasts and the Cape Horn group of islands.

At about the same time as a little wooden house was being got ready at Port Stanley for erection at Ushuaia, my father was recalled to England. The committee of the South American Missionary Society [1] had decided that, to carry on his work, it was desirable that he should take Holy Orders. Accordingly, on the last day of October, 1868, he sailed from the Falklands in H.M.S. *Brisk*, a barque-rigged corvette. He was then twenty-five years of age and had been in those distant lands for twelve years.

5

The little wooden house for the new Mission was shipped from the Falklands to Ushuaia, where it was erected on the beach. Its measurements were, I believe, about twenty feet by ten, and it was divided into three rooms. On the 14th January, 1869, Mr. Stirling was landed there, and the *Allen Gardiner* sailed back to the Falklands, leaving him alone with the Indians. In this enterprise he had two companions: Jack, the young Yahgan who had been to England with him, and Jack's newly acquired wife. There had been some trouble among the settlers at Laiwaia, and Jack had left there to go to Ushuaia. Mr. Stirling took occupation of one of the three rooms, Jack and his wife were given the second, and the third was used as a kitchen.

The *Allen Gardiner* returned during the following month. On the 13th February Mr. Stirling wrote to his children:

" I caught a glimpse of the *Allen Gardiner*. Oh, delightful moment! My eyes almost sprang a leak and my heart beat with joy."

He must have been very lonely. He went on to say in his letter that

[1] Formerly the Patagonian Missionary Society. The change had taken place in 1864.

when the vessel arrived one of the Yahgan members of the crew said to him:

"I am very glad. I think my countrymen kill you, but you have wigwams all round your house."

By this he meant, writes Mr. Stirling, wigwams of really friendly natives.

Mr. Stirling remained at Ushuaia over six months. He lived with the natives, as my father afterwards described it, "in comparative peace; daily instructing them, and organizing various employments." During this time he learned that he was to be made Bishop of the Falkland Islands, the largest diocese in the world, embracing the whole of South America.

6

On my father's arrival in England he was ordained deacon by the Bishop of London. Before returning to his labours at the other end of the world he travelled about England, lecturing on the Fuegians and the country in which they dwelt. At Bristol he met Mary Varder, one of the daughters of Mr. and Mrs. Stephen Varder of Harberton. On the 7th August, 1869, they were married in the church of that little South Devon village, and two days later left England in the S.S. *Onega*. Notwithstanding splendid weather, my mother suffered from sea-sickness during the whole voyage. They dropped anchor in Rio de Janeiro on Wednesday, the 1st September, and saw slave labour for the first time—as my father wrote in his diary, "a truly pitiful sight." Three days later they embarked on the *Arno*, a paddle-boat that plied between Rio and the River Plate. The weather was very rough, and sea-sickness was general. "Dear Mary," wrote my father, "was very sick indeed. . . . The motion caused by the paddles is much more unpleasant than that caused by a screw."

They reached the River Plate on the 9th September, and landed in Montevideo. On the 18th Mr. Stirling arrived in the *Lotus*, on his way to England. He gave my father a very encouraging account of the new settlement at Ushuaia. My parents stayed in Montevideo until the 24th September, when they took two passages on the *Normanby*. She was a guano-carrying barque and was manned, for the most part, by American negroes. The master, Captain McKintosh, was most kind, and gave up his berth to them for the whole of the trip to the Falklands. On the 6th October they reached Port William, whence a cutter took them in to Port Stanley, which was a tiny hamlet in those days.

In Stanley my father purchased necessary provisions before they continued their journey to Keppel Island. The trip, which they made in the schooner *Selton*, generously placed at their disposal free of charge by her owner, Mr. Dean, took three days.

The party at Keppel consisted at that time of a Mr. and Mrs. William Bartlett and their children, a Mr. Phillips, a Mr. Jacob Resyck and three Yahgan lads, whose names were Shifcunjiz,[1] Gyammamowl and Cushinjiz. Mr. Bartlett was a hard-working farm bailiff. He and his wife had come from England with Mr. Despard and my father in 1856. He had planted gardens and cared for the stock—sheep and cattle—at Keppel Island ever since. He was assisted by Mr. Phillips, a farm labourer, who was lame and had lost two fingers from his right hand. Mr. Jacob Resyck was a coloured man. An earnest Christian, so taciturn as to give the impression that he was either deaf or simply morose, he was in charge of the spiritual welfare of the little community, and gave lessons to the three Yahgan lads and the Bartlett boys.

When my parents reached Keppel, they found that Mr. Bartlett, unaware that they would arrive so soon, had left a week before on the *Allen Gardiner* to superintend the planting of the native gardens at Ushuaia. My mother was introduced to the rest of the party, including Shifcunjiz, Gyammamowl and Cushinjiz, who were decently clad and clean. Cushinjiz, afterwards known as James, belonged to the eastern end of the Beagle Channel, and will appear later on in my story. These three young men prepared their own meals and lived in a little house that Father, in earlier days, had shared with them in order to acquire a knowledge of their language.

In my father's diary five days after my parents' arrival we find reference to the two women hard at work getting their homes in order and tending to the needs of their menfolk, who were working in the garden, where " vegetation is beginning to shoot and polyanthus and daffodil are in full bloom." Father and Resyck spent some time giving instruction to the children and natives. On Sunday, the 17th October, 1869, he wrote : " Pleasant weather, calm and bright. We have a very happy and peaceful time. Took my dearest Mary to our little cemetery and gave her particulars of each person interred there."

Father was also occupied making an inventory of Mission goods at the settlement. There were other activities besides. They had a net, and

[1] Very many Yahgan names end with " . . . jiz," which has no meaning by itself, but as an affix means " born at."

appear to have caught all the fish they needed. Father and Mother would go with one or more of the Indians and a couple of pack-horses with crates to the penguin rookery, where they would work very diligently, and return in the evening with anything from 800 to 1,600 eggs. These, after their own needs had been supplied, would be packed in barrels and other receptacles, to be shipped later in the *Allen Gardiner* to Fireland— a welcome gift to the natives, who, having lived extravagantly on penguins' eggs in the past, had kept the number of these birds within limits, whereas in the Falklands, which had no aboriginal inhabitants, the penguins had steadily increased throughout the ages. It is possible to preserve these eggs so well that I have eaten two penguins' eggs fried without being aware that one was fresh within a few days and the other a full year old. One of the chief occupations at Keppel Island was the cutting, drying and storing of peat, their only fuel. Those barren, wind-swept, yet generous islands gave this commodity as lavishly as they did fish and sea-birds.

On the 14th November the *Allen Gardiner* arrived back from Fireland with Mr. Bartlett and two young Yahgan couples as passengers. She had encountered very bad weather. The main boom had been snapped off, the topmast carried away and the mate severely injured. Mr. Bartlett reported happily on the progress at Ushuaia, where a good deal of land had been enclosed, dug and sown; and nearly an acre of potatoes planted, under his direction, by the Yahgans, most, if not all, of whom had had some training on Keppel Island.

The *Allen Gardiner* remained at Keppel for some days, then sailed for Port Stanley with my father aboard. He went partly on business and partly to welcome some new arrivals: John Lawrence, James Lewis and their wives. The Lewises had brought with them their little son, Willie. Father had met these two men in England nearly a year before. Mr. Lawrence was by trade a nursery gardener, Mr. Lewis a carpenter, and as it had been rightly thought that such men would be exceedingly useful in training the natives in the ways of civilized men and in making Christians of them, they had, with my father's approval, been engaged by the committee. Father reached Port Stanley in time to greet his two new assistants and their wives, and they all returned to Keppel on the Mission schooner.

Natives are often good mimics. Father mentions in his diary that one of the recently arrived Yahgan couples, Quisenasan and his wife, Cushinjizkeepa,[1] were " frequently seen walking so nicely arm in arm; it was a pleasant sight." I know where they learned that. The second Yahgan

---

[1] Another common ending, meaning " woman born at."

couple, Laiwainjiz and Pakawalakihrkeepa, had a baby son on Christmas Eve. At the earnest request of his parents, he was named Shukukurhtu-mahgoon (Son from a House Thatched with Grass). This cottage on Keppel bore the imposing name of Fireland Villa. The bungalow in which Mother lived was called Sullivan House, after a former governor of the islands.

Father now had a new duty—giving lessons in Yahgan to Messrs. Lawrence and Lewis. In the middle of March, 1870, he paid another visit to Tierra del Fuego in the *Allen Gardiner*, in which the Yahgan lad Cushinjiz (later James) was now serving as steward, and doing very well indeed at it. On the trip, Father occupied himself making tin drinking-mugs for the Fuegians, cutting out and making trousers for them, and, for a change, studying algebra or walking the deck—when possible.

At Banner Cove on Picton Island as many as twelve canoes came along-side at once with some seventy persons. Father went on shore and spoke to the natives. " I showed them what a just claim God has upon our lives and affections and how good are all His commandments." Falk-land geese and penguin eggs were distributed, but Father writes, " All the canoes seemed well supplied with fish and the Channel teemed with bird life."

The natives were most persistent in their begging for more. When Father reproved them, Cushinjiz joined in and backed him staunchly. But this was his country. He had been long at Keppel, and now wanted to rejoin his own people. So early the next morning Father and the second mate put him ashore with a box of goods and injunctions to spread the Bible story and the good precepts he had learnt. Then the vessel set sail again for Ushuaia.

Ushuaia had not been visited by any white man since Mr. Bartlett had left over five months before. Nevertheless, the sixteen native families there had not been unduly molested by their countrymen. They had exerted themselves to improve their little settlement and had refrained from digging up and eating the potatoes Mr. Bartlett had helped them to plant—even the new ones, which were reaching a fair size, though already nipped with frost. There had been some divergence of opinion amongst them, but they had abstained from violence.

Not so, however, at the Laiwaia settlement on Navarin Island, which had been started in January, 1868, with Okoko, Pinoi, Lukka and Jack. After Jack had left, the others had been overwhelmed by the jealousy of their poorer fellows. There had been fighting, and at a nearby spot a man had certainly been killed. George Okoko, head man of the settlement, had had his house burnt down when he was out fishing. He had hastened to dig his potatoes (four sacks, all that his enemies had left him) and had escaped to Ushuaia, where, though feeling safer in the company of the settlers, he had wisely taken no part in their labours, but had kept quiet and awaited developments.

The *Allen Gardiner* had brought building material for the new Mission residence, which was to be called Stirling House. Father felt justified in leaving it under the protection of the Yahgans settled there, so it was landed and carried to the top of a hill a third of a mile away, to be erected later. Father and the natives dug out a thirty-foot-square foundation site for the house, then went to work in the woods on the north shore of the harbour, cutting posts so badly needed in the Falklands. These were put on board the schooner till she had a good load. They would be sold to help defray the cost of running the Mission vessel.

Many Yahgans from distant parts gathered at Ushuaia. Father exhorted them not to be envious of those who had gardens and had learnt to work, and not to obstruct or annoy them, because their own turn was coming. Mission work and training would soon be organized at Ushuaia, and they would be given the opportunity of planting their own gardens and improving their standards of living in other parts of their country as well.

Penguin eggs and a limited number of Falkland geese were given to all Fuegians they met before the *Allen Gardiner* again set sail for Keppel. On the trip Father wrote, " Last night was very rough and I was in constant fear of being pitched out of my bunk, so lively and vigorous were the vessel's motions." Later she was " so lively that I could not walk the deck." At eight o'clock in the evening of the 8th May the schooner dropped anchor in Committee Bay, Keppel Island. Mother and all were well, so Father was soon off again on a visit to Stanley, and on the 25th of that same month we find him on his way back to Ushuaia.

After the milder climate of the Falklands, he was surprised to see so much snow and ice at Ushuaia. He found the little group of Yahgan settlers had been troubled by the envy of their less fortunate kinsmen. There had been, however, no fatal clashes or sickness, and the building material had not been stolen or destroyed.

George Okoko's strength of character had brought him to the front, and he was now the leading figure at Ushuaia. The potatoes had been dug, and had proved a fine stand-by during the ten weeks' absence of the

Allen Gardiner. A further amount of cargo was discharged and carried up the snowy hill to be added to that lying at the site of the future station. The really settled Indians were each given a saucepan and a knife, and some biscuits and beans were divided amongst them. When a quantity of potatoes from Keppel Island had been distributed generally, the schooner again set sail for Keppel.

While they were anchored that night near the east end of Gable Island in the Beagle Channel, four canoes came alongside. In one of them was Cushinjiz. He was still decently clothed, but must have given away all he could afford, for every native had some garment. He seemed happy, and had no wish to return to the Falklands. He sent Mother the gift of a basket, and one of the other Keppel ladies two huge sea-shells, such as the Yahgans used for drinking-vessels.

In August of that year, 1870, Father took my mother to Stanley and left her in the care of a Mrs. Hanson. Towards the end of the following month he sailed in the *Allen Gardiner* for Ushuaia in the company of James Lewis, Jacob Resyck, Gyammamowl (one of the three Yahgan lads) and Quisenasan and his wife. They had a rough passage, but reached Ushuaia on the 10th October, and immediately started work, road-making and completing the digging out of the foundations of Stirling House, which my father had begun five months earlier. There were soon twenty canoes there with over one hundred and fifty natives aboard them.

On Wednesday, the 16th November, Father left James Lewis and Jacob Resyck to carry on the good work—teaching, advising, persuading, building, gardening. The resident population of Ushuaia was then eighty-two, but Father's instructions to his two assistant missionaries were to employ only the seven most trained and civilized natives in his absence. Otherwise they would soon run short of provisions. He explained this to the other natives, and advised them to continue for the time being to hunt and fish as before. The truth was that these natives, totally unused to steady work, needed constant and close supervision; and the more there were of them together, the less each individual would do. It was no use merely telling them to do a thing; one had to show them right down to the smallest detail, then watch them to make sure they were doing it in the right way.

Back in the Falklands, after a voyage during which Father recorded that " even the Yahgans on board were seasick and I find the motion unfits me for mental exertion," he remained in Stanley until, on the 5th December, 1870, he was able to write in his diary, " This morning at three o'clock my dear wife was happily delivered of a daughter. I directly wrote a note to father and mother [Mr. and Mrs. Varder] to give them information of the joyful event and took my letter on board the schooner *Foam,* which was getting under way."

A month later Mother, Father and baby Mary were on the *Allen Gardiner,* bound for Keppel Island. It must not be imagined that these trips of the Mission vessel were simply for sport or pleasure. Frequently passengers and families were landed on different islands where they had their little homes; thus many avoided either a long wait in Port Stanley, or the discomfort of less seaworthy vessels or open boats.

My father's next visit to Ushuaia was in January of the following year. When the schooner neared Gable Island, Cushinjiz came alongside and aboard. He was accompanied by Gyammamowl and Quisenasan, who had joined him on the island. They had planted large gardens and prepared still more land for planting next season. They had heard nothing but good news of the two missionaries left at Ushuaia.

Two days later, when Father arrived at Ushuaia, he was well pleased with what had been done there and the quiet that reigned in the settlement. James Lewis and Jacob Resyck, who had used as their abode the little house on the beach in which Mr. Stirling had resided, were well advanced with the erection of Stirling House. Again wood was cut for shipment to the Falklands, and on the 13th February the *Allen Gardiner* sailed away with Mr. Lewis as her only passenger. Father, established in the unfinished Stirling House, remained with his coloured helper, Mr. Resyck, to carry on the good work.

Father must have brought a few sheep for mutton on that last voyage, for he says that one was drowned and there were thirteen left. They had to be shut up at night and shepherded on account of the native dogs. The summer days in Fireland are long. Father was up at 4 a.m. and, having let the sheep out to graze, seems to have carried on working all through the day, ending at night by writing, studying the language, visiting sick Indians, and performing a variety of other tasks. I find in his diary: " My whole being is in a state of excitement. Earnest and frequent are my prayers to Him who alone is able to keep, guide, comfort and bless us. I feel that God only is my strength and source of my good. . . . Brother Jacob came over and kindly made me a cup of coffee." I imagine Father was weary and needed it badly, though he never mentions such weakness in his diary.

Friday, the 14th May. The nights grow long at this season, and at

7 a.m. they breakfasted by lamplight. Then, to their surprise, they saw
the *Allen Gardiner* at anchor in the harbour. She had come in at 3 a.m.,
with Mr. and Mrs. Lewis aboard. With them were their little boy and
his baby brother, who had been born on Keppel Island. He was baptized
by my father in Stirling House on Sunday, the 28th May, by the name of
Frank Ooshooia,[1] in the presence of Jacob Resyck, the captain of the *Allen
Gardiner* and most of her crew.

My father now vacated Stirling House and took up residence aboard
the schooner, landing every day to teach or work about the settlement
with the natives, or in the forest across the harbour. By the beginning of
June he was back on Keppel Island, and on the eleventh day of that month
he baptized the first-born child of Mr. and Mrs. Lawrence by the name
Emma Louisa.

On the 17th August, Father, Mother and my sister Mary set out from
Keppel on the *Allen Gardiner* on the last lap of the long journey from
England to Ushuaia.

[1] So spelt. Frank Lewis afterwards altered it to Ushuaia.

CHAPTER THREE

My Parents Come to Ushuaia. The Surrounding Country. My Mother's First Sight of Stirling House. The Other Settlers. Their Fuegian Neighbours. The Alacaloof. The Yahgans. Some Facts about Kelp. The Importance of Fires. The Fire-Stone of Tierra del Fuego. Fires Kept Burning in Canoes. The Origin of " Fireland." The Ona Tribe.

I

ON THE FIRST DAY OF OCTOBER, 1871, MY PARENTS DISEMBARKED AT USHUAIA after four days' sail along the Beagle Channel westward from Banner Cove.

Ushuaia [1] means in the tongue of the native inhabitants of that locality, " Inner Harbour to the Westward." Well sheltered from the prevailing westerly winds by a double peninsula, the harbour is situated on the north shore of the Beagle Channel. The peninsula, which extends some two miles to the south-eastward, is, for the most part, a nest of hills covered with wild grass and bushes. Small lakes nestle in its valleys, and its southern shore, facing the Channel, has a rampart of clay or conglomerate cliffs.

On the northern side of Ushuaia harbour, less than a mile across, the mountains rise steeply from the water's edge. Except for a few small areas close to the shore that have been cleared by the Indians for wigwam sites, unbroken beech-forests clothe the mountainside up as far as the line known as the upper tree level, just short of two thousand feet above the sea. Above the forests are masses of rock patched with snow and some glaciers which rise over a thousand feet. This range of mountains runs east and west from Ushuaia, the nearest high peak being Mount Olivia, which rises to over four thousand feet. There are deep, narrow gullies where the mountain streams, and the few large rivers that have found their way through the coastal range from their sources among the mountains of the interior, rush down into the Beagle Channel. The western part of the range is more desolate than the east. Its highest peak, Mount Darwin, rises to seven thousand feet. Many glaciers reach out into the sea in winter and summer alike, and vessels passing along the Channel sometimes find difficulty in forcing their way through the masses of ice. Eastward the

[1] Pronounced " Oo-shoo-wai-ya ": " Oo " as in " foot "; " shoo " as in " shoot "; " wai " as in " wily "; and the final " a " as in " fat," with the shadow of a " y " before it.

mountains become lower, till at San Diego they seem to dive under the Straits of Le Maire and reappear for a breather in the shape of that menacing cluster of splintered rocks called Staten Island, before taking their final plunge into the Atlantic Ocean.

Of Staten Island Anson wrote in 1741:

". . . I cannot but remark that though Tierra del Fuego had an aspect extremely barren and desolate, yet this island of Staten-land far surpasses it in the wildness and horror of its appearance. It seems to be entirely composed of inaccessible rocks without the least mixture of earth or mould between them. These rocks terminate in a vast number of ragged points, which spire up to a prodigious height, and are all of them covered with everlasting snow. The points themselves are on every side surrounded with frightful precipices, and often overhang in a most astonishing manner. The hills which bear them are generally separated from each other by narrow clefts which appear as if the country had been frequently rent by earthquakes; for these chasms are nearly perpendicular, and extend through the substance of the main rocks, almost to the bottom; so that nothing can be imagined more savage and gloomy than the whole aspect of this coast."

A terrible picture indeed, yet it would be misleading to give only the more melancholy aspects of the Fuegian scenery. On a calm evening in autumn, when the leaves of its northern forests are red and the dark mirrors of its waters are broken only by the wake of some diving bird, the beauty of Ushuaia harbour is hard to exaggerate. But when my mother first set eyes upon it, it did not hold out so pleasant a welcome.

As they were rowed ashore from the *Allen Gardiner*, this Ushuaia, of which she had heard so much, was new, strange and rather frightening. Behind the shingle beach the grassland stretched away to meet a sudden steep less than a quarter of a mile from the shore. Between shore and hill were scattered wigwams, half-buried hovels made of branches roofed with turf and grass, smelling strongly, as she was to find later, of smoke and decomposed whale-blubber or refuse flung close outside. Round the wigwams dark figures, some partially draped in otter-skins, others almost naked, stood or squatted, gazing curiously at the little boat as it approached the beach.

Some canoes lay hauled up on the shingle, and in others women were fishing or paddling alongside the schooner, trying to barter fish or limpets for knives or those great delicacies introduced by the foreigners, biscuits and sugar. These Paiakoala [1] were wanderers, attracted by the wish to see what the white men were doing at Ushuaia.

On the summit of the thornbush-covered hill in the background she

---

[1] Beach people of the Yahgan tribe. . . . *oala*, though never used alone, means " folk " in its broadest sense. I have even heard Yahgans use *amuroala* to describe guanaco (*amura*) collectively.

saw her future home, Stirling House, a five-roomed bungalow of wood and corrugated iron. It was not yet completed, and looked very lonely perched up there all by itself.

Though it was now mid-spring, snow lay about in patches, and on calm nights ice still formed in the sheltered harbour. Across the harbour, right from the very shore, the leafless trees stood out against the snow, except where some sombre evergreens hid the ground and broke the monotony. Above tree-level the snow gleamed pure and white to the very peaks of the mountain range.

In that country my mother was to spend the greater part of her life, and if she thought wistfully at times of her native Devon, with its kindly climate, its rich, generous fields and its friendly neighbours, no one knew it. In looking after my father, in raising her family, and in mothering every living creature that needed her care, she was too busy for regrets, and was not, in any case, the kind of woman to complain. She had chosen a life that would have daunted a lesser spirit, and in it she herself found happiness, as she certainly brought it to others.

2

James Lewis, his wife and the mulatto, Jacob Resyck, had been anxiously awaiting the arrival of the vessel; and if they were delighted to see her again and get news from the outside world, Father was equally glad and relieved to find them and the children safe and well.

Stirling House was now divided into two sections, one for my parents and the other for the Lewises. Resyck lived by himself in Stirling Cottage, which had sheltered the brave Bishop so long. It was later removed in sections from the beach to the hill-top. The partitions were taken out and a tiny belfry built on one end of it. For some years it served as a church and meeting-house until, in due course, a more adequate building was erected.

As my father had told my mother during that swift courtship in Bristol, Ushuaia's nearest contact with civilization was the Chilean convict settlement at Punta Arenas (Sandy Point), a hundred and twenty miles away, over impassable mountain ranges and across the Magellan Straits. By sea the distance was double, and to reach Punta Arenas a vessel had either to brave the tide-rips of the Straits of Le Maire and the Atlantic Ocean, or face the prevailing westerly winds and beat up the Beagle Channel, out through Desolation Bay into the Pacific, round Brecknock Peninsula, where the waves sound like great guns as they break into the

mouths of the caves; then in through Cockburn Channel, past the Kirke
Rocks and across the Magellan Straits to Port Famine and Punta Arenas.
The frequent stormy winds and thick weather in those narrow, rock-
bound channels made the sea trip from Ushuaia to the Chilean settlement
hazardous. The journey by land was utterly impossible; in fact, in spite
of many attempts—which, now the track is open, seem rather feeble—it
was over twenty years before anyone succeeded in crossing the island
from the Beagle Channel to the northern side. The Mission settlement
was obliged, therefore, to accept the Falkland Islands, nearly four
hundred miles away, as its only link with the outside world.

Thus did a tiny, but resolute, party take up their abode in the Fuegian
archipelago, a collection of islands infinitely more numerous than is shown
on any chart and covering an area of two hundred miles from north to
south and three hundred and sixty miles from east to west; their
neighbours not their friends and relatives, but anything from seven
thousand to nine thousand primitive children of Nature, the Fuegian
Indians.

These Fuegians were divided into four distinct groups, each with its
own language and customs: the Alacaloof, the Yahgan, the Ona and the
Aush (or Eastern Ona). The western parts of the archipelago were the
home of the Alacaloof. Brecknock Peninsula, a rough, precipitous headland thrusting out into the Pacific and ending in London and Sidney
Islands, formed a natural boundary between them and the Yahgan tribe,
whose territory extended from Desolation Bay, along the southern coast
of the main island as far as Spaniard Harbour, and took in all the southern
islands down as far as Cape Horn. There is no record of their ever
having crossed to Staten Island. The Ona inhabited the interior of the
main island and its northern and eastern coasts. The Aush were to be
found on its south-eastern tip.

The Alacaloof were a tribe of canoe Indians. They lived almost
entirely on birds, seal, fish and limpets. As did their neighbours, the
Yahgans, they made bark canoes. They also made dug-outs, which were
much larger than the bark canoes. Father found one that measured
twenty-nine feet in length and well over three feet in depth. For these
the Alacaloof used not only paddles, but also oars of primitive design, with
wooden rowlocks. They were dexterous in the use of bows and arrows,
spears and slings. Adventurers, both Alacaloof and Yahgan, had passed
round the Brecknock Peninsula in their canoes, and inter-marriages between the two tribes occurred from time to time.

The Yahgans were the southernmost inhabitants of the earth. Their lands included the harbour and settlement at Ushuaia. They lived close to the shore, and spent much of their time in canoes. When Father was studying their language he chose his tutors, whenever possible, from the very heart of their country, hoping thus to learn the language in its purest form, unadulterated by contact with neighbouring tribes. This most central part was the Murray Narrows, aptly called by the natives Yahga-shaga (Mountain Valley Channel), and the inhabitants of that area were called Yahgashagalumoala (the People from Mountain Valley Channel). This was shortened by my father to Yahgan, by which name the whole tribe later became known to the outside world, though amongst the natives themselves it was confined to people of the Murray Narrows district. The tribe's own name for itself was Yamana (People). In the same way, the Ona, which was the Yahgan name for them, called them-selves Shilknum; and the self-styled Aush were known to the Yahgans as Etalum Ona (Eastern Ona).

The Yahgans were fearless cragsmen and splendid sailors, but seldom ventured far inland, for, in addition to certain wild-men-of-the-woods—strange creatures of their own imagination—they had a mortal fear of the Ona. In any case, there was little to attract them amongst the snowy mountains and boggy valleys of the interior. As they lived almost entirely on fish and limpets, they had very few skins with which to clothe themselves. Some otter- and fox-skins were available, but hardly enough to go round. For the few Yahgans who lived on the shores of Navarin Island and the north shore of the Beagle Channel, skins were to be had from the guanaco, a species of wild llama with a reddish-yellow wool. Fur-seals were scarce, and the hides of the hair-seal were generally eaten or cut into thongs (*mun*), often used for lowering bird-hunters over cliffs. The Yahgan word for a poor person was *api tupan* (body only); it will be gathered from the preceding that many of the young Indians qualified for the epithet.

Father once measured some thirty grown Yahgan men. The tallest of them was five feet five inches and the shortest just under four feet eight, the average height being five feet two and a quarter inches. Yet, in spite of their short stature, they were strong, and FitzRoy says frankly that he forbade his sailors to wrestle with the natives, who, being the stronger, would learn to despise the white man. The Yahgan women were short and fat, with tapering limbs and little hands and feet.

Men and women wore a tiny apron made of otter-skin, which was supposed to hang down in front. They also had a second primitive garment of the same material, generally too small to wrap themselves in, which they wore flung over their shoulders, or tied to their bodies as a protection against the wind. The women wore many necklaces of delicate shells, beautifully polished and neatly strung together. They also used short sections from the leg- and wing-bones of birds strung on plaited sinew.

Although they employed slings for stones, and bows and arrows, the chief weapon of this tribe was the spear, of which they made three types for different purposes.

There was a fair division of labour between the sexes. The men gathered the fuel and fungus for food, whilst the women cooked, fetched water, paddled the canoes and fished. The men tended the fires, made and mended canoes and prepared material for them. They also attended to the hunting—otter, seal, guanaco, foxes and birds—and speared the large fish. Being in charge of the canoes—for it was only on long journeys, or when in a hurry, that the men helped with the paddles —the women were always good swimmers, but it was a very rare thing to find a male Yahgan who could swim. The women were by no means slaves, for what they caught was their own. The husband used only what his wife gave him, and she did not ask his permission before making gifts to her friends.

Members of this tribe often lived in places where for many miles there were no beaches on which it was possible to haul up their canoes. They were compelled, therefore, to anchor them off the rocks in the best shelter to be found. This anchoring was done by the women. After the canoe had been unloaded and the husband had gone up into the forest to collect fuel for the fire, the wife would paddle off in the canoe a few fathoms into the thick kelp (a large species of seaweed), which makes a splendid breakwater. She would grasp a handful of the kelp's rope-like branches and secure them to the canoe, which was thus safely anchored by their roots, then slip into the water, swim ashore and hasten to the fire to dry and warm herself.

These Yahgan women swam like a dog and had no difficulty in getting through the kelp. I have never seen a white man foodhardy enough to attempt this dangerous feat. They learnt to swim in infancy, and were taken out by their mothers in order to get them used to it. In winter, when the kelp leaves were coated with a film of frost, a baby girl out with her mother would sometimes make pick-a-back swimming difficult by climbing onto her parent's head to escape the cold water and frozen kelp.

There are different species of sea kelp. The kind mentioned here gets its roots around rocks, but will grow only where it is possible for its branches to reach and spread over the surface of the water. In some places it grows so thick that seagulls, ducks and herons can perch on the leaves. It is found on rocky shoals fringing the coast, in as much as fourteen fathoms of water. These vegetable ropes sometimes attain a length of over two hundred feet. The leaves grow to three or more feet long. They are proportionately broad, and leathery in texture. At their bases are pods full of air, which keep the plant afloat. Unless an oarsman is expert, it is difficult to row through thick kelp. It will wind itself round propellers and render them temporarily useless. Fish and all kinds of lesser sea life abound in these kelp forests, which flourish on all the coasts, except where there is sand or mud. A small boat or canoe running before a storm may find safety in a thick kelp patch until the storm abates, but this plant, though it has thereby saved many a life, has also caused numerous deaths by entangling swimmers a few yards from the shore. The Yahgan name for it is *howush*. A forest of kelp separated from the shore by deep water is *palan*. The spot at Ushuaia where my parents had made their home was called Tushcapalan, which means "the Kelp Island of the Flying Loggerhead Duck."

Living, as they did, practically naked in this raw climate, the greatest comfort these people had was fire. Their favourite tinder was *dunda*, the filmy web from the puff-ball, a ground fungus. If this was lacking, they used fine bird's down or insects' nests. The tinder was kept dry in the bladder of a seal or guanaco. To ignite it they employed iron pyrites fire-stone—far more effective than flint for producing sparks. This fire-stone was not common. There was only one source of supply in those parts—Mercury Sound on Clarence Island, a region where Yahgan and Alacaloof mixed. In a snug harbour a well-worn trail led to a large deposit of refuse, evidence that the natives had worked there for centuries. The heaps of chippings were huge, and to this day there are to be seen the rounded masses of iron pyrites from which, with great labour, both Yahgan and Alacaloof obtained their supplies. Those of the islanders who could not reach Mercury Sound would give handsome presents in exchange for the fire-stone, rather than use the much-inferior flints available in their own localities.

In practice, the Yahgans seldom needed flint or tinder. Fires were

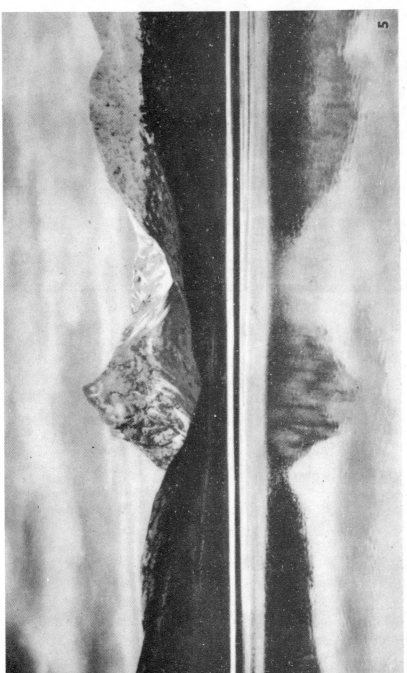

The view across Ushuaia harbour, looking north-eastward from the beach where my mother first landed.   The conical peak is Mount Olivia.

Temporary Yahgan wigwam.

By courtesy of Dr. Armando Braun Menendez. Photo by the French Scientific Expedition of 1882.

Men and women wore tiny aprons.

From "The Land of Magellan" by courtesy of the author, Mr. William S. Barclay.

Civilization advances.

By courtesy of Dr. Armando Braun Menendez. Photo by the French Scientific Expedition of 1882.

kept up night and day, and if a woman was careless enough to let her fire go out, she would fetch burning embers from a neighbouring wigwam to avoid having to coax another fire into life with *dunda* and fire-stone. Round the wigwam fire, parents and children crowded for warmth and food. Mussels, limpets, fish, crabs, birds and seal were the main diet. Whatever the hour of the day, there was always something cooking over the fire, for these people had no regular meal-times and no name for any special meal. As long as food was available, they ate when they were hungry.

Fires were also kept going in the canoes when these were in use. There was little danger. Sea-water leaked through the seams and kept the interiors of the canoes perpetually damp. The fires were built on little heaps of sand and moist turf in the centre of the canoes. On reaching their night's camping-ground after a day in the canoes the Yahgans would carry embers or blazing torches ashore. When they re-embarked the following morning, or if the women went off for a few hours' fishing, fire was carried back to the canoes. Thus, except when men went hunting and passed the night away from home, it was rarely necessary to kindle a new fire.

There is another interesting point about the fires of the Fuegian Indians. In the numberless sheltered nooks round the shores, at points where canoes could be safely beached, were Yahgan families living in their wigwams. If a distant sail appeared, or anything else occurred to startle those who had remained at home, they would send out a warning to those away fishing by piling green branches or shrubs on the wigwam fire. At the sight of the black signal smoke the fishers would hurry back home. The early explorers of that archipelago would see these countless columns of smoke rising at short intervals for miles along the coast. This is doubtless the reason why they named those regions Tierra del Fuego. It is possible, however, that some tract of grassland on the northern part of the island may have been seen burning.

3

The Ona tribe, as has been mentioned, inhabited the interior of the main island and its northern and eastern coasts. It occasionally happened, however, that some of its members ventured into Yahga-land as far as the eastern end of the Beagle Channel. The only weapons used by the Ona were bows and arrows, and they lived almost entirely on guanaco meat. They clothed themselves in the skins of these animals, and used them also for their shelters. They were as different from the Yahgan and Alacaloof as Redskins from Ancient Britons. The canoe Indians greatly feared this remote, almost legendary tribe, inhabitants of a rugged land of forest and mountain where no white man had ever trod and into which no other Fuegians had penetrated more than the fringes.

It was my destiny to be born at Ushuaia. Even as a child, I was obsessed by a passionate longing to explore those ranges of mountains that hemmed us in and join the wild tribe of which I had heard such fantastic tales from our Yahgan playmates. Later in these pages it shall be told how I achieved that ambition.

CHAPTER FOUR

*My Brother Despard and I are Born at Ushuaia. Yekadahby Comes to Ushuaia.
The Second Allen Gardiner. The Settlement is Cut Off for Nine Months. My
Brother William and my Sisters, Bertha and Alice, are Born. Mr. Whaits is Introduced. The Growth of the Settlement. A Road is Built. The New Village.
Yekadahby Makes Jam. The Edible Berries of Tierra del Fuego. Fuegian Dwellings
and the Rings of Shell and Bone that Form Around Them.*

I

BY THE END OF 1874, THREE YEARS AND TWO MONTHS AFTER MY FATHER
had brought my mother to Ushuaia, the members of the little settlement
had grown in number. Mr. and Mrs. Lewis had gone back to Keppel
with their two small sons, but their places had been taken by the Lawrences, who now had two children. My mother had presented Mary,
now nearly four years old, with a brother. He had been named Thomas
Despard, and had been the first white native of Ushuaia. The second
white native had been the Lawrence's second child, a boy. Three months
after him, on the last day of December, 1874, there came into the world
the third white native of Ushuaia—myself.

Another new and valuable addition to the settlement was Auntie.
She was my mother's sister, Joanna Varder, a sturdy, active, energetic
young woman, the same height as my mother and her junior by several
years. On a certain occasion, some time before Despard was born, there
had been a discussion among the four remaining Misses Varder in the
family home at Harberton in Devonshire, on the subject of Mother's
difficult position. None of the others had seemed eager to go to her
assistance, but Joanna is reported to have said:

" Polly needs help, and if none of *you* want to go to her, *I'm* going ! "

And she had gone. A steamship had taken her to Montevideo, where
she had changed on to a sailing-vessel. This had carried her to the Falklands. After a short stay in those islands she had finished her long journey
from England to Ushuaia in the *Allen Gardiner*, and had arrived at the
settlement before I was born. In spite of my talent for crying and overfeeding, with the usual unhappy results, Auntie seemed to think I belonged to her, and my mother was too wise to undeceive her.

The Yahgan for " aunt on the mother's side " is *yekadahby*, which
means literally, " little mother." It was no wonder, then, that Auntie

Joanna came to be known as Yekadahby.[1] She was, as I have said, a valuable addition to the settlement. She had spent much of her life on my grandfather's farm at Harberton and had become an authority on the preparation of butter, junket, cheese, jam, and strawberries and cream; and an expert at rearing chickens, ducks and geese.

Unlike my mother, Yekadahby was never troubled by sea-sickness, nor was she nervous in a sailing-boat, whatever the weather—as long as my father was at the helm.

2

The little schooner, *Allen Gardiner*, had done grand service for many years, but her running costs were high, and eventually she had to give place to a smaller vessel, more in keeping with the slender means of the South American Missionary Society. So, seven months before I was born, she made her last trip as Mission vessel from Ushuaia. On her arrival in the Falklands she was sold. Her new owners renamed her *Letitia* and, so that the name of a brave man should be perpetuated, her successor became the *Allen Gardiner*.

The new *Allen Gardiner* was a North Sea fishing-yawl of forty-one tons burden. She was purchased in England by the Society, and soon afterwards set sail for Tierra del Fuego under the command of Captain Willis. He was a broad and sturdy little man, barely more than five feet tall, with a bristly brown beard and moustache, both trimmed in a fashion that was all his own. His eyes had a merry twinkle, and his fund of good stories made him a great favourite with children. The mere sight of him would make them laugh in anticipation, and his mischievous wink intimated that he understood and fully sympathized with their struggle against the tyranny of grown-ups.

Despite her diminutive size, the new *Allen Gardiner* was a splendid sea-boat. She made good going on her long journey south. When large ships passed her, their crews would hurl at her such insulting remarks as :

" Does your mother know you're out? "

I am sure that Captain Willis and Charlie Gibbert, the one-eyed mate, were not slow in flinging back appropriate replies.

[1] This name was used only amongst ourselves. I forget what the Yahgans called her. Father and Mother were known as Tanuwa and Tanuwakeepa, terms of respect used generally, but not necessarily, for old people. We brothers were known collectively as Tushcapalanjiz or Ushuaianjiz. Doubtless we had individual names, but I do not know them. Father was nicknamed Dogfish, perhaps for his sharp nose, and Mother was referred to as Shiny Face, a characteristic that was considered beautiful.

This exchange of vessels caused the settlement at Ushuaia to be cut off from the outside world for longer than ever before. There had been times when it had been five, six, even seven months; on this occasion it was nine. Anticipating that there would be some delay, and not wishing to incur the expense of specially chartering a vessel, my father had given instructions to the captain of the first *Allen Gardiner*, before she had left Ushuaia on her last trip as Mission vessel, that, even if the yawl was delayed in her arrival at the Falklands, no other ship was to be chartered to wait on Ushuaia for ten months.

Time went by. Then on the 19th March, 1875, nine months after the departure of the schooner, my father wrote in his diary:

" At 5 p.m. on the 15th we were electrified by the announcement that a ship had been sighted. Daily, for five weeks, we had been expecting the new *Allen Gardiner*, and some of us were growing anxious for her safety. We have not been in want or any trouble through the long space of nine months since the *Gardiner* left us . . ."

But this ship coming over the horizon was not the North Sea fishing-yawl; it was the *Letitia*, the old, original *Allen Gardiner*. The good people on the Falklands, worried by the non-arrival of the yawl, and fearing for the safety of their friends at Ushuaia, had gone against my father's instructions and sent off the schooner to their aid. Perhaps it was as well that they had. Nine months is a long time.

The yawl did at length reach the Falklands, and began to make regular trips between there and Ushuaia with the doughty Captain Willis. It was to be fully twenty years before that efficient, sunny-tempered little sailor gave up his task of maintaining contact between Tierra del Fuego's white settlers and the outside world.

3

My mother had three more children after me. The first was William Samuel, who was born when I was eighteen months old. He was followed by Bertha two and a half years later, and three years after that, Alice arrived. She was a real Devonian, the fairest of us all, and the only one with Mother's blue-grey eyes.

Will, as a child, was small, compact and full of mischief—a contrast to my own more timorous character and my tendency, in growth, to run to seed. When baby Bertha was added to the family, a wheelbarrow took the place of a perambulator and, as we were allowed a great deal of free-dom in our wanderings, Bertha had many adventures in it. It was a wonder the child came through it alive. By the time Alice took her turn as passenger the charioteers had grown stronger and wilder, and Alice's survival remains an even greater mystery.

Meanwhile, the Ushuaia settlement was growing. It was, in fact, assuming the proportions of a village. This expansion was largely due to the efforts of one man. His name was Robert Whaits. He joined the Mission with his wife and young daughter when I was about a year old. He stood some five and a half feet tall and had kindly grey eyes and greying hair and beard. As well as being an earnest Christian and greatly valued by my father for his companionship, he was a hard and conscientious worker, a skilled carpenter, wheelwright and blacksmith. Before long he had Yahgans working with two or three pit-saws in the forest across the harbour, preparing timber for the new village.

With a great deal of labour, a road was constructed by my father with a gang of the less civilized natives. It ran up from the shore and through the centre of the village, which was perched on the summit of the hill. On the right-hand side of this road, as one walked up from the beach, were built several houses of corrugated iron lined with wood. The first that one came to was occupied by Mr. and Mrs. Lawrence and their children when Stirling House became too small for the two increasing families. Eighty yards farther along was Stirling House, and about the same distance beyond that was the building known as the orphanage. This home for parentless Yahgan children was in the care of Mr. and Mrs. Whaits. Farther on still was Stirling Cottage, which in those days also served as church, meeting-house and schoolroom. It was not until later years that this was replaced by a larger church with two or three rooms for a catechist at one end of it. The faithful, silent Resyck had left Ushuaia shortly after my mother's arrival there. Beyond these residences were a cowshed and yard, outhouses and wood-sheds. Near the orphanage was a carpenter's shop with a forge adjoining. As my brothers and I grew from infancy into boyhood that forge of Mr. Whaits' held a great fascination for us. We loved to watch the sparks and listen to the little ornamental tap that followed the heavier blows of his hammer. But what we admired above all were his trousers. When at work he always wore some kind of corduroy or fustian trousers which, apart from their delicate clothy odour, made a whisking sound as one leg swished past the other when the wearer walked briskly, as Mr. Whaits always did. However hard we tried, my brothers and I could not achieve that " frou-frou, frou-frou " of his. I remember our joy when my mother, learning no doubt how well the material lasted, procured some of it and, with the help of Yakadahby and a sewing-machine, made corduroy trousers for the three of us. When we found that, after a little practice, we could "frou-frou" as impressively as Mr. Whaits, we all felt very grown-up and important.

On the other side of the village street was a row of Yahgan huts built by the natives under the supervision of Mr. Whaits. There were also two or three model cottages, in which lived the most civilized of our Ushuaia natives. They had roofs of shingle or corrugated iron, and glazed windows. Each had its own little fenced kitchen garden; and some of the residents had even flanked their front doors with beds of flowers.

All the gardens in the settlement were fenced, not so much as a protection against attack as to keep out the cattle. Stirling House had a good kitchen garden at the rear, whilst in front were thriving flowers and fruit-bushes. Some years we would get a fair crop of potatoes; at other times early frosts would cut down the plants when they were in flower. Swedes, turnips, carrots, cabbage, lettuce and cauliflower did well, but we could get very little produce from the garden before midsummer. For fruit we had strawberries, currants, gooseberries and raspberries, all imported by the Mission. Our great stand-by was rhubarb, which did very well indeed.

Yekadahby was kept busy when the jam-making season came round. Such produce as was not suitable for jam she would turn into pickles to last us throughout the long winter and spring, when the garden produced nothing. Besides cultivated fruits, there were wild berries to be had from the surrounding country-side.

There are several kinds of edible berries in Tierra del Fuego, but only two of them are used for the table. The first is the more abundant. Strongly resembling a grape in taste, it has little juice by comparison, being full of hard seeds. It is larger than a big blackcurrant and is of a dark blue colour. The Yahgans called it *umushamaim* (*umush*—thorn-bush, *amaim*—berry); my father refers to it in his journal as the sweet barberry. It grows on a thorny bush (*Berberis buxifolia*), one of the four shrubs of the genus *Berberis* in Tierra del Fuego.

We children used to enjoy our barberry-picking excursion with Yekadahby. Besides eating off the bushes till our faces were purple with the juice, we gathered ample supplies for puddings, jelly and wine. I shall never forget those wonderful boiled barberry puddings we used to eat with cream, or the scent of the bushes in blossom-time, when the flowers looked like small yellow roses.

The other table berry is the wild strawberry, which is not to be confused with the wild strawberry that is found in great abundance in the Andean regions of Patagonia and southern Chile. The Fuegian variety is called by the Yahgans *belacamaim* (rain berry). These berries are plentiful in certain places, but only for a short season. They look like small raspberries, having little lumps all over them, which give each fruit the appearance of a cluster of tiny berries glued together. They grow buried in tree-mould or moss, and are easy to overlook; one can walk over a bed of them without knowing it. The little stalk on which the berries grow forms a loop, and the green star which protects them is generally level with the moss, with the fruit below the surface of it. The stalk bends over as the fruit develops, for the flower looks bravely up towards the sun. These wild strawberries are delicious with sugar and cream, or eaten where they grow, but in that district are seldom plentiful enough to be collected for making jam.

There are other wild berries besides these two table varieties. There is the wild blackcurrant. It tastes very good, but it is unwise to eat too large a quantity, for it is strongly laxative. The bush when in flower has a scent as delicious as the barberry. Since the larger bushes never produce any berries, it is to be concluded that they are the males of the species. Another is the *sepisa*, the smallest of Tierra del Fuego's edible berries. It is known in the Falklands as " diddy-dee," and grows close to the ground in such masses that the berries can be collected by the handful and buckets rapidly filled. In the season at Ushuaia we used to gather them for the domestic geese and chickens, though the chickens did not much care for them. There must be two or more species of *sepisa*; some of the berries are bright red, others nearly black. Then there is the white *shanamaim* (swamp berry). It has scarcely any plant, and grows, like the wild strawberry, half buried in moss, but, unlike the wild strawberry, it is to be found only in swamps.

The last of the berries to be mentioned here is the *goosh*. Sir Francis Drake's chronicler refers to " a kind of wild grape," which members of the expedition enjoyed when they discovered Cape Horn. Undoubtedly this fruit was the *goosh*, which grows abundantly on those outer islands and is at its best in spring, the season when those adventurers landed on that island and claimed it for Queen Elizabeth. The *goosh*, usually a deep red, grows on a bush that sometimes reaches a height of five feet. On exposed rocky hilltops these berries may be found in great profusion, though in such places the bushes are stunted. Like the *shanamaim*, the *goosh* has a somewhat spongy texture and enough air space within to save it from bursting in the winter frosts.

When my early days in Tierra del Fuego had long been left behind, I saw in the rock garden at the Chelsea Flower Show in London some *goosh* bushes bearing fruit. The man in charge told me that they were *pernettya* from the Magellan Straits and were highly poisonous. I thanked him for the information and, with his permission, collected several of the fallen berries. Then, under his horrified gaze, I ate them and departed. He must have scanned the newspapers for days afterwards in search of the report of my death.

The *goosh*, the *shanamaim* and the *sepisa* were much valued as food by the Yahgans. In the season it was a common sight at Ushuaia to see large baskets filled with them in the cottages of the more civilized and the wigwams of their primitive brothers at the eastern end of the village.

It is a strange fact that, even in Ushuaia, the inhabitants had followed, however unintentionally, what is said to be a general rule—that the wealth and luxury of a town spread westward, while poverty is to be found in its eastern quarters. The eastern and north-eastern slums of Ushuaia were made up of wigwams, each in its own hollow in the ground. This hollow gave some natural protection, which was assisted by the wigwam's most inadequate roof of branches, turf and grass. With every change of wind, the ever-open doorway would be shifted round to the lee side of this humble dwelling. All refuse, such as mussel and limpet shells, bones and so on, would be thrown out close to the door, and in time a protecting rim, many feet in height, would form round the hollow. Kindly Nature would then step in. Wild currant-bushes, followed by the slower-growing thorn-bush and other shrubs, would take root in this circular rubbish-heap, and flourish exceedingly. A tall, broad-leafed perennial grass, rightly called *ucurhshuca* (house-grass) by the Yahgans, for it grows only in these places, would come to lend a hand, forming picturesque screens round these unsightly hovels.

As time goes by, the work of man and Nature leaves its mark indelibly on the land. Along the Fuegian coast in centuries to come the site of many a simple prehistoric village will still be as clear as Stonehenge, for there will remain ring after ring of shell and bone, often eight feet above the hollows they surround, to show where generation after generation of Yahgans once had their homes.

Porous land, when such could be found, was generally chosen for the village site, so the hollows seldom held water, unless heavy rain had fallen on frozen ground.

During recent years an American archaeologist, Mr. Junius Bird, excavated certain village sites. At considerable depths he found stone tools and weapons inferior to those used by the natives of our time. He drew the conclusion that he had delved a thousand years into the past and that during that period even those primitive tribes had been advancing, slowly but unmistakably, in knowledge.

CHAPTER FIVE

Perilous Days and Nights. Quarrels Among the Natives. Hatushwaianjiz is Murdered by Cowilij. Hatushwaianjiz's Friends Seek Retribution. My Father is Threatened with a Spear. Tom Post is Prevented from Committing Murder. Harrapuwaian Plots to Take Father's Life. Henry Lory Fights at a Disadvantage. Ritualistic Ceremony for the Settling of Differences. My Father Tries to Prevent Bloodshed and my Mother Goes Through some Terrifying Moments. Usiagu Steals a Knife. Meekungaze Seeks Raspberry Vinegar. The Reappearance of Fuegia Basket.

I

OF THE ORIGIN AND DEVELOPMENT OF THE USHUAIA MISSION, MY FATHER said, in lectures delivered many years afterwards:

" The language of these natives was learned [at Keppel Island] and reduced to writing; the natives were instructed in Christian knowledge and the arts of civilized life, with the happiest success, by divers employees of the same Mission; and being thus prepared by some five years of constant intercourse with these people in repeated visits to their country in the Mission schooner, and by having taken some sixty of them for a longer or shorter stay to the Mission station in the Falklands, we considered it safe and wise to begin to live amongst them in their own country: thus aiming to develop the work among them more rapidly. Our Superintendent, now Bishop Stirling, was the brave man to do this and he made it alone; and lived six months with the natives in comparative peace; daily instructing them, and organizing various employments. It then fell to my lot to resume the work from which I had been called home for a space of nine months. Since then, the year 1869, these natives have been quietly progressing in knowledge and the arts and good manners of civilized life, treating us with respect and conducting themselves exceedingly well. The powerful lever that did this was knowledge brought to their minds by means of their mother tongue and also the extensive employment of the people in various works of creating a civilized settlement . . . "

During his fifteen years in charge of the Mission at Ushuaia, my father was the leading figure, the judge and law-giver. When reading his diary, or the reports of his lectures, one would imagine that nothing worth calling an adventure had ever happened to him, yet there were times when his own life, the lives of his dear ones or the safety of the settlement were in danger. Many stormy nights he spent in an open boat among those islands; and many times he had to risk everything in his attempts to reprove and thwart the most turbulent evil-doers.

For my mother those were anxious years. I can imagine how she must have felt when fierce quarrels broke out among the Indians, and Father went off, alone and unarmed, in the hope, not always fulfilled, of preventing bloodshed. I can imagine, too, her fears when he was at sea in an open boat—in later years accompanied by one or more of their sons—while she sat listening on some stormy night to the fierce gusts of wind tearing at the house, and prayed for the travellers who were long overdue. Hers must have been the harder part, waiting helplessly, and hiding from others whatever fears she felt.

These boat-trips of my father's sometimes kept him away for ten days at a time. They were seldom plain sailing. Fine weather in those latitudes rarely lasts long, and squalls and rain sweep down from the mountains with little or no warning. Even before I was eight years old, he sometimes took me with him. If the weather was abnormally cold I would be thrust into a sack partly filled with dry grass or straw. This was tied under my armpits, and gave surprising protection, except when it got sodden with spray or rain. I remember more than once being out all night, wet and cold, and feeling very sorry for myself. Beating up the Beagle Channel, the boat would seem tiny and the water dark and merciless. I would look over the windward rail at the phosphorescent white of a breaking wave and feel a chill of dread lest it should swamp our little craft. But I should have disliked even more to have been left behind in Ushuaia.

My sole comfort was the presence of my father. Though he had a reputation for recklessness, and even the Yahgan crew sometimes refused to go out with him, his calm nearness always allayed my fears. I think he was never happier than when steering a sailing-boat with the crew lying along in the windward bilge for ballast, and the lee rail nearly level with the water. At such times, with his hand on the tiller, he would start singing for sheer joy. When the weather was specially nasty he favoured " Glide Along, my Bonny, Bonny Boat " or such hymns as " Fair Waved the Golden Corn " and " Yes, God is Good in Earth and Sky."

2

Those were the perils of the sea. The land, too, held its hazards.

The frequent quarrels amongst the Yahgans started generally with suspicion, slander, jealousy over women, or stealing from buried supplies of whale-blubber. A sharp word to someone else's child might bring some long-standing grievance to a head. Angry shouts from their wigwams would bring the opponents to their doors, where the most outrageous threats and insults would be exchanged, the hysterical actors frequently stamping and choking in their rage. Sometimes the excited parties approached each other brandishing sticks or furiously flinging stones, usually without aim, simply to show the other how angry and strong they were. When honour was thus satisfied they could retire exhausted to the bosom of their families to listen, maybe, to flattering remarks on the way they had routed the enemy.

At other times the encounter was more serious. Sticks and stones would be used in earnest and the fight would become general. Frequently many were injured in these party struggles, sometimes fatally. Between individuals savage fights would be fought, either with the bare hands, or with one or both of them holding a rough stone, not to throw, but to strike with. It was not uncommon for a strong savage to twist his enemy's neck or injure his spine with fatal results. In such cases the victor was very often rough-handled by his people, in anticipation of the trouble his action was sure to bring from the victim's community.

An extract from a letter written by my father a short time after Mother's arrival in Ushuaia gives a good picture of such an incident and throws, in addition, a sidelight on Yahgan social customs.

" In the morning," wrote Father, " when all were in a hurry to *mukka*,[1] Hatushwaianjiz [Man Born in Bone Harbour] was in Cowilij's wigwam, cooking and eating some mussels; Cowilij, who was jealous on account of his young wife, suddenly seized the lad and, as is the usual practice here, bent back his head, with apparent intent to break his neck. The lad told me that Cowilij had hurt him, but I little guessed the extent of his injury. The lad had been hurt in the neck and chest, but we did not expect him to die, which he did early on the twentieth of March, in spite of the kindness shown him by those who were in the wigwam with him. . . .

" Cowilij returned with the rest of the whalers on March 21st, and escaped into the woods when he heard of what had taken place. . . . It seems that before Cowilij made his escape, Hatushwaianjiz's mother arrived . . . and together with her [younger] son gave the murderer a good beating. Cowilij escaped alone, his two wives—one aged about sixty and the other seventeen—remained behind. He, however, presented himself the same day, and had to make distribution of his blubber. . . .

" On April the 8th sixteen canoes arrived prepared to avenge the death of Hatushwaianjiz. I was asked to speak to the people, which I promised to do; and accordingly, when they landed went to meet them, to explain matters and restrain them from injuring innocent persons. [Cowilij had taken to the woods again.]

" Every native who felt it was possible for him to become involved in the affray presented him or herself armed with a paddle, a stout stick, or other weapons, such as spears, stones and slings. On landing, the men and women from the canoes lost no time, but went straight towards the wigwams, where they met those who, being connections or relatives of Cowilij, were, according to Fuegian usage, exposed to the revenge of the avengers.

---

[1] The act of going by canoe to fetch whale-blubber. The Fuegians obtained nearly all their supplies of whale-meat and blubber from stranded whales, which had either drifted ashore after falling victim to killer whales in deep water, or had been stranded in their desperate efforts to escape those fierce creatures. My father heard of only one occasion when the Yahgans actually did a whale to death. A whole fleet of canoes was used, and the attack lasted over twenty-four hours.

"The two parties were known to each other by their painted faces, the avengers having their faces covered with white spots on a black ground, the others, white bands across the face on a red ground. . . . I intercepted them and laid hold of the arm of the foremost one. They listened a very short time whilst I told them that only one was guilty and he was away, and that, as the lad's death happened long after the injury was given and he had been kindly treated by all who were here, they should not injure innocent persons. Then they hurried on to where they saw the natives met ready to receive them. About six of them, the principal actors, had large round stones in their hands. Meakol, being the son of Cowilij's sister, was, in his absence, the chief object of their attention. He separated from the other natives and presented himself. The avengers made straight for him and threw the stones on this or that side of him, he avoiding them by his agility, leaping about with his hands placed against his ears. The stones thrown, the two parties joined, the avengers threatening, the others bearing their threats, but always ready to defend themselves if need be. Three persons were slightly hurt, and with a great deal of fuss and pretence the affair passed over, much to our comfort. . . .

"Gifts were angrily demanded, and in order to appease the avengers, the others, but especially Meakol, were obliged to relinquish everything that was coveted and seized as a right.

"The matter as regards the others was over, but Cowilij, for years after, if ever he had happened to fall in with any near relative of the murdered lad, would have been subjected to violence, though his life would have been spared."

When things had quietened down, and some of the visiting canoes had left, my father declared the rest of the day a half-holiday for the workers at the settlement. On the following day, though some of the visitors still remained, he felt it was safe to leave the settlement and go across the harbour into the forest with the wood-cutters.

But more trouble was on the way. A second party of avengers—this time from the murdered boy's native place—was reported heading by land for Ushuaia. My father threw aside his work and went out to meet them with a few of the settlement Yahgans. When he came face to face with the advancing party of angry natives, one of them rushed at him with spear raised and made a violent thrust at his chest. The point did no more than touch his body, and was probably intended to intimidate him and stop him from interfering. Father, however, stood his ground, and matters threatened to take an ugly turn. Fortunately, one of the Ushuaia Indians, who was in no way related to the murderer's family, persuaded the avengers, at some risk to himself, to abandon their projected attack.

It was in the forest across the harbour that my father nearly lost his life on another occasion. He had at that time a Newfoundland dog that was always his close companion. One of the wood-cutters was a powerful fellow nicknamed Tom Post, mentioned frequently in my father's journal. He was a man of violent temper and frequent fights. Exceedingly disinclined to work, he was not content with doing little himself, but enjoyed obstructing the others. On the occasion in question my father rebuked him sternly, and had just turned away from him when the dog sprang at Tom Post. Father indignantly dragged the dog off the Indian and cuffed him soundly. Later the other workers said to him:

" You did wrong to be angry with your dog. Tom Post was going to kill you with his axe."

Tom Post was not the only Indian at the settlement with notions about axe-murders. Harrapuwaian was ugly, strong and quarrelsome, even for a Yahgan. He added another wife, stolen from a man who feared him, to those he already possessed. My father took him to task and, backed by the general opinion of the natives, forced him to relinquish his last acquisition.

Harrapuwaian was furious and plotted revenge. His plan leaked out, and Father was informed that he intended to come to the front door, under the pretext of asking for a biscuit, and, when Father turned to fetch it, pull out a hatchet from his otter-skin covering and hit him a deadly blow on the head.

Father, with his usual optimism, doubted this story, thinking his informant might have a grudge against the accused, or that Harrapuwaian had been merely boasting of the things he would like to do. But his doubts were abruptly dispelled when Harrapuwaian duly presented himself at the front door and asked for a biscuit.

Instead of turning back into the house, my father made a grab at Harrapuwaian's wrist and demanded:

" Why do you come here with a hatchet? Give it to me."

Without a word Harrapuwaian handed it over. It had been specially sharpened for the deed. After talking for a while with the Indian, Father returned it to him, telling him that when he came visiting in future he had better leave it at home.

3

Unlike the Ona beyond the mountains, the Yahgans disapproved of homicide. The epithet *walapatuj* (murderer) was an insult amongst them. A Yahgan might kill his opponent during a quarrel, but deliberately planned murder was rare. I recall only one case—that of an Indian who cut the thong on which his companion's life depended when they were bird-hunting together, and caused him to crash to the foot of the cliff. This crime, it was said, was committed in order to get the victim's wife. The accused, an exceptionally powerful Indian, happened to be named Sassan, which sounds rather like " assassin."

Fighting between angry men, even when more or less civilized, can hardly be carried on with perfect fairness, and certainly the first fight I ever witnessed between two Yahgans was no example of sportsmanship.

We boys were playing on the roof of an outhouse when our attention was attracted by two natives across the road. One of them was Lory (baptized Henry), a friend of ours, to whom I shall refer again later. After a vociferous shouting match, the two men began belabouring each other with sticks. Lory soon began to bleed; his adversary's stick had a sharp nail driven through it, with the point sticking well out on the other side. An excited crowd gathered round the pair. Lory rapidly became a dreadfully slashed and gory spectacle.

Then Father appeared on the scene. A squadron of police could not have quelled the uproar more quickly. He ordered the angry men to desist and berated both warriors, but especially the one who had used the nail. Then he turned his scorn on the onlookers for not having stopped the unequal combat. It is possible, though, that if they had attempted to intervene, they would have taken sides and the *mêlée* would have become general.

That was a personal, unrehearsed skirmish. The Yahgans usually had a more ceremonious way of settling their differences; an age-old ritual. There is an account of such a formal reckoning of scores in my father's journal of Saturday, 2nd May, 1874. Apparently there had been an accident involving a member of a neighbouring community, and it was suspected that responsibility lay with one or another of the Ushuaia Indians.

" A calm, cold day; frost last night," wrote my father. " To-day seventeen canoes arrived, with people from many places. There was a little commotion made by the newcomers on landing, which was feared by some would prove serious. I must describe it. Last night, unknown to any of the people here, the above arrived and put up at Hamacoalikirh.[1] Some of the people here heard the voices of many *shadatoo*, i.e., a loud tremulous shouting, as is the manner of those who have blood to avenge. Not knowing what might have occurred elsewhere, and who might unhappily find themselves deeply concerned, many were anxious. However, before the people landed here this morning, we learned from a fishing canoe which came in before them, that there was nothing serious to fear.

" The canoes kept together and the men landed, all disguised with paint and charcoal, so that I could not readily recognize many whom I knew well. The women and children remained in the canoes, put out a little from the shore, and moved very slowly forward. The men came along, many armed with clubs. One man, Lasapowloom [or Lasapa], a vigorous, active young fellow, acted the champion and challenger, and stood prominently forward to meet the foremost and most excited

---

[1] The point of the peninsula separating Ushuaia harbour from the Beagle Channel. By itself " ikirh " has no meaning, but as an affix it means a point or headland.

of the opposite party. Like the man who confronted him, he had a broad band of white from his chin downward, and his head was bound with the skin of a kelp gander with the white down on it, and his hair was also whitened. He had a white stone in either hand. His antagonist, who came leaping along making much noise, was armed with a club. He kept on demanding that *Iacasi* [1] would let him kill someone, as though he thirsted for blood. He held his club ready to use and they both spoke excitedly and loudly to each other. Presently, Lasapa threw one of his stones a full yard behind his opponent's back, and ran after his stone to pick it up again. Looking to where I heard much noise, I saw two other highly painted fellows engaged in loud vociferations and earnest gestures, each with an arm round the other's neck, and bobbing their heads each to the other. The rest stood quietly looking on, and presently the people dispersed to the various quarters to which they had been invited meanwhile.

"I was highly amused," concluded Father, "to hear that Lasapa, acting the part he did, was, according to custom, called *Towwora*, or ' Storm of Wind '; the man who met him was called *Tumutowwora*, or the one who ' invites the storm to rage against him '."

But the exacting of vengeance was not always a masquerade. A party of natives had their wigwams at a place called Ushaij, over two miles from the Mission station, across low hills covered with grass and bushes. The place was situated near the south-western side of the peninsula, close to the beach facing the Beagle Channel. A member of another community was killed at Ushaij, and our natives, deservedly or not, were blamed for his death. A message reached Father that the expected fleet of canoes was approaching from the west and south, on no friendly errand. An armed party of Yahgans had already set out from Ushuaia to engage the attackers. Father hastened after them in the hope of preventing bloodshed.

Hour after hour passed and he did not return. At last my mother could bear the anxiety no longer. Taking a revolver, which she greatly feared and had never fired, she commended the children to the care of Yekadahby and the Lawrences, and started out into the gathering dusk. About three-quarters of a mile from the Mission there was a huge rock near the footpath. Just as she had got past it she saw a party of natives approaching. They were howling as they do for the dead and, by the light of their primitive torches, she saw that they were carrying a corpse.

She feared the worst, and her knees refused to support her any more. But one of the mourners, a Yahgan named John Marsh (probably after some benefactor in England), who had been to the Falklands and spoke

---

[1] A collective word for seals, penguins, mollymauks and other sea-birds, and deep-water fish, which came in the autumn in pursuit of the vast schools of sprats. A time of superabundance for the natives. The arrival of *Iacasi* was as welcome as a harvest festival and might last two months.

English after a fashion, hurried forward to meet her with the reassuring words :

" Him no kill, Ma'am. Him come to-morrow."

He handed her a leaf torn from Father's pocket-book. The note, which she read by the light of a torch, told her not to worry; that he had resolved to remain where he was for the night, as he feared fighting would break out again if he came away.

The mourners were some of our own natives from Ushuaia, returning to the settlement with one of their number, who had had his neck broken in a savage struggle with one of the attackers. Greatly relieved by my father's note, Mother followed them back to Ushuaia.

4

As time went by and the settlement increased, not only in size, but also in the scope of its activities, signs of the Mission's moral effect on the Indians began to become increasingly apparent. There were frequent cases of confession and genuine repentance. These were not due to fear of punishment in this world or the next. The Yahgans lived for the day, taking no thought for the morrow, much less for something that might happen to them after they were dead. Father never used threats of horrible torments awaiting them in a future life, in order to frighten sinners into the fold, nor did he pet and praise them unduly, much less give them any reward for acts of confession or repentance.

Yet these gestures of humility occurred. A certain Iaminaze came from afar to return a saucepan that he had stolen. Who knows what mental struggles had kept this rascal awake at night before he made up his mind to get into his canoe and make a trip of several days in order to return his treasure?

Then there was Usiagu, who stole a knife. Of him my father wrote in his journal :

" On Friday evening immediately after tea I went down to visit the different Indians living on the shore, who were known by the term Paiakoala (Beach People), a name given to those who came and went, as distinct from the more respectable who were settled and had gardens. I went into Usiagu's wigwam last of all. One of his three wives had some fish for me which I asked Usiagu to bring up to the house, so after some very friendly conversation we came up at 8.30 p.m. I left him in the kitchen till I could bring a light. I came to him as soon as I could, gave him some biscuit for his fish and sent him away. I had occasion to use the knife shortly after and could not find it."

A day or two later came the sequel. He wrote :

". . . Usiagu came to the door saying he had a dreadful pain in his stomach. I let him in, and immediately he began to retch most violently. Before I could pass him

· to get a light he gave me my knife which he stole last Friday evening. He pretended to have vomited it up, which of course I would not credit. However, when he came to the kitchen I saw that the violent retching had brought great profusion of tears which had run down his face."

This incident happened while my mother was still in the Falklands and Father was living alone in the unfinished Stirling House, with Jacob Resyck the only other civilized man in the country. There was another incident during that period. It concerned Lukka, one of the four first settlers at Laiwaia. He now had a wife and family, and was a frequent visitor to Ushuaia. He quarrelled violently outside Stirling House with another Indian named Meekungaze, and the two of them began to fight. Father came between them and, getting Lukka into his room, kept Meekungaze from him. Meekungaze was furious, and would not listen to reason, but behaved like a madman. On the following day, however, he came to make his peace with Father. His baby was unwell, and he begged anxiously for medicine. Father gave him a little sweetened raspberry vinegar, and he went away delighted. The baby, of course, recovered.

5

It will be remembered that forty years before the Ushuaia Mission came into being Captain FitzRoy had given four young Fuegians a holiday in England. One of them had died, but three of them had been brought back to Tierra del Fuego—York Minster and Fuegia Basket, who had been married at Wulaia, and the rascally Jimmy Button.

There is a postscript to that episode.

A party of Yahgans from the outer coast between the South-West Arm and Brecknock Peninsula paid Ushuaia a visit. These Alisimoonoala, as people from that desolate, stormy land were called, looked down —with some reason, perhaps—on the Wiisinoala (Creek People) from the more sheltered waters, for they considered them wanting in hardihood and inferior to themselves in vigour and strength.

Among this wild-looking party was none other than Fuegia Basket. It was my father's first meeting with her. He found her strong and well; short, thickset and with many teeth missing from a mouth that was large even for a Fuegian. When he tried sounding her memory, she recollected London and Miss Jenkins, whose special charge she had been. She also retained memories of Captain FitzRoy and the good ship *Beagle*, and recalled such words as "knife," "fork" and "beads." When my mother showed her her two children, Mary and Despard, she seemed greatly pleased, and said, "Little boy, little gal." All else she appeared to have forgotten, including the art of sitting on a chair, for when offered one she squatted beside it on the floor.

When Father talked to her in Yahgan, he learnt that her husband, York Minster, had been killed in retaliation for the murder of a man; and that the youth of eighteen by whom she was then accompanied was her present husband. She herself was over fifty years of age. The discrepancy in ages was quite usual among the Yahgans, who considered it correct and advisable. It enabled the older men to add desirable damsels to their own households; and the younger men to have in their homes elderly women of vast experience to attend to their needs, give them good advice, handle their canoes and assist them in many ways beyond the capabilities of a mere child of marriageable age.

When she had been in England she had received religious training, but now, though Father did his utmost to revive her memory, all recollection of it had faded entirely from her mind.

She had spent much time with the Alacaloof, and spoke their language as well as she did her own native Yahgan. Probably she had not heard a word of English since she had landed at Wulaia and become York Minster's bride. By the time of Father's meeting with her, her two children by York Minster were grown up. She was pining for them and, the call of home being too strong for her Alisimoonoala companions, they left Ushuaia after a week's stay and went back to their own country.

It was to be ten years before my father met Fuegia Basket again. On the 19th February, 1883, when on an expedition to the west, he learnt of her whereabouts from some natives on London Island. He went to see her. She was then about sixty-two years of age, and nearing her end. He found her in a very weak condition and an unhappy state of mind, and did his best to cheer her with the beautiful Biblical promises in which he himself so firmly believed.

Finally he left her, satisfied that she would be well cared for. Besides her daughter, who attended her closely, she was back again amongst her own people. She had two brothers with children of their own, would lack for nothing that their circumstances could provide and was unlikely to fall victim to *Tabacana*. This was a custom sometimes resorted to in those latitudes: hastening the end of aged relatives by strangulation. The natives had recourse to it only in cases of long-continued insensibility and utter weakness preceding death. *Tabacana* was kindly meant; it was carried out openly and with the approval of all except the victim, who was too inanimate to do anything about it.

CHAPTER SIX

Yahgans Give Presents and Receive Rewards for Services Done. The Wreck of the San Rafael.

GENEROUS PEOPLE IN ENGLAND USED REGULARLY TO SEND LARGE CON-
signments of clothing for distribution amongst the natives. These
articles were generally somewhat shop-soiled, and many of them, particularly shoes with high heels and flimsy garments intended for ladies
with slender waists, were of no use to the sturdily built Yahgan women.
There was, nevertheless, a great deal of useful clothing in these shipments.
This was distributed at stated times amongst the natives, who on such
occasions assembled in great numbers at Ushuaia.[1]

Despite the efforts of Mother and the other ladies of the Mission to
make the clothes fit, some extraordinary fashions must have appeared in
the neighbourhood. One would think our good ladies would have had
enough to do in attending to the needs of their husbands and children,
without holding continuous "Mothers' Meetings" with the Yahgan
women, whom they taught to sew, knit and darn.

One of these women was taken ill, and during one of Mother's visits
to her shortly before her death she produced from the poor mound of
odds and ends that served her as a pillow a treasure which it was evident
she greatly prized. It was a little bag filled with buttons of all colours and
sizes, doubtless collected in the course of years and kept with miserly care.
These buttons she gave to Mother as if bestowing something she could
not take on her last journey. The pathos of this act touched Mother, and
I remember many years later being shown the little bag and its contents.

Another example of Yahgan generosity, without any idea of reward,
was the sending by James Cushinjiz of presents for the ladies on Keppel
Island.

The motive for giving gifts to the Fuegians was not entirely philan-
thropic. Frequently they were sent out from England for distribution
among some special group of natives as a reward for services rendered to
shipwrecked crews.

[1] It is of interest to put on record that a fine lawn grass, not indigenous to the country,
made its appearance and spread rapidly around the Yahgan settlements. Father was
strongly of the opinion that the seed had been brought adhering to the soles of used
tennis shoes.

85

One of my earliest recollections is of some boxes. They appeared huge to me and contained hatchets, knives, fish-hooks and some great slabs of Navy cocoa. How well I remember Father using a saw to divide the blocks of cocoa, and with what enthusiasm we youngsters collected and ate the delicious sawdust!

Father summoned a gathering of the Yahgans and distributed these gifts to those who had brought news of a shipwreck, at the same time exhorting the others to do all they could to assist distressed mariners. He told them that these sailors had powerful friends who not only sent such rich gifts from their far-off land in gratitude for assistance given, but were also able to send an expedition of a very different kind if any of the Indians ever behaved badly towards shipwrecked crews. The Yahgans welcomed the hatchets and knives, but would not use the fish-hooks. They had their own methods for catching fish.

That the Yahgans could give useful help is shown by the following incident, which is retold here with the aid of my father's correspondence on the matter.

On the 4th January, 1876, the San Rafael, a sailing-vessel bound from Liverpool to Valparaiso with coal, caught fire and was abandoned to the south-west of Cape Horn. The crew took to the two boats, which lost touch with each other during the first night. Twenty-seven days later the mate's boat with eleven survivors was picked up by a New Zealand vessel bound for England. They had suffered greatly, and one man had died of exposure. The boat carrying the master, Captain James McAdam, with his wife and eight men, found her way to Rous Peninsula on the south-west coast of Hoste Island, not far from False Cape Horn.

Here are some extracts from the report my father sent to the Governor of the Falkland Islands, and which was later published in London. It was written on the 22nd May, 1876, on board the Allen Gardiner on her return voyage from the scene which he describes.

"On April 22nd a large party of Indians reached Ushuaia from New Year's Sound. They brought news of the death of nine men and a woman by starvation on an exposed part of the coast. . . . They brought proof of their statements in the clothing they wore, and an English sovereign they offered for sale. The report was briefly as follows: An Indian, Cushooyif, from his canoe had seen signs of the presence of strangers on a rugged islet. Being unaccompanied by any to help him, save his wife, he was afraid to land or even approach near, but went eastward in search of helpers.

"After some time a small number in one or two canoes approached. The men landed and walked up, and found a shipwrecked party with only two men still living, but very weak, rigid in limb, emaciated and unable to walk or stand. The natives were affected to tears, and lit a fire for the two sufferers, one of whom was stronger than his companion and still retained his senses. The Indians fetched them water and gave them a shag [sea-bird] and left them. The poor men had neither fire, water, nor food, and their skin had largely peeled off. Much clothing was taken by the natives, but only such as they found lying around, and we learned afterwards that what they took on this visit was given them by the poor man to whom they gave drink and food. We also learned that the natives tried to straighten his legs, and offered to convey him away in their canoe, but in vain. He drank twice and tasted the shag, but could not eat, being too far gone and too weak to avail himself of the natives' kindness. He, however, gave away many things, beckoning them to take what they chose. The natives then left, as they could neither moor their canoe to the kelp in such rough waters, nor haul it ashore on the steep rugged coast.

"We heard that bad weather prevented their return for some days, and when they were at last able to land they found the whole party dead. They took away what they chose, but did not denude the dead."

The *Allen Gardiner* happened to be in Ushuaia at the time, so immediately set sail. She had an exceedingly stormy voyage to the outer coast before they found a spot, some distance from the scene of the disaster, where the vessel could lie safely at anchor. From there my father, accompanied by Captain Willis, two seamen and four Indians, proceeded by boat. The seamen remained in the boat to keep her off the shore, whilst the others, awaiting their opportunity, jumped out and scrambled up the steep rocks. There they found the bodies of the woman and all nine of the men. "The dead," wrote my father, "were lying orderly, so placed by their sorrowful companions, but the natives had placed some of the bodies as we found them."

Searching for anything by which to identify the corpses, Captain Willis found a note on four loose leaves of a pocket-book. It had been written by Captain McAdam, and was addressed to John Fleming, his stepson, at 84, Canterbury Street, Everton, Liverpool.

"In latitude 54° 30' S, Long. 71° W. Feb. 15th, 1876.

"DEAR JOHN,— When you receive this your Mother and me will be no more we have been 41 days in this desolate island on very low diet your Mother and me is very weak I am almost blind I can scarcely see the paper I am writing My watch and your Mother chain I give to Willie my Albert to yourself and you must wear your Mother's ring The earings for Jessey My instrument cloths & gold watch & three pounds twelve shilling to assist in maintaining Willie, and I hope you will be as a father to him kind and giving him good advice, the furniture to yourself their is two chronometers one telescope one night chronometer marked Webster & telescope you must take to the office and you can see if there is any money due for me if there is it will have to go for the maintainance of William and his Mother joins with me in hoping he will be a good Boy and not forget his God and we hope that you & Jessey may live long together in happiness and peace in Fear of the Lord, and now we send you our last kind loving blessing and may God Bless you all is the sincerest wish of your Parents.

"JAMES McADAM TO JOHN FLEMING."

After this an official Notice to Mariners was published, advising them how to reach Ushuaia and stating in which parts of the Fuegian archipelago the natives could be trusted and in which parts it was advisable to avoid them.

In the report of a missionary meeting in London on the 1st March, 1877, the following passage appears :

" Bishop Stirling, writing from Stanley, gives us the pleasing intelligence that Her Most Gracious Majesty the Queen has been pleased to convey to the Rev. Thomas Bridges and Captain Willis her warm thanks for their conduct in regard to the crew of the ill-fated *San Rafael*, who, as our readers will remember, were starved to death on Rous Peninsula, Hoste Island; and that, by the advice of Lord Carnarvon, the Board of Trade have ordered presents to the value of 1£ to be given to each of the Indians connected with the discovery of the dead and dying seamen. The Bishop has recommended, through the Governor of the Falklands, that the sum of 20£ should be given to Mr. Bridges to purchase gifts for those whom he thinks deserving of them. The Governor has endorsed the recommendation. . . ."

CHAPTER SEVEN

My Father Falls Ill. We Go on a Visit to England. After Fifteen Months There We Set Out Again for Ushuaia. At Punta Arenas We See H.M.S. Dotterel *Blow Up in the Harbour. The* Allen Gardiner *is Slightly Damaged, but We are Able to Finish our Journey Home.*

WHEN I WAS IN MY FIFTH YEAR, FATHER BECAME EXCEEDINGLY ILL, THOUGH he carried on his work as long as it was humanly possible. At last, however, he was obliged to go to Punta Arenas to get advice from Doctor Fenton of that town. The doctor's examination led him to fear that my father had contracted cancer of the stomach. Bishop Stirling, on hearing this, decided that the invalid must go to England at once.

Towards the end of September, 1879, our whole family packed into the cabin of the little Mission yawl *en route* for Punta Arenas, whence we embarked for England on the *Galicia*, a " floating palace " of 3,829 tons, belonging to the Pacific Steam Navigation Company.

The ship's doctor, a large, stout man, vaccinated us all on board. I still remember the horrors of that operation, and my feelings for the doctor did not improve during the voyage.

Our cabin was in the stern of the vessel. Near the bow were a number of steerage passengers, who seemed to live on boiled potatoes served in their skins. The galley-boys brought them in a pot or bucket, and when they poured off the water the people charged in and seized their share. Still, they seemed a cheery crowd for all that, and even danced, which was something quite new and strange to me. The Yahgans never danced, but when seated swayed their bodies in unison to monotonous " chants " not worth calling by that name. There were animals and chickens on board, to be killed during the voyage, and also a milch cow.

Before we had left Tierra del Fuego, John Marsh, the Yahgan who had reassured my mother on her meeting with the returning party of mourners, had made me a toy boat, entirely on his own initiative. During the voyage it was decided that, in return, it would be right for me to make him a nice warm knitted comforter, which was commenced without delay. " Under—over, under—off." What a monotonous tune for a four-year-old to repeat indefinitely! And I am afraid I sometimes hated John Marsh and his wretched boat. When I dropped a stitch, Mother or Auntie would pick it up, and perhaps knit a row at

89

lightning speed, just to encourage me; but if they had done more it would have been bad for my character, so the task dragged on. However, a young lady of sweet fifteen—who did not care a scrap about my morals—upon learning the object of my endeavours, took pity on me, and occasionally added many inches to my scarf. At long last, except for a few knots and little odd baggy bits, a fine garment was produced, which I proudly presented to my old friend on our return to Ushuaia.

We reached Birkenhead two months after leaving Ushuaia, and I thought it must rain all the time there, for while we were in Liverpool it poured continuously. I remember Father taking us to a railway station where a new kind of illumination was being tested. People said it was too bright and would be injurious to the sight, and I devoutly hoped our sight had not been harmed already. Father explained that it was allied to lightning, of which we had seen plenty coming through the tropics, and that it was called electric light.

We went to Grandfather's home at Harberton, near Totnes, in Devonshire, where we met various uncles and aunts. I remember a great barn, cows, pigs, chickens, ducks, geese and turkeys; an orchard, a forge and a wheelwright's workshop with a circular saw driven by a water-wheel. What an enchanting place we children thought it! One day we went to visit an aunt and some cousins at their farm some three miles from Harberton. After dark, as we were returning home in a pony-trap, to me it seemed that the clouds were standing still, and that the moon was rushing through them. This thought filled me with grave anxiety. Even at that early age the extreme caution which was natural to me began to assert itself. Hearing lock-jaw mentioned, I made enquiries, and someone told me that the person attacked could neither talk nor eat, and so died slowly of starvation. Mother, on seeing how frequently I opened my mouth to its utmost capacity, enquired the reason, and when I told her, laughed at me and said that it might lead to a dislocated jaw, which would bring on the same result. Hemmed in on both sides by dangers, I did not know which way to turn, until an aunt did away with my fear by assuring me that lock-jaw never attacked anyone under the age of forty-five!

Father refused to oblige the doctors by dying as they had predicted, but instead travelled about a great deal lecturing on the Mission work amongst the Indians of Tierra del Fuego. My brother Despard and I were put to an infants' boarding-school, and my sister Mary to a girls' school in Bristol.

After fifteen months in England, Father was so much better that we were able to depart for Ushuaia, and on the 23rd March, 1881, we embarked on the *Iberia*, another floating palace of 4,671 tons. Mary remained at school in England. Friends of my parents insisted that they ought to leave us boys to be properly educated, and were even offering to pay our expenses. It was a serious problem for Father and Mother to face, but they felt that they could not leave us, so back we went to the land of our birth.

I remember very little of our return voyage, except that we saw some negroes at one of the ports of call diving into the water for pennies. On the 23rd April we arrived at Punta Arenas, where the *Iberia* left us and proceeded on her way up the west coast. Approaching the Straits of Magellan we had sighted H.M.S. *Dotterel*, a British cruiser, on one of the periodical visits undertaken at that time by such vessels. Later we had sighted the *Allen Gardiner* beating tediously into the Straits. When H.M.S. *Dotterel* overtook the little sailing-vessel she took her in tow, and both arrived in Punta Arenas on the night of the 24th.

More than once in its short, sanguinary history Punta Arenas has been practically wiped off the map by what might be called internal combustion. By 1842 the original convict settlement—a group of log huts in a high wooden stockade—had attained a population of over six hundred souls, after at least one serious rising of the convicts. Following a long interval without a visit from the north, a new Governor had arrived, to find the place reduced to ashes and skeletons, without a living soul to be discovered there. It had looked as if a horde of Vandals had destroyed it and the Tehuelche Indians of Patagonia had finished it off.

A new settlement had been formed, and the population had increased to about a thousand persons, most of them convicts and their soldier guards. Then, in 1877, there had been a third rising, in which the guards had undoubtedly joined. Of course there had been bloodshed, and the mutineers and convicts, dreading future reprisals, had scattered northwards into Patagonia—most undesirable immigrants, and anything but a good influence on the Tehuelches. Most of them had been captured later. Others, as is the way with that kind of people, had ended by killing each other off.

Punta Arenas had survived this third blow, and within four years had developed into a little town—the southernmost town of the world—with a population of nearly two thousand, a church, a diminutive fort, a score or so of small houses and, of course, the prison. This advance was largely due

to the fact that every month at least four P.S.N.C. liners, either westward-
or eastward-bound, touched at this port. It was almost the only spot
in the whole of Patagonia where the Tehuelches could dispose of their
pelts and feathers. And, last but not least, it was about this time that
someone whispered, " Gold ! " [1]

We lodged with old friends of my father's, and had a front room on
the top floor of their two-storeyed house, which looked out across a
stretch of open country towards the sea. On the morning after our
arrival, seeing the Mission vessel at anchor in the harbour, Father and
Auntie went on board early, and had breakfast with Captain Willis.
The *Allen Gardiner* was meanwhile brought alongside a hulk for loading.
The *Dotterel* was anchored nearby.

We four children—Despard, Will, Bertha and myself—happened to
be in the front room with Mother, watching the movement in the harbour, when suddenly, at nine o'clock in the morning, there was a terrific
explosion, followed by the bursting open of our windows and the rising
of a huge cloud of black smoke with leaping tongues of flame and dark
shapes, which might have been men, shooting into the air. We stood
horrified; Her Majesty's Ship *Dotterel* had blown up.

It was dead calm in the harbour, and for some time the smoke covered
everything with a black pall, while we strained our eyes for a glimpse of
the *Allen Gardiner*, fearful lest she had shared the fate of the other ship.
At last the smoke lifted, and there was our little vessel lying safely at
anchor as before. Her two small boats were hurrying from her side,
while others were putting off from the shore to search the spot where, a
few moments before, that fine vessel had lain so peacefully.

A dozen men were picked up, and the Mission boats rescued four of
them, all officers. Among them was the commander, who was taken into
the *Allen Gardiner's* cabin, where some garments were found for him.
As he was very tall, his scorched head blackened the ceiling of the cabin,
leaving marks we children looked at with awe when they were pointed
out to us later by the steward. The clothes of Captain Willis—or even
of my father—will have been a sad misfit.

The commander had been in his bath when a minor explosion had
shaken the vessel, and he had dived into the sea through the porthole.

---

[1] The opening of the Panama Canal was a great misfortune for Punta Arenas, for
it diverted much shipping from that port. But the exporting of wool and frozen mutton
has since restored her lost prosperity, and nowadays the working people there are probably
the best paid, and least contented, in Chile. The population in 1946 was approximately
35,000.

As he had come to the surface the real blast had occurred, and the flames had scorched his hair. When he had found himself alive and uninjured and had thought of his lost men and vessel, the poor fellow had wept.

Several loose pieces of metal had fallen on the deck of the *Allen Gardiner* and considerably dented it, and the hulk had crushed in her bulwarks when the swell made by the sinking vessel had caused the other ship to roll.

To this day, in the old cemetery at Punta Arenas, is to be seen a stone placed there to the memory of getting on for two hundred men who perished that morning.

On the 27th April we left Punta Arenas on the forty-one-ton Mission yawl, but instead of reaching Ushuaia in a few days (she once did it in sixty hours), the trip took seventeen days. Father, who was given to understatement where weather was concerned, wrote, in a letter to the committee, that they were delayed by " exceptionally bad weather, strong head-winds with constant sleet and snow," and that " one dark, stormy night violent squalls prevented our reaching a port and an anxious night was safely passed outside."

Captain Willis, however, in his report gives a far more graphic description of the difficulties when, " in blinding hail and sleet, with double-reefed sails, the sea was so turbulent and the gusts so fierce that we had to wear ship and run into Cockburn Channel in search of the shelter which it was too dark for us to find, so kept dodging about in the lee of the Kirke Rocks till ten o'clock the next morning."

It was during those worrying periods that we learnt how Captain Willis kept his bristly moustache and beard trimmed. He would fiercely bite off, masticate and apparently swallow as much of it as his tongue could collect. We never saw him spit it out, so let us hope his digestion was good.

When he came below to study the chart with Father, though fortunately a diminutive man, he seemed, dressed as he was in streaming oilskins and sou'wester, to fill the tiny cabin. We greatly admired his clothing as well as his sturdy expression, but I am certain that he found Father's proximity and unruffled calm soothing to his troubled nerves.

On the 14th May we arrived safely back in the place of my birth.

CHAPTER EIGHT

*Parental Discipline. Boyhood Adventures. Despard is Given a Shot-Gun.
Games with the Indian Boys. Yahgan Methods for Catching Fish and Birds. The
Gift of the Leeloom. The Islands in the Channel are Stocked with Rabbits. Hunt-
ing the Sea-Otter and the Guanaco with Dogs.*

I

IN SPITE OF OUR MANY MONTHS' ABSENCE IN STRANGE SURROUNDINGS, IT
did not take us long to settle down into the old way of life in Ushuaia.

Father and Mother were the very best parents any children could
have had. Mother had trained us well from our earliest years, and instant
obedience came natural to us all. I can remember my father saying to
her :

"Never tell the boys to be quick or to hurry. The very fact that
you have called them or sent them anywhere should be enough to make
them come or go as quickly as they can."

Though we almost worshipped Father, we were not without fear of
him, for, despite the fact that he hardly ever laid violent hands on any of
us, he had a habit of which none of us approved. If he considered a
rebuke was insufficient, he sentenced us to bread and water, perhaps for a
whole day. Sometimes we were even condemned to penal servitude—
with hard labour. This punishment consisted in picking up buckets of
stones in the garden, or weeding, or sorting potatoes, during hours when
we might have been at play. I think the bread-and-water ration hit me
worse than the hard labour; I was so very fond of eating.

Mother was far too true a wife to help us with comfort or pleasanter
food when we were in disgrace, whatever may have been her inclinations,
but the sorrowful look she assumed on these occasions was more punishment than the bread and water. We were not obliged to eat this meagre
fare or anything else, but food disdained at one meal would be sure to
appear on the scornful one's plate at the next. The bread-and-water
criminal was expected to be cheerful at these sad times and to join in
conversation with the virtuous, without showing a morose or sulky disposition. This method was certainly unpleasant for the rest of the family,
but not so bad as knowing that someone of whom you were fond was
undergoing another kind of punishment in the next room.

When we wanted anything very special we used to confide in Mother. If she thought well of it, she would either suggest that we went straight to Father with our request, or tell us to leave it to her. She would then engineer the matter herself, generally with success.

Father gave us boys a tremendous amount of liberty and abstained from continually warning us against getting wet or running into danger. We spent up to four hours a day at lessons and had, in addition, certain duties to perform, such as gardening, or cutting firewood; but the rest of our time—apart from penal servitude—was our own.

Despard had some carpenter's tools, which he jealously kept in good order. With these he used to make toy boats, picture-frames and, later on, useful articles of furniture. He was never satisfied with his last job, but always yearned to improve on it and make something better.

Will was a sturdy little chap, active and fearless. He would climb trees, would go up to the crow's nest or the cross-trees of a cutter or a schooner at anchor in the harbour, or even shin up the top-mast. I remember how he once performed a Blondin act by walking right round the bulwarks of a vessel, using his hands only when getting past the stays. He was most independent, and seemed to have no respect for me, in spite of my superior age and far greater size. If ever I attempted to chastise him for his own good—if, that is, I could lay hands on him, for he was very hard to catch—I had Despard as well to reckon with. Another of Will's ardent supporters was little Minnie, the younger daughter of Mr. and Mrs. Lawrence. When Will and I were engaged in any kind of prank, Minnie would watch us from the window, and her eyes were always for Will. She had not the slightest sympathy for me when I was worsted in some scrap with him, or admiration if I happened to be victorious. So Will went his evil way unchecked.

On one occasion he pushed me off the veranda of Stirling House into the gooseberry bushes below. My roars of pain and rage brought Mother on the scene. She took Will to task, saying severely:

" You might easily have killed your brother."

This stern reproof made a lasting impression on the little fellow, and often from the safety of a high branch, or from the roof of an outhouse, where he had taken refuge, there would come his jeering shout:

" I might easily have killed you if I'd wanted to. Mother said so."

A really bad character was Will!

One of our favourite playgrounds in those early days was a swamp. The inner harbour at Ushuaia was very shallow. At low tide quite half of it was a mud-flat largely made up of decayed kelp and the decomposed remains of shoals of stranded sprats. When the tide was out this mixture gave forth a scent which, I believe, modern scientists call " ozone." Stretching for nearly a mile westward from the head of the creek that formed the inner harbour was a large swamp. It was covered by a spongy growth—called *shana* by the natives—and in it were pools and many small streams trickling through it into the creek. In these streams and pools were tiny fish, about the size of a whitebait, which the Indians knew as *yeemush*. We boys used to catch these with open canvas or scrim. Besides fishing, we hunted in the swamp for birds' eggs, beetles or imaginary treasure. Occasionally we would find a duck's nest, though generally some sharp-eyed Yahgan had got there before us. These activities invariably left us in a shockingly messy condition, and a wooden tub in front of the kitchen fire was in frequent demand before we were allowed to go to bed.

2

When we grew in years and had passed through the stages of little bows and arrows, slings and catapults, we were given, to our great delight, " Star " air-rifles. There were thousands of sparrows and finches, as well as some thrushes, which used to come from the woods to steal our strawberries and currants; and we were given permission to hunt these little pests. If we brought in a sufficient number, well plucked and cleaned, Mother or Auntie would make a fine pie of them, which tasted all the better for our having shot the birds ourselves. At other times we roasted them by a fire out of doors and enjoyed them greatly.

Thus we learnt very early to handle a gun, and also to approach game. Despard was far ahead of the other two of us, being very much a man for his age, while I was just the opposite. On his tenth birthday, Father gave him a shot-gun. Armed with this, and followed by his faithful henchman—myself—he would roam the country within a radius of three or four miles of the settlement, in search of game, mostly geese and duck. In summer in those regions there are four distinct breeds of geese, numerous kinds of duck and, in addition, woodcock, snipe, partridge, plover and other game birds. They were scarce and wild enough to make shooting a very good sport. Never in my life have I felt prouder than when, laden with an assortment of birds, carefully spread out to show the various types, I followed this successful hunter home from the field.

Besides playing and hunting by ourselves, we were allowed to join in the pursuits of the Yahgans. Their games were simple, yet required considerable skill. Sometimes of an evening an Indian boy would set off running, dragging behind him a worn-out basket on a string. This basket would be about the circumference of a steel helmet, but much deeper. We had spears, and used to join in trying to spear the moving basket. It was great fun, and eventually we became quite proficient.

What we were never much good at was spearing fish in the water. I would often be rowing or paddling, with a Yahgan standing in the bow with his spear, when a fish, well under the surface, would cause a ripple to rise some distance behind it. The refraction was so great that when I saw the spear strike the water I was sure it had missed; but there was a fish, perhaps as large as a salmon, transfixed and wriggling helplessly at the end of the spear.

For spearing birds and fish the Yahgans used bone spear-heads, often over a foot long, with many barbs, such as are shown in the pictures opposite page 128. For dislodging shell-fish and limpets from the bottom, and sometimes for crabbing, a four-pronged wooden spear-head, firmly bound to the shaft, was used; but for larger game a great bone spear-head, as much as eighteen inches long, with a single huge barb, was fixed loosely into a groove at the end of a stout shaft, which was often over fifteen feet long, carefully shaped and tapered to a point. A thong was attached to this spear-head, and tied firmly to the shaft, about a third of the way from the front end. Thus, when the spear-head entered the body of a seal, porpoise or, on exceedingly rare occasions, a diminutive whale, and the creature rushed forward, the shaft came loose and was towed through the water by the thong. The shaft would swing round nearly at right angles to the direction in which the victim was swimming, and the latter's speed was consequently much reduced, enabling the pursuer in his canoe to overtake the exhausted quarry and get home other spears, which, in time, would end the struggle.

The devices these Indians had for obtaining food were many and ingenious, varying greatly according to season and locality. I have space here for only a few.

One way of catching *alacush*—the flapping loggerhead (or steamer) duck, a huge bird frequently weighing over twenty pounds—was as follows: at the edge of a wood on the shore a man would build a little bower, or simply hide in the bushes. If he had no captive decoy bird he would very cleverly imitate the cry of the drake. When he saw any of these birds near he would repeat the cry or induce the captive bird to do so. The other birds, filled with curiosity, would draw nearer and nearer. The hunter had a long, slender rod, with a fine noose attached, which he used dexterously. Before long one of the birds would put his foot or neck into it and be drawn in. The others, not seeing any enemy, would become excited, but would soon return, as their curiosity was not satisfied and they still heard the decoy bird. The noose and rod would be carefully thrust out again to bag another victim.

For catching shags (cormorants) the Indians had a very successful procedure. They tied to stakes short lines baited generally with a small fish, which these birds invariably swallow head first. Inserted or securely bound to this bait near the tail were three or four finely pointed pieces of hard wood about an inch and a half long, with the ends opening slightly outwards. These points drew inward on being swallowed with the bait; but the shag, finding the bait attached to something, would try to vomit it up. The sharp points would open and stick into the gullet of the unfortunate bird.

Another way of catching these birds was to approach in the darkness of night the cliffs on which they roost. The natives would cover over the fires in their canoes, but would have prepared torches of bark beforehand. Suddenly these were ignited and at the same instant the covers thrown off the fires. When the astonished birds were thus startled from sound sleep they would flop down in a semi-conscious state into the sea, where the occupants of the canoes would kill all they could.

There was a third method. Before the shags returned to some distant islet where they used to pass the night in large numbers, two or more natives would hide themselves under the stones or driftwood, so that the birds could not see them. Then the canoe would leave with the rest of the party, after fresh water and firewood had been put ashore, in case bad weather should prevent the return of the canoe on the morrow. Evening would draw in and the birds assemble. Dull and even rainy weather was always chosen, and when it was quite dark the men would creep forth from their place of concealment with the utmost caution. They would seize an unsuspecting bird firmly over the wings so as to keep the head imprisoned, thus preventing a flutter or a cry, and kill it by biting its neck or head, holding the bird till it was quite dead. They then laid it down, and treated another and another in the same way, till, through some mishap, the alarm was given and the startled birds made off. These shags sleep soundly, with their heads under their wings, and sometimes several hundreds might be taken. I have heard of natives being marooned for days on account of bad weather making it impossible for the canoes to return to these exposed islets where the sea-birds congregate. For fishing, the women had their own method. In some cases they used a fish-line made of their own hair plaited. Near the bait was a perfectly rounded stone with a little groove cut in it to hold the line. Neither Father nor I ever saw or heard of these stones being shaped by the natives in our time, for earlier generations of Indians seem to have left such quantities that enough could always be found in the old wigwam sites to make unnecessary the tremendous labour of shaping stones anew.

The canoe, securely fastened in a kelp patch, would have one gunwale almost level with the water, and over this the women lowered their lines. They baited them with the tails of small fish. These would be swallowed by the luckless victim, which was then drawn up without any jerks. Unaware of danger, and reluctant to lose its food, it would hang on, but no sooner was it within a few inches of the surface than the skilled hand of the fisher grasped it, and deposited it in the basket with its fellows. The bait having been drawn out of its mouth, the line was thrown over for the next victim. For catching fish such as mullet and smelt they had another way, in which all joined wholeheartedly. At high water these fish would go up into narrow creeks, of which there are a great many in that country. Near the mouth of these creeks are ramparts of stone built by the ancients, with spaces left in the centre. The ramparts may be three or four feet under water at high tide. Days before, the natives would have collected a large supply of branches on both sides of the creek. The tide being high, they would come very quietly, so as not to alarm the fish, and lay these branches thickly along the top of the rampart, weighting them with stones. Across the centre gap they would place their net of sinew. If they had no net, branches would be used for this purpose. As the tide fell, the water would drain through, and the unsuspecting fish would find their retreat cut off. Even if they discovered a flaw in the barricade, a native was waiting there with his spear to prevent their escape. Sometimes, in this way, a ton or more fish might be taken at once, but it would be a long time before a like number would assemble in that same creek again.

Two classes of conger-eel (*tukupi*—pronounced " tuckuppi ") live in the cavernous pools. The natives would seek them at low water and locate them by the refuse of food outside their lairs. The Yahgans would thrust in their spears, searching for the fish, which would try to avoid them, keeping head-on to their enemy. The natives would repeat their thrust, and at last draw them out, speared generally in the head. Where they found one, they would be sure to find its companion. These scaleless fish resort to their holes only in summer, probably to rear their young. They are fat, and make good eating.

There are two kinds of cockle which live in the kelp-beds, nipping between their shells the leaves of the plant. They can change their abode at pleasure, darting about with a jerky motion by alternately opening and closing their shells, which are semi-transparent. They are very choice eating, and the most important kind is called by the Yahgans *shaapi*. They are occasionally found in great shoals, and for long periods may be very scarce indeed.

3

In 1880 a group of ladies, chiefly from Lee, near Southampton (Lee-on-Solent), subscribed for the purchase of a boat for my father. She arrived at Ushuaia in due course; a fine whale-boat. She was a real beauty, thirty feet long—two feet longer than the largest American whale-boat of her class that we had ever seen—and as she had a centre-board and ample beam, there was room to double- or treble-bank her five long oars. There was a still longer oar for steering, which could also be done by means of her rudder, with either tiller or yoke. She had a single mast with large mainsail and jib, and was christened *Leeloom*, which meant, in the Yahgan tongue, that she came from Lee.

For my father the *Leeloom* was a welcome and most useful gift. He was enabled to make frequent trips to outlying Yahgan settlements. He usually took Despard and me with him, so in time we learnt to handle a sailing-boat in any kind of weather.

On some of these boat trips Father took passengers of a different species. In the Beagle Channel, and others farther south, there are innumerable islands, mostly rocky, but with a good deal of bush, grass and wild celery growing on them. Father realized that these islands, if stocked with rabbits, would yield welcome food for the natives and for any shipwrecked crews who might be stranded there. Accordingly, he brought some rabbits from the Falklands. He took good care that they did not escape on the main island, nor did he release them on the larger islands in the Channel, lest they should become a pest to future farmers. But on any small island that he considered suitable he would land two or three pairs. Where there was good sandy soil and bush they thrived and increased exceedingly. Some years later H.M.S. *Sirius* anchored off one of these islands, and the whole ship's company landed in two batches on consecutive days. Hunting the descendants of the couple of pairs set free there by my father provided them with plenty of exercise, and over six hundred rabbits were caught—one for every man on the ship.

On other islands results were not so spectacular. Sometimes the rabbits were exterminated by birds of prey before they had had a chance to multiply; sometimes they found the land too wet or rocky for burrowing; and sometimes the natives hunted them with dogs until none remained.

The Yahgan hunting-dogs were small. Large dogs would have been unsuitable for accompanying canoe people cruising among the islands of Fireland, so their dogs were not much larger than a big fox-terrier. They were, however, both fierce and strong, and of a very mixed type, some being much more shaggy than others. All had prick-ears, and might have been a very stunted cross between an Alsatian police dog and a wolf. Black and white or grey were their usual colours; hardly any of them were brown. They were untrained, ill-natured and quarrelsome, but, though always expecting a blow, snuggled in amongst the family close to the fire and mixed happily with the children in the sometimes crowded canoes.

In certain places on the exposed coasts where the ground is enriched by kelp and other refuse blown in from the ocean, there are thickets nourished by abundant moisture and closely pruned from above by continuous gales. These are often so dense that a person may walk on the top of them. It is surprising to find, after walking thirty or forty yards from the beach on what appears to be a coarse and springy turf, that in reality one is treading on tree-tops, six or eight feet above the ground. This illusion is enhanced by the moss and turf which form on the tree-branches while they are still struggling upwards towards the light.

In these dark thickets—where the land is quite unsuitable for burrowing—hide the sea-otters, much valued by the Yahgans for their flesh and skins. The small dogs would go busily in to hunt them out. The otter is strong, but his safety lies in the water. The Yahgan, knowing by the excited barking where the otter would be likely to break from the bushes, would wait there and spear him, or hit him with a club, as he emerged. Even if the intended victim managed to reach the water he would be short of breath from the chase through the thicket, and his first dive would be a brief one. He could then be speared on coming to the surface to breathe.

When the coast was not too precipitous, and the canoes were cruising along near it, the dogs often wandered along the shore in the hope of finding something fit to eat. They might startle a bird from its nest, or an otter, and in parts of the country where guanaco were found one of these creatures might attract the dogs' attention. In pursuit of guanaco they were dogged and persevering but had no chance of overtaking their quarry, except when the snow was deep and had a frozen crust that would support a dog, but not a guanaco. When a guanaco thus got into difficulties and the dogs swarmed over him, the ravenous pack did not bother to kill him before beginning to devour as much of him as they could swallow, whilst the Yaghans hurried to reach the spot before their share of the meat should be too greatly diminished.

In parts of the Beagle Channel and Navarin Island the thick forests clothe the mountain-side from snow-line to high-water mark, and in winter the guanaco are forced to seek their food in these thickets. Heavy timber generally falls downhill, rather than along it, so it is much easier in the forest parts to proceed up or down these mountains than along the sides. In winter, when the snow was deep, the natives landed their dogs in such places, and the frightened guanaco started working their way uphill, keeping well ahead of the dogs; but soon the snow grew deeper and deeper, and the animals, unable to proceed farther, rushed downhill at great speed, until they reached the beach. Before long, however, some rocky promontory barred their path, and they had to choose between a steep ascent and a repetition of their recent experience, or taking to the water. The guanaco are good swimmers, but the canoes were generally nearby, and the latter course—which they often chose—proved fatal, for many would be speared by the happy Indians.

Unlike wild cattle, guanaco never banded together in mutual defence. A single animal might occasionally make a brave stand against one or even two medium-sized dogs. His teeth were quite as good as theirs, and he used both forefeet and hind feet most ably in a fight. He could not, however, defend himself against a number of dogs; he would be so dazed with fear that he would be unable to fight them all, and would soon fall exhausted.

Pups from some bitch that had distinguished herself in hunting would be in great demand amongst the natives, who hoped that they might take after their mother. But no attempt was ever made to improve the breed by selection of both parents, and the dogs were as undisciplined as were the native children.

Indians have been known to keep an otter, a fox or a bird for some time as a pet, and loggerhead drakes used as decoys were occasionally found, but the pet mortality rate in these parts was high, for if they did not die from neglect or rough treatment by naughty children, the dogs were sure to get them.

The dogs themselves were sometimes reduced to starvation, and would get into a garden and gnaw frozen swedes or cabbage-stumps, but, unlike the dogs on certain Polar expeditions, they rarely made a joint attack on one of their own kind and killed it for food. I have known only one such instance.

CHAPTER NINE

Italian Scientists Visit Ushuaia. My Father, Despard and I Go with Them in their Ship, the Golden West, to Sloggett Bay, where We are Wrecked. We Land and Pitch Camp in the Snow. We are Visited by the Eastern Ona. We are Rescued by the Allen Gardiner. The Story of Spanish Joe. Two of the Eastern Ona Return with Us to Ushuaia. My Father Attempts to Cross the Mountains into Ona-land.

I

IN MAY 1882 CAME AN ITALIAN SCIENTIFIC EXPEDITION ON THE SCHOONER *Golden West*, which they had chartered in Punta Arenas. The vessel was commanded by a grey-bearded Englishman, Captain Pritchard, with two stalwart Portuguese, Moustache and Gerryman, as first and second mates. As befitted the leader of such an expedition, Lieutenant Bové, an officer of the Italian Navy, was rather tall and grand; Signor Lovisato, supposed to be a mineralogist, was small, dark and dynamic; Signor Spegazzini, a botanist, with his magnificent beard and vast paraphernalia, made a great impression on us youngsters; and Bové's servant, Reverdito, completed the party.

They expressed a desire to visit some remote parts of the region. Father agreed to accompany them, for it not only gave him an opportunity of visiting outlying groups of natives, but also freed him from anxiety as to possible friction between them and their foreign visitors. He took Despard and me with him. Also included in the party were two Yahgans from Ushuaia.

The weather at first was fine, and we were frequently becalmed, landing at several spots to visit the natives, or to please the visitors. One of the places at which we anchored was Banner Cove. Shortly after, we were joined by the *Allen Gardiner* on her way from the Falklands to Ushuaia, so Father was busy that night with his mail. Near Banner Cove we had picked up a Yahgan from those parts called Paiwan, who spoke some Aush (Eastern Ona) and was acquainted with the country about Sloggett Bay, whither we were bound.

When at last we arrived at Sloggett Bay there was a heavy roll coming in from the south. It was early winter, when southerly gales are frequent and the seas come up unbroken from the Polar ice. Landing was out of the question, on account of the surf, so we anchored under the lee of a rocky islet which we hoped would shelter us. The weather, however, instead of improving, grew worse, and we rolled about there for three days and nights.

On account of this rough treatment, the vessel began to leak badly. Father urged the captain to " beat her out," and the latter replied that it would take the " sticks " out of her, by which, no doubt, he meant the masts. Had he taken my father's advice and failed, I should not be writing this story, for at the extremes of this open bay are promontories where the mighty breakers would soon have pounded the vessel to bits, and not a life could have been saved. One of those headlands is well named " Devil's Yacht."

The waves sweeping round on each side of the islet behind which we had sought shelter were so overwhelming that the hawse-pipes broke away, and the chains were making matchwood of our vessel as she jerked at them. They must have been good chains, for I remember well the terrific force with which the vessel was brought up after some particularly giddy plunge. We could not lie there another night, so, late in the afternoon, under staysail only, we drove ashore. A line of unscalable cliffs loomed ahead of us through the driving snow, but fortunately the sea broke on the beach at their feet, and not right up against them, as it would had the tide been higher.

The *Golden West* was an American schooner, with a long, overhanging forefoot. She drew only about five feet in the bow, and she ran in on a big sea. Father, with Despard and me, remained as long as possible in the cabin, and I do not remember his showing either impatience or excitement as he held me by the hand and hurried forward.

The men who had crowded in the bow of the vessel, some even on the bowsprit, were jumping overboard and running up the beach, whilst Moustache and Gerryman did heroic work in assisting weaker men out of the backwash, which was too strong for some of them.

The steersman—who had been tied at the helm and had a knife with which to cut his bonds—sped past us and sprang ashore in fine style. When we reached the bow Father took me by the wrists and swung me out as far as possible towards Mr. Reverdito and Gerryman, who had run down to help. I fell into a seething mixture of seaweed, pebbles and foam, but was grabbed at once and dragged into comparative safety at the foot of the cliff. Father and Despard—the only two left on board— were now in great danger, for the vessel had been drawn farther out and flung nearly broadside on to the sea.   Father caught at a rope that was hanging from the foremast and wound it round one of his arms.   Then, with Despard clinging to him, he came swinging in over the beach. Despard let go and landed well up the beach, but the rope must have drawn too tight round Father's arm, so that he could not release himself at the right moment and was swung back against the rigging.   When the vessel reeled towards the shore again he swung out in a wide curve, and this time landed safely.   His hand and arm, however, became much swollen, and his wrist never quite recovered from the strain.

Thinking the tide might still be rising, some of the leading men, feeling, possibly, that their lives were of greater value to humanity than those of the common herd, crowded on a rock that jutted out from the cliff about six feet above the shingle.   I saw that they held revolvers in their hands.   I did not grasp the meaning of this at the time, but noticed that the sight greatly displeased Father, for when he joined our group he called to them in no kindly manner to come down, as the tide was falling.

On reading Father's version of the wreck of the *Golden West*, I feel I must have been mistaken in imagining it was more than a rather exciting picnic.   Of the landing he writes :

" The vessel, tried by the jerking of her anchors, made much water.   Fearing that the strain on the cable might cut the vessel down if we spent another night such as the last, it was determined to run her ashore.   This was accordingly done, and well done; the surf was considerable, bursting in the bulwarks and smashing the boat that was to windward.   The weather was very unpleasant.   My dear boys received abundant care from all, and were helped up the beach when I threw them overboard."

After we landed I was made to run backwards and forwards at the foot of the cliff, feeling very sorry for myself, until some of the men were able to board the vessel and obtain fuel with which they managed to light a fire on the beach.   A snow-storm from the south, which had lasted several days, had brought up the biting air from the Polar ice.   This wind joined with the spray in giving us a shower-bath that lasted intermittently until, after over two hours, one of the three natives, who had been exploring, returned and told us that the tide had fallen far enough for us to reach a place where the cliff could be scaled.   His companions had gone ahead to select a site for our encampment.

The Indian led us to a spot where a tiny stream ran down a little gully. Great icicles had formed there, but we had the ship's lanterns, as well as the snow, to light our way upward.   The other two exploring Yahgans had already started fires in the snowy scrub, and soon, with my wet clothes removed, I was turning round and round, roasting myself in the welcome glow. All my troubles were now over, as besides warmth there was ample to eat. A sack of flour has to soak a long time before the water penetrates to the centre of it, and there were plenty of undamaged tinned provisions saved from the wreck.

Some days later it was decided that a party should set out to fetch help from Ushuaia in our one surviving whale-boat, which had been patched up with canvas and tar. Moustache, who was to be in charge, was highly flattered when Father sent Despard along under his care. Father did this because he did not trust the armed white men. If any considerable number of Yahgans appeared, these men might become alarmed and start shooting. Despard's presence would prevent such an incident. The Yahgans would recognize him and he would be able to talk to them in their own tongue, thus reassuring the men in the boat.

By then the weather was clear and calm, but cold, for even in the daytime the thermometer never rose as high as freezing point. The sea, however, had subsided sufficiently for the launching of the boat to be attempted.

There was still a considerable surf on the beach, and in spite of many willing hands to run the boat into the water at the most favourable moment, she was very nearly swamped, and some of the men were forced to swim beside her out beyond the breakers. Then they all started baling, some using their boots for the purpose, and when they had lightened the boat they rowed away amidst cheers from the party assembled on the beach.

That night they managed to reach Banner Cove under oars, but had not gone far next day when it came on to blow. The party had to take refuge in a little cove near the north-east point of Navarin Island.

On the third day, however, in spite of a light head wind, they managed to reach Ushuaia before midnight. The oarsmen were completely exhausted, and one or two had to be carried from the boat. The *Allen Gardiner*—which fortunately was still there—soon set out to fetch the rest of us, but was delayed by contrary winds.

The days of waiting at Sloggett Bay were fully occupied, for though the *Golden West* was being battered to pieces under the lashing of succeeding tides, we spent our time salvaging provisions, as well as ropes and sails; these last making it possible for us to develop our encampment into an orderly canvas village.

Writing in his diary four days after our landing, Father says: "We have made our camp quite comfortable and at last have got our clothing and bed-clothes dry." So, quite inadvertently, he does acknowledge that we had got wet.

A day or two later smoke signals were seen some three miles beyond a river that flowed into the bay, about a mile to the east of our encampment. These may have been made by some other shipwrecked crew, but the signallers were judged to be Aush. Father went off with Paiwan and another Yahgan to try to make contact with them. On reaching the river they found it so unevenly frozen that they did not care to venture on it, and returned to the camp.

Next morning two tall figures clad in guanaco skins appeared, walking briskly towards our encampment. Bold fellows they must have been, for they might easily have been received with a hail of bullets. I had noticed the haste with which fire-arms and ammunition had been distributed amongst the sailors when the Indians had first been sighted.

Father spoke some warning words to Captain Pritchard, then hurried out with Paiwan to greet the visitors and escort them to our fireside. They were soon joined by nine others, who had doubtless been watching to see how their companions were received. These Aush had crossed the river on the ice that Father and the Yahgans had feared to trust the previous day. They came in style, painted and in their best attire. Each wore tied over his brows a triangular piece of skin from the head of a guanaco, with its short, close, blue-grey fur. From the front this head-dress appeared conical in shape and produced a pleasing and imposing effect. The men came provided with bows and arrows in skin quivers. These they speedily bartered for knives. Father distributed among them a barrel of bread, and, seated round our camp fire, had much conversation with them. He writes that they were very well-built, tall, powerful men. Their feet were encased in moccasins made out of skin from guanaco's legs. Some of the visitors understood enough Yahgan to translate our remarks to those who knew none at all. Paiwan's knowledge of Aush, though scanty, was also helpful. Some of the Indians had their legs covered with severe scratches which had evidently bled freely, and which we thought had been acquired when chasing guanaco through thorny bush-country. Later we learned that these wounds were self-inflicted, as a sign of mourning.

While we were waiting for the *Allen Gardiner* I amused myself by playing on the beach. Like many boys of my age, I carried a toy magnet in my pocket. On this I now collected a mass of magnetic iron sand, which in its turn became magnetized and held together. In due time the magnet, with this sand clinging to it, found its way into my treasure-box at Ushuaia. Its reappearance from there three years later led to interesting consequences, which will be described in a later chapter.

At last the *Allen Gardiner* appeared in the offing. I was one of the first to be put on board. Captain Willis refused to anchor, much less pass the night, in the place he called "Suicide Harbour," and for two days we lay on and off, while the ship's boat plied backwards and forwards with the stuff we had salvaged from the *Golden West*. The weather was cold and miserable. Finally all was ready and we set off back for Ushuaia. With us came, at Father's invitation, two of the Aush, who had all become most friendly and trusting.

During those two days of waiting in Sloggett Bay and the return voyage to Ushuaia the *Allen Gardiner's* cook was kept busy, with a crowd of thirty on board instead of the normal six or seven. This diminutive, sprightly little man, who combined the duties of steward with those of ship's cook, was known as Spanish Joe; and though he must have been overworked and worried, he allowed me to sit on the wood-box in his tiny galley and sizzle scraps of meat on the top of his rusty stove. By letting me prepare these dainties for myself he found the way to my heart.

2

Fifty years later, when I was crossing a thinly populated stretch of Patagonia, I stopped at a little farm. They told me of the presence there of an aged tramp, who claimed to have known my father. Greatly interested, I sought him out in the cook-house, where he was resting. As I approached the building a tiny, white-haired imp of a man hurried out to meet me. He was very excited, and spoke such a mixture of English and Spanish, interlarded with many swear-words in both tongues, that it was hard to understand him. He seemed surprised, almost hurt, that I did not recognize him, then told me that his name was Spanish Joe.

Out of the almost forgotten past came a picture in my mind of the cold, crowded deck of the yawl and the warm comfort of the galley where I had been made so welcome; and the jabbering of this agitated bit of flotsam, coupled with the memory of his exceeding kindness of long ago, touched me deeply. I felt that I owed him a debt on which interest had been accumulating for half a century.

When I arrived back at my home, some forty miles farther into the mountains, I sent a lorry to the farm to collect him and the pack that contained all his worldly goods. When he reached my home he was allotted a little room and a seat, not in the men's dining-room, but beside the cook-house fire. When he felt inclined to work he chopped firewood for the cook, and being, like all sailors, clever with needle and thread, he was soon well off in my old clothes, mercilessly cut down.

When I told the peons his story, they, led by the kind-hearted cook, treated him like a Chinese idol, till one winter's morning, some years after his arrival, he failed to turn up for his coffee and mutton chops, and was found dead in his bed.

But that is by the way. I must go back to the days of my youth.

3

When the *Allen Gardiner* had landed us all safely back at Ushuaia, the Italians carried on with their work. When they had gathered all the information they needed they left us.

Father spent many hours in conversation with the two Aush men. Their language was remarkable for its excessive jerkiness and strong gutturals; and he found that their words, though simple in structure, were difficult to pronounce, and even more difficult to write down. Nevertheless, he managed to collect a great number.

The sight and proximity of these stalwart fellows in their guanaco-skin robes and head-dress attracted me greatly; and when one day they disappeared without a word of farewell, all my thoughts went after them on their journey back to their own tribe. My imagination was fired with a longing to join them. Such has always been my craving. When I was very young, stories of little boys being adopted by wolves fascinated me; and once when I caught sight of a fox that gazed at me from the edge of a wood and presently slipped silently away into the forest, I longed to follow him. My father once read us a story called " Settlers in Canada," in which a painted Redskin Chief called Angry Snake carried off the youthful hero and adopted him. This so filled me with envy that I yearned to live in the woods, far from whatever civilization existed in Ushuaia.

It is not, then, to be wondered at that I was furious when, some twenty months after the wreck of the *Golden West*, Father went off on an expedition into the mountains—and left me behind. Instead he took Despard with him. With five Yahgans they crossed Ushuaia harbour by boat and, to my immense mortification, disappeared into the forest.

Father was anxious to follow up the Ainawaia valley—renowned throughout Yahga-land as the source of supply for flints or agate, used by the natives for arrow-heads and cutting implements—and then to penetrate as far as possible into the hitherto unexplored interior and try to make contact with the elusive, almost mythical, forest Ona, whom both Yahgan and Aush greatly feared. This was not his first attempt to get through the mountains from Ushuaia. The first had been made before my time, and had been given up because of the fears of his Yahgan companions.

This second attempt was also unsuccessful. At the head of one mountain valley their path was completely blocked by glaciers, which obliged them to retrace their steps and to climb to the summit of a mountain. There they found a deep and impassable gully separating them from the Ona country beyond. All they could then hope for was a view of this mysterious land to the northward, but continuous rain and cloud blotted out everything.

Twice on that trip my father fainted. He should never have attempted such an arduous expedition. Even on that mountain-top, when all attempts had failed, he still wanted to try again, but he was almost forcibly turned back by the devoted Yahgans, who combined anxiety for the life of their leader with the traditional dread not only of the legendary inhabitants, but also of imaginary wild-men-of-the-woods.

Five days after leaving Ushuaia they were back home again. Father wrote in his diary:

" Thus ended our attempt to open up communication with the Ona and their land."

In the light of later knowledge, it was as well that they did not meet a party of those mountain men. They would not have welcomed an invasion into the very heart of their sanctuary, and would undoubtedly have picked off the members of the expedition one by one with their arrows, whilst remaining themselves unseen.

During that same year (1884) the schooner *Rescue* arrived at Ushuaia, bringing our former acquaintance Bové, now Captain, with his young wife and an Argentine officer named Nogueira. This latter gentleman had been sent by his Government to inspect the land for which the South American Missionary Society had asked a concession. In addition, he was supposed to carry out a general survey of the country around Ushuaia. These visitors remained as our guests, and on the following day the *Rescue* resumed her voyage.

In March Captain Bové and Nogueira started inland, taking as their guides the same five Yahgans who had been with my father on his exploration two months earlier. Before they started Father gave them the benefit of his experience on the two former attempts, advising them as to the best route to take.

The party landed on the eastern side of the Hushan River, whence, after breakfasting, they began their journey. Their course lay up the valley between the Hushan and Machinan Rivers, and thence to the north-west. In due time they managed to push on some distance farther than Father had succeeded in doing, but were still hampered by forest and rugged mountain, and by weather so overcast, and visibility so poor, that they failed to get a good view of what lay beyond. Although by the time they returned they had been away eight days, they had observed no guanaco, nor shot game of any kind, and they had seen no vestige of the Ona tribe.

CHAPTER TEN

French Scientists Come to Hoste Island to Photograph the Transit of Venus. Dr. Hyades Cures Sickness in Ushuaia and Performs Operations without Anaesthetic. My Brothers and I Assist the Scientists. Yekaifwaianjiz Turns Frenchman. My Father Falls Exceedingly Ill and is Attended by Dr. Hyades. He Leaves his Bed within Two Days. Shipwrecked Germans. Adventure in the German Long-Boat. We are Detained at Lapa-yusha and I Learn what it is to be Hungry. Robbed by Yahgans. The Sealers from Diego Ramirez.

I

THE ITALIAN EXPEDITION OF 1882 WAS FOLLOWED BY A SCIENTIFIC MISSION sent by the French Ministry of Marine. They arrived in Fuegian waters in a gunboat, the *Romanche*, and set up their temporary home at Orange Bay, on the southernmost peninsula of Hoste Island, one of the most desolate spots to be found in that rugged, rain-washed land.

On the shore of this sheltered cove, which lies about ten miles north of False Cape Horn, the Frenchmen speedily erected huts from the framework, boards, windows and corrugated iron brought with them in the *Romanche*. They also built shelters for their telescopes and other instruments.

The primary object of this visit was to observe and photograph the transit of Venus, which was expected to take place the following year. Apart from this undertaking, the scientists were as busy as ants. For these fine men there was no spectacular race for glory or any startling adventure, but only incessant work under generally trying climatic conditions. For all that, they carried on cheerfully through what must have been to them, unaccustomed as they were to the rigours of the country, the greatest hardships.

Having a fine meteorological observatory, they noted weather conditions, studied the vegetation on land and sea, and the infinitely varied life that inhabited both. For every branch of science there were professors or students. There were also two medical doctors, who made a study of the Yahgan natives. In this my father was able to help them greatly.

This assistance did not put them in his debt, for the first act of kindness came from them. At the time of their arrival at Orange Bay there was sickness at Ushuaia. During a single month no fewer than eight of our small population died. Hearing from natives of the coming of the strangers, my father visited them in the *Allen Gardiner* in the hope of finding among them a doctor who would return with him to Ushuaia.

He was well received. It was readily agreed that one of the two medical men, Dr. Hyades, should go back with him. The *Allen Gardiner* left Orange Bay that same afternoon. Dr. Hyades spent four days at Ushuaia, visiting the natives from morning till midnight. During that time he performed four surgical operations without anæsthetic. One of these was on an old fellow called Palajlian, who had one eye removed and the other operated on, in the hope of saving his sight. Father records that the patient clutched his hand convulsively, but refrained from showing, even by a moan, any sign of pain.

Dr. Hyades went back to Orange Bay with his mission successfully completed.

2

When we boys visited Orange Bay, the wooden bungalow, with duckboards across the bogs, made an ideal place for us to play. On my first meeting with the Frenchmen, the realization of their learning, enhanced by their coloured spectacles and beards of different shapes and hues, filled my boyish mind with awe. But we soon discovered that those dreaded scientists had a great sense of humour.

They found that we could be of service to them. They wanted specimens of everything they could get—plants, stones, birds' eggs and insects. They gave us bottles of alcohol for killing bugs, grubs, beetles and spiders, whilst Despard was entrusted with some still more deadly powder with which to kill butterflies, moths and other winged insects before pinning them on a board. What fun we had! Despard had his shot-gun and secured many specimens of birds. He was given instruction in the art of stuffing them. We also helped to overcome the scientists' language difficulties. Several of them spoke English, but none of them the Yahgan tongue; and we boys were proud, when given the opportunity, to explain to them what some Indian had been trying in vain to make them understand.

My father, too, gave them all the help in his power. It was only through him that they were enabled to take casts of the natives, who, without his previous assurances, would never have allowed themselves to be smothered with a thick coating of plaster of Paris. He records how one of them gripped his hand and would not release it, while, with quills in his nostrils to breathe through, the whole of his face was covered with the composition.

It must not be thought that the scientists had a monopoly of interesting observation. If they studied the ways of the Indians, the latter evinced an equal curiosity about them. Many of the natives were great mimics, and would watch and imitate strange mannerisms which attracted their attention. One of these was Yekaifwaianjiz. He was not a particularly handsome Indian, though tough and hardy, even for a Yahgan from the outer coasts. White men called him Jack-knife. He himself preferred Yekaif, considering that the abbreviation gave him distinction. On several occasions he had been out with American sealing-schooners and returned to his home when the season was over, enriched with gifts and a great supply of seal-blubber and oil. On these trips he had picked up a dreadful mixture of Spanish and English words, and, no doubt to show his superiority and give emphasis to his speech, he mixed them horribly with his native tongue, even when speaking to his own people.

For all that, he was an intelligent, willing fellow, and now spent much of his time with the Frenchmen, who were glad of his help as guide and interpreter. Thus he soon learned a number of spicy French exclamations to add to his stew of Yahgan, Spanish and English. Some of the habits and little tricks of speech that he had noticed in the visitors and had taken pains to imitate—at first, no doubt, for his own enjoyment and the amusement of his fellows—grew on him as time went by. At every opportunity when talking he would spread his hands, palms upwards and towards his hearer, and, drawing backwards, shrug his shoulders with a gesture a comedian might well have envied. Eventually these ultra-French motions became so perfectly natural to him that he could not have avoided using them even had he tried.

3

Dr. Hyades was again to prove a friend in need. Father became extremely ill from the same trouble as had driven him to England four years earlier. It was a happy chance that when this grave attack occurred he was on a visit to Orange Bay in the *Romanche*. In his diary for the 30th August, 1883, he made this entry:

"Weather bad. Prepared to go ashore after dinner, but had to void it all. Afterwards I was reading by the fire, feeling inclined to vomit and faint. I lay down, but had to go away to vomit. I brought up blood, but getting more faint returned to the saloon in haste, rang the bell and lay on the floor. Seeing a man as I lay, I was just able to. call out 'Le Docteur,' then lost my senses. . . . When I came to, the good doctor was beside me, a pillow was under my head and a wet pad on my forehead. My pulse was not perceptible for five minutes. Twenty minutes later I was taken to my bed, but had to lie down hastily to prevent fainting. Pulse ceased for 14 minutes. To allay the hæmorrhage I took peroxide of iron and ice. Had a mustard plaster over my stomach and one on each calf. Am very grateful to my God and Father for his kind providence in giving me this timely warning when having good medical aid at hand. Receive every kindness."

The next morning, in spite of his utter weakness, Father went on shore and talked with the natives. The kind French doctor went with him. After two hours, Father was again overcome by faintness, and was forced to return to the ship. He took to his bed, but for only two days. His only nourishment for the next six weeks was milk, beef-tea and lime-juice.

4

The transit of Venus was duly recorded by the French scientists. Fortunately, though rain and cloud are the rule in those parts, when the hour for which they had prepared arrived the sky was clear, and they were able to observe the planet through their glasses and photograph her as she crept across the face of the sun.

With their main task ended, they got ready to return to France, where they were later to publish nine or ten bulky volumes of information about Fireland—records destined to grow in value as the years roll by.

While their preparations to leave Orange Bay were in progress, we at Ushuaia were greatly excited at daybreak one morning by the sight of three boats coming into the harbour from the eastward. They looked like the three bears that Mother and Yekadahby had told us boys about in our childhood, for one was very big—so big and so crowded with men that we wondered if they were pirates—the next somewhat smaller and the last smaller still.

Our boyish expectations were not realized, for there were only twenty-three men in all three boats, and they were not pirates, but twenty-two members of a shipwrecked crew and our old Yahgan friend, James Cushinjiz. The crew—all Germans—were from the *Erwin*, a barque of 1,300 tons, which, bound from Liverpool to San Francisco with a cargo of coal, had caught fire after rounding Cape Horn.

Many miles to the south-west of the Ildefonso Islands the crew had abandoned the vessel, and none too soon, for ten minutes after they had taken to the boats an explosion in the hold had blown the decks off, and she had become a sheet of flame.

From the ship's deck they had been able to see the snowy peaks of

Tierra del Fuego over the horizon, so they set the boats on a north-easterly course. In the month of July, which corresponds to the English January, the South Pacific is a cold waste of waters when viewed from an open boat, even when the weather is calm and the Cape Horn rollers lack their renowned " greybeards." No less forbidding was the distant coast, with its reputedly savage inhabitants.

Before they had abandoned ship, however, one of the officers had noticed on the chart a reference to the settlement at Ushuaia, with directions as to the best way for shipwrecked crews to reach that haven. Accordingly, following those directions, they had worked their way along the outer coast of Hoste Island, past False Cape Horn, and steered northwards across the mouths of Tekenika and Ponsonby Sounds, passing unseen quite near the settlement at Orange Bay, where the French scientists were preparing to depart for their native land.

The German crew had not been able to find the southern entrance to the Murray Narrows, for the rugged mountains had seemed to block their way, and among the many creeks and gullies they had essayed to enter, they had failed to find the one that would have let them through into the Beagle Channel. Less than twenty miles of comparatively sheltered water had separated them from Ushuaia when they had given up the vain search. Concluding that the chart must be wrong, they had headed south and east through Nassau Bay, round Navarin Island and into the Beagle Channel from the east.

The first mate was the only one of the party who spoke English. When hailed by an Indian in that language, he had been able to understand, and they had found in James Cushinjiz a willing guide to pilot them to Ushuaia.

In the whole ten days since they had left the *Erwin* they had only ventured to land three times to make a fire and warm themselves. Fortunately, the weather had been remarkably fine, otherwise they would very likely have been lost, as many have been on that exposed outer coast. What a joyous sight our little settlement on the hill must have presented to that shipwrecked crew !

Everything possible was done to give comfort to this large party. They had suffered greatly from cold and exposure. Many were in a bad state from frost-bitten feet. The bo'sun, who had been hurt before leaving the ship, was in a very serious condition when he was carried ashore.

During the considerable time they stayed at Ushuaia before being taken to Punta Arenas they made themselves useful at the settlement. The ship's carpenter, a willing and able fellow, was soon at work with his assistant, repairing the *Leeloom*, which had recently suffered considerable damage, and others of our boats that needed overhauling.

The first mate, a tall, fair-haired and most kindly man, had a large natural-history book with fine pictures of animals in it, both modern and prehistoric. He must have set great store by his book to have brought it away with him from the burning vessel. Before leaving Ushuaia he made me a present of the precious volume, and for many years it was one of my most jealously guarded treasures.

Not all the men, however, were so attractive as the mate. One day, when a party of the crew were cutting firewood, he pointed out a huge, red-bearded ruffian, and said to Father, "None zo bad ahss jee," giving the final word the strong guttural sound of the Spanish *hota*, which has no counterpart in the English alphabet. His voice and earnest manner took our fancy, and "Nonezobadahssjee," word of unutterable scorn, with a fierce choke for its last syllable, was added to our Anglo-Yahgan vocabulary.

Eventually, when the *Allen Gardiner* took them to Punta Arenas, she was too small to accommodate their boats as well, so these were left behind, and doubtless wiped out the debt owed by these people for their trip and the provisions they had used during their protracted stay with us.

Their long-boat was a great, clumsy craft compared with the *Leeloom*, but wishing one day to bring a good load of grass for the calves from one of the islands, and also to land some rabbits there, we took her, on account of her carrying capacity, for a day's outing. She had no centre-board and, instead of mainsail and jib like the *Leeloom*, had a large lugsail, which none of us fancied.

We landed the rabbits on an island near the middle of the Beagle Channel, some seven miles from Ushuaia, and loaded many sacks of grass aboard the long-boat. We did not, however, immediately set off back for Ushuaia, because the wind had got up and we should have had a full gale in our faces. We lay in a sheltered place all day, until at sunset the wind, as is often the case, began to die down. Taking advantage of this, we put off and started to beat up the Channel. We were not to be let off so easily as we had hoped, for when we got out into open water the lull ended and the wind sprang up as strongly as before. Night came on, dark and stormy, and with reefed sail we were not able to fetch back to the island from which we had started. Between us and Navarin Island

angry waves swept down the open Channel, so we headed for the rocky
northern coast. The mountains, rising abruptly from the sea, looked like
an unbroken wall, and the night grew so dark that we could not see their
outline against the sky.

By this time we were shipping a good deal of water, and it was plain
that we had either to find some sheltered spot to land for the night, or
else run before the wind to Shumacush,[1] about eight miles farther east.
The latter alternative, besides taking us into still rougher water, would
have meant a long return journey on the following day, or whenever the
wind chose to abate. There was, however, no sign of an opening in the
rocky wall, so Father consulted with the Indians who were with us, and
when one of them, a native of that district, kept pointing to a spot that
we could not distinguish, wisely relinquished the tiller to him. Besides
fishing by night and hunting for sleeping birds, the natives were in the
habit of travelling in the dark hours, as there is generally less wind then
than in the day-time. Their eyesight in the dark was amazing.

When the Indian took the tiller he dropped off a point or two, thus
increasing our speed and, it seemed, hastening us to certain disaster; for
ahead, against the rugged coast, glowed white a continuous line of angry
breakers. Suddenly two rocks like the backs of whales loomed close to
the boat, one on each side. We were drenched with spray as, still under
a press of sail, we slipped between them into a perfectly sheltered basin
with a narrow shingle beach, and a deserted wigwam at the farther
corner.

In no time we had a good fire going and, though saturated, found
comparative comfort. Next day we reached home, allaying the grave
anxiety that Mother and all our friends had felt; for our boat had been
sighted on her first tack after sunset the previous day, before the final
storm had hidden us from sight.

I have since visited Simachi, our haven on that memorable night, and
would think twice before driving a sailing-boat between those rocks in
broad daylight, much less on a night such as the one I have described.

5

Early in the following spring, Father went on a trip in the *Leeloom*
to the eastern part of the country, again taking Despard and me with him.
We had been away nearly a week, and were homeward bound, when we
reached Lapa-yusha (the Coast of Conch Shells), a place on the south

[1] Now called Punta Remolino (Whirlwind Point)—and with reason.

shore of the Beagle Channel, some thirty miles from Ushuaia. There we found a considerable settlement of Yahgans.

We had pitched our tent in a sheltered place and landed our goods, when these people told us that a seal had found its way into a nearby lagoon. Father took a small rifle, which he had bought from the French expedition, and set out with the idea of shooting the animal for the natives. My brother and I, with our native crew, followed him, on the chance of seeing some sport and tasting the meat. The seal, however, gave us the slip by diving down through the channel which joined the lagoon to the sea. When we returned empty-handed, we discovered that our camp had been raided, and all our food and blankets stolen. The only thing that remained was a small tin containing a pound of sugar, which had escaped the notice of the thieves. Father went to the Yahgan wigwam nearby and accused the natives of thieving. They denied all knowledge of it, and tried to put the blame on a small party from another place, who, they said, had been seen passing while we were away. That is the only instance I remember of such a robbery, though other natives had endless opportunities and must have been sorely tempted.

The situation was serious. The weather had worsened, and we could not leave Lapa-yusha. Both tide and wind were against us. Because of the continuous westerly gale, the tide did not fall low enough for us to get shell-fish. There was nothing for us to eat—except the pound of sugar, which was divided equally among the eight of us. On the second day we were fortunate enough to catch a penguin, which had rashly strayed far from the sea; but one penguin will not sustain eight persons for long.

The difficulty at Lapa-yusha lay not in embarking, but in the direction and strength of the wind when once away. We left there on the night of the second day, and had to fight every inch of the way to Ushuaia against contrary winds. We took three days to cover the thirty miles home, beating backwards and forwards across the Channel when weather permitted, or rowing up close to whichever shore afforded us the best shelter.

That was the first time in my young life that I knew the pangs of hunger.

6

The crews of the *Golden West* and the *Erwin* were not, by any means, the only ones to seek succour at the Mission station, or to benefit by the friendly bearing of the natives towards white people. Some time after the *Erwin* party had left us, a whale-boat appeared at Ushuaia, manned by a tough-looking crew. They had been left by a sealing-schooner on Diego Ramirez, a desolate, rain-swept island standing alone sixty miles south-west of Cape Horn, and not belonging to the Tierra del Fuego archipelago. The object of these men on Diego Ramirez had been sealing, but, their vessel being long overdue, they had chosen a spell of fine weather and crossed the wide strip of ocean to await the schooner at Ushuaia. They had left a note on Diego Ramirez for the captain of the vessel, which was called, to the best of my recollection, the *Surprise*.

The leader of the party was the mate, Mr. Smith, a name shared by another member of the crew, a pleasant, good-looking young fellow, who also answered to " Chips." Whilst they waited for their vessel, which arrived in due course and took them away, " Chips " and Despard worked together in the building of a nine-foot punt. We boys claimed that Despard built it with the help of young Mr. Smith, though that worthy craftsman would probably have put it the other way about, even if he had been gracious enough to acknowledge that Despard had helped him at all. Be that as it may, the punt was to prove very useful, as will be seen in the next chapter.

CHAPTER ELEVEN

Argentina at Last Remembers her Most Distant Outpost—Ushuaia. My Father Hoists the Argentine Flag. The Sub-Prefecture is Established. A Terrible Epidemic Breaks Out. My Brothers and I Keep the Helpless Yahgans Supplied with Fish.

I

THE FUEGIAN ARCHIPELAGO, WITH AN AREA OF APPROXIMATELY 27,600 square miles, is divided between Chile and Argentina in the ratio of two to one respectively. Chile's portion includes: firstly, all that part of the main island to the west of a line beginning at a point on the Beagle Channel twelve miles to the west of Ushuaia, and running northward to Cape Espíritu Santo, at the eastern entrance to the Magellan Straits; and secondly, all the islands south of the Beagle Channel. The remaining third of Tierra del Fuego, including Staten Island, belongs to Argentina.

Up to the time of which I am now writing, neither Chile nor Argentina had shown any active interest in their southernmost dependencies. My father had dreaded the advance of civilization—more for the sake of the native inhabitants than his own—yet he had realized that, sooner or later, both countries would establish authority in their own areas. With this in mind he had, for some time past, included Spanish lessons in our daily curriculum.

One Sunday afternoon in September, 1884, sixteen years after the Mission had begun work at Ushuaia, we were startled to see four vessels coming up the Beagle Channel, evidently bound for our harbour. Three of them were steamers; the fourth a sailing-cutter in tow.

Our peaceful little village was in a turmoil at once. Such a sight had never been seen before, and the excited natives crowded round my father and Mr. Lawrence, demanding to know what this visitation portended. Thoughts of war and an imminent attack against our beloved home filled some of us younger ones with fear.

The vessels continued their sinister advance, and finally dropped anchor in the harbour. The largest of them was the transport *Villarino*, the second a gunboat, the *Paraná*, and the third a Government tender, the *Comodoro Py*—all of the Argentine Navy.

Accompanied by Mr. Lawrence and Mr. Whaits, my father went out to meet them in the whale-boat with a Yahgan crew. When they drew near to the *Villarino*, her commander, Captain Spurr, called out in English:

" The other ship, Mr. Bridges."

He waved towards the *Paraná*, on boarding which Father and his friends were most kindly welcomed by the leader of the expedition, Colonel Augusto Lasserre. He explained to them that the object of this visit was to establish a sub-prefecture in Ushuaia and so inaugurate Argentine rule in the most southerly part of their domain.

When the visitors went ashore they were delighted with what they saw there. They had spent the previous six months at Cape San Juan, on Staten Island, erecting a lighthouse and establishing a sub-prefecture. As Staten Island is probably the wettest and most desolate outpost of the Fuegian archipelago, and as that winter had been unusually severe, the cheery Mission station at Ushuaia, with the natives already busy preparing their gardens for planting, milking their cows and tending their calves, must have presented a striking contrast to the dreary place they had just left.

An Argentine flag was placed in my father's hand by Colonel Lasserre. Father lowered the flag that had flown a welcome to all comers for so many years,[1] and hoisted in its stead the flag of the country in which he had made his home. There was a salvo of twenty-one guns from the ships in the harbour; and on land the Yahgans sent up a cheer in their own boisterous fashion.

The inaugural ceremony was attended *en masse* by all the Yahgans in the neighbourhood. My father, on behalf of the Mission, promised cordial assistance to the Argentine Government. He also spoke for the assembled natives, expressing their allegiance to the country that had taken them under her protection, and their desire for law and order.

In replying, Colonel Lasserre guaranteed the continued independence of the Mission and the ready assistance of the Argentine Government, which, he said, officially recognized the worth of the Christian and humane work of the English missionaries.

2

After consultation, a site for the new sub-prefecture was selected at Alacushwaia (Bay of Flapping Loggerhead Ducks), on the north shore of the harbour, and the necessary building work was immediately put in

---

[1] A composite affair, not unlike the Union Jack, used to avoid any suggestion that the Mission had imperialistic aspirations.

hand. A beacon light was set up near the sub-prefecture and another established on our side of the harbour, with our Yahgan, John Marsh, in charge of it.

The sub-prefect, Mr. Virasoro y Calvo, was wisely chosen and had been educated in England. Under his control were twenty men. Several of these were English sailors, which facilitated communication between the sub-prefecture and the Mission. We boys did our best to augment this with our simply awful Spanish, and were always delighted to serve as interpreters between these smart new arrivals and our dowdy old Yahgan friends. I recall that one of these English sailors was a fair, good-natured man by the name of Fred Greethurst. He was well over six feet tall, and was known to all of us as Longfellow.

On the 4th October the *Villarino* left Ushuaia by the western channels, and Captain Spurr was glad to avail himself of the services of two Yahgans as pilots. A fortnight later, with his mission accomplished, Colonel Lasserre prepared to follow in the *Paraná*. He wished to go to Punta Arenas by the intricate, little-known channels with which Father was well acquainted, so he invited him to accompany them. Father was pleased to accept, for we needed supplies from Punta Arenas. The tender *Comodoro Py*, which was to go with the gunboat to Punta Arenas, would be returning from there to Ushuaia with goods for the sub-prefecture, so Father could bring back his purchases at the same time. The *Comodoro Py* was over a hundred tons register, and besides accommodation for captain, mate and crew, had sleeping-berths for several passengers.

When the two vessels left Ushuaia, the *Paraná* carried, in addition to my father, our old Yahgan friend, Henry Lory, and six other young men of the same tribe.

As one steams westward from Ushuaia, the scenery on either shore grows more and more wild and desolate. Approaching Gordon Island it is grand in the extreme, for on the northern shore of the North-West Arm, which separates Gordon Island from the main island, vast glaciers appear. These originate far inland, fill the valleys that intersect the Marshall Range and culminate in precipices of ice, washed, winter and summer, by the sea.

From the glaciers much drift-ice breaks away, sometimes in such quantities as to prevent the passage of vessels along the North-West Arm. On such occasions the vessels have to use the South-West Arm, on the other side of Gordon Island. The *Paraná* and *Comodoro Py* were not forced to take this course. Nevertheless, a great deal of ice was encountered, and during an exploring expedition the gunboat's steam-launch was badly damaged. Happily, no lives were lost.

There were two official pilots on board the *Paraná*, but neither had ever been through these tortuous channels before. Navigation devolved, therefore, on Father and Henry Lory. For a time they shared duties. Then Lory was seized with a violent fever, so Father had to carry on alone. He was on the bridge continuously. Some of the channels they passed through, where the waves caused by the vessel washed the nearby precipices of rock, gave some anxiety to the ship's officers, but after a week of thick weather the *Paraná* and her tender came safely through to Punta Arenas.

But all was not so well with the Yahgans aboard. During the voyage the six young natives had been attacked by the same deadly fever as had struck down Henry Lory. Dr. Alvarez, the ship's surgeon, had diagnosed it as typhoid-pneumonia; and this was confirmed by Dr. Fenton when they reached Punta Arenas. A cottage was hired for the sufferers, and Father, assisted by a sailor from one of the ships, acted as nurse. But in spite of every care and medical attention, only one of the patients survived. Poor Henry Lory was among those who died.

These six deaths from this virulent disease greatly worried my father, for before he had left Ushuaia in the *Paraná* several of the natives had been smitten with the same complaint, though no one had had the slightest idea that it would develop into anything so dreadful. Dr. Alvarez had prescribed for them, and left medicines in the care of Mr. Whaits. But medicines had not saved Henry Lory and the five Yahgan boys—and my father was desperately anxious about us all at Ushuaia.

Immediate return, however, was not possible. The *Comodoro Py* had been sent off to assist a French steamer, which had been wrecked near the eastern entrance to the Magellan Straits. Father awaited her return with ever-growing impatience and disquiet.

3

Meanwhile at Ushuaia his worst fears were being realized. After the departure of the *Paraná* and *Comodoro Py*, the natives went down with this fever one after the other. In a few days they were dying at such a rate that it was impossible to dig graves fast enough. In outlying districts the dead were merely put outside the wigwams or, when the other occupants had the strength, carried or dragged to the nearest bushes.

In Stirling House and the Lawrences' home down the road all the children were struck down at once. In the orphanage Mrs. Whaits had thirty Yahgan children on her hands, all victims of the epidemic. My mother and Yekadahby, neither of whom had ever heard of typhoid-pneumonia, formed a different opinion from that of Doctors Alvarez and Fenton, and dealt with us accordingly. Mrs. Lawrence and her sister, Miss Martin, who had come to live with them at the settlement, agreed with the diagnosis of Mother and Yekadahby—and so did Mrs. Whaits. They all decided that it was measles.

None of the grown members of the Mission party, who had all had measles in their youth, contracted the complaint, which goes to prove that this time the ladies knew better than the medical men. It is astonishing that this childish ailment, contagious in civilized communities, yet seldom fatal, should wipe out over half the population of a district and leave the survivors so reduced in vitality that another fifty per cent. succumbed during the next two years, apparently from the after-effects of the attack. It must be that our ancestors, for generations past, have suffered from periodical epidemics of measles, and we, in consequence, have gained a certain degree of immunity from it. On the other hand, the Yahgans, though incredibly strong, and able to face cold and hardship of every kind and to recover almost miraculously from serious wounds, had never had to face this evil thing, and therefore lacked the stamina to withstand it. It is hardly to be wondered at that the doctors failed to recognize it for what it really was, when it appeared in such a virulent form.

By the time my father got back from Punta Arenas in the *Comodoro Py* the epidemic had passed its peak, though the natives were still dying fast. I remember his going off, Sunday and week-day alike, with pick-axe and shovel on his shoulder, and returning, completely exhausted, late at night. At one settlement, a short distance away from the village, he found a whole family dead, with the exception of one small infant, whom he brought home. Mother and Yekadahby cared for it till some native woman was able to take it over.

In this pitiful task of grave-digging, my father had the assistance of Fred Greethurst—Longfellow—whose services were made available by the kindly sub-prefect, Mr. Virasoro y Calvo.

4

The surviving Yahgans were still in a very weak state. In the month of November, which corresponds to the English May, there was no garden produce except such potatoes and other root-vegetables as had been stored from the previous harvest—a necessarily small reserve, as husbandry was unusual among those improvident and generously communistic people. The Mission distributed as much food as could be spared, but, with so many hungry mouths, it was a meagre allowance.

Luckily, my brothers and I were able to help in this emergency. There was at Ushuaia a trammel-net—an ingenious contrivance of floats and weights that was anchored off shore and entangled fish, large and small, in its meshes. It was left in sheltered waters, and if, on returning to collect the catch, one noticed that any of the cork floats were sunk or much out of line, one could be sure that there was a big fellow or two in the net.

While the Yahgans were still unable to get about, we three brothers had quickly recovered from our mild attack of measles, and were able to look after the trammel-net. For this we used the punt that had been built some months before by Despard and Mr. " Chips " Smith. Weather permitting, we used to visit the net in the punt at least twice a day, and procured a regular and most unusually bountiful supply of fish. Most of them were mullet, which sometimes reached two and a half feet in length. There was also a fine kind of smelt (*yeemacaia* in Yahgan; *perjerrey* in Spanish). Later in the season, in pursuit of the sprat shoals, came such voracious ocean fish as the *hahpaim* (one of the mackerel family), which we valued highly for food. It was built for speed, and measured as much as three feet from its swallow tail to the tip of its pointed nose. These and others of their kind would sometimes tear the net or drag it adrift from its moorings.

On every trip in the punt we came back with more fish than two of us could carry slung from an oar on our shoulders. Frequently we had to make three or more journeys from the beach to the settlement with our booty. With the exception of those needed by the Mission party, these fish were divided amongst the natives, and we were indeed delighted with ourselves for being the means of bringing these vital supplies to our unfortunate friends—or all that were left of them.

CHAPTER TWELVE

*Governor Felix Paz. We Go to School. Serafín Aguirre Becomes Our Idol.
My Father and I Explore the Land of the Alacaloof. A Strange Meeting near
Wellington Island. Chonos Dandies. A Queer Coincidence. Day-Dreams in
Ushuaia.*

I

THE FOLLOWING YEAR, 1885, WAS A MOMENTOUS ONE FOR DESPARD, WILL
and myself, for during it there came to Ushuaia three important person-
ages : a Government official, a schoolmaster and a convicted murderer.

The official was Captain Felix Paz of the Argentine Navy, who became chief of administration when the sub-prefecture was succeeded by
a governorship. He was rather fair, below medium height, and quick
both in temper and action. He brought with him several horses, and
gave my father one of them; a chestnut with a distinguished Roman
nose. Governor Paz was exceedingly kind to us boys. He made a
companion of Despard, and would take him sailing in his canoe. Sometimes he used a larger boat with two masts, and Despard and I would
comprise the crew. We handled the sails under the Governor's orders
and, as he was a naval officer, received first-class training in navigation.
Curiously enough, my brother Will did not care for boating in those
days. Though so bold in other ways, he was inclined to be nervous in a
sailing-boat. In later years, however, he was to do far more sailing than
either Despard or myself.

The schoolmaster was a Mr. Armstrong. He arrived in the *Allen
Gardiner* on the 4th March, 1885. He was over six feet in height, and
when we learnt that he was to be our schoolmaster, his huge size and
ominous name filled us with dread. With his advent, life at Ushuaia
changed for the worse. We had regular school hours, both morning and
afternoon, and were expected to be clean and neatly dressed.

I never approved of Mr. Armstrong. He was a University man and
quite a sport, yet he and I were seldom in harmony. He hated sneaks
and milksops, and had I attended an English school I should undoubtedly
have been dubbed a milksop—or something worse, if anything worse
existed. One of the sailors of the *Allen Gardiner*, comparing me, with
my great size and extreme caution, to Will, so small, venturesome and

Yahgan children.

A Yahgan binding a fish-spear head to the shaft.

By courtesy of Dr. Armando Braun Menendez. Photos by the French Scientific Expedition of 1882.

Throwing a fish-spear. This man was an exceptionally well-grown Yahgan from the outer coast.

By courtesy of Dr. Armando Braun Menendez. Photo by the French Scientific Expedition of 1882.

A Yahgan canoe. These were made from bark, usually that of the evergreen beech (*Nothofagus betuloides*).

From "Los Onas."

Family group.
Taken on the visit to England in 1880.
From left to right: Despard, Will, Mother, Bertha, Father, the Author, Mary.

naughty, had christened me "Lady Jane." This name of unspeakable
scorn stuck to me like tar. Even Mr. Armstrong stooped to use it—
until I vindicated myself in battle. The conflict in question took place in
the depth of winter. We were playing with some native boys, one of
whom hurled a snowball with a stone imbedded in it at one of my smaller
companions—with sad results. Swift reprisals were unavoidable. I
emerged victorious. My nose bled splendidly. Mr. Armstrong must
have witnessed the affray from a window—or perhaps my face still bore
tell-tale smudges, even after I had cleaned myself up—for in school that
morning, after giving me an unconvincing lecture on the evil of fighting,
he announced that he would never call me "Lady Jane" again.

He was at Ushuaia about a year. Before he left us he married Mrs.
Lawrence's sister, Miss Martin. He later entered the Church. His
influence on us boys was unquestionably beneficial, yet I, for one, was
glad when he went.

The third important personage, the convicted murderer, was a much
more exciting and romantic figure. He was a gaucho called Serafín
Aguirre, and he came to Ushuaia with Governor Paz. He must have been
a protégé of the Governor's, for, although nominally serving a term of
imprisonment for homicide, he was allowed a great deal of freedom. He
came from the province of Tucuman in Argentina and, though scorning
steady work, was a grand man with cattle and horses. Dark and dignified,
he stood nearly six feet tall, and combined great strength with dexterity.
By grasping a cow's lower jaw with one hand and a horn with the other,
he could throw her to the ground with the greatest ease.

We learnt a lot of Spanish from Aguirre, but many of the words would
have caused us to be ejected from a respectable drawing-room, or even a
stable. We were fascinated by this picturesque stranger, and made up
our minds to be gauchos when we grew up. We procured little *lazos*
and *boleadoras* and practised on hens, dogs or any other unfortunate
creature we could find. As we grew older and more and more sinful,
we used to arrange for the calves to escape through a gap in the fence or
a gate left open by some unknown person, so that we could have the fun
of lassoing them and bringing them back into the enclosure. I suppose
pranks like these took the place of football, cricket and boxing enjoyed by
schoolboys in other parts of the world.

Another of our boyhood misdemeanours was smoking. Finding it
difficult to get cigarettes or tobacco, we used any rubbish we could obtain :
dried tea-leaves, lichen from the trees—even dry horse-dung was con-

sidered better than nothing. Our smoking club was in the cow-house loft, where straw was stored. Hidden in the rafters we kept such cigarettes as we could get and our other smoking materials. Our pipes were hollowed-out swedes or turnips with straws thrust through them. A larger turnip with three or four straws sticking out of it, according to the number of warriors present, was the Pipe of Peace, to be smoked with due ceremony after some specially heated argument. Despard had too much sense to join us in these follies, though he certainly knew what was going on. The arch-criminal in this and everything else was Will. Apart from Fred Lawrence (an addition to our neighbours' family whom I have not previously mentioned), Will was the youngest of our party. Nevertheless, he was the ringleader, yet, being quite small and junior, always got off lightly when anything went wrong, on the unfounded supposition that he had been led astray.

Our smoking activities were never found out, though our fondness for eating mint, which we did to disguise the scent of tobacco, or whatever rubbish we had been smoking, caused Mother some surprise. This immunity was due partly to luck and partly to a natural aptitude for looking after ourselves. Once when the Governor came across the harbour to protest against our being allowed to go sailing alone in the *Leeloom*, Father told him that we had the bump of self-preservation very well developed. We certainly had.

Despard, being older than the rest of us, had more opportunities for horse-riding. We younger ones had to confine our attentions to the calves. We scorned, I am glad to say, to mount calves not strong enough to jump and throw us off. We learnt, from painful experience, that the only way to stick on for any length of time was to mount facing the tail and hang on to that.

Later, under Aguirre's tuition, we graduated as horsemen. Will, with his daring and high spirits, naturally became Aguirre's favourite. At first, being so small, he rode pillion behind our hero, but before long he was riding alone, and no horse could go fast enough to please him.

With my more meditative and placid turn of mind, I preferred less boisterous forms of amusement. I discovered an attractive pastime in plaiting hide and making worked buttons. In this and other handicrafts I was instructed by Aguirre. Altogether, in spite of the awful language he taught us, I think we got more good than harm from that tough rascal.

2

My father had always been anxious to get further acquainted with both the Alacaloof and the Ona, not only to bring to them the benefits of Christianity, but also to make a study of their completely different languages. With the recent inauguration of Argentine rule in the eastern part of that region and the growing influx of white population, he saw that civilization of one kind or another was bound to reach the Ona and Alacaloof eventually; and he felt that it must be brought either with the Bible, the gin-bottle or the rifle, and that the first was surely the best way. With these ideas in mind, he set off in the *Allen Gardiner* to explore the little-known channels among the western islands, the home of the Alacaloof. To my immense delight, he took me with him.

This *Allen Gardiner* was not the yawl, but her successor, the third vessel to bear that honoured name. She had only recently been acquired; a diminutive schooner-rigged, auxiliary-screw steamer, nothing like as good a sea-boat as the yawl, but far handier in calm weather and among the narrow, intricate channels, where the wind came off the mountains in irregular gusts that we called " woollies " on account of the spindrift they whirled from the water.

We had on board two Yahgans from that rough region round the shores of Brecknock Peninsula, the borderland between the Yahgans and their western neighbours. The first was Acualisnan, nicknamed Wapisa (whale) because of his girth, and the other was Sailapaiyinij, an active little man whose mother was an Alacaloof. Both men spoke the Alacaloof tongue fluently.

Since the first explorers set foot in Fireland there had been many sanguinary clashes between the Alacaloof Indians and the whites; and, though we saw smoke and distant canoes as we steamed through some of the inner waters—so hidden that they might well have been called fastnesses—no natives cared to come alongside.

To overcome this reticence, when an Alacaloof encampment was sighted my father would put off with his two Yahgans in the dinghy. He was, of course, unarmed, and such was his confidence that he always took me with him. His trustfulness was justified, for we received nothing but kind and friendly treatment from the various groups with whom, through our interpreters, we became acquainted. At one place we induced three young natives—distantly related, I believe, to Acualisnan—to join us on the *Allen Gardiner.*

After exploring the grand but gloomy channels south of the Straits of
Magellan, we proceeded northward, where we met with less wind and
milder weather.   Some of the channels we passed through were hardly
more than clefts in the rocks, which stood up like irregular walls thousands
of feet high on either side of us.   The climate there is so wet that moss
and trees cling to the faces of these almost perpendicular cliffs.   On a still,
clear night the stars in the narrow strip of sky overhead shine with double
brilliancy and their reflection is multiplied again in the sombre depths
below.

In one of these narrow fiords, not far from Wellington Island, a canoe
came alongside our steamer.   The people in it did not wear even the
scanty apron that was customary among the Fuegians.   One man had
instead a flat-topped, wall-sided bowler hat as his only garment, and
another a collar, once white, tied round his neck, for the lack of a stud,
with a strip of hide.   Neither Acualisnan nor Sailapaiyinij could understand their language, but one of the three young Alacaloof was familiar
with it, so we had the unusual experience of carrying on a conversation
through two interpreters.   We learnt that these were Chonos from
farther north.   Father expressed his surprise at meeting them in those high
latitudes.

We turned southward and made for Punta Arenas, where, with
Acualisnan, Sailapaiyinij and the three young Alacaloof, we went ashore,
in order to impress them with the power and importance of the whites.
With the five natives all dressed in civilized clothes, we went for a walk
through this most southerly town of the world.   Our little party attracted
much attention.   One group of well-dressed people, who should have
known better, stood in a doorway pointing at us and making humorous
remarks in Spanish about the appearance of our Indian companions.   My
father, who was no respecter of persons, immediately called a halt, pointed
back at the discourteous ones and commented in Yahgan on the bright
colouring of their clothing and the size of one of them, who was even
more enormous than our champion fat man, Acualisnan, likening him to
a stout penguin and Acualisnan to a thin cormorant.   When his words
were translated into Alacaloof, they raised such a shout of derisive laughter
that the enemy retired discomfited.

On the way back from Punta Arenas to Ushuaia we drew near to the
nest of mountains called Clarence Island.   Acualisnan told us that it was
not, in fact, one island, but was split into two or three parts by a channel
that ran right through it.   With Acualisnan as pilot we followed this

channel's devious windings—and Acualisnan Channel on the Admiralty charts now perpetuates his name.

After leaving our three Alacaloof friends among their own people, enriched by presents, and with a warm invitation to visit us at Ushuaia, we started homeward.

Before our first contact with the Alacaloof on this trip there had occurred an accident that might even have proved fatal. We had on board the *Allen Gardiner* a murderous old pin-fire shot-gun, loaded with ball cartridge. When some wild ducks had been sighted, the gun had had to be reloaded with shot. One of the cartridges had jammed, and, while Father had been trying to lever it out with a knife, it had gone off. The bullet had remained lying on the deck where the muzzle of the gun had been resting, but the metal cartridge had flown back with such violence that it had left a nasty scar on Father's left temple, and his face had been so badly burnt by the powder that we had feared at first that he might be blinded. Such was, fortunately, not the case. His eyebrows and most of his hair had been singed off, the skin of his face and whites of his eyes had been speckled with powder-grains, but he had not been seriously injured.

When we reached Ushuaia we found Despard in exactly the same unhappy plight. At the same hour on the same afternoon, when three hundred miles had separated father and son, Despard had been making squibs, and the mixture had exploded in his face. It was the only accident of its kind that ever happened to either of them during their lifetimes. A queer coincidence.

3

High on the mountain opposite the Mission village was a bright green gap in the forest, with a stream flowing through it. It was probably a patch of saturated moss, but as I gazed at it from across the harbour, I preferred to imagine that it was a paradise of grass and wild flowers. In my frequent day-dreams I planned to live up there by and by, far from the crowded village. I would have a few goats, I decided, and a little garden. I should be able to look down on the distant Mission and, when the fancy took me, row across the harbour to swop some of my goat-cheese for sugar and other luxuries. I should not need bread; I had had quite enough of that when in disgrace.

In later years I was to grow more ambitious. I determined on Gough Island, south of Tristan da Cunha, for my future abode; and a lovely shipwrecked damsel crept into my dreams. But that was not yet. The fancies of my early boyhood centred, as I have said, around the bright green gap in the forest across the harbour, or on the sunny northern slopes of the range which, for weeks on end in winter, cast its freezing shadow over our homestead.

And I was not the only one to think of a new, wider life beyond the familiar confines of the place of my birth. That sick, indomitable man, Thomas Bridges, my father, had his brave dark eyes fixed on a fresh horizon.

CHAPTER THIRTEEN

*My Father Plans a New Venture. He Resigns his Position as Mission Superinten-
dent. He Visits President Roca in Buenos Aires and Obtains a Grant of Land.
He Goes to England and Brings Back Supplies and Building Material for our New
Home. We Move from Ushuaia to Harberton.*

I

LET US TAKE A BRIEF SURVEY OF WHAT HAD BEEN DONE AMONGST THE
natives. In twenty years a handful of missionaries had transformed these
irresponsible savages into a law-abiding community. Not only at
Ushuaia, but also in numerous little creeks and sheltered coves along the
coast, there had come into being Yahgan settlements with gardens, which,
when cattle was kept, had been fenced. One Indian, Samuel Mahteen
by name, owned twenty head of cattle. In the shelter of a wood near
Ushaij River, over two miles to the west of Ushuaia, he had built a
modest house and had enclosed a garden in which such fruit and vegetables as the climate allowed did well. On at least one occasion he and
his bright little wife entertained our whole family, including Mother and
Yekadahby, with strawberries and cream round his rustic table.

There was progress, too, in other directions. Canoes, for instance.
For numberless generations the Yahgan canoes had been made of bark.[1]
This soon rotted, lasting a year at the most, when the natives were obliged
to make new ones, or run the risk of their foundering in a storm. Now,
with tools supplied by the Mission, the Indians made dug-out canoes
from logs. These, though not such good sea-boats, had great durability,
could be beached on stony coasts, where the bark canoes had to be
anchored off shore, and, once constructed, freed the owners from the
heavy task of constant replacement.

Under the careful direction of Father and his fellow-workers, there
had grown amongst the Yahgans a keen sense of law and order and of
property rights. Murder was now almost unheard of and, owing to the
strength of public opinion and increased civic consciousness, lesser crimes
had greatly diminished. There was no police force, nor was it needed,
for the unwritten laws emanating from the Mission were respected by the
mass of inhabitants of that region.

[1] Usually from the evergreen beech (*Nothofagus betuloides*), called by the Yahgans
" shushchi."

These were the people whom Charles Darwin had labelled, if not the missing link, then the next thing to it.

With all this achieved, it was still plain that, when the white man—of a very different type from those who had lived so happily amongst the natives—came to the country, as come he would, these children of the wilds would not be able to hold their own; liquor would be introduced and, powerless to continue their simple existence, the poor Fuegians would go to the wall.

Father had long tried to get the Mission to establish a place where employment would be found for all those willing to work. He wanted the Society—of which he was general superintendent in the Falklands as well as in Tierra del Fuego—to obtain from the Argentine Government a grant of land on which to settle and succour the natives, employing them in farming or other works. He submitted his proposals to the committee in London, but did not receive unanimous support, the general opinion being that an Anglican Mission should confine its activities to evangelical work. Apart from that, it was found, on seeking advice, that the Argentine authorities would not be inclined to give a grant of land to a foreign society with its headquarters in London.

My father was disappointed, but not defeated. He realized that the early phases of the Mission work had passed and that, if the committee would not, or could not, follow the only line that would protect the natives against the invasion he foresaw, he must break away and take the matter into his own hands.

At this stage came the surprise visit of Colonel Lasserre from Buenos Aires and the devastating outbreak of measles. What a change! Hamlets deserted; gardens overgrown with weeds; cattle slaughtered for needed food—or even sold for liquor or exchanged for a third-rate gun; but, worst of all, a frightened, weakened tribe in mourning. Not only was it now plain to Father that the old Mission was doomed; another very human consideration must have influenced him. He had six children, all eminently suited to wrest their living from the land of their birth, but not equipped to stand their ground amongst children who had had the advantage, not unmixed, of having been brought up in more civilized surroundings.

He was assured that, though the Argentine Government would refuse to make a grant of land to a society in England, they might make such a concession to an individual who had spent his life in Fireland, especially when his children were Argentine citizens by law and, with their knowledge of English, Yahgan and Spanish, would form an increasingly useful link between the Fuegians and the Argentine authorities.

With these thoughts in mind, my father began to look round for a site for the new settlement. He eventually decided on a spot some forty miles east of Ushuaia. It covered an area of about fifty thousand acres and included some islands in the Beagle Channel, the largest of which was Gable Island.

For many years he had corresponded with students and scientists in different parts of the world, but since the advent of the sub-prefecture in 1884 and the setting up of the Governor's headquarters in the following year, his correspondence with the officials of La Plata Museum, near Buenos Aires, had become greater than ever before. Besides this useful contact, he had made many good friends among the naval officers who had visited Ushuaia, and had become well known, by repute, to a number of influential persons in Buenos Aires. Through these channels he caused enquiries to be made. The response was encouraging; the Government would be most unlikely to refuse his formal request for the land on which he had set his heart.

So certain was he of the justice of his claim and the generosity of the authorities that, on the strength of these verbal and unofficial assurances, he took the most reckless plunge of a life already packed with venturesome acts. He resigned his position as superintendent of the Mission.

Immediately there was a general outcry. Friends in the Falklands and elsewhere loudly expressed the opinion that he was heading straight for bankruptcy and deplored the fate that awaited his unfortunate wife and family. They pointed out with great relish that, even if the land were his—which it was not—he would be trying to do what no man had ever done before in the country south of the Magellan Straits: to wrest a living unassisted from the soil.

At a committee meeting in London a prominent member of the Society compared my father to a rat forsaking a sinking ship, but piously added the rider that he had undoubtedly been " instigated by the Evil One to his ruin."

Not everyone was antagonistic, however. He was backed by every member of the family. That staunch little sailor, Captain Willis of the *Allen Gardiner*, lent him, at a fixed rate of interest, his whole life savings —seven hundred pounds—when no one else would finance what they considered to be a crazy venture.

Once started, Father allowed no grass to grow under his feet. He took the whale-boat and, with Despard and myself, sailed down the Beagle Channel for a close inspection of the country we already called Downeast. In the comparatively sheltered water to the east of Gable Island there is a cluster of creeks and harbours. One of these was provisionally chosen, but a second, somewhat farther east, was later judged more suitable. The first we called Thought Of (for obvious reasons); the other was known to the natives as Ukatush, the exact meaning of which we never established, and was now named by my father Harberton, after Mother's birthplace. A map of the district is facing page 274.

Round the shores of this harbour were many sites of ancient Yahgan villages, and one was chosen as the place for our future home. The Yahgan name for it was Tuwujlumbiwaia (Black Heron Harbour).

Pending Father's formal application for the Downeast land, James Cushinjiz, who belonged to those parts, was put in charge of the new venture. He was given provisions and authority to employ up to six of his countrymen in the making of an enclosure for cattle and a fence across the isthmus to prevent animals from wandering off the peninsula into the vast forests at the back. He was also instructed to make huts for himself and his helpers and to cultivate more land. Father purchased eight cows and a bull from natives who were willing to sell them.

On the 10th July, 1886, he wrote in his journal:

"Left Ushuaia in the *Allen Gardiner* for Sandy Point [Punta Arenas]. There I propose taking passage for Buenos Aires to present my request for land, which having obtained, I then D.V. go to England to charter a vessel and bring out such goods as I require for my station. I leave the people with much reluctance. I went round to wish them all good-bye, as I hope to see them again in about six months and to live among them for many years. I was much comforted by the expressions of their goodwill."

He arrived in Buenos Aires on the 23rd of that month. During his stay in the capital he was the guest of Dr. Moreno, head of La Plata Museum, who treated him with great kindness and introduced him to many influential friends, including his uncle, Antonio Cambaceres, the President of Congress. My father also became acquainted with Dr. Moreno's father-in-law, Rufino Varela, who, as Father says in his journal, "spoke English well and did all that was possible to forward my cause."

Antonio Cambaceres went with him on several occasions to Government House and introduced him to various ministers, senators and deputies, among them the ex-President, Bartolome Mitre, and the then President, Julio Argentino Roca.

General Roca, an enlightened and progressive statesman, had been a soldier as well as a politician. In his day he had led more than one punitive expedition against the turbulent pampa Indians, who lived in the grassy, woodless lands between the Andes and the Atlantic; and he had done more than any of his contemporaries to bring those fierce tribes to order. Thus he was able to appreciate the courage shown by a far more humble soldier who, without weapons or military backing, had invaded the territories of an equally lawless people, his only buckler an unshakable faith in his divine errand.

He received Father warmly. In some respects they were not unlike each other: about the same height; both lean and wiry, with small, eager, almost hungry faces surmounted by broad, high foreheads; both with neatly trimmed beards and moustaches. There the resemblance ended, for President Roca was fair, though nearly bald, and had pale blue-grey eyes, while Father had a head well covered with jet-black hair, then streaked with white, and eyes of the darkest brown.

The President spoke good English. He had, of course, been told the object of Father's visit, but began their interview by asking many questions about that little-known land down south and Father's life among its native inhabitants. Then at length he said, as if Father came not as a suppliant, but as a valued creditor:

" How can my government compensate you in some measure for the life of self-sacrifice you have led, and the humanitarian work you have accomplished? "

My father answered:

" By giving me a piece of land where I can settle and make a home with my children, born in the country."

A map was produced and the block solicited was marked on it, with the extent of eight square leagues, which in those days was valued at fifty pounds a square league. President Roca expressed the belief that, with the consent of the Minister of the Interior and the Minister of Lands and Colonies, he would be able to grant this tract direct, without taking it to Congress. He promised Father there and then that it would soon be as surely his as the coat he was wearing.

It transpired that the President, even when backed by his Ministers, could not legally make a grant of land, so the matter had to go through Congress. Pushed by Father's good and efficient friends, it passed both Chambers in three hours with very little opposition. Even then there was still much to be done before the title-deeds could be made out. The land had to be located, surveyed, measured and staked, and a correct map made of the whole. This would be a tremendous task; the endless creeks and inlets, with swamps draining into them, and the numerous irregular islets, combined with the difficulties of getting from place to place, would keep the Government surveyor busy for a very long time.

But President Roca promised Father that as soon as the deeds were ready he would sign them; so, on the 1st October, just over two months from the date of his arrival in Buenos Aires, Father felt that matters were sufficiently advanced for him to leave for England, to buy the materials and stores for our new home.

2

Twelve years later, soon after the death of my father, Roca was elected President for the second time. While making a tour of the southern limits of his domain, he visited our home. His party numbered nearly fifty. Mother received him and was able to supply tea for all, with strawberries and cream in real Devonshire style. The President spoke of my late father with the greatest appreciation and told us how, remembering his promise, he had insisted that the title-deeds of the land should be produced for his signature. They had appeared on his desk on his final day in office, and had been the last deeds to which he had put his signature during his first term as President; not only the last, he added, but the ones that had given him the greatest satisfaction to sign.

At about the time of Roca's visit to our homestead, Father's life-long friend and helper, Mr. Lawrence, was also granted nearly 19,000 acres at Punta Remolino (Shumacush), on the Beagle Channel. He settled there with his family, though remaining in the Mission service till his death at a good old age.

Julio Roca was a great, kind and wise leader. In my opinion, his grandest deed was during a frontier dispute with our neighbour, Chile, towards the end of his last term as President. I have lived for years on one side or the other of the frontier then at issue and have crossed it in a hundred different places far removed from each other; and, from a stockman's point of view, do not consider the land in question to be worth as much as a fair-sized *estancia* in the Province of Buenos Aires. Yet, swollen with national dignity and hoarse with voicing sovereign rights over desert, bog, rock and glacier, the peoples of Chile and we of Argentina were ready to fly at each other's throats and tear one another to pieces. Then, when war seemed inevitable, Roca put his pride in his pocket. He met President Errázuris of Chile in the little town of Punta

Arenas, where the two men were able to settle the issue as all such disputes should be settled, and brought to their peoples many decades of peace and friendship, in place of who knows what bitterness and strife.

In the city of Buenos Aires, on a pedestal of grey marble, stands a great bronze monument to President Roca. He sits in his general's uniform astride a mighty stallion, but though grand in appearance, he looks tired. His stallion, too, instead of prancing in some impossible attitude, gives the impression of a steady walk. Its arched neck and shortened curb show that it has still the strength and fire to carry on, but there is something in its mien to suggest that it has already done a long day's work. The supreme simplicity of that monument is enhanced by the fact that it bears no eulogies in gilded characters. Instead, on the plain marble, are the four letters " ROCA."

3

My father reached England from Buenos Aires, and was able to purchase everything we should need for a long time to come. A large wooden frame-house was constructed in my grandfather's carpentry-shop in Devonshire. All that was then required was a ship, the finding of which caused Father much trouble and anxiety. After a great deal of difficulty, he managed to charter the *Shepherdess*, a brigantine of some 360 tons burden, for which he had to pay fifty shillings a day. The captain was not an easy man to handle. He belonged to some peculiar religious sect, and claimed that, after a riotous youth, he had suddenly realized the wickedness of his life and, bursting into tears, had proceeded to sign the pledge. This reformation was signalized by a blue-and-white ribbon sewn on the lapel of his jacket.

When the vessel's load had been completed with bricks, limestone and some coal for sale at Harberton to passing steamers, they set sail for Tierra del Fuego. On board were two carpenters from Devonshire and a Mr. Edward Aspinall, who was to take over my father's duties as superintendent of the Ushuaia Mission. There were other passengers, too: a young South Devon bull, four Romney Marsh rams, a couple of Devonshire pigs and two collie dogs.

Despite the captain's strict principles, he was not disinclined to augment his own income at my father's expense and, secure in the knowledge that payment was by the day and not by the mile, saw to it that the voyage was a protracted one.

4

My father had said that he would be back in six months. These went by, and still he did not return. At Harberton, James Cushinjiz and his companions consumed the provisions that had been left there for them, but there was very little work done to show for it. This laziness on their part was put down in large measure by their benevolent foreman to the after-effects of the measles. Some calves were born, and Cushinjiz kept the cattle tame.

Meanwhile the family waited anxiously at Ushuaia. The six months dragged on to seven, eight, nine, until finally my mother could bear the suspense no longer. Leaving Yekadahby in charge of my sisters, Bertha and Alice, she boarded the *Allen Gardiner*, which was in port at the time, and sailed for Harberton, taking my brothers and myself with her.

We hoped to find my father already arrived at Harberton, but we were doomed to disappointment. The *Allen Gardiner* could not stay for long at Harberton, and Mother was reluctant to return to Ushuaia. Mr. Robbins, the ships' engineer, came to our assistance in this emergency, and within two days had built a one-roomed hut from some scantling and corrugated iron that had been left in the care of James Cushinjiz on an earlier trip. We called it "Robbins' Cot."

We planned to take occupation of our primitive home on the following day and to live there until Father arrived, or, dreadful thought, had to be given up for lost. The night was passed on board the *Allen Gardiner*.

The morning broke bright and cold—and there, some three miles away, looking huge under her square sails, was the brigantine. She had taken one hundred and eight days on the voyage from England.

And so, reunited after so many weary months, did we take up our new life at Harberton.

PART II

HARBERTON
1887–1899

Harberton harbour, looking eastward from the settlement, with Picton Island appearing to seal the entrance to the harbour. In the background on the right is Navarin Island.

A view of Harberton taken from near the homestead, looking north-north-west, with Pink Mountain in the central distance.

Guanaco in their winter haunts.

From Gable Island, looking east-north-east. In the distance is No Top Hill.

Looking north-north-east from the eastern Guanaco Hill. In the foreground is the *Lakooma* lake.

CHAPTER FOURTEEN

Our New Home at Harberton. We Exterminate the Pigs. Evening Pastimes in the Homestead. Books from England. Skating on the Lakes. I Find an Excuse to Skate on Sundays. The Shepherdess Takes Fencing-Posts to the Falklands. Despard Contracts Typhoid.

I

COUNTLESS CENTURIES AGO THE SEA-LEVEL IN FIRELAND MUST HAVE BEEN as much as twenty feet higher than it is to-day. In many places where there is a clay formation there are undulating hills that end suddenly in very steep banks, from the foot of which the land, often rocky, slopes more gently to the sea. These banks, eroded by time and now covered with vegetation, were once sheer cliffs washed by the sea. There is no doubt that in days gone by the innumerable peninsulas that now form part of the Fuegian mainland were separate islands. At Ushuaia there is a quarter-mile isthmus, the native name for which is Yaiyuashaga. It is overgrown with grass and bush and has been above sea-level maybe for thousands of years, yet *ashaga* means in Yahgan, not a neck of land, but a channel. This description not only confirms that the sea has fallen during the course of the centuries, but also strongly suggests that the natives were in the country before the geological change took place.

On one of these peninsulas was to be our home farm; and near the beach on one of the moderate slopes mentioned in the previous paragraph was to be our new settlement, with the steep bank rising behind it to a height of some fifteen feet, above which the hill sloped upwards more gradually, to be crowned by a forest of evergreen trees and thick undergrowth covering an area of roughly twenty acres. The exposed hills round about were covered with grass or with dwarf deciduous beech trees,[1] scrub of the same species, and the thorny bushes that yielded the fruit for those delicious barberry puddings.

Creeks running in from the sea thrust their heads well into the main forest. Their shores were impassable for horses and bad enough for a man on foot, for numberless huge trees had fallen from the forest to lie

[1] *Nothofagus pumilio.* This tree seldom exceeds a height of forty-five feet or a girth of eight feet. It grows as a bush on dry or boggy land and is leafless for seven months of the year.

with their branches in the mud, which in those sheltered creeks was as soft as cream and no man knew how deep. The trees came down to the water's edge, so that timber did not have to be dragged, with great labour, overland. Logs for fuel or for sawing into boards could be loaded at high water on a boat, or formed into rafts, for shipping to the homestead. This served the dual purpose of providing wood for the settlement and clearing a track.

Throughout that first exceedingly severe winter at Harberton the *Shepherdess* lay safely anchored in the harbour while her cargo was unloaded. There were no docks, derricks or landing-gear; no lighters, only boats. Everything had to be carried or dragged up the stony beach. The ground was frozen like rock, and everything might be buried under a foot or two of snow over-night. The sailors of the *Shepherdess* considered their work done when they had got the cargo out of the vessel. The two carpenters from Devonshire, who stayed at Harberton for a. while, were both good fellows, but not exactly suitable or willing dock labourers. The Yahgans were willing enough, but lazy when steady work had to be done. They were a dying race, who seemed to know it. They certainly did the best they could. That romantic gaucho, Serafín Aguirre, who had come with us from Ushuaia, was wonderful with cattle or horses, but hated any kind of labour; he was too proud. There remained my father, who was a very ill man, and his young but sturdy sons.

For the mountain of perishable goods unloaded from the *Shepherdess* some form of protection was essential, and much of the timber of the frame-house from Grandfather's shop in Devonshire had to be used for this purpose. Greatly to Father's sorrow, the new homestead could not be built entirely of that material, but had to be completed with wood sawn on the spot. We lived in Robbins' Cot till spring, when three rooms of the new house could be used. It was over a year before the building was finished.

In the spot where it stood, with the land sloping upwards behind it to the north-east, our new home received the benefit of the summer sun till well on in the afternoon. Then the sheltering hill at the back cast its heavy shadows over the place, and the hills and woods across the harbour would stand out with marvellous clearness as daylight faded. This was the hour when Father and Mother, arm in arm, would take their evening stroll, until the dusk crept over the land and the air grew chilly. Then it was that the reflection of the hills on the calm, darkening water made a picture of peace beyond my power to describe.

It was April, 1887, when we moved from Ushuaia to Harberton. Father and Mother were then both forty-four years of age. Despard was fourteen, I twelve, Will ten, Bertha eight and Alice, the baby, five. Mary, the eldest of the family, was sixteen and still in England. Yekadahby, of course, came to Harberton with us. Aguirre brought with him a buxom Yahgan woman, whom he had actually gone as far as marrying. It certainly was on her account that Father gave Aguirre a job, and, needless to say, we boys were delighted to have our hero with us again.

Also from Ushuaia came a number of Yahgan families, glad to move their homes and settle in a new place, where they could continue to enjoy the protection of the man who had always been such a friend to them. Their numbers varied, but frequently there were over sixty. All who wanted to work were provided with employment, in exchange for which they were given bread, sugar, coffee and clothing. The sawyers and other semi-skilled workers were given a modicum of cash to purchase other things for which their contact with white men had given them a liking. At times of *Iacasi*, when the sprat-shoals lured the large, voracious fish and penguins in from the ocean, the Yahgans would take to their old life. They would be out all day in their canoes, spearing penguins—and there might be only one or two left working in the settlement. But when food was scarce we would have as many as twenty helpers, either working on the many acres of land that the needs of this large family compelled us to cultivate, or cutting boards and scantling for building work. A few of them had learnt to use a pit-saw at Ushuaia. They soon trained others, and it was not long before we had three pit-saws going at Harberton.

The pigs from Devonshire—one of them a white sow—were joined by two black sows, Majorca and Minorca, from Ushuaia. Later all three had litters: Majorca eighteen, Minorca fourteen, and the Devonshire sow a modest eight. These animals were self-supporting during the summer, but in winter-time had to be fed. Bushland was torn up and planted with swedes and turnips to satisfy their appetites. As time went by the original four increased to over a hundred, which began to run wild and make extensive demands on our foodstuffs. This was fine from Father's point of view, because it enabled him to employ all the Yahgans who had the slightest inclination to work; but as some of the toil in the fields fell to my brothers and myself, we did not share our parent's satisfaction. We much preferred hunting guanaco and birds, or fishing with a net, to growing vegetables and cooking them for pigs. It was therefore with relief and delight that we greeted Father's decision to reduce their numbers. The extermination proved to be an exciting job; and smoked and salted hams were soon abundant, not only in the homestead, but also in the huts and wigwams of the Yahgans.

The Romney Marsh rams brought on the *Shepherdess* were large, but coarse-woolled, animals; and as wool rather than mutton was the chief marketable product, they were not in every respect an asset. It was Father's intention to obtain more sheep from the Falklands. The bull, of the light red, short-horned South Devon breed, was remarkably tame, and quickly grew to a tremendous size. As our herd increased, the longer-horned Criollo bulls would stand around him, bellowing their hate and fear, but ready to draw back humbly the moment he offered combat. The cows, his offspring, all good milkers, were a very fine strain, existing to this day in those regions.

2

Though the day's work was far more strenuous than ever before, our home life at Harberton was much the same as it had been at Ushuaia. During the evening we would discuss the doings of the day and what should be undertaken on the morrow. Sometimes we played dominoes or an exciting game of " Snap," in which everyone took part. Despard played draughts or chess with Father. My own favourite recreation was mathematical problems, which I attempted to solve, not in the hope of improving my mind, but simply because I took pleasure in puzzling over them. These and other pastimes were enjoyed in the sitting-room, but part of the evening was spent in the kitchen in occupations of a different kind. Guns had to be cleaned and oiled, gear to be made for horses, hide to be plaited and buttons worked, and new moccasins made almost weekly, for that type of footwear never lasted long.

My parents had a fair collection of books. Some well-wisher in England had once bequeathed the sum of twenty pounds to be spent on literature to enliven Father's long winter evenings, but the person entrusted with the purchase of suitable books had had queer ideas regarding his need in this respect. When the case had arrived and had been opened, it had, alas! been found to contain Baxter's *Saint's Rest*, Cruden's Concordance, and a number of other equally huge, dingy and wearisome tomes. Fortunately our library contained reading-matter of a more diverting nature. We had the bound yearly volumes of *The Leisure Hour* and *Sunday at Home*, many of the stories from which were read aloud to us by our parents. Father, by nature, was tough and resolute to the point of obstinacy, yet sometimes he was so affected by a touching story that he would grow husky and be unable to continue reading. Mother, on the other hand, managed to carry on steadily through the most moving episodes.

From time to time we boys received from good friends in England *The Boys' Own Paper* and *Chums*. The stories we liked best were those in which boys of our own age drove their dirks deep into the bodies of ferocious pirates, or, chased by bloodthirsty Redskins, galloped incredible distances on the most impossibly tireless ponies. Father was somewhat scornful of these exciting tales, so we did not usually read them aloud; it seemed a shame that such fine literature should be wasted on his unbelieving ears.

At the evening's end Father would read a chapter from the Bible and sometimes give us an interesting talk on it. Then he would offer a short prayer, generally one of thanksgiving, after which we would go to bed.

3

Our most popular winter sport was skating. Near Harberton there were several lakes, and when the wind had swept the snow from them we could enjoy ourselves on the ice. I myself had no special skill in jumping or running, but I was a really fast skater, and never met anyone, either then or in later years, who could beat me. Whilst others were whirling about in graceful fashion, I would be dashing around a good-sized lake as hard as I could go. Speed was all I cared about. My favourite skates had long, narrow runners with a hook curved up in front. A Newfoundland captain, who once came skating with us and seemed to know all about the sport, told me that I ought to try for a speed championship. Long afterwards someone found a *Whitaker's Almanack*, in which skating records were given. I started to race the world champion's time over a measured mile; and if any confidence can be placed in the stop-watch available at the time there was not much to choose between us.

When we were boys at Harberton we used to play such games as " Touch-about " and " Bobbies and Thieves," marking on the larger lake a boundary beyond which we were not to pass—a great handicap to me. We often skated at night; and I shall never forget the beauty of the moonlight on a lake encircled by the vast, silent forest.

Mother did not like us to skate on Sundays, but I conceived a plan to overcome this difficulty. In those days foxes were very numerous.

To snare them we did not use a spring-trap, which, besides being costly, was a cruel device. We employed instead a home-made box, known as a " Maltese Church." As a preliminary I set traps at the extreme end of one of the lakes, and every day for a week skated out to bring back such foxes as had been captured. When Sunday came round I pretended to be worried about any unfortunate animal that might have been imprisoned overnight. Mother agreed that I should inspect the traps, whereupon I explained to her how I could do the journey much more quickly and with less effort on skates, as I had been doing all the week. She had no alternative but to agree to this as well—and that was how Sunday skating began.

4

For every day of the winter when the *Shepherdess* lay at anchor in Harberton harbour, fifty shillings slipped away on the vessel alone. When spring arrived, Father, seeing an opportunity of making some badly needed money and, at the same time, giving remunerative employment to his beloved Yahgans, decided to use her for conveying a load of fencing-posts to the Falkland Islands, where, there being no natural timber, they would fetch a good price.

Once again he had the captain to reckon with. Knowing that the vessel was bringing in a steady two pounds ten a day, he pursued his policy of procrastination by refusing to move from Harberton to any port not marked on the Admiralty chart. This meant that the *Shepherdess* could not be used for collecting suitable timber for posts from various points along the coast. Father explained to him that he could explore these places in a boat before taking the ship there, but the man flatly declined. The result was that, instead of leaving for the Falklands with a full load of some thirty thousand posts, the *Shepherdess* set sail with less than four thousand in her hold.

Shortly before she left, with Father aboard, Despard had gone east, in the hope of getting a guanaco. Finding a pool of clear water, he had taken a drink, and had noticed that the water had had a bad taste. He returned home the day the *Shepherdess* put to sea and, complaining that he did not feel well, was put to bed. At first it was supposed that he had caught a cold, but he grew rapidly worse. In a state of great anxiety, Mother decided to get medical aid from Ushuaia. She sent off James Cushinjiz with an urgent letter to Mr. Aspinall, the new superintendent of the Mission.

James, with a few Yahgan companions, set out in the *Bertha*, a fine boat brought by Father from England. It was a fierce day for an open boat when they started to beat up the Channel.

The weather continued stormy, and it was several days before the *Bertha* appeared again at Harberton. Worn out with anxiety, my mother received James, who told her sadly :

" Too much big wind, ma'am. All day, all night, we no come Ushuaia."

" Oh, James! " said Mother. " How could you come back to tell me that? "

James brightened up at this and answered :

" Steamer close by, ma'am. He come now."

As he spoke the *Comodoro Py* appeared rounding the point at the entrance to the harbour.

James's opening remark had been literally correct, intended not only as an excuse for being away so long, but also to impress her with the heroic efforts of himself and his companions. The vile weather had prevented him from getting nearer than ten miles from Ushuaia. They had landed at Jones's Point and had made three signal smokes, which had been observed at Ushuaia. The *Comodoro Py* had been sent out to investigate, had taken my mother's letter back to Mr. Aspinall and had then started for Harberton with the Government doctor aboard. By driving the boat before the gale, James Cushinjiz had kept the lead all the way home.

In those far-away places the patient is either dead or better by the time the doctor arrives, and Despard was not dead. The doctor diagnosed the case as typhoid fever, and blamed it on the water that Despard had drunk from the pool—and well he should. During the previous winter a large dead fish—reputed to have been a shark—had drifted onto the beach to the east of Lanushwaia (Woodpecker Harbour). A party of Aush had found this fish and had made a grand meal off it. As a result, many Indians and dogs had died. News of this had come to Ushuaia. While the *Comodoro Py* had been on the way to render assistance, the surviving Aush had disposed of the bodies of their companions. The ground had been too hard to dig graves, so the corpses had been sunk in a pool.

No wonder Despard had contracted typhoid.

CHAPTER FIFTEEN

Father Buys Sheep and Cattle. in the Falklands. Governor Paz Sells Us Horses. The Exploit of Cosmos Espiro and Juan Fariña. A Stormy Trip in the Bertha. Father Buys More Sheep. They are Landed on Gable Island. Fuegian Foxes. Despard Builds a Boat.

I

WHEN THE SHEPHERDESS REACHED THE FALKLANDS, THE CAPTAIN—SURE, it seemed, of his ultimate salvation—enjoyed himself as sailors will, and in consequence there was some delay. Notwithstanding this, the four thousand fencing-posts were sold for a good price. Had it been possible to load the vessel up to the hatches, Father would have made a fine profit on that trip.

It had been his intention to bring back sheep on the return voyage to Harberton. He encountered difficulties, however. Among sheep there is a disease known as scab. It is caused by a tiny parasite hardly visible to the naked eye. Once a flock is infested with it the task of eradication is tremendous. Father found scab was rampant in the Falklands when he reached there. He dared not take the slightest risk of importing such a plague into a land where it was unknown, even at the required price of four shillings a sheep.

On the only two islands where he was certain no scab existed the prices demanded were from eighteen shillings to a pound for a ewe and five pounds for a ram. Even at these prices he was only able to obtain three or four hundred animals. One of the sheep-farmers was making room for more sheep on his land by killing off cattle that had run wild long before. Father bought seventy of them, delivered to the water alongside the ship, at thirty shillings each.

With the sheep and cattle safely aboard, the *Shepherdess* sailed for Harberton. Father's foresight in returning with an almost empty ship was amply justified by events. The Harberton sheep-farm started clean. For over fifty years there was no need to dip the flocks there; and thanks to the surrounding sea and mountains, our sheep have never been contaminated by neighbouring flocks.

The sheep were landed from the *Shepherdess* on the smaller islands in the Channel. Half of the cattle were put on Walanika (Rabbit Island), which was well out in the Channel and from which the animals would not be able to escape. The remainder were taken to Harberton and put ashore. A fence had been built across the isthmus that connected the double peninsula with the mainland, thus providing a safe prison. At first the cattle were weak from the hardships endured on the voyage, but when they found themselves on solid earth again it was not long before they became strong and dangerous.

Their presence stressed the need for horses; ill-natured cattle have no respect for a man on foot. The only horse we possessed was the chestnut with the Roman nose that had been presented to my father by Governor Paz. Formerly this animal had belonged to the Tehuelche Indians of Patagonia, who, as he was remarkably swift, had used him for chasing guanaco, with the result that the moment he felt a rider on his back he was off like the wind.

From Governor Paz my father now purchased ten more animals, four of which were riding-horses, two mares and the remainder foals. To these we were enabled to add another seven in consequence of an extra-ordinary achievement on the part of two brave men.

One day we were astonished beyond words to see a solitary horseman riding along the north shore of Harberton from the east. This was so unexpected that we should hardly have been more surprised had the horse and rider come swimming in from the ocean. We put across the harbour in a boat to meet this tall, lean man. He introduced himself as Cosmos Erasmus Espiro, a Greek. Shortly we were joined by his companion, Juan Fariña, who appeared with a troop of five horses and a mare.

Espiro and Fariña, who was Chilean—or maybe Uruguayan—had ridden down the north-east coast of Fireland and, crossing farther east, where the mountains are lower, had come sloping up to Harberton. The trip, which had gold as its object, had taken them three months. They told us that they had been obliged to shoot Ona Indians on sight, for fear of allowing them to come too near.

There was less forest in the country they had traversed than there was farther west, and the hills were not so abrupt, yet there were leagues and leagues of swampy moor where the only way to proceed with horses was to keep in the streams that wound through the bog. These streams usually had stone bottoms, though on both banks the peat—impassable for horses—was piled up high; and in many places the bushes met and interlaced across the stream.

These two men had made an amazing journey, and were the first and only men ever to bring horses through that track. They were glad to sell the animals to Father and to proceed onward to such civilization as Ushuaia afforded.

2

One day the *Allen Gardiner* called at Harberton in urgent need of meat, and Father gave them twenty wethers for mutton, on condition that on their return from Keppel Island—where there was no scab—they brought us the same number of breeding ewes. When the vessel next anchored in the harbour we were advised that they had the sheep they owed us on board. So anxious was he to avoid bringing scab into the country that Father determined to land these animals on a separate island, and keep them in quarantine for a year.

That afternoon, though the weather was threatening, we put the twenty new arrivals in our best boat, the *Bertha*, and set off for Yekhamuka, a suitable island in the Gable inner channel, some eight miles from Harberton. The crew consisted of Despard, myself, a couple of Yahgans, and a young sailor from the *Allen Gardiner*, who was eager for a treat.

We beat up against an ever-increasing north-westerly wind, and landed the sheep at dusk. Then, while Father went to see if there was water for them in a little hollow, the rest of us hurried to stow flat rocks for ballast in the bottom of the boat and take a reef in the mainsail, for we saw heavy cumulus clouds rolling over the mountains from the north, and knew that it was going to blow.

Father returned and, taking the tiller, told us to push off and hoist the sails. Then, annoyed to find that we had taken in a reef without orders, made us shake it out again at once, so, with a wind on our quarter, we were soon rushing through the water towards home, under full sail. At the mid-point of our journey the shallows at the mouth of the river Lasifharshaj forced us to keep a good distance from the shore. By this time it was quite dark, but my brother and I saw a white line bearing down on us from the windward side, and had the halliards in our hands, ready to let go. Father obstinately held on until the last moment, when he told us to take a reef in the mainsail, and immediately afterwards ordered two reefs. Then, almost in the same breath, when we were nearly smothered in a " woolly," came the order, " Down mainsail! " I think we obeyed that command before it was given, but such was the force of the wind that ere the mainsail could be stowed we were ordered to down jib as well. With a small corner of this last showing, we flew through the water, and just managed to fetch up in the shelter of Rabbit Island, where the boat could be safely moored. We were, of course, saturated, but fortunately someone had dry matches. Soon with grass and driftwood we made a fire, though the wind blew away most of the embers and all the heat. We roasted, as best we could, a wild goose we had brought with us. There were no trees on the island, and we had no blankets, so, having eaten the half-cooked bird, we lay near the fire, such as it was, and tried to get some sleep. Next morning the gale subsided and we got back to Harberton. The folk there were much relieved to see us coming safely home, for it had blown exceptionally hard during the night, damaging part of the house, which was not finished, ripping the roof off our wood-shed, and moving one of the boats that lay bottom-up near the beach.

3

When the *Shepherdess* eventually returned to England, my father's finances were extremely low. There was an abundant supply of provisions and clothing, as well as building materials and tools. There was also the coal he had brought from England in the hope of selling it to passing ships. Also on the credit side were a number of sheep, cattle and horses. Those were the assets, but the liabilities were heavy. The supplies would not last for ever. Our losses in cattle and sheep had been considerable during the severe winter. The price of wool in our nearest market— London—was fourpence a pound. The local market for meat was poor and uncertain. In hard cash, reserves were running perilously low.

But Father was not a man to be easily dismayed. He had determined that the Harberton enterprise should succeed. Already he had taken risks to that end—and he was fully prepared to take still more. With a substantial part of the residue of the joint fortunes of Captain Willis and himself, he chartered a schooner called the *Rippling Wave*, which had already been engaged in bringing sheep from the Falklands to the Magellan Straits and Rio Gallegos in Argentina, caused the vessel to be thoroughly disinfected, and brought in her from the Falklands fifteen hundred scab-free sheep.

This flock was landed on Gable, by far the largest of our islands. It is about six miles long and, in places, nearly three miles wide. All along its western end the cliffs rear themselves to a height of over three hundred feet, looking like a succession of gigantic, steep-roofed cottages built close together and standing end on to the channel. Hence the island's name.

Up to that time there had been a great number of foxes on Gable Island, and as this flock of sheep was the first ever to be landed there, Father was anxious for their safety. When these fifteen hundred loudly bleating strangers appeared, however, the foxes seem to have taken fright and swum panic-stricken to the mainland. The distance across in the narrowest place is about a quarter of a mile, but at one point rocks could be used to break the journey and so reduce the longest swim to something like a hundred yards. No foxes reappeared on Gable for over twelve years.

The Fuegian fox is about four times the size of its Patagonian brother, which, in its turn, is a trifle smaller than the English variety. The larger breed is found not only in Tierra del Fuego, but also far north along the Andean range. When the big Fuegian foxes eventually returned to Gable Island after their long absence, having meanwhile discovered on the main island how harmless these noisy invaders were, they caused havoc among the flocks. By taking it by the throat, they could kill the strongest sheep with ease. Father once shot a vixen on the island. She was carrying a nest of small live birds in her mouth and was evidently on the way to her cubs, so that they could have the fun of killing them.

We did what we could to exterminate foxes. Once we sent a bale of over three hundred selected skins to London. There they were classified as wolf-pelts and sold by auction for prices not exceeding half-a-crown apiece. Someone got a bargain.

4

Despard's favourite haunt had always been the carpentry-shop. If left to himself he would toil there throughout the day, as though for a wager. Having, in his time, made innumerable toy boats, he now aspired to make a real one, clinker-built with copper fastenings. When he asked Father's permission, the reply was:

" It will be a waste of time, boards and nails, Despard. To undertake such a work, you would need at least a year's apprenticeship under an expert boat-builder."

Besides these objections, Despard's help was needed on other jobs, and Father could not well spare him; but Despard, sure of himself and eager to prove his ability, promised always to be available when required. In addition, he undertook to saw his own boards without Yahgan assistance and to pay for the copper nails. At last Father gave way.

Despard and I already knew how to use a pit-saw—a tool not often seen nowadays. Two sawyers are necessary. A log is laid on planks over a pit. The top sawyer takes up his position on the log and guides the saw. The bottom sawyer stands in the pit and gets all the sawdust into his eyes, ears and mouth. The saw does its work on the downward stroke and has to be lifted clear of the cut for the next stroke to be made. Operating a pit-saw is considered hard work, even for grown men, yet Despard and I contrived to produce a fine pile of boards, which my brother then smoothed down with a plane.

Our boat (it will be noted that I claim my share of glory in its completion) was built on three stout frames. The ribs were steamed, bent into the correct shape and fitted into position. Then, when the thwarts were also in place, the frames were removed.

Father wisely left us quite alone at the task, though he watched our progress with interest. One day he stood for a time observing us, then said to Despard :

" I shan't need you again, Sonny, till that boat is finished. It will be a good one and I hope you will let me use it sometimes."

And a good one she proved to be. We rigged her with a sliding gunter. Old man-of-war sailors will remember that rig, though it is a rarity to-day. We called her the *Esperanza*.

CHAPTER SIXTEEN

Mary Returns to Fireland. On Keppel Island She Meets her Future Husband. We Hunt Guanaco. Tales Round the Camp-Fire. The Sea-Lion's Son. Wasana is Turned into a Mouse. Ghosts of the Departed. The Lair of the Dreaded Lakooma. The Floating Island. The End of Women's Leadership. I Write for the Press.

I

IN 1888, THE YEAR FOLLOWING OUR REMOVAL FROM USHUAIA TO HARberton, my sister Mary came back to Tierra del Fuego. She was accompanied on the voyage by a lady who was on the way out to take charge of the orphanage at Ushuaia. After the usual delays and changes of boats, they arrived at the Mission settlement on Keppel Island, there to await the *Allen Gardiner* for the last stage of their journey.

At that time on Keppel, besides Mr. and Mrs. Bartlett and their children and a handful of Yahgans, there was a young Scottish missionary whose name was Wilfred Barbrooke Grubb. He was not a catechist or parson, but nevertheless a Christian and, in addition, an inveterate adventurer and born pioneer. He was no taller than Mary, who was of my father's height; was neither dark nor fair; and his mouth and jaw might have given him the face of an arch-criminal had it not been for the kindly, mischievous expression and the merry twinkle in the eyes.

On that almost desert island these two young people were thrown together for over five weeks before the *Allen Gardiner* arrived to take Mary and her chaperon away to Fireland.

Despard and I had finished our " education " before the family had left Ushuaia, and now, with good reason, considered ourselves working men, but Will, Bertha and Alice could still benefit from the teaching that Mary was able to pass on to them. The two girls were good, attentive scholars, particularly Alice, who had always been a searcher after knowledge. She was very fond of reading, and loved word-pictures of wild scenery such as are to be found in Scott's poetical works; though, to tell the truth, the thing both she and Bertha loved best in all the world was to be out of doors, helping their brothers.

This being the case with the girls, it was hardly to be expected that Will could sit happily at a table wielding pen or pencil, with the selfish hope of personal benefit in some distant future. Outside there were horses to ride, missing cattle to be hunted up, canoes to paddle, birds to shoot, and fish to be caught; all for the immediate good of the firm. I need hardly say that he magnanimously chose the latter course, finished his education in double quick time and manfully joined the working party out of doors.

Mary was loved by all and admired for the brave way she put up with an existence that must have seemed terrible to her after the safety and comfort of England. She kept her secret well. Not even Mother guessed it till the next trip of the *Allen Gardiner*, some three months after Mary had rejoined us. Then a letter from Wilfred Grubb came for my parents. Inside it was another letter for Mary, which was to be handed to her if my parents consented to her becoming engaged to Wilfred. That letter to them must have been as honest and sincere as was the man who had written it, for after a talk with Mary they handed over the letter addressed to her.

There then began between the two lovers a correspondence as regular as our intermittent mail would allow. Soon after their engagement, Wilfred volunteered to work among a tribe of natives, untouched by civilization, who lived in the upper Paraguayan Chaco. The rest of the splendid story of Mary and Wilfred has its place later in these pages.

2

The years went by at Harberton. Father had told us in the early days there that our future depended entirely on our own exertions, and that we must either put our shoulders to the wheel, work hard and be independent, or resign ourselves to working for wages during the rest of our lives. He set us a fine example, for, though he could not hide how ill he was, he remained cheerful and never spared himself. Through the long summer days we worked strenuously from dawn to dusk, and when bedtime came we were tired out, though none of us would acknowledge it, even in our thoughts. With the advent of winter our labours diminished, for even though we rose and breakfasted by candle-light, we could put in only six or seven hours work before night came on again. Besides this amelioration of our lot, we had another reason for welcoming the winter months.

As the mountains grew white and the snow spread from their peaks to their feet, growing continually deeper, we knew the guanaco would be coming down to their winter haunts. This meant that we could hunt them within reasonable distance from the beach, from where we could ship the meat home by boat. Till after mid-winter the guanaco remained fairly fat. We always looked forward eagerly to those early months of winter, when they were in good condition and there was plenty of soft snow to silence our footsteps through the woods. This was the sport we loved.

Hunting guanaco in the thick woods was an art. They were always on the alert, and unless the hunter moved with the utmost caution he would be seen or heard by these timid, watchful creatures, and their warning cry—it sounded like a derisive laugh—would precede him through the woods and put all other guanacos on their guard.

One morning Despard and I, having slept out, started our hunt early, on some steep land about thirteen miles to the west of Harberton. Before very long we spied a guanaco on a knoll about half a mile away. He stood among some burnt trees, and was evidently on the watch. He must have seen us move, and remained so long motionless that it was difficult to believe that his long neck was not a piece of dead wood showing up with the other charred stumps against the sky. Finally, without moving his body, he turned his head for a moment, probably for advice, for soon two others joined him. There they stood, alert and vigilant, then disappeared. We were too far away to hear the warning cry, but soon we saw a long procession of guanaco steadily ascending a distant mountain ridge.

In these modern times guanaco are not in such a hurry to run away. They have become accustomed to sheep, horses, cattle and harmless shepherds—in some places, even to automobiles. But fifty years ago, when natives and white men hunted them for meat, they were exceedingly shy. Whenever they were feeding in a valley, there was always one sentinel who, instead of eating with the others, surveyed the surrounding countryside from some high vantage-point.

We often used to go in a boat with a few Yahgans to one of the many coves on the main island or on Navarin Island. We would land before nightfall, fix up the boat's sails as a shelter for the night, and the next day scatter through the woods in search of guanaco. At first we had old-fashioned muzzle-loading fowling-pieces, for which we moulded bullets from lead salvaged by the natives from wrecked vessels. The day's bag of guanaco was seldom less than three. This hunting was doubly good sport, because we knew the meat to be urgently needed at home, where there were many mouths besides those of the family to feed. In early winter we salted and smoked the hams for use in the spring, when the guanaco grew lean, and the summer, when they were away in their mountain haunts.

Sometimes, when the Yahgans considered that the terrain or the state of the snow would give dogs an advantage over the fleeter guanaco, they would take a few with them. The dogs seldom met with much success, usually managing to frighten the game away. When the day's sport was over, the dogs would be tied up near the camp. If during the night one of them whined in his sleep, the Yahgans were delighted. When a dog hunted in his dreams, it was a sign that we should have good luck on the morrow.

Another excellent omen, even more propitious, was the sharp, shrill cry of the tiny owl, *lufcuia*. He would perch on some branch where the firelight barely flickered, looking like a little fluffy ball with a strangely human face, seemingly taking a great interest in the goings-on in the encampment. Soon would come a succession of metallic chirps, like a knife struck on steel or stone to sharpen it.

" He knows," the Yahgans would say. " We shall get meat to-morrow."

The little prophet was not disturbed, and generally proved to be right.

Those long evenings round the camp fire, fifty years ago. . . . After discussing the day's hunt and planning for the morrow, it was time for story-telling. When the Yahgans found an interested listener, they enjoyed searching their memories for the tales they had heard long since —and still firmly believed; tales that I am certain were not invented on the spur of the moment for my entertainment.

There was the story of How *Syuna* the Rockfish got his Flat Head. Some miles to the east of Lanushwaia (Woodpecker Harbour) there is a flat shingle point, and east of this still is a steep, rocky coast with sheltered coves here and there, suitable for canoes. The best of these little harbours is Wujyasima (Water in the Doorway), once a favourite site for Yahgan wigwams.

Once upon a time a young girl left her home at Wujyasima and walked alone round to the shingle point, where she began to play, running down the beach after the receding waves and back again as the breakers rolled in. Watching her unseen was a lustful old sea-lion; and when a great wave swept her off her feet, she found the creature by her side. Like all Yahgan women, the maiden was a good swimmer, and therefore sought to evade him. But by keeping between her and the shore, and forcing her farther and farther out to sea, he at length exhausted her, and she was glad to rest her hand on his neck.

Now that her life depended on him, the maiden began to feel quite friendly towards her strange escort. He swam with her for many miles until they reached a great rock, in which there was a cave. The girl knew that she could never swim home without help, so she decided to accept the inevitable, and took up residence with the sea-lion in the cave. He brought her abundance of fish, which, as there was no fire, she ate raw.

Time passed and a son was born to them. In shape he resembled a human child, but he was covered with hair, like a seal. The boy grew quickly, and was company for his mother, especially when he learned to talk. This the old sea-lion could never do, yet, because he was always so kind and considerate, the young woman grew exceedingly fond of him.

Nevertheless she longed intensely to see her own country and people again. She managed to make her wishes known to him, and one day all three of them set out for Wujyasima. At times mother and son swam beside their protector; at others he towed them through the water at a great pace; and sometimes they rode on his back.

At last they landed on the shingle point. The sea-lion flopped up the beach and lay down to rest in the warm sunshine, while the mother, taking her queer little son by the hand, walked to Wujyasima. In the village she found a number of her relatives, who had long given her up for dead. When she told them her story, great was their surprise and deep their interest in her funny little hybrid son.

After the first excitement had died down, the women of the village suggested that they should go in their canoes eastward along the rocks, to look for deep-water mussels and sea-urchins, which have the size and shape of flattish apples, with hard shells covered with stiff, spike-like bristles. The young mother accompanied them on this excursion, while the men and children remained behind in the settlement.

The children began to play games, in which the little visitor joined boisterously. The men, however, longed for meat, and knowing there was a seal lying on the beach, one said :

" Why do we sit here hungry? "

So they took their spears and, creeping up to the old sea-lion, killed him. Laden with meat, they returned to the village and began to cook the meal. The children sniffed the delicious odour of roasting seal and gathered round the fire. When the time came for the meat to be distributed, the young visitor received his piece with the rest. He tasted it and cried with delight:

"Amma sum undupa!" ("It is seal meat!")

Then, eating as he went, he ran to meet his mother, who was just returning. The canoes came alongside a steep rock, which at that state of the tide served as a jetty, and the women stepped ashore with their baskets of sea-urchins. The little boy ran up to his mother and offered her the last morsel of his meat, saying it tasted good. In a flash she realized what had happened. She snatched a large sea-urchin from her basket and struck her child on the forehead with it. He fell into deep water, instantly changed into *syuna* the rockfish and swam away.

The other women went up to the wigwams and feasted on roasted seal meat, but the mother refused to eat, and mourned alone for her lost son and his kindly old father. She never afterwards took a husband from among her own people.

If you examine a *syuna* you will find that its head is flat and that it is covered with the little pit-marks left by the bristles of the sea-urchin, which goes far to prove that the story is true.

3

Another tale of transformation concerned a very small Yahgan whose name was Wasana. At any assembly of these quarrelsome, though not warlike, people there was bound to be much shouting, boasting and angry threatening, that often ended in a fight. At one such meeting Wasana was distinguishing himself by vociferous bragging and ridiculous menaces, when he suddenly realized, by a movement of his adversary, that he had gone too far. Panic-stricken, he turned to flee from the wigwam, but as he stooped to get through a low door at the back, his enemy could not resist the tempting target, and made a violent thrust at it with his fish-spear. Wasana raced away screaming shrilly, with the spear dragging behind him. He was turned into a mouse, and the spear became his tail.

As I have previously mentioned, the Yahgans believed in wild-men-of-the-woods, the chief of whom, the Hanush and the Cushpij,[1] were extremely savage and strong. They were said to have a bald spot on the back of their heads where they had rubbed them against the rough tree-bark. In addition to these dangerous creatures, the Yahgans acknowledged the existence of ghosts. These were the spirits of the dead, and

[1] The final "j" is a strong guttural like the "ch" in the Scottish "loch."

bore a greater resemblance to our civilized conception of a phantom than those about which I was to learn later from the Ona.

When the occupants of a canoe were drowned not too far from the shore, a relative would go alone to the beach nearest the scene of the accident. Here he would light a fire close to low-water mark, sit by it and wait. When the flames died down and there were only embers left, the spirits of those who had been drowned, transparent but recognizable, might come out of the sea to warm themselves, in perfect silence, by the still-glowing embers.

Sitting alone by the dying fire, thinking of his departed dear ones and expecting a visit from them, a superstitious Indian might very well conjure them up in his mind and firmly believe he had seen them. Conversely, even if he knew that his experiment had failed, he might still be tempted to invent a little story to interest his waiting friends in the wigwam and, in course of time, grow to believe it himself.

4

There are certain caves, lakes and bays where the Yahgans believed that the monsters called *Lakooma* lay in wait for the unwary human, and many strange stories were told about them.

Some six miles east of Harberton is a nest of bluffs about five hundred feet high. They are called the Guanaco Hills, and among them are numerous lakes, five of them of considerable size. During the winter these lakes freeze over, and for two or three months, if the ice is covered with snow, herds of cattle can pass over them without danger of breaking the ice.

In one of these lakes lurked a *Lakooma*. It was said by the Yahgans that any person venturing near the bank ran the risk of being seized by a gigantic hand, which would be thrust out of the water to grab the unlucky one and drag him into the lake to be devoured.

One winter, when everything was frozen hard, I was crossing that same lake alone, with a load of guanaco meat on my back. Suddenly I realized that I was walking on thin ice, when all should have been thick and solid. Right ahead of me was a large hole. I made a wide detour, and crossed the rest of the lake with the utmost caution. I had been on the brink of the *Lakooma's* lair.

Unlike the story of the sea-lion's son, the *Lakooma* legend may be based on natural causes. There are no hot springs in Tierra del Fuego, but there are strong springs that, coming from a great depth underground, seem warm in winter and icy cold in summer. It is highly likely that the *Lakooma* lake contained a comparatively shallow area, below which was a powerful spring that, by forcing up water of a higher temperature, prevented ice from forming evenly on the surface.

Possibly the local legend arose through some native less fortunate than I being drowned there; or maybe the sight of a hole in that thick surrounding ice gave some fanciful Indian the notion that it was a breathing-place for an under-water monster. There are many other places in Yahga-land where *Lakooma* are said to dwell. One I know of is where a rock and current have caused a whirlpool, which may, at some time, have been responsible for the loss of a canoe with all on board.

5

It has been stated that all primitive tribes have some legend of the Flood. I have diligently searched for some Ona story about it, but have found none. On the other hand, the Yahgans have various versions of such an occurrence. The stories differ according to locality, each narrator setting the scene in his own district. Without doubt some of these stories were influenced by an awareness of our Bible account, or by prompting and wishful thinking on the part of certain hopeful missionary listeners. There is, however, one story that I am certain is close to its original form. It was related to me by the Yahgans who belonged to the eastern end of the Beagle Channel.

They said that long ago the moon fell into the sea, which rose in consequence with great turmoil, just as water in a bucket will rise when a large stone is dropped into it. The only survivors of this flood were the fortunate inhabitants of Gable Island, which broke away from the ocean bed and floated on the sea. The mountains round about were soon submerged, and the folk on Gable Island, looking in all directions, saw nothing but ocean to the far horizon. The island did not drift. It was anchored in some way; and when the moon rose out of the sea and the water subsided, it settled down again in the same place as before, with its burden of human beings, guanaco and foxes. From these, the world was peopled again.

The Yahgans were certain that they were the only Fuegian tribe descended from those who came through the flood on Gable Island. How the Alacaloof, Aush and Ona survived the disaster, the Yahgans did not try to explain.

The chief interest of this legend lies in the natives' obvious comprehension of the moon's tremendous size. In passing, they were also well aware, before being told by the white man, of the influence exerted by the moon on the tides.

6

Like many other native tribes, the Yahgans believed that at one time the women ruled, by witchcraft and cunning. According to their story, it was not so very long ago that the men assumed control. This was apparently done by mutual consent; there is no indication of a wholesale massacre of the women such as took place—judging from that tribe's mythology—among the Ona. There is, not far from Ushuaia, every sign of a once vast village where, it is said, a great gathering of natives took place. Such a concourse was never seen before or since, canoes arriving from the farthest frontiers of Yahga-land. It was at that momentous conference that the Yahgan men took authority into their own hands.

This legend of leadership being wrested from the women, either by force or coercion, is too widely spread throughout the world to be lightly ignored.

7

I have one other camp-fire story—of a very different kind. I went alone with some natives on a guanaco-hunting trip. For supper we shared some sandwiches that my mother had wrapped up in a copy of the *Liverpool Weekly News*. While glancing through the newspaper, I noticed an article on Tierra del Fuego and the settlers there. The author had some interesting tit-bits for his readers. According to him, there was on Cape Horn, or some adjacent island, a strong barrel with a lock on it. Keys to fit this lock were held by the settlers, and also by the captains of certain ships. We, the settlers, placed all our correspondence in the barrel; and it was picked up in due course by the captains when their ships passed that way, for posting at their next port of call. Any incoming mail was left in the barrel for us to collect. Only thus, asserted the author, were we kept in touch with the outside world.

Better still was a description of the natives' cannibal feasts, at which they ate their useless old women. This gruesome story lost nothing of its horror when I translated it for the benefit of my companions. They fairly rocked with mirth. Then the face of one of them, Halupaianjiz, became grave.

" Why," he asked me, " do these people tell lies about us? We do not say bad things about them. You ought to write and tell them the truth."

I promised to do so—and kept my word. The following winter I received some copies of the *Liverpool Weekly News*. In them was my article, which I read out to my Indian friends, who enjoyed hearing their virtues translated from an English newspaper. The editor also sent a kind note inviting further contributions and, to my surprise and joy, a money-order. This, the proceeds of my first literary effort, went to swell the family's sadly depleted fortunes.

CHAPTER SEVENTEEN

The Wild Bull on Gable Island and How it is Finally Killed. The Case of the Home-Sick Cattle. Instances to Show that the Cow is More Intelligent than the Horse.

I

SOME TWELVE YEARS PRIOR TO THE PERIOD WITH WHICH I AM NOW CONcerned the Ushuaia Mission had put cattle on Gable Island and given a few to certain Yahgans who lived there. There had subsequently arisen the discord that wealth and worldly goods sometimes engender. Quarrels over the ownership of some of the cattle had led to fighting, in one case to murder. So three years before we had come to Harberton the animals had been removed from the island. Only two, a heifer and a young bull, had eluded capture. The heifer disappeared after a time and the bull remained alone, soon to earn a sinister reputation for cunning and ferocity.

Once, when meat was needed at Harberton, Despard and the gaucho, Aguirre, were sent to kill it. My brother was armed with his rifle and Aguirre with lasso and knife. To assist them in the task, our two best horses were swum across to the island. They spent some days there, but failed to find the bull. When the other cattle had been taken away, he had changed his habitat from the more open country where they had hoped to find him to the eastern end of the island, which was exceedingly broken by rocks and little swamps, besides being largely overgrown with thick scrub that made travelling fast on horseback most difficult.

They returned to Harberton with their object unaccomplished. Soon afterwards Aguirre, smitten with the gold fever, joined a band of miners and, after more than one sanguinary adventure, came to a violent end.

Autumn arrived, but although the land in shady places was already frozen hard, the guanaco had not yet come down to their winter quarters, and there was no fresh meat at Harberton. Then, to our tremendous joy, my brothers and I received orders from Father to kill that bull. What a lark! We took a bell mare and a small troop of horses, swam them to the island and, choosing three of the most active, started on our quest.

Will and I had left our muzzle-loaders behind. We knew that the round, home-made bullets would flatten on the bull's skull and that the clumsy weapons would hinder us in pursuing—or escaping from—this legendary monster. Instead we acted as beaters and pinned our hopes of a kill on Despard, who was armed with his Winchester rifle.

We rode eastward. A fall of snow earlier in the day soon put us on the track of the bull, but in many places his haunts were so thickly wooded that we had to follow him on foot. It was a whole day before we caught sight of him—and discovered that, more wily than fierce, he was, in reality, following us. For several days the fun continued. When we were not chasing him, he was chasing us. We had started the hunt with only a few rounds of ammunition, and had to conserve it. A leaden bullet from the Winchester carbine of those days needed to be well placed to bring down a bull on the defensive. In that kind of country an excited rider on an equally excited horse might spend a lot of ammunition before making such a shot. So Despard held his fire.

These tactics were kept up until the bull, disgusted no doubt with this disturbance of his quiet life, took to the water in a place where the main island was nearly a mile away. Leaving Will to watch him, Despard and I raced our horses for the boat, delighted at the unsporting prospect of shooting our quarry at close range in the water. In the hope of intercepting him, we were rowing frantically when Will came riding along the coast, signalling and shouting to us that the bull had turned back and gone into a thick wood.

We went ashore and, mounting our horses, surveyed the country. Then Despard climbed onto the low branch of a large evergreen tree, whilst Will and I, having led his horse to a place of safety, returned to tease the bull. Will, an expert in the art, soon succeeded in raising the creature's ire and, hotly pursued by the infuriated beast, raced his horse under the branch on which Despard was perched. A shot in the spine at point-blank range brought the creature down, and a second in the brain put an end to his troubles.

We arrived back at Harberton at midnight with the boat heavily laden with beef. Our clothes were stiff with dirt and gore, but we were as proud as kings.

2

As previously related, a number of indignant cattle from the Falklands were landed on the Harberton peninsula. One day it was reported that four of these animals were missing. There were several thick copses on the peninsula, and these were combed over and over again without success. The fences across the isthmus ran well out into the water on both sides, and the possibility of the missing animals having swum round them was considered. It was not until three days had elapsed that tell-tale tracks revealed that the creatures had not negotiated the fence, but had swum the harbour at its mouth, where it was over a quarter of a mile wide, and taken to the great forest beyond.

From the direction of their tracks—which we followed until heavy rain obliterated them and compelled us to return home—these four animals were making a bee-line for the Falklands. Information that reached us years later confirmed that they had continued their course in the same direction, deviating from it only when they encountered insurmountable obstacles. One of them must have perished on the way, but the other three managed to reach the sandstone cliffs that guard the Atlantic coast. From there they could proceed no farther towards the Falklands, and soon fell victims to the arrows of the Ona Indians.

On their voyage from the Falklands to Tierra del Fuego these cattle had been dragged aboard and dumped into the dark hold of a sailing-vessel which, owing to contrary winds, had tacked about in all directions. After more than a week they had been hoisted from the hold by their horns and lowered into the sea, to swim to the nearby beach. How did they know at Harberton the exact direction of their Falkland home? It is over three hundred miles as the crow flies. Even with the best magnetic compass in the hands of an expert mathematician, it would be hard to calculate the meanderings of the *Shepherdess* in the confines of her hold. Yet the animals knew their course, and only the Atlantic prevented them from continuing on their way. No doubt animals have something better than a magnetic compass stowed within their brains. Primitive man had the same instinct, though perhaps less highly developed, whilst in civilized man it has almost disappeared.

I have hunted wild horses and wild cattle on Picton Island. The horses were trapped without undue difficulty, but in the cattle I noticed many instances of cunning—I am tempted to say thinking-power. They would disappear over a rise at a run, and immediately they were out of sight of their pursuers would double back and peer from a different spot to see whether they were being followed. When hunted till desperation forced them to face their tormentors they would never turn and wait in their tracks, but would double back and wisely choose a spot suitable either for defence or further flight, thereby putting the hunters at a disadvantage.

Tame beasts are no less intelligent. A cow in a thousand-acre field, not wishing to be separated from her new-born calf, will hide it in a thicket and then spend many entire days at the most distant end of the field, only going to attend to her little one at night. If, in the farmer's attempts to find the calf, he purposely detains the cow for twenty-four hours, she will not hasten to the calf on the moment of her release, but will remain another whole day as far from it as possible, and not approach the thicket in which it lies until the second night is well advanced. Meanwhile, the calf, though well able to run about, will remain where its mother left it, and, should she fail to return, would, I imagine, eventually die of starvation.

As for working oxen, dragging heavy logs through bad forest tracks and lifting them over fallen timber—their prowess needs to be seen to be believed.

When cattle strayed in Fireland they were usually to be found scattered in little groups near clumps of *leña dura*,[1] an evergreen of which they are extremely fond. This bush sometimes has a trunk as much as a foot in diameter.

The larger animals would hook their horns on a branch—perhaps as thick as a man's arm—and, lifting their heads as high as possible to obtain a better leverage, force the branch down until it snapped. As the green leaves came lower, the smaller animals would snatch what they could till the branch broke, when the big one would drive them off. Having eaten the choicest leaves, he would move away in search of another suitable tree; whereupon the small fry would rush in to devour his leavings, keeping an eye open for the next descending branch.

Spring is a hungry time for roaming cattle. The previous season's grass is so mildewed and sodden that it is not fit to eat, and the new grass has not yet appeared. It is then that the cattle turn to the deciduous beech.[2] At that time it is in bud and the tender young leaves hold out

---

[1] "Hard firewood" (Spanish), called *iacu* by the Yahgans. I do not know its English or Latin name. Cattle and guanaco thrive and grow fat on it throughout the winter and spring; sheep and horses touch it only when starving. The flower is insignificant and the seed is like a tiny acorn very highly coloured (red and yellow). It seldom reaches a height of twenty feet and is always an undergrowth. My father describes it as a shrub.

[2] *Nothofagus antarctica*. This tree, known to the Yahgans as *hanis*, reaches a height of a hundred feet, with a girth of twenty feet. It is most abundant on the drier eastern foot-hills, whereas the evergreen beech (*Nothofagus betuloides*) is found chiefly in more rainy country. Their leaves are somewhat similar, but those of the evergreen are stouter in texture and of a darker green. The evergreen is the more aromatic and is sometimes found in clumps in forests of the deciduous variety. The three species of beech—evergreen, deciduous and dwarf—the Fuegian cypress and the Winter's bark are the only trees to be found in Fireland. The stems of the cypress, which grows only in the wet, mild western parts of the country, were valued by the Yahgans and Alacaloof, who used them for spear-shafts. Winter's bark—named after Captain John Winter, who first brought it to England in 1579 from the Magellan Straits—was called *ushcuta*

great attractions. The deciduous beech grows tall, with its leaves high up. A strong animal, usually a steer or a bull, will choose a young tree, hook his horn on it and push forward with all his strength. It would be expected that he would lower his head, but he is wise enough to lift it as high as possible. Sometimes in his efforts to bend the tree he will almost rear up on his hind legs. As the tree commences to come down he will get astride it and, with his body holding it down, slowly walk forward, eating as he goes, till he reaches the top, where his followers, reaping the fruits of his hard work, have been snatching a hasty meal. Having eaten all he wants, he walks off the upper end, thus allowing the tree to spring up again, nearly as straight as before.

Such a sapling may be four or five inches in diameter at the stump and thirty feet to the highest branch, and frequently they fail to recover from this rough treatment. Cattle are not always to blame for bent trees. Sometimes a mass of snow freezing on their branches will bring their tops to the ground and hold them there for the rest of the winter, or until a thaw sets them free.

Horned cattle are not alone in their intelligent way of dealing with the deciduous beech. It is surprising how well even the polled Angus and other hornless cattle use their strong necks to bring down the branches.

Horse-lovers—or horse-worshippers, as one might call the female of the species—have often been indignant when I have been bold enough to claim that cows have far more sense than horses. Anyone who has hunted both wild horses and wild cattle will agree with me; and the instances I have just quoted may help to prove that we are right.

---

by the Yahgans. Its Spanish name is *canelo*, but here I think we have a misnomer, for *canelo* is the Spanish for cinnamon. In Ona-land it is unknown. It may attain a height of over forty feet and a girth of ten feet, but it is never found alone in a forest, being really an undergrowth in forests of deciduous or evergreen beech. This beautiful conical tree, with its large leathery leaves of a bright shining green, looks quite out of place among its hardy small-leafed companions. It seems to have lost its way and wandered from some warmer clime. This idea is supported by the fact that its daisy-like flowers open very late in summer, and the tiny pods they leave when they fall mature in the following season, so that on the same branch can be seen this year's flowers and last year's seed, which fall at the same time in autumn. The wood has little strength and, being of a porous nature, sinks when green, but when dry it is extremely light. The young trees grow straight and slender to a good height and, like the cypress, are often used as spear-shafts. The bark is smooth and about an inch thick, greenish outside, but red within. It is highly pungent and might be ground and used as pepper. Walking through thickets of Winter's bark, one's eyes may smart, and if the wood is put on the fire, the cook will soon be in tears. If the ripe black seed—smaller than a grain of rice—is taken from the pod and crushed, there results a drop of white liquid which, if it touches the tongue, makes one wish that one had taken a tea-spoonful of mustard instead.

CHAPTER EIGHTEEN

The Gold-Rush to Sloggett Bay. How Came the Gold to Tierra del Fuego? We Sell Beef to the Miners. Despard and Will Score Over our Rival Traders. The Tragedy at Lennox Cove. I Meet an Apparition and Profit by the Encounter.

I

IT WILL BE REMEMBERED THAT WHILE WE WERE WAITING FOR THE RESCUE ship after the wreck of the *Golden West* I played alone on the beach at Sloggett Bay and collected a mass of magnetic iron sand, which clustered together and clung to my toy magnet. Captain Felix Paz of the Argentine Navy, first Governor of the territory, took a kindly interest in us little boys and the stories we told him about Fireland. One day, as a special mark of favour, I showed him my box of treasures. When he saw the black sand clinging to my magnet he became greatly excited and demanded to know where I had found it. On hearing my answer he immediately sent off the *Comodoro Py* to Sloggett Bay. She brought back sacks of pay dirt in which gold was found.

This was the first gold struck on the south coast of Tierra del Fuego, although miners were already prospecting on the northern shore, near the eastern entrance to the Magellan Straits.

The news of this discovery spread slowly, for communications were very bad in those days, but little by little a drifting population of prospectors and miners began to scatter along the coast. They explored the southern shores of the big island and Lennox, Navarin and New Islands. Here and there they found gold that paid well for the working, though probably no beach was quite as rich as that on which the *Golden West* had been driven ashore. In one single morning a party of miners there collected a heap of pay dirt with over a hundred pounds' worth of gold in it.

About this time someone blessed, or otherwise, with a vivid imagination started an interesting story that actually found its way into print. It seemed that my father was nothing but an avaricious adventurer, thinly disguised as a missionary, who long ago had found gold. Helped by the innocent natives, who had no idea of its value, he had collected over a ton of this precious metal and had shipped it in his whale-boat to some place near Harberton where, assisted by his rascally little sons, he had cached it in spots not known even to the Yahgan natives. Thus, with this splendid reserve to fall back upon, the Bridges family had found it easy to gain a foothold in this new territory. This story accounted—to the satisfaction of those who were envious of us—for the success already beginning to crown Father's efforts to make a home at Harberton in the face of almost overwhelming difficulties.

We had heard and read about the behaviour of gold-miners in other places, but were agreeably impressed by the ones who came our way. They were an inoffensive crowd of men gathered from all parts of the world. Many of them were navvies from the Dalmatian coast. To-day they would be called Yugoslavs. Accustomed to a diet of brown bread, tomatoes, onions, olives and wine, some of them fared badly on salt meat and beans. Scurvy was common. Generally we found them honest; and their family relations interested us greatly, particularly when some huge and powerful boy of twenty cowered at the threat of a beating from his uncle, a tiny, wizened old man, perhaps three times his age.

The gold-mining industry in southern Tierra del Fuego reached its zenith about 1893. By that time there were some eight hundred men working at it. They were scattered in small groups along the different beaches, usually in places exposed to the ocean rollers. It was, in fact, only where the sea had done most of the washing for them that the miners found it paid to work. At the foot of conglomerate cliffs, where the waves broke at high water—or had done in ages past—were deposits of shingle and sand. These yielded so little gold that they were not worth washing, so were shovelled away. From a foot to as much as twenty feet below these surface deposits was the bed-rock, on which gold lay mixed with black magnetic iron sand. This pay dirt was carefully collected, all crevices and hollows being explored with a teaspoon or a penknife. Now and again would be found nuggets as large as two or three sovereigns, but usually the gold came in tiny flakes as small as the scales of a sprat—and not much heavier. A hundred of these " colours " (as they were called) might be worth little more than a shilling.

Sometimes the loose surface shingle was so deep that even a large party of miners had hardly reached bed-rock before the rising tide ruined their work and stopped them from going on. A deep hole with a rich bottom was a temptation to undermine the walls. More than one miner's life was lost in that way.

2

Many engineers and experienced prospectors, who had come from the snows of Alaska and Australian sands, found pay dirt near the mouths of Fireland's rivers. They looked towards the mountains whence those rivers flowed and, with pack and shovel on back and hopes running high, tramped into the hills. But when they had left the alluvial deposits of conglomerate behind they found not a single trace of the precious metal; nor, to my knowledge, has any gold-bearing quartz ever since been discovered in those mountain ranges.

How came that gold where they found it? It was not inland. It was not in the sheltered channels or along any coasts or islands west of Cape Horn. It was on the southern side of Navarin Island, the outer coasts of Lennox and New Islands, and in Sloggett Bay, where the ocean currents—different from those of to-day—may have swept vast fields of ice up from the Antarctic or round the extreme point of the American continent. When ice forms in shallow creeks or river mouths many inches of mud and grit become frozen to the bottom of it. The high tides of spring break the ice into blocks, which drift out to sea. Some disintegrate, but others get caught in currents that bear them along and leave them stranded on distant coasts. As summer advances, the block-ice melts—and many a ton of mud is deposited on the shore, miles from its place of origin.

And if that place of origin should have been a vast gold-bearing shoal in the Southern Ocean, was that not how the pay dirt found its way to Tierra del Fuego?

3

The advent of the miners was a godsend to us. By bringing us trade, it helped my father to establish the Harberton settlement with something more than the savings from a missionary's meagre salary. We sold them beef. We could have sold them far more than we did, for the demand was great, but we had to limit the number of animals slaughtered, in order not to deplete our small herd. When there were no more to spare we had to stop selling.

Even at the height of the gold-rush the price never rose above sixpence a pound, if collected from our farm. Many of the miners had boats in which they could have fetched the beef, but they were not keen on using them in those treacherous waters. They much preferred us to deliver it to them. I do not remember what freights we charged to the different beaches, but I know they were not exorbitant. We were far from being good business men, and Father had some queer, old-fashioned ideas about not taking advantage of others.

The task of delivery fell to Despard and Will. We had acquired a useful lifeboat from a wreck. It was thirty feet long, had two masts rigged with spritsails and was ideal for the purpose. With a crew of Yahgans they ran regular trips to the mining-camps with loads of beef.

They were not without competitors for the miners' custom. On one occasion they reached Sloggett Bay, to find that a schooner had arrived from Punta Arenas on a trade-filching expedition. With many sides of beef hanging in the rigging, it was anchored in the uncertain shelter of that very islet that had proved such fickle protection to the *Golden West* ten years before. On account of the heavy rollers on the beach, the schooner had been unable to make contact with the shore.

My brothers drew in as near to the outer edge of the breakers as they dared and dropped a small buoy, with a line attached, into the water. The buoy drifted ashore, was grabbed by the expectant miners congregated on the beach, and supplied the means of establishing an endless rope, to which the quarters of beef were tied and safely hauled ashore through surf and sand.

Meanwhile the rival schooner, having waited in vain for the sea to abate, set sail for less dangerous beaches, with the unsold beef still pendant from the rigging.

4

Nearly a hundred miners were working at Lennox Cove, where the shingle covering the bed-rock was not only many metres deep, but was also so shifty that it was extremely difficult to shore up the sides of the pits they dug. Nevertheless, their labours were rewarded. The layer of pay dirt on the bed-rock was so rich that one party of seventeen men took out seventy kilogrammes of gold (more than seven thousand pounds' worth) in three months. We heard that this party were leaving with their spoils for Punta Arenas, and as, when starting work at Lennox Cove, they had run somewhat into our debt and had not since paid off the score, Despard took one of our boats to Lennox to collect the amount due before the lucky miners had a chance to squander their hard-won gold on the primitive entertainments that Punta Arenas had to offer.

The weather was threatening, and, as the outer coast of Lennox Island is exposed to the full force of the sea, Despard put into a little cove on the sheltered side. He left his Yahgan crew with the boat and walked across the island, which was mostly moor and thicket, to Lennox Cove. He was welcomed by the happy party, some of whom were on the point of leaving in a schooner then anchored in the offing. The debt was gladly paid.

The members of the party about to take passage—eight or nine in number—had difficulty in getting on board the schooner. Repeated attempts to launch a whale-boat failed. Finally the captain of the schooner jumped into the sea and swam ashore with a line. Soon a stout rope was attached to the bow of the whale-boat, which, though it quickly filled with water, was hauled through the surf, with the miners and the courageous captain clinging to her. When they were all safely aboard, the vessel set sail for Punta Arenas.

By the following day the sea had somewhat subsided, and the rest of the party, anxious to spend their gold, decided to leave in a whale-boat. They offered Despard a passage round to the point where he had left his Indians. The wind now blew from the west, and by going round east of the island they would be sheltered, but the off-shore wind would be gusty. Despard warned them about it, but the men were too delighted with the wealth they had acquired and intoxicated with the thought of good times to come to listen to him. They repeated their invitation, and my brother replied that he would go with them only if he went as captain. He must have seemed a presumptuous young fellow, for they laughingly told him that they were quite satisfied with their present captain, who was a wonderful man and held a sailing-master's certificate. So Despard stood and watched the whale-boat go.

Turning a point when running before the wind under full sail, they let her jibe and she capsized. Despard saw six of the men struggle on top of it and cling there, looking, at that distance, like birds on a drift-log. They did not stay there long. The wind got under the sail and turned the boat clean over again. After that my brother could see only one solitary figure clinging to the overturned boat as it drifted away out to sea. There was nothing that could be done to rescue him, and in that icy water, however strong he might have been, he could not have long survived.

Those unfortunate men must have sunk like stones, for each probably had sewn in his clothes over nine pounds weight in gold.

5

One evening at dusk I was returning home along the edge of a wood when I was suddenly startled by a strange apparition. The lower part of it was white—and it was coming along the path towards me. I stepped behind a stump and stood perfectly still. The apparition drew nearer until I could recognize it for what it was : a little man in his underpants. The remains of his trousers were wrapped round his feet—the clumsiest pair of moccasins I ever saw.

He was a Spaniard. When I spoke to him, he told me that he had been with other gold-miners on an eight-ton cutter that had been wrecked in a rocky part of Moat Bay, about twenty miles east of our meeting-place. All of them had managed to land safely, but the cutter had been smashed to pieces against the rocks and had sunk near the shore. The others had decided to walk to Sloggett Bay, where there were mining-camps, but this poor little chap had elected to make for Harberton. Thinking to reach our homestead in a day, he had started off with scarcely any provisions. Night had overtaken him. Wet and hungry, he had used his last match to light a fire, put his boots to dry and settled down for the night. When he had attempted to put them on in the morning, he had found it impossible; the leather had been completely cooked.

I asked him to whom the sunk cutter had belonged, and was vastly interested by his reply.

He came back to Harberton with me. While he was eating a hearty meal I sought out my brother Despard and told him what I knew. No one, I said, would think of salvaging anything from the cutter on that exposed and rocky coast. In calm weather, with boat-hooks and a grappling-iron, a couple of fellows—such as ourselves—might fish up some very useful odds and ends without anyone being the wiser or the worse off. Despard quite agreed with me, and on the next calm day we started off for Moat Bay before daybreak.

Just where the cutter had sunk was a rock wall, against which the ground swell rose and fell, instead of breaking heavily as it was doing in the shallower water a little farther east, where some of the wreckage had drifted onto the beach. The things we most coveted were lying with the smashed remains of the vessel on the shingle bottom near the foot of the wall. We could see them clearly from our boat, though the water was twenty feet deep. With our grappling-iron we hooked out several lengths of rope, a loose hatch-cover and a large iron pot. Farther out was a small kedge-anchor that we wanted very badly. After many vain attempts we managed to get it on board, together with a length of chain.

We filled up the boat with other useful articles from the shore and set off back for Harberton so laden down with booty that we had less than eight inches of freeboard. We had twenty miles to go, but we were happy. That cutter had belonged to our most unscrupulous rivals in our trade with the gold-diggers.

CHAPTER NINETEEN

The House at Cambaceres. I Look After the Cattle. I am Nearly Gored by a Bull.
I Build Fences on No Top Hill and Lose Twenty Pounds in Weight.

I

SOME OF THE HALF-WILD CATTLE BROUGHT BY MY FATHER FROM THE FALK-lands had been landed on Walanika (Rabbit Island), so that they might not wander off and get lost in the woods on the main island, or get drowned in some of the dangerous swamps that abounded there. To these had been added the bull calf from Devonshire and some eight or ten yearlings from Harberton. It had soon become evident, however, that, with the increase of rabbits on the island, the cattle were not getting enough to eat.

It was decided, therefore, to transfer them to the mainland. The spot chosen was a double peninsula not much more than two miles from Harberton as the crow flies, but about three miles by sea and, going round swamps and creeks, five by land. The long inner harbour that formed this peninsula was known to the Yahgans as Lanushwaia [1] (Woodpecker Harbour or Creek). In 1851 Captain Allen Gardiner and his ill-fated little party had called it Bloomfield Harbour. Father now named it Cambaceres, after Antonio Cambaceres, the President of Congress, who had been such a good friend to him.

Before Serafín Aguirre was smitten with the gold fever, advantage was taken of his great strength and dexterity with the lasso to catch the cattle on Walanika. For a consideration, a small schooner put the animals across to Cambaceres. The isthmus that joined the double peninsula to the mainland was not much over a hundred yards across, so a Yahgan was installed there with his wife, to prevent the cattle from wandering away and getting lost.

Aguirre went off in search of gold, while business took my father to Punta Arenas. About a fortnight after the cattle had been landed the Yahgan guardian came to report that they had all got away and, in spite of his efforts, he had been unable to get them back. It seemed that he

[1] " Ush " as in " usher," not as in Ushuaia, which appears thus on the maps, but should really be spelt Ooshoowaia.

had gone for a two days' picnic, and that the cattle had taken full advantage of his absence.

What an opportunity for us! Horses and fun! The animals had scattered, and it took us several days to find them and get them all back again. Here I saw my chance; the Yahgan was disqualified, so I must be allowed to take his place. This was agreed to on Father's return. Cambaceres was started with a leaky wigwam and a tent. Later we had a two-roomed shack, and when we began dairy-farming, Despard built, with the help of Will and myself, a good-sized bungalow of sawn board and corrugated iron. We also put up a cow-shed and corrals right across the isthmus.

The land behind Cambaceres became our principal cattle-farm, and as time went by Harberton saw less and less of me. I was more often at Cambaceres or camping in the woods. Will also had an outdoor job. He was given charge of the sheep on our various islands and in the western region of our land. Despard was kept fully employed at Harberton. In the daytime (and sometimes by lamplight at night) he had his carpentry and other work around the homestead, and in the evenings greatly relieved Father of the book-keeping and the business side of the growing concern. My parents may have feared that I should take to the woods altogether, for I was summoned back to Harberton for two consecutive summers to look after the cattle there, while Despard and Will worked at Cambaceres.

My busiest time at Cambaceres was during the spring round-up, after the animals had been left to themselves all the winter. They were increasing rapidly, and by that time there were over three hundred for me to look after. The animals roamed over thirty thousand acres, more than half of which was covered with trackless forest, through which wound numberless valleys so swampy, or so full of fallen timber, that only in a few places were they passable for driven cattle. It would have taken an army of men, all used to forest work, to round up that herd all at once. The most I could manage was about seventy per cent of the entire herd, which by 1898 numbered six hundred. I had previously listed them under some forty different groups: according to sex and approximate age; whether horned or polled, with any peculiarity; whether red, dun, black or brown; whether spotted, streaked or speckled. If, as had happened once or twice, there had been two animals so alike that it would be difficult to tell them apart, I had marked either the horn or the ear. Then at the round-up I would check against my list such animals as I had mustered in the corral, and put a pencil mark against the missing ones. If they turned up later, the ticks were rubbed out. Some of the absentees died in swamps or during bad weather. The rest were stolen. I could prove nothing, but it was significant that all the cattle that disappeared were those that haunted our eastern boundary. They could not stray beyond this of their own accord because of a fence that I shall describe later in this chapter, and I was sure the Aush and Ona were not responsible. I had much more cause to attribute the thefts to certain white men who ran meat to the miners, and wrote off the loss against an iron pot, a length of chain and an extremely useful little kedge-anchor.

In this task of looking after the Cambaceres cattle I had one Yahgan assistant, a lad named Tom. I also had the help of my sisters, whenever they could come. With my aunt, Yekadahby, they were often to be found at Cambaceres. They loved the outdoor life and the riding, especially when there were wandering cattle to chase. Bertha became an expert at rounding-up. She could recognize every animal in the herd. Besides myself, the only other who could do that was Tom. After spending a day in the woods, he would give me details of all the animals he had come across, and so enable me to erase more ticks from my stock-list.

2

In the land at the back of Cambaceres a few of the cattle wandered far into the forest, and some of the calves grew up outlaws. If any of them reappeared we did our best to catch them. Some of them might be over two years old and were very wild, even dangerous.

Once, when Yakadahby and Will happened to be with me at Cambaceres, Will and I captured one of these animals—a young bull—outside the corral, and decided to slaughter it. This was usually done either by shooting or by pithing—that is, severing the spinal cord with a knife—which is almost as quick a death. To assist us in the task, we always made use of two posts planted a few inches apart near the corral. When Will had lassoed this bull, with the other end of the rope fastened to his strong cow-hide saddle-girth, he slipped the rope between the posts and by urging his horse forward, dragged the bull towards them.

With the bull's head close to the posts, it was time for me to administer the *coup de grâce*. The bull was furious at being treated in this way for the first time in his life, but, as the lasso was an exceptionally strong one, I thought it would be a fine idea to show how brave I was by pithing him.

When I approached him on foot, knife in hand, he gave a violent jerk

in my direction—and the lasso snapped close to the ring.   In a flash he was
right on me.   I had no time to dodge or even fling myself face downwards
on the ground.   I stumbled backwards to avoid his horns and, as he passed
right over me, received a blow from his nose in the lower ribs.   This
winded me completely and left me standing on my head.

It seemed a long time before my feet came to the ground.   Dazed and
shaken, I scrambled up.   The bull was a hundred yards away, charging a
boat on the beach; and twenty yards from the house, right in the open,
stood Yekadahby with a broom in her hand.   She had been watching from
the house, had seen me fall, snatched up the nearest weapon and rushed
full-tilt to the rescue.   These women!   I doubt if I should have the pluck
to go out with a broom against an angry bull.

The animal took to the sea and swam the entrance to the inner harbour.
That evening we shot him near the Varela River.

3

By the autumn of 1894, Will, with his Yahgan lad, Teddy, and a
sturdy, jovial young Spaniard named Modesto Pernas, had divided Gable
Island into three parts.   By taking advantage of certain lakes and running
fences from one to the other, they had effected a great saving in time and
material.   The lakes, of course, when frozen and covered with a little
snow, were no barrier to sheep, but during that period of the year barriers
were not much needed.

In addition to this major division of the island, they made fields for
the sheep, and corrals in which to gather them at shearing time.   The
fences were made of posts and rails, all of which had to be cut and brought
from the forest.   In the winter the ground was frozen as solid as stone, so
the post-holes had to be dug and the posts planted in the summer-time.
Even then it was heavy and tedious work, for the land, except in the
swamps, was hard and rocky.

Between us we had also erected fences on the mainland.   We had
enclosed the several peninsulas by fencing across their isthmuses—a line
extending from the Cambaceres inner harbour to the shore opposite the
Harberton settlement, and on round the three west creeks, across Thought
Of peninsula, to the Lasifharshaj River.   Whenever there had been a
suitable forest we had made a good sheep-fence of logs by arranging them
as a child does his wooden bricks.   This had used a lot of timber and had
been heavy work, but no nails had been needed and, as no post-holes had
had to be dug, we had been able to carry on all through the winter, our

only tools some good sharp axes. Thus approximately two thousand acres had been enclosed, with only two miles of fence.

In that winter of 1894, which was summer-time in England, Will and I planned two more big fencing jobs. For these we had to divide forces; his work lay westward, while mine was to the east. Assisted by his Yahgan boy, Teddy, and the valiant Modesto Pernas, it was his purpose to make a long fence just inside the edge of the forest on the western margin of our farm. When it was completed we would be able to transfer sheep from the islands, which were beginning to get over-stocked.

I myself was to have the help of the other Yahgan lad, Tom. Considering the task before us, it seemed a tremendous undertaking. From a rocky headland ten miles eastward of Harberton rose No Top Hill; long and narrow, with wooded sides, steep without being precipitous. Above the timber line were the rounded moors from which its name was derived. On the moors were small lakes here and there. In some places were out-crops of rock, in others patches of sharp gravel mixed with soaking moss and mud. The boundary line of our land ran from north to south across the middle of No Top; and it was my intention to make a barrier to prevent our cattle from wandering farther eastward.

Accompanied by Tom, I set out in Despard's boat, the *Esperanza*, taking with me a small tent and bedding, together with such provisions as biscuits, flour, rice, sugar, salt, coffee, and plenty of swedes and carrots from the garden. We always aimed at a Spartan diet when on these trips away from home, so, judging most of these things to be expensive luxuries, I made up my mind, before we started off, to live almost exclusively on the garden produce and such guanaco meat as I could obtain.

It was an ideal winter's day, calm, but freezing hard, when we rowed the ten miles from Harberton and landed on the shingle beach beside the rocky promontory. We unloaded the boat, laid the cars on the beach for the boat to slide over and hauled her up to a spot where she would be safe from the highest tide. So that she might not get filled with snow and ice, we turned her over. Having done this, we hacked a narrow path through the thick wood at the foot of No Top and carried all our goods up to a point through which I considered the fence would have to pass, and immediately started felling trees.

As a man and a boy cannot move heavy logs, even with levers, without a great deal of effort, we had to work carefully so that the trees fell across each other, thus interlacing to form a natural log fence. By leaving the branches on to be crushed down by the weight of other trees, we formed a barrier impassable to cattle and one that even a guanaco would not attempt to cross.

The direction of the fence, to within half a mile or so, did not matter in the least, so Tom and I were free to follow the forest where the timber was best suited to our purpose. As we worked our way farther up No Top, we came to more stunted trees, which made our progress slower. Sometimes we had to carry, roll or drag logs downhill to build them up in places where fire had long ago destroyed the forest. In some of the hollows where snow lay very deep, we had to build in such a way that, when the snow melted, the fence would sink down properly criss-crossed and not disintegrate. Our only tool was the axe and, because we used no nails, the construction presented some tricky problems calling for not a little skill.

It was one of Father's axioms that a change of work is as good as a rest, so instead of doing fencing on Sundays, Tom and I went after guanaco meat or to inspect the cattle. I had purposely left my dogs behind at Harberton, in order that their barking would not frighten guanaco away, so we were able to secure meat without having to go very far for it.

The mountainside we were fencing faced south, and was so steep that for a full four months of winter it never saw the sun. Consequently it was an excessively cold place. A steep rock standing out of the woods, not much over a mile from where we worked, and well up the mountain, caught the sun for a short time in the early afternoon. One Sunday when we were not in need of meat I went up there and climbed the rock to get a sight of our old friend. His warmth was rather feeble, but nevertheless I was greatly cheered by the experience.

Having brought our fence up to the foot of a cliff above which it was most unlikely that cattle would pass, we launched the *Esperanza* and rowed back to Harberton for a couple of days' rest. After this very welcome break, with the delights of well-served meals, a comfortable bed and a chair to sit on, I returned with Tom to No Top, to start work on a very long cattle-fence on the western side. When the gap between the mountain and the Eastern River had been closed we should have a great triangle bounded by sea, mountain and river. The last two were not absolutely impassable, but they would be very useful to check the animals' wanderings.

There was a fair depth of snow on the ground. On arriving at the spot decided on for our encampment, Tom and I constructed with poles a conical-shaped wigwam with very steep sides. The prevailing winds were westerly, so the doorway opened to the east. Against the walls we piled branches and tree-bark, leaving a small opening at the top. Such a wigwam is no more than a large chimney, and when the wind did not blow too fiercely we could enjoy the warmth of the fire inside without being troubled by the smoke.

I had an alarm-clock, given me by an ex-miner called Bertram, who worked for us for some time at Harberton. This aroused us two or three hours before daylight. We would boil some guanaco meat, with a handful of rice and chopped swede to thicken the gravy. We would then breakfast off the soup, reserving the meat for our midday meal, in order not to waste the precious hours of daylight by further cooking. Unless the weather was damp and muggy, which was seldom, the meat was frozen by lunch-time. We would make a fire to thaw it out and stand by the fire while we ate it. This seldom took more than ten minutes, and when it was finished, we would swing our axes again till it was too dark to carry on. Then we would go back to the wigwam to roast meat and eat enormous quantities. Biscuits we rationed to one a day each; and tea or coffee we had only once a day, either in the morning or at night. Sometimes in the evening our clothes had to be dried—or there was mending to do. I made a new pair of moccasins every week and, with a supply of hide brought with us, made head-stalls and other saddle-gear until finally sleep overcame me.

From our mountainside we could see the Harberton settlement across six miles of forest—a gladdening sight. In calm weather we regularly heard the crowing of the cocks. One perfect morning, breaking the deathly silence, came the sound of music floating gently on the still air. So clear was it that I recognized the tune—the Austrian National Anthem, later to be adopted by Germany. Tom and I looked at each other in amazement to hear such a sound in such a place. When, weeks later, we returned to the homestead, I made enquiries, and learnt that there had been no singing at Harberton on that date, but a large party of Austrian miners had gathered in the open air at Afluruwaia (Puerto Toro) on the east end of Navarin and, in celebration of one of their country's feast-days, had sung their National Anthem. The distance from there, across water and forest, was over eighteen miles.

During that winter, whatever the weather, I went to work every week-day, but in bad weather did not take Tom with me. Apart from the fact that he was a boy and did not have the incentive to work that possessed me, I wanted to find a roaring fire to roast myself by when I got back. There were times when the wind, laden with snow, howled through the woods; others when the snow fell calmly through the night till every twig was bent double with its weight. Perhaps the beginning of a slight thaw would liberate masses of snow, which, in tumbling down, brought lumps of ice that had frozen amongst the branches above, and could really hurt. On such days I might take an empty sack to protect my shoulders, and would go to work wearing only moccasins and a pair of trousers. I would work furiously till the exercise no longer kept me warm and I grew chilled right through from the slush and masses of melting snow that had poured on me from above. Then back to the fire to warm myself, happy in the reflection that I had earned my day's keep.

One Sunday morning before daybreak we heard a strange call. At first we thought it to be some young bull wandered far from the herd, but soon realized that it was someone in search of our encampment. I answered the call lustily, and soon saw in the moonlight the figures of Despard and my sisters, Bertha and Alice. I was delighted to see, not only them, but also the good-sized bundle that Despard had on his back; it promised luxuries.

Knowing that I would be sure to leave camp at daybreak, either to hunt or to see how the cattle fared, they had left Harberton on the Saturday afternoon, slept for a few hours at Cambaceres and started into the woods soon after midnight.

They told me that at Harberton they had watched the gap we were making in the forest, with its dark line of fence against the snow, growing day by day as it climbed the mountainside till it reached the foot of the cliff.

Throwing economy to the winds we were soon feasting royally on the dainties Mother had sent: bread, butter and some of Yekadahby's jam; coffee and condensed milk. To my joy, Despard also produced from his bundle something that was not often seen at Harberton, let alone on No Top: a bunch of onions. What an improvement for our monotonous guanaco stew!

After we had eaten and chatted and they had admired the stretch of fence near the encampment, I saw them off on their way back to Cambaceres. Before we parted, I told Despard that I should soon be moving my encampment farther south, as the fence was growing in that direction and every day Tom and I had to walk farther to our work. It was my intention, I said, to build a little log-hut and roof it with guanaco hides.

I suggested that when it was ready Bertha and Alice might come and stay a week or two with me in the woods. The girls went off in high glee.

The log-hut was duly constructed by Tom and myself. It was not much larger than a big packing-case and was built on the edge of a frozen lake. When it was finished I went to Harberton to fetch my sisters. Mother consented to their vacation, and they returned with me to No Top. We brought the dogs with us, and every night saw a race across the frozen lake after an imaginary fox—an exciting chase that my sisters and I enjoyed as much as the dogs. With these and other diversions, the work on the fence became more of a pleasure; and in one last delightful fortnight Tom and I finished our winter's work by bringing the fence down a deep gully and joining it with the river.

Will finished his work on the westward fence at about the same time. Meanwhile Despard had not been idle. He had built an eight-ton lighter, in which later we were able to ship to or from the islands either a dozen horses, or over a hundred sheep at a time. I believe Despard, in a different way, worked harder than either of us, although he lived in more civilized surroundings. He ate beautifully cooked meals at a table and slept at night between sheets, yet he could not share with us our carefree life in the woods. For all that, he was not of a jealous disposition, so I do not think he envied us. I am quite certain that neither of us envied him.

It was not long after I arrived back at Harberton that I began to feel the effects of my over-rigid economies on No Top. I had lost both strength and energy and from well over fourteen stone had come down to twelve and a half. The store account for Tom and myself for three months worked out at six shillings a month each. One gets thin on a diet of lean guanaco meat, especially when one works too hard.

CHAPTER TWENTY

My Father Obtains Permission to Occupy Picton Island. Will and I Shoot Wild Cattle. Christian Petersen Cooks an Early Breakfast. Our Splendid Wigwam is Burnt to the Ground. Tom has an Accident and I am Suspected of Murderous Intent.

I

IN THE AUTUMN, TWO YEARS AFTER THE INCIDENTS RELATED IN MY LAST chapter, Will and I were planning our winter campaign of fencing and hunting, when Father, who had just returned with Mother from a trip to England, sprang a surprise on us. He told us that he had purchased a hundred acres of land on Picton Island, on which to build a homestead, and in addition held an official authority from the Governor of Punta Arenas to occupy the whole island. He had decided that, when winter came, I should take a good boat to Banner Cove, with men, provisions and tools, and start a settlement there. I was to fence as much land as possible, so that our surplus animals could be shipped there the following summer— and I was to capture the wild cattle and horses, of which there were quite a number on the island. Years earlier, the Chilean Government, wishing to establish its claim to the island, had landed cattle and some mares, and placed a Captain-of-the-Port in charge. This man had soon deserted his post, the cattle had run completely wild over the whole island, and Chile had, so it appeared, lost all interest in the enterprise. The Governor had told Father that the cattle were ours for the catching.

Despard took over the care of the sheep- and cattle-farms, thus leaving Will to accompany me on this new venture. We crossed to Banner Cove, about eighteen miles from home, late in the month of April, after the livestock had been settled safely in their winter quarters. We had five companions. Two of them were our Yahgan boys, Tom and Teddy. The third was José Radic, a strong, hard-working, semi-savage Austrian miner. He had quarrelled violently with his fellow-miners and now intended to pass a quiet winter, doing enough work to pay for his keep. In spite of his lack of polish, he was a good fellow and a grand man with an axe. The fourth was Olaf Aslaksen, a Norwegian sea-captain who had occasionally commanded the *Allen Gardiner*. He had recently married in the Falklands and was anxious to give up the sea and settle down with his wife on a shore job. My father thought he might be a good man to leave in charge of the island after the preliminary work had been completed. He was lightly built and barely of average height, though exceedingly active and wiry.

The fifth was Christian Petersen, a tall, stooping Danish sailor, flotsam from the mining-camps in the north. Petersen was an old man. He was almost bald, with a noble forehead, anxious, watery-blue eyes and a white beard about a foot long. He had probably seen better days. With a few strokes of a pencil he could draw a speaking likeness. His other hobby was a concertina, which he played at every opportunity. He spoke, with apparent authority, on rubies and other precious stones, of which he claimed to have found traces in different parts of Tierra del Fuego; but the fortune of his dreams, though for ever almost within his grasp, had continued to elude him. Of late years, he told us, he had served on several vessels as ship's cook. Father was sorry for the old man and had insisted that we should take him in a similar capacity to Picton. I had protested against this. Petersen could not last much longer, and it was hard to dig a grave in frozen ground. But Father had won the day.

We beached our boat at Banner Cove and built the finest wigwam I have ever seen. We used poles nearly thirty feet long and covered them with a layer of evergreen beech (*shushchi*) branches over a foot thick— enough to keep out even the rain of Picton Island, which was twice as heavy as at Harberton. The branches were pressed down by weighty logs. Of the same material we also made—fortunately, as things turned out—a separate dormitory, with raised bunks of saplings and mattresses of *shushchi*. This was real luxury, for *shushchi*, when drying, gives off a pleasant sylvan scent.

We laid a log across the floor of the wigwam. Beyond that line was Petersen's domain. I told him that if anyone crossed it—including myself —he was to be ordered back to his own quarters. I had brought my old alarm-clock; and Petersen received instructions to be up in good time, so that we could have food and warmth before dawn allowed us to begin work.

These preliminaries having been attended to, we settled down to our winter's task. I spent a whole day in the woods, blazing the trail for a timber fence, then Radić, Aslaksen, the two Yahgan boys, Will and I got busy felling trees, while our ancient chef pottered about in his cook-house, producing some of the worst meals it has ever been my misfortune to have set before me.

For these meals the principal item was beef, with which, by courtesy of the Chilean Government, Picton Island abounded. Procuring it, however, was not without risk and excitement. Once, when meat was needed, Will and I, dressed only in trousers, shirts and moccasins, went off at the first sign of daybreak. We had not gone two miles before we found cattle-tracks, and, topping a ridge, saw two bulls and two cows hastening away. It was a waste of ammunition to shoot them from behind with the old-fashioned Winchester, but the leading cow, turning somewhat, gave me a chance at the heart, and a lucky shot brought her down. The other cow seemed not to have heard the shot. Seeing her companion fall, she got excited and charged the dying beast. Will brought her down in the same way.

The bulls crossed a little stream at the foot of the hill and went scrambling up the opposite bank.

There is a spot behind the horns, just where the head joins the neck, where a shot, even with a rook-rifle, will bring down a bull; but the area has no greater diameter than a hen's egg, and takes some hitting at a distance. I now chose instead the long line of spine, took aim at the leading bull and fired. To my surprise, he dropped like a stone.

His companion, a fine jet-black animal, looked round angrily to find out where all the trouble came from. He caught sight of Will and me and came at us full-tilt up the hill. We held our fire and waited. When he was about forty yards away we opened fire. Every bullet must have hit him, but he never flinched. He was getting dangerously close, and we were just considering taking evasive action by scrambling up the nearest tree, when he sank down unconscious and died. Our pride at this fine kill was not unmixed with admiration and regret for the fallen hero.

2

Apart from the rain and the prevailing cheerlessness, there were several incidents to mar our stay on Picton. Once, having retired to bed after a heavy day's fencing, we were awakened by the rattle of the old Danish cook's tin and his usual call of, " Bwekfast wetty ! "

It was pitch dark, with a miserable drizzle falling, as we bundled into the kitchen, feeling far more sleepy than hungry. Petersen's cooking had to be eaten to be believed. As I had already told him, I strongly doubted that he had ever been a ship's cook, for he would certainly have been flung overboard by the sailors, even of a Mission vessel. However, despite the cooking and our own unnatural weariness, we managed to consume our breakfast, and waited for daylight. At last, as no dawn appeared and the alarm-clock showed it to be after nine, I thought of another timekeeper: the tide. It should have been high at about eight o'clock. I took a torch from the fire and went down to the sea-shore, to find that the tide had not even started to come in. We spoke severely to the cook and went back to bed.

We should have been warned by this occurrence, yet the next time it happened we actually went off to work, over a mile away, and had to wait for two hours round a fire before it grew light enough to swing an axe. There could now be no doubt that someone was tampering with the clock when the rest of us were asleep. We suspected Radić, the Austrian. He had a queer sense of humour, his highest form of entertainment being to throw bones covertly at the aged Petersen, whom he hated for his bad cooking and laziness. No doubt he was eager to get the old fellow into trouble. I had a heated argument with Radić on the subject, but was never able to prove that he had been the culprit.

More trouble was to follow. One night we reached our encampment after dark, keenly looking forward to a good supper round the fire. We found Petersen, a truly pitiful figure, standing beside a heap of ashes that had once been our palatial wigwam. He had spilt fat in the fire. But worse than the loss of our wigwam was that all our provisions had either gone up in the blaze, or had been rendered quite unusable. The only thing the poor wretch had saved was his beloved concertina.

Our companions now expressed the view that we should return to Harberton. Will and I stood out resolutely against this suggestion. We had come to do a job, and we were not going back home until it was finished. If we had no other provisions, we still had beef. The others agreed with a bad grace and, in an atmosphere of mutual hostility, the work on the fences continued until, a fortnight later, there came the culminating disaster.

We arrived in the morning at the spot where we had left our axes the night before. The Yahgan lad, Tom, took up his axe in one hand and carelessly swung it at a branch above his head. He missed it. The axe slipped from his grip, somersaulted in the air and, sharp as a razor, buried its head deep in his breastbone.

The poor boy grasped his chest with both hands, but uttered no cry. We pulled off our shirts and bound him up as best we could, drawing his shoulders as close together as possible, to keep the wound closed. We got him to the nearest beach, fetched the boat with all our goods on

20

Yekadahby.
Miss Joanna Varder.

An Ona from the north.

board and, through a day of rough weather, made Harberton the same
night.

Tom, who had fainted several times on the voyage, was put straight
into my bed, where Father did what he could for him.   The axe had sunk
into his brisket to its full width.   It had gone right through the bone,
leaving only membrane uncut.   He must have contracted congestion of
the lungs, and for many nights either Despard, Will or I sat up with him.

But his condition steadily improved.   The wound healed up, leaving
one side of his chest a trifle sunken.   When a vessel bound for Ushuaia
put in at Harberton with a doctor on board, we asked him to have a look
at our patient.   After an examination, he insisted that an operation
should be performed, and that he should take Tom to Ushuaia for that
purpose.   None of us believed that this was necessary, but we could not
dispute the doctor's authority, so Tom had to go.

About a fortnight later we received a note to go and fetch him, as he
was much better.   When we arrived we were presented with a bill that
was, to us, exorbitant.   It solved the mystery of Tom's urgent trip to
Ushuaia, but it did not explain the fact that we found no difference in
the shape of the lad's chest.

The story of this accident got about, with the doctor quoted as the
authority for the details.   Such a cut, it was said, could never have been
made by an axe.   It was undoubtedly a stab, and the murderous hand that
had held the knife was mine.

CHAPTER TWENTY-ONE

The Aush Give the Ona a Bad Name. We Hear about Kaushel, the Man-Killer.
My Brothers and I Try to Cross the Mountains. Two of us Try Again. I am
Visited at Cambaceres by the Ona and Become Acquainted with the Notorious Kaushel.
Bertram is Warned. Such is Youth.

I

DURING THE EARLY YEARS AT HARBERTON WE HAD OCCASIONAL VISITS
from a small party of Aush. Some of its members we had first met at
Sloggett Bay when the *Golden West* had lain broken on the beach. Two
or three of the party spoke a good deal of the Yahgan tongue. One
woman, Weeteklh, was of Yahgan origin. She had a large family, and
later settled with them and her Aush husband, Missmiyolh, at Harberton.

These Aush had an even greater dread of their northern and western
neighbours, the Ona, than had the Yahgans—and with reason. Through
many generations they had been forced to evacuate far better land farther
north and retire to the thickets, swamps and moors near the south-eastern
extremity of the country, to which unfriendly region they were now
restricted. Because of their fear of the Ona, these visitors to Harberton
always crossed the ranges well east and came along the coast. They told
us that the Ona were very bad men and had slaughtered many Aush.
They spoke of one terrible man, a killer of extraordinary strength and
daring, whose name was Kaushel. They also spoke of a great lake in
Ona-land. It was, they said—though few had seen it—as long and wide
as the Beagle Channel.

In spite of our good understanding with these occasional visitors, they
always seemed restless. They stopped with us only for a few days, their
purpose being to exchange fox-skins and other articles with our Yahgans
for knives and hatchets. When one party left, late one autumn, two
ancient crones stopped behind, intending to winter at Harberton. They
looked equally wrinkled, and it was hard to say which was the elder,
though it turned out that Yoiyimmi, the shorter of the two, was Saklhbarra's mother. In spite of their age, they carried themselves upright
when walking without a load and stepped out with the grace of gypsies.
Yoiyimmi had the rare distinction among these people of being a great-

grandmother. Of her grandson and his family much will be told in the pages that follow.

Each of these two aged women had her full rows of teeth, but a first glance at either of the wrinkled faces gave the impression that it was toothless—especially in the case of Yoiyimmi. She was quite a jolly old lady, and would laughingly open her mouth to show neither incisors nor canine teeth, but two complete rows of molars, polished smooth and ground down till they were almost level with the gums. Most of the aged folk amongst the Fuegian tribes were in the same happy condition, and in the early days I never heard of an Indian having toothache. I believe they were unacquainted with that malady.

In order to pick up their language, I used to spend all the time I could spare with Yoiyimmi and Saklhbarra. Had I known then that Aush was spoken by fewer than sixty natives in all Fireland, I would not have bothered. On Sundays I would generally go and kill a guanaco, bringing down a load of meat for them. They would eye my rifle with the utmost suspicion, as though it were some evil living thing, and would even cover their faces to express their horror of it, so I learned to put it aside when I went to sit down with them for a chat.

We got on very well, and before spring, with the help of a number of words collected by Father long before and those that I picked up from these women, I was beginning to make myself understood by them. One day, when spring was well advanced, mother and daughter disappeared without a word to anyone. But they would fare well, having a supply of half-dried meat, besides being as much at home in the woods as were the very foxes.

After a while these visits of the Aush ceased altogether, and for several years we saw no more of them. Doubtless they had clashed with the Ona.

2

Often in the late summer, when the wind blew from the north, there would come the pleasant scent of vast forest fires; and smoke, mingling with the clouds, would take the glint out of the sun and show it up like a dull red ball. Occasionally we saw, up some distant wooded valley, thin spirals of smoke rising into the clear air; and at times we found places nearer home where Ona hunting-parties, or solitary wanderers, had made their fires.

There were other signs to tell us that, although we did not catch sight of the Ona, they were nevertheless not far away. Wandering cattle, after being away from the settlement for weeks, would return terror-stricken to the corral and hang around the homestead for days. There were disturbing stories, too, of fatal encounters between the Ona and mining or farming pioneers who had encroached on their domain in the northern part of the island.

It became increasingly evident to us that, sooner or later, we ourselves must come to grips with these mysterious, phantom-like people. In winter there was no need for caution. The snow lay so deep amongst the mountains that the guanaco sought the coast. In consequence, the Ona would not trouble to leave their own country beyond the ranges, because there would be no guanaco in the hills. But the summer-time, when the guanaco were back in their old haunts—that was when we might expect them, and we hoped our first meeting would not be announced by an arrow in the back while we were cutting timber or walking in the forest.

Though we could not enjoy the idea of being shadowed, it did not trouble us much. What did concern us were the skirmishes between the Ona and the white invaders. Our intentions towards the Ona were friendly, but these bloody fights with others of our kind were certain, in the long run, to make them number us among their foes. With this thought in mind, I was continually urging my brothers to come with me on a tramp through the mountains. I felt that if I could only make contact with these elusive people, the few words of the Ona language that I had managed to pick up would enable me to convince them that we at Harberton were not out to destroy them, but to make them our friends.

Ultimately my brothers were persuaded. We could not go exploring in the summer-time; there was too much work to be done. But when our sheep and cattle had been settled on their winter pastures there was opportunity for adventuring. Late one autumn, Despard, Will and I started off for the north. After our summer's work, we were all in good training. We carried our rifles (all three of us had Winchesters by then), a small tent, billy cans and spoons, some sugar, salt, biscuit and tea, together with a good quantity of rice. I have always found that rice is better value, weight for weight, than any other food. With a handful of rice, salt and a little wild celery, a thrush—or any other bird—can be transformed into a savoury stew, while berries and a pinch of sugar make a fine pudding for a hungry man.

On the first day of our trip we covered about ten miles of tangled forest and swamp not yet frozen. It rained most of the time, and we struggled forward soaked to the skin. Close to the foot of a second range of mountains we found a dry ridge with somewhat open forest, and a lake on the northern side of it. We decided that this was a good camping-place—and there were indications that others had thought the same. There were traces of a large Ona encampment. Over a dozen fires had been lighted. In the ashes we discovered charred guanaco bones, which had first been broken open to remove the marrow. The Fuegians always threw bones on the fire, to prevent their hungry dogs from breaking their teeth or choking themselves.

Of the Ona we saw nothing. Nevertheless there was a distinct possibility that they were spying on us, so throughout that night we took spell about and kept watch. The tent proved useful, for it rained continuously; but as we were not able to dry our clothes in the rain, we slept wet and cold. Next morning we pushed on round the lake and up the mountain-side, the summit of which was completely hidden in clouds. Presently the rain changed to snow. Then a gale sprang up and we could see no more than a few yards ahead.

Winter was very near, and this foul weather might continue for a long time. It would have been madness, under such conditions, to go farther into rugged and often precipitous country, all of which was unknown to us. So Despard and Will decided to return home. Knowing full well that this resolution was wise and irrevocable, I protested loudly against it, but the others were adamant, and when Despard became threatening, I had no alternative but to return with them to Harberton.

3

Fifteen months later Despard and I decided to start a second venture some miles to the west of our first attempt. From hills near Harberton farm we could see a considerable extent of moorland. It was in the depth of winter, and the moorland shone white with snow, with dark patches of evergreen trees. We fancied the snow would be frozen, with a crust strong enough to bear us, and also that we might find good hunting. The last item was what attracted Despard, rather than the wish to explore beyond the range.

Progressing through thick forest for the first five miles, we found the undergrowth bent double with snow, which, on the moors beyond, was very deep and powdery. In many places we sank through to our waists, discovering to our surprise that frequently the bog beneath was wet, not frozen. In the evening we found an excellent place to camp; a circular clearing, only a few yards across, in the middle of a very thick patch of evergreen forest. There was plenty of dead wood round about, and we collected a fine heap of it. Dead standing trees are attacked by rot only at their bases. The upper trunk and branches will remain dry and healthy for a very long time, but near the ground, where it is subject to damp, the wood rots right through in a few years. So it is often possible, when fuel is needed, to break off dry logs, nearly as thick as a man's body, at the junction where air and water meet. After sweeping most of the snow from the spot selected for our fire, we laid a mat of green branches on what seemed like frozen ground, piled the dead wood on top and put a match to the fire.

This trip we were travelling light. We had no tent, and had brought only our rifles, some biltong (sun-dried meat) and biscuits. We had seen no guanaco that day, so, having eaten sparingly of our rations, we lay down in our blankets beside the fire, which we intended to keep going all night.

About two o'clock in the morning I got up to replenish the fire—and was struck by the amount of water about. I went to our wood-heap and brought back a large log on my shoulder. I was just about to throw it on the fire when the ground gave way under my feet and I found myself up to the waist in water. The fire went with me. As the last of the embers hissed themselves into darkness, I sank still farther into the soft mud.

Our lovely clearing was nothing but a deep pool, so sheltered by trees and protected by snow that it was only slightly frozen. Our fire had weakened the ice so much that the combined weights of myself and the log had been too much for it to bear. I managed to scramble out with Despard's help and, though all around us was as black as could be, we found our wood-pile, and soon got another fire going on more solid ground. I spent the rest of the night trying to dry my clothes without burning them.

The next morning Despard expressed the definite opinion that we had gone far enough. I knew that he was right, but boastfully retorted that we had not accomplished the object of our journey. As on the previous occasion, he refused to listen to me. I offered to go on alone, but he would not hear of it. So back we went again to Harberton.

In all that snow-covered moor we had not seen the tracks of either fox or guanaco, but about two miles from home Despard shot an exceptionally fine specimen of the latter; so, if I had failed in my own purpose, Despard had not been entirely unsuccessful in his.

4

One lovely evening at Cambaceres, towards the end of 1894, two tall Indians appeared on the crest of a hill some four hundred yards away from the house. My sisters, Bertha and Alice, were with me at the time. They could both use a rifle, so I left mine with them and went out to speak to these strangers. I had a small revolver hidden on my person and carried a handkerchief full of biscuits.

To show their peaceable intentions, the men had placed their bows and quivers on some nearby bushes. They were both well-grown, powerful, resolute-looking fellows, and their guanaco-skin robes, triangular head-dress and paint made them look even larger than they really were. The taller, about six feet high, was, I learnt later, called Chalshoat. Although his companion was two inches shorter, there could be no doubt that it was he whom I should address, for I guessed at once that this was the famous Kaushel. Though he smiled in an amiable way in answer to my manifestations of friendship, there was a dignity about the man that one could not help feeling.

We sat down together. I started eating a biscuit, then offered them a share. Having heard stories of Ona being poisoned, I made a rule always to consume some of any food I gave them, in case anyone might be taken ill afterwards and then blame it on me. We tried hard to talk, but the only thing that emerged clearly was that we all wanted to be friends. Kaushel's voice, considering the harsh, guttural language he spoke, was gentle. At last I intimated that the sun was down, that it was time for sleep and that they should return the following morning. I do not know how much they understood, but we all rose, and they, adjusting their robes with a fling quite inimitable and as natural as it was graceful, turned and went back to pick up their bows and quivers from the bushes.

It had been an amicable meeting, yet I thought it prudent to send my sisters back to Harberton. The night being calm, they left in a small boat after dark. Next morning before daybreak, Bertram, the ex-miner who had given me the alarm-clock, and who happened to be at Harberton, arrived with the boat, bringing a note of encouragement from Father.

As usual, I started out early on horseback to bring in the cows from the nearby hills. I went a little beyond what was necessary, to see if the Ona were about or to pick out their camp-fire smokes. Surely enough Kaushel, Chalshoat and others appeared, scattered in groups of twos and threes, every one with bow and quiver. I dismounted and, leading my horse, approached a small group. Soon about twenty Indians had gathered round, and we sat down in a circle.

This time I had purposely left my revolver at home, realising how useless it would be if taken at close quarters by more than one of these strong fellows. They were a fine-looking set of men, with earnest though friendly faces. They commenced to speak amongst themselves, and soon I guessed that a serious debate was going on. Several of the older men put in a word here and there, but the two leaders of opposite opinion were Kaushel on one side and Kushhalimink—by far the biggest Ona I ever saw—on the other. These men spoke in low voices, but when they wished to emphasize their words their gutturals sounded even harsher than usual. They did not shake or nod their heads, for those signs of disagreement or consent were never employed by the Ona. No one ever interrupted a speaker, and there was a gravity and a pleasing dignity in the manner of their debate, which obviously concerned myself. Years later they gave me the details.

It seemed that huge, good-natured Kushhalimink wanted to take me away with them. Apart from having taken a fancy to me—as a small boy might to a captured squirrel—he thought I would be able to make or obtain rifles and ammunition and help them defend their country and destroy their enemies. Kaushel objected to this proposal, suggesting that probably I would have neither the means nor the knowledge to manufacture the articles they needed, and that if they did take me away with them, there would be no chance at all of my procuring them. He maintained that I was now very well-disposed towards them, but that both I and my people would resent the kidnapping, and they would thereby make enemies on both sides of the mountains.

Kaushel's arguments proved to be the more convincing, and the debate was concluded. Having my morning's work to attend to, I rose with a friendly gesture, mounted my horse and rode back to Cambaceres. On my return to the house I found Bertram awaiting me with great anxiety, having seen a number of Indians on the distant hill. Before coming south he had dug for gold in northern Fireland, and his experiences there had imbued him with a deep distrust of the Ona. Bertram believed in the old adage : the only good Indian is a dead one.

Some hours after I had left the party on the hill, Kaushel, followed by a band of men and lads numbering over a score, appeared walking rapidly towards the house. After their first two meetings with me, these Ona were now so friendly and familiar that they carried their bows and quivers as naturally as an Englishman might carry his umbrella. Clad and painted as they were, they made an impressive picture. Bertram, full of foreboding, was watching with me from a window where we could not be seen from the outside. At last he could stand it no longer. Cocking his rifle, he exclaimed excitedly :

" I'll shoot that devil that's ahead. They mean mischief."

I was not yet twenty, but from that moment I was a boy no longer. My rifle was as ready as his, and I said :

" Bertram, you're a dead man if you do."

And he knew that I meant it.

Telling him to stop well back in the house and on no account to shoot unless I was attacked, I left my rifle and went out to receive our visitors. There was nothing brave about this, for after having met them in the morning, I felt there was not the slightest danger. This incident shows how easily a rash action might have given us such a bad start with the Ona that we might never have regained their confidence and affection.

I remained some time with the party outside the house. Presently we were sitting on the turf, trying once again to carry on a conversation. Kaushel knew two or three words of Yahgan. They had no meaning for him, but he kept repeating them parrot-wise to show his amiable intentions. I tried my smattering of Aush, which caused them some amusement. Although they did not understand me, they recognized the language I was trying to speak.

Bertram, who had wisely refrained from mixing with the party, felt that all was well, though he still kept near to his rifle. Presently he opened the door of the house and showed himself in the doorway, with his rifle out of sight. The Ona displayed immediate relief; until that moment they had been somewhat nervous in their manner, knowing that someone was lurking in the closed house, and perhaps wondering how many the building contained, and what was being planned against them.

I made a sign to them to remain where they were, and went into the house to get a bucket of milk and some biscuits. The milk they would not touch until I had taken a good drink myself. Even then they only sipped it until, at Bertram's suggestion, I added sugar and boiling water.

Later in the day there appeared a long, straggling line of women, carrying huge, neat, cigar-shaped bundles. With them came their children, and dogs on leash. They rested nearby, and soon all had had a taste of milk and biscuit. Then the whole party went on together to

Harberton, where they camped on the edge of the main forest opposite the settlement.

Thinking it advisable to look well after the cattle while these people were about, I refrained from visiting them there. After a few days' friendly intercourse with the Yahgans and my own people, they departed quietly for their forest home without returning to Cambaceres.

On the following morning, when, from a hill, I saw in the distance the Indians' smoke rising from the tree-tops, I longed to escape from my humdrum life and go with them on their perpetual hunt. I knew nothing then of their treachery and murderous attacks on each other, and in my young heart would have loved to join them with a supply of rifles, to share their struggle against the advance of so-called civilization into the romantic land that was theirs. Such is youth!

CHAPTER TWENTY-TWO

*Capelo, the Ona, Goes to Buenos Aires. He Returns to Find his Wife had Dis-
appeared, and Plots Revenge. The Massacre of the Miners. Capelo Comes to Cambaceres. He Goes on to Harberton. Don Lavino Balmaceda Reports to the Police.
The End of Capelo. My Brothers and I Fear Reprisals.*

I

A MARITIME SUB-PREFECTURE HAD BEEN ESTABLISHED FOR SOME YEARS AT
Thetis Bay, near Cape San Diego. The officer in charge was very good
to the natives and sent a young Aush, with his father's consent, for a trip
to Buenos Aires on the government transport, which visited that port
about once every two months. They named the lad Emilio, and when he
returned he spoke quite a lot of Spanish and seemed impressed by the
wonderful things and the numberless people he had seen.

It occurred to the sub-prefect—whose wife was with him at Thetis
Bay—to try the same experiment with a young Ona they had named
Capelo,[1] who, after Emilio's grand experience and safe return, was eager
to go. Capelo, however, had a young wife whom he was afraid of
losing, so the sub-prefect's wife promised to take care of her till his
return.

Capelo departed happily; but when, some months later, he came
back, his wife had disappeared. He was told that, other Indians having
plotted her abduction, for safety's sake she had been taken to Staten
Island, and that she would be returned to him when the steamer made its
next visit. He was far from satisfied with the story.

The steamer came again, but Capelo's wife was not on board, so he
went away brooding. For some time he lurked in the neighbourhood
with a few members of his tribe, hoping for an opportunity of carrying
off the sub-prefect's wife, to hold her as hostage till his own was returned.
The people at the sub-prefecture, however, suspected that there was
danger, and consequently kept good watch. One day a young man went
out with his shot-gun for birds, and Capelo caught him unawares with an
arrow. He took his gun and the few cartridges he had, as well as his
clothes, then went with his Ona party northward along the coast, where
they happened to meet a number of mountain Ona, who were always

[1] Spanish for a cardinal's hat ; a name given him probably on account of the conical
head-dress of the Ona.

game for any exciting enterprise. Two of these mountain men were
Chalshoat, who had come with Kaushel to Cambaceres, and Halimink,
of whom much will be told before my story is done.

Accompanied by a gang of over twenty willing followers, Capelo next
fell in with a party of miners who were encamped in the shelter of a clump
of trees, where a little stream flowed out on the sea-coast, and wooded
hills rose on either side. The miners had only three horses, one of which
was tethered nearby, while the others were left free to graze. The men
had gathered round their fire, while Capelo with his party lay watching
them from the wood, some three hundred yards away. Then Capelo,
dressed in civilized clothes, walked out into the open alone and came down
unarmed, as if to make friends with the miners, who received him well.
The leader was called San Martin. He was, I believe, a Spaniard. With
the exception of a dark little Argentine gaucho, the rest of the men—four
in all—were Dalmatians, who, like most of the early miners in those parts,
came from a Dalmatian colony at Punta Arenas. Big-boned, heavily
muscled navvies, they were eminently peaceable and seldom carried either
daggers or revolvers. San Martin had a revolver, and the little gaucho a
long knife in his belt.

Capelo told the miners that he had five companions who were hungry,
having been unsuccessful in their hunting. San Martin told him he could
fetch them, provided they came unarmed, and he would give them food.
Thereupon Capelo returned to the forest, where he selected five strong
fellows, who, leaving their weapons behind, returned with him to the
miners' encampment. One of these five was Chalshoat, strong and of
great endurance, but slow, both in mind and body. Capelo instructed the
rest of his men to gather in the forest as close as possible to the miners'
tent, and rush in with their weapons as soon as a disturbance began.

The miners were preparing a pot of stew for their visitors when Capelo
gave the signal, whereupon each Ona grappled with the man assigned to
him. Capelo chose San Martin and brought him to the ground before he
could draw his revolver. Chalshoat attacked the gaucho, but the little
man dodged his clumsy opponent and darted off towards the tethered
horse, pulling his knife from his belt as he ran. He slashed through the
thong by which the horse was tied and, leaping on its bare back, raced
away.

Meanwhile the rest of the Ona, armed with bows and arrows,
had joined the struggling party. Three of the whites were arrowed
at once. One miner broke away and managed to reach the beach,

where, the tide being high, panic-stricken he took to the water; but an arrow ended his troubles. San Martin was soon tied hand and foot, and although he pleaded for his life, Capelo, after due consideration, cut his throat.

The booty was divided among the Indians, Capelo keeping the lion's share. This done, the party moved some twelve miles to the north-west, camping at a place called Najmishk, which was well chosen for strategic reasons. Here other natives swelled their numbers to over eighty men. They knew that one man had got away, and that he would spread the news of the massacre, so, fully expecting a revenge party to appear, they prepared for its reception.

Scouts were stationed at points of vantage and Capelo chose for his ambush a spot overlooking a patch of soft land through which horses could barely flounder. On one side was a precipice and on the other impenetrable scrub on the edge of the wide forest. In this thicket the natives cleared little paths through which they could race unseen from without; and in some places made hidden breast-works of branches. Their armament of bows and arrows was strengthened by at least five fire-arms, each of which had cost some human life.

More than two uneventful weeks passed and Capelo, who had assumed supreme command over his untamed countrymen, had now grown over-bearing and made himself both hated and feared. The impatient warriors had time to remember ancient feuds, and feelings ran so high that it is a wonder that they did not turn upon each other. Soon the party broke up into small groups, most of them retiring to their ancestral hunting grounds, whilst Capelo, hoping to replenish his diminished stock of ammunition, came south.

That was the Ona version of the story, given me years later by instalments.

2

At Cambaceres one evening, some two months after Kaushel's appearance there, the dogs warned us of the approach of visitors. My aunt, Yakadahby, and my two sisters, Bertha and Alice, were with me at the time. Looking out of the window, we saw two unarmed Ona walking towards the house. One of them, Chalshoat, looked well in his Ona dress and paint, but the other—a rather stocky, powerful-looking stranger—was, to my surprise, dressed completely in white man's clothing; and I did not like his looks at all. He introduced himself in broken Spanish as Capelo, said he had been in Buenos Aires and now proposed to encamp on the edge of the forest, less than half a mile away across the inner harbour.

Whilst he was speaking, I saw that a few others were already appearing out of the woods and selecting places where they proceeded to erect their shelters. Naturally I had no objection to this, yet I did not want a number of them near the house at that time of night, so I took a small bag of biscuits and, with my two visitors, went to their encampment. There were eight men in the party altogether, of whom two besides Chalshoat had visited us before, and with them were a few women and children. All but Capelo were dressed in their usual guanaco-skin robes and paint. In their encampment I saw a bundle of clothes, a rifle, revolver, shot-gun, field-glasses and two hounds of a very different type from the usual Ona dog. From this I deduced that some white man's encampment had been sacked in his absence, or that murder had been committed, and I returned home at dusk with grim forebodings.

As soon as night fell my aunt and sisters left for Harberton. As usual, the boat lay on the western side of the second isthmus, out of sight from the house and also from the place where the Ona were encamped.

That night I slept in my clothes, including my belt and revolver, with my rifle in its usual place beside my bed. As day was breaking I heard the dogs barking and a thunderous hammering on the door. I approached noiselessly and, flinging the door wide open, stood back in the dark room, revolver in hand. The outline of a huge figure loomed out of the dusk, and it was fortunate for the caller that he spoke before stepping forward into the house, for I was frightened; and an armed man when in that state is doubly dangerous.

" Ich shvimmed it," he said, and I knew that Father had sent a recently employed German, whom I had not yet seen, to keep me company. His name was Robert Schmidt.

My sisters must have left the boat in Varela harbour and Schmidt, coming at night, had failed to find it. Rather than walk round the Cambaceres inner harbour, which was fringed with thick forest right to the beach, the tide being high he had " shvimmed " the Varela River at the mouth, and then walked on to the long point, to swim the entrance of the inner harbour, thus reaching the house.

Schmidt was one of the strongest-looking men I have ever seen and I was well pleased to have him with me. Later in the morning, Capelo, with some of his companions, came to the house, and so I went outside to meet them, warning Schmidt on no account to get excited and not to start shooting unless I was attacked, in which case he was to be very careful not to plug me instead of my assailants.

Capelo, after telling me how hungry they always were and how hard it was to keep the camp supplied with guanaco meat without ammunition for his rifle, asked me to give him some in exchange for bows and arrows and some coils of hide. His story did not ring true, so I told him I could not give him any ammunition, being very short of it myself. When he heard my refusal, the look that crossed his face made me glad Schmidt was in the house behind me, and that the natives were aware of the fact.

The Ona did not wait long at Cambaceres, but soon moved on to encamp on the Harberton peninsula, half a mile from our settlement and about half that distance from the edge of the main forest. Their choice of a camping site struck me as a good sign when I heard of it, for surely, if they had been troubled by guilty consciences, they would have en-camped in the forest or close to it, rather than choose a place where it would be so easy to cut off their retreat. They were soon in touch with Father, who gave them gifts of food. Using Capelo as interpreter, he induced the four youngest men of the party to join some Yahgan natives in clearing bush on a piece of land near the homestead.

In a sheltered harbour on Navarin Island, some six miles away across the Beagle Channel, Don Lavino Balmaceda, a gentleman adventurer, who had been exiled from Buenos Aires for his political activities, had made his temporary home. He had a few sheep, did some timber-cutting and indulged in seal-hunting expeditions, by which means he had found, so he firmly believed, a short, straight road to fortune.

One Sunday, when the Indian Capelo had been at Harberton for a week, Señor Balmaceda paid us a visit. I was often at the homestead on Sundays, and now with Father, my two brothers and our visitor, went to see the Ona encampment. I was anxious to pick up what I could of their language, so never lost an opportunity of going amongst them. We were all on friendly terms with this party, and my brothers surprised them by their expert handling of the bow and arrow.

We were sure that some crime had been committed, but knowing what the natives had suffered at the hands of certain whites, were inclined to remain strictly neutral. My personal sympathies were all with the original lords of the land, so Balmaceda, probably guessing what my feelings were, kept his own counsel. In the evening, the weather being fine, he left, apparently for his settlement, whilst I returned to mine, where Schmidt still kept me company.

A few days later a rattle of rifle-fire disturbed the quiet of Harberton, and the four young Ona who were clearing brushwood near our house vanished into the scrub. Fortunately Father had gone at that moment to see how they were getting on and, as I learned later, the Indians realized that he was as much surprised by the sudden noise of shooting as they were.

It seems that Balmaceda, when he had left Harberton ostensibly to return to Navarin Island, had hurried instead to Ushuaia, to advise the authorities of what he had seen at Harberton. Almost at the same time news arrived at Ushuaia *via* Punta Arenas of the massacre of San Martin and his party. Without saddle or bridle, the little gaucho had galloped north-west some forty miles along the coast of the Atlantic to Rio Grande, where a settlement was just being started. There the horse had collapsed and died. There was no direct means of communication with Ushuaia, and nearly two months had elapsed before the news reached that station.

The Chief-of-Police at Ushuaia, tall, energetic Don Ramón L. Cortéz, was sympathetic towards the Ona, but had his duty to perform. Accordingly, accompanied by Balmaceda and a squad of armed police, he left post-haste by boat. They landed in a creek a short distance west of Harberton and stole down to the narrow isthmus, thinking to cut off all possible retreat. They took the encampment completely by surprise, but the only man there with the women and children was Chalshoat. Capelo, the man they most wanted, was visiting the Yahgan village with two other members of his party. Never dreaming he was in any danger, he had left his rifle and other possessions in the encampment.

The police followed them to the village and were close upon them before they realized it. The Chief-of-Police was anxious to avoid bloodshed, and, on meeting Capelo at the entrance to a Yahgan hut, ordered him to give himself up, but Capelo, who was exceptionally strong, sprang at him and tried to wrest the revolver from his grasp. At this moment one of the policemen, firing at point-blank range, shot Capelo dead. One of his two companions was taken prisoner; the other tried to escape and was shot by the police. This was the volley that had been heard at the settlement.

The few women and children who, at the time of the police raid, happened to be absent from the camp, successfully hid themselves and slipped away at night.

The dead having been buried, Chalshoat and the other prisoner,

Ona Indians.
Original lords of the land.
These five men do not figure in my story. They were photographed by Mr. A. A. Cameron, by
whose courtesy the picture is reproduced.

Ahnikin, Shishkolh, Halimink, Chalshoat, Puppup. Under the eye of the camera, Halimink finds it impossible to retain his beaming smile.

By courtesy of Col. Charles Wellington Furlong.

Kaushel and his family.
Kiliutah, Minkiyolh, Kohpen, Kaushel, Kiyotimink, Halchic (wife of Kiyotimink), Keëlu, Haäru.
The horizontal lines across the faces are red paint.

Photo by the late Governor Godoy.

together with some ten or twelve women and children, were taken to
Ushuaia, where they were kept under guard for some time, until vigilance
slackened—purposely, I expect—and they were allowed to slip quietly
away.

3

When we heard the whole story about Capelo we were relieved that
he was dead, for he had been most anxious to get ammunition, and sooner
or later would have made some desperate move to obtain it. Knowing
the revengeful nature of the Indians, we were anxious as to their reactions
to this affair. I continued looking after the cattle at Cambaceres as before,
but was now, to say the least, extremely nervous. Amongst the mountains, less than a day's walk away, parties of Ona were hunting either game
or one another. It was not unlikely that they would decide to hunt me.
They had a grudge against the whites who were invading their country
from the north, and now probably believed, after the shooting affray at
Harberton, that we in the south were in league with their enemies.

Despard had become father's right-hand man at the homestead,
though he was always ready to join Will or myself when we needed help.
Will, though in charge of the sheep (the most important part of the farm),
would often come with Despard to give me a hand with the cattle. When
the three of us chanced to be riding through wooded country we would
advance along the footpaths nearly a hundred yards apart, in order not to
be caught together in an ambush. If we spent the night in a hut and the
dogs barked, we put out the lights at once and cautiously went outside to
investigate.

That year the coming of winter was a great relief to me, for then the
Ona went back to the part of their own country that had not yet been
invaded by the white man. I felt that, on account of the deep snow and
the absence of game, neither Indians nor any others were likely to pass
through the mountains, and therefore I could slacken my vigilance. One
day when I was staying at the homestead I went off on foot in hopes of
getting a guanaco. The snow lay fairly deep on the ground, and about
three miles from home I came on two guanaco, which I shot. As they
were in good condition, I hung three halves on a tree, out of reach of the
foxes, and carried one half home on my shoulders. Next morning I
suggested to Will that we should go for the rest of the meat. Together
with Missmiyolh, the Aush, who was glad to get some food for his
numerous family, we set off, taking a different track from the one I had
followed the day before. We found the meat undisturbed, but someone

had been there—and the footprints were certainly not Missimyolh's or those of any of the Yahgans at the homestead. Examining the tell-tale track in the snow, we saw that this stranger had followed me to the edge of the wood overlooking Harberton and then turned off to the right, heading into a vast, dense evergreen forest. Leaving our loads, we followed his trail for some distance. He had evidently been walking fast. It had been snowing ever since we had first seen his footsteps, so now they were difficult to follow, and, as night was coming on, we turned back, resumed our loads and went home.

These footprints made me nervous. If the Indian who had followed me was not an enemy, why was he down here stalking me at that time of year?

I had a tough bull's hide from which I had been cutting a thong round and round the edge until there remained only an oval piece in the centre. The ordinary cattle known as Criollos have very much thicker hides than the finer breeds such as Devons, Herefords or Durhams, and, judging from the thickness of this hide, that bull must have been a very ordinary Criollo indeed. It occurred to me to make of this material a waistcoat the full length of my body, so, taking the hide mentioned, I hammered it until it was somewhat softened. I had started on the job when Missmiyolh came along with his bow and two or three arrows in his hand. When moving about the settlement he always had these weapons with him, without their usual flint heads, in case he should find some sea-bird along the shore and thus add a tasty morsel to his family supper.[1]

I told him that the tracks I had seen in the snow had made me wise and that I would wear this new coat when walking alone. He looked at me quizzically and said:

" Will that stop an arrow? "

Outside our back door the snow had been shovelled away, and was heaped up yards high close by the track. I placed the beginnings of my arrow-proof waistcoat firmly against the snow, as it would have rested against my body. Missmiyolh took one of his arrows, stepped back to about ten yards' range and let fly, with the result that nearly two feet of arrow stuck through the waistcoat into the snow.

So ended my coat of mail.

---

[1] They did not waste flint or glass heads on birds; the sharpened hardwood point was sufficient.

CHAPTER TWENTY-THREE

Kaushel Returns to Harberton. Tininisk, the Medicine-Man, and Kankoat the Jester. A Double Abduction. The Mountain Men Visit Harberton. Talimeoat, the Bird-Hunter. The Ona Hide their Gratitude. Iodine Becomes a Magic Paint. An Unsolicited Testimonial. An Ona Courtship.

I

ON THE 29TH DECEMBER, 1895, ALMOST A YEAR AFTER CAPELO'S DEATH and two days before my twenty-first birthday, a number of Ona camped in the forest near Harberton. They did not visit the settlement, but a messenger came to ascertain from our Yahgans the state of our feelings towards the Ona. We learnt that Kaushel, the remarkably fine man whom we had already met, was one of the party. These people had come from the north, not, as on Kaushel's former visit, from the east. Ever since Capelo's death we had expected a revenge expedition, and were very glad when they showed themselves again, evidently nervous, but apparently with no hostile intentions.

I had come from Cambaceres to celebrate my birthday, and went with Father on a visit to the Ona encampment on the other side of the harbour. We crossed in a boat and walked up to the woods, on the edge of which four Indians were seated. They were unarmed and so, of course, were we. They rose to their feet as we approached. One of them was Kaushel. Another—a lithe, good-looking youngster—turned out to be his eldest son, Kiyotimink. The son was about six feet in height, a good two inches taller than his father, who, though by no means fat, weighed all of fifteen stone.

They conducted us to the encampment, fifty yards from the edge of the woods—a spot well chosen for observation and, if necessary, for speedy flight. Our arrival caused a stir in the camp, where there were ten men and from thirty to forty women and children. Kaushel pointed out his wife, Kohpen. Men and women were well painted, mostly with white spots or stripes on a red background. There was plenty of guanaco meat hanging in the trees nearby.

Kaushel took us into his guanaco-skin shelter,[1] while the other Indians

[1] These Ona shelters (*kowwhi*) were not tents, but merely skins sewn together and tied to sticks planted in less than half a circle to windward of the fire. The sticks were very light and sloped towards the fire at an angle of nearly forty-five degrees. There was no further roof. *Kowwhi* were seldom as much as five feet high. Some of them were over six yards across ; they were drawn closer in very bad weather.

clustered excitedly round it. Kaushel spoke volubly and with the most friendly gestures, but, try as we might, we could not understand a word of it. I fancied that I had learned some six hundred words of Aush and now, specially anxious to impress Father, did my best to speak in that tongue, which is completely different from the Ona language.[1] To Kaushel it meant nothing, but I was delighted when I was able to understand a reply in Aush from Kohpen, his wife. She had originally belonged to the Eastern Ona tribe.

My efforts to make myself understood by her with my modest vocabulary caused some amusement, yet the conversation was of the greatest value, for before we parted from Kaushel and his people we were able to assure ourselves that the four young Ona who had escaped the police during the raid on Harberton had subsequently convinced their people that Father's amazed reaction to the rifle-fire was ample proof that, whoever had instigated the raid, it had not been the Bridges family.

I walked the woods more boldly after that.

2

Relief appears to have been mutual. Following upon the visit of the venturesome Kaushel, the belief must have spread through all the mountain country that we could be trusted, for we were frequently called upon, both at Harberton and Cambaceres, by small parties of Ona. Usually they did not stay with us more than a week or ten days, but there was one group from Kaushel's country in the east, comprising some six or seven families, who remained camped near Harberton for almost a month. The hunting-grounds of this party lay between No-kake Mountain and the Atlantic coast, along which they extended from Cape Santa Inés (called Shilan by the Ona), past Cape San Pablo to Policarpo Cove, thus trespassing across the borders of the Aush. In summer they hunted southward as far as the hills overlooking Sloggett and Moat Bays. I will call them the Cape San Pablo party.

Second only to Kaushel as an outstanding figure in this group was the

---

[1] Here are five words with their equivalents —

ENGLISH	SHILKNUM OR ONA	EASTERN ONA OR AUSH	YAMANA OR YAHGAN
Shelter (Home)	Kowwhi	Hahli	Ukurh
Man	Chohn	Hink	Ua
Woman	Nah	Nimmin	Keepa
River	Shike	Iyual	Wayan
Water	Choh	Utn	Sima

medicine-man, Tininisk. In company with a few Aush, he had paid Harberton several flying visits during the past year or two, and was as much an Ona as an Aush. He had a considerable influence over the scattered few of both those border tribes. This was the more remarkable because, except for his infant son, he had, as far as I heard, no surviving male relations, not even cousins, uncles or nephews, though his wife's relatives were an exceedingly tough crowd. A fine, athletic figure, broad-chested, yet slender, Tininisk stood about five feet ten. His eagle eye, retreating forehead and beak of a nose gave the impression of some bird of prey. This was far from the truth; Tininisk was a most good-natured and reasonable man. I was to know him for twenty-five years and never found him otherwise. When we became more familiar with each other he was pleased and flattered when I suggested that his forebear must have been a hawk or an eagle. Once, when comparing his profile with that of another of his tribe, I remarked jokingly that the second man probably had an ancestral duck to thank for the shape of his bill, and even the victim of the gibe joined heartily in the laugh that followed.

Tininisk's wife was called Leluwhachin. She was well-grown and pleasant-mannered; and the only Ona woman I ever met to be credited with magic powers. Many Yahgan women were considered to be witches, but Leluwhachin was unique as a sorceress among the Ona. Originally she had belonged to a group who roamed the ranges behind Harberton and Ushuaia; an elusive group who had a very bad name amongst their eastern and northern neighbours.

Another member of the Cape San Pablo party was Kankoat, who could well have been called the Jester. He was son of Saklhbarra and grandson of Yoiyimmi, the two Aush crones who had passed a winter at Harberton. His father, an Ona, had died during Kankoat's childhood, and the boy had been cared for, in some measure, by Kaushel's wife, herself an Aush and probably related to Kankoat through his mother's people. I never heard Kankoat claiming close relationship to any man, though I think he felt nearer to Kaushel than to Tininisk. Kankoat was a likeable fellow, but no beauty. Twenty-five years of age and of medium height, he had a bright, willing disposition and an attractive, impish grin that seemed to intimate that he sensed some hidden joke in everything. He was a widower with a son, about four years old, who was his pride and joy. The little boy was looked after by Kankoat's sister, Chetanhaite, a girl of thirteen.

The winter of 1897 was making its approach when the Cape San Pablo party suddenly made up their minds to leave Harberton. I was disappointed, for I had hoped they would winter with us and give me the pleasure of hunting with them, and the opportunity to learn more of their language, beliefs and customs. Before they left, I sought out Kankoat and suggested that he should stay behind at Cambaceres with Chetanhaite and his son. When the winter snows brought the guanaco down from the mountains and work at Cambaceres was slack, he and I would go hunting together. Kankoat readily agreed to this proposition. Tininisk, however, was not anxious to lose so brave a warrior, scout and hunter. Kankoat would greatly help to keep the party supplied with meat, as well as heartening them with his gaiety—if that were needed.

Kankoat was away from Harberton on the day that Tininisk and the others packed up and left. Chetanhaite stayed behind at Harberton to await her brother's return. In her charge was Kankoat's little son. But at the last minute the wily Tininisk carried the boy off with him, knowing that Kankoat would follow. On their way eastward the party passed near Cambaceres and, after looking in on me for a friendly chat, pitched camp a mile and a half to the east.

Kankoat appeared the following morning with his sister. With sorrow he informed me that, although he would have much preferred to stay with me, he would now have to go with Tininisk, who had kidnapped his son. He longed for his child, wanting him to grow up by his side, so that when he himself grew old and helpless there would be someone to support and defend him.

It was time for me to take a hand, so, advising Chetanhaite to hide in a great clump of wild currant-bushes near the Cambaceres house, where Yekadahby happened to be alone, I sent Kankoat back to Harberton, where he would be out of reach of Tininisk's persuasive tongue, if not his magical powers, and set off myself for the Ona encampment.

They must, I think, have guessed my errand, for when I dismounted from my horse, Tininisk was seated with the kidnapped boy beside him, whilst his wife and several other women completed the group. I told the medicine-man what I wanted and why, but he remained unyielding. Some of the women began to wail loudly at the suggestion that this beloved little boy might be taken from them. The foremost in these protests was an Aush woman named Honte, who had lived for some time with an Italian from the sub-prefecture at Thetis Bay.

Seeing at last that further argument was useless, I returned to where my horse was tethered. Near it had gathered a group of small boys, all stark naked, to discuss this strange animal. Among them was Garibaldi, the four-year-old half-breed son of Honte.

Giving way to an impulse, I snatched up Garibaldi in spite of his protests, mounted quickly and called to Tininisk as I passed his shelter that he should have Garibaldi back in exchange for Kankoat's son. Then, to the accompaniment of the struggling infant's yells and the shrieks of indignation from the enraged women, I galloped off.

Back at Cambaceres I turned Garibaldi over to Yekadahby, who soon found him a little garment and had him eating happily beside the kitchen fire.

My plan worked. Before very long Honte arrived with Kankoat's child, who, in spite of his vigorous objections, was left in our care, while Honte went off with her own offspring. On her departure, Chetanhaite came out of the bushes and set off happily for Harberton with her nephew on her back.

So Kankoat remained with us for the winter, after all. When Tininisk reappeared at Cambaceres in the course of time it was evident that he bore neither Kankoat nor myself the slightest grudge; in fact, he referred to the incident as a great joke, in which I had come off the winner.

3

I have mentioned that Tininisk's wife, Leluwhachin, had once belonged to the group who roamed the ranges behind Harberton and Ushuaia. The boundaries of their territory were not clearly outlined and did not limit their wanderings, for besides the mountains between the Beagle Channel and Lake Kami—that great inland water of which the Aush had spoken and which is now known as Lake Fagnano—they regarded their hunting-grounds as extending as far to the north-east as the Atlantic coast, where a strip twenty miles wide gave them access to the ocean. Here they killed seal, sea-birds and *dahapi*, the large, scaleless fish known to the Yahgans as *tukupi*, which are abundant during summer and autumn amongst the rocks on those wide sandstone beaches.

The members of this party, whom I will call the mountain men, were as undefined as the boundaries of their territory. They usually numbered fewer than fifteen men and their families, but if disagreement arose the party might split in two, or one member might go off with his family and not return until the ill-feeling had subsided, or the cause for it had been removed. These mountain men had always borne an extremely bad reputation among their eastern and northern neighbours.

Soon after Tininisk's departure we were surprised by the arrival at Harberton of some eight of the mountain men, with their wives and families. These Ona seemed to come and go like shadows, but this time, as winter set in, it was evident that the party from the mountains intended to remain with us till spring. The staple food that we could always procure was meat. Fortunately we also had a good supply of swedes, carrots and cabbages, as well as a fair amount of potatoes. The Indians, however, had acquired a taste for such luxuries as flour, rice, coffee and sugar, and we knew it would be ruinous for us, as well as exceedingly bad for our visitors, to continue giving them these things, unless they made some real effort to give us something in return.

These men had never done a steady day's work in their lives, and if left alone accomplished next to nothing; so I regularly went with them to clear tracks and make huge heaps of firewood for future use. Though the guanaco-skin garment, flung loosely round the body so that it could be discarded the moment the wearer needed to move noiselessly through the forest, was ideal for hunting, it was not convenient for working in the snowy woods, where both hands were needed for axe or saw. The workers, therefore, had to be supplied with clothes; and every evening, on returning to the homestead, they received a generous ration of food to take home to their families.

The Ona had no hereditary or elected chiefs, but men of outstanding ability almost always became the unacknowledged leaders of their groups. Yet one man might seem leader to-day and another man to-morrow, according to whoever was eager to embark upon some enterprise. Social rank among the Ona was best defined by the jovial Kankoat in later years. A certain scientist visited our part of the world and, in answer to his enquiries on this matter, I told him that the Ona had no chieftains, as we understand the word. Seeing that he did not believe me, I summoned Kankoat, who by that time spoke some Spanish. When the visitor repeated his question, Kankoat, too polite to answer in the negative, said :

" Yes, Señor, we, the Ona, have many chiefs. The men are all captains and all the women are sailors."

Of discipline there was none. It is certain, however, that the most ruthless, the strongest, either physically or mentally, or the one who excelled in treachery or cunning, was bound to influence the common herd. The principal figure in the party of mountain men who came to winter at Harberton that year was a man who combined the last-mentioned qualifications with eloquence, a keen sense of humour and a bright, happy smile, as though his heart were full of kindly thoughts. He was a most attractive little fellow, about thirty years of age, light and active, standing no more than five and a half feet tall. His unique characteristic was that he always walked on tiptoe. Even when carrying a load his heels seemed to press only lightly on the ground. He had joined with Capelo and Chalshoat in the massacre of San Martin and his party of miners. He was a brother of Leluwhachin, Tininisk's wife, and his name was Halimink.

Various other members of the mountain group have their places in my story. It is necessary to mention only two of them here. They were father and son, Talimeoat and Kaichin. Talimeoat, a few years older than Halimink, to whom he was closely related, was some three inches taller, lean and silent. He was famed, as had been his father before him, for his daring as a cragsman and his successful hunting of the shags (cormorants) that infest certain of the great sandstone cliffs on the Atlantic coast of Fireland. His favourite haunt was Cape Santa Inés. Kaichin was still a mere boy, but already following in his father's footsteps. He promised to make a good hunter and was to grow into an excellent tracker, as will be seen in a later chapter.

Winter is not the time to enjoy clearing tracks or cutting firewood, so there were frequent hunting trips, with the result that guanaco soon grew scarce in the woods near Harberton. When a good supply of meat was needed we would take a large boat and go off for two or three days. The coast of Navarin Island was our favourite hunting-ground. There being no natives in the interior of the island, the guanaco led a more peaceful life in summer than did their brothers on the mainland. Consequently, when the winter snow drove them into the lower forest, they were in better condition than the others. These Navarin guanaco came from the same stock, but were larger than those on the northern side of the Beagle Channel.

On one of these excursions to Navarin Island I was accompanied by nearly a score of Ona, among them Talimeoat and Kaichin. We moored the boat in a sheltered cove, then scattered in all directions in search of guanaco. The day was really too calm and still for successful stalking, and our difficulties were increased by the fact—as we soon discovered to our disgust—that a party of Yahgan Indians had recently hunted in the district with dogs, a practice that always disturbed the game over a much wider area than bows and arrows, or even rifles, would do.

In twos and threes we returned to the camp empty-handed, to face the

prospect of a hungry night. For reasons of economy—and hunters'
pride—we took few, if any, provisions on these trips. Finally only two
of us were missing—Talimeoat and his son. It was getting late before
they appeared, and I was greatly cheered to see that they carried meat.
My Ona companions were too dignified to show their joy.

After skinning a guanaco, the Ona generally divided the carcase into
six pieces, in order to make the neatest possible bundles. In this instance
Talimeoat set to work to sub-divide it further, and very deliberately
distributed it piece by piece. He tossed each portion in the direction of
the man for whom it was intended, but the recipient was the only one
who showed no interest in the proceedings. He would be arranging the
fire, or drying his moccasins, or gazing vacantly into space, till someone
drew his attention to Talimeoat's bounty. Then he would pick it up
without any sign of pleasure and, scarcely glancing at it, put it down by
his side. At last we had all been supplied, leaving Talimeoat and Kaichin
with not a scrap between them—not even the brisket, which was always
considered the killer's portion. After a short while several of the others—
who may have purposely been given a larger share than the rest—divided
their portions and tossed some of it back to the successful hunters. This
was the correct Ona procedure in such circumstances, though probably
Talimeoat and his son had already had a feed of nice warm fat, fresh from
the interior of the animal.

Here is a similar example of apparent ingratitude that I encountered
on another occasion. With a single Ona companion, I had had a long,
trying day in the worst of weather, but he had accepted it cheerfully and
worked willingly with me from dawn to dusk. When I arrived home
I was so pleased with him that I presented him with my hunting-knife
and sheath. He received it in silence, with a far less friendly expression
than he had worn at any moment during that wet and wearisome day.

My mother had come to the door to welcome me. I turned and said
to her:

"Not much thanks one gets for giving a present like that. The man
was positively annoyed."

"You wouldn't say that," she answered, "if you had seen the look
he gave the knife, the moment you turned to speak to me. He seemed
to love it."

What an effort the good fellow must have made to hide his feelings
and to refrain from showing childish pleasure until my back was
turned!

4

The reticence that was natural to the Ona Indians is exemplified in another anecdote, this time concerning a young fellow called Teëoöriolh. One day, with the help of a party of Ona, I was moving a heap of large posts down a nasty track to a spot where a yoke of oxen with a sledge could come and drag them away. Passing two or three times with a load on my shoulder, I noticed that Teëoöriolh was sitting by the side of the track with a rather mirthless smile on his face. He appeared oblivious to the fact that the rest of us were extremely busy, so I asked him:

" Why are you not working? Are you tired? "

He put his hand to his collar-bone and made it click.

" My bone is broken," he replied.

To have complained, or even to have mentioned it without being asked, would have been unmanly.

I put a pad under his armpit and tied his elbow close to his side with a sash, but this treatment was not quite satisfactory to him; it was too simple. I remembered that I had a bottle of iodine in the house, so I took Teëoöriolh along there and applied the tincture lavishly to the injured part. What a marvellous balm that was! So red and scented! Teëoöriolh went away rejoicing, and was back at work again within a few days. Soon the fame of this wonderful medicine of mine spread throughout the country. The Indians would come with the most flimsy excuses for a touch of this magic paint, which was regarded not only as a cure, but also as a preventive against any possible pain or accident in the future.

I was to discover that I had yet another wonder-worker; this time a certain magic soap, the miraculous effects of which the manufacturers have been too modest to claim themselves.

One of the Ona had been working on Picton Island, frequently for long spells. During one of these protracted periods of absence his wife gave birth to a son who had fair skin and hair and blue eyes. (Here I must make it quite clear that my own eyes are brown and that, in those days, my hair was nearly as dark as an Ona's.) Naturally I wondered what the good husband would say when he returned home to find this remarkable addition to his family.

In due season he came back from Picton Island. A day or two later he came to see me and begged for a cake of soap; not the ordinary soap, but the magic soap of the colour of dark glass and shaped like the egg of an upland goose. I did not understand what he was driving at, but he was very much in earnest. He told me that while he had been away his wife had borne a son as dark as was usual among the Ona at birth, but that by the time he set eyes on him, the tiny child's skin and hair had changed to a wonderful fairness. When questioned about this incredible transformation, his wife—supported in her story by two women who had attended her—attributed the miracle to a cake of magic soap that had been given to her by my sister, Alice. Some of the soap, she had gone on to say, had got into the baby's eyes, which had at once become as blue as the sky.

The proud father was so impressed by these wonders that he came seeking another cake of soap. Suspecting that he wanted to try its effects on himself and might be foolish enough to doubt his wife's story if the experiment failed, I hastened to tell him that the particular cake of soap given to his wife by my sister must have possessed some special virtue not to be found in any other tablet. He went away disappointed, but satisfied.

I suggested to Alice that we should take a photograph of the happy trio and send it to the manufacturers, in case they wished to use it as an unsolicited testimonial to the merits of their wonderful product. Alice, however, thought it would not be quite the thing, so the photograph never went to Messrs. Pears.

5

Another sidelight on Ona customs was thrown by the courtship by Teëoöriolh of the daughter of Missmiyolh. In an earlier chapter I have described how Missmiyolh, the Aush, came to live at Harberton with his Yahgan wife, Weeteklh, and their extensive family. Missmiyolh was a quiet, happy little man. I was never able to discover how he had acquired a Yahgan wife, nor how Weeteklh, doubtless brought up to fish and paddle a canoe, had accustomed herself to tramp the forest and bog of Eastern Ona-land, laden with all the family's goods—and sometimes a couple of babies as well. Missmiyolh was an excellent stalker, silent and alert. He frequently went into the woods on his own with his bow and arrows and, thanks to clever stalking and woodcraft, his family seldom lacked for meat. In hunting he had one remarkable characteristic. If, when walking at speed through open forest, he encountered an interlaced thicket or log across the track—maybe no more than three feet from the ground—he would stoop with his body horizontal and pass beneath the obstacle without changing pace.

On his trips away from Harberton, Missmiyolh never made his camp close to the real Ona. He preferred—possibly on account of his Yahgan-speaking wife—the society of the canoe people, by whom he was greatly esteemed. When at Harberton he had no fear of the Aush's historic enemies, for there all ancient quarrels between the groups and tribes seemed to be forgotten by mutual consent, but though on excellent terms with the Ona, he never went hunting with them.

Missmiyolh and Weeteklh had a daughter whose name I forget. She was the eldest of their daughters and was, at the time of which I speak, quite fifteen years of age and fast developing into a decidedly pleasing young woman—particularly to Teëoöriolh, who was about nineteen; a bright, good-looking young Ona of medium height, well-mannered and, like all mountain men, lithe, active and silent. True he was not of the same tribe as Missmiyolh's daughter and there was a great difference between the languages they spoke, but young people in love have a way of overcoming such hindrances.

At the time, in an effort to master their language, I was associating as much as possible with the real Ona and, in consequence, somewhat neglected my Aush friends. One day, so that he might not think himself ignored, I called on Missmiyolh and, as usual, was offered a seat by his fire.

Presently I noticed that the daughter of the house was nursing, almost caressingly, a bow. I had never seen a woman handling a bow in this or any other manner, so speculated on the reason. Looking about, I then saw Teëoöriolh waiting in the shade of a large tree a hundred yards away. He was not facing us, but was apparently interested in some object in the distance. While the girl fondled the bow, her mother commenced to talk to her. I could not follow all she said, though I understood it to be some kind of plaint to the effect that she needed her daughter's help with the brood of smaller children. Evidently the matter was taken very seriously, for presently Missmiyolh put in a few earnest words. At last, seemingly with reluctance, the girl handed the bow to her little brother for him to return it to the waiting Teëoöriolh, who took it and stalked off without a backward glance. When I asked Missmiyolh the meaning of all this, he told me that it was a proposal of marriage. It was not unexpected, as the young man had sometimes brought choice gifts of meat on returning from the hunt. He added that, apart from her duty to her mother, it would be good if she married into that mountain group, as he himself was alone and would welcome their protection.

Two or three months afterwards I found the girl had gone. I was told that Teëoöriolh had again passed his bow and that this time she had gone to return it in person. This, Missmiyolh informed me, was the correct and ancient way of proposing. I saw it, alas! in only that one instance. Most of the marriages I knew amongst those primitive people were brought about either by conquest or by abduction.

In the early days at Harberton, before we were familiar, except by name, with Halimink and Kaushel, three seemingly harmless brothers had visited us in company with Tininisk, the lovable Kankoat and other Aush and Ona from the borderland of the two territories. The first of these brothers was an ugly medicine-man named Koh, which is the Ona for "bone." The second was Kanikoh, diminutive and exceedingly active. The third was by far the stoutest fellow among our visitors from the east. I do not know his Ona name, but, possibly to make it rhyme with those of his brothers, some white wag had dubbed him Tisico, which is the Spanish for "consumptive." Kanikoh and Tisico had, I believe, two wives each, and Koh probably had three. We looked upon these brothers in the same friendly light as on Tininisk and Kankoat—in fact, we bracketed them in the same group, the Cape San Pablo people.

When Halimink and his companions from the mountains began to visit Harberton, it seemed plain that they were on good terms with Tininisk, Kankoat and the three brothers. Their encampments were often pitched near together and they frequently joined forces to go hunting.

Then Koh, Kanikoh and Tisico came no more to Harberton. When asked about them, Tininisk and Kankoat were dumb, as behoves those who mourn for the dead. The best answer we got from any of the others was :

" Where are they? We have not seen them."

We noticed, however, that several of the mountain men had acquired new wives, who had previously belonged to the Cape San Pablo party. It was years before I gathered the details.

Tininisk, Koh, Kanikoh and Tisico had joined up with Halimink and company, who were Tininisk's wife's people. The meeting had become quite hilarious, when Tininisk's three companions had realized too late that evil was determined against them. Koh and Tisico had fallen victims to the first flight of arrows. Little Kanikoh had slipped away and run for his life. As he had stooped to pass under a low branch, an arrow from Halimink had got him in the left side of the groin and had finished with its barbed head sticking out of his neck close to his right collar-bone.

Kankoat had not been with the party at the time of this massacre. Tininisk had taken no part in the killing, but it is certain that he had been the Judas. Had it been possible to ask those mountain men why they had killed the friends who had trusted them, the straightforward answer would have been :

" Why shouldn't we? They were not our people and we wanted their wives."

The numerous widows had cut their hair in mourning, but if the funeral and wedding bells were not intermixed, there had been hardly a pause between one and the other. The women of a party vanquished in a *battue* would have been unwise to refuse to follow their new husbands when those victors had " blood in their eyes." The fear would soon subside; women captives were wooed and made much of, to prevent them from running away. When badly treated, women took the first opportunity to give their captors the slip, though, if they were caught by their new husbands before they could get back to their own people, they ran the risk of being soundly beaten or arrowed through the legs with arrows from which the barbs had been removed—generally. A wife of long standing, if she obstinately refused to do her husband's will, was just as likely to be thrashed or arrowed. The clumsy, blundering Chalshoat shot his arrow a little too high when he once administered such punishment, and killed his wife. The women never forgave him for that.

Halimink, who already had one wife, had gained a second from the massacre just described. She had been one of the wives of Koh—the third, I imagine—and her name was Akukeyohn (Afraid of Fallen Logs). I have noticed Halimink, with a mischievous grin on his face, lay unnecessary stress on the word *koh* when speaking to Akukeyohn. She would put on a vexed, but coy, expression. Her anger was obviously only skin deep, for Halimink was a good husband to his favourite wife, and Koh had been by no means attractive.

CHAPTER TWENTY-FOUR

The Brig Phantom. *Dan Prewitt Comes to Harberton. The* Belgica *Goes Aground Off Cambaceres. We Become Acquainted with Frederick A. Cook, Doctor and Anthropologist. He Photographs the Ona and Rewards Them in Niggardly Fashion. He is Shown my Father's Dictionary and Offers to Get it Printed. I am Invited to Join the Expedition, but the* Belgica *Sets Sail for the Polar Regions without Me.*

I

LOCAL FREIGHTS AND PRICES WERE VERY HIGH, AND THE FINE SUPPLY OF goods brought out by the *Shepherdess* had been exhausted by 1897. Something had to be done about it. The gold-rush had been most opportune and we had not worked in vain, so Father went to England and purchased for nine hundred pounds an ancient brig of 300-tons register called the *Phantom*. This vessel was partially laden at Cardiff with provisions and merchandise, but the greater part of her cargo was coal, which we were now sure of disposing of to passing steamers.

Father noticed that England was getting over-stocked with young fellows who seemed to have nothing to do, so he had a large cabin built in the after part of the brig's hold and made it known that he was prepared to take ten young men back with him to South America. He wanted only those who were ready to apply themselves to any kind of work that was given to them, in exchange for which they would receive two pounds a month and their keep. At the end of two years they would be free from all obligation to us and would be given their passage home. If they elected to stay in Tierra del Fuego, either with us or elsewhere, they would receive a cash payment in lieu of the passage money.

There was no lack of volunteers. Father selected ten of them, but when the captain of the *Phantom*, whose name was Davis, saw them, he refused to leave Cardiff unless Father went with him to keep order. This meant for Father another long trip by sail. There were several hard cases amongst that party, but the toughest of the lot was Dan Prewitt, a short, thickset man with a scarred face and some missing front teeth. After having bullied his nine companions into submission, Prewitt proceeded to gain the homage of the ship's crew by the only form of argument they could all understand.

Lasifharshaj Valley.

Falls on the River Lasifharshaj.

Another view of the River Lasifharshaj.

A glimpse of Lake Kami through the trees.

Ewan Valley.

The mouth of the Ewan River. Beyond Tijnolsh is Cape Santa Inés.

No one was killed on board, and the *Phantom* arrived safely at Harberton. Most of these young fellows had the idea that, once in South America, all they had to do was to get broad-brimmed hats and pretend to be Buffalo Bill. How glad we were when six of them determined that Britons never would be slaves, and left us! Four remained, and did well. Only one decided to return to England, though he stopped much more than the two years agreed upon. The one who was to stay longest with us was Dan Prewitt.

When he arrived at Harberton, Dan tried the same technique as he had employed on the brig—until he came up against an Ona whose nickname was Dante. When Prewitt launched his attack, Dante merely embraced him, brought him to the ground and was reaching for a stone with which to crack his skull when Will, who chanced to be near, intervened. Prewitt never again laid violent hands on an Ona. After this bad start, he settled down to a more peaceable way of life. Strong and trustworthy, he soon grew to be well liked and respected by the Indians.

There were frequently friendly tussles at Harberton. I enjoyed wrestling with the Indians—both Ona and Yahgan—and when opportunity occurred I would take on white men, maybe a Norwegian sailor or a Dalmatian miner. Results varied, though I was fully aware that I would have no chance against even a second-rate professional. In numerous matches with Kankoat the Jester, I managed to hold my own, but doubt if I could have worn him down had we been fighting in earnest. In the rough wrestling of the Ona, the unwritten rule was that the struggle should go on until one or other of the opponents refused to wrestle any more. Another of my friendly adversaries was an exceptionally stout Yahgan named Waiyellen, who had been given the name of Clement, so that, as was the custom, Waiyellen had become his surname. I could throw this man five times out of six, yet he himself frequently managed to throw Kankoat, who was for me the more doughty opponent. Which raises the interesting question: Which of the three of us was the champion?

Clement Waiyellen had been long with the Mission, both at Ushuaia and on Keppel Island. Like all Yahgans, he was a born sailor, and on many a rough trip served under my brother Will; and, like many other sea-faring folk, he developed a liking for strong drink, which, as civilization and trade advanced, was sold at practically all the stores in Ushuaia. In later years, after my father's passing, we bought a twenty-five-ton cutter, the *Juanita*, in which we delivered cargoes of meat to Ushuaia;

and we had so much confidence in Clement that he was trusted to captain the cutter on these trips. He would receive money for us at Ushuaia or would take cash with him to purchase things we needed.

On these occasions this good Yahgan would not touch a drop of liquor and would faithfully render an account of his transactions on his return to Harberton. Once, when an Ushuaia trader taunted him beyond endurance for his self-imposed sobriety, our captain, instead of succumbing in the way the tempter had hoped, hit him a k.o. blow with a heavy ship's rowlock and, in consequence, remained in prison till Will went and bailed him out. The injured man learnt a good lesson, but took some time to recover his senses.

After these trips to Ushuaia, the tremendous effort poor Clement had made to keep straight would leave him in a condition of mental and moral exhaustion. He might then ask for ten days' leave and find his way back to Ushuaia for what one of his companions in folly—an Englishman—used to call " a roll in the gutter," which often ended in jail.

So passes out of my story Clement Waiyellen, a man whose loyalty to the trust we rightly reposed in him, and whose staunchness under the terrible temptation to which that dying race of his had given way, are now placed on record.

2

Early in the morning of New Year's Day, 1898, I looked out of a window of the Cambaceres house. Across the outer harbour to the southward, about half a mile away, lay a little vessel on a shoal. She was well aground and leaning over at a steep angle. I walked down to the beach, pushed our boat into the water and rowed out to the vessel.

She had been aground for some time, and the tide was falling. Those on board had lowered a boat, attached a kedge-anchor to the stern of it and were paying out the anchor's chain from the sloping deck of the ship. Four men in the boat were rowing furiously, and a number of others on deck were encouraging them even more furiously in French. By the united efforts of all concerned, the boat had struggled about twelve yards from the vessel. By that time the heavy chain was lying on the sea-bed and held the boat like an anchor, so that with every stroke of the oars she bounded forward, and between strokes sprang back exactly the same distance. It did not seem to have occurred to any of them to load the chain in the boat, pay it out as they rowed away and end up by dropping the anchor.

S.S. *Belgica* was as curious as her crew; a strange, hybrid craft, neither steamer nor sailing-vessel, but a little of each. Her deck, lying over at an angle she would never attain when under sail, was littered from end to end with a strange assortment of goods. High stacks of coal-bricks, coils of ropes, sledges, skis and canvas tents all added to the confusion.

As I watched the crew's efforts with the kedge-anchor, a man appeared on deck and hailed me in English with a slight American accent. He was a smartly dressed, personable fellow, not much over thirty and full of life; rather below medium height and slimly built. He introduced himself as Dr. Frederick A. Cook, surgeon and anthropologist, member of a party of scientists on a Belgian expedition to the Antarctic. He told me that the *Belgica*, a stout wooden vessel, had been specially fitted out for the undertaking.

I suggested to him that, as the vessel had gone ashore at high tide, she might float off with the evening tide if we lightened her as much as possible. I offered to go to Harberton and fetch the eight-ton lighter Despard had built. We could bring her alongside the *Belgica* and relieve her of her deck-load of coal before high tide. Dr. Cook spoke to the captain in French. My proposal was agreed to, and the doctor and I set off for Harberton.

We returned with the lighter and a mixed crew of Yahgans and some of our best Ona. Two loads of coal were landed on the nearest suitable beach and, with the rising tide and a favourable wind, the *Belgica* drifted off the shoal undamaged. Even then her troubles were not over. The wind was blowing so hard that it was nearly two hours before she could gain the shelter of Cambaceres harbour.

Probably men whose minds are devoted to science should not be expected to be practical, and there ought to be no condemnation of a little act of carelessness when they landed from the *Belgica*. They left their boat with the painter coiled on board, and she took the first opportunity to drift off with the rising tide. She was soon recovered, but I could not help thinking that, in the desolate regions for which they were bound, the consequence of similar neglect might well be tragic.

Dr. Cook and the other scientists on board the *Belgica*, though on their way to explore the regions of the South Pole, were nevertheless interested in everything they encountered *en route*. I mentioned to them that a party of Ona, real forest warriors with long hair, skin-robes and paint, were encamped less than a mile from Cambaceres. Our visitors were immediately anxious to take photographs of them. On the following morning I escorted them to the camp. Knowing that the Ona would be nervous, I went on ahead of the scientists to allay the Indians' fears. I found them on the point of departure, but managed to persuade them to stay for another hour.

The Ona of both sexes did not like the little magic eye of the camera winking in their direction. I did my best to reassure them; and Dr. Cook was thus able to take some fine photographs, particularly of the women, with their huge loads done up in the orthodox, cigar-shaped fashion and a child or two stowed on top.

With his exposures made, Dr. Cook produced from his capacious pocket a sock containing about two pounds of small, hard sweets of many colours, each with a little seed in its centre. He handed a pinch to each of the numerous natives, then put the remainder, perhaps half a pound, back into his pocket with the remark:

" I think they have all had a taste."

The Indians did not know what to do with these queer little beads, so I took a few from Dr. Cook, put them in my mouth and started to crunch them up, despite the risk to my teeth. The natives followed my example. Feeling that this reckless hospitality of the anthropologist might not seem adequate recompense for what they had done at my request, I took a couple of the Ona to the house and gave them a sack of flour. This was always a welcome gift; with it they made a kind of damper.[1]

Before they left our shores to continue their voyage south, I took the scientists to Harberton and introduced them to my father. Dr. Cook was most interested in the Yahgan–English dictionary on which, by then, Father had spent over thirty years of work and thought. Publication was discussed. One of the chief difficulties lay in the printing. Father had used Ellis's phonetic system, but had had to adjust or add to it, to suit the Yahgan pronunciation of various words. Dr. Cook assured him that there was a society in the United States who made a speciality of American aboriginal languages. This society had the necessary facilities to print the work and, Dr. Cook expressed himself quite confident, would be glad to do so. He offered to take charge of the dictionary there and then, but Father feared that the precious volume might be lost in the Polar ice, and would not part with it. He promised to hand it over to Dr. Cook on the return voyage of the *Belgica*.

I was relieved at this refusal, having no great admiration for the sea-

---

[1] Bread made of flour and water, without yeast, and baked in ashes.

manship of captain and crew.   They had run aground on a shoal buoyed
by kelp, with a point of land running out towards it from the shore.   An
experienced sailor would have kept his ship well away from such dangers.
Their attempts to get out the kedge-anchor had not inspired any greater
confidence, nor had the incident of the drifting boat.

For the same good reason, I declined a pressing invitation to join them
in their expedition to the Polar regions.   The prospect of adventure
tempted me sorely, but I was reluctant to place my safety in such un-
practised hands.   Apart from that, I had my work to do and my contacts
with the Ona to consolidate.

So the *Belgica* sailed from Tierra del Fuego with neither the dictionary
nor myself aboard.

CHAPTER TWENTY-FIVE

Introducing Slim Jim, Whose Ona Name is Unpronounceable, and Minkiyolh, the Son of Kaushel. With These as Guides, my Brothers and I Penetrate at Last into Ona-Land. We Enter Regions in which No White Men Ever Trod Before. My Father's Passing.

I

AMONGST THOSE OF THE MOUNTAIN PARTY WHO HAD SPENT THE PREVIOUS winter at Harberton was a younger brother of Talimeoat, the bird-catcher. His name was Jalhmolh, but to escape the effort of pronouncing it,[1] we called him Slim Jim. Standing about five feet ten, lean and wiry, with prominent nose and high cheek-bones, he had a full share of the nervous alertness noticeable in all the mountain men. His shaggy head of hair, generally impregnated with red clay, gave him a wild but not unpleasing appearance. I always found him a good and willing companion, my only grouse against him being that, unlike myself, he could stride up a steep, boggy mountain slope with the same apparent ease and speed as he walked down it. He would, like most of his kind, hold back a branch rather than let it spring in the face of the person following him. I actually saw him go to this trouble when it was only his wife behind him.

Wrestling is a popular pastime among the Ona, and I often had friendly bouts with Slim Jim. He would make a great show of force, yet seldom took advantage of the many opportunities to throw me that my inexperience gave him. Nevertheless, I am certain that he told his companions that, with practice, I would become a good wrestler, and thereby help them in their struggles against other Ona groups.

Besides Kiyotimink, his eldest son, our friend Kaushel had a second boy whose name was Minkiyolh. He was a good-looking, undeveloped lad of seventeen, nearly as tall as Slim Jim and decidedly intelligent. The other Ona suspected him of studying magic. He was frequently absent-minded, would talk to himself in a queer, high-pitched voice and would burst out laughing for no apparent reason. In addition to these peculiarities, he was given to bragging of his strength and prowess—a

---

[1] " J " as in Spanish or the " ch " in the Scottish " loch," and each " lh " like the Welsh double " l " in Llanelly. The reader is advised not to attempt it.

thing no self-respecting Ona, however he might excel in these particulars, would think of doing.

In early March, 1898, Despard, Will and I, with Slim Jim and Min-kiyolh as guides, set out to accomplish what we had already twice failed to do: cross the mountain range into Ona-land. We had tried once in late autumn and again in the depth of winter, both times without guides. This time we were sure of success. March, the first month of autumn, is frequently the most lovely of the year, with calm, still days; in Slim Jim we had a guide whose home was those mountains and bogs; and one of our great deterrents, fear of the mountain Ona, was now a thing of the past. We each took a rifle and an unlined robe of guanaco-skin to sleep in, burdening ourselves with nothing else—not even a tent.

The first five miles were through tangled, mostly evergreen forest. Many fallen giants barred our way, and their descendants, growing on and around them, choked each other as they strove upwards towards the light. My brothers and I were looked upon as expert forest men among the whites, yet our guide led us through that wooded belt in less than half the time we should have taken by ourselves. Slim Jim slipped along without a moment's hesitation, following some trail invisible to us, which led him to an excellent ford across the Varela River, in wading which he hardly slackened his pace. Beyond the river we ascended a steep bank that took us out of the woods on to the moors.

Late in that perfect afternoon we found ourselves crossing a high, barren moor, flanked by ramparts of rock. The hollows still harboured patches of winter snow. Suddenly the moor ended and a sharp descent ahead disclosed a valley down which a stream flowed northward. We were over the divide—and Ona-land lay just ahead.

The valley—for the most part wooded—widened out farther down into a great forest, stretching out unbroken until, in the far distance beyond it, water glittered in the light of the declining sun. It was our first sight of Lake Kami, six miles across at its widest point and in length from east to west over forty. Beyond it, to the north-west, were mountains crowned with snow, their steep slopes wooded right down to the water's edge. They were more scattered than the ranges between Kami and the Beagle Channel, and we caught entrancing glimpses, in one of the wider valleys, of Lake Hyewhin with its wooded islands.

Evidently the Indians appreciated our admiration of the land they loved. Slim Jim dropped his rather aloof, stoical manner, and pointed out different spots. He named them, and in some cases added some item of historical or legendary interest. With only a sketchy knowledge of the Ona tongue, it was hard for us to understand all he told us.

We were loth to cut short the contemplation of this picture, but at length started to descend the mountain, scrambling down a shale slope that streamed with water from melting snow-drifts. At the foot, where the forest began, we camped for the night.

The following morning we were off early, with Slim Jim leading at the same relentless pace as he had kept up the day before. In order to avoid fallen trees and thickets, he was continually wading along or across the ice-cold stream already mentioned; and he proceeded at such a speed that if we paused to tie a moccasin, the only way to catch up was to run. But Slim Jim was not hurrying; this swift, unbroken pace was his normal travelling speed. In later years, when I journeyed for days alone or criss-crossed the country with a party of Ona men, I could do the same as effortlessly as he; but on that first trip into Ona-land I was a novice at the game. Only occasionally did Slim Jim deign to pause. When emerging from the stream, he would stop for a moment to squeeze the water out of his moccasins without stooping, by treading with one foot on the other. Then on he went again, silent and watchful.

After two hours of this we left the stream and passed into unbroken forest. The trees, though of the same species, were taller and appeared of sounder quality than those we were accustomed to farther south. We crossed a ridge known to the Indians as K-Jeëpenohrrh (Narrow, Promi-nent Ridge),[1] and had, through a gap in the trees, a fine view of the rolling, wooded hills stretching mile after mile northwards, till lost in the distance. Standing out alone, away from the main range, we could see a table-land, tree-clad almost to the summit. This, Slim Jim told us, was Heuhupen, once, long years ago, a powerful witch. I was afterwards to learn more of Heuhupen's latent powers.

On the northern side of that isolated table-land is an extraordinary treeless slope of great boulders that must have slipped from the mountain and either destroyed the forest or, by their presence, forbidden it to grow. They are most difficult to cross and I have seen no similar pile anywhere else.

As we passed near Heuhupen a troop of guanaco rushed by. Despard brought one of them down, and our supper was assured. We spent

[1] The initial " K " is clicked out alone without the support of any vowel, as one would pronounce " kick " if it had no " i " in it. In this instance it means " It is "; at other times it corresponds to our apostrophe " s "—e.g., *Sinu K-Tam* (Daughter of the Wind), the humming-bird.

that second night among wooded hills near the east end of Lake Kami.

The next day we went on northwards, but now our guides were growing nervous, apparently expecting to meet an enemy. Presently, in a burnt patch of forest at a place called Goljeohrrh (Dead Standing Tree Ridge), Minkiyolh, the visionary, called out:

"Who are you? Why don't you speak?"

He professed to have caught sight of an Indian watching us, but there was no answer. More reliable evidence was produced by Slim Jim, who found some tracks showing that people had been there lately. These greatly increased his anxiety, and throughout the day we were on the alert.

A few miles after leaving the beach of Kami we found the streams were running northward towards the Atlantic. Here were wide stretches of open country. The valleys were wet, and all the dry land was completely honeycombed by little rodents called tucu-tucu (*apen* in Ona), which resembled mouse-grey guinea-pigs and were never found south of the mountain range. These little creatures were so numerous that they had dug up the whole countryside. There was no grass; they had either eaten it or destroyed it by gnawing at the roots from below. These digging activities made walking difficult and very tiring. Despard, Will and I were getting footsore. Though used to wearing moccasins, the effort of keeping up with Slim Jim and so often crossing stony mountain streams at speed was telling on our feet.

Towards midday we came to another rocky ridge called Shaikrh,[1] which stood above the surrounding forest and gave us a splendid view. To the north a grassy valley stretched away for many leagues towards the Atlantic, with wooded hills on either side. The stream that formed in this valley joined a larger river, the Ewan, some ten miles away. The snowy mountains, though a long way behind us now, could still be seen over the forest land.

On Shaikrh we held a pow-wow. We had accomplished the avowed object of our trip. We had penetrated through the mountains and had walked some distance along the shore of that grand lake of which we had so often heard. We had explored the country beyond it and we had gone into regions never before trodden by white men. Yet I was still

---

[1] A word allied to *haikrh*—"to see," "to look out." There were other similar vantage points with much the same ending to their names. The ending *ohrrh*, as in K-Jeëpenohrrh and Goljeohrrh, meant "ridge" or "nose."

not satisfied; I wanted to go on.   Mine was a lone voice.   Despard and Will spoke of the ever-pressing work on the farm that our absence had brought to a standstill.   They mentioned, too, that Father might want to load the *Phantom* with timber as yet still lying in the forest.   They went on to say that summer was not the season for prolonged holidays and that we ought to go home.   Boastfully I retorted that, in spite of these things, I would continue the advance northward without them, if one of the Indians would go with me.   Had either Slim Jim or Minkiyolh agreed to this, pride would have forced me to go on, but I should have had my heart in my mouth.   Luckily for me, my exhibition of courage went unchallenged; the Indians were afraid of meeting an enemy, and would not proceed farther.   Perhaps Slim Jim, who had left his young wife in Harberton, exaggerated the perils, but his arguments prevailed.

We went down Shaikrh by a different track and camped not far from our sleeping-place of the night before.   Despard, Will and I took turns to keep watch.   It was getting on for autumn and the night seemed very long.   Nothing happened, however, and we went home by a far more mountainous route than that by which we had come, thereby avoiding some of the innumerable river crossings we had encountered on the outward trip.   We reached home after an absence of five days.

2

Despard and Will had been right.   My father did want to load the brig with timber.   I had not long been back at Cambaceres when I received an urgent message from him, instructing me to go to a suitable place at the eastern limit of our land, taking a number of bullocks with me, and to drag out a shipload of logs destined for Buenos Aires.

These orders were carried out.   The brig was loaded, and on the 15th April, 1898, the eve of a voyage from which he was not to return, Father wrote in his diary:

> " Left home, all there being well, at 3 p.m. in our life-boat, rowed by my sons and some men, and got on board the brig lying off Owiyamina at 4 p.m., with a load of essentials for the voyage which we hope to begin to-morrow morning. Calm evening."

The *Phantom* sailed on the following day with Captain Davis in command.   They reached Buenos Aires on the 5th May, but were prevented from docking by hidden mischief-makers, who feared that new timber coming into the country might harm their interests.   They eventually docked on the 13th May and, in spite of much hindrance and obstruction, managed to discharge two hundred and sixty tons of timber.

The brig was reloaded with cement for the naval base at Bahia Blanca, and left Buenos Aires on the 13th June. On Monday, the 20th of that month, Father recorded in his diary:

" Since last entry we have had a very trying time. On Friday and Saturday for over thirty-six hours we had a terrific gale from west and west-south-west, before which we had to run for at least fourteen hours. When the decks were too much flooded, again we had to head up as the seas grew over high and long, and running became too dangerous. We were deluged with water. Everything movable was on the move and in a great state of confusion. The men were frequently knocked about and the breakages and losses were many, both below and in the rigging and sails. I did not undress for forty-eight hours.

" Yesterday morning it moderated, but heavy water continued to curl over upon us till the afternoon, and our vessel still rolls a good deal. Happily no one has been injured; our vessel being deep she is not very weatherly and makes much water.

" 3 p.m. Monday, 20th June: Again in sight of land, about where we were when we turned before the gale on Friday night. Wind N.E. and lowering sky, and though so early it is dusk already."

3

At Harberton we received no tidings of Father for nearly two months. Then, about the middle of August, we saw the brig, almost becalmed, about eight miles away. Anxious for news, I put off in a boat and rowed out to her. Father was not on deck. I went below and spoke to Captain Davis in his cabin. He told me that Father had passed away. He had been landed at Bahia Blanca after a severe hæmorrhage. Accompanied by a Salvation Army officer, he had gone by rail to the British hospital in Buenos Aires. There he had stayed until, at his own request, he had been moved to a friend's house, where he had died on the 15th July, 1898, in his fifty-sixth year.

I spent a very short time in the cabin with Captain Davis. When I came on deck, I saw they had hoisted the flag at half-mast. Hoping it had not been seen at Harberton, I asked them to take it down, and rowed hard for home.

But dear, anxious Mother had seen the flag through the telescope and, full of foreboding, had watched me row back without Father in the boat. As I entered the house, her first words were:

" Is there bad news, Sonny? "

I took her in my arms and answered:

" No, Mother. Father has just gone on ahead, that's all."

Yes, Father had gone on. Yet in his influence and his example of faith and fortitude he is with us still. Once when very ill he had said :

" I live in my children."

Though I cannot claim that I have adhered faithfully to his high ideals, it is my one hope that the sons of whom I have since become father have inherited some of the qualities of their grandfather.

CHAPTER TWENTY-SIX

My Brothers and I are Left to Fend for Ourselves. Kiyotimink's Dogs Bring Hydrophobia to Fireland. Kiyotimink Dies of the Disease. Kaushel Falls Sick of a Tumour and Attributes his Misfortunes to a Malignant Power. Dr. Cook Returns to Harberton and Takes Away the Yahgan Dictionary.

I

WHEN OUR FATHER DIED, DESPARD HAD JUST TURNED TWENTY-SIX. I WAS twenty-three and Will twenty-one. There and then, we made up our minds that it was useless to mourn; that it was for us to carry on the work he had begun, to keep together, to look after Mother, Yekadahby and the girls; and to pursue his aims for the property he had left us and the betterment of the natives' way of life. So, although his loss was grievous, things went on without check at Harberton and Cambaceres. Despard took full control at the homestead, Will had charge of the sheep westward and on the islands in the Beagle Channel, and I continued to look after the cattle in our eastern acres.

Besides our loyal colony of Yahgans, more and more Ona came to settle with us at Harberton. One of these was Kaushel, the fearsome killer of whom the Aush had spoken in awed and frightened tones. We had grown fond of him, and were glad when he made Harberton his headquarters. He brought with him his wife, Kohpen, and his four sons and two daughters. The second son, Minkiyolh, continued to be erratic in his behaviour and gave us to think that we might have serious trouble with him eventually. The eldest son, Kiyotimink, was of a different stamp. He was married to a young woman called Halchic, and both of them were fine specimens of the Ona tribe. The other two sons, Keëlu and Haäru (Upland Goose), were still quite small boys, Keëlu not more than ten and Haäru about two years his junior.

There was to be an exhibition in Buenos Aires, and the then Governor of Argentine Fireland, the well-loved Don Pedro Godoy, was anxious to send two or three Ona to take part in it. He appealed to us to find suitable Indians. Our automatic choice was Kiyotimink and Halchic. They much appreciated the honour, and in due course embarked on the transport with their guanaco-hide shelter, bows and arrows, dogs and chattels. With them went Kiyotimink's small brother, Keëlu, and, as guardian and

237

interpreter, Don Ramón Cortéz, the Ushuaia Chief-of-Police. He had picked up some words of the Ona tongue and, always kindly disposed towards the native inhabitants, was a good man for the job.

The party arrived at Buenos Aires and encamped in Palermo Park. From the point of view of the exhibition, their visit was a great success, but there was a pathetic sequel. During their stay in the capital there was a dog-fight in which some of Kiyotimink's animals were bitten. Rabies was suspected and the other dogs were destroyed, but Kiyotimink protested so fiercely against his own dogs being killed that he was allowed to bring them back to Tierra del Fuego. On the return voyage he was himself bitten by one of them.

We were not told all this until after the party had landed at Harberton with their dogs. Then Don Ramón Cortéz warned us that hydrophobia might break out, gave us the approximate dates when it would be likely to develop in Kiyotimink and the dogs, and cautioned us to be watchful.

Kaushel and his family, most happy at being united, and rich in gifts brought back by the wanderers, went off with the dogs on a hunt. When they came back to Harberton, Kiyotimink was not with them. He had died in a manner never before seen by the Indians. Simultaneously rabies had broken out among his dogs. Some died of it, others were killed, but not before the disease had spread to other dogs in the neighbourhood.

One day, when out riding, I noticed a dog springing about like a mechanical toy and falling over on its back in a jerky way, as if worked with wires. The animal made no attempt to attack me or my horse, neither did I try to diagnose the case. Instead, without dismounting, I put a bullet through its head.

Kaushel mourned with an abandon as true and deep as that of any white man. His sadness became more pitiful when both he and Kiliutah, the elder of his two daughters, fell sick—not of hydrophobia, but of other maladies. They believed that all their troubles were due to the machinations of some wizard. I was staying at Harberton at the time, and comforted these poor folk by daily visits. I anointed them with iodine and turpentine—remedies they held in high esteem. The rains that autumn were exceptionally heavy, so I put a little roof over their inadequate shelter. Kaushel asked me to take it away, because he liked to look at the stars when lying awake at night.

On one occasion I was sitting by his bed, which was spread on the ground, when a mad dog rushed out of the bushes and leapt on the bed.

Kaushel immediately disappeared under his covering of skins, leaving me to deal with the animal, which was in the convulsions of hydrophobia. I was badly frightened, but resisted the temptation to run. I grabbed the dog by a hind leg and, whirling myself round and round to keep the poor creature at arm's length, got to an axe stuck in a stump close by and put an end to its sufferings.

It was some time before this dreadful plague was finally stamped out in our locality.

2

Despite my mistrust of the seamanship prevailing on the *Belgica*, she returned from the Polar regions during the following summer, nearly eighteen months after her visit to Cambaceres, without the loss of a single man. She put in at Punta Arenas, from where Dr. Cook came down in a cutter to Harberton, with the intention of securing my late father's dictionary. We remembered how Father had given his assurance that the manuscript would be handed over when the *Belgica* came back from the Antarctic, so we now entrusted that brisk young American surgeon with the priceless dictionary and grammar, together with a great pile of papers relating to the Yahgan language.

Before he went back, I took him to see Kaushel and his daughter, neither of whom had grown any better. Poor Kaushel, who, in his prime, had stood out, by sheer force of character, far above all the other men from Cape San Pablo, was still convinced that the misfortunes of himself and his family were due to some malignant power and that some horrible thing had been planted inside him by an enemy magician.

Joön, the Ona word for a magician or wizard, also meant doctor, so when I introduced Cook by that title, Kaushel invited him to feel the creature that was gnawing at his vitals. The doctor examined father and daughter. He diagnosed Kaushel's complaint as a tumour in the stomach, and Kiliutah's as tuberculosis of the hip-bone. Both, he informed me, were incurable at that advanced stage. He left with me a large phial of pills, probably containing opium or some similar drug. With these I dosed them. The girl, who suffered greatly, grew to watch eagerly for my visits, and her eyes would brighten perceptibly when I drew the bottle from my pocket. They both lingered for some months, and died within a few days of each other. The drugs held out till the end.

Dr. Cook most obligingly visited other sick natives, including Kankoat's little boy, who had contracted serious eye trouble. Things had gone too far to save one eye, but the doctor preserved the sight of the other, to the delight and relief of Kankoat. The child was thereupon nicknamed "Nelson."

After the doctor had taken measurements of a number of Indians and had pronounced the Ona to be the finest, though by no means the tallest race he had ever seen or heard of, he prepared to leave. In spite of all his kind help, I repaid him with an act of horrible meanness which I should not be able to confess had not he himself played a still dirtier trick on me in the end.

The cutter, in which he was leaving for Ushuaia, had anchored in Thought Of, and to see him off, it was necessary to walk across the Harberton peninsula. I went with him, bearing my full share of his luggage. Cook was carrying a good fur-lined overcoat he had used in the Antarctic regions. Pleased with the result of his visit and the prospect of getting away, he said how grateful he was for my help and how he longed to give me some memento. Mentioning the overcoat, he said what a pity it was that it would be too small for me. Although of the same opinion, I answered :

" I'm not so sure of that. Just let me try it on."

He could hardly refuse, so replied with a laugh :

" You're welcome, but you're twice my size. You'll never get into it."

By that time I had taken off my own coat. I managed with an effort to squeeze my bulk into Cook's overcoat and even button it across my chest. One could say of it that the arms came well below my elbows and the coat almost reached my knees.

" My, Doctor ! " I exclaimed joyfully. " It fits me like a glove ! "

Which was perfectly true.

Having thanked him warmly for the gift, I saw him on the little vessel, which bore him away, together with that heirloom, our priceless dictionary, which started that day on the first stage of the almost incredible wanderings that are described in the appendix on page 529.

When Dr. Cook arrived back at Punta Arenas, he sent me two pairs of snow-shoes that he had used down south. They were a great improvement on my own amateur copies of the Canadian tennis-racket type, being lighter and stronger, and I was very grateful to him for such a present.

Four years after the Belgian expedition, Cook went exploring in Alaska, and subsequently declared that he had ascended Mount McKinley, which rises over twenty thousand feet, the highest summit in North America. In 1907 he turned his attention to the North Pole, and two

Cape Peñas, the scene of the massacre.

Another view of seals at Cape Peñas.

Undisciplined nomads, armed only with bows and arrows against repeating rifles.

By courtesy of Mr. A. A. Cameron.

Kautempklh and Paloa, northern men. The valiant Kautempklh fingers his chin, a gesture peculiar to him when deep in thought.

Puppup and Ishtohn (Thick Thighs). Ishtohn's rather fancy robe is from the forelegs of yearling guanaco.

By courtesy of Col. Charles Wellington Furlong.

Shishkolh of the Najmishk group with Ahnikin (centre) and Puppup.   Puppup's heightened paleness shows white through the branches.

By courtesy of Col. Charles Wellington Furlong.

years later announced that he had reached it. Commander Peary
questioned this assertion, the matter was investigated and the claim of
Dr. Frederick A. Cook, surgeon, anthropologist and Arctic explorer, was
utterly discredited.

In the midst of these and other activities, he still found time to arrange
for the publication of the Yahgan dictionary—and try to pass it off as his
own work.   A few days after he left Harberton, I sold the fur-lined overcoat for twenty grammes of gold, so I considered that the sack of flour I
had given on his account to the Ona Indians a year before had now been
paid for.   As for Father's dictionary, for an irreplaceable manuscript such
as that, two pairs of snow-shoes and a bottle of soothing drugs were a poor
exchange.

CHAPTER TWENTY-SEVEN

A Long Stern Chase. With Seven Ona Companions I Set Out to Cross the Island. Puppup Steps Warily. We Reach Najmishk and Pass On to Rio Fuego. A Police Sergeant is Kind to Us. I am Shaved for the First Time. I Fail to Meet Mr. McInch at Rio Grande. We Start Back for Harberton. Ona Woodcraft. Shaiyutlh Spreads a Panic and Makes Himself a Laughing-Stock. I Arrive Safely Home.

I

A BUNCH OF ABOUT TWENTY HEAD OF CATTLE FROM THE HERD I WAS LOOKing after had disappeared some two years before, having been chased too much by Ona dogs. I heard that these cattle had gone up the valley of Lasifharshaj River, and so made an attempt to get them down during the summer. The thick forest, however, and the swampy moors beyond, made it impossible to use a horse to advantage—and the cattle continued to run wild. I knew that when the snow lay deep on the high moor known as Flat Top, the animals would be greatly restricted in their wanderings, so determined to get them down in winter-time. With this object in view, I set off with three Ona lads, all belonging to different groups.

Two of these groups, the Cape San Pablo party and the mountain men, have already been introduced. The third was the Najmishk group, whose hunting-grounds lay around Cape Santa Inés, north of the territory of the Cape San Pablo people (Tininisk, Kankoat, Kaushel). An important Najmishk figure was the medicine-man, Te-ilh (Mosquito), who had a son named Chauiyolh, and it was this young man who was one of my three companions in the cattle hunt. The second was Minkiyolh, the queer second son of Kaushel. The third was one of the mountain party, a lad who, though not large, was fast developing into a strong, square-jawed, resolute man. His name was Ahnikin, and he was a brother of Teëoöriolh, the young man who had broken his collar-bone. There was a younger brother, still a boy, whom we called Old Face. Their father I never met, but I knew their mother, a great strong woman from Najmishk or farther north. They were connected in some way with Tininisk's wife, Leluwhachin, and her brother, Halimink; I am not certain of the exact relationship.[1] The father may have been a brother, half-

---

[1] The Ona, in order to show their friendly feeling, often claimed a closer relationship than actually existed. The plurality of wives brought in numbers of half-brothers. Exact relationships were, in consequence, often complicated or obscure.

brother or cousin of Leluwhachin and Halimink. Ahnikin often addressed me as *Yain*.[1] I had once looked after him when he was sick and thought to be dying. After he recovered, he firmly believed that he owed me his life.

On the morning of the third day out we left Chauiyolh with our provisions and scouted round the whole day. Finding nothing but very old cattle-tracks, we returned to the encampment at night, to discover that Chauiyolh had decamped with all our provisions and my spare ammunition—in fact, with everything we had except my guanaco-skin sleeping-robe.

Ahnikin, Minkiyolh and I had eaten nothing all day. Fortunately, a large owl became interested in the fire we lighted and perched on a branch near enough for me to bring him down with my Winchester. These eared owls, though they look huge, are mostly composed of feathers, and one of them did not make a very substantial meal for three hungry men. However, we made the best of it, and the next day started off early, hoping to get a guanaco or one of our wild cattle. Though as yet little snow had fallen, the country was desolate, even the guanaco seeming to have deserted it. That afternoon the two Indian lads agreed that Ahnikin should follow up a small stream and find a place to encamp, while Minkiyolh and I made a detour up the river valley in the hope of finding meat of some kind.

We were turning empty-handed and hungry towards the place agreed upon for the encampment, when we came on the fresh tracks of a solitary male guanaco, which we followed some distance. After a while we heard a slight rustling in some saplings ahead as the animal bounded off. I caught a glimpse of him and fired, wounding him badly. I would have given him another shot, but Minkiyolh said:

"He is going towards the encampment and will soon die. Why should we carry him?"

The wounded animal, however, seemed to get a new lease of life. Turning downhill, he crossed the Lasifharshaj, which was nearly three feet deep by forty yards wide and had a strong current. As he was scrambling

[1] A case in point. *Yain* meant "my father." *Ain* (father) was never used by itself, but only in such combinations as *Yain, Main* (your father) *Yikwakain* or, in an abbreviated form, *Yikwain* (our father) and *T-ain* (his father). "Mother" was *Ahm* or *Kahm*, hence *Yahm, Mahm, Yikwakahm* (or *Yikwahm*) and *T-kahm*. The initial "T," corresponding to the English "his," was spat out by itself, as one might say "table" without the "able." Thus *T-oli* (his robe), *T-hah* (his bow) or *T-kos* (his face). This last was often used as an exclamation, as the speaker turned away after some childish quarrel or facetious argument—"His face!"

up the opposite bank, I gave him the shot I should have fired ten minutes earlier. Then, telling Minkiyolh that it was his fault the guanaco had crossed the river, I said that he could now go and fetch it.

Close to the banks, or in places where there was little current, thin ice had formed, but in the middle there was a strong current. Minkiyolh dropped his robe and waded across. He took the dead guanaco by the leg and dragged it into the water. When he reached the middle of the river, it was flowing so powerfully that he had to let go of the animal, which went drifting down stream.

Without waiting to see how Minkiyolh got out, I ran along the bank, finding it hard to keep the animal in sight. Ahead was a large bend in the river, but a little daylight was visible through the trees, so, hoping to gain on my quarry, I cut across the isthmus. It was growing dark, but when I came to the river-bank again, I spied the guanaco drifting down towards me at a great rate, quite near the shore. It would have passed a yard or two out of my reach, so, putting my rifle on the bank, I stepped carefully into the water, for the bank went down steeply. The guanaco was still beyond my reach, so I took one more step. I got one hand on the animal, but my feet were no longer touching the bottom.

The current swept me some way down stream before I could get into shallow water and drag my booty ashore. When at last I succeeded, I had all the meat I needed—and no means of cooking it. My matches and clothes were wet and, in that dark forest, I could not tell to within a mile or two where my companions might be encamped. I took off my garments, wrung the water out of them and went back for my rifle. Then I cut open the guanaco and fed on the warm fat.

As it was freezing hard, I knew that I must keep moving. The edges of my trouser-legs were already stiff with frost. I cut the brisket from the guanaco and started off with it to look for my companions, with little hope of finding them. After a while, to my unspeakable relief, I saw a spark of light glimmering in the dark woods on the other side of a deep gully.

I crossed over and, coming to a glorious fire, found that Ahnikin and Minkiyolh had resigned themselves to a hungry night. When they saw the brisket of meat I was carrying and the blood on my hands they cheered up wonderfully and, lighting a torch, went off at once to bring the rest of the guanaco before the foxes found it. In the meantime, I stripped and fairly roasted myself, turning round and round in front of the fire, at the same time drying my clothes.

Many years have passed since that night, yet when I see a single distant light twinkling through forest branches, I recall the thrill I experienced when, after two hungry days, with my clothes stiffening on me, I caught that first glimpse of my companions' cheerful fire across the wide, wooded gully.

2

After about three days we found the wandering cattle, which, as they had not seen a human being for two years or more, rushed off through the woods at a great pace. I knew from experience that a man on foot can wear down even wild cattle if he follows them long enough. They must stop to feed, and in that desolate country it took them a long time to get even the poorest meal.

Minkiyolh, who was an erratic fellow, was soon tired of his job. Complaining that he felt ill, he left for their encampment at Harberton, whilst Ahnikin and I followed the cattle for three days and the greater part of three nights, a little snow on the ground giving us enough light to walk by. In this way we gave the cattle no time to rest or feed.

One evening a young bull, at last resenting our interference, made a sudden charge at us. Fortunately, there were trees we could dodge round, and as he rushed past me I shot him in the shoulder. It was very nearly dark, so we followed him cautiously, and soon heard sounds that told us he was at his last gasp and would not need a final bullet.

Ahnikin, who was carrying our small bundle of spare moccasins, a little guanaco meat and some odds and ends, now found that he had lost my knife. He had, however, an iron spoon with him, so we rubbed one edge of the handle on a stone till it was sharp enough to skin and cut up the bull. Having done this, we hung up such meat as we did not need and festooned it with branches, out of the reach of foxes and protected from vultures. Then, camping close by, we settled down to eat roast beef and delicious scraps of fat and intestines.

A little snow had fallen at intervals, and the next day we were able to keep the cattle in sight, but could not drive them in the direction we wanted. We followed them up a wooded valley till they came out on a moor above the level of the forest. Here the snow was very deep and packed hard enough for us to run over the crust, while the cattle were continually breaking through. Thanks to this circumstance, in a short while we were well ahead of them. Seeming to realize that the game was up, they turned and raced back on their own tracks into the forest, with Ahnikin and myself running and yelling behind them.

The night had turned very wild, blowing from the south and snowing heavily. Finding a little shelter under a rock, we made a fire and, after eating our roast, lay close together, rolled up in our robes, and went to sleep. Next morning there was over two feet of fresh snow, and it was still falling, though the wind had abated. In the sheltered forest, the branches were bent double with their weight of snow, and all traces of the cattle had been obliterated.

We went along the edge of the woods where the snow had drifted deep, until we came to a spot where Ahnikin was certain that the cattle had entered the wood. For me it was just a white world, with all landmarks blotted out. The woods looked almost impenetrable. Ahnikin went ahead with a stick, touching the laden twigs so that they sprang up and shook off their burden of snow, which would otherwise have descended on him. Sometimes he paused for a moment to choose between two gaps in the forest, either of which the cattle might have used. After a time he pointed out a broken stick which, upon examination, proved to have some cow-hair on its jagged end. This kind of thing happened two or three times, and after following for well over a mile we came to the bank of the river, and soon found the hungry cattle hunting for a little food. It was amazing how young Ahnikin had followed that invisible trail.

The cattle seemed now to know that they were beaten, and that evening we put them through the boundary fence, joining them with a troop of tame animals we had left there for that purpose. We reached the homestead about midnight.

This episode was one of many somewhat simliar excursions, but I have chosen it from all the others. It shows how the human frame when in training can wear down animals. It gives an idea of the country amongst the mountains at the back of Harberton. And it also provides an insight into the characters of two Ona who are to be often mentioned in the pages that follow.

3

Towards the end of November, 1899, I left Harberton on an expedition that I hoped would take me right across the mainland of Tierra del Fuego, from the Beagle Channel to the Rio Grande, a matter of sixty miles. I took with me seven Ona Indians, all of whom had agreed to go as far as I chose. They were Ahnikin, Minkiyolh (who was not very welcome, but refused to stop behind), that live wire, Halimink, Kankoat the Jester and three others, the name of one of whom was Puppup. This Puppup was Chalshoat's brother and a cousin of Talimeoat, the shag-hunter of Shilan, and was one of the mountain men. He stood about six feet tall, was gentle in manner and appearance and was credited with limited magical powers, which he used only for relieving suffering. Rather pale for an Ona, he enhanced the peculiarity by the application of more chalk and white ash than was usual among his people.

My companions carried bows and seal-skin quivers full of arrows. I had my Winchester, with a good supply of ammunition. Like the Indians, I carried a robe. Normally my dress was shirt and trousers, guanaco-skin moccasins lined with soft grass, and the conical Ona head-dress of blue-grey fur taken from the head of a guanaco. On this excursion, having in mind the civilization I should encounter on the other side of the island, I abandoned the head-dress for a more conventional cap and wore a jacket over my shirt. We took with us a small tin pot, billy cans, a few tin mugs and some iron spoons, as well as small quantities of biscuit, rice, sugar, coffee and salt.

We followed at first the same course as my brothers and I had pursued on our trip with Slim Jim, but after a while sloped away eastward through a nest of mountains. It was a short cut, but a difficult track. The Indians told me that, over one part of it, dogs had to be carried. We came eventually to a wide valley, well up the mountain, where the upper edge of the northern forest began. Here we camped for the night.

I believe my companions had taken that track in the expectation of finding abundant guanaco. The absence of these creatures, combined with the tracks of dogs, had suggested other hunters in the neighbourhood, and that night there was anxious discussion as to who those hunters might be. Next morning we were off early, and moved with caution through the forest. Before long the natives noticed certain signs that I myself would never have distinguished. Birds and guanaco often disturbed the leaves, so there were no clues there; neither could I see any human foot-prints. So invisible were the signs and so wary our advance, that I began to think that my companions were intending to scare me into returning to Harberton. Then, just as my doubts were becoming a conviction, one of them pointed out a dead goose hanging from a tree. It was out of the reach of foxes and festooned with branches to protect it from the vultures. Someone would be coming back for it. My companions redoubled their vigilance as we moved forward. Puppup was leading. We followed in single file with about three-yard intervals, walking almost on tiptoe.

Suddenly our leader stopped dead and stood motionless except for the slightest sign with his hand. The rest of us froze where we stood, listening intently.

Someone else had been just as sharp and silent as we had been. After a moment or two a voice, harsh with excitement, called out in Ona :

"Who is that? Speak quickly."

Young Ahnikin recognized the voice. It belonged to a man of the Najmishk group, with which he was connected and, at that time, on fairly good terms. He answered at once, and said that with him was Lanush-waiwa.[1] Ahnikin signalled to me to follow him, and he and I stepped forward.

Very near us, just beyond a thick growth of young beech trees, were scattered ten or eleven Ona. They had been hidden behind some larger trees, and were resuming their robes and replacing arrows in their quivers when we appeared among them. Some of the party I had met before. Among those who were strangers to me was one Shijyolh, a stout man of medium height, whose fox-skin mantle gave him a fine appearance. As I talked with his companions, I noticed that Shijyolh kept looking at me with a shy curiosity, as a small child might look at an unfamiliar visitor. I found that he had never seen a white man at close quarters before, and was inclined to fight shy of them.

After we had exchanged a few friendly words, Ahnikin told them the names of the rest of our party. We then called these to join us, and all proceeded northward together until we came to the south-east side of Heuhupen, the table-land that, if Ona legend could be relied upon, had once been a witch. Here there was a sheltered stretch of level grassland, some ten acres in extent, ringed by bold hills covered with unbroken forest, and with a stream running through it. On the edge of this grassland was the Ona encampment, bustling with women, children and dogs. They had plenty of meat, and soon some choice pieces were cooking for us. We, in our turn, boiled enough rice and sugar in our billy cans to give everyone a taste. Te-ilh, the father of Chauiyolh, the young man who had decamped with our provisions, was not with the party, and there seemed to be no other outstanding man among them. I

---

[1] One of the names by which the Ona knew me. It is an Ona corruption of Yahgan, meaning, The Man from Woodpecker Creek. Alternative titles were Khueihei (Obstinate or Persuasive, according to circumstances) and, after I had been deprived of a finger in 1908, Goöiyin u Whash Terrh Komn (The Mountain Fox who Lost a Claw). There were others, both complimentary and opprobrious.

attached myself chiefly to Shijyolh and was quite sorry when, having finished eating, we felt it was time to move on.

The next day we set out to follow the Ewan River towards the Atlantic coast. We had gone some distance when we heard a dog give one sharp bark, which was instantly checked. We made ourselves as inconspicuous as possible and remained motionless for some time. Then, with the utmost caution, we moved towards the spot from which the sound had come. We encountered neither dog nor man. Halimink and the others decided that we had been seen by natives who wished to avoid us, and we resumed our journey.

We followed the Ewan River throughout the day, and camped not far from the Atlantic Ocean. The next morning we forded the river at its mouth. This was a tricky manoeuvre. Although the water was calm and there was very little current, the tide was high. None of the Ona could swim. Ahnikin and Halimink were much shorter than the rest of us, and even Kankoat could not possibly have waded across without a taller man to hang on to. The feet of all three of them did not touch the bottom, but with their hands on our shoulders they purposely raised themselves as high as possible, so as to give us a firmer foothold, and we all got safely across.

The tide was too high for us to pass along the beach under the Ewan Cliffs, an imposing sandstone formation such as I had not seen before. We went up stream a little way and, after climbing a steep hill, crossed an extent of beautiful parkland and approached the coast again. Here we came upon a sweep of shingle beach nearly six miles long. At low water the tide, which had a rise and fall of over thirty feet (five times as much as at Harberton), went nearly a mile out, uncovering a level sandstone flat. Just above high-water mark, along the shingle beach, a steep bank rose to a height of thirty feet or more, except where little streams had cut paths through it. Beyond the sweep of beach we could see a higher range of coastal hills, ending in the cliffs called Najmishk, in the neighbourhood of which Capelo, the renegade, had prepared his defences against an attack that had not matured.

Close to the top of the bank and a quarter of a mile in depth was a tangled, stunted forest, but behind it was a narrow open space like a road, over four miles long, running parallel with the coast. The name of this natural road was Shaiwaal. A legend concerning its origin is recounted on a later page. We walked along Shaiwaal and reached Najmishk. There we found signs of an encampment with every indication of having been evacuated in haste.

Fearing an ambush, we took to the beach.   The tide had fallen, and we were able to pass along under the shadow of the cliffs, which were over three hundred feet high.   Here and there were great boulders of a harder nature than the sandstone cliffs from which they had fallen. There were also pools left by the tide.   In such pools the Ona women were accustomed to catch the large, scaleless fish called *dahapi*.   The women caught them by stabbing them with small spears, always through the head, for *dahapi* invariably put themselves on the defensive and face their attackers.

After passing Najmishk, we came to another break in the cliffs, where a stream ran out of a fine, well-grassed valley.   Beyond was a long lower cliff called Waken.   After this we crossed another stream, then left the beach for a splendid stretch of grassland—the widest extent of open, level country that I have ever seen.   We splashed across some shallow lakes, but the greater part of the flat was well grassed.   I peopled it, in imagination, with cattle and horses; the land seemed far too wet for sheep.

Some three miles ahead of us, the flat ended in low hills, and the forest of dwarf deciduous beech again drew near the coast.   We rounded this point of wood to see, about a mile and a half away, two log-huts roofed with corrugated iron.   They were built on a little knoll that commanded a good view in our direction.   These huts were the Rio Fuego police-station, the foremost outpost of civilization as it advanced southward from Rio Grande settlement, some seven leagues away.

With the forest not far on our left, we walked on briskly.   When we were half a mile distant from the police-station, we noticed a stir : rifles and ammunition-belts were being passed round in haste among a group of about ten policemen.   I told my companions to sit down and, leaving my rifle in their care, walked on alone.   Knowing that my appearance was rough, to say the least, I felt quite nervous of my reception.   As a safe-guard, I flourished a letter of introduction from Despard to Señor Pessoli, the district Chief-of-Police, whose acquaintance he had made at Ushuaia. I reached the log-huts and stepped up to the sergeant in charge.   I told him my name, which was familiar to him, and handed him the letter.

Without losing the military dignity proper to one who represented his country on that isolated frontier, the sergeant became kindness itself. After a little chat, he told me that my Ona companions could come over and camp in a wood close by, provided they deposited their weapons with the police during our stay.   I assured him that they were old and trusted friends and he did not press the point.

We were the first civilized party—if such we could be called—to have crossed the no man's land direct from the Beagle Channel. Miners had occasionally passed along that coast, but since the fate of San Martin's party and the failure of one or two other individuals to return, these expeditions had been discontinued. So visitors at the police station were a rarity. They made us more than welcome and, from their modest rations, produced nicely cooked food for us all.

The sergeant proposed to escort me next day to the farm settlement known as La Primera Argentina, which was to the south of the Rio Grande. This farm was one of the two huge tracts of land, one on each side of the Rio Grande, owned by Don José Menendez. The settlement on the north side of the river was called La Segunda Argentina. The energetic and far-sighted Don José had, in the early days, sent the second of his five sons, then scarcely more than a boy, to Australia, where he had studied sheep-farming for some years. With the experience thus gained, combined with his own force of character, the young man was afterwards able to direct the development of the vast farms which that remarkable family acquired—and still own—in Tierra del Fuego and other parts of the world. At the time of which I am now writing he was manager of La Segunda Argentina, which, at that period, was the smaller of the two. His name was Don José Menendez Behety, the last being his mother's maiden name. He was known to all as Josecíto.

The manager of La Primera Argentina was called "The King of Rio Grande." For reasons that will emerge as my story proceeds, I will not give his real name, but will call him Mr. McInch. He was an unscrupulous, hard-drinking Scot, whose early attempts to start sheep-farming in northern Fireland had been greatly hampered by Ona depredations and was, in consequence, their sworn and relentless foe. His treatment of the Indians was not looked upon with favour by his employer—or by Josecíto—but his predecessor, who had honestly tried milder methods, had been unsuccessful and had had to quit.

In the projected trip to Rio Grande, the sergeant's principal intention was to exhibit me to Mr. McInch, whom I had not met. With this in view, the sergeant looked me up and down and decided that, were he to be seen riding into the settlement on the morrow with such an apparition, the report would have flown through the country that he had captured a desperate criminal. I had never shaved in my life. Why should I? My father never did, and the thought of it had never entered my head. Now, at the sergeant's urgent request, I consented to submit to my first shave.

That terrible ordeal at the hands of the police barber I shall never forget. To have a complete stranger scraping away with a sharp razor so close to my jugular vein filled me with terror. It needed all my self-control not to stop the operation half-way through. By a supreme effort, I managed to hold myself in check until the job was successfully concluded, then faced the lesser perils of a hair-cut.

My face and head were now beyond reproach. Not content with this, the good sergeant found something else to worry about—my moccasins. There were no London policemen on the establishment, so none of the regulation pairs of boots were large enough for my out-size in feet. Then the sergeant had an idea : a huge Austrian miner, who was working on the draining of a swamp not far from the track that would take us to Rio Grande, would certainly have a pair to fit me. I was not at all happy about this, knowing how uncomfortable boots can be after one has become accustomed to moccasins; but, to please the sergeant, I consented.

Next morning the police gave us coffee all round. I told my Ona companions to see if they could get a guanaco to relieve the strain on our hosts' larder, then set off for La Primera Argentina with the sergeant and one of his men. They had supplied me with a splendid horse with a pace known as *sobre-paso* or *pasuco*, an easier gait than that of our smaller mountain ponies. However, never in my life having ridden twenty miles without encountering obstacles to overcome, I found the long, level stretch monotonous. Fortunately for me, the gigantic Austrian had shifted his encampment, so I was allowed to go on with my comfortable footwear.

To the sergeant's chagrin, Mr. McInch was not there at La Primera Argentina to inspect this curio that had just strolled out of the woods. Notwithstanding his absence on business, I was able to look over the farm settlement. It was only seven corrugated-iron houses, or shacks, but the shearing-shed was the finest I had seen up to that time. We afterwards had lunch at the settlement, then galloped back to the police station at Rio Fuego.

I was pleased to hear on my arrival that my Ona friends had complied with my request and bagged a guanaco. They had not gone far in their hunt before the genial Kankoat had successfully arrowed one, much to the surprise and admiration of the police, who had hunted the surrounding district with dog and rifle till the guanaco had grown scarce and wild.

We left Rio Fuego at daybreak the following morning. As our track would lead us for fifteen miles along the beach, the sergeant wanted me to send my companions on ahead and overtake them on horseback with a squad who would return with the horse to the police-station. It was a tempting offer, but my communistic principles when dealing with the Ona forbade me to accept. They always tried to walk me off my legs, yet I can claim that I never kept them waiting.

It was our intention to return to Harberton by a different route. It would take us past the conical mountain called No-kake, which, like Heuhupen, stood out apart from the main range. On our journey, my companions spent some time scouting. They could not understand why we were being avoided by other parties of Ona. Our progress was also impeded by the unevenness of the ground. Where dry, it was full of tucu-tucu underminings; where wet, it was overgrown with coarse grass and reeds. All this changed when we reached the mountain country.

In the afternoon of the second day we noticed tracks that gave Hali-mink and the others cause for worried discussion; but on the third day we found moccasin tracks, clear even to myself, that set all their fears at rest. The tracks led down the mountainside, in the opposite direction to our own line of march, and, from the strides and bounds of the man who had made them, he might have been pursued by the Devil himself. With their uncanny aptitude for detecting clues and drawing from them the right conclusions, my comrades soon decided that the tracks had been made about a week previously and that the wearer of the moccasins had been one Shaiyutlh (White Moss). This young Ona was a close relation —either brother or cousin—of Shijyolh, the stout man in the fox-skin robe who had been so interested in me during our meeting a few days before. Shaiyutlh had been at Harberton when we left, and my comrades now deduced that, on seeing the departure of an armed party, none of whom belonged to his own—the Najmishk—group, he had made northward by another track with all speed, to warn his people of the bloodthirsty expedition that was on its way in their direction.

This ingenious inference ultimately proved correct. Shaiyutlh had acted exactly as they had surmised. As he had raced through scrub and bog, his fertile imagination had painted vivid pictures of our murderous intentions, so it was not surprising that we had been shunned by people we should otherwise have met, though scouts had spied continually on our movements. It was fortunate that Shaiyutlh had chosen the eastern track; otherwise we should have missed that interesting encounter in the woods with Shijyolh and party. When all this became known by those who had been concerned in this game of hide-and-seek, it was turned into a great joke at Shaiyutlh's expense, he himself seeming to enjoy it as much as anyone.

Greatly reassured, Haliminkk, Kankoat, Puppup and the others resumed the march homeward. Towards midday we came to the highest pass in our journey. It was of bare rock patched with snow and high above tree level. We noticed a guanaco coming briskly along a ridge towards us, enjoying the security his wide view gave him. We were anxious to take some meat back to Harberton, so hid ourselves among some rocks about fifty yards from where the guanaco was likely to pass, and waited.

It seemed about a minute later that I was startled by an explosion. Puppup was shaking me into wakefulness, imploring me to shoot the guanaco before it got away. I had fallen asleep as soon as I had sat down. The guanaco had turned aside before coming within bowshot and Minkiyolh, wishing to distinguish himself, had taken my rifle and fired. Puppup, having no confidence in his temperamental young countryman's marksmanship, had instantly aroused me; but while I was trying to clear my vision and Minkiyolh was aiming for a second shot, the animal fell dead among the rocks.

We were soon off again, after partaking of certain scraps of fat, which it was the Ona custom to eat off a recently killed animal. Thinking of their families, whom they would meet next day at Harberton, my friends left nothing of the carcase for the vultures.

That afternoon we passed the eastern end of the lake near which my brothers and I had encamped on that stormy night years before, when we had first attempted to cross into Ona-land. There were two or three small islets on the lake. On these, gulls from the sea, twelve miles away, laid their eggs and hatched their young. There were no fish to speak of in the lake, so the devoted mothers would fly to the sea, fill their crops and return to disgorge the food into the hungry gullets of their little ones. Not far from the lake were a few scattered trees, on which we saw three or four eagles perched. The quantity of dead gulls, skeletons and feathers lying around the trees showed how the eagles had taken advantage of tired mothers flying home with supper for their young.

We reached Harberton the following day—and what a welcome I received! Mother was for ever telling me that I looked either tired,

haggard or thin—or all three at once. These tramps certainly emaciated me, yet I was beginning to learn the folly of making up for the privations of the trip by eating too heartily on my return. I had, therefore, developed the habit of restraining my appetite at table just before getting to the stage when I would be unable to eat another mouthful.

CHAPTER TWENTY-EIGHT

*Kankoat Performs an Amazing Feat. I Take my Revenge on Him. Minkiyolh,
the Son of Kaushel, Runs Amuck. I Study Magic under the Tutorship of Tininisk
and Otrhshoölh. I Decide not to Become a Medicine-Man.*

I

MY TRAMP TO THE ATLANTIC COAST WAS FOLLOWED BY A HAPPY, UN-
eventful period, during which our ties with the Ona drew even closer.
We had, it is true, many childish disagreements. These were of intense
interest to me ; they revealed so clearly the workings of the primitive
mind. I had also many opportunities of observing their well-developed,
though curious, sense of humour. The leading joker was, of course,
Kankoat.

There was one occasion when Kankoat and I went hunting together
in early summer-time. We left our encampment and ascended the
wooded mountain known as No Top till we came out on the moor,
where patches of winter snow were melting in the sunshine. The ascent,
now more gentle, still continued for about a mile, when we commenced
going down on the mountain's northern slope. Here, on a grassy bank
close to the upper edge of the woods, we surprised two full-grown male
guanaco. I shot them both.

It was said of Kushhalimink, that huge fellow with the vast expanse
of chest who had wanted to take me away when Kaushel and his party
had paid their first visit to Cambaceres, that he was so lazy that when he
killed a guanaco, however large it might be, he would not even open it,
but would carry it home entire, so that his wife could skin and cut it up,
and so save him the trouble. Other Ona, of less indolent disposition, did
the job for themselves—and this Kankoat now proceeded to do, whilst I
went down to the nearby scrub for a load of firewood. Near the kill, I
was soon roasting pieces from the interior of the animals—delicacies that
some people would call offal.

Unless in a violent hurry, the Ona divided a guanaco in a particular
manner. The brisket, which was generally regarded as the hunter's
portion, came off first. Then the ribs, each side with its shoulder and
front leg attached, were removed close to the backbone, leaving that still
fixed to the neck. Next one of the hind legs was cut off like a ham.

The other hind leg remained attached to the trunk, which, when separated from the neck just where the second rib would have been, was the heaviest portion. The animal was thus divided into five sections, not counting the brisket. The second heaviest section was the piece that included the head, neck and backbone.

If it was intended to carry the meat more than a short distance, the Ona hunter would make a neat bundle of it, and would then tie it up with a thin hide called *moji*, which he always carried with him. The *moji* was coiled in a fashion similar to that known to Boy Scouts as a sheepshank. The ends were fastened to the bundle something over two feet apart. Unlike the sheepshank, the centre loop of the Ona knot, instead of having three lines across it, had considerably more—any odd number from about fifteen upwards, according to the length of the *moji*. These lines were fitted over the carrier's shoulders and across his chest, so that he was enclosed in a network. The burden rested on his hips, and he walked with his body stooping forward. The advantage of this mode of packing was that the weight, by being rested on the hips, tired only the legs, whereas on the shoulders it would have fatigued the whole body. It was particularly suitable for carrying heavy loads a long distance.

I now supposed that Kankoat's plan was to carry most of the meat down till we found trees on which to hang it out of the reach of foxes, then return and take a moderate load to the encampment. It was, therefore, with surprise that I saw Kankoat, having finished cutting up the two guanaco, pack every scrap of meat, the skins, blood [1] and even the feet, into two huge bundles in the manner just described. By the time he had finished, there was not enough left on the ground to make a meal for a hungry mouse.

In Tierra del Fuego a grown guanaco will provide over a hundred kilos (2 cwt.) of meat and bone, so, with the skins and other odds and ends, our two parcels each weighed far more than that. I chose what seemed the smaller and, lying down on my back on top of it, pulled the *moji* tightly over my shoulders. With a mighty effort I rolled over face downwards on the mossy land. Then I got on my hands and knees, straightened my body, and, using my rifle, butt down, as a support,

[1] When an animal is shot through the body, and the stomach, intestines, heart, etc., have been removed, there is always a lot of blood left in the carcase. As containers for this blood, the Ona used the membranous sacs from the guanaco's interior. The blood was scooped by hand into these receptacles, the ends of which were then securely tied. Having no means of boiling water, the Ona always roasted these black sausages, which were very appetizing.

managed to rise to my feet. Kankoat did likewise, then, to my astonishment, instead of walking downhill into the forest, turned and started up
the mountain, straight for our encampment.

For a long time past I had been doing my utmost to prove to my
Indian friends that, even at their own game, I was pretty well their equal.
So now I did not question Kankoat's choice of direction. I followed him
doggedly, toiling along slowly behind him. Kankoat was a good six
inches shorter than I and was certainly two stone lighter than my own
fifteen; yet, though in good training at the time, after three-quarters of
a mile of upward struggle, I decided I was beaten. I saw a convenient
rock, of the height of a table, that would enable me to alter my load
without rolling on the ground, and managed to gasp out:

" Why do we hurry? Let us rest by this rock."

Kankoat did as I asked. Realizing that I could not face another bout
like the last, I told him I was going to leave some of my meat for the foxes.
He advised getting rid of the neck portion, which contained most bone
and weighed nearly half a hundredweight. Following his suggestion, I
took this piece out of my bundle and left it on the rock. Then, having
readjusted the *moji*, I was ready to start off again. Kankoat proposed that
I should now take the lead, which I did, feeling quite sprightly at the
reduction of my burden.

Glancing back after a while, I noticed that my companion was lagging
a good way behind and took mean pleasure in the thought that, even if
not quite his equal, I was not so very greatly his inferior. As soon as I
reached the upper forest and found suitable trees in which to hang the
meat, I threw off my load and waited for Kankoat. He soon joined me.
As he lay down on his load and slipped the *moji* off his shoulders he said:

" My back is broken."

When he undid his bundle, I saw that it now contained the piece I had
left on the rock. He had covered a mile of wet clay and stony moor
with a load weighing well over three hundred pounds.

And the joke was on me.

2

There was another example of Kankoat's impish humour. I had
been working with him and some other Ona, one of whom was Chalshoat, the strong, heavy, dull man who had been taken to Ushuaia after
the shooting of Capelo and had since regained his freedom. We had
been clearing some fallen timber in the forest. It was getting rather late

in the day and I knew that my companions felt it was high time to stop, so we stuck our axes into logs and made ready to start for home. Just before we left, the merry Kankoat made a remark that was clearly not intended for my ears. The others laughed in agreement, whereupon Kankoat led off at the steady run that the Ona could keep up indefinitely. It was obviously their intention to run all the way home, up hill and down dale, and leave me far behind.

Not to be outdone so early in the proceedings, I got up near the front of the line and ran with the rest. Then, when an idea came into my head, I began to pant audibly and slackened my pace. One after another the happy rascals passed me. Chalshoat brought up the rear and did not try to hide his smile of conscious superiority as he lumbered past.

This was my country more than theirs. I knew that to the left of our winding track lay, just ahead of us, a low, boggy moor, by cutting across which, the distance could be shortened considerably.

I kept Chalshoat in sight till a hollow on our left showed me it was time to leave the track. After fifty yards of thicket I was out on the swamp and running for all I was worth. It was heavy going for five hundred yards. Then I reached a wooded hill on the ridge of which ran our track. I scrambled up the hill onto the track, where I lay down. I had nearly recovered my breath when I saw my friends approaching, with Kankoat still running in the lead. I closed my eyes and began to snore. When Kankoat pulled up alongside me, I judged it time to wake with a start. Sitting up rubbing my eyes, I said with a yawn :

" Why have you kept me waiting so long? I went to sleep."

Kankoat grinned. This time the joke was on him.

3

Kaushel, that grand old Indian, died at last as Dr. Cook had predicted, having been, before his illness, the only able-bodied man to enjoy free rations at Harberton without working for them. His daughter, Kiliutah, died also, from tuberculosis of the hip-bone. When Kiyotimink, the eldest son, had lost his life by hydrophobia, his young widow, Halchic, had been taken to wife by Kankoat, himself a widower.

Minkiyolh, the second son, he of the strange behaviour, had married a well-grown girl called Yohmsh, who was a sister of Halchic. Minkiyolh, a good-looking young man, very nearly six feet tall, was keen on the acquisition of knowledge and the study of magic, but he was not fond of work. Although rightly proud of his heroic, yet modest, father, he could not understand why, when living at Harberton, he was expected to work for his living, while his parent had received a free ration during his lifetime. Perhaps because Minkiyolh was Kaushel's son, we put up a little house for the young couple. In this they kept their goods, using it as a living-place only in very rainy weather. At other times they wisely preferred to shelter behind a wind-screen, as their ancestors had done before them.

They had been married about two months when Minkiyolh began to act even more strangely than he had done before. The story soon went round that he was bewitched. He seemed to see queer things. Occasionally, with a frightened look, he would emit wild cries, staring horror-stricken at some object no one else could see. On one stormy night, after such an attack, he suddenly sprang to his feet and ran away stark naked, without even putting on his moccasins. He ran a long way before his pursuing friends could overtake him, then collapsed and had to be carried home. I felt certain at the time that all this was play-acting, to call attention to himself and build up fame as a highly endowed magician.

One day he came to our house at Harberton, saying he was hungry and wanted to work. I gave him something to eat, then set him to chop firewood in the wood-shed. When later I went that way, dusk was falling and, as I passed the darkening shed, I heard a weird cry. I looked round just in time to see Minkiyolh fling an axe at me with all his might. Fortunately only the handle hit me, but Minkiyolh followed up the attack by rushing at me. He was nothing like my weight, but had the fierce strength of a madman. Even his teeth were a danger. To avoid these I got my forearm under his chin and we came to the ground together. But I was on top, and when some other Indians came running up, we tied him hand and foot.

Suddenly he went quite limp, almost as if he had fallen asleep. He had not been hurt in our struggle. I had not been so lucky. My right thumb had been put out of joint. I made clumsy efforts to pull it back and at length tied it by a strap to a rafter in the wood-shed, then jerked on it by suddenly bending my knees. Fortunately it came back with the first jerk, though it has never been the same thumb since.

Despard, Will and I discussed what to do with this incubus, Min-kiyolh. Obviously we could not keep him tied up for the rest of his life, nor could we shoot him, which would, in truth, have been the best solution. The only alternative was to set him free—unless we could get someone to take him off our hands. We knew that a transport, the

Santa Cruz, was loading timber at the recently established saw-mill at Ukukaia,[1] twelve miles to the west of Harberton, and thought that, if we could catch her before she started off, the kindly Captain Mascarelo might agree to take Minkiyolh to an asylum in Buenos Aires.

Accordingly Minkiyolh was freed from his bonds, put into a boat and rowed to the saw-mill. Will was in charge and told us that Minkiyolh slept all the time. Captain Mascarelo took him on board the transport and bore him off to Buenos Aires. Some months later the transport was back again—with Minkiyolh. The Argentine doctors had examined him and pronounced him perfectly sane. Captain Mascarelo told us that the young man had behaved well during the whole trip; and it is probable that both he and the doctors considered it to be a case of much ado about nothing.

On his return, Minkiyolh talked far more than he had ever done before. He boasted to the Ona of his exploits, and the wonders he had seen in the capital. He pretended to read a Spanish newspaper, holding it upside down, and translated into the Ona tongue, for the benefit of his audience, tit-bits from his vivid imagination. In these translations his friendship with the President of the Republic was often mentioned and the listeners were told that Minkiyolh had been elected their chief and leader. On learning that even the guanaco were claimed by the President, but that, thanks to Minkiyolh's intervention, the Ona would be graciously allowed to use them for meat, one veteran in the audience remarked that if he saw the President's brand or ear-mark on a guanaco, he would abstain from killing it.

In spite of his new line in tall stories, Minkiyolh seemed to have profited by his visit to Buenos Aires. He was now much more inclined to work and settled down to a peaceful home-life with Yohmsh, showing no inclination to return to his old peculiar standard of behaviour. Later he took a second wife, Ohmchen (Comb), the younger sister of Yohmsh, and in course of time the affair of the wood-shed and other strange incidents in his past life became nearly forgotten.

4

Tininisk, the medicine-man who had kidnapped Kankoat's little son, often paid us visits at Harberton. Being a *joön* of repute, he preferred chanting or instructing us in ancient lore to work and drudgery. I always listened with proper respect to his legends and beliefs, but openly

[1] Now Port Admiral Brown.

told him—and other medicine-men—that their magic could do me no harm because I was not afraid of it and that, in my opinion, it could injure only people who feared it.

When talking on this subject with Tininisk or with his fellow-magicians, I would bare my chest and invite them to put all their powers into causing me pain. Under pressure, they acceded to this request and made the most excruciating efforts to throw some evil thing upon me. Once or twice, after much hard work on their part, they succeeded in making me wince, but in the end admitted that I was quite impervious to their machinations.

Some of these humbugs were excellent actors. Standing or kneeling beside the patient, gazing intently at the spot where the pain was situated, the doctor would allow a look of horror to come over his face. Evidently he could see something invisible to the rest of us. His approach might be slow or he might pounce, as though afraid that the evil thing that had caused the trouble would escape. With his hands he would try to gather the malign presence into one part of the patient's body—generally the chest—where he would then apply his mouth and suck violently. Sometimes this struggle went on for an hour, to be repeated later. At other times the *joön* would draw away from his patient with the pretence of holding something in his mouth with his hands. Then, always facing away from the encampment, he would take his hands from his mouth gripping them tightly together, and, with a guttural shout difficult to describe and impossible to spell, fling this invisible object to the ground and stamp fiercely upon it. Occasionally a little mud, some flint or even a tiny, very young mouse might be produced as the cause of the patient's indisposition. I myself have never seen a mouse figure in one of these performances, but they were quite common. Perhaps when I was there the doctor had failed to find a mouse's nest.

I asked Tininisk whether he could explain to me something of the origin of his magical powers. I gathered from his ambiguous replies that, in some way, the moon was helpful in these matters; and that it was possible for a medicine-man to get into touch with spirits out of the reach of ordinary folk, and even to see things happening far away. I inferred also that the power of a *joön* was not constant; at times he might be very strong, at others quite impotent.

Seeing that I was anxious to learn, Tininisk at last volunteered to try to instil some of his magic into me. Three magicians were present at the session: Tininisk, his wife Leluwhachin and Otrhshoölh. This last, whose name meant White Eye, was also one of the Cape San Pablo people. In appearance he was rather similar to Tininisk, lean, lightly built and eagle-visaged, with a stern, but not at all disagreeable or discontented, expression. In height he was quite five feet ten. Leluwhachin, though never admitted to the secrets of the Lodge (to which I shall refer later), was looked upon as sharing her husband's occult powers. As I have already mentioned, no other Ona women of my acquaintance had these attributes, although they were frequently to be found amongst the Yahgan women.

My inception took place by a small fire, with the usual shelter of guanaco skins spread on the windward side. After giving me a harangue on the serious nature of my undertaking, Tininisk suggested that I should strip. I did as instructed, and remained half reclining on my clothing and some guanaco skins while he went over my chest with his hands and mouth as intently as any doctor with his stethoscope; moving in the prescribed manner from place to place, pausing to listen here and there. He also gazed intently at my body, as though he saw through it like an X-ray manipulator.

Then, the two men dropping their robes and Leluwhachin her cape, though retaining her *kohiyaten*,[1] they literally put their heads—and hands —together and produced something that I could see. It might have been the lightest grey down teased out into the shape of a woolly dog about four inches long, with a stout body and prick-ears. With the trembling of their hands and possibly their breathing, they gave its movements a semblance of life. I noticed a peculiar scent that seemed to accompany this object as, with their three pairs of hands held together, they brought it to my chest with many guttural sounds. I did not feel the pressure of the thing against my body, but without any sudden movement it was no longer in their hands.

This performance was repeated three times and, though each time a new puppy was supposed to be put into my body, I felt only the touch of the magicians' hands.

Now came a solemn pause, as if of expectation. Then Tininisk asked me if I felt anything moving in my heart; or if I could see something strange in my mind, something like a dream; or if I felt any inclination to chant. The truthful answer was an unequivocal " No," but I put my

---

[1] Woman's garment of soft guanaco skin, worn with hair outwards. It reached from just below the breasts to the knees and was wrapped about one and a half times round the body, being tied securely in position with *moji*. Hence *kohiyaten* (hip-tied).

denial as mildly as possible. I told them that I thought the magic puppies had not found in me a comfortable resting-place and might either have perished or returned whence they had come. I added that I would wait till the morrow. If by that time I had felt nothing strange within me, we should know that I was not an apt student.

It would certainly have been interesting to continue these studies. Had I done so, I might have been able to explain certain things that I shall describe later in this book. These have always remained mysteries to me. On the other hand, further instruction under Tininisk and the others would not only have forced me to frequent lying, at which I was not very clever, but would also have made me a creature apart from the honest Indian hunters I so greatly admired. They feared the sorcerers; I did not wish them to fear me, too.

There was another reason: self-preservation. Medicine-men ran great dangers. When persons in their prime died from no visible cause, the " family doctor " would often cast suspicion, in an ambiguous way, on some rival necromancer. Frequently the chief object of a raiding party, in the perpetual clan warfare of the Ona, was to kill the medicine-man of an opposing group. No, I would not become a *joön*, to be blamed, maybe, for a fatal heart attack a hundred miles away.

When I met my instructors next day, I told them, after a thoughtful silence, that I felt no effects, either good or bad, from yesterday's ceremony, and that I considered it best to give up the study of the black arts.

CHAPTER TWENTY-NINE

Trouble between the Ona and the Northern Settlers. The Silesian Mission. Hektliohlh, the Caged Eagle, Dies in Captivity. Paloa Defies the Police. A Party of Ona are Massacred by Mr. McInch and his Followers. Kilkoat Plots Revenge. Kiyohnishah Steals some Sheep and Places Me in a Difficult Position. I Am Assisted by Ahnikin and Halimink.

I

IN THE EARLY EIGHTEEN-NINETIES THE NORTHERN PART OF ONA-LAND HAD been found to be excellent for sheep-raising, and vast tracts had been sold or leased to different companies and individuals on both sides of the Argentine–Chilean frontiers. The Argentine government had made a grant of land on the Atlantic coast north-west of Rio Grande to the Silesian Fathers under Monseigneur Fagnano, who had established a mission there for the benefit of the Indians. The same society had been given Dawson Island by Chile for a like purpose. Except for this, no provision had been made for the ancient native races, lords of the land from time immemorial.

I need hardly state that the white invaders soon found it impossible to start the farms they had planned in a country over-run by these wild, undisciplined nomads, of whose language and customs they were totally ignorant. A story—widely circulated and not yet forgotten—tells that certain of the newcomers paid a pound a head for every Indian killed. Personally I believe this to have been done by one individual only, who left the country over forty years ago. He was not in the service of anyone who owns land there at present and, except by a very few, his name is not remembered. He was not the man whom I have called McInch. Two famous hunters of Indians who were said to be in his employ met with violent deaths. Of one of them, Dancing Dan, I shall have more to say later.

These unfortunate natives, though, as a rule, vastly superior physically —and in some ways mentally as well—to their enemies, were hopelessly handicapped by having to provide for their numerous families. They were split into small groups continually fighting with each other. There was a complete lack of discipline and this, combined with the fact that they were on foot and armed only with bows and arrows against men who were mounted and armed with repeating rifles, made their case hopeless. Even so, those same invaders found it dangerous to follow the Indians into the wooded part of their country farther south.

It is said that some of the settlers paid five pounds for every Indian taken off their hands and transported to a mission. This may be looked upon as a meritorious act, clearing the country of predatory vermin and, at the same time, helping to reform the savages and make useful citizens of them. On the other hand, it could be regarded as condemning free natives—rightful owners of the land—to a kind of penal servitude.

Hektliohlh was one of the finest Indians I ever met. I have heard him called a giant, though I doubt if he stood over six feet three inches. Together with a party of men, women and children, he was captured without bloodshed. This, I have been told, was due to the courageous action of a Scottish shepherd who, though unacquainted with the language, went over to them unarmed when they had been surrounded and, by his courage and friendly gestures, induced them to surrender. I do not know this man's name.

Hektliohlh and the others were taken by steamer from the northern part of the country to the government settlement at Ushuaia, where there were already several captives from other parts of Ona-land. Hearing that they were there, Despard and I went to see them and found amongst them a few mountain men with whom we were acquainted. One of these—and I have a particular purpose in mentioning him here— was a half-brother of Halimink and uncle to young Ahnikin. His name was Yoknolpe. The Governor kindly agreed to set Yoknolpe and the two or three other mountain men free. The northerners, for whom Despard and I could not vouch, had to remain in captivity. They were well treated and after a time allowed—it may have been purposely—so much freedom that some were able to get away and return through the mountains to their own country.

Some four years later I was on a little steamer which touched at the Silesian Mission on Dawson Island, where, it was said, about seven hundred Ona were confined. The women were employed making blankets and knitting garments under the training of the Sisters, and a number of men were working in a saw-mill cutting timber, largely for shipment to Punta Arenas. When I went into the saw-mill and made a remark to these fellows in their own language, they crowded round me. Many of them were splendid specimens, but, though not the tallest, Hektliohlh stood out alone amongst them for his looks and bearing.

These Indian workers were " decently clad " in discarded or shop-soiled garments, generally some sizes too small for them. Looking at them, I could not help picturing them standing in their old haunts, proud and painted, armed with bows and arrows and dressed, as of yore, in *goöchilh, oli* and *jamni* (head-dress, robe and moccasins).

Some of them knew me by sight and many others by report. I am afraid that the work came to a standstill and the lay brothers showed some annoyance at the interruption, so I retired. Later, however, when they broke off work, I was able to have a talk with Hektliohlh. Having escaped from Ushuaia, he had been captured once again, this time by settlers, and handed over to the Silesian Mission. He seemed to have nothing whatever to complain of with regard to his treatment, but was terribly sad at his captivity. Looking with yearning towards the distant mountains of his native land, he said :

" Shouwe t-maten ya." (" Longing is killing me.")

Which was actually the case, for he did not survive very long. Liberty is dear to white men ; to untamed wanderers of the wilds it is an absolute necessity.

2

Paloa was a quiet, middle-aged Indian, rather below medium height, who belonged to the northern edge of the wooded land. With his brother and a few women and children, he was crossing some open country when a small party of mounted police rode out of a valley.

The Ona, wherever they happened to be, always kept in their minds the nearest spot where they could hide in case of need. It might be a forest, a thicket or the bed of a stream. For Paloa it was a cave in a rocky hilltop. He speedily retired there with his little party. He and his brother hid the women and children in the cave, which was very like a dry well with a narrow opening towards the sky. The two men remained in the entrance, hidden by the rocks, but with a good view all around. They were both armed with bows and had plenty of arrows, but the brother would be of little use as a marksman ; his arm was weak from a wound..

When the horsemen rode up, Paloa let fly an arrow. It wounded a policeman. The ground was very rough for horses, and the white men, believing that a considerable number of Indians lurked in the rocks, were loth to dismount. They fired back from their saddles.

An Ona hunter, when looking over a rock for game, will throw his head well back, so that only his nose and eyebrows are exposed to his quarry's view, instead of his forehead and hair.   Paloa knew this, but half his bow had to appear over the rock before he could discharge an arrow. Because of their excited horses, the firing of the police was erratic, but a lucky shot splintered Paloa's bow just above his hand, which was injured, though not seriously.   His brother passed him his bow and Paloa bravely continued to shoot off arrows until the enemy retired baffled.

The policemen returned to the attack the following day with large reinforcements—to find that the birds had flown.   Paloa and his party had escaped to the forest when night had fallen.

I heard the tale of Paloa one night round the camp-fire.   It was recounted amidst jokes and laughter.   I also had the other side of the story.   In this second version, there had been not one, but twenty bow-men hidden among the rocks.   In time, the number of Indian warriors grew to " about a hundred."

3

There were those who did not pay others to do their dirty work, but attended to it themselves.   One of these was Mr. McInch.

It had been an age-long custom among the Ona to go from time to time to certain places on the Atlantic coast and kill seal for the blubber and skins.   On one such occasion a considerable number of Ona ventured to Cape Peñas, a prominent headland where the seal came ashore in hundreds.   Between their forest home and the sea, there were leagues of dangerously open grassland for the party to cross, but the craving for oil and fat seal-flesh was too great a temptation after living for months on lean guanaco meat.

Mr. McInch was warned of the intended hunt by a renegade Ona who had deserted this group for the whites and now harboured a grudge against them.   Armed with repeating rifles and eager for excitement, Mr. McInch and a band of mounted white men encircled the headland, thereby cutting off the retreat of the luckless sealers, who, when the tide rose, were driven from their refuge at the foot of the cliffs into the range of the enthusiastic man-hunters.

I do not know how many natives were killed that day.   Mr. McInch claimed afterwards that they had shot fourteen.   He maintained that it was really a most humanitarian act, if one had the guts to do it.   He argued that these people could never live their lives alongside the white man ; that it was cruel to keep them in captivity at a mission where they would pine away miserably or die from some imported illness; and that the sooner they were exterminated the better. McInch was a most forthright type of man. He never boasted and never made any attempt to appear better than he was. About five feet nine inches in height, he had a broad red face, light red hair and green-blue eyes that really seemed to blaze. He was dynamic in his movements, tenacious and without moral scruples. At times he could look boyishly happy. He had been a soldier and, as a young man, had gone with Kitchener to Khartoum. Even in later years, after continuous hard drinking, he was a wonderful shot with his rifle. At the period with which I am now concerned he was in the middle thirties.

Among those fortunate enough to escape from this massacre was Paloa's cousin, Kilkoat, a tall, lean, hungry-looking Ona who is not to be confused with the merry Kankoat. He escaped with his life by a fraction of an inch; a bullet grazed the side of his head just above the ear, leaving a permanent mark. He left behind him on the headland the lifeless bodies of four near relations, and from a hitherto harmless man changed into a dangerous fugitive, nursing an intense hatred for the white invaders.

He sought out his wife and child and with them lurked in the wooded lands. One day, when they were encamped among the trees not far from the beach, Kilkoat left his family and went off hunting. On his return he found his little camp deserted. He concluded that his wife had gone down to the sea-shore to look for fish in the pools at low water, and went after her. In a reedy swamp between the forest and the shore, he found her dead body with the child, still alive, tied to her back.

She had been shot from behind. The bullet had grazed the child just below the ribs before it had passed into her body. The child survived; I have seen the marks left by the bullet.

Now more than ever Kilkoat thirsted for revenge. It was not long before a party of miners came prospecting within ten miles of the spot where his wife had been killed. Kilkoat watched and waited, until one day he saw a man armed with a rifle walk off alone along the beach, hoping, no doubt, to get something for the pot.

Kilkoat hid behind a rock near which the man had passed, in the expectation that he would return by the same route, which he did. Kilkoat let him go by and, at close quarters, shot him through the back with an arrow. Then, taking his victim's Winchester rifle and ammunition, he hurried away.

4

Under the increasing pressure from the north, the visits of the Ona to Harberton and Cambaceres became more frequent. As the parties from farther afield grew more numerous, we had to be careful not to give cause for jealousy to those who considered they had a prior right to our affection. This was particularly so when a strange party's arrival coincided with that of persons well known to us. When this happened, we would occasionally find dead sheep with arrows sticking into them and so conspicuously placed as to leave no doubt that our older friends sought to throw suspicion on the newcomers.

Soon after Kilkoat had slunk off into the forest with the rifle of the man he had murdered, two such separate groups were at Harberton. Near the homestead were camped Halimink and Ahnikin with six or seven other frequent visitors from the mountains, while a short distance away, with their wives and families, were some twenty more men from farther north. We had met most of these before, but they were not on quite such a familiar footing as the mountain men. I will call them the northern group. Of the party then at Harberton were Kilkoat and his cousin Paloa, the little man who had fought the police single-handed, but foremost among these visitors from the north was a stout, powerfully built, good-natured fellow, close on six feet tall. His name was Kiyohnishah (Guanaco Dung).[1]

While all these Indians were staying with us, I was going through the woods with Halimink, the happy-smiled walker on tiptoe, about two miles from home, when he pointed out a branch some five feet from the ground. There were a few shreds of sheep's wool adhering to it. He remarked quizzically:

" Are your sheep as high as that? "

Halimink was a sly rogue, but somehow I did not suspect him of trying to deceive me. I was never in a hurry to accept their statements

---

[1] This was in no way insulting. The Ona used four types of names: 1. Ancient names, not necessarily ancestral, whose meaning had been lost with the passing of the years. 2. Names of places that were frequent haunts of their bearers, but not always (as with the Yahgans) their places of birth. 3. Names of things or creatures, e.g., Koh (Bone), Te-ilh (Mosquito), Haäru (Upland Goose), Yohn (Guanaco) and Kiyohnishah. 4. Epithets descriptive of personal peculiarity of manner, feature or accident, e.g., Ishtohn (Thick Thighs), Kostelen (Narrow Face) and Shilchan (Soft Voice). There were others that would be considered highly objectionable by our standards, though the natives, through constant use, seemed unconscious of their meaning. It is for this reason that I cannot give the English equivalent of some of the Ona names mentioned in this book. (See also footnote to page 331.)

or innuendoes against each other. This time, however, it looked as if the evidence had not been planted there for my benefit, but that someone had made off with one of our sheep on his shoulder.

A few days later, Shaiyutlh (White Moss), the young man who had spread panic through Ona-land when my companions and I had crossed to Rio Grande, took me on one side and told me in strict confidence that he had seen Kiyohnishah kill two sheep at a place six miles westward.

For a man to allow his family to go hungry is, in my view, far worse than stealing a sheep. For all that, even the lesser crime was not to be tolerated. If two sheep had been killed—whether by Kiyohnishah or by those who wished to see him in disgrace—the matter had to be investigated. The first step was to make sure that the sheep had, in fact, been killed and that White Moss's story was not a product of his imagination, of the fertility of which we had already had proof.

I talked the matter over with Will. He suggested that he should go with White Moss to the spot where the sheep were reputed to have been killed and endeavour to collect enough evidence to be able to accuse the thieves without having to expose White Moss and Halimink as talebearers.

Shortly after Will had set off on horseback—a not unusual proceeding —young Ahnikin came to the house to tell me that Kiyohnishah and his party were breaking camp, preparatory to leaving Harberton for good. I was anxious to be understood and trusted by all these people, feeling that, if they feared us, they might soon become our enemies, so I hurried off with Ahnikin to the encampment, having left my coat at home to show that I had no concealed weapons.

Kiyohnishah's camp was alive with the bustle of departure. I walked up to him and asked him why he was leaving in such a hurry. He promptly replied, no doubt with Capelo's fate in mind:

" Because you intend to kill us and have sent your brother to Ushuaia to fetch soldiers."

I told him that my brother would be back before sunset; that he had not gone to fetch soldiers, but only to see if any of our sheep had been killed.

" Will," I said, " is not a bird. He cannot fly. If, as you say, he has gone for soldiers, they cannot arrive here for several days. If Will does not return to-night and you still mistrust us, there is the great forest where you will be safe from pursuit. You will have plenty of time to leave without haste to-morrow morning."

Kiyohnishah realized from my reference to sheep that I had heard the story. He now blamed the killing onto his dogs and admitted that he had brought the meat home to his people, who were hungry. I told him that, if this should happen again, he must not hide like a fox, but come like a brother, bringing with him the skins, and tell me what had occurred. I assured him that I should not be angry, but would ask him to give me a couple of fox-skins or, if he had no fox-skins, to chop firewood until the sheep were paid for. Evidently Kiyohnishah was inclined to believe what I said and seemed to be calming down, when Kilkoat and his cousin, Paloa, came out from behind a windbreak, followed by other relations. They were much excited and looked threatening, for Kilkoat had his rifle in hand, whilst the others had their bows and arrows.

Kilkoat shook his rifle and his followers their quivers, a typical Ona gesture to intimate that they had plenty of arrows, which they were ready to use. Kilkoat, hoarse with indignation at the thought of his wrongs, shouted to Kiyohnishah not to believe me; that I, like other white men, was a liar and now spoke gently because I was alone and wanted to delay their departure till others should arrive and help me to kill them.

At that moment I noticed to my regret that Ahnikin, who often called me *Yain* (my father), had slipped away, leaving me to face this danger alone. Feeling far from comfortable and knowing that I could not safely retire, I sat down on a log, suggesting to Kiyohnishah that he should do likewise; but he remained standing. It was no use trying to reason with the angry Kilkoat, but I asked Kiyohnishah if he thought I should have come unarmed and alone to visit them in the woods if my intentions had been bad, and I invited him to name the Indians whom I was supposed to have injured or killed. Kilkoat and his friends were still greatly excited, so I began to wonder how the matter would end, when I noticed that something was attracting their attention.

On the edge of a thicket barely two hundred yards distant, wrapped in their robes, with bows and quivers in hand and a band of red paint the full width of a man's hand drawn right across each face from ear to ear, stood Halimink, Ahnikin and six or seven others of that tough mountain gang. When Ahnikin had, as I thought, deserted me, he must have run at speed to tell his little party, who were encamped some distance away, that I was in danger.

The paint alone was a threat, but not to me, and this demonstration seemed to have a calming effect even on the turbulent-spirited Kilkoat, as well as his supporters. A few minutes later I told the northern men not

The Lawrences' homestead at Punta Remolino.

Punta Remolino.
(Whirlwind Point.)

Western's Pass, looking southward towards Harberton.

40

41

Tininisk, the wizard from Cape San Pablo.
From "Los Onas."

Pahchik of the northern group with his wife
and child.

42

43

Halah of the northern group with his wife
and children.

Yoknolpe, finest hunter of all the mountain
men. I never saw him painted in this manner.
From "Los Onas."

to be foolish, but to come with me to the homestead. Then, calling on the other party to join us, I walked off with Kiyohnishah, followed by over two dozen others.

We went to the store, where we got a large sack of dried figs and another of walnuts, which were carried to a suitable spot and divided up amongst the party. Then we sat around on the grass, eating and chatting, in both of which occupations Kilkoat joined.

My brother and White Moss returned that evening, and a few days later Kiyohnishah with his people departed happily to their own country, and Halimink and his party went back to their mountain home.

I hoped that these people would settle their differences and become good friends, but there had to be much bloodshed before, some six years later, this came about.

THE HARBERTON HOME

(*Looking South, left to right.*) The old Home, with store attached; hen house beyond, Gardener's house at the back: boat house: engine house, with saw mill and shearing plant: men's house: stable: married men's houses: large sheds for keeping sheep dry during rain squalls at shearing times. On the hill is the cow house. The distant mountains are on Navarin Island.

My father built the old Home and mother lived there twenty-three years. It was the centre from which we radiated and to which our minds returned. It was a wooden house, sheathed in tarred felt and covered with corrugated iron. It was the wonder of the country, but when the rocky bank on which it was built was excavated (blasting powder had to be used), the wooden piles removed and a brick cellar substituted, our pride in it was complete. My brother Will lives in it now, also the manager, Douglas Henderson, with his family, and it is a striking monument to the founder if that were needed.

HARBERTON

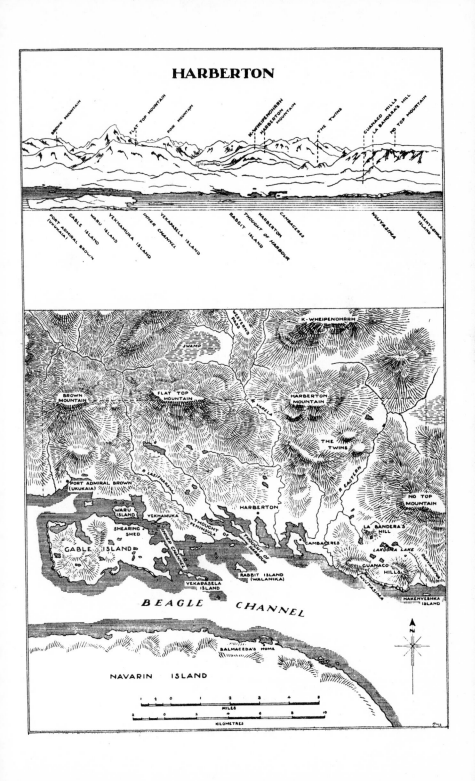

PART III

THE ROAD TO NAJMISHK
1900–1902

CHAPTER THIRTY

We are Invited by the Ona to Live in their Country. My Brothers are Reluctant to Accept, because they are Both about to be Married. Hoping for Adventure I Decide to Start a Settlement at Najmishk and Begin Work on a Road to It. Minkiyolh again Becomes a Menace. We are Visited by Houshken, the Joön of Hyewhin, who Demonstrates his Magic. He is Shown some White Man's Sorcery.

I

IN THE PRECEDING CHAPTER WE SAW EXAMPLES OF THREE METHODS OF approach to the Indian problem in the Tierra del Fuego of the 1890s: the first, extermination; the second, heart-breaking captivity; the third, friendly co-operation based on patiently fostered goodwill, with sympathetic acceptance of the Indians' right to live their lives after their own fashion in the country that was their birthright.

None of the white invaders, whether Mr. McInch and men of his kidney or the Silesian Mission, had had the wonderful advantages enjoyed by my brothers and myself. They had not been born in the country. They had not been brought up to look on the Indian as an intelligent comrade, with whom to work side by side. To them the Fuegians were not individuals, each one to be treated not only on his merits, but also as a fellow human being, but a horde of dangerous, untamed natives, to be wiped out as speedily as possible or, as a less violent expedient, stripped of their hereditary finery, put into a white man's cast-off clothing and expected to work for their living, unless they died as the splendid Hektliohlh had died—as a wild bird in a cage dies—of longing for freedom.

Was it any wonder, then, that the Ona, slowly retreating from the north, should look southward, beyond the boundaries of their own country, for help? Before long, all the lower northern lands would be settled by strangers, and the Ona would have nowhere to go when winter snows drove them—and the guanaco—from the mountains. As their position grew more desperate, party after party came to Harberton with the same entreaty: would we help them by blocking the advance of the ever-encroaching white man from the north?

It was not their plan that we should take up arms and throw back the intruders, but that we should go and settle in Ona-land. Their feeling was that if we secured the land, it would still, nevertheless, be theirs.

The absorbing passion that filled the very being of all these men was their love for their own country. All they wanted was freedom and security. If we gained possession of the land, they would get both; if others walked in, they would get neither. That was their resigned philosophy.

It was indeed flattering to hear one group vying with another in extolling the merits of their own hunting-grounds. Had we accepted all the invitations we received, we should have occupied many thousands of square miles, from the rocky thickets and boggy moors of Cape San Diego in the east, past the snow-capped mountains across the Chilean frontier to the west; and from the wooded, precipitous heights and sponge-like bogs south of Lake Kami to the sea-bird-haunted sandstone cliffs on the Atlantic coast.

I myself was strongly in favour of securing as much land as possible in the Ona country, not only to oblige my Indian friends, but also because I hoped for adventure and—let it be added—felt there was money in the project. My brothers, however, did not share my enthusiasm.

Despard's considered opinion was that it would be both expensive and risky to start a farm over the range. We should not be owners, but squatters, with no assured continuity of tenure. If the land on which we settled were subsequently put up for sale, the wealthy companies who owned vast tracts farther north would always be in a position to bid higher than we could. Access, said Despard, would be more difficult than at Harberton. Our only port would be Rio Grande, which could be used only by small vessels in the summer-time. Moreover, he added, there were the Ona to be taken into account. They had no scruples, and, even if they refrained from murdering us, would certainly not hesitate to steal our sheep. In short, if we wanted to see a return on our money, we could find safer investments elsewhere.

Will's contention was that we already had plenty to live on and that, if expansion were ever called for, we could improve on the land we already had. By clearing bush and draining swamps, it could be made to carry twenty or even thirty per cent. more stock than at present.

It will be seen from these arguments that neither of my brothers was anxious to take any chances. They were not interested in any hazardous enterprise, preferring an assured future to the unpredictable outcome of further adventuring. There was a very simple reason for this: both of them had recently become engaged to be married.

Will had been the first. The girl of his choice was Minnie, the younger daughter of Mr. and Mrs. Lawrence, who had shared with us those early days at Ushuaia. I remember how, when we were little boys, she had no interest in anyone but Will and little sympathy to spare for the victims of his mischievous pranks.

Years after my father had given up his superintendence of the Mission and we had moved our home to Harberton, the Lawrence family had gone to Shumacush (Punta Remolino), where the ageing missionary had received a grant of land from the Argentine government, in recognition of his lifelong service in the cause of civilization.

Our sheep-shearing station was about twenty miles east of Punta Remolino, but the track was so winding that on horseback the distance was very much greater. For a young fellow able to run for miles without a break along steep and rocky paths, it was quicker to go on foot than on horseback.

On those summer days we worked extremely long hours. Saturday was the same as the rest of the week. Will would carry on till the Saturday's work was finished, then stride off in the direction of Punta Remolino, breaking into a run the moment he was out of sight. During the short summer night he might snatch a little sleep on the track, but would nevertheless appear at the Lawrences' homestead as soon as the smoke rising from the kitchen chimney showed that someone was astir. He would spend a happy day there, leaving when the family retired for the night and joining us early on Monday morning, ready for another day's work. Noticing that he sometimes looked rather haggard by Monday night, we remonstrated with him, urging him to leave early on Saturdays, so as to have a good night's rest at Punta Remolino. But Will had a pride of his own. He was determined that neither Despard nor I should ever have cause to feel that he was dancing attendance on his sweetheart and, in consequence, neglecting to do his full share of work at home.

Despard's courtship was not proving such a strain on him, in so far as he could not run to Buenos Aires and back over the week-end. On a visit to the Argentine capital he had met Christina, a daughter of Professor Reynolds, one of Father's oldest friends there. When he returned home, he told us that he and Christina had become engaged.

Now both my brothers were hoping soon to get married. When Will used the argument that the land we already owned could be made to carry as much as thirty per cent. more livestock, I countered by saying that, if we all three married, we should, with any luck, increase our own species at a far greater rate than that, and consequently Harberton would rapidly become too small, not only for ourselves, but also for our ever-growing family of Ona, all of whom had to be supported and supplied with work.

At first my reasoning was of no avail. Neither of them would join me in the venture. The ding-dong discussion lasted for many months, and it was not until the autumn of 1900 that we reached our final compromise. It was agreed that I alone should be actively concerned in the new farm. I was to be free to devote my whole time to it, without giving up my share in the old home. The new farm would be regarded as a separate concern, with its own account in the ledgers. I was to be allowed credit facilities by way of cash, goods, horses, cattle and sheep, all of which would be charged at full value to the account. My brothers undertook to look after Harberton without my help and to share in the expenses of the new farm. They would also participate in the profits, if any. Each of us was to receive a salary of two hundred pounds per annum, mine to be charged to the new account as long as I devoted my whole time to the farm across the mountains.

These essential preliminaries having been settled, I was able to proceed. After some thought, I determined on Najmishk for my settlement. It was some miles to the north of the hunting-grounds of my old friends Halimink and the other mountain men, and was well within the territory of the Najmishk group, some of whose members we had met during the trip that had taken us across the island to Rio Grande. But it was no use starting a farm at Najmishk until we could bring cattle, sheep and horses from the homestead at Harberton to the Atlantic coast. A track would have to be made across the moors and through the forest from Harberton to the open land beyond, and even then there would still be numberless deep, meandering streams and swampy valleys to be bridged before the track would be fit for pack-mules and horses, or even sheep.

To make miles of the timbered track known as corduroy road across the bogs at the back of Harberton was far beyond our powers, but there were many streams winding on stony bottoms across the moors. These we could use during summer and autumn at such times as they were not in flood. I spent many days crossing and recrossing the land between Harberton and Lake Kami before I finally decided where we ought to make our track. There were some big decisions to be made. For instance, at one point there were three passes available through the mountain. Two of them were decidedly lower than the third, yet I ultimately chose the highest and, at first sight, the most difficult. How well those Ona men had explored the country before me is shown by the fact that this third route closely followed the path we had taken on our first tramp with Slim Jim, who had ignored the more inviting gradients of the other two passes.

To avoid certain swamps, I resolved that the track should not come out on the Atlantic coast at Najmishk, but at a spot six miles to the south-east, on the other side of the mouth of the Ewan River. The track would end on the beach along the north-western foot of Tijnolsh Hill, which terminated in a cliff half a mile from the mouth of the river. The rest of the journey from Harberton to Najmishk could then be made along the shingle beach. As the crow flies, the distance from Harberton to that part of the Atlantic coast was just over fifty miles, but the nature of the country would compel my track to wind its way through many miles more than that. Its approximate course is shown on the map facing page 510.

On one of these exploratory trips of mine, I took with me Minkiyolh, the eccentric young man whom the Buenos Aires doctors had judged to be perfectly sane. After a strenuous day, we camped for the night. We made a good fire and collected branches to lie on. While I was arranging my bed, I happened to glance across the fire at Minkiyolh. He had his eyes fixed on me. I have seen many a trapped fox watching the hand about to deal his death-blow. Minkiyolh's face now wore that same expression. A cold shiver of fear ran down my spine, for I knew that the man was as hopelessly insane as he had been on the night he had attacked me with an axe. But now there was no one to help me, and only the dark, silent forest for witness.

I felt that he knew what was passing through my mind; his lip curled in a thin, mirthless smile. I had my Winchester rifle, but at close quarters could hardly have used it, even as a club; and I could not very well shoot him in cold blood through sheer funk.

I gathered enough firewood to last through the night, then sat down with my guanaco-skin robe flung over my shoulders. Seeing that I was not preparing for bed, Minkiyolh asked me if I was not sleepy. I replied:
" Mahshink shoön me ya." (" Sleepy not am I.")

At this, he settled down on his own bed of branches. I believe he slept a good deal during the night, but at other times he was certainly shamming; his breathing was unnaturally heavy and the firelight glinted on his almost closed eyes.

It was a great relief when daylight came, after the long hours of forcing myself to keep awake. When we set out for home, I suggested that Minkiyolh should lead the way. We arrived without incident. His conduct afterwards was quite normal and gave me cause to wonder whether I had given way to an attack of nerves, that night in the woods. He still continued to use Harberton as his headquarters, but would often wander off by himself, sometimes to the Ukukaia saw-mill, where the men found him amusing and his knowledge of Spanish and vivid imagination made him popular. Occasionally he went as far as the Lawrence homestead at Punta Remolino, in quest of admiration and a few free meals.

On one such excursion to the saw-mill, he took his young brother Keëlu, who had accompanied the ill-fated Kiyotimink on his trip to the exhibition at Buenos Aires. Minkiyolh came back from the saw-mill alone. His story was that Keëlu had wandered away from him and must have been drowned in the Lasifharshaj River. Knowing how cautious and capable these young Ona were, no one believed this story, though there was no proof to the contrary. Young Keëlu was never seen again.

Some months afterwards, Minkiyolh visited Punta Remolino. He came away from there in the company of a mulatto, whose body was later found on the beach, which lent itself to the supposition that he had been drowned. Minkiyolh appeared at Harberton looking haggard and distraught. When I asked him where he had been, his answer was evasive. When the mulatto's body was found, Minkiyolh was interrogated. He said he had parted company with the other man soon after leaving Punta Remolino. Once again nothing could be proved against him, so he was allowed to go free.

2

Having decided on the course the track was to take from Harberton to Najmishk, I began work on it. To make room for more sheep, we had disposed of half our herd of cattle and had engaged Contreras, a half-Indian cattle-man from central Chile, to look after the remainder. I was, therefore, free to devote my whole time and energies to the new task, in which I counted on the assistance of my old Ona friends. We started work from Harberton and for the first five miles had to cut through a thick tangle of undergrowth and heaps of large fallen logs. In addition we had to build several corduroy bridges across gullies where the roots of stunted trees formed a treacherous floor over apparently bottomless pools and swamps.

We had broken off one morning for our midday snack when Hechelash, the dwarf, appeared unexpectedly amongst us. He was an ugly little fellow of the northern group, barely four feet tall, thick-set, with big head and bulging stomach, and would have been hideous but for his ingratiating smile, which was at once pitiful and attractive. He may have been somewhat lacking mentally, but was good-natured, unless goaded beyond endurance by some wag, when he would attack his tormentor like a wild creature. Hechelash had no enemies and on that account was often sent [1] forward by the northern men as messenger to some other group.

This time he brought a message from Houshken, who was known as Hyewhin *Joön* (the Doctor of Hyewhin). I had heard much of this elusive magician of the northern group. Imbued with powers above all other wizards, he haunted the wide forests between Lake Hyewhin and the greater Lake Kami. By keeping much to himself, he had enhanced his prestige with the common herd. Amazing stories were told of his magical powers. Besides this, he was a famous hunter and was supported by his powerful brothers, Kiyohnishah (Guanaco Dung), who has already been introduced, and Chashkil, a tall, sturdy young man, and a strong party of relatives that included Kautempklh, a most valiant old warrior. Kautempklh was a very attractive man, whose cheerful good-nature was evinced by his whimsical smile, which would occasionally give place to the keen, fierce look of an eagle. He was of medium height, still very active and, it was said, had never been in a fight without killing his man. With these qualifications, he had acted as leader on more than one of the northern party's raiding expeditions.

The message now brought by Hechelash was to the effect that Houshken was about to pay us a visit. When my Ona companions heard that the great *joön* was near at hand, they wanted to go home. I persuaded them to remain where they were, not only because I was anxious for the work to proceed, but also to show our visitors that we were not frightened of them. Keeping a sharp look-out, we worked steadily on through the afternoon until Houshken appeared in the company of Chashkil, Kautempklh and four or five other stalwart fellows. All were well painted and looking their best in their skin-robes and head-dress, and moccasins with the dark stripe from the guanaco's foreleg running up the instep—the mark of a good moccasin. Every man carried his bow and quiver.

[1] This word has to be used with discretion in relation to the Ona. Certainly Hechelash travelled proudly round with messages from group to group, and boys were sent on errands by their parents, but nobody, were he magician or strong man, gave any orders, except, possibly, in actual attack.

I had met several members of the party before, but not Houshken. He was every bit as tall as myself, lean and broad-shouldered. His glance was searching, yet kindly. His eyes were exceedingly dark—almost blue-black. I had never seen eyes of such colour before and wondered whether Houshken was near-sighted. When I enquired of his friends later, I was told that he could not only see as well as any hunter, but also could look through the mountains at what was going on beyond them.

I had a short, friendly talk with Houshken and his party before they returned to their encampment. They told me that they did not intend to remain long in our neighbourhood, as winter—which was often ushered in with a heavy fall of snow—was drawing near. They had brought with them only a few women, all capable of travelling fast.

It snowed some inches that night. The next afternoon I was told that the newcomers had increased their numbers somewhat and were encamped on the edge of the forest, just over a mile from the Harberton settlement. In the evening, Will and I went to visit them. As these people had come openly, I had no fears, but Will took the precaution of tucking his revolver —with which he was an excellent shot—under his left armpit, inside his loose pilot-coat. Thus he could stand with folded arms—a favourite pose of his when at rest—grasping the weapon with his right hand, ready to shoot through his coat should anyone be foolish enough to embrace him from behind. We took with us a very fine young hound as a gift for Houshken.

I had already taken a great liking to the Doctor of Hyewhin. I gathered that he had never before seen a white man at close quarters, which may have accounted for the long, searching look he had given me in the woods. We presented him with the dog. In spite of his dignity, he could not help showing pleasure, for he remained silent, holding the dog in his arms and pressing it against his body as one would a child. Our conversation—as was always the case at such meetings—was slow, with long pauses between sentences, as though for deep thought. I told Houshken that I had heard of his great powers and would like to see some of his magic. In order to impress him, I told him we would show them some white man's magic in return. It injured nobody and would be performed, I promised him, on the following night. Houshken did not refuse my request, but answered modestly that he was disinclined, the Ona way of saying that he might do it by and by.

After allowing a quarter of an hour to elapse, Houshken said he was thirsty and went down to the nearby stream for a drink. It was a bright moonlight night and the snow on the ground helped to make the scene of the exhibition we were about to witness as light as day. On his return, Houshken sat down and broke into a monotonous chant, which went on until suddenly he put his hands to his mouth. When he brought them away, they were palms downward and some inches apart. We saw that a strip of guanaco hide, about treble the thickness of a leather bootlace, was now held loosely in his hands. It passed over his thumbs, under the palms of his half-closed hands, and was looped over his little fingers so that about three inches of end hung down from each hand. The strip appeared to be not more than eighteen inches long.

Without pulling the strip tight, Houshken now began to shake his hands violently, gradually bringing them farther apart, until the strip, with the two ends still showing, was about four feet long. He then called his brother, Chashkil, who took the end from his right hand and stepped back with it. From four feet, the strip now grew out of Houshken's left hand to double that length. Then, as Chashkil stepped forward, it disappeared back into Houshken's hand, until he was able to take the other end from his brother. With the continued agitation of his hands, the strip got shorter and shorter. Suddenly, when his hands were almost together, he clapped them to his mouth, uttered a prolonged shriek, then held out his hands to us, palms upward and empty.

Even an ostrich could not have swallowed those eight feet of hide at one gulp without visible effort. Where else the coil could have gone to I do not profess to know. It could not have gone up Houshken's sleeve, for he had dropped his robe when the performance began. There were between twenty and thirty men present, but only eight or nine were Houshken's people. The rest were far from being friends of the performer and all had been watching intently. Had they detected some simple trick, the great medicine-man would have lost his influence; they would no longer have believed in any of his magic.

The demonstration was not yet over. Houshken stood up and resumed his robe. Once again he broke into a chant and seemed to go into a trance, possessed by some spirit not his own. Drawing himself up to his full height, he took a step towards me and let his robe, his only garment, fall to the ground. He put his hands to his mouth with a most impressive gesture and brought them away again with fists clenched and thumbs close together. He held them up to the height of my eyes, and when they were less than two feet from my face slowly drew them apart. I saw that there was now a small, almost opaque object between them.

It was about an inch in diameter in the middle and tapered away into his hands. It might have been a piece of semi-transparent dough or elastic, but whatever it was it seemed to be alive, revolving at great speed, while Houshken, apparently from muscular tension, was trembling violently.

The moonlight was bright enough to read by as I gazed at this strange object. Houshken brought his hands farther apart and the object grew more and more transparent, until, when some three inches separated his hands, I realized that it was not there any more. It did not break or burst like a bubble; it simply disappeared, having been visible to me for less than five seconds. Houshken made no sudden movement, but slowly opened his hands and turned them over for my inspection. They looked clean and dry. He was stark naked and there was no confederate beside him. I glanced down at the snow and, in spite of his stoicism, Houshken could not resist a chuckle, for nothing was to be seen there.

The others had crowded round us and, as the object disappeared, there was a frightened gasp from some of them. Houshken reassured them with the remark:

" Do not let it trouble you.   I shall call it back to myself again."

The natives believed this to be an incredibly malignant spirit belonging to, or possibly part of, the *joön* from whom it emanated. It might take physical form, as we had just witnessed, or be totally invisible. It had the power to introduce insects, tiny mice, mud, sharp flints or even a jelly-fish or baby octopus, into the anatomy of those who had incurred its master's displeasure. I have seen a strong man shudder involuntarily at the thought of this horror and its evil potentialities. It was a curious fact that, although every magician must have known himself to be a fraud and a trickster, he always believed in and greatly feared the supernatural abilities of other medicine-men.

My brother was impressed by the ceremony, but had not enjoyed such a good view as I had. Old Kautempklh and other natives had crowded in on him and he had not been sure when he might be obliged to press a little harder on the trigger of the revolver tucked under his left arm.

3

Next evening I kept my word by staging some white man's sorcery. Houshken's party and a number of mountain men came to the homestead, where we had fixed up a magic-lantern in a barn. Besides members of the family who attended the performance, we had a visitor from Buenos Aires. His name was Percy Reynolds, and he was a brother of Despard's *fiancée*, Christina. He was later to become my brother-in-law by marrying my sister, Bertha.

Among the native audience were a good many women. To reassure them, my youngest sister, Alice, sat with them. The magic-lantern was hidden in a back room behind a screen, so that none of our visitors could see it, and was operated by Percy, with Bertha as his assistant. The first pictures to be shown on the screen—a bed-sheet—were of a highly coloured and mildly interesting character. They met with a favourable, but not very excited, reception. The next slide showed us Bluebeard in all his terrible grandeur. By some contraption, he was made to roll his eyes dreadfully as he waved his scimitar. To add to the horror, Percy moved the lantern or fiddled with the focus in such a manner that Bluebeard leapt forward at the agape assembly. This time there was a more decided reaction. There was a hasty retreat for the door. Proven warriors, whose deeds of daring might fill a book, backed away from that frightful apparition. Alice and I tried to check the rush. Houshken was beside me and drew back, visibly frightened, till I put a reassuring hand on his shoulder and said a few calming words. Our old friend Chalshoat, for once wiser than the rest, showed great presence of mind by seizing Alice by the arms in a grip of iron and holding her firmly between himself and the threatening monster. Unfortunately, the Ona word for " picture " or " shadow " was the name of one of their ghosts, so the assurance that this was only a picture would have been no better than telling a frightened child that it was only a bogey-man.

The light was turned on, and at last we managed to calm the Indians and entice them back to view less alarming scenes. We allowed some of them to inspect the apparatus and see how the shadow pictures worked. Then we all went outside for a display of rockets, squibs and Véry lights. The evening was concluded by a repast of biscuit, cocoa and dried fruit.

The following night Will and I again visited the party from the north. Will engaged in a friendly wrestling match with Houshken's tall and robust young brother, Chashkil. The two were fairly equal and made a good show, but did not carry the bout to the extremes customary in sterner Ona encounters, when the struggle continued until one or other contestant was worn out and refused further challenge. Houshken and I, now firm friends, sat close together, watching with dignity while our young men indulged in this sport. Another of our party was a particularly good-looking man called Ohtumn, whom I had met several times before. He was a pleasant-natured fellow, about six feet tall and perhaps thirty years of age.

While Houshken, Chashkil, Ohtumn and the others remained at Harberton, there was much friendly visiting between them and our other Ona friends, Halimink, Ahnikin and men of the mountain group. With such excitement going on, it would have been hard for my helpers to concentrate on the humdrum daily work on the track, so I did not trouble them with it, but joined with great pleasure in the general happy social intercourse. Nevertheless I was not sorry when, after a five days' stay, our visitors started making preparations for departure. Houshken told me that winter was near and they must return to Lake Hyewhin while swift travel was still easy. I invited him to return the next summer and promised to visit him in his own country, which he assured me was very beautiful.

When he and his party finally left us, the mountain and northern men were, to all appearances, on the best of terms. They talked gaily together. Presents were exchanged, and we ourselves gave Houshken and his party some knives and provisions, so they departed well content. I had every reason to believe that the feuds of long ago would be forgotten now. My people, especially Ahnikin, encouraged that conviction by the friendship they had shown towards our visitors. I looked forward to my next meeting with Houshken and Ohtumn, by both of whom I had been most agreeably impressed.

But, alas! I was never to see either of them again.

The south shore of Lake Kami, coming out of the woods from Harberton.

On the track. Will, wearing a beret, fixes a pack-horse.

(*Left*) The track. Good horses were needed on either side to keep abreast of cattle trotting along it. (*Right*) Through the track with sheep.

No. 46.—*By courtesy of Mr. William S. Barclay.*

(*Left*) Te-al, who looked after my sister, with her husband, Ishtohn (Thick Thighs). (*Right*) Yoiyolh, the little medicine-man; Kilehehen; Kautempklh, father of Te-al, with a younger daughter in front of him. Beside her is the daughter of old Hechoh, who is looking over her shoulder. On the right are Minkiyolh and his two wives, Ohmchen (Comb) and Yohmsh, with her baby. The proud mother has fitted him out with a *goöchilh* in anticipation of his future prowess as a hunter.

CHAPTER THIRTY-ONE

Work on the Track Continues. A Guanaco Recluse. A Legend Explained.
Kewanpe Shows her Gratitude in Charming Fashion. The Crime of Halimink and
Ahnikin. The Ona Attitude towards Murder. Tininisk, Otrhshoölh and Te-ilh
Feel Safer.

I

WHEN HOUSHKEN LEFT, WE WENT BACK TO WORK ON THE TRACK. THE DAYS
were fast drawing in and we were spending too much time going backwards and forwards to Harberton, so we decided to camp out and return
to the homestead only for week-ends. The Ona shelters (*kowwhi*) were
made from guanaco hides sewn together. All the hair was plucked or
scraped off and the hides scraped thin for lightness. My own protection
from the weather was a canvas sheet of no great weight, so it was an easy
matter to move on our encampment as the work progressed.

Enthusiasm for the job slackened after the excitement of Houshken's
visit and often there were only six or seven men with me. We were
going through a nasty spell of weather, the snow-laden branches making
work disagreeable. But soon the weather changed for the better. After
the early warning of its approach, winter held off for a time. A thaw,
with a northerly wind and drizzling rain, cleared most of the snow, and
there followed a series of delightful, cloudless days and still, clear nights,
when the stars seemed to stand right out and away from a dark blue sky.
Perhaps it was this welcome change in the weather that revived my Ona
companions. They came along in greater numbers and all worked well.
Only two familiar faces were missing. Some time previously, those fine
young men, Jalhmolh (Slim Jim) and Teëoöriolh, Ahnikin's brother, had
both died after a few days' illness. Pneumonia had, I believe, been the
cause. This tragic double loss had affected us all deeply.

The thaw was followed by a frost. The bogs, streams and patches of
snow became frozen hard, facilitating swift travel over swamp and moor.
I took this excellent opportunity to carry on my exploration of many a
mountain valley, on the chance that some low pass might have escaped my
earlier notice. The country, though beautiful, seemed void of all life.
In spite of the perfect weather, the guanaco had deserted their summer
haunts; doubtless they knew that the season was well advanced.

My guide on one of these excursions was Halimink's half-brother, Yoknolpe, whom Despard and I had rescued from captivity at Ushuaia. He was a taciturn man, slender, active and watchful—the finest hunter of all the mountain men.   As he and I were trudging up a rugged valley, he paused and froze where he stood.   Something had caught his eye.   I was close behind him, and did not move or speak till he slowly drew back and we crouched together.

On the sunny side of the valley clung a large, thick clump of evergreen beech and on the edge of it stood a solitary guanaco, almost indistinguishable in colour from the yellow reeds behind it.   Guanaco meat was always welcome and our camp was only five miles away, so we went after it.   Approach was difficult over the open moor, but Yoknolpe's quick eye soon picked out the best route and we got near enough to the unsuspecting animal for me to shoot it.   I made a fire and roasted a few tit-bits, while Yoknolpe skinned the body and made our bundles ready.   After we had eaten, he seemed in no hurry to depart, but went scouting about in the thicket.

The object of his search proved to be a small cave, with the ground near the entrance trampled like a corral.   This home of the animal I had just killed was dry and clean inside.   In the dust could be seen the place where he had been accustomed to sleep.   These guanaco recluses, braving the long winter in the mountains alone, were very rare.   I was sorry that my hand had removed the sole lord of that wild spot.

That night, discussing the matter round our camp-fire, I suggested that the hermit might have remained there alone in the cave to study guanaco magic.   Instead of laughing, my companions agreed, with serious expressions on their faces, that this was quite likely.

There is a belief among certain white men that guanaco, when old and infirm, go—as elephants are said to do—to lay their bones amongst those of their fellows in a selected dying-ground.   There is a much more matter-of-fact explanation for the accumulated masses of guanaco bones to be found in Patagonia and Tierra del Fuego.   In severe winters these animals forget their differences and join in large groups wherever there is less snow and more chance of finding food.   This tendency to congregate is increased by the fact that it is easier to follow beaten tracks than to break fresh ground through very deep snows.   In Patagonia and northern Fireland, where there are no forests, a fierce blizzard may force guanaco to seek shelter in some clump of bushes where the wind, sweeping over the hills, piles up deep snow all around them.   They will eat the bushes, however hard and thorny, but very soon, having lost all their strength and with a white world of snow stretching for leagues in every direction, they give up hope and, one by one, lie down and die.

After one very severe winter, not many years ago, I counted the bodies of no fewer than fifty-two guanaco lying in an area of less than an acre on the stumps of the hard bushes they had gnawed to the very ground. Only a few miles from the same spot, a friend of mine once counted over two hundred in like condition.

Hence the legend of the guanaco cemetery.

Sheep often meet with a similar fate. They will crowd for shelter into a bush. Then the snow will come and completely bury both sheep and bush. The warmth of the animals' bodies will melt the snow, which will re-form around them in an insurmountable ring of ice. The sheep will eat the bush, gnawing the wood down to the roots, and then starve. The roof of snow will have long ago melted and the lighter snow in the surrounding country disappeared, but the sheep will no longer have the energy to break through that still-frozen ring.

2

Yoknolpe had a wife whose name was Kewanpe. She was a daughter of Te-ilh (Mosquito), the Najmishk *joön*, and here is a story about her. The episode happened soon after the shooting of the guanaco recluse.

Two or three men had stayed near Harberton to do the hunting for the encampment there, but meat had been scarce and we learned that the women were not satisfied at being deserted so long. So it was agreed that the men who were helping me with the track should go hunting in the forest near Lasifharshaj River, some miles to the westward. Once decided, the men set off down the track we had cut. I was glad of an excuse to spend a day or two at Harberton, but for some reason stopped overnight in our encampment and started off alone for the homestead the next morning.

About two miles from Harberton, I saw a woman with a small bundle on her back walking rapidly towards me. It was Kewanpe with her infant child. I stood still till she saw me and stopped. Knowing that she and Yoknolpe were on good terms, I was surprised to see her heading for the mountains alone at this time of year, and asked the reason for it.

" My baby is ill and will die," she answered, " unless I can get to my father Te-ilh, who is a great medicine-man. My husband hates my father, and I must get away quickly before he comes back from the hunt. Last year my other baby died.   My father could have saved it, but my husband would not let me go to him."

I could not advise the woman to return home, as she would have held me to blame if the child died, so I went my way and she hers.   The following day I returned to our encampment in the woods.   Late that night Yoknolpe turned up with his half-brother, Halimink, and asked if I had seen his wife pass that way, as he had called at their encampment and found that she had left with the child.   I told him what he probably knew already by the tracks : that I had met her on the road and that she had gone north to her father's people, adding that he should not be angry with her, as her object in going was to save his child's life.   Halimink, who would rather have been eating meat by his own fireside than hunting a runaway woman, said :

" That is not so.   She has gone back because she hates to be with our people."

But I maintained that he was wrong and that she had gone to try to save the baby's life.   The angry husband did not wait for more argument, but, followed by his brother, hurried off into the night, knowing they must overtake the mother before she reached her father's encampment, where, if she arrived first, they would be powerless and in some danger. She had no means of knowing exactly where Te-ilh might be encamped, nor was there any special track that her pursuers could be sure she would follow.   However, three or four days later, the two men, Kewanpe and the baby arrived back at our encampment.   When I enquired, Yoknolpe told me the child was better and that they had overtaken the mother before she could join the Najmishk party.

Kewanpe now remained with us.   One evening soon afterwards, when I was sitting in front of my little fire, she came over with a nicely baked guanaco head.   The top of the skull had been neatly removed to expose that delicacy, a roasted brain.   She asked me gently :

" Oush ta yohn k-koyerh haiyin yorick? "   (" Does my elder brother long for guanaco brain? ") [1]

I answered, " Karr ya t-haiyin."   (" Much I it long for.")

The woman stood watching me in silence while I finished it, then, producing a bladder containing seal-oil, invited me in almost the same words to take some of that.   I knew the taste of the stuff, so I said with a sigh of repletion :

| [1] " Oush | ta | yohn | k- | koyerh | haiyin | y | orick? " |
| " Is it that | perhaps | guanaco | 's | brain | longs for | my | elder brother? " |

" Omilh me ya." (" Satisfied am I.")

She turned and went back to her fire; and I knew that her husband had told her that I had spoken in her defence when he, with his angry brother, had started to follow her trail.

3

The lovely days could not be expected to continue for ever. Winter was long overdue and soon a heavy fall of snow would smother everything for months. Before many days were out, we should have to stop working at the track on the Harberton side of the range. Several of my Ona assistants now became very anxious to return with their families to their own country before winter began in earnest. This proposal suited me well, for it was difficult to employ Indians to advantage in the depth of winter, besides having to find food for them.

Halimink and Ahnikin proposed to go with the rest, but suggested to me that they should spend the winter working at the portion of the track that was to run through the low forest near the shores of Lake Kami. The snow seldom lay deep there for long, and they would be able to put in a good deal of useful work before spring allowed a resumption of our labours on the Harberton side. I was, of course, fully in agreement with this, but received their next proposition with less enthusiasm. It was to lend them fire-arms. They expressed fear of attack from the northern men who, besides being far more numerous than they, had obtained two rifles some years before from white men they had killed. One of these weapons was in the possession of Kilkoat. As Halimink and Ahnikin would not feel secure against attack, and would not be able to devote proper attention to their work without being adequately armed themselves, they asked me for rifles.

These fellows had been so docile and well-behaved since the killing of Koh and his brothers that I eventually consented and, after much admonition—to which they listened with respectful attention—lent them a couple of old rifles that they had often used when hunting near Harberton. I also gave them a limited supply of ammunition and warned them to keep well within the limits of their own country.

The sky was taking on an ominous leaden hue when, with some axes, the two rifles and a fair load of provisions, the party started off with wives and children, to hasten over the barren land and gain the shelter of the forest that clothed the northern slopes of the range. They had not been gone long when great snowflakes began to fall. By the second day a southerly gale sprang up, and it was with the greatest difficulty that they managed to reach a place where they could camp for the night. The men had to carry all the smaller children and help some of the women with their loads.

4

Late one evening in July, in the depth of that winter, two tough, haggard-looking Indians arrived at Harberton and knocked violently at our back door. When I went to open it, they were standing on the ice-covered clearance, with the shovelled snow piled up high behind them. They were dressed in their moccasins and head-dress, carried bows and quivers and clutched their only garment of guanaco skin around their naked bodies.

Both men were known to me. One was Halah, a strong, square-jawed, determined fellow; broad of shoulder and about five feet nine inches in height. The other was Chashkil, the brother of Kiyohnishah and the great medicine-man, Houshken, the *Joön* of Hyewhin. Knowing the conditions prevailing in winter-time on the moors and mountains that these two gaunt and weary men had had to cross, their visit to the homestead filled me with grave misgivings. Theirs was no trivial mission. I asked them the reason for their long journey and, excited yet dignified, they told me their tale.

Halimink and Ahnikin had gone north with the rifles I had lent them; from their own hunting-grounds into the lands of the northerners. They had encountered a small party, which had included Houshken and Ohtumn, the pleasant, good-looking man who had so impressed me on my meetings with him. Halimink and Ahnikin had approached openly with smiles of friendship. Remembering the happy days they had all spent together at Harberton, Houshken and the others had been convinced of their good intentions. Then, when all precautions had been thrown aside, Halimink and Ahnikin had suddenly opened fire on them, killing both Houshken and Ohtumn.

More shooting would have followed had not Halimink's rifle jammed after the first shot. The murderers had made good their escape, Ahnikin having taken with him Houshken's elder daughter for his wife. Kilkoat, the stormy petrel, had not been one of Houshken's party.

That was the tragic story told me by Chashkil and Halah. These two courageous men had run the gauntlet through their enemies' country to find out if their people could still count on a welcome at Harberton or whether, as some of them suspected, I had lent the rifles to Halimink and

Ahnikin in order to reduce the numbers of the northern men. Most of them did not really believe this, but wanted to hear a denial from my own lips. Another reason for this visit was to ensure that I heard their version of the story first.

Naturally I disclaimed all evil designs against Houshken and his followers. With this earnest declaration Chashkil and Halah seemed content, but they upbraided me bitterly for having supplied the fire-arms with which the crime had been done. They did not tarry long at Harberton. When they departed, I was left with the sorrowful knowledge that, in one deadly stroke, Halimink and Ahnikin had undone all the good work of the past and sown the seeds for a new era of bloody factional warfare.

5

Among the Ona it was not looked upon as wrong to kill a man of another group. The Ona axiom was, "If I do not kill him, he will certainly kill me if he thinks he can gain anything by it." It was also quite in order to kill a man of another group to get his wife, even though the slayer had a wife already. In addition, it was an accepted practice to slaughter at the same time as many of the victim's friends as possible, thereby reducing their power to retaliate on some later occasion. Yet these killings were not indiscriminate. They were man-to-man affairs. When the fight took place at the encampment, the women and children who could not bolt pulled the loose guanaco skins over their heads and yelled with fear and indignation. Any infraction of the rule against killing women and children was frowned upon. I recall one raid (it shall be mentioned later) when, in the absence of a warrior, his two little sons were killed instead. Members of the assassin's party were loud in their disapproval of this unseemly deed.

Undoubtedly the principal reason for these murderous attacks was to procure additional wives. A second reason—often used as an excuse for the first—was to destroy the *joön* of the other group. I have recorded on an earlier page how I was reluctant to become a witch-doctor, for fear I might be blamed for a fatal heart attack a hundred miles away. Sudden death from illness was always put down to witchcraft. It was assumed that the magician of a rival party had introduced into the anatomy of the deceased some creature or evil presence that had slowly devoured his vitals until he had died.

The local medicine-man might spend nights and days in tremendous mental and physical effort, while the bereaved relatives hovered round, listening avidly to his ejaculations as he received inspiration from embers, ashes, the land of shadows, or anywhere else. Ona magic was not merely on land or in the sky; it was everywhere. At the termination of this exhausting performance, the " family doctor " would direct suspicion, obliquely or by implication, against some rival *joön*.

This was a very useful arrangement for the local medicine-man. He not only pleased his clients, but also ridded himself of a dangerous competitor—or paved the way for it. The relatives found it equally satisfactory, because it gave them an excuse for a punitive expedition—always a welcome diversion—and also a chance to acquire desirable young women from the families of their victims.

Here, in the murder of Houshken and Ohtumn, was a case in point. The motive for this crime of Halimink and Ahnikin was revenge for the deaths of Slim Jim and Teëoöriolh, who had been Ahnikin's brother. Houshken's fame as a wizard must have been the envy of lesser exponents of the black arts; and the favourable impression he had made at Harberton had doubtless added fuel to the flame of their jealousy. What more easy than for Halimink and Ahnikin to seize the opportunity afforded by the deaths of Slim Jim and Teëoöriolh to remove for ever a neighbour as dangerous to Tininisk, Otrhshoölh and Te-ilh as Houshken?

A glance at the comparatively recent history of witchcraft in England, Europe and America should persuade one not to judge the Ona too harshly. They were in the act of taking, in one generation or less, the stride from prehistoric man to a civilization that has taken us thousands of years to accomplish, if we can be said to have accomplished it yet.

CHAPTER THIRTY-TWO

Halimink and Ahnikin Ask for More Ammunition. The Elusive Te-ilh and Why He Avoided White Men. With the Coming of Spring, Work on the Track is Resumed. The Honesty of the Ona. Our Camp is Visited by Kiyohnishah, who is Rightly Indignant.

I

EARLY IN THE FOLLOWING SPRING, HALIMINK AND AHNIKIN TURNED UP alone at Harberton. They casually asked for a further supply of ammunition and for Halimink's rifle to be repaired. When I taxed them with it, they freely admitted the murder of Houshken and Ohtumn and claimed praise for the exploit. They were surprised and disappointed when I not only refused to give them ammunition, but also insisted that both rifles be returned to me forthwith. This lack of sympathy was beyond their comprehension, and it was not until I had warned them that, if they did not comply with my request, our friendship would be at an end and I should have no further dealings with them, that they surrendered the fire-arms. I gave them some provisions and told them that I would join them a little later on in their own country, so that we could carry on the work they had started near Lake Kami.

They were not pleased with me. Complaining indignantly that I had taken the rifles away from them so that their enemies could kill them more easily, they went off back to Lake Kami, leaving me to speculate upon the reception I should receive when I met them there.

2

It was a certainty that the northerners would not take the killing of Houshken and Ohtumn lying down. Sooner or later Kiyohnishah, Chashkil, Halah, Kilkoat and the others would come south, bent on revenge. This meant danger not only to Halimink and Ahnikin, but also to the Najmishk folk, with whom they were connected.

Te-ilh of Najmishk, father-in-law of Yoknolpe, was credited with no little magical power. Physically he was immensely strong. Not more than five feet six inches in height, he had an expanse of chest and shoulders that I have seldom seen equalled. I met him only three or four times, for he was exceedingly wild and avoided any contact with the whites. This was due to an encounter on the Atlantic coast near Najmishk with a party of miners. Te-ilh, another man called Koiyot and two companions had approached the miners' encampment. The miners had signalled them to advance and, when they had drawn near, had opened fire on them with rifles. The two other men had been killed, but Te-ilh and Koiyot had gained the shelter of the woods.

The miners had claimed afterwards that they had shot the Indians because they had tried to steal a hand-saw. It was a feasible story, for a saw was greatly valued by the Ona; it could be broken up into a number of pieces and turned into knives and other tools. It is more probable, however, that the shooting had been done to prevent the Indians from going away and coming back with reinforcements; or—which was even more likely—that the two men had been shot because they had been wearing fox-skin robes, which were always much coveted by white men.

After this narrow escape, Te-ilh kept well away from the northern *cristianos* and ventured only three times to Harberton and then did not stop long. I was sorry not to get better acquainted with this sturdy fellow. From all reports, he was quite an exceptional man.

Koiyot became much better known to me. Like Te-ilh, he was short, broad and inclined to corpulence. Neither of them conformed to the fine Ona standard of manly beauty.

3

Spring had come. The snow had nearly all gone from the low land, and all the forest trees except the dwarf beech showed signs of bursting into leaf. It was time to get in touch with our wandering friends across the range and to carry on work at the track. I knew how glad they would be to have some civilized food after the hard winter, so decided to take as much as could be carried of rice, sugar, ground maize, fat and coffee.

I chose as my companions the merry Kankoat and the dull, lumbering Chalshoat. In addition to the food, we would have to carry cooking and eating utensils, a dozen large axes and some shovels. Kankoat took it upon himself to arrange our respective loads. I was amused to see how he divided them. All the heaviest items were added to Chalshoat's burden, so that, although Kankoat and I were called upon to carry well over a hundred and twenty pounds apiéce, Chalshoat's load exceeded ours by half as much again.

When all was ready we set out. The first five miles through the woods were not bad going, but in the hollows on the moors beyond there were still large patches of snow. One great drift we encountered was over forty feet deep. Where the snow was shallow, we would often break through with a jerk into the water below. But Chalshoat followed doggedly on without a word of complaint.

On the fourth day we found, near Lake Kami, the beginnings of the track through the woods that had been put in hand by Halimink and Ahnikin during the winter. A useful attempt had also been made at laying a corduroy bridge across a swamp. That same afternoon we met Halimink and another Indian. They had been expecting us and had no doubt seen us before we saw them; but, according to Ona custom, they gave no indication that they had come out to meet us. Instead they strolled across our track and just " happened " to fall in with us in a casual way.

After a chat we went to their encampment, where we spent the night. They had plenty of lean guanaco meat, but were glad to see the food we had brought with us. Men, women and children all shared our stew and the coffee that followed.

They were living in constant fear of a return attack by Kiyohnishah and his party. Knowing as they did that their enemies would come in overwhelming numbers and try to take them by surprise, they were scattered about the wooded country in twos and threes, keeping a sharp look-out. Their hope was that the numbers of different tracks in all directions would delay the enemy and give themselves time to scatter still further. These tactics, together with a perfect knowledge of their own country, would enable them to travel faster than their pursuers and maybe, by choosing their own ground, do some damage to the northern band as they fled. They would have to desert their families, though some of the younger women might go with them. The older women and children would be safe enough from their enemies. As has been said, the killing of women and children, even small boys, for revenge was practically unheard of in those days.

That night we sat late around the fire, making our plans. Halimink knew, to within a few leagues, where his friends were likely to be found, and we agreed that he should go off the following day and collect them together at a pre-arranged spot. This he accordingly did and it was not long before ten or so of the old brigade were collected there with their families. Among them were Talimeoat, the bird-hunter, and his tall, pale, gentle-mannered cousin, Puppup. We began cutting our track

southward through the woods towards Kami, which was only three or
four miles away.

Apart from the risk of attack, our chief anxiety was food. There
might be only ten or twelve willing fellows, but their households—the
old men, women and children—brought the mouths to be fed up to five
times that number; and fifty or sixty people could not be fed for long on
food brought by three men, even though one of them had been the stalwart Chalshoat. For this reason we were obliged to live almost entirely
on guanaco meat, to procure which we frequently had to go a long
distance. I found that living in this frugal fashion, especially at that time
of the year, when the meat was exceedingly lean after the rigours of the
winter, kept one as strong and active as ever, but inclined one to be lazy
and unwilling to exert oneself. Even the vigorous Ona noticed this.
When I could give them stews, with rice or beans and vegetables, and
follow up with sweetened tea or coffee and ship's biscuits, there was a
marked improvement in the energy they displayed.

I placed our treasured civilized foods into the care of one of the
families, who doled it out as and when I required. This was my usual
practice on such expeditions and never once did I have cause to complain
of theft or unauthorized use. I once left a bag of biscuits hanging under
the branch of a tree in a spot frequently passed by Indians. On the
advice of one of them, I left my footprints by well treading the ground
around the tree, so that everyone should know to whom the biscuits
belonged. When I came back ten days later, other footprints than mine
were near the tree, but the tempting food had not been touched.

We were drawing near to Lake Kami with our track when Hechelash,
the dwarf, arrived with a message from Kiyohnishah, saying that he and
a few of his party would visit us on the following day. This introductory
procedure left nothing to be desired, but it was no friendly message;
Kiyohnishah and his people had a grudge that sooner or later had to be
settled.

We had known for some time that we were under observation.
Tracks had been seen and also tired guanaco that had been chased by other
dogs than ours. So this message was no surprise to us. What did
astonish us was that, when Kiyohnishah and his friends duly kept their
appointment, they did not come alone, but brought women and children
with them and, furthermore, set up a temporary encampment in full
view, two hundred yards from us, across a little stream.

I was puzzled what to do. I had my repeating Winchester rifle with

me. If I carried it in my hand when I went out to speak with Kiyohnishah, they would think that I did not trust them; and might also be
tempted to take it from me by force, to use against their enemies. Alternatively, if I left it behind, Halimink or one of the others might seize the
opportunity thus offered and open fire with it on the northern men. I
solved the problem by emptying the magazine, stowing my whole
supply of ammunition in my pockets and going out to welcome the newcomers with empty hands.

Kiyohnishah came a short distance to meet me. With him were his
brother, Chashkil, and Halah, who had come with Chashkil to Harberton
during the winter. My party remained behind in our encampment,
looking over the tops of their tents, which they had arranged as shields.
Guanaco skins hanging loosely, with the fur towards the enemy, would
check an arrow in its flight.

By nature, Kiyohnishah was a good-tempered, reasonable man,
qualities shared by his brothers, Chashkil and the late Houshken. Now,
in his dignified way, he was angry; rightly indignant with Halimink
and his fellow rascals for having so treacherously slain Houshken and
Ohtumn; and with me for having so foolishly trusted them with the
rifles with which the cowardly deed had been done. He called on my
party to come out and speak like men, upbraiding them for their cowardice
and perfidy. From behind their defences, they answered him back, but did
not emerge into the open; an extremely feeble performance, I thought,
for my sympathies were with the visitors. It was my habit to remain
strictly neutral in these inter-group squabbles, but this time I was concerned
in the affair and derived no satisfaction from the part I had played.

As the long-range interchange of epithets continued, some of the
visiting children began to play on a log that bridged the stream between
the two camps. One of them was Kiyohnishah's small son. Happening
to glance in that direction, I saw the child fall off the log into the water.
I ran there as fast as I could and pulled the little fellow out.

The father was not many yards behind me when I did it, and I have
thought since that that incident may have been the reason why he refrained
from challenging me to a rough wrestling match—that much-favoured
Ona method of venting anger.

The party moved off quietly before nightfall. Yet the issue had not
been decided; the reckoning merely deferred. I was left with a feeling
of dread hard to define. It seemed as if the shadow of a crime hung over
our encampment in those quiet woods.

CHAPTER THIRTY-THREE

*Heuhupen Sends the Rain and We Defy Her. I Go Wife-Hunting with Halimink.
Ona Method of Welcoming the Belated Hunter, with Some Account of Fuegian
Torches. Halimink, Chalshoat and I Attempt to Ford the Varela River.*

I

MANY OF THE MOUNTAINS IN ONA-LAND, ESPECIALLY THOSE SEPARATED
from the main range, were human beings long ago and should be treated
with respect. That was the Ona legend. It was considered extremely
bad manners to point at any of them. At such rude behaviour, they
might wrap themselves in cloud and bring on bad weather. One of
these was Heuhupen, the table-land that had once been a witch.

We had cut through a considerable tract of timber-land still wet with
winter snow, had carried our track southward along the eastern shore of
Lake Kami, and were now striking into the great forest of deciduous
beech that clothed the northern slopes of the range. Our axes gave out
sounds such as had never been heard in those regions before; they were
breaking the silence of ages.

Ahead of us, about two miles away, was Heuhupen, her flattish top
reaching just above upper tree level. Her steep sides were forest-covered,
except where the great slide of rock, which I had noticed during the trip
with Slim Jim, had left her bare of trees. Her two daughters, less conspicuous than she, stood out on either side of their mother. I have
forgotten their Ona names.

We carried the track past Lake Kami and worked on towards these
mountains. After a day or two, the sky became overcast and it began
to rain. I had my sheet of canvas, and the natives their *kowwhi* stretched
over sticks planted on the windward side of the fire. In these shelters it
was possible to lie or crouch and keep fairly dry, but in a downpour that
showed no signs of stopping, it became wearisome after a time. When
the rain had continued throughout the second day, my Ona companions
began to voice the suspicion that Heuhupen, objecting to her peace being
disturbed by the sound of our axes, had influenced the weather against us.

Everything possible was done to stop the rain. We went outside our
windbreaks, one, two or three at a time, brandishing flaming firebrands
and shouting in a derisive yet threatening manner at Mohihei and Kow-

koshlh, two long-since departed medicine-men who had once had great influence with the fresh westerly breeze, which could blow the rain away. "Pwhrah, Mohihei! Pwhrah, Kowkoshlh!" was our cry. "Pwhrah!" was a shout of ridicule, often accompanied by laughter; it was used as a jeer when someone had made a particular fool of himself. Mohihei and Kowkoshlh were always invoked in that order—never Kowkoshlh first. When night came the men removed the flint or glass heads from their arrows and inserted specially prepared glowing embers in their places. These they then discharged with full force and a wild, but different, yell of defiance in the direction from which the rain came. As these primitive rockets sped on their way, the breeze of their flight would cause them to flare up, lighting the glistening foliage overhead with a bright glow that made against the surrounding blackness a brief, attractive picture. In response to the entreaties of the Indians, I fired, with the appropriate shouts, two or three of my treasured bullets in the required direction, but our united efforts were of no avail.

We had no influential witch-doctor with us at the time;. Puppup made claim to being a magician of only extremely limited powers. When politely invited to help when all we others had failed, he smilingly answered:

"Goötn me ya." ("Disinclined—lazy—am I.")

However, he kept a sharp look-out for the slightest sign of Kenenik-haiyin (the westerly wind). When he thought the moment was near, he arose with the greatest dignity and took a piece of burning wood (not a torch), with which he went through the same performance with regard to Mohihei and Kowkoshlh as we had done, but with even louder gestures and cries than those that we had used in vain.

The following morning the rain stopped and we were able to put in some hours of useful work. Then, in the afternoon, Heuhupen wrapped herself in her mantle again and down came the rain once more. Mohihei and Kowkoshlh had reacted to the taunting of Puppup and had summoned Kenenikhaiyin; but Heuhupen was stronger than all of them. The suspicions during the first downpour now became a certainty: Heuhupen, who had once been a witch, was displeased with the noise we were making. We must make a big detour to the west. It would lead us through more broken country than the route we had proposed to take and would make the road to Najmishk much longer, yet Halimink, Kankoat and the others felt that it was the only thing to do. I listened with respect to their arguments, feeling I had no more right to ridicule, or even ignore, their age-old superstitions than they had to scorn our religious services and customs. As they spoke, I wondered how I should answer if, in later years, I was ever asked why we had not followed the obviously better and straighter road. Would I reply that the mountains had objected to the noise of our axes and had sent heavy rain, so that we had been obliged to make the detour to secure fine weather?

I had no desire to go the long way round. I played for time. I told my companions that I remembered some very heavy rains on occasions when we had given the mountains no cause for offence by the sound of our axes. I suggested that we should talk the matter over the next morning.

We awoke to find the weather was perfect. A fresh breeze from the west soon shook the moisture from the branches. I waited till the sun was well up, then called my helpers around me. I suggested to them that the women should shift the encampment close to the foot of Heuhupen, where there was a lovely glade in which we had camped before. We ourselves would go close to the mountain and start working hard, as though not afraid to make a noise. If it came on to rain again, I promised we would make the track well to the westward. If, on the other hand, the rain held off, we should know that, when it did come, it came of its own accord and not at the behest of Heuhupen.

After some debate, they agreed rather reluctantly to this proposal. The women moved camp and we workers put in a noisy and highly successful day with our axes. I need not mention with what anxiety I watched the sky, and the summit of Heuhupen, during that and the following days. But fortunately the weather held and all was well.

2

We were, whilst making the track, a happy party, moving our encampment from time to time, as the work advanced southward. My store of civilized food had dwindled away to nearly nothing, and now we were reduced to living almost entirely on guanaco meat. The two kinds of tree fungus found growing at that time of year have hardly any food value. The very young deciduous beech trees yield an edible sap. By stripping the bark from the saplings when the trees are coming into leaf, a woody liquid can be scraped off. It does not take long to collect a pint of it, but even a hungry person can enjoy only a small quantity, on account of its acrid taste, which roughens the tongue and throat.

After the day's work, we often amused ourselves by wrestling. The earnestness with which the little boys applied themselves to it entertained

Kaichin on the road to Ushuaia at a later date.

The Governor's house at Ushuaia.

By courtesy of Col. Charles Wellington Furlong.

Aneki (Left-Handed), Koniyolh, Ishiaten (Scratched Thighs), Kostelen (Narrow Face), Shilchan (Soft Voice), brother of Aneki.

From "Los Onas."

Standing: Kilehehen, later my adopted father, and Shishkolh. Seated at the back: Kautempklh, Halah, Hechoh (the only Ona glutton I ever met) and, against the tree, Pahchik.

Aneki, Kostelen and Shilchan. Notice Shilchan's second arrow held in readiness in his left hand. This was a general practice.

From "Los Onas."

us greatly. But during all our work and play, we were haunted by the knowledge that Kiyohnishah and his band were only waiting for an opportunity to strike some deadly blow. In consequence our nerves were strained, and a sound at night—the sudden barking of a dog or the cry of a startled bird—was enough to alarm us. We kept together and nobody strayed alone far from the encampment. When the guanaco grew scarce in that district and the need for meat to feed many mouths became urgent, we were faced with a problem. Should some of us stay at the encampment and carry on the work while others went for a few days' hunting? This would weaken our party by division. Two or three men could not work and keep a sharp look-out at the same time. A shower of arrows might then be the first warning of a visit from unfriendly Indians attracted to the scene by the ringing of the axes. The alternative was for all of us to go hunting, leaving the women and children behind.

After due discussion we decided on the alternative; it was not only a safer arrangement, but also gave us all a little relaxation from tree-felling. None of us would have been too willing to remain at work while the others hunted.

With the intention of staying away for two or three days, we started off together, walking at speed to put as many miles as possible between us and that disturbed area before we scattered for the hunt. About two miles from our encampment, however, a lone male guanaco was sighted. It was moving swiftly away and already well beyond bow-shot, but a bullet from my rifle brought it down. The women at the encampment were already short of meat, so it was decided that, to relieve them of a diet of tree fungus and sap, Halimink and I should return with the guanaco, while the others went on to procure a good supply of meat.

When Halimink and I got back to camp with our load early in the afternoon, I was not sorry to take a rest. I took off my moccasins and lay down in my little shelter on the couch of dry grass and fragrantly budding twigs that the women, unasked, always gathered for my bed. Halimink rejoined his family in a larger kowwhi a few yards away.

From the sounds I heard, I gathered that all was not well with the Halimink household. Instead of lying down with an exaggerated air of exhaustion, intended to impress the women with the heroic efforts we had made to bring supplies in time, my friend's voice became harshly raised and he started running round the encampment, darting from one kowwhi to another, excitedly questioning the women in turn.

The reason for all this commotion was the disappearance of Akuke-yohn, widow of Koh and the younger of Halimink's two wives. As soon as we had left camp that morning, she had packed up a small bundle and slipped away, with the apparent intention of deserting her lord and master. Halimink could gain no information as to the direction she had taken. Impatiently breaking off the useless babbling of the women, he suddenly turned and, with a resolute expression, hastened off into the forest.

Knowing that he would certainly be killed if sighted when alone by almost all members of any other group, I did not imagine that he would go far, so was not surprised when, some ten minutes later, he appeared beside my couch. As I sat up he said:

" My wife has left me and I must follow her. Do you grudge lending me your rifle, in case I meet bad people in these woods? "

I did not remind him how he had misused the rifle I had lent him less than six months before, but said instead:

" Am I able to defend myself with bow and arrow, like an Ona? If I lend you my rifle, I shall be as helpless as the women in the encampment."

" Maybe," he replied dolefully, " you are too tired to come with me, and I shall be killed."

Even had I been very weary, I could not have acknowledged such weakness; nor could I resist so plaintive an appeal thus cleverly made. I put on my moccasins, took my rifle and told him to lead on.

Our encampment was surrounded by miles of unbroken forest of the tall deciduous beech known to the Yahgans as *hanis*, to the Ona as *kual-chink*, and to the learned as *Nothofagus antarctica*. Here and there were stony ridges where the trees were dwarfed for lack of soil. In most other places there was an enormous amount of fallen timber which, long in decaying, lay about in all directions. The gaps these fallen giants had left overhead encouraged the rising of another generation of trees that swarmed up, choking one another to death in their struggles towards the sunlight.

Through this tangled maze we went off in search of the younger Mrs. Halimink; a quest that was made more difficult by the countryside for a considerable distance around the encampment having been criss-crossed and criss-crossed again by women searching for tree-fungus, sap or fire-wood, and by adventurous youngsters hopefully preparing for the days when they would become distinguished hunters. But this did not trouble my light-footed little companion, who followed a trail quite invisible to me, and slipped round, under or over every obstacle at such a speed that I had as much as I could do to keep up with him.

As I stumbled along behind him, my mind was filled with unkind thoughts about Akukeyohn. Instead of reclining near the fire, plaiting or ornamenting some piece of hide gear for the horses, or chatting with the women and noting down Ona words, I had to go hurrying through these thickets. I had seen many Ona women with numerous scars (principally on their heads) said to have been inflicted by irate husbands, and two or three times during my years with them I heard cries and the sounds of blows, but whatever my inclinations, I did not think it wise to interfere between husband and wife. On this occasion I had not the slightest desire to raise my voice in protest against anything Halimink might do if, in some incredible fashion, he managed to track down the fugitive. I was very angry with that young woman and positively gloated over the thrashing she was in for at the hands of her exasperated spouse. I was even indignant enough to have enjoyed administering the chastisement myself.

We hurried on for over an hour, then Halimink stopped with a puzzled expression. I took the opportunity to suggest that his wife had more likely gone south to Harberton than in the north-easterly direction that we were following. He gave me a long, quizzical, rather pitying look and deigned me no answer. Presently a bright thought seemed to strike him. He walked back some ten paces to a spot where we had stepped over a large fallen tree that lay across our track. We got on the log and I followed him along it to the far end, where in the tree mould, plain even to my eyes, were two little heel-marks where the young lady had jumped down.

We went cautiously forward, not because the trail was difficult to follow, but for another reason. After going about a hundred yards, Halimink stopped and beckoned to me. In a little hollow, with her bundle under her head, lay the younger Mrs. Halimink fast asleep.

My friend sat down noiselessly on a log near his wife, whilst I, in order not to embarrass him or the lady, kept in the background, pretending to be absorbed in the movements of the little forest birds that had recently arrived to spend the summer with us. I expected to hear a burst of re-criminations from Halimink, followed by shrieks of indignation, or wails of woe from his wife, but no such sounds reached my ears. Instead I heard a hearty laugh from Halimink, which awakened his wife and made me draw near to find out the cause of his merriment. In answer to my question he said:

" I was thinking that if you had a wife and she ran away, you would never be able to find her again."

So Akukeyohn did not get her beating after all.

3

Our comrades came back with good supplies of guanaco meat which kept us going for a while, but all too soon it became necessary to go hunting again. The northern men seemed to have left the district. No sign of them or their camp-fires had been seen for some time. It was decided, therefore, to reverse our former procedure and divide forces. Two small parties of hunters went off in different directions, leaving the rest of us to carry on with the work.

At dusk, with a light drizzle loading the budding undergrowth with water, one of the parties returned—empty-handed. Night fell and the darkness was as black as pitch. We gave up hope of the second party returning that night and made our supper by scraping the meat off the few bones still hanging up and breaking them open for the marrow.

Our fires were getting low, and some of us had already drawn our robes around us and settled down for the night in the driest spots we could find beneath our inadequate shelters, when a feeble glimmer of reflected light was noticed high up on a nearby tree-trunk. Presently the light flickered and went out, but soon it reappeared on the shiny trunk. There could now be no mistake; it was the reflection of a torch, waved in the air from time to time to make it flare up. Our second party of hunters was returning.

The dogs grew excited and began to bark. Soon we saw our be-draggled friends, heavily laden with meat, approaching through the tangled woods, with the torch, dexterously manipulated by the leader, lighting up the whole scene like some illuminated picture. At a sugges-tion from Kankoat, we all started barking like dogs to welcome the successful hunters. The Ona were good mimics and now, accompanied by the real dogs, they raised babel in those silent woods. Women and children joined in the chorus.

Mixed with the joyous barking, one could hear angry growls and whining from some of the human dogs. I noticed Kankoat and another man snarling at each other and baring their teeth in such realistic fashion that they might have been on the point of flying at each other's throats.

This performance in honour of hunters who had pushed on through the darkness and vile weather with vital food for their families and friends, instead of camping comfortably for the night, had a name that I cannot recall. I have been present on only four such occasions. The second time, Yoknolpe (Halimink's half-brother) and I were the hunters. The joyous reception, so seldom indulged in, was ample reward for having carried on well into the night with torches through the soaking forest, rather than light a fire, feed abundantly and stay there till daylight, whilst our companions back in camp were on short commons.

The Ona torches are worthy of description. When light was needed for a journey through the night, the hunter groped around until he found a sloping tree with dry bark on its under side. With pieces of this bark he got a fire going. By the light of the fire he collected more dry wood, standing it on end round the little flame to create a draught. When a good-sized blaze had been got going, it lighted up the surroundings sufficiently for the hunter to find the necessary strips of bark for his torch. Three such strips were required, each three feet long and about four inches wide. These were tied together at intervals, with short transverse pieces of stick as thick as a man's finger to keep them apart. The torch was then lighted from the fire and the hunter proceeded on his way, periodically waving the torch in the air to keep the flame alive.

The Ona hunter carried tinder and flint in a waterproof bladder tucked under a thong tied round his waist. After my experience during the cattle-hunt behind Flat Top, I adopted a similar procedure by carrying my matches in a corked metal cartridge-case in a belt worn against my body. Then, even if I lost my clothes, I still had my precious matches. And what, it may be asked, of the white hunter who finds himself without matches in the wintry woods and must have a fire? Does he rub two sticks together till they ignite, or does he shoot off his gun into a heap of dry grass or twigs? The first needs some science and special wood, and as for the second, in practice the blast from the gun blows the fuel away. A better method is to take the driest available piece of cloth, or spider's web or any light fluff, then work the bullet out of a cartridge (which may not be easy) and put the tinder in its place. The heap of dry grass or twigs is next collected and the shot fired. The tinder may come out of the gun smouldering, in which event it can be applied to the heap and blown into flame.

4

As work on the track proceeded, our axes became increasingly in need of a good grinding and we all longed for sweetened coffee, biscuit, etc., so it was decided that I should go with Halimink and Chalshoat to spend a few days at Harberton, taking with us five blunt axes to put in order, and bring back fresh supplies of provisions. The truth was that I was badly in need of some days of home life after living solely on guanaco meat, which, as already stated, is always lean after the winter. Out in the forest I had begun to dream that I was at tea with Mother. Bread and butter, cake and other delights of civilized life, such as Yekadahby specialized in and loved to place before the returned wanderer, were spread on the table. . . . And what a disappointment it had been to wake up and find it was only a dream.

It was late spring. The rain was falling steadily when the three of us left camp and there seemed no likelihood that it was ever going to stop. The snow was melting on the mountains at a great rate and the rivers were in flood. We avoided crossing them whenever possible, but were eventually confronted, when only four miles from home, by the Varela River, which was impossible to negotiate other than by fording. I did not like the look of it at all. The river was in full flood. The dark water swept along branches of trees; and occasional lumps of ice rushed down at great speed. Halimink and Chalshoat, both overbold, thought we could ford it, but I was not so sure. There was no alternative, however, so we determined to try.

For one man to have attempted it alone would have been madness, for the current would have swept him away; but for larger parties the Ona had a method of their own. Our first step was to cut a pole about eight feet long. Next we took off most of our clothes, not to keep them dry—they were already saturated—but because clothes, especially trousers, are a terrible drag in swiftly flowing water. Besides myself, Halimink also wore trousers on that trip. The more conservative Chalshoat was robed in guanaco skin. As time went by, the Ona were slowly adopting the dress of the white man, but Chalshoat loyally clung to his ancestral garb. I was carrying my rifle and one of the axes; the others, two axes each. These and the clothing we made into three bundles, which we tied with *moji* high up on our shoulders.

The Ona procedure for crossing rivers in flood was as follows: one of the best men took the pole and stepped into the water, where he stood half facing up stream. Holding the pole with both hands as far apart as possible, he rested one end of it on his shoulder and the other on the bottom of the river. This was intended to break the force of the torrent and to divert the onrush of bits of ice and driftwood. This man's function was, by keeping his body rigid, to form a bulwark against the current. The rest of the party then lined up in the broken water below him, grasping each other firmly. When all were in place, the leader lifted the pole out of the water and dug it into the river bed a little nearer to the opposite bank. Meanwhile the others exerted all their strength to brace him during this tricky manoeuvre. When the pole was solidly planted in its new position, the others edged forward—and the whole process would be repeated over and over again. The second man in the line was almost as important as the first. He had to concentrate on keeping his foothold, with both hands bracing the body of his companion. He might even need to place one hand near the knees of the man he was supporting and the other against his waist. With the rush of the river, the water on the up-stream side might be up to their armpits, while on the lower side it was hardly above their knees. The men farther down stream were less important, yet each had to do his utmost to support the man breaking the force of the water above him. The last man of the line was sometimes also provided with a pole, but it would have been of little use if all the other men had been wrenched from their foothold. A string of men may cross a torrent in this way, on occasions when it would be utterly impossible for one man to cross alone and when even a horse would be swept off its feet. At the same time, it can be a dangerous proceeding. I heard of one incident in which several Aush lost their lives while attempting it.

Halimink, though the shortest of our party, bravely took upon himself the role of leader. I was second, with Chalshoat on the down-stream side of me. With Halimink holding the pole in the required manner, we started off from the bank. In swirling water it is most difficult to force one's feet down to the bottom and our progress was slow and arduous. We had almost reached the centre of the stream when disaster nearly overtook us. Chalshoat, though remarkably strong and enduring, always seemed to fail at the last moment. It was he who had let his intended victim escape when all the rest of San Martin's mining company had been massacred by Capelo's band. Now, when we were practically half-way across, Chalshoat lost his footing.

He was on the down-stream side of me and, instead of being a support, he clutched wildly at my body, while his feet, kicking away in the water, tried vainly to find bottom.   I suppose I should have acted unselfishly by letting go of Halimink and gone drifting away down stream with the struggling Chalshoat.   If I had, I should not be writing this story now. Instead, I put Halimink's life in danger by hanging on.   It was a mystery how that little fellow held his position until Chalshoat, with great difficulty, regained his feet.

After this narrowly averted tragedy, we decided not to proceed, but to return to the bank from which we had started.   We managed to regain the safety of dry land and, carrying our clothes, for we expected to take to the water again, walked down stream, hoping to find a better place to cross.   A short distance below, on the other side of the Varela, was a low point running some way into the water.   On our side was a steep bank, on the top of which, twenty feet above the water, was a tree.   The full force of the river flowed under this bank; on the opposite side the point made it less turbulent.

The tree sloped towards the water.   We discussed the question of forming a bridge by felling it.   It was fifty feet high and, by chopping it on the further side, we could make it fall—not right across the river, but far enough out for us to gain the quieter water.   There was the danger, of course, that it would be swept away, possibly while we were scrambling down the trunk, but the risk was worth taking.   Four miles away was Harberton, with all its home comforts.   The alternative was a night in the dripping, cheerless woods.

We got to work with the axes and cut into the tree until its great weight brought it crashing into the river, splitting it down into the roots, so that it stayed anchored to the bank.   The topmost branches were now in the water, just beyond the main rush of the torrent.   The pressure of the current against the lower branches immediately threatened to wrench the tree from its hold on top of the bank.   Before it could be carried away, we hastily slithered down the steeply sloping trunk, out on to the thin branches, and dropped waist-deep into water calm enough to let us wade ashore.

It was indeed good to be home that night!

CHAPTER THIRTY-FOUR

The Stranded Whale at Cape San Pablo. The Whale-Eaters are Fallen Upon by the Northern Men and There is Great Slaughter. The Slaying of Te-ilh. Shishkolh's Revenge. A Wrestling Tournament between South and North. The Ona Respect the Rules of the Game. I Meet Chashkil in Single Combat. We Fight until Chashkil is Sleepy.

I

A SHORT TIME AFTER THE VISIT TO HARBERTON JUST RECOUNTED, OUR working party in the woods was joined by some of our friends from Najmishk and also by Tininisk, the medicine-man, accompanied by others from his country. One evening, two young Ona emissaries arrived at our encampment. They evidently brought important news, but were too proud to blurt it out in a hurry. We, on our side, had too much dignity to show undue impatience—not that the scent that accompanied them did not give us some clue as to the information they had to impart.

This they shortly confirmed. A huge whale had been stranded on the shores of Tininisk's country, near Cape San Pablo. This meant little to me, for I did not care for the taste of whale. A whale is such a huge, warm-blooded mass that, long before it can cool, it goes putrid. Even the oil is strongly tainted. But for the Ona Indians it was a gift from the gods. How attractive to them in the spring, when guanaco meat was so lean and poor, was the thought of unlimited supplies of blubber and oil! More often than not, a whiff of whale from leagues away was their first intimation of this vast treasure of food, and they never wasted time in hastening to the scene.

Tininisk and others from those coastal areas wanted to leave at once, the *joön* being probably attracted more by social expectations than the prospect of an orgy. A stranded whale drew visitors from all around, and he wished it to be known to all that Tininisk, the great and puissant wizard, was still lord of his ancestral domain.

All my helpers were ready for a break. They soon tired of axe-work on streaming mountainsides under continual squalls of rain, and welcomed any sort of diversion. So I declared a general holiday. I had anticipated that the whole party would go to Cape San Pablo, but some

313

of them preferred to enjoy their short vacation elsewhere. Halimink, Ahnikin, Yoknolpe, Talimeoat and others of the mountain men put safety before whale-blubber and decided to go hunting in their wooded country, where they would be free from the avenging hand of Kiyohni-shah. It was just as well for them that they did.

I divided up our provisions, giving the hunters the lion's share, on condition that they returned to work as soon as possible. Then we moved off in three directions: I to Harberton, the hunters to less disturbed areas of their own lands, and the whaling party—among them the gentle Puppup and his family—eastward to the coast.

Near the stranded whale they found gathered from the surrounding country about a hundred and fifty Ona, some thirty of whom were men. Chief of them was Te-ilh, the strong, short-statured medicine-man of Najmishk, who had been fired on by miners and charged with stealing a hand-saw. With him was the corpulent Koiyot, who had escaped with him on that occasion, leaving their two companions dead on the ground. Another participant in the whale-feast was Shijyolh, also from Najmishk and a relative of Te-ilh. He was the shy man in the fox-skin mantle whom I had met on my trip across the island to Rio Grande. With him now were his wife, his two small sons, aged nine and six, and his brother, whose name was Shishkolh.

The whale-eaters had made two encampments not far apart and were all on the best of terms. They made Tininisk, Puppup and the rest of the party welcome, and all settled down to revelry. Abundance of food and strength of numbers gave them a feeling of safety. They grew care-less, no look-outs were posted; so that they were in no position to defend themselves when, early one morning, Kiyohnishah and his men fell upon them with rifles and bows and arrows.

Kiyohnishah had not been idle since the death of his brother, Housh-ken. He had travelled far around the wooded borders of the northern sheep-farms and had collected together a band of some sixty followers, with whom he attacked the unsuspecting whale-eaters. Of his party were Chashkil, Paloa, who had defied the posse of police, the embittered Kilkoat with his stolen rifle, and Taäpelht.

This Taäpelht was a brother-in-law of Puppup. Of medium height and lightly built, he was renowned throughout Ona-land for speed and courage. He was famed, also, for certain exploits. Alone and armed only with bow and arrow, he had killed one of the two notorious white hunters of Indians, reputed—as I have mentioned on a previous page—

to have been paid a pound a head for every Ona they slaughtered. In Fireland this hunter had a nickname. Not wishing to hurt the feelings of his descendants, even if illegitimate, I will not use it here, but will call him Dancing Dan. I never saw him, but have heard that he was small, very active and a deserter from a British warship that had anchored at Punta Arenas. If Dancing Dan was not a good horseman, he was certainly a reckless one and would go tearing over the roughest country. In shooting he was equalled only by his companion—I might say leader— whose name I also withhold. Taäpelht was also responsible for the serious wounding of two other well-known white men—both in the same skirmish. The first was the King of Rio Grande, the unspeakable Mr. McInch. Taäpelht's arrow had got the Scotsman right across his broad shoulders and its extraction had been a painful process. The barb had had to be dug out with a knife before the arrow could be withdrawn. The second victim, a few minutes later, was no less a person than Don Ramón L. Cortéz, the Chief-of-Police, who had approached too near the thicket in which his quarry had been hiding and had received an arrow in the neck.

In addition to Kilkoat's rifle, Kiyohnishah's party had at least one other stolen fire-arm. They took the whale-eaters completely by surprise and there was great slaughter. Among those who lost their lives that morning was Te-ilh, the wild and strong. Some of the men escaped into the woods: Tininisk, Shijyolh and his brother, Shishkolh, and my old friend, Puppup.

Assuming that their enemies would respect the Ona rules of warfare, these fugitives left their wives and families behind in the encampment. On this occasion the rules were broken. One of the fierce avengers, baulked of his prey, arrowed the two little sons of Shijyolh—an unheard-of crime.

Puppup had been a little distance from the encampment when the storm had broken. He raced across an open valley, hoping to gain the wooded hills beyond. But there was after him a man who could run faster than he; a man who called:

"Don't run away, Puppup! I do not hate you. I am your brother-in-law."

When he realized that it was Taäpelht behind him, Puppup stopped. They rested together for a while, then returned to the scene of the carnage. The attacking party had been followed at a short distance by a number of active young women, who had kept pace with them on their forced march.

Though I have no details, I can imagine that they took good loads of blubber and oil on their return journey to the north. Kiyohnishah seemed to have come purely to avenge the death of Houshken. Wonderful to relate, they took none of the women away with them when they left—not even Ahli. Tall, good-looking and childless, Ahli was the wife of one of the men who had just been killed, but originally she had come from the country of the slayers.

When the coast was clear, the fugitives returned to their shelters; and feasting and merry-making gave place to mourning. Of all, perhaps Shijyolh and his wife were the most bereaved. Shishkolh, when he saw his dead nephews and friends, longed for revenge. His glance rested on Ahli, who had once been of the northern group. He enticed her a short distance from the encampment, then, at close range, drove an arrow through her body, so that she died.

This deed of Shishkolh was criticized afterwards by Ona men of whatever party as severely as the murder of the two unfortunate children of Shijyolh. It was, they protested, an act unworthy of a man. Halimink said when he heard of it:

" The woman had no bow or arrows."

Shishkolh's thirst for revenge, however, was still unquenched. On a later occasion he went on a solitary raid. When out scouting, he noticed a distant smoke and drew near to the enemy encampment. Getting as close as he dared that stormy night, he discharged one arrow with all his might, then ran for his life. The dogs rushed out barking and the camp was immediately in an uproar. They could have had no idea that it had been a one-man attack and must have slept little that night.

Long afterwards others told me of this escapade, to the undisguised amusement and delight of all, though the hero did his best to look modest.

2

Three months after the bloody affair near the stranded whale, I was at Harberton. With me there were a number of Ona from the south, including Halimink, Ahnikin, Kankoat, Tininisk, Shishkolh, and Koiyot, with the small remnant of the once numerous Najmishk party. We were all greatly surprised one day to receive a visit from Kiyohnishah and well over a score of northern men.

I was glad to see them. Kiyohnishah was a fine, good-natured fellow, and my sympathies, since Houshken's death, had been with him and his people. I still hoped to bring the factions together, for it was plain that these murderous vendettas would have to stop, unless they wished to be exterminated to the last man. There could be no chance of survival for them unless law and order prevailed ere long in that part of Fireland still free from the white invaders from the north.

The newcomers asked for work, which the rules of the farm forbade us to refuse to natives, whether Ona or Yahgan. It was soon apparent, however, that that was not the real object of their visit, which was to meet their enemies on neutral soil, and to challenge them to a series of rough wrestling matches—not the gentlemanly bouts with which it was our habit to amuse ourselves.

Halimink and party numbered barely twenty against these formidable visitors. The Ona from the forests and mountains of the south, though keen and quick, were generally of lighter build than their neighbours from the better lands in the north, where the *apen* (tucu-tucu) and other strength-building foods were more plentiful than in their own boggy country. Thus, when they met in wrestling matches, the heavier northern men—who were also more numerous—generally had the best of it. Against Halimink and his friends were now ranged such stalwarts as Kiyohnishah, Chashkil, Halah, Paloa, Kilkoat, Taäpelht and that kindly old warrior, Kautempklh. In support of them were other valiant wrestlers, including the dwarf, Hechelash, and his two equally diminutive brothers, Yoiyolh and A-yaäh.

The two parties had no confidence in one another. Halimink and his people moved their camp from the edge of the main forest and crowded their windbreaks almost into the Yahgan village, whilst Kiyohnishah and the newcomers pitched theirs in the shelter of a clump of trees, a quarter of a mile away from the homestead. Yet, though there was mutual mistrust, these foes from time immemorial, who had suffered so many wrongs at each other's hands and could not have met in their own land without bloodshed, now came together on neutral soil and observed to the last detail the rules of the game laid down by ancient Ona custom.

The day before they proposed to meet, Kiyohnishah sent his messenger with the official challenge. I kept in close touch with both parties. My brother, Despard, knowing how hard I should find it to abstain from joining in any tussle that might be going on, warned me that this was to be no ordinary wrestling match, and that there was no knowing what I might be letting myself in for if I joined either side. I reluctantly promised him that I would remain a strictly neutral spectator.

At about two o'clock in the afternoon of the following day—during the morning of which the intending participants had eaten nothing—the challengers walked out from the coppice where they had been encamped. Followed by their womenfolk, they came unarmed. As was the general custom on such occasions, the intending wrestlers wore only their robes, having left behind their *goöchilh* and *jamni* (head-dress and moccasins). Fine patterns of painting were not indulged in, but bodies and faces were well smeared with red paint.

Halimink and his fellows were ready. They must have been on the look-out, for they managed to arrive simultaneously at the appointed spot: a grassy hollow between the two encampments. On one side of this space one party stood, and opposite them, some ten yards away, the other party assembled. As onlookers increased, the ends of these two lines drew in, to form a ring around the champions. The women, children and old or sick men were on the outer edge of this ring, while the fit men, all of whom would sooner or later be drawn into the struggle, formed the inner circle. Bearing Despard's good advice in mind, I wandered impartially from point to point among the spectators while the wrestling proceeded.

The contest opened with speeches. Very earnest and fierce were the challengers as they stated their grievances in a few stern words. Their voices were hoarse with emotion, yet, unlike the Yahgans, who were quarrelsome, but unwarlike, they refrained from shouting or screaming threats. They expressed their scorn in no measured terms of the treachery of their opponents, to which Halimink's party suitably responded. Terms such as " Whash-win " (like foxes) and " Wishn-win " (like dogs) were ferociously exchanged. Now and then, some bereaved wife or mother would join in the abuse in a high-pitched voice, or break into prolonged howls of woe.

The wrestling was initiated not, as was customary, by the challengers, but by one of the opposing team. This was Shishkolh, who, with the killing of Te-ilh and his two little nephews still fresh in his mind, would not listen to these insults any longer. He dropped his only covering and, though no great wrestler, stepped forward with his left hand outstretched towards Halah, the square-jawed, broad-shouldered, determined man who had, with Chashkil, brought me news at Harberton of Houshken's murder.

With the wrestling thus begun, other contestants joined in and occasionally two or even three bouts were being fought simultaneously in the ring. Shishkolh's was the correct form of challenge, but a challenger could not be sure of a fight with the man of his choice; any impatient young warrior might step in front of his friend and do battle in his stead. Normally, the man challenged grasped his opponent's outstretched left hand with his own right hand, then they embraced, each with his left arm below the other's right. After that ceremonious preliminary, the bout would develop into a wild struggle, all kinds of tripping with feet or legs being allowed, each man seizing every opportunity to get the other at a disadvantage.

For all the apparently haphazard rough-and-tumble, there were certain strict unwritten rules in these encounters. In this and other meetings of the Ona, I never saw eyes or ears attacked. If a handful of hair was grasped, there were protests from the offender's own people. I have seen a wrestler throw his hand round the back of his opponent's head, take a firm grip of his nose and try to twist his neck. I have also seen a fist or hand forced hard against a neck, with the intention of interfering with the circulation. But I never saw a grasp made on the throat, or that low-down upward jerk of the knee that may knock the other fellow out completely. A man was entitled to hurt his adversary by clutching him with strong finger-nails, but direct scratching was disapproved of. That mode of warfare was the prerogative of the women. Biting was also taboo. During the match that afternoon, Halah—gasping for breath in Koiyot's mighty embrace—pressed his teeth against the other's shoulder, at which one of his own people exclaimed:

" Oush ta wishn? "   (" Is it a dog? ")

The mountain men were wiry, quick and clever, but the opposing party, besides averaging a greater weight, were considerably more numerous. This was a serious matter, for there was less time for Halimink's men to rest between bouts. When a man retired from the ring for a breather, he might be instantly challenged by someone who had already rested, and would be lucky if one of his own people was ready to step in front of him to take on the task. Even men who had little chance threw themselves fiercely into the fray, in the united attempt to wear down the resistance of the other team. Hechelash, for all his dwarfish proportions, fought valiantly. His podgy, round body made him difficult to lay hold of; and I was not the only spectator unable to repress a laugh at his savage antics and distorted face.

The onlookers kept silent when their favourite did anything good, as if to say, " It is just what we expected." The opposition might greet the same feat with, " Haik ni chohn ! " (" He is a man ! "), which intimated that, inasmuch as their champion was strong, the other must be formidable indeed to have thrown him.

As the afternoon drew on, the green turf in the hollow showed many streaks of red, some of paint, others of blood. Neither party would, or could, acknowledge defeat; and the wrestling continued spasmodically until, one by one, the warriors wrapped their robes around them and quietly left the ring. When none was left to wrestle, the contest was considered over and the meeting broke up with no further interchange of angry words.

Those brave southerners, especially Ahnikin, Koiyot and Kankoat, had put up a splendid fight against much larger men, but they had undoubtedly got the worst of it. Nevertheless, after a few days they sent a return challenge. When I expressed my surprise to Halimink, he exclaimed scornfully:

" Are we afraid of those men? "

It was the rule, always rigidly observed, that however unsuccessful a team might have been, another meeting must be sought with the original challengers. In this instance, Halimink's party fared as badly as they had done in the first contest, but this did not deter them, on subsequent occasions, from exchanging fresh challenges with the northerners.

I trust that my description of these wrestling matches will demonstrate that these so-called savages were more gentlemanly in their respect for the rules of the game than many a white sportsman.

3

As the summer went by and work on the track had to take its turn with other important tasks in that busiest season of the year, warnings began to reach me from here and there that Chashkil's thirst for revenge had not been satisfied either by the massacre near the stranded whale or by the wrestling contests that had followed. The chief object of his rancour was not one of his own kind, but myself. This young man, once so pleasant in his manner, had become embittered by the murder of Houshken, his brother, for which—rightly, alas!—he held me directly responsible. His purpose, I gathered from my informants, was not to kill me, but to challenge me to a wrestling match, in which I was to be severely punished. This kind of individual duel was not unknown among the Ona. I have heard of one being fought for a wife.

I thought that Chashkil's enemies were probably exaggerating his

MARY.

56

BERTHA.

enmity towards me. Feeling, however, that, if the challenge did come, I should have to accept it, in order to maintain my position among these good sports, and knowing, moreover, that it would be no friendly tussle, but a struggle till one or other acknowledged defeat, I went into training. In addition to working, as usual, long hours with the axe and carrying heavy logs, I spent part of every evening wrestling with various Ona friends, at whose hands I received some fairly rough treatment. Young Ahnikin, who for his size was extraordinarily strong, was my chief tutor, with Kankoat a willing substitute.

In the early autumn there came ample justification for these precautions. With Ahnikin, Kankoat, Halimink and several others, I was away to the west of Harberton building corduroy bridges across some swamps, when five or six Ona arrived in the locality with their families and made their encampment half a mile from ours. Soon after pitching camp, some of them left it and sat down together on a little knoll a quarter of a mile away from us and in full view. One of them was Hechelash, the dwarf; another was a man called Pahchik, who had been of Kiyohnishah's party at the Harberton wrestling tournament; and a third was Chashkil.

It was evening. The little group remained there motionless for a considerable time. Then Hechelash rose to his feet and, trying to assume the dignity of a king's messenger, came to our camp. The intimation he brought was that Chashkil wished to wrestle with me on the morrow.

I, too, had my pride. Not wanting either party to get the idea that I was excited, I answered:

" We must work in the day, but about this time in the evening I will wrestle."

I was glad that the period of waiting was over. By giving satisfaction to the aggrieved Chashkil, whichever way the game went, I should prove my manhood to the people whose esteem I valued so highly and, at the same time, supply the only peaceful method of healing the breach between myself and the northern men. By all Ona precedents, this challenge should have come from Kiyohnishah. He was Chashkil's senior and had become head of the family on the death of Houshken. I conjectured that he now held back because I had rescued his little son when he had fallen into the stream.

When Hechelash had gone back to his party with my reply, Ahnikin warned me—not for the first time—that Chashkil was fierce and strong, and that I must expect a whirlwind. He considered that my only chance would be to save my strength during the early part of the struggle, at the cost, perhaps, of many a fall. By letting my opponent feel my weight continuously, said Ahnikin, I might be able to wear him down until I could employ my reserves of strength with telling effect. Ahnikin also counselled me to refrain from eating before the encounter.

I went against this last piece of advice by taking a little food early the following morning. After that I abstained, and took care not to tire myself by working too hard. At seven o'clock in the evening, Chashkil arrived. He was accompanied by his little party of men, with their women following behind.

Halimink had chosen the site for the match. It was in a small hollow near our encampment, and Halimink had ostentatiously gone over it beforehand to make sure that no stones projected through the turf. It was an ideal spot; one that might have been chosen in olden times by two of our ancestors about to fight a duel to the death. Close by to the west lay twin lakes, each many acres in extent, divided by a narrow strip of bushy land, and mirroring in their quiet depths on that perfect evening the scattered clumps of trees, now taking on their autumnal tints. To the north lay the great forest; the wooded slopes of Flat Top, with Mount Cornú, eternally snow-capped, beyond. Southward were three bold, wood-crowned hills, their steep sides dropping abruptly into the yellow *shana*, upon the bridging of which we were, at that time, engaged. These moss-covered swamps gave the three hills the appearance of islands in the sea.

In the hollow, Chashkil's followers joined with my own party in forming a ring around the principal figures: Chashkil and Pahchik, who filled the role of second, Ahnikin and myself. Chashkil looked very grim in his paint. He wore his robe, which he would throw off when the bout began, and was barefooted. I was also barefooted, but, as a sop to civilization, wore trousers and belt. This promised to give Chashkil the advantage of something to grip, while I should have nothing but his naked body, made slippery by the paint. The Ona were so solidly built that their weight greatly surprised men of science; and Chashkil, though his appearance did not suggest it, certainly weighed well over thirteen stone. I had the advantage there, for I was close on fifteen.

Chashkil opened the proceedings by giving me the chance to draw back. He asked if I was afraid to wrestle with him.

I answered, " Am I a child? "

Pahchik muttered something that I did not quite catch—I think he compared me with a woman—then said aloud to Chashkil:

" Throw him hard and he will soon give up."

Ahnikin and I exchanged a glance; Chashkil was receiving advice that fitted perfectly into our scheme.

No time was lost. Chashkil threw off his robe, stepped forward and held out his left hand in the orthodox Ona manner. I took it with my right and the wrestle began. Ahnikin had in no wise exaggerated the whirlwind qualities of Chashkil. His onslaught was of the fiercest and I carry to this day at least one of the many marks his strong nails left upon me. It was his obvious intention to end the struggle quickly. In this I prevented him, at the expense of fall after fall.

There were no rounds as civilized sportsmen understand them, but from time to time we would break away from each other by mutual consent and take a rest. These breaks sometimes lasted only a few seconds, at others as long as ten or twelve minutes. We might remain standing, while our seconds clasped our robes around us, for the evening grew chilly; or we might lie on the ground till one or the other of us stepped forward to resume the contest. Whichever of us felt it would be to his advantage would be the challenger and would be at once engaged by the other.

I followed Ahnikin's advice until I had suffered a dozen falls or more, Chashkil concluding, no doubt, that Pahchik's opinion of my woman-like abilities was justified. When I felt that his strength was beginning to ebb, I took the offensive. I gave him little time for rest between bouts. His initial attempts to finish me off had told upon him and his defence began to lack vigour. After a prolonged ding-dong battle, during which I threw him several times in quick succession, the match ended abruptly. At the end of one break of a few seconds, I reached out my hand. Chashkil drew back. With the words, " Mahshink me ya " (" Sleepy am I "), he resumed his robe and walked off the field, with his companions and womenfolk at his heels.

It was almost midnight. The full moon was nearly overhead. I was very sore and hungry. We gathered round the fire to eat. While my friends discussed the match in detail, I listened in silence, hiding my conceit as best I could. In spite of the result, I claim—and with no mock modesty—that Chashkil was the better man. Besides the difference of nearly two stone in our weights, the poor fellow had been under other disadvantages. He had been badly advised, had nursed a grievance and had been leading a hunter's irregular life. I, on the other hand, had acted on Ahnikin's excellent counsel, had no grievance to nurse and had been working hard and steadily for a long time.

Our visitors did not hurry away. We often ate and talked together. I am certain that Chashkil no longer bore me a grudge. The score was settled. He never challenged me to wrestle with him again.

CHAPTER THIRTY-FIVE

The Track is Finished. Escaped Convicts. Kaichin, Son of Talimeoat, Astonishes His Excellency, the Governor. Aneki, the Left-Handed, Performs a Miraculous Feat. The Unmatched Woodcraft of the Ona. Talimeoat Hunts Cormorants. I Dine with Him on Tijnolsh Hill. Talimeoat Sighs.

I

WORK ON THE TRACK TO NAJMISHK CONTINUED SPASMODICALLY UNTIL IT was finished. It was now possible, during five months of the year—that is, from the beginning of December to the end of April—to ride on horseback, or drive pack-mules or sheep, all the way from Harberton to the Atlantic coast. When the track had been roughly completed, Will and I had tested it by riding through it with a troop of horses. We had noted the places where our tough little cobs had found the going difficult, and I had afterwards put matters right. Nevertheless, it was far from being a comfortable route or, in any sense, a surfaced highway. Approaching the mountains from the Harberton side, one had to cross the Varela river more than a hundred times. In some places the water, with a strong current, would be up to the horse's body, but as one got nearer the source, the Varela dwindled to a small stream and progress became easier. After crossing the mountain—or rather the high moor to which we gave the name Spion Kop—the track led into another stream, later called Rio Valdés. This, as it flowed northward, growing steadily wider, had to be forded nearly as often as the Varela before the track finally left it and wound its way through the main forest of Ona-land and emerged on the beach of the Atlantic coast at the foot of the cliff called Tijnolsh, six miles south-east of Najmishk Hill, the place chosen for the new settlement. As the crow flies, it was not much more than fifty miles from Harberton to Tijnolsh, but with the winding and often zig-zag nature of the track, the distance on horseback was nearer a hundred. On foot this could be shortened by twenty miles by cutting out the turn by the Ewan River and splashing through places unfit or impossible for a horse. With the Ona men as companions, I could leave Najmishk in the morning and reach Harberton in the evening of the following day—a matter of forty miles a day. We were not racing, nor were we fatigued at the finish, though all of us invariably carried some small burden.

My sister Alice was keen on seeing the Atlantic Ocean from the cliffs I had described to her, so she determined to cross with me on one of my early trips. Always having had a great sympathy for the Indians, she was also anxious to gain some insight into the lives of the Ona in their own land. She could ride or walk all day without fatigue, could find— without any help from me—a comfortable place to sleep in the woods at night, and could coax a fire to burn in almost any circumstances.

She and I travelled in what, to me, seemed luxury, for we had a little tent and rode on horseback. My own destination was Rio Grande, where I had some business to do, but when we reached Najmishk, Alice was reluctant to go any further with me. A white woman coming down from the woods, a region supposed to be inhabited by savages, would have created quite a sensation among the frontier folk of Rio Grande, and Alice did not care to be regarded as either a tomboy or a heroine.

A considerable party of Ona and their families were encamped near Najmishk, so Alice decided to stop with them, while I went on alone to Rio Grande. She said she preferred the company of the Indians to that of some of the white men she might meet if she came with me. My business at Rio Grande was at the police station on the other side of the river, which meant that I would not be able to get back until the following day, so I pitched our little tent by the Ona encampment, placed my sister in the care of Te-al, the wife of Ishtohn (Thick Thighs) of the northern group, and daughter of the famed Kautempklh, and resumed my journey.

When I came to Rio Grande and told some white men there that Alice had stopped behind with the Ona, they were horrified, obviously thinking I was mad to have left her. But I had not the slightest anxiety for her safety. In spite of the horrible tales of murder and treachery that I have had to tell in these pages, the Ona Indians had some very fine qualities. My father's advice that we should treat their women as we would wish them to treat ours had never been forgotten by any of us; and we never had cause to regret it. On arriving back at Najmishk late in the evening of the day following my departure from there, I found that Alice had had a pleasant and most interesting time with her hosts, and that Te-al had been a devoted companion during my absence.

Where our path emerged on the beach below Tijnolsh cliff, I planted a signpost that gave directions in English and Spanish for finding the way to Harberton. I intended this for the benefit of travellers or shipwrecked sailors, pending the setting up of my new establishment at Najmishk. I did not foresee that the first to take advantage of this new facility would be a troop of soldiers, who would ride out from Rio Grande, not against rebellious Ona Indians, but in search of escaped convicts.

In the year 1883, before the national flag had been hoisted by my father at Ushuaia, the Argentine government had founded a convict settlement at Port Cook on that desolate pile of rocks, Staten Island, which lies off the south-east point of Tierra del Fuego. For criminals sent there from the sunny pampas and towns of northern Argentina, the change of climate had been so hard to bear that many of them had succumbed. This sad state of affairs continued until the turn of the century, when the government mercifully determined to move the convict station to the more pleasant surroundings and milder climate of Ushuaia, which, by that time, had a civilian population of about two hundred.

While this removal was in progress, the number of guards on Staten Island was, of necessity, greatly diminished in proportion to the convicts awaiting transportation. Seizing this opportunity, the convicts made a bid for freedom. They attacked the guards, killing some of them and overpowering the others, then took their rifles and ammunition and set off in boats across the Straits of Le Maire.

Shortly after these happenings, we heard that at least two of the boats had landed safely on our shores and that some forty armed and desperate criminals were on the eastern point of Fireland. As Harberton was the nearest permanent settlement to their landing-place, the authorities warned us of possible attack and we went about our business with increased caution. Soldiers were shipped from Argentina and were landed at Rio Grande. Supplied with horses by the police, they rode east along the coast, came upon my signpost and got through to Harberton. From their subsequent remarks I gathered that they did not like my " road " at all.

As soon as he learned that the escaped men had landed on the main island, the Governor [1] came from Ushuaia to Harberton and invested me—and, I think, Will—with the high-sounding title of Honorary Commissary of Police. He then asked—or rather ordered—us to direct the Ona to help in the hunt for the criminals. A party of my Indian friends were nearby. I told them the kind of men who were now invading their country and endeavoured to enlist their aid. To my surprise, they

---

[1] Don Esteban de Loque. Governors held office for three years, and several had come and gone since Captain Felix Paz had reigned in Ushuaia. Don Esteban de Loque, a captain in the Argentine Navy, was married to an English wife and later became Argentine Consul-General in London. He was succeeded at Ushuaia by Don Manuel Fernandez Valdés.

raised objections. Their spokesman was that influential medicine-man, Tininisk; and his words show how far removed from savages were these Ona hunters.

"We have no quarrel with these strangers," he answered earnestly. "They have not killed our friends or relatives, and we care nothing about other people they may have killed in their own country."

I replied: "You are not asked to kill them, but you don't want to have these people wandering about in your country, for soon they will do you harm. You are only asked to find them and take the soldiers to where they are encamped."

Tininisk saw the force of this argument. He and his companions agreed to lend their assistance; and, thanks almost entirely to them, all but seven of the prisoners were in captivity again within a few weeks of their escape. Three of these seven defied arrest and were shot; the others have never since been traced.

Many months after the escaped convicts had been lodged in the new prison at Ushuaia, three of them slipped away again. After the police had searched for them in vain, our Ona were requisitioned once more. Tininisk, who spoke a good deal of Spanish, went with two others on the quest. They soon located their quarry, who had travelled many leagues in a westerly direction. Without being seen, the Indians returned to Ushuaia and guided the police back to the spot. Meanwhile the escaped men had moved on, but they were soon overtaken and either captured or shot.

For this admirable piece of woodcraft, the Indians received from the authorities a reward that was, in their opinion, inadequate, so that when later on another dangerous convict escaped from Ushuaia, they were even more disinclined to respond to an appeal for help than they had been on the first occasion. By that time the Governor was Don Manuel Fernandez Valdés. When I gave the Ona his message, in which he asked for an experienced tracker to go to Ushuaia as soon as possible, they repeated their previous argument that they had no interest in white men's quarrels.

Finding Tininisk, Talimeoat, Halimink and the others so obstinate, I glanced from face to face in search of someone inclined to be more helpful. My roving eye picked out Kaichin, the son of Talimeoat, the bird-hunter. He was a bright lad of about sixteen and his eager expression suggested to me that he would enjoy going on this adventure. I said to him:

"You are not disinclined to go, Kaichin?"

He did not reply, but glanced at his father questioningly.

I said to Talimeoat: "Oush ma tushnain?" ("Do you grudge him?").[1]

"Dowu," he answered. "Kau chohn ijen, tani telken." ("No. Now he is reaching manhood, not a child.") [2]

With this intimation that the lad could please himself, I took Kaichin along to the homestead, supplied him with everything he might need, including a letter of introduction to his Excellency, and despatched him to Ushuaia, a fifty-mile tramp over very rough country.

In my note to the Governor I said that, though he was so young, I believed Kaichin would be quite equal to the task. His Excellency did not entirely share my conviction. Besides its resident population, there were at Ushuaia at that time as many as five hundred convicts with their guards, and a considerable number of soldiers. The convicts were employed, for the most part, in cutting firewood under supervision in the surrounding forest and carrying it to a huge wood-pile on the beach in front of the prison buildings, ready to be shipped to Argentina in the government transport, *Santa Cruz*. Civilians were also felling timber and dragging the logs to the beach with yoke oxen. When not at work these animals wandered over a large area and had to be searched for by their owners when they were needed. As a result of all these activities, together with the normal coming and going of the village community, the woods around Ushuaia were a labyrinth of tracks of every description. From these Kaichin was now called upon to pick out the trail of the escaped convict.

His Excellency was doubtful of success and would have preferred a tracker of more experience. However, he was a kindly gentleman and decided to give Kaichin a chance to prove his worth. He sent him along to the soldiers' quarters with orders that he should be well treated and allowed to carry out his task in his own fashion. The boy was shown a photograph of the missing man and was allowed to examine a pair of shoes that the prisoner had worn. He was also supplied with details of his size and height.

For some days little was seen of Kaichin, except when he turned up, with great punctuality, for his evening meal in the army cook-house. He had a smattering of Spanish, but was so uncommunicative when questioned about his activities that the belief soon spread that he was

---

[1] "Oush | ma | t | ushnain?"
   "Is it that | you | him | grudge?"

[2] "Dowu. | Kau | chohn | ijen, | tani | telken."
   "No. | Now | man | arrives, | not | child."

wasting his time, while enjoying the privilege of good food and comfortable quarters. Then, one evening, he did not put in his customary appearance at the cook-house and was no longer to be found at Ushuaia. It was thought that he had slipped away to rejoin his own people.

His return was as stealthy as his departure. A week later the Governor found him sitting outside his house, waiting, as was the Ona custom, to be spoken to. Somewhat derisively, his Excellency asked to be told the present whereabouts of the escaped prisoner. In his broken Spanish the young Indian replied with great decision:

"Este hombre no escapa nada." ("This man did not escape at all.")

That was all the Governor could get out of Kaichin. Finally he impatiently dismissed the lad, who started to walk away, then turned round to repeat the same laconic phrase before proceeding to the military lines for his supper.

Don Manuel Valdés dismissed the matter from his mind as the evasive talk of a child, and took no action. He was to be sharply reminded of young Kaichin's five-word report when, that same evening, the missing man was discovered, quite by chance, hiding in the wood-pile immediately outside the prison. He had been lurking there for nearly three weeks and must have either stored provisions beforehand or been supplied by a confederate. No doubt he had hoped to stow away on the *Santa Cruz* when she called to collect the firewood.

Kaichin's temporary disappearance was subsequently explained. His tracking had taken him as far as the Lawrences' homestead at Punta Remolino, fifteen miles to the east, and the same distance westward of Ushuaia, to a saw-mill at Lapataia. Who knows how many human tracks Kaichin had followed, as he had circled round Ushuaia in an ever-growing radius? Who knows how many parties of woodcutters and men out searching for oxen had been spied on by that silent shadow? Yet from all that confusion of footprints he had established to his own satisfaction that not one of them had been made by the man he sought.

Many other instances showing the highly developed instinct of these people crowd into my mind. I will recount but two of them, both about the same man. The wizard Otrhshoölh (White Eye) of the Cape San Pablo group had two brothers, both very much younger than he. One was named Aneki (Awkward or Left-Handed), the other Shilchan (Soft Voice). My two anecdotes concern the elder of the two, Aneki. He stood nearly six feet tall and, though he weighed over fourteen stone, his walk, which I had often noticed with pleasure, was so swift and tireless that it might have been called a glide.[1] One Sunday at Harberton, Aneki and I rowed across the harbour with the intention of destroying some half-wild dogs that were worrying the cattle on the Varela peninsula. From the top of a little hill near the centre of the isthmus, I managed to shoot three of these nuisances, but when I fired at a fourth, which was trotting by the river nearly two hundred yards away, Aneki grunted:

" Ma tairucush." (" You it missed.")

The next day I was in the same neighbourhood with Aneki and some other Ona. We came by land and approached from a different direction from our route of the previous day. The spot where the dog had been when I fired was much trampled by cattle and sparsely covered with tufty grass and a very few small bushes not much over a foot high. Aneki took a glance at the hill on which we had stood, then made straight for a piece of ground, where he began prodding into the grit with a pointed stick he carried. In a very short time he unearthed the thing he sought. He picked it up and handed it to me with the words:

" Mak yahn." (" Your arrow.")

It was the battered bullet I had fired at the dog. Aneki must have seen it disturb a twig or throw up some particles of grit, but how he knew exactly where it was to be found is beyond my comprehension.

My second story of Aneki relates to a time when we were having a nasty spell of weather, and the snow-laden branches made working on the track disagreeable. As we were getting short of meat, we decided to go for a day's hunting. Several men went off to Harberton for the day, while I and three others, Aneki being one of them, went north-westward in search of guanaco. Soon it began to snow in earnest. After we had walked a mile, we crossed a guanaco track going at right-angles to our path. It was still easy to follow, though the fresh snow was fast obliterating it, but the guanaco had been walking quickly and we had to trail him for about two miles before we overtook him where he had stopped to feed, and I was able to shoot him.

We each took a portion of meat and I led the way back along the track by which we had come, the others following behind. There was not a

[1] Aneki was, I believe, ambidextrous, but he was certainly not awkward. He was far from being the only Ona to belie his name. Children were often called after some long-deceased ancestor, or because of some childish peculiarity out of which they grew in later years. One of the group in photograph No. 52 is Kostelen. The reader can judge whether this man deserved to be called Narrow Face. To quote two more examples, Otrhshoölh had, when I knew him, quite normal eyes, and Akukeyohn, as has been seen, was no longer afraid to walk on fallen logs. Shilchan, on the other hand, did have a soft voice. (See also footnote to page 270.)

breath of wind and it was snowing so heavily that, even had we been in the open, visibility would have been down to about fifty yards. In the wood we were practically blinded. My companions did not know that country; being covered with a thick growth of evergreen beech, it was little frequented by their quarry, the guanaco. After we had gone a short distance, Aneki asked:

" Why don't we go straight home? "

I was quick to accept the hint.

" You had better take the lead," said I, and dropped meekly behind.

Without any hesitation, Aneki led us as straight as was possible through that kind of thicket directly to our deserted little camp. So smothered was it in snow that I almost stumbled into my shelter before realizing we were there. Aneki had led us as if he had been able to see the place all the time.

Amongst white men, even those who spent their lives in camp and forest, I was looked upon as a first-class scout, yet by comparison with even the least skilled Ona, I was the merest beginner. I have stalked deer in the Paraguayan Chaco in the company of natives of those parts; with a Mashona guide I have hunted buck in the bush veldt of Southern Rhodesia: but I have never seen anything to equal the woodcraft of the Ona trackers of the Fuegian forests.

2

Talimeoat, father of Kaichin, though lean and wrinkled, was not an old man. He had a whimsical expression that I found attractive. Renowned throughout Ona-land as a cormorant hunter, his favourite locality was Cape Santa Inés (Shilan). When he was a boy, he and his father used to crawl along an exceedingly narrow ridge that connected the main Shilan cliff with a sandstone pinnacle, as precipitous as a church steeple, called Tukmai; but by the time the old man died, erosion had worn the ridge so thin that no one—not even Talimeoat—cared to venture on its knife-like edge, and the cormorants now roosted there in peace. But along Shilan and on Tukmai there were numberless ledges and holes where the sea-birds still roosted.

In daylight Talimeoat would make a preliminary exploration of some ledge or hole. Around his waist would be tied a strong seal-hide thong, the other end of which would be held by his trusted friends on the clifftop above. When he had satisfied himself as to what would be feasible in the darkness, Talimeoat would wait for a black, drizzling night, when the birds were sleeping soundly with their heads tucked under their wings. Then he would be lowered once again—naked, of course—down the cliff-side. It was dangerous work, for the rain and droppings from the sea-birds made the ledges terribly slippery. He would feel his way cautiously along a ledge, knowing that the slightest sound would give the alarm, and as he encountered sleeping birds, would seize them firmly with both hands and, in Yahgan style, bite their heads or necks until they were dead.

It was seldom that Talimeoat returned empty-handed from these excursions. The trees round his camp were usually festooned with scores of shags, plucked, singed and ready for cooking. When they visited him in autumn or winter, less expert hunters could always depend on the gift of a fine, fat bird from the famed Talimeoat.

There was a safer way than Talimeoat's to catch cormorants. At high tide the sea came in close to the cliffs, but at low water it was a mile or more away. Choosing a dark, wet night when the tide was well out, the Indians, armed with sticks, would scatter in silence about the beach with torches and bundles of inflammable shrub. Up on top of the cliff would be stationed the old people and children, also with torches and fires ready to light at the moment agreed upon.

When everyone had got quietly into position and all was ready, the blaze was started. Torches were waved so that they flared up brightly, the fires and shrubs were lighted, and the whole party simultaneously raised a great hubbub. The frightened shags, suddenly awakened by the uproar, flew from their ledges and, either thinking that the tide was still high or else too panic-stricken to think at all, came crashing down on the beach. With their robes held like shields—for these heavy birds can strike tremendous blows—the Indians fell on their bemused victims with their clubs and sometimes killed so many that they had to return again and again to the beach before all the shags had been carried up to the encampment.

Much the same method was used for duck-hunting in shallow lakes. The hunters would blacken themselves and their torches with charcoal and, with torches blazing, approach the lake openly, but in complete silence. The torch-bearers and their companions would wade into the water, where the ducks, startled and dazzled by the lights, would swarm round them, making no attempt to escape. They would be caught one by one and held under the water until they drowned, or gripped between their captor's knees while their necks were twisted. Soon there would be a large number of dead ducks floating on the lake, and the hunters would return heavily laden from their foray.

Not long after his son's convict-tracking adventure at Ushuaia, I visited Cape Santa Inés, where Talimeoat and his household were encamped with four other families—including those of Tininisk and Halimink—on the top of Tijnolsh Hill. Away to the north-west was the Atlantic coast with its lines of rolling breakers stretching league after league into the distance. To the southward were the wooded hills and, in the far background, the snowy range of mountains. Because of their constant fear of surprise attacks, the Ona considered a good view of the surrounding country to be preferable to the protection from the weather offered by more sheltered spots. They felt more secure in a low, scrubby wood on a wind-swept hilltop than in the more comfortable haven of a valley. Another reason for this choice of a high position was water. Whenever possible they camped near a spring, the water from which was much more to their taste than that from sluggish streams meandering down the valleys of Ona-land. They kept their supply of water in skin bags hanging from the branches of trees near the encampment.

Talimeoat's shelter was the first I came to when I reached the summit of Tijnolsh Hill. When I glanced in, I found him inside with Kaichin. He told his son to pass him a robe, which he folded up and placed near him, where the smoke from the fire would not be troublesome. Then, patting the robe, he said to me:

"Wahwurh pay naäiyim." (" Come sit here.")

I accepted the invitation with alacrity, for hanging in the branches nearby were at least thirty large and oily sea-birds. They had been opened and the feathers plucked or singed off. In colour they were nearly black. The adjoining abodes of Tininisk and Halimink were also well adorned with cormorants.

Talimeoat summoned his wife and ordered her to prepare a bird for me. As she reached for one, he said:

" No, not that one. It is thin."

Her second selection was greeted by:

" That bird is old."

With ostentatious care he discussed with his wife the relative merits of different birds until at last they decided on one that was, in their opinion, superior to all the others. Talimeoat, the perfect host, then superintended the cooking.

When roasted in an oven or boiled in a pot, a cormorant tastes and smells too fishy to be appetizing, but when baked over embers until it is crisp, it has a delicious flavour, the memory of which makes my mouth water still. For preparing a bird for baking, the Fuegians had a special method, which Talimeoat's wife now put into practice. Under the watchful direction of her husband, she stretched the great bird out on sticks, which kept it spread like a boy's kite while it baked over the fire.

As we waited for our meal to cook, Talimeoat and I talked together. We were soon joined by Tininisk, Halimink and other friends who gathered round to hear what news I brought. Amongst other things, I mentioned young Kaichin's achievement at Ushuaia and commended him warmly. An Ona did not boast of his exploits and Kaichin had told his people nothing of the affair when he had rejoined them. Talimeoat listened to my remarks in silence and made no comment afterwards, but I knew that he was pleased. After a while, Tininisk said:

" You had better sleep in our shelter. Here there are many children."

His use of the word " our " instead of " my " was his polite way of saying that his house was also mine.

When the cormorant was crisply baked, Talimeoat's wife attended to the carving. For this she used a knife made from a piece of barrel-hoop, a type of implement common among the Indians in those days, when they largely depended for their supplies of metal on jetsam salvaged from the beach. The bird had been jointed when it had been spread out before roasting, but, even then, to divide it adequately without table or dish called for quite elaborate measures, entailing the employment of teeth and toes. To leave both hands free for the carving, she held the bird by gripping one of its legs with her teeth and its head between her big and second toes. For even larger birds, both big toes would often be needed.

By the woman's side was a little heap of fresh green branches, on which she piled the joints as she dexterously divided them. By the time she had finished, all that remained were the thin neck and backbone—and even those would not be wasted.

The carving finished, the meat was distributed. New arrivals were always served first, because their need was usually the greatest. If the visitors had recently eaten—a most unusual occurrence—they would say, as soon as they saw preparations for cooking:

" Karrhhaiyin shoön me yikua." (" Hungry not are we.") [1]

---

[1] " Karrhhaiyin " is a composite word. " Karrh " means " stuff," in this instance " food "; " haiyin " means " want, like, love, yearn after," but not in the sexual sense. (See footnote to page 292.)

The Ona were not greedy people. They had healthy appetites, as is natural in those who go long periods without food, but they never over-fed themselves for the sheer love of eating. In all my years with them, I met but one who could have been called a glutton. He was the ancient Hechoh, known as Shaipoöt u Hahhen (the Old Man of Shaipoöt).

A remark frequently to be heard at the end of an Ona meal was: "Omilh me ya." (" Satisfied am I.")

The word "Omilh" denoted only one kind of satisfaction, that resulting from a sufficiency of food. On that evening when I ate cormorant by Talimeoat's camp-fire on top of Tijnolsh Hill, I was among those who could say with truth, when all that remained were the bare bones:

"Omilh me ya."

3

Talimeoat was a most likeable Indian. I was much in his company. One still evening in autumn, just before business was to take me to Buenos Aires, I was walking with him near Lake Kami. We were just above upper tree level, and before descending into the valley, rested on a grassy slope. The air was crisp, for already the days were getting short and, with weather so calm and clear, there was bound to be a hard frost before sunrise. A few gilt-edged, feathery clouds broke the monotony of the pale green sky, and the beech forest that clothed the lake's steep banks to the water's edge had not yet completely lost its brilliant autumn colours. The evening light gave the remote ranges a purple tint impossible to describe or to paint.

Across leagues of wooded hills up the forty-mile length of Lake Kami, Talimeoat and I gazed long and silently towards a glorious sunset. I knew that he was searching the distance for any sign of smoke from the camp-fires of friends or foes. After a while his vigilance relaxed and, lying near me, he seemed to become oblivious to my presence. Feeling the chill of evening, I was on the point of suggesting a move, when he heaved a deep sigh and said to himself, as softly as an Ona could say anything:

"Yak haruin." (" My country.")

That sigh followed by those gentle words, so unusual for one of his kind—was it caused by a vision of the not far distant future, when the Indian hunter would roam his quiet woods no more; when the light wraith from his camp fire would give place to the smoke from saw-mills;

Spion Kop, looking north-north-east. It was near here that Ahnikin and I passed an uncomfortable night.

A sprinkling of snow on the high moor near Spion Kop. In the centre distance, more darkly shaded, is Harberton Mountain, with Mount Misery on Navarin Island behind it.

Looking westward along the divide, Spion Kop.

when throbbing engines and hooting sirens would shatter for ever the age-old silence?

If such were his thoughts, I shared his emotions to the full. I was powerless to stop the inevitable encroachment of civilization, but I was determined to do my utmost to soften the blow of it. I was going to Buenos Aires, but I should come back, not to Ushuaia or Harberton or Cambaceres, but to Najminshk in the heart of the Ona country, where I could help, by every means at my command, the hereditary lords of the land, the people whom I was proud to call my friends.

CHAPTER THIRTY-SIX

*Despard Brings his Bride to Harberton. Mary Goes to Live in the Paraguayan Chaco.
I Visit Buenos Aires and am Alarmed by the Traffic. My Argentine Lawyer
Endeavours to Provide Me with Feminine Companionship. With Great Relief I
Return to Fireland to Take Up my Life with the Ona Indians.*

I

I HAD NOT LEFT FIRELAND SINCE, AS A BOY OF ELEVEN, I HAD GONE WITH MY
father on his voyage of exploration to the western islands, the home of
the Alacaloof. On our homeward journey we had touched at Punta
Arenas. Since then, my contacts with civilization had been confined to
Ushuaia and Rio Grande.

My brother Will was in much the same position. Despard, on the
other hand, had been several times to Buenos Aires and had also made a
second trip to England with Father. As has been recorded, it was on
one of these visits to Buenos Aires that he had become engaged to Christina
Reynolds.

Some months later he had gone off again to Buenos Aires. There
was no regular mail in those days and, except for the rare occasions when
they brought us cargo—or they needed meat—vessels were never sighted
nearer than off the coast of Navarin Island. Thus we had no idea how
our wanderer fared or when we might expect his return.

One day, when Will was away visiting Minnie Lawrence at Punta
Remolino, I was working in the woods near Harberton with a dozen
Ona. We started our labours at daybreak and went on until it grew too
dark to work any more, when we downed axes and walked home. I
went into the back kitchen with the intention of kicking off my moccasins
and having a preliminary—and greatly needed—wash, before going to
my room to change out of my tramp's attire into clean, dry clothing.

The door from the kitchen to the sitting-room was wide open. As I
entered the kitchen, I heard voices coming from the other room. Among
them were the familiar tones of Despard and a feminine voice that was
strange to me. Knowing that my uncouth and barbarous appearance
would be no pleasing sight for a lady, I immediately made to withdraw
from the kitchen and escape to my bedroom unseen. But I was too late;
Despard caught sight of me, advanced upon me and dragged me into the

338

sitting-room to be presented to his wife. If I gave her a rude shock, Christina did not show it. She knew what was customary in such circumstances and, coming right up to me without hesitation, she did it. From that moment, I became her willing slave.

While my gang of workmen and I had been busy in the woods, a steamer had slipped into the harbour, landed Despard and his bride and gone on her way without our knowing anything about it.

Despard and Christina made their home at Harberton. Not long afterwards, Will also married and brought his wife to live at the homestead. As I had told my brothers during our argument on the question of settling in Ona-land, the Harberton accommodation was likely to become too cramped for the growing family in the near future.

I have described how my sister Mary met Wilfred Grubb on Keppel Island, how they became engaged, and how Wilfred subsequently volunteered to work among a tribe of natives in the upper Paraguayan Chaco, which can be justly described as the Last Spot on Earth. For ten years Mary and Wilfred corresponded as regularly as the intermittent mails would allow. During this long period my sister saw little of her nomad *fiancé*. She stayed for several years with us at Harberton, then spent some time in England. On her return from there, she and Wilfred were married in Buenos Aires, a fortnight before the wedding of Despard and Christina.

Mary and Wilfred went back together to the Gran Chaco, that vast region of forest, lakes and swamps that lies between the Pilcomayo River and its tributary, the Paraguay, where large areas are inundated when the rivers flood, and the climate is abominable. Here, away from their own kind and among barbarous tribes, they were to spend the best years of their lives.

Wilfred Grubb was a grand man. Much of his life has been described in four books,[1] but the best stories about him will never be printed. When I visited him in later years, he told me some of them—and most of them were against himself—as we reclined close to the camp-fire, preferring the pungent smoke to the mosquitoes, while, from time to time, some painted and befeathered Indian silently took from him his home-made pipe, stacked it again and handed it back to him.

[1] *An Unknown People in an Unknown Land*, by Barbrooke Grubb.
A Church in the Wilds, by Barbrooke Grubb.
Barbrooke Grubb, Pathfinder, by Norman J. Davidson.
Barbrooke Grubb of Paraguay, by C. T. Bedford.
All published by Messrs. Seeley, Service & Co., Ltd.

I must confine myself to recounting here but two of Wilfred's experiences. The first was when he was far from home one day with an Indian named Poet (Little Frog). Wilfred was walking in front when suddenly a blow like a terrific whip-lash struck him in the ribs. Poet had shot him with an arrow from behind. The culprit ran off shouting with fear, for it was believed by those people that if the spirit of a murdered man could get into the body of the murderer, the two spirits in one body would make a madman. This undoubtedly saved Wilfred's life, for Poet did not wait to finish him off. The arrow was not poisoned, but had been specially prepared. The head had been made from the blade of a knife, nine inches long and sharpened on both edges, and Wilfred was able to withdraw it. He lay there till the next day, when an Indian found him and cared for him until, two days later, two of his fellow missionaries arrived on horseback. After untold hardship, he reached the British hospital in Buenos Aires, where clots of blood had to be drawn from his lung. He refused an anæsthetic.

Poet had spread the story that Wilfred had been killed by a jaguar. When the true story became known, he said that he had felt obliged to kill Wilfred on account of a dream he had had. His fellows summoned a great meeting at which it was decided that Poet must die. Three village chiefs each told one of their young men to stab him to death; which was done.

The second adventure occurred far to the west across the Bolivian frontier, some distance north of the spot on the Pilcomayo River where Bolivia, Argentina and Paraguay meet. With some companions from the Lengua tribe of the Paraguayan Chaco, Wilfred was exploring an unknown part of the country, when they came upon an arrow tied to a twig in the path they were following. It was pointing against them and was a warning that they had been seen and were not welcome. When his companions refused to proceed further, Wilfred went on alone. He soon discovered that he was being shadowed, then found himself surrounded by a strange tribe whose language he could not understand; and realized that his life was in danger.

He knew that both religion and superstition generally spread over countries far beyond the boundaries of language. Fortunately for him, he had already been admitted into the secrets of the Lengua Lodge, so, being a great mimic, he now took a stick and carefully drew on the ground the figure of an enormous beetle, over which he crouched in the approved Lengua style and, with certain motions of hands and body, commenced a chant.

The ruse succeeded. Here was a wizard who knew the mystic rites of the Lodge! Soon a woman was found who had strayed or been stolen from the Lengua tribe. She acted as interpretress, and Wilfred—reported in numbers of newspapers to have been killed by the Indians—spent months in their company. In the harvest season he went with them to the great sugar plantations of the Leech brothers in Jujuy, where, through him, a branch of the Mission was later established.

In Paraguay Wilfred started a company called the Chaco Indian Association. The shareholders were exclusively the Chaco Indians. They traded in cattle and skins, and the assets were valued by an expert at £52,000. Paraguay is a Catholic country, whereas Wilfred was a Protestant of very low church. Nevertheless he was summoned to Asuncion, the capital, invested with the rank of honorary colonel and given the title " Protector of the Indians."

Mary went to Edinburgh shortly before her first daughter, Bertha, was born. When the child was a very few months old, they both returned to Wilfred in the Paraguayan Chaco, where I visited them soon after. Later I met Wilfred again. Encouraged by the Leech brothers, he had decided to start a branch Mission near their place at San Pedro, Jujuy.

2

It was in 1902, a year after the marriages of Mary and Despard, that I went to Buenos Aires. I was then in my twenty-eighth year. The reason for this journey was to secure the rights to the Harberton property, which still remained in my father's name. I was accompanied by Mother, Bertha and Alice. We travelled on the government transport, *Santa Cruz*, under our old and faithful friend, Captain Mascarelo. The voyage to Buenos Aires took thirty-one days. When we docked, I was alarmed by the vast number of people in the capital, all striving after something different and getting in each other's way. For years I had avoided going even to the village of Ushuaia. I had grown as wild and as apprehensive of white strangers as the wary Te-ilh of Najmishk. If, when on my way to Harberton for a few days' rest after weeks at Cambaceres or in the woods, I had noticed from some hilltop that a vessel was anchored in the harbour, I would turn back and return to the place from which I had come, rather than meet visitors. So, to put it mildly, I did not like Buenos Aires at all.

We were met at the docks by Despard's parents-in-law, Professor and Mrs. Reynolds, and their son, Dr. Robert Reynolds. We took cabs and drove to their home—undoubtedly one of the most frightening journeys of my life. I had ridden many an untamed colt and been out boating in the roughest of weathers, yet never had I been so perturbed as when I found myself being whisked along through what seemed a confused whirl of traffic, with a strange—and, for all I knew, undependable—driver in control of the horse.

When we reached our destination, Bobby Reynolds, who had noticed my reactions, remarked:

"I cannot understand you at all. You are a bundle of nerves, and from what I have heard of your life down south, I imagined you would have been just the opposite."

I felt very small indeed when I answered:

"This is the first time I have been in a coach since I was six years old."

The business that had brought us to Buenos Aires moved very slowly and at times stood still altogether. The main difficulty was that we, the children of Thomas and Mary Bridges, had no means of proving our identities. Father had jotted down our names and dates of birth in the family Bible, but that was not accepted as sufficient evidence by the authorities. Finally I engaged an Argentine lawyer, who was most anxious to be of every service to us. His first step was to seek out such of our old acquaintances at Ushuaia as were now resident in Buenos Aires. While these enquiries were in progress, this frank and honest man went out of his way to show that he was at my disposal not only in legal affairs, but also in those of a social nature.

He was extremely concerned for my personal happiness during my stay in the capital. To this end, he showed me some very nice photographs of girls of his acquaintance. Whether I preferred them large or tiny, blonde or brunette, he was prepared to give me the necessary introduction. Bluebeard's unfortunate wives could not have been more varied in type than the collection from which I was now asked to choose. He also offered me cards of invitation that had been left at his office by well-intentioned people who were prepared to show me round the town and teach me how to "live." All these efforts of his were prompted by pure kindness of heart; and when I declined his repeated offers with thanks, he obviously came to the conclusion that I was either mentally or physically deficient. In spite of, or possibly because of, our vastly different outlook, I developed a real affection for this conscientious friend; and, though he regarded my puritanical ideas as a huge joke, I am sure he liked me, too. He argued that a life of abstinence in the midst of plenty was wrong. It is interesting to add that, some years later, he assured me that he had quite altered his ideas on the subject.

The frail sisterhood of Buenos Aires were also set on giving me a good time. It is not the slightest credit to me that I did not fall for them, for I found their advances repellent to a degree. Mrs. Potiphar had a better chance with Joseph than even the loveliest of them had with me. Even those awful wax figures in the shop windows, with their painted lips and unblinking gaze, made me avert my own eyes and hurry past. So unnatural were they—and yet so human—that I could not meet their glassy stare.

More respectable forms of entertainment had a different effect on me. I vividly recall a dance to which I was invited by some friends. From among the onlookers, I watched the couples waltzing. I had never before seen men and women in evening dress. This was supposed to be a children's ball, yet a great many of those children were quite grown up. The girls, with their radiant faces and their brightly coloured, not too abundant clothing, looked magically beautiful to me. With the music and the lights, they dazzled me—and made me sad. I realized, for the first time, how much grace and gaiety I had missed; pleasures of early manhood that would never come to me again. I saw then that, right through life, I should be unlike other men; unable to throw myself wholeheartedly into such a joyous party as I was then watching. Yet, as my thoughts turned from civilization to the snowy forests and windswept heights of my native land, I echoed the words of *The Sick Stock-rider*, by Adam Lindsay Gordon.

" I'd live the same life over if I had to live again."

Our industrious lawyer's enquiries bore fruit. He was not long in discovering that several old friends of ours now held important positions in Buenos Aires. One of these was Mr. Virasoro y Calvo, who had been the first sub-prefect at Ushuaia and was now manager of a large national Bank. Another was a gentleman who, as a young naval officer, had been a member of that memorable expedition of 1884, when the Argentine government had, for the first time, taken cognizance of their most distant territory. Now he was no less a personage than the Minister of Marine.

With these to testify that the family of six children were known to them and were their parents' legitimate heirs, matters began to move forward with greater momentum and were soon sufficiently advanced to allow Mother, my sisters and myself to return to Fireland.

I was glad to get away from the turmoil and rush of the city, and to fill

my lungs with good cold air when we entered the Magellan Straits and saw on the southern horizon the white peaks I knew so well. The dream of my earlier years was about to come true. I was going to make my home in Ona-land among my Indian friends. Soon I should be able to say with Talimeoat and all those others—Halimink, Puppup, Kankoat, Yoknolpe, Taäpelht and the rest—those words of the shag-hunter of Tukmai as he had looked across Lake Kami towards the setting sun :
" Yak haruin."

PART IV

A HUT IN ONA-LAND

1902–1907

CHAPTER THIRTY-SEVEN

I Start the Farm at Najmishk and Call it Viamonte. We Use the Track to Take Tools and Provisions There. We Build a Hut and Begin to Fence the Land. I Ignore the Advice of Mr. McInch. Ahnikin and I are Caught in a Blizzard and Spend a Sleepless Night in the Snow.

I

IT HAD BEEN DESPARD'S OPINION—AND ONE THAT HE HAD EXPRESSED IN the most forcible terms—that to start a farm over the coastal range would be an expensive and hazardous business. He had based his argument on three main points : difficulty of access, the inclination of the Ona Indians towards murder and treachery, and the opposition of the wealthy sheepfarmers of the north. The first of these objections had now been, to a large extent, removed by the construction of the track from Harberton to Najmishk. The second was a risk that I had been taking for some time past and was quite prepared to continue taking. The third was a danger of a different kind.

There was no doubt in the minds of my brothers and myself that the great and powerful landowners in the north would not welcome our intrusion over the mountains. We felt sure that, having already occupied all the best sheep country near the ports, they—or others of their kind—would soon be looking for fresh land to annex—and the fertile country around Najmishk had doubtless not escaped their notice. At that time the general belief was that the region was unsuitable for sheep, but they could not have failed to realize that it was ideal for cattle and horses.

But " Nothing venture, nothing gain " was my motto ; and heartened by the memory of my father's heroic plunge when, in spite of ill-health and advancing years, he left Ushuaia and moved to Harberton, on I went. I cannot compare my life with that of my father, who came across the wide ocean to do his Master's work, yet there was a certain similarity— were it no more than that between Mount Everest and an anthill—between his venture and my own. When he had first gone to Ushuaia, he had settled where no white man had settled before. When he had left there, the first few rough shacks had developed into a flourishing village, and a centre of government had been established there. During the years the family had lived at Harberton, that, too, had expanded in the same way and, though hardly worthy to be called a village, was already self-supporting and boasted enough white men's dwellings besides our own to earn the name of hamlet.

I needed someone who could take charge at Najmishk at such times as I was absent at Harberton or elsewhere. The unsettled state of affairs in Ona-land at that time made it out of the question for an Indian to be left unarmed in charge of the stores of provisions and tools; some enemy would be bound to come along and kill him. And after my unhappy experience with Halimink and Ahnikin, I dared not trust the Indians with rifles, for fear they went on the war-path again. Whatever my hopes that the wrestling matches at Harberton had ended the long-standing quarrel between the northerners and the southern men from the mountains, Najmishk and Cape San Pablo, there was still the ever-present threat of bloody reprisals by one faction or the other.

Apart from these considerations, I knew from experience the impossibility of placing one Ona in authority over another. They were accustomed to a most communistic way of life. Everyone did as he liked; as much, or as little, as he pleased. If a difference of opinion arose, one man would either murder the other fellow out of hand, or drift off with his own family—and maybe a few sympathisers—to hunt in another district.

So I looked round for a white helper—and decided on Dan Prewitt. Of all the ten young men who had come out with my father in the *Phantom* in 1897, Dan Prewitt was the only one who had not drifted away from Harberton. He was a very good fellow, short, sturdy and dependable; and was well liked by the natives. He was, in fact, just the man to have by my side at Najmishk and work in harmony with my Ona friends, who were as keen as he to assist me in my new venture.

2

With the track ready for use, the next need was for horses. Good riding horses from the Harberton farm were valued on an average at the fantastic price of a hundred Argentine dollars—about eight pounds—a head, but untamed mares they would let me have at fifteen dollars each. I bought forty-two of these and went to work taming them. This gave me very little trouble, as they were already well accustomed to being driven into enclosures. I selected the best of them for riding purposes, intending to use the remainder as pack animals for conveying our stores to Najmishk. For these we made pack saddles, then loaded them to such good effect that, when Dan and I left Harberton with a party of our Ona friends, we were able to take with us nearly a ton of tools and provisions.

With our long line of laden animals, the journey to Najmishk was not an easy one. As has been mentioned, it entailed about two hundred crossings of the Varela and the Rio Valdés. In places the gradients were exceedingly steep. The mares had to scramble up, digging in their hooves and taking advantage, wherever possible, of the thickets on either side of the track. There was one point where the track led sharply upwards from a stream. Horses travelling in the other direction—that is, down the wet and slippery incline—made a *tumbadero* [1] of it, gathering their hind legs under them, planting their forelegs in front and glissading down for a distance of forty yards, until they reached a ledge where, in carrying out this manoeuvre, they soon piled up a mass of mud. A plunge through this brought the animals to the top of a second *tumbadero*, which led them slithering down into the stream at the foot of the hill. Though well used to steep land, our mares had a terrible job to scramble up these *tumbaderos*. In the final struggle at the summit of these and other very steep inclines, they might have to dig their chins into the earth on the brink, bunch their legs for one last effort, then, with a heave, come out on top of the bank with their knees on the ground.

In spite of these and other difficulties, we reached Najmishk on the fourth day out from Harberton with all forty-two mares and the whole of our stores intact.

3

I have said that the track came out on the beach along the north-western foot of Tijnolsh Hill, which ended in a cliff half a mile from the Ewan River. Some six miles to the north-west, past the mouth of the Ewan River, beyond the grand headland known as the Ewan Cliffs and a five-mile sweep of shingle beach, was the wooded hill (it would be as correct to say " hills ") of Najmishk. Rather rounded, but with several knobby lumps on top, with between them a few narrow, grassy glades, two or three of which had ample springs or tiny streams, Najmishk ended, as did Tijnolsh, in a cliff. This was about a mile long and with an average

---

[1] Slide (Spanish). Literally, a tumbling place in a gymnasium. The word is used by lumber-men to describe places so steep that logs have to be released and allowed to roll or slide down them.

height of some three hundred feet. In two places near its centre, where the height was no more than two hundred feet, two of the tiny streams just mentioned dribbled over the cliff at its lowest points. It was between these streamlets that Capelo had prepared the ambush into which the whites had refused to walk—or ride.

At the east-south-east end of the cliff was a grassy bank about a hundred and twenty feet above sea level. On this, at a spot nearly a quarter of a mile from the beach, and on the edge of the sheltering woods that practically covered the four hundred acres of Najmishk Hill, we made our first settlement. We started with a windbreak behind some huge wild currant bushes, later building a one-roomed hut with an un-glazed, wooden-shuttered window and an earthen floor. In this we fitted a couple of bunks, but Dan Prewitt was the only one to make use of the accommodation. I myself preferred my couch of branches and dried grass to the leeward of a windbreak near my Ona friends, who camped nearby; and the second bunk became a depository for such provisions and tools as could not be stored elsewhere in the tiny hut.

This was the modest beginning of the new settlement. I called it Viamonte, the picturesque Italian name of an historic Argentine general, which also means "Through the Woods," thus suiting the place admirably. With its inception, I began an abode with the Ona in their own country that was to last, with occasional breaks in the depths of winter, until the First World War called me away from the land of my birth.

4

There rallied around me in those early days at Viamonte all that remained of the sadly diminished Najmishk party—Koiyot, his two nephews, Ohrhaitush and Yoshyolpe, the brothers Shijyolh and Shish-kolh, Shaiyutlh (White Moss), Ishiaten (Scratched Thighs) and three or four other useful lads, among whom was Kautush. This boy Kautush was a stepson of that fine old man, Kautempklh, of the northern group. His mother was a Najmishk woman. His father had been killed some time before by one of the northern men. From that same northern group, eager to help in my new enterprise, came Paloa, Dolal, the son-in-law of Talimeoat, Kostelen (Narrow Face) and Ishtohn (Thick Thighs), the son-in-law of Kautempklh; and from the east, the joyous, faithful Kankoat and a young Aush lad by the name of Tinis, who had a withered arm. These enabled me to keep in touch with some fifty wandering hunters on whom I could count if needed.[1] The mountain men—Ahnikin, Hali-mink, Yoknolpe and the rest—seldom paid us a visit, and then only for an hour or two, as they felt safer further south. They had treacherously broken a peace of some years' standing and had brought disaster on the Najmishk party, whilst they themselves escaped scot-free. Ahnikin, the stormy petrel, well aware that Kiyohnishah (Guanaco Dung) would never forgive him for the murder of Houshken, now preferred to spend most of his time at Harberton. Kiyohnishah, Chashkil and one or two others of the northern group who had been conspicuous in the massacre at the stranded whale also avoided meeting those they had injured, and refrained from visiting us at Najmishk.

5

I was not in agreement with those who believed that the Najmishk area would be unsuitable for sheep, and proposed to bring as many as I could from Harberton. But before I could do this, the necessary land had to be enclosed. Our first task, therefore, after having installed our-selves at Viamonte, was to build fences. We started a timber fence at the top of Najmishk cliff and began to carry it down through the wooded part of the country. On this we worked until winter had well set in, when I felt that I could safely leave Dan Prewitt in charge at Viamonte while I spent a month or two with the family at Harberton. As his right-hand man, Koiyot was appointed.

After a pleasant month at Harberton, I decided to pay a visit to Viamonte. I had no fears for Dan's safety, but wanted to see how he had fared. Perhaps an even stronger attraction was the lure of the gleaming mountains. Mother, with an eye on the weather, was anxious when she heard of my intention, but I managed to reassure her, optimistically promising to be back in ten days' time. Seeking a companion on the trip, I asked young Ahnikin whether he would like to come with me, and was very glad when he accepted. He was a tough, resolute fellow, as he had proved when he had kept with me throughout that prolonged cattle hunt behind Flat Top after the others had deserted us.

[1] The frequent repetition in these pages of a score or so of names may give the impression that they were the only Indians to inhabit those parts in the early years of this century. This was far from the case. Besides those already mentioned, I could name a great many others with whom I lived and hunted. With wives and families, there was a wandering population of well over two hundred and fifty souls. Were I to name them all (if I could remember them), this book, already lavishly sprinkled with names that have given me much trouble to render phonetically in English—so guttural is the Ona tongue—would be intolerable to all but the most indulgent reader.

We started off together from Harberton, both wearing snow-shoes. Amongst the mountains we saw an occasional fox-track in the snow. In the great forest, before reaching Lake Kami, we came on the tracks of over thirty of them, all travelling together in the same direction. Ahnikin told me that on rare occasions, when driven by hunger, foxes gathered in packs to hunt guanaco. I myself had never before witnessed this wolf-like trait in foxes. Nor had my father. He had spoken of having heard Yahgans telling of foxes hunting in packs when weather was extremely bad, but he had added that he was inclined to doubt it.

Near Lake Kami on our third day out, the snow became shallow and hard-frozen, so we hung up our snow-shoes on trees, to be collected on our return journey, and pressed on to Najmishk, which we reached by noon on the following day. Dan Prewitt was glad to see us. He was in good spirits and well pleased with his henchman, Koiyot. His only complaint was that he felt his position as my deputy at Viamonte was not properly understood at Rio Grande, where he had gone on one occasion for provisions. I considered it advisable to clear the matter up before returning to Harberton, so the next day, leaving Ahnikin at Viamonte, I took a horse and rode along the coast to the port, where I spent the night as the guest of the hospitable, but otherwise deplorable, Mr. McInch.

This uncrowned king of Rio Grande was indeed a most curious mixture. He who took open pride in having persecuted and murdered the Indians—albeit for their own good—hated to see a sore-necked yoke-ox, or a horse being unduly spurred; and a remarkable understanding existed between him and dogs. He would sit chatting with visitors on the verandah of his house or the store, while his sturdy Irish terrier lay snoozing at his feet, but with one eye fixed on his master. The host's manner towards his guests would be warm and kindly, and his friendly attention would not waver were one of them to become uppish. His eyes would shift with the same benign light from the self-assertive one to the dog and back. An imperceptible flicker of an eyelid—and the terrier would fly at the legs of the startled offender. He would then be hauled off by his enraged master, who would declare that he had never seen him behave like that before and wondered if the creature was going mad.

Mr. McInch had long ago recovered from the effects of Taäpelht's arrow and produced for my inspection one of his most treasured possessions: the tiny glass arrow-head that had nearly cost him his life. This he was proposing to have made into a tie-pin.

| Chalshoat (Puppup's brother) | Chalshoat's daughter | Puppup's second wife | Puppup | Puppup junior | Puppup's first wife | Her daughter |

The first Mrs. Puppup was the mother of the second Mrs. Puppup by a previous husband. The two children were also hers, but by Puppup. Subsequently both wives—mother and daughter—had children by Puppup almost at the same time. The girl on the right became the wife of Martin, who is mentioned in later chapters. The perpendicular lines on Miss Chalshoat's face are not tear-stains, but lines of yellow clay to show that she feels moody and does not wish to be bothered.

From the library of Dr. Armando Braun Menéndez. It is believed that the original photograph was taken by Col. Charles Wellington Furlong.

(*Left*) Grandmother and child, both with hair cut in mourning. Behind them is the *kowwhi* (shelter), with a bow, a basket, guanaco meat hanging from a stick, and on the right, hanging from the pole, a *moji*. (*Right*) Chalshoat and Puppup (standing).

By courtesy of Col. Charles Wellington Furlong.

The same *kowwhi* as the one above, with two men, two women, children and dogs. Ona men always held their bows and quivers as in this picture. These are northern Ona from near Useless Bay. The mountain Ona rarely used baskets as seen here; they used skin bags instead. The man on the left has a bracelet of plaited sinew on his wrist—an unusual adornment. The slim pole slanting up below the basket is probably a woman's fish-spear.

This photo is reproduced by courtesy of Mr. A. A. Cameron, who took both this and No. 61 above over fifty years ago.

By the following morning a bitter wind from the south had sprung up. Mr. McInch strongly advised me to remain at the Primera Argentina settlement, but, with the purpose of my visit achieved, I preferred not to listen to his warnings and started out on my horse with the powdery snow blowing into my eyes. A Scottish shepherd, who had his shanty a few leagues away, left the settlement and rode with me until the parting of our ways. Before we separated he produced a bottle of whisky and kindly offered me a swig to keep out the cold. In those days I considered this a weakness, so refused, whereupon he took one himself and we said good-bye. I was the last to see him alive. His saddled horse turned up riderless at Rio Grande some days afterwards, and later his frozen body was found in the snow. He had been quite sober when he had left me.

I reached Viamonte without mishap. The weather showed no signs of improvement and I began to regret having promised Mother to be back at Harberton within ten days. Knowing that she would grow anxious if I did not arrive on time, I started off on foot with Ahnikin before dawn on the seventh day.

We found our snow-shoes where they had been left, and by that time we needed them badly, for driven by an ever-increasing contrary wind, the snow was getting very deep. On the evening of our ninth day out we found ourselves at the head of the long valley that runs into the mountains from the north. It was sheltered from the wind, but, for that very reason, the drifts in many places were over twenty feet deep, and there was no possibility of getting a fire on the ground. We collected a lot of branches and, laying them on the snow, made our fire on top of them. The fire soon melted a deep pit into which it sank, giving us more smoke than warmth. We had some meat which we thawed and roasted after a fashion. We also managed to cook some rice, sugar and fat in our billy cans. I had a skin robe and sleeping-bag, whilst Ahnikin had two robes. In these we passed a fairly comfortable night.

Next morning the outlook was far from cheerful, but there was nothing to make us wish to remain where we were. Nor did we care to go back the way we had come. When the snow cleared ahead of us for a moment, we could see it drifting in clouds over the ridge of Spion Kop, less than half a mile away, but we determined to push on, for though well aware that on that high moor, with the gale in our faces, it would be really nasty, a mile or two further on we should find some shelter and soon be in an evergreen wood, where we could make a good fire.

The snow was soft and deep on this sheltered side and without our snow-shoes we could not have advanced at all. At last we crossed the top and for a short distance tried to face the blizzard. Sometimes we had to open our eyes with our fingers, for the eyelashes froze, and we had to pinch our noses continually. We turned a little to the eastward then, but could not see the ground we were walking on. At last a rock gave us some shelter and we rested awhile, hoping that the wind might calm down, but it began to grow dark and still the storm continued. We were utterly blinded with snow, and being already off the track might have walked into some death-trap if we had tried to go back, and we certainly could not go forward, so we trod down a place in the snow and prepared to spend the night there. My companion remarked, not very cheerfully, that the foxes would find us there when the snow melted in the spring. I asked if we were two old women, but added:

" We must not go to sleep. If my head nods, hit me hard till I am awake, and I will do the same to you."

We were not really cold, though our robes were heavy with snow and somewhat damp, but I was afraid that if we slept we might be buried like sheep, for in the shelter of that rock the snow was piling up at an incredible rate. When sleep seemed to be overpowering us, we would get up and wrestle strenuously with each other until we were awake and warm; and so we passed the night.

The storm was over before daybreak and the stars began to appear. We put on our snow-shoes and made for the wood of evergreens, where we got a roaring fire going. After a good hot meal, we started off again and reached Harberton after nightfall on the eleventh day. Our arrival was a great relief to the family. The terrible weather had caused them grave anxiety on our account. That morning Will had been on Gable Island, digging out buried sheep. He had seen the smoke from our fire and, thinking it might be a distress signal, had come to Harberton with Kankoat, ready to set out in search of us next morning.

Ever since my father had been able to converse with the Yahgans, he had heard them speak of dreadful winters long ago. With his own experience limited to Fuegian winters of no tremendous severity, he had consigned these stories to the jumble of legend and fable, a subject in which he took small interest. But the stories had persisted, some of the older men claiming to remember when the frozen channels had made it impossible to use canoes for catching fish, their principal food, and the solid ice on the beaches had cut off all supplies of mussels and limpets;

when guanaco in their hundreds had died of starvation and only a few had survived.

Making due allowances for exaggeration, my father had eventually reached the conclusion that these stories were substantially true and that, some fifty years before the advent of the Mission at Ushuaia, there had been a succession of hard, prolonged winters, of which there had not since been so serious a repetition. He had warned us that what had happened once might well happen again and that we must be prepared for heavy losses—even the total destruction of our flocks and herds.

This winter was one which made us believe that the Yahgan story-tellers had not been romancing. I do not recall anything previous to equal it, as, before it finally left us, it was to give us a most unpleasant surprise. To all appearances, it ended about the usual time. Then, when the trees and bushes had come to leaf and numberless birds had returned to their nests, it came again. On October the 6th there was a fall of more than three feet of snow, followed by a protracted period of hard frost. Out of over four thousand lambs at Harberton, less than four hundred survived, and a great many of their mothers perished as well. Thousands of forest birds—finches, thrushes, etc.—were driven out of the snow-laden woods. They landed on the beaches when the tide was out and, unused to the exposure, remained there with outspread wings until they drifted away to their deaths on the rising tide. Even the wild up-land geese lost all their energy and power of flight. They lay on the snow vainly endeavouring to rise and were so helpless that one could walk over to them and pick them up. There was a small cave on the little island in the Cambaceres inner harbour where we had occasionally picnicked. When we went to it later that year, the cave was so carpeted with dead birds that had sought refuge there that we did not care to use it again.

Though all the Yahgan country suffered, it seems that Harberton got the worst treatment in that death-struggle of departing winter. Except for continuous icy wind from the south, the Atlantic coast felt it hardly at all.

CHAPTER THIRTY-EIGHT

The First Sheep-Shearing at Najmishk. I Wrestle with Chorche. Kiyohnishah and his Party Come Again to Harberton. Some Account of Ona Customs. Sundry Ways to Obtain Two Wives. Ona Infants. Halimink Controls his Natural Curiosity. Correct Behaviour for Father and Son-in-Law. The Ona Mourn their Dead. An Ona Burial. Painting and Tattooing. Native Clothing. The Propriety of Ona Women. Kewanpe Overcomes her Modesty. The Family Doctor. A Cure for Lumbago. Ona Bows and Arrows. Flint-Knappers Ancient and Modern. The Hunters' Code of Honour. How the Ona Hunt a Guanaco. Unexpected Discomfiture of the Terrible Tigre. Discourteous Habits of the Guanaco. Dr. Holmberg is Disappointed.

I

DESPITE OUR LOSSES DURING THE WINTER, WILL HAD ENOUGH SHEEP LEFT at Harberton and Gable Island to enable me to start my farm. The following summer, with Ona companions, I drove the first 2,300 across to Viamonte—not all at once, but about five hundred at a time. Each drive took six or seven days, with two days for the return trip for the next batch. The whole undertaking was carried through without a hitch, though trouble was sometimes experienced in man-handling the sheep in the streams.

There was much excitement among the Ona in those parts when the time for the first sheep-shearing in their country came round. A number of them congregated at Najmishk, some to help and others to watch. Most of those of our Ona friends who had learnt to shear were busy with Will at Harberton, so that many who were eager to try their hands at Najmishk were the merest novices. It would have caused a civilized sheep farmer some astonishment to see a bunch of fine, painted, stark-naked Ona trying to shear the sheep with hand-shears. The women who had gathered round the corral, in the apparent belief that the whole show had been got up for their entertainment, watched with undisguised glee the struggles of the unfortunate animals in the strong hands of those willing but incompetent apprentices, while I did what I could to teach them the correct procedure. To this day I wonder what the wool-buyers thought of the patches of red paint that were inadvertently transferred from shearers to fleeces.

A fat, good-natured young fellow called Chorche, who was nearly as tall as I and weighed every ounce as much, insisted on holding the sheep in a most irregular way, thinking, no doubt, that he was being very clever. After I had rated him several times he grew vexed and, with a cheeky remark, advanced towards me, evidently with the intention of wrestling. He was the challenger, but I forestalled him by holding out my left hand. When he held out his right, instead of embracing him in correct Ona style, I seized him by the wrist, drew him forward, dived my head and shoulders under his right arm, then gave an upward heave. Taken by surprise, Chorche turned a complete somersault and landed on his back behind me, to the accompaniment of roars of laughter from the men and shrieks of delight from the women.

Chorche got up rather shaken and not at all pleased. I was expecting a rough-and-tumble on the spot, but he did not return to the attack. That evening I gave him the satisfaction of a wrestling match by Ona rules. We found that there was not much to choose between us. There was not the slightest ill-feeling on either side, and Chorche and I had many a friendly tussle after that.

It was a mean trick for me to play. The Ona were quite unacquainted with such jiu-jitsu tricks (though I fancy that this simple throw, effective only when used as a surprise, belonged to wrestling before jiu-jitsu was conceived) and I should not have employed it.

2

Meanwhile shearing operations were also in progress at Harberton and on Gable Island. In addition to the usual families of the southern groups, Harberton received a visit from Kiyohnishah, Chashkil, Pahchik and a dozen other stalwarts from the north, all with their wives and children. With a like number of the southern folk, they were taken by Will to Gable Island, where all joined in the shearing. They pitched their encampments near each other and seemed on better terms than ever before. Working well together, they laughed at the same jokes; but still they met of an evening in none too friendly wrestling matches, with Halimink, Kankoat, Ahnikin and other old friends engaging once again with their heavier opponents, Chashkil, Halah, Pahchik, Kautempklh and the rest.

After the shearing they all prepared to leave on their autumn wanderings, when the guanaco were in good condition and there was an abundance of wild goslings and other game. Similarly the gathering at Najmishk dispersed. The Ona were born wanderers and never stayed long in one place. Most of them came and went at Viamonte just as they had done—and continued to do—at Harberton and Cambaceres, which was now in charge of Contreras, the Chilean half-breed. Our nearest neighbours at Viamonte were, of course, the Najmishk people, whose leading figure, Koiyot, acted as Dan Prewitt's principal assistant in the care of the sheep and mares.

Koiyot's wife was called Olenke. She and her sister, Walush, had once been the wives of Koiyot's brother. It was said that Koiyot had broken his brother's neck in wrestling, in order to obtain Olenke and Walush, who had been, for a time, his second wife. Walush had had two sons by Koiyot's brother—Ohrhaitush and Yoshyolpe.

From Olenke and the other women of the little party I received every attention. All Ona women were friendly souls and there were always girls willing to fetch water or fuel. Frequently, on arriving back late in the evening, I would find a fine *dahapi* or two, fresh caught in the pools among the rocks on the beach, hanging up near my shelter, with no clue as to the donor; or I might discover a nice roasted fish waiting for me on hot embers near my couch. Chief of the good fairies were Ijij and her daughter Koilah. They were a good-looking pair. Ijij may have been thirty-five and the daughter looked barely twenty years younger.

A story told of Ijij was that, in company with some other women, she had been returning from the beach with fish, when they had met a friendless man whom they all hated. His teeth had been chattering and he had been numb with cold; his robe had been soaking wet. At Ijij's suggestion, the women had done him to death with their fish-spears and rocks. That was the story, yet it may have been that the unfortunate man had had a seizure on the beach and his body had been battered and bruised by being washed against the rocks, and torn by voracious birds. Who knows?

Ijij never seemed to have a permanent husband, and years later my little friend Koilah might well have been called a prostitute. Notwithstanding this, I can affirm that, during my life with the Ona, I do not remember one single instance when any of the women passed the rules of propriety, rules that might have been laid down by the Pilgrim Fathers. In their homes both men and women were correct in their behaviour and well-mannered. One could spend weeks living amongst them day and night without being annoyed or repelled by their conduct. With the exception of the crazy Minkiyolh, I never heard an Ona brag of his strength or prowess. When flattered or praised unduly, a man would feel self-conscious and check the speaker, perhaps adding :

"Yi shwaken shi ma." ("You might annoy me.") [1]

For a long time my chief occupation at Viamonte was the fencing of the land, working only with Ona companions. Nevertheless I found time to go off on hunting expeditions and to travel about Ona-land, increasing my knowledge of the language and customs of these brave, attractive, treacherous people. Before continuing with my main theme, I think I should digress for a few pages in order to describe some of these customs of a race now virtually extinct.

I have told how young Teëoöriolh wooed and won the daughter of Missmiyolh, the Aush, in the correct and ancient fashion. This, in my experience, was a notable exception from the all too common practice of acquiring wives by conquest or abduction. Another method—not unknown in civilized communities—was an arrangement between the parents without reference to the wishes of the young people concerned. In these cases, if the prospective husband was some years older than his future bride, instead of waiting for her to reach the necessary age, he would take another and much older woman for his first wife. This matron would instruct him in all the duties of a husband, then, when the girl was old enough, would meekly give her pride of place. She would not necessarily forsake her erstwhile husband, but would remain a member of his household, attending to his needs in a manner far more efficient than could have been expected of the inexperienced damsel who had superseded her.

The Ona had no marriage ceremony of any kind. The woman was taken into the man's home—and that was that. Sometimes a newly united couple would be conspicuous by their absence from the encampment for a day or two; on the other hand, if there was a disappointed rival, they might feel safer near their own people. It was always left to the man to take the initiative, yet, for all their apparent subjugation, the Ona women had their rights and customs. For instance, it was not considered proper for a new wife, whether a young girl or a mature woman, to give herself away too cheaply. On the contrary, she would frequently put up a good fight and, on his next appearance, the bridegroom might have a badly scratched face and maybe a black eye as well. I remember one man asking me to attend to a really nasty bite inflicted on his

---

[1] " Yi | shwaken | shi | ma."
" Me | annoy | in case | you."

forearm by his bride, a strong, determined woman of considerable experience.

Very few Ona had three wives; custom limited the number to two. The second wife was often the younger sister of the first wife, whose lot, without some assistance, was not a happy one. In the normal course or married life, it would not be long before she found herself with a couple or helpless children to carry on her back in addition to the sundry goods and chattels that it was her wifely duty to move continuously from place to place. In these circumstances, it was a natural thing for the young sister to lend a hand, and automatically she became wife number two. It was a husband's privilege to go to his father-in-law and demand another of the old man's daughters as his second wife.

Some wives, of course, were not sisters to each other. The husband might have obtained them from different places and by different methods. There were cases in which the husband treated his unfortunate first wife in an abominable fashion, in order to please his second wife. By lavishing his attentions on the younger woman, he hoped to induce her to stop with him rather than seize the first opportunity of giving him the slip. Such a man was young Ahnikin. His first wife had been the daughter of Kaushel (sister to Kiliutah and Minkiyolh, the madman). His second wife was the elder daughter of Houshken, whom he had murdered. In order to win this girl's affection, Ahnikin treated his first wife with the utmost brutality—so much so that she ran away from him and sought a protector among the whites. Then his second wife died, leaving him a widower, and he had to look round for another wife. The outcome of his search is dealt with in a later chapter.

Ahnikin had obtained his second wife by killing her father. Another popular Ona way of getting a wife was to kill her husband. This method is best illustrated by the case of Puppup. Before I became acquainted with them, the mountain men began to experience a shortage of wives. Though many of the older ones were in happy enjoyment of two wives, some of the others—among them the gentle Puppup—had no wife at all. To remedy this deficiency, they decided on a raid to the north-westward. For this expedition a strong party was got together. It was not limited to wife-seekers, but included a number of men already adequately endowed in that respect, but who refused to remain behind when such an adventure was afoot.

Off went the raiders, out of their forested domain into the more open country of their unsuspecting neighbours. Advancing with the utmost caution, they managed one evening to locate a party of the other group. They waited until daybreak, then fell on their victims, who were hopelessly outnumbered. Few of the men escaped death by the arrows of the mountain warriors, who, with no loss to themselves, carried off to their own country enough desirable women to make the foray well worth while. Puppup was one of those to win a wife—a young woman in an advanced state of pregnancy.

Most of the kidnapped women managed to make their escape before very long, but several of them elected to remain with their captors. The kindly Puppup was one of the favoured few. In due course his wife gave birth to a daughter, the child of her murdered first husband. When this girl grew up, she automatically became the second Mrs. Puppup, and mother and daughter lived very happily together. Both had children by Puppup at nearly the same time, and I noticed that they passed the babies from one to the other for nourishment without troubling which belonged to whom.

When Ahnikin's second wife, elder daughter of Houshken, had died, her younger sister should, according to Ona custom, have gone to Ahnikin, but Houshken had promised during his lifetime that she should be the wife of Hinjiyolh, the athletic and well-grown only son of my old friend, Tininisk. The married life of Hinjiyolh was tragically short. Six weeks after she had given him a daughter, his wife died from some other cause. Some two months later, I happened to pass near Tininisk's camp in the woods and caught sight of his wife, Leluwhachin. I noticed with surprise that she was feeding her grandchild, a bonny little girl, as a mother would.

" How is it possible," I asked her, " since you have gone so long without having a child of your own, that you are now able to feed this baby? "

" Because I wanted to," she answered. " The little one needed the milk or she would have died." She smiled as she added, " Do you think she is thin? "

The child did splendidly and they called her Matilde. When she grew up, she married Garibaldi, whom I had kidnapped when he was four years old and later exchanged with Tininisk for Kankoat's little son.

Ona infants were seldom weaned until they were about three years old. Nursing mothers were supposed to eat only certain parts of the guanaco. These were put on one side for them and custom forbade them to eat any other portions of the animal. When a troublesome child objected to being weaned, the mother would anoint herself with a few drops of gall. The guanaco has no gall, so the gall from a seal, a fox or a bird was used. The child's grimaces of disgust and disappointment would have amused any onlooker, but it soon learned wisdom.

When a baby, apparently well, cried incessantly, the mother, showing signs of impatience, might utter a prolonged shriek into each ear. Generally the child stopped crying. Deafness among the Ona was almost unknown. With a thirsty child, a mother would spare it the shock of ice-cold water by warming it first in her own mouth, then letting it run into the mouth of her little one.

Twins were practically unheard of and babies rarely arrived in quick succession. A newborn baby was generally wrapped up in the softest fox-skin. An eye-shade of pliable guanaco hide with the hair scraped off was tied round the forehead just over the eyes. It was painted a very dark red and looked something like a jockey's cap.

The cradle, *taälh* (which also means " fern "), resembled a ladder in construction and held the baby upright instead of in the supine position preferred for their children by civilized mothers. The *taälh* had two side pieces between four and five feet long. These were pointed at one end for sticking into the ground and were joined together by rungs, each a foot in length, tied at short intervals across the upper part. Having first been well wrapped up, the child was laid on the cross-pieces, with a skin several times folded as a cushion, and securely bound to the *taälh* with strips of hide. An injured limb could scarcely have been more tightly bandaged, and, when watching this operation, I always found it hard to refrain from interfering, so anxious was I for the infant's circulation. With the child thus attached, the *taälh* was stood upright and the pointed ends pushed firmly into the ground, ensuring that the baby was kept out of the way of dogs and safe from being trampled on by careless children.

The birth of a child imposed certain restrictions on the father. It might be some days before he knew whether the latest addition to the family was a boy or a girl. Sometimes, however, he was given a clue. One winter I was working with a party of Ona, among them Halimink, cutting firewood in the west creek at Harberton. We were returning home one evening and were approaching the native encampment, when we saw Akukeyohn, the younger Mrs. Halimink, carrying a huge load of firewood. Her husband said, as though questioning:

" Has my wife had a boy child to-day? "

Some two days later, when I met Halimink again, I asked him if the child was a boy or a girl. He said:

"I have not seen it yet."

As these people were living by the same fire, under the same guanaco-skin shelter, I was much surprised at this, but learned later that it was not the correct thing for the father to show any curiosity about the matter, nor was he supposed to address his wife after the birth of a child until spoken to by her. She had been carrying that heavy load of wood so that the child she nourished might be very strong when it grew up. For that reason, Halimink had thought the child was probably a boy, and his surmise proved correct.

The story of Akukeyohn's next baby also throws some light on Ona motherhood. The various parties used to come to Harberton by different paths, two or three of which converged near the east end of Lake Kami before separating again on approaching the mountains. Accompanied by a few Ona men and one or two active women, I was on a hurried tramp, bound for home. In the dangerous neighbourhood just mentioned, we were joined by Halimink and Akukeyohn. He was anxious for our company through this part, where his enemies might be passing, and I was surprised to find him near there in those unquiet times.

In the afternoon of our first day together, his party seemed to lag behind—or possibly I, looking forward to spending the following night at Harberton, was walking too fast. Halimink came up to me and said:

"Why don't we camp here? This is a good place."

I answered, for it was about five o'clock in the afternoon:

"Why should we? The sun is still high."

He said simply: "My wife is about to have a baby."

I did not argue any more. We made our encampment and went on with the usual business of cooking, drying clothes, fixing moccasins, etc. Halimink arranged a little shelter some fifty yards away. There the women collected, while he came across to spend the night with us. He went over at dawn to the other shelter, and soon after sunrise we were all ready to start, Akukeyohn having a small additional bundle on her back. We crossed many a mountain stream that day and climbed steep hills till, after midday, Halimink separated from us, feeling that he was far enough into his own country to proceed at leisure.

Children were treated kindly by all. Though these people never kissed each other, I have seen men pressing their children's little bodies to their lips. Children were much valued by their parents. When the men grew too old to hunt, their sons could be depended upon to supply them with food and to defend them. They might always get another wife, but children were not so easy to replace. Even brothers were far more greatly valued than wives; a brother would fight by a man's side and avenge him if he were killed.

There was a code of behaviour governing fathers and their sons-in-law when sharing the same home. I once spent a day or two at a small encampment near the Chappel River, where old Kautempklh was living with his daughter Te-al and her husband, Ishtohn (Thick Thighs). I noticed during my stay with them that the two men appeared to be quite unaware of each other's existence. They never exchanged glances when speaking. Any remark they made was addressed to the fire or the sky or the young woman, who acted as an intermediary and seemed to take an equal interest in both of them. When, after an absence from the encampment, Ishtohn came in with a portion of guanaco meat, he said nothing at first. After a while he observed to the empty air that the rest of the animal was hanging in a tree near a little cliff called Kaäpelht and went on to express some anxiety as to whether the foxes might get it during the night. Kautempklh made no sign that he had heard. To preserve his dignity, he let ten minutes go by before asking his daughter to hand him his moccasins. This she did without a word, having carefully put a little soft grass into each, which I thought a very pretty action. Kautempklh put them on and, taking his *moji*, bow and arrow, went off towards Kaäpelht. He returned at dusk with the remainder of the meat.

This was apparently the correct procedure when father and son-in-law lived together, and surely it was a good arrangement, for they could never quarrel. Nevertheless, they could still feel hurt with one another, even though they never exchanged a word. Years later, when Kautempklh lay dying, Will paid him a visit. During their chat, the ancient man complained bitterly that Ishtohn was lazy, for he had not yet dug a grave for him to lie in.

According to my father, the Yahgans did not wound themselves in mourning. Among the Ona, it was the custom for the chief mourners to scrape their legs and arms with sharp stones, glass or shells. Sometimes they made very severe cuts, and many carried the scars of self-inflicted wounds for life. Koiyot had a great cicatrix over a foot long right across his chest. It was said that this had been done as he stood beside the dead body of his brother, whom he had killed while wrestling. It is possible that that tremendous gash had been made when he had realized what he had done. Some men, I have been told, wounded themselves so grievously that they died in consequence. I know of no such instance.

When an Ona died his bow and arrows were broken up and burnt. This performance—and the scraping of limbs—often started before the invalid had passed away. Both Talimeoat and Kaushel (some years before the illness that finally carried him off) were able to boast that they had recovered after being so ill that their bows had been burnt and all their friends had cut themselves in mourning, which left them weak from loss of blood that had run down to the ground. I recall how those two rascals, in speaking of it afterwards, chuckled at the way they had cheated the would-be mourners and death itself.

Bodies were buried in graves dug in the ground. I have told how when Kiyotimink, son of Kaushel, died of hydrophobia, his young widow, Halchic, was taken to wife by Kankoat. It was not long, alas! before poor Kankoat was again a widower, for Halchic died in childbirth—as far as I knew or heard of, the only Ona woman ever to do so. Ijij, the chief midwife who attended her, went for some time in fear of being killed by the bereaved husband.

The corpse was wrapped up well in guanaco skins and in a shelter-skin (scraped skins sewn together). A few light sticks of the full length of the body were wrapped in with the coverings to keep it stiff and make it easier to carry on the shoulders. Only five or six men besides myself went to the burial, the women stopping behind in the encampment to wail and cut themselves. We took a couple of spades and a pick-axe, and carried the corpse about a third of a mile to a spot chosen by Kankoat. The ground was hard, so when we had dug about three and a half feet down, we put the corpse in the grave and filled in the earth and stones. As we were about to leave, Kankoat gave one long wail that would need Robert Service or Jack London in their tales of the wolf-lands to describe.

If, on account of deeply frozen ground, it was not possible to dig a grave, the body was burnt and the place afterwards avoided, not for fear of ghosts, but because it brought thoughts of the departed too vividly to mind.

Halchic's child survived and must, I think, have been a girl. Had it been a boy, Kankoat would have taken far greater interest than he did. I know nothing of the child's subsequent history. Since making the acquaintance of Kankoat and his little boy, Nelson, whose second eye had been saved by Dr. Cook, I had discovered that Kankoat had an even younger son. I did not know the boy until he was about four years old; he had probably lived with some foster-mother in Tininisk's generous household. He was called David.

To mention the dead by name was as offensive to the Ona as to the Yahgans. It was equally objectionable to use a man's name when speaking of him in his presence. The courteous method was either to indicate the man in question by a gesture of the hand, as was the Yahgan habit, or to make use of such circumlocutions as " Toni Nana " [1] (the father of Nana [2]), " T-kai Kautush " (the mother of Kautush), " Hyewhin Joön (the doctor of Hyewhin), " Tamshk u hoiyipen " (the hunter from Tamshk) or " Tijnolsh u kbowtn " (the successful hunter from Tijnolsh). That was the Ona way.

In their signs of mourning for the dead, whether the loss was from sickness, accident or murder, Yahgans and Ona both shaved the crowns of their heads, leaving only a fringe of hair round the bald pate. When their only cutting implement was a flint, this must have been an uncomfortable and rather tedious operation. This tonsuring, which was done as closely as their blunt implements allowed, was carried out by women as well as men. A visitor, on seeing the growth of hair that had taken place since the head had been shorn, could make a fair guess as to when the bereavement had happened and regulate his behaviour accordingly. The safest plan was to adopt a thoughtful attitude, unless the rest of the party showed signs of hilarity.

Both Yahgans and Ona used paint as a sign of mourning: Yahgans black, Ona a very deep shade of red. Their painting procedure was very similar. The chief colours were red, white and yellow. The first was the most popular. It was made from the red clay called *akel* in the Ona tongue. This was well mixed with grease and then burnt. The resulting powder was mixed again with a very little grease and rolled into a ball so dry that it could be easily powdered again. This was generally carried in a little skin bag or the bladder of a seal or guanaco. Yellow paint was made from *koöre* [3] and prepared in the same fashion. White

---

[1] The Ona for " his father " and " his mother " were *T-ain* and *T-kahm* respectively (see footnote to page 243), but, when avoiding mention of the parent's name, especially when he or she was present, *Toni* and *T-kai* were used.

[2] Halimink. Nana was his eldest son by his first wife. At that time he was a boy of ten or twelve. Bullet-headed and even shorter than his father, Nana later became a reckless horseman and tamer, as well as a useful shepherd, but he had the dangerous temper of the mountain gang.

[3] Yellow clay. According to Ona legend, which is dealt with in detail in a later chapter, *Koöre* was once a man and his wife was a guanaco. These animals continually

paint was either chalk (*kaithtrrh*) or ash and was the favourite adornment of Puppup. Black paint was obtained from charcoal.

There were various ways of applying the paint. A neat instrument for making rows of small spots, either red or white, on face or body was a section of the jaw-bone of a porpoise. When the skin had been painted red or white, according to taste, the other colour would be daubed lavishly on the row of blunt teeth, many in number, in the jaw-bone, which would then be pressed gently against the skin. To obtain larger spots, a finger dipped in the paint sufficed. This simple method could also be used to draw white, red or yellow lines. Yellow paint, when applied in perpendicular lines on either side of the mouth, advertised, by the grim, surly expression that it gave the face, that the wearer was feeling moody and wanted to be left alone. Speaking for myself, one glance at the unsmiling face with its yellow disfigurement was always enough to ensure that I, for one, respected the gloomy one's wishes. How much better it would be if certain white men in similar mood would follow the Ona custom in this matter, instead of answering a friendly greeting with a vacant stare or a boorish growl! An alternative way of painting lines was to plaster the palm of one hand with paint and then make furrows across by scratching it off with the nails of the other hand, the fingers being held close together. This was done in one continuous movement and, the thumb not being used, left three little ridges of paint running parallel across the palm. Further scraping of the margins would bring the number of ridges up to five or more. These were then transferred to the face or body by pressing the hand on the part desired.

At times when exotic spots like those of a leopard were called for, a friend of the warrior would take powdered paint in his mouth and blow it out hard between his teeth onto a prepared background of a different colour. Some of the men excelled in this and achieved quite artistic results on the persons of their fellows.

Ona hunters painted themselves and smeared their bows and quivers, in order to be less conspicuous; yellow clay to resemble withered grass, chalk to match the whiteness of snow.

As for tattooing, the Yahgans never practised it and the Ona only to a small extent. They raised a tiny piece of skin with the point of a knife or a needle (in the old times they probably used a thorn), trying to avoid

---

roll in the yellow clay and, when irritated by burrs or some skin trouble under the wool, rub themselves fiercely—it is said even passionately—against it. One finds places where guanaco go regularly to roll and have worn hollows in the *koöre*.

much bleeding. Beneath the skin they then buried a speck of charcoal as large as a pin's head. With the healing of the flesh these specks grew somewhat larger and took on a bluish tint, marking the man for life. The spots were arranged in a straight line of perhaps a dozen, about a quarter of an inch apart. I never saw any attempt at a pattern. The tattooing was done on the arm or the leg. Only in two or three cases did I see it on the face. There was no matching; no corresponding marks on both arms or both legs.

In common with the Yahgans, the Ona plucked all hair from face and body except the eyelashes and the hair on the head.

3

The Ona men cared nothing for being clothed, considering that a man should be ashamed of his body only when it was mis-shapen or over-corpulent. If a man were unduly fat, they said, he must be greedy and so bad a hunter that his wife had to feed him on fish. Their only garment was the *chohn k-oli* (man's robe). This covered a man well from neck to knees. It was never fastened in any way, but was held in position with the left hand, in which the hunter also carried his bow and quiver. In warm weather the right arm and shoulder were generally exposed and free. Fox-skin robes were prized as much by the Ona as they were coveted by the white miners. Usually the robes were made from guanaco hides. Only the back and sides of the animal were used for this purpose, and two full-sized skins were needed. The skins, when trimmed, were scraped thin on the meat side, the shavings being collected and used by the hunter for food. Though not very appetizing they staved off the pangs of hunger, for they were chewed a long time before being swallowed. The robes were worn, of course, with the fur outwards. With the skin side against the body there was no danger of harbouring vermin, from which these people in their native state—except for those who grew careless from sickness or extreme old age—were remarkably free.

A man when fully dressed wore on his forehead, as has been already described, a triangular piece of blue-grey skin from the head of a guanaco. This *goöchilh* stood up about four inches above the crown of the head and was held in position by a band of plaited sinew. From the front, the *goöchilh* appeared conical in shape; actually it did not cover more than the forehead and temples.

They had another head-dress called *ohn*, but it was very seldom used;

I have seen only four or five of them in my life. They were made from small feathers fixed to a band, which was worn round the head with the feathers pointing downwards. As was to be expected, by far the finest *ohn* belonged to Talimeoat, the bird-hunter. The other *ohn* were made of feathers tastefully selected from any suitable bird, but Talimeoat's *ohn* boasted feathers only obtainable from the heads of certain blue-black, white-breasted shags, a species far from common in Fireland. The feathers were cylindrical and about two inches long; and each bird yielded only three or four of them. Talimeoat had worked a large collection of them into a beautifully neat braid of guanaco sinew and, though he seldom wore it, was modestly proud of this visible proof of his hunting prowess.

I have never seen an Ona wear a conspicuous feather head-dress. The Yahgans sometimes did, using black or white feathers, doubtless to emphasize the colours with which the wearer was painted. No women of either tribe ever wore head-dress. If one of them had a headache, she might tie a piece of hide tightly round her brows, but that was all.

Occasionally when an Ona started on a long run, into which he intended to put his utmost speed, he would take four or five small feathers from a swallow and attach them to a sinew, which he then tied round one of his upper arms. I have been told that when Ona met for league-long races (none of which I ever witnessed), some of the fastest runners—Taäpelht, Ishtohn (Thick Thighs) and Koniyolh [1]—used this token to increase their speed and endurance. I have forgotten its name.

On his feet an Ona generally wore *jamni* (moccasins), made preferably from the skin of the guanaco's legs and worn with the hair outwards. Water will not soak into or through a skin from the outside, but will pass very quickly through from the inside, by the same processes as perspiration when the live animal wore the skin. In his *jamni* an Ona might walk for hours through icy water, often above the knees. When he camped for the night, he would wring the water out of his *jamni* and replace them on his feet, to which they would cling so closely that soon the feet would become very warm, though the fur outside might be frozen stiff. With his *jamni* on his feet and his robe swathed tightly round his body, he would pass a comfortable night, despite the fact that the temperature might be many degrees below freezing point, with his bare legs

---

[1] Second in fame for speed only to Taäpelht, from whose part of northern Fireland he came. About five feet ten in height, he was slightly built, good-looking, with the nose and eyes of an eagle.

exposed from ankle to knee to the stars. I myself could wade for long periods through ice-cold swamps with only moccasins on my feet and my trousers tied round my neck to keep them dry, yet I could never sleep at night with my legs at the mercy of the frost. The barrel of my rifle has often stuck to my hands as if with glue and, when fixing up boards, I have had to leave off because the nails clung to my fingers as if drawn to a magnet; but I have never seen those things happen to an Ona working by my side under the same conditions.

When sunshine by day and frost by night had formed on the surface of the snow a crust of ice not strong enough to support a man, the Ona made use of *ishmkil*. These were leggings made of guanaco hide with the hair scraped off. Only one man of a party wore *ishmkil*. He would walk in front of his companions, breaking through the frozen crust. When he tired of this onerous task, he would relinquish the lead to another man, who would take over the *ishmkil* from him and tie them to his own legs. *Ishmkil* was a curious word for these leggings, for in practice they reached only a short way above the knees, and *ish* was the Ona word for thigh (compare Ishtohn—Thick Thighs). The Ona for leg was *kahtch*.

4

The women wore a diminutive apron of guanaco skin with the hair scraped off. Over this they wore a *kohiyaten*, the fur-covered petticoat described in the footnote to page 263. In addition to the *kohiyaten*, the women wore a skin robe similar to the men's, but smaller. It was called *nah k-oli* (woman's robe) and, unlike the men's robe, was fastened around the shoulders like a cape by means of two strips of hide. When a baby travelled on its mother's back, it was carried, for warmth, inside the *oli*, on the outside of which was spread *moji* to form a little net resembling a miniature garden hammock. If the mother had some other burden, the child would be seated on top of that, but still inside the *oli*. Women never carried children any distance in their arms.

If it happened that skins from guanaco legs were not plentiful enough to supply all needs for moccasins, the women's footwear came from other parts of the animals' bodies. When not on the march, they seldom wore them at all.

The Ona men devoted more care to their personal appearance than did the women. Notwithstanding this, the women were most particular over certain matters. Whereas the men were able—by virtue of the Ona rules of propriety—to perform their ablutions (if such they could be called) in full view of the community, the women carried theirs out in private; either screening themselves with a robe, or seeking the shelter of a thicket. Only once did I see the women disturbed by a Peeping Tom. He drew too near and teasingly made some sound of pretended admiration, at which the women—whatever their real feelings might have been—expressed great scorn and indignation. The culprit, it need hardly be added, was Kankoat the Jester, who was always ready for any sort of fun.

The women would discard their *oli* at any time without hesitation, but would not further uncover themselves in public, or even in their own homes. They would shorten their *kohiyaten* if need arose, but would not discard them. One afternoon in spring I was walking north with a party of about twenty Indians—men, women and children. We came to the river that flows out of a considerable lagoon into the south-east corner of Lake Kami. The warm weather, melting the mountain snows, had brought the river down in spate, so we camped on the southern side of it, hoping that the night frost would stop the thaw and lessen the rush of water by morning.

Morning came, but a damp mist had kept the frost away and the river, which was perhaps fifteen yards wide, had hardly gone down at all. To get round the lagoon meant a walk of many miles through soaking under-growth, so, as none of the Ona could swim, I left my clothes with them and swam the lagoon a little further up, where there was no current. I had left all ready and at the ford one of the men flung a stone across with a strip of hide attached. To the other end of the hide was tied my strong lasso, which we then firmly secured on both sides of the river.

The wind was cold and I was glad when the first man came across with my bundle of clothes on his back. Holding the lasso for support, the men now came across one at a time, carrying the children and the women's bundles. On the up-stream side the water piled against their bodies above the waist; on the lower it was not much over their knees.

The women had gathered close to the water and were contemplating the circus with laughing interest. Knowing their turn was coming, they simulated timidity, so I called out to them:

"Don't be silly! Take off your *kohiyaten* and we will all look the other way."

But would those modest creatures do it? Not a bit of it. The husbands had to go back and bring them over, and although they fastened them as high as their sense of propriety would permit, the women got their skirts very wet as they waded alongside the men, hanging on to them and perhaps to the lasso as well.

There is another anecdote that will fit in nicely here. It shows how an Ona woman, so modest and shy, could emulate Lady Godiva and overcome her natural modesty for the public weal.

Not far from Ewan Cliffs on the Atlantic coast was a thick, circular clump of trees, less than an acre in extent, surrounded by a stretch of open country. In this strategic position a small party of the mountain men were encamped with their women and children. Two of the men were the half-brothers, Halimink and Yoknolpe; one of the other sex was Yoknolpe's wife, Kewanpe, a fine type of young Ona womanhood. It was she who had offered me guanaco-brain and seal-oil in token of her gratitude.

They had not long pitched camp when a look-out warned them of the approach of a group of their northern neighbours, who were evidently looking for trouble. Halimink and the others hastily prepared a defence against flying arrows by collecting every available robe and shelter-skin and hanging them loosely around the encampment. When their enemies drew nearer, they retired into their fortress and prepared to resist attack to the last man.

From a safe distance, the unwelcome visitors exchanged a few doubtful compliments with the defenders. Some arrows were shot by both parties, but it was at long range and no one was hit. Halimink invited the visitors to come nearer, but they prudently held back. Growing impatient at this state of stalemate, the men behind the arrow-shields decided to bait a trap. They instructed Kewanpe to strip and walk out a little way towards the northern men. Never having been on the stage, she doubtless protested as much as she dared, but finally complied and walked out naked into the open, withal as unwillingly as any well brought up young woman should.

As she emerged into view of the visitors, Yoknolpe shouted from behind his defences:

"If it's a woman you want, come and take this one."

Possibly to Kewanpe's chagrin, none of the northern warriors would accept the risk of running in to catch her, and after a time the besiegers retired. It speaks well for them that none of them fired an arrow at the tempting target.

5

To get back to my subject: Ona clothing. Children of both sexes wore robes like their parents'. For small children, the soft skins of the very young guanaco were used. These, however, got sodden with rain too rapidly to be of much use in bad weather. When the temperature permitted, the boys ran about stark naked, but the girls, though discarding their robes, always retained their tiny aprons. I have heard an Ona sternly reprove his wife for allowing their little daughter, a child of six or seven, to play without her apron. It was the *wearing* that was important; if in the child's gambols her apron worked its way half round her body, it would have been of no account and would have brought no comment from the father.

With the steady infiltration of the white man into Fireland, many of the Ona relinquished their ancestral robes and took to civilized garments. The chief reason for this was a change of employment. The robes were eminently suited for hunting, but were a most inconvenient attire when both hands were needed for sawing wood or carrying out other work not dreamed of by the Indian of former generations. Although I was the first to acknowledge the necessity for this, I always encouraged my Ona friends to change back into their robes and paint when the day's work was done. This painting was really the cleanest habit, for the old paint was energetically rubbed off before the new coat was applied. I encountered criticism on this score, particularly from the Silesian Mission at Rio Grande. They held that it returned a clad and civilized Indian to a state of nakedness and painted barbarism.

In time, there were comparatively few Ona who had not adopted white man's clothing. One of these was Chalshoat, who clung to his robe, moccasins and head-dress until the day of his death, thirty years after he had come to Cambaceres with Kaushel and my long association with the Ona Indians had begun.

6

I have given an account in a previous chapter of the methods used by the native doctors for curing sickness and disease. Serious illness was always attributed to witchcraft, usually on the part of the medicine-man of a rival group. One or more doctors might do what they could for the patient. They would fix their eyes on him like men possessed. Then the chief actor would pounce down and begin biting and sucking at the seat of the pain. With teeth and nails he might cause the patient to bleed somewhat, then, by pressing his hands on other parts of the body and bringing them towards the small wound thus made, appear to draw to that spot the evil thing—a small flint, some mud or a tiny live mouse—

that lurked inside the sufferer, so that it could be sucked out through the break in the skin, thrown violently on the ground and stamped on. On occasions no wound was made. With his hands the doctor would sometimes force the evil thing into an arm or a leg and, following it down to the hand or foot, suck it out without breaking the skin. This performance might be repeated many times on the same patient. If all the sickness was eventually drawn off, the invalid would recover. If anything remained, the enemy *joön's* malign influence was judged too powerful for the local doctor to overcome, and the patient died.

If the malady was not serious—maybe pains in the body or a strained muscle—the doctor would massage the affected part with his bare feet. Beginning gently, he would increase the pressure until at last, if the patient could stand it, the *masseur* would be treading with his full weight on the centre of the pain. The patient would direct him where to tread. If the pain of the weight became unbearable, he would start a warning hiss, which might increase in intensity. Many of these medicine-men weighed as much as fourteen stone, and it was really painful to watch one of them moving slowly over the stomach of a sixteen-year-old lad or a grandfather of sixty. Generally the whole performance was carried out with good humour and laughter, giving the sufferer an opportunity to show his stoicism. I have heard some white men maintain that they had seen these doctors spring into the air and land again on the patient's body. I have never witnessed this myself and am inclined to doubt it.

For back-ache—possibly lumbago—the patient would lie on his face while the doctor stood on his back and worked his way slowly up and down. At sheep-shearing time, when the day's work was long and hard, I often saw men being trampled on by one of their companions, in order to relieve themselves of that tired feeling.

7

Ona hunters had their own code of honour. No man, however unsuccessful he had been, would ever ask a more fortunate hunter for a portion of his kill. But, as we have seen in an earlier chapter, on the occasion when Talimeoat and his son were the only ones to return laden to the encampment, a hunter was tacitly expected to share his kill with his hungry friends. I was once with a party of six or eight Ona, putting the finishing touches to the track. Among my companions were Kankoat, who took life as one huge joke, Koiyot and Otrhshoölh (White Eye), the medicine-man of Cape San Pablo, who was getting on in years.

We had finished our job and also our provisions and had been attacked by some epidemic of feverish colds, which had put us off successful hunting. We reached the beach of Lake Kami early in the day, but it was too late to make Harberton that night, so we determined to try for meat. Two or three of my companions went off into the nearby woods, while Koiyot, Otrhshoölh and I went to look for guanaco on the mountain called Kashim, which stands at the north-east corner of the great lake, opposite her sister Heuhupen.

Passing along the miles of shingle beach at the east end of the lake, I took a chance shot with my rifle at a large *oiyi* (crested grebe) far out on the lake, and happened to kill it. The onshore breeze would slowly bring the bird in, and as we might have a long walk before us if we failed to find guanaco soon, we could not afford to wait, so Koiyot and I left Otrhshoölh to take the bird home when it drifted ashore, and went on our way.

We returned empty-handed to the encampment late that evening and found that those who had hunted nearby had had no better luck than we. Hungry and weak with fever, Koiyot and I looked around for Otrhshoölh and the crested grebe. Otrhshoölh was there, but of the crested grebe there was no sign. A few ounces from that fat, tasty bird would have been most reviving, but both of us were too proud to enquire about it. I felt that the grebe must have been eaten by our companions while we were away, but was surprised, for such was not the Ona custom.

We ate a few poor roots and tree fungus, and early next morning started for Harberton. Otrhshoölh was now carrying a bundle of reeds as unobtrusively as possible. The woods seemed deserted and neither guanaco nor bird gave us a chance shot. We did, however, come upon the skeleton of a guanaco and got some marrow from such bones as the foxes had failed to break. Our colds were better and my companions seemed in excellent spirits. As the afternoon drew on, one or other of them would give vent to a most perfect imitation of the wailing cry of the *oiyi*, as expressive as the mew of a hungry cat, and a smile would flicker over the face of everyone but Otrhshoölh, who pressed on silently with his innocent-looking bundle of reeds.

All save the *joön* from Cape San Pablo were evidently enjoying themselves greatly, and soon the unusual cry grew more and more frequent. It was not until the sun was getting low in the west, and Harberton was almost in sight, that I tumbled to it. Poor old Otrhshoölh was a good husband and father and had wrapped up the grebe in the reeds, so that his wife and family might share in the delicacy. I had indeed misjudged my companions, who, though very hungry, had kept his secret until it was too late to stop and cook the bird. Until the day of his death, a few years later, humorous rascals such as Kankoat found it hard to repress that long drawn out wail when they felt old Otrhshoölh might be within hearing.

An Ona starting off on a hunting trip would take certain necessities with him: a knife, often made in those days from the hoop of some barrel that had drifted ashore; a *moji*, that length of thin hide for tying up his load of meat when he got it; tinder and flint for fire-lighting, kept dry in a bladder tucked under a piece of thong tied round his waist; and, of course, his bow, quiver and arrows.

The Ona bows and arrows were beautiful pieces of workmanship. The bow was made from the dwarf deciduous beech (*Nothofagus pumilio*), which, when fully grown, is something over a foot in diameter. Just below the bark the wood is white, but the heart of the tree is red. Only the white wood was used for the Ona bow and, as few trees had white wood in sufficient quantity and quality for the purpose, a suitable tree was not easy to find. When a choice had been made, the tree was felled and a log, a trifle over four feet in length, cut from it.[1] This was then split to produce a piece free from knots and without any red wood in it. In section, the bow began as an isosceles triangle, further cutting reducing it to a shape resembling an elongated pear. The apex of the triangle would be nearest the bow-string. From the apex to the base was about two and a quarter inches; and the base, which was the younger, more springy wood close to the bark, was about an inch and a quarter across. When fashioned by a good bow-maker (the experts were called *k-haäl-chin*), the wood was not smoothly rounded, but had some twenty-five flat faces, each of which diminished in width as the bow grew thinner from its centre to its ends. In making the bow, the bending of it edge-ways was a most difficult task. The finished article was most ingenious, combining strength with lightness.

Arrows were made from the yellow wood of the barberry bush. Good arrows could be obtained from the species bearing the edible berry, but the best wood was that from the holly-leafed barberry, which was to be found in southern Ona-land. This forest shrub has a large prickly leaf,

---

[1] When I was with them, one or other of the party always had an axe or hatchet for tree-felling. Before the white man came, they must have mauled their way through with sharp stones and with much labour; it would have been difficult to burn through the green trees without damaging them. I have seen one stone that had evidently been bound to a piece of wood and used as an axe by the ancient Firelanders.

and its berries, unlike those described by my father as sweet barberries, are not pleasant to eat. The arrow-maker would select a stick of wood nearly two feet six inches long, peel off the bark, split the wood into four pieces and remove the pith. In this early stage, the arrow was sure to be crooked, but warming by the fire and bending with the fingers as the work on its proceeded made the finished article perfectly straight. The preliminary scraping was done with the edge of a flint or a piece of broken glass, the object being to shape the arrow so that the point of balance was slightly nearer to the head than to the feathers. From this thickest part, which was a third of an inch in diameter, the arrow tapered in both directions to an end diameter of about a sixth of an inch. After scraping, the arrow was rubbed down on a particular kind of stone which, from long use, became corrugated like a stove-brick. The final polishing was done with fine powder scraped from the stone and applied with a piece of softest fox-skin.

The feathers and head were neatly bound to the arrow with the same material as was used by the Ona for all other binding and sewing jobs— the sinews of a guanaco; not the coarse sinews that run the whole length of the body, but the finer ones just under the skin of the back. The sinew was moistened before use. It shrank as it dried, thereby holding both head and feathers firmly in position. The end of the binding was prevented from coming loose by means of a tiny piece of pitch called *teik*.

Two feathers were used for each arrow. They were taken from the wings of the goose, the swan, the crested vulture or, much less frequently, the huge black vulture known as the turkey-buzzard and those breeds of oceanic birds that sailors call mollymauks. Even from the first three, few feathers were deemed suitable and many wings were discarded. Only the wide vanes of the feathers were used. They were cut down to about two inches long and the same binding did for both. To avoid ruffling, the end of the arrow was given an identical slope to that of the feather-barbs.

The Ona word for a feather was *sheëtrh*, but the feather most used for their arrow was called *shosheëtrh*, for that meant a feather from the left wing. If the barbs of a left-wing feather and a right-wing feather are cut off and the two compared, the transverse slant of the stumps will quickly show why a right-handed man can make a neater job of the binding when he uses a feather from the left wing. I remember right-wing feathers being put aside for one or two men who could use them.

A small nick to fit the bow-string was cut in the feather end of the arrow. It ran parallel with the feathers and with the width of the arrow-head. The original Ona arrow-head (*heurh*) was made of flint, but when empty bottles began to be strewn along the path of the white man, the Indians found it easier to make their arrow-heads of glass. The Ona knapper would smash a bottle and select his fragments, which would not be those that the uninitiated, seeing the other shapes available, would have expected him to choose. Whether the arrow-head was to be of glass or flint, the method was the same. The fragment was held in one hand in a piece of fox-skin doubled up to form a pad. The knapper's only tool was a dry bone from the leg of a guanaco or a fox, with one end jaggedly broken off for chipping. By his side was a rough, rounded stone, on which, as the work progressed, he frequently struck the bone to keep it sharp. With this primitive apparatus, he would produce a tiny, barbed, perfectly made arrow-head. Very often he would be working on two or three arrow-heads at once. While he chipped at one of them, the others would be held in his mouth to keep them slightly warm. When the piece he was busy with grew too brittle, he would put it in his mouth and transfer his attention to one of the other pieces. The finished heads were close on an inch long and slightly less than half an inch wide.

During one of my subsequent visits to England, I read an article on "The Flint-Knappers of Brandon." This so interested me that I drove to that little Suffolk town to see English knappers at work. Besides examples of present-day flint-chipping, I was shown a collection of arrow-heads covering a period of over eight thousand years. These had been found in or around some of the three hundred and sixty-six quarries known to have existed in that district. With this collection were some flint arrow-heads made by the most expert of modern masters of that craft. Not one of these exhibits compared in quality of workmanship with the arrow-heads of the Ona Indians.

I was interested to learn that the Brandon knappers, when doing very fine work such as arrow-heads or flint ornaments, also used the pad and dry bone method, though they did not hold the flints in their mouths to prevent them from becoming brittle.

The Ona quiver was neatly made from seal-skin, with the hair outside. It was never attached to the hunter's body, but was carried under his arm. Near the top of it was a loop of the same material, so that the quiver could be hung up when not in use.

The bow-string was always made from twisted sinew from the front part of the foreleg of the guanaco. When hunting in wet weather, the Ona carried it in the bladder in which he kept his tinder and flint. It was attached to the bow at the last possible moment; a wet bow-string is useless.

To discharge an arrow, the Ona held the bow in his left hand with the arm slightly bent. The arrow was held against the bow-string between the thumb and forefinger of the right hand. The nick was pressed firmly against the bow-string, but not with the full force of the pull, for the thumb and forefinger also gripped the string. When the bow was at full stretch, the two middle fingers were used as well. At the moment of the arrow's release, the hunter would suddenly straighten his left arm to give another two inches stretch, while a forward jerk of the whole body seemed to impart to the arrow a greater impetus. An arrow wound bleeds much more than a bullet wound. A bullet tears its way in; an arrow cuts.

The hunter discarded his robe before using his bow and arrows. When after guanaco, which were his commonest prey, he would get as near as he could under cover and there leave his robe and quiver, to make the final approach with two or three spare arrows held crosswise in his mouth. The best moment to discharge an arrow was just as the animal realized its danger and turned to bound away. Then the arrow could be planted just behind the ribs in such a way that it drove forward through the animal's body without encountering any bones till, piercing the vital organs, it brought it down in its tracks. Such was the power behind the Ona arrow that I have seen a guanaco with the feather of the arrow just visible in the flesh behind its ribs and the barbed head protruding at the base of its neck. In Paraguay and Brazil, the natives have far better and more springy wood than that from the dwarf beech of Tierra del Fuego, yet I have never seen—either in those places or anywhere else—an aboriginal weapon to compare in workmanship with the Ona bow and arrow.

With an arrow or bullet straight through its intestines, a guanaco might run for miles before lying down to die. The hunter might discharge other arrows after the retreating creature. Arrows were too valuable to lose, so the hunter would follow the wounded guanaco until he caught up with it. If he found the animal resting, he might wait patiently until it grew weaker before approaching to finish it off. He would then go back to search for the arrows that had missed their mark. In this way, the Indians developed almost incredible powers of memory and sight.

It is interesting to note that an arrow, once it had been used to kill a

man, was never used again. It generally remained in the body of the
slain.

8

Before taking up again the threads of my main story, I will jot down a
few notes about that animal, mentioned so many times in these pages, the
guanaco.

When I was a youngster at Ushuaia, the Governor had a huge dog,
half bulldog, half mastiff, which he called Tigre. This monster, whose
fierce appearance had been enhanced by the removal of his ears and tail,
and by the addition of a spiked collar round his great neck, was responsible
for the deaths of several dogs that had dared to oppose him, and finally
became so dangerous that he had to be shot. Before that timely removal,
Tigre had an adventure that must have haunted his dreams until his dying
day.

Another possession of his Excellency was a guanaco, very tame and
not yet fully grown. It had come from Rio Gallegos in Patagonia as a
gift from the Governor of that territory. One day this young guest
abused his host's hospitality by jumping the fence into the kitchen garden.
He was enjoying a feed of fresh, green vegetables when the Governor
caught sight of him. This combination of impudence and theft raised
his Excellency's ire so much that he summoned the terrible Tigre, opened
the garden gate and snapped:

" Chumbale! "

This amounted to an invitation to Tigre to " eat him up," and the dog,
nothing loth, plunged forward like a cross between a hippopotamus and
a tank, while my brothers and I, who were there at the time, waited
breathlessly for the dreadful fate about to overtake the unsuspecting
guanaco. At first he did not seem to appreciate his peril. Then, when
Tigre was almost upon him, he raised his head with his mouth full of
young lettuce—and sailed into the air.

All four feet came down simultaneously on the dog, while the guanaco's
teeth sought for a hold on his opponent's tough, round body. Tigre
made an effort to stand up to this whirlwind, but after a few fruitless
attempts to grab at him, he lost his nerve and rushed back to his master,
panic-stricken and yelping for protection, with his enemy pounding after
him as he ran.

Ever after that event, though Tigre might be out looking for trouble
and ready to challenge any other foe, the sight of that guanaco was enough
to send him straight to the shelter of his kennel. As it grew older, the

guanaco became as big a nuisance as Tigre, but did not share the same fate. Instead he was sent to the Zoo at Buenos Aires.

I quote this incident to show that the guanaco is not the poor, defenceless creature of popular belief. Even a tame guanaco can be a dangerous beast. In the Botanic Garden at Edinburgh, Scotland, they once had a male guanaco from Patagonia that very seriously injured one of the keepers, who, though a powerful man, would undoubtedly have been killed had his companions not promptly run to his rescue. At the very best, the guanaco is a disagreeable, ill-mannered brute. He chews the cud like a cow, mixing it with saliva, and has the unpleasant habit of spitting out great quantities of the nauseous blend, with unerring aim and in a most insolent manner, right in the face of his visitor.

The long, sharp, canine teeth in the jaws of the grown male might almost be called tusks and, though the student of animal dentistry may say that it is not possible to have more than two canine teeth in one jaw, the guanaco seems to have them in pairs. Perhaps there is a special name for the extra teeth.

While I was on a visit to Buenos Aires, I was invited to lunch by Dr. Holmberg, the director of the fine Zoological Gardens in that city. During our conversation, I happened to mention that there were certain small differences between the guanaco of Patagonia and those on the main island of Tierra del Fuego, and also between the latter and those on Navarin Island. Dr. Holmberg did not attempt to disguise his incredulity. He said that they had a number of Patagonian guanaco in the Zoo and that there had been put with them a Fuegian guanaco so resembling its brethren from Patagonia that not even the keepers could tell them apart. He had been at great pains to assure himself that there was no dissimilarity whatever between the two types.

I took this as a challenge and we went out together to take a look at the troop—about fifteen of them. It did not take me long to decide that there was not a Fuegian guanaco amongst them. I suggested to Dr. Holmberg that the animal he had mentioned had either died or escaped. He smiled at my obstinacy and persisted that the Fuegian guanaco was there before me. He added that it had been sent from Ushuaia as a present to the Zoo.

That explained it. This claimant to Fuegian origin was the same redoubtable warrior as had put the formidable Tigre to flight; the animal who had first seen the light at Rio Gallegos in Patagonia. He must have been at least seventeen years old.

CHAPTER THIRTY-NINE

Koiyot Becomes my Adopted Uncle. The Delinquency of Contreras, the Cattle-Man. The Dreadful Massacre by Lake Hyewhin. The Valiant Kautempklh again Gets his Man. Dario Pereira Discovers his Courage. Contreras Finds He has Made a Bad Bargain. I Out-General Halimink and Ahnikin.

I

IN THE YEAR FOLLOWING THE STARTING OF THE NEW FARM AT VIAMONTE, I left Dan Prewitt in charge there and went to Gable Island to help Will with the sheep-shearing. I took with me several of the Najmishk people, including Koiyot and his wife, Olenke. When we reached Harberton, we found that Kiyohnishah (Guanaco Dung) and his party had come once again for the sheep-shearing. Halimink, Yoknolpe, Ahnikin and other mountain men were also there, and soon we were all working together in outward harmony. Among Kiyohnishah's party were his brother, Chashkil, and a younger brother, a lad whose name was Teorati. There were also Kautempklh, his son-in-law Ishtohn, Heche-lash the dwarf and Kilehehen. This last named was a cousin of Kau-tempklh, but lacked his dynamic charm.

We had a fairly peaceful time, with only one incident that need be mentioned here. We had to ship a number of lambs across from Gable to the mainland. These wild little creatures were gathered in batches on the beach for shipment and were prevented from escaping by means of lamb-nets, which were held in position by the women, who took great delight in the task. The sight of the frisky little lambs jumping up against the nets and falling back again caused the women the utmost glee.

On one such occasion, we had driven a consignment of lambs down to the beach. The encampment was a furlong away, and the willing Koiyot ran off to fetch the women to help us. In a few minutes he was back with them, all eager for a little excitement. Olenke, his wife, was not among them.

When the job was finished and the lambs were all aboard the lighter built by Despard some years before, Koiyot came up to me, looking extremely grave. He asked me to go with him to the encampment, as his wife's leg was broken. I hurried there with him, to find Olenke lying on the ground holding her leg, on which, six inches above the knee,

382

there was an enormous bruise. When she saw me, she grated the ends of the broken bone together to make them click. Nearby her lay a wooden club.

I asked how the accident had happened and Koiyot told me that he had hit her with the club. Seeing the poor woman lying there so helpless, such a wave of anger swept over me that I put all my strength into a punch that caught the unsuspecting husband on the side of the head and sent him reeling.

It was a foolish thing to do. If Koiyot had attacked me in turn, it would have served me right. I believe he would have got the better of me, for, though four inches shorter, he weighed as much as I did and would doubtless have worn me down in the end. Fortunately he did not fling out the left arm of a challenger, but meekly helped me to do what I could for Olenke. We prepared a couch on which she could lie with her feet slightly higher than her head. To prevent the shortening of the injured limb, I intended to attach a small weight to the ankle and hang it over the foot of the couch. While I was anxiously considering this step, I heard to my great relief the siren of a steamer.

I guessed it to be the government transport anchoring at the sawmill at Ukukaia on the mainland. Leaving Koiyot with his wife, I ran back to the beach to find Will. He immediately set off in a boat for medical aid, and returned that evening with the ship's doctor, who brought with him a kind of wire boot, in which Olenke's leg was encased without delay.

It seemed that when Koiyot had arrived at the encampment to fetch the women, Olenke had refused to come. Earlier in the day they had quarrelled over some other matter, and now Olenke would not budge. Had Koiyot had his bow and quiver with him, Olenke would probably have been arrowed through the leg, but the nearest weapon had been the wooden club—a stout pole about five feet long. This Koiyot had seized and, with one terrific wallop, brought the poor woman to the ground. Koiyot was no weakling, so a certain heavy-handedness was to be expected when he lost his temper.

After the surgeon had fixed up Olenke and she was comfortably settled, Koiyot came to me with a humorously rueful expression, took my hand and, putting it to the side of his head, said:

" Feel that."

The bump felt like a soft goose-egg. He went on invitingly:

" Would you like to fight me now? "

I answered him with the nearest Ona equivalent to :
" No, thank you."

I felt rather ashamed of having given way to my feelings and attacked this good fellow like an angry child. After all, Olenke was his wife, not mine; and it had been on my behalf that he had hit her, on her refusal to help me when I had called for her aid. Luckily all turned out well. The surgeon made such a good job of the broken leg that Olenke, when she was on her feet again, was able to walk with hardly a limp. She became the most spoiled of wives. Koiyot was to be seen helping her with her load long after she was able to carry it herself; and often, feeling, perhaps, that he was growing less attentive, she would put on an extra limp when her husband glanced that way.

As is frequently the case, this rough encounter between Koiyot and myself seemed to put our association on a new and more intimate footing. I took to calling him Yi Poöt, which meant " my uncle on the father's side." The name stuck and, as the years went by, Koiyot became known, even in civilized Argentine circles, as " El tio del Señor Bridges."

2

With the shearing finished, the parties dispersed to go their various ways, leaving me to hope once again that their murderous raids on one another were now things of the past. But, alas! more trouble was brewing.

Most of the responsibility lay not with an Ona, but with a Chilean half-caste cattle-man—Contreras. When I had handed the Cambaceres herd into his care, Contreras had been without a wife. At first he had seemed content with this state of affairs, but as time had gone by he had grown tired of the lonely life at Woodpecker Creek and had looked around for a mate.

More often than not, there were one or two Ona at Cambaceres to give Contreras a hand with his work. On one occasion, one of these helpers happened to be Ahnikin—and it was to this square-jawed, vengeful, treacherous young man that Contreras confided his longings. Ahnikin, who had never been able to disguise his hatred for those he had injured by murdering Houshken in cold blood, now saw the chance to strike a bargain. He promised Contreras that he would supply him with a fine young Ona wife in exchange for three rifles and plenty of ammunition.

Unable to resist this tempting offer, Contreras secretly obtained three Winchester ·44 repeating rifles from departing miners on their way to civilization, and slipped away from Cambaceres without a word to any of us, taking the rifles and some ammunition with him. One of the rifles went to Ahnikin, the other two to Halimink and Yoknolpe. Contreras travelled with the party as far as Lake Kami, where they pitched camp. The single ambition of the mountain men was now to go after Kiyohnishah's people and wipe them out with their newly acquired fire-arms. So, leaving Contreras with the women, they set off in search of their enemies. Besides Ahnikin and his uncles (or half-uncles) Halimink and Yoknolpe, the revenge party included Kankoat and the sixteen-year-old Kautush, whose father had been killed in a previous clash with the northerners by a man named Kawhalshan. Kautush, who was much at Harberton, was a very intelligent boy and was regarded by us as one of the most civilized of the Ona. A number of men from Najmishk also joined in this raid. One of them was Shishkolh, uncle of the little boys who had been murdered at the whale-feast.

They located the northerners near Lake Hyewhin and waited for daybreak. With Kiyohnishah there were his two brothers, Chashkil and the young Teorati; that splendid old fellow, the ageing Kautempklh; his cousin, Kilehehen; Pahchik, Halah, Kilkoat, Paloa and Kawhalshan, the slayer of Kautush's father. Besides these men, there were a number of others, as well as a considerable following of women and children, among them the wife, two daughters and two little sons of old Kilehehen. Their only fire-arm was the rifle that Kilkoat had taken from the man he had murdered some years before. In spite of a broken stock and other faults, it was still usable.

As day dawned the attackers advanced on the sleeping encampment. The dogs began to bark, but their warning came too late. Taken completely by surprise, Kiyohnishah sprang to his feet. As he looked over the top of his *kowwhi* to see what the dogs were barking at, a bullet from Ahnikin's rifle blew his brains out. This was followed by a fusillade of shots that brought down six or seven more, among them Chashkil, who died as swiftly as his brother. Kawhalshan fell with a broken leg. Kautempklh, Kilehehen, the boy Teorati, Kilkoat with his rifle and a few others dived into the woods, while the women hid their heads and wailed.

Kawhalshan, lying helpless on the ground, was prodded slowly to death with a blunt arrow by young Kautush, who, as he despatched the wounded man, shouted at him again and again:

"You killed my father."

That was the only instance of which I ever heard of an Ona being done to death by slow degrees by one of his own kind. And we had thought Kautush was civilized. . . .

Halimink and his band of murderers scattered through the woods in pursuit of further victims. Some of these had not fled far and there was still fight left in them. Paloa snatched Kilkoat's rifle and brought Kankoat to the ground with a bullet through the hip. Kautempklh, who was said to have never been in a fight without killing his man, arrowed Yoknolpe at close range, picked up his rifle and made his escape.

Ahnikin, seeing his uncle, of whom he was extremely fond, lying dead, pursued the slayer, but had to watch out for an ambush, so the wily old Kautempklh got safely away, as did his cousin, Kilehehen. When Ahnikin returned to the scene of the massacre, he found a group of the bereaved women cutting up the body of Yoknolpe and feeding it to the dogs. Ahnikin's bad blood was up. He raised his rifle and shot down at least seven of the women—an unforgivable crime. Ever after that, even the women of his own party would frequently cover their faces, as though in fear, when he passed by. When he finally left the corpse-strewn encampment, he forced the elder daughter of Kilehehen to go with him, leaving the mother with the younger girl, a child of thirteen, and the two little boys.

In this fashion did Ahnikin provide himself with a new wife and so relieve the tedium of a widower's life.

Many other young women were taken by the conquerors, amongst them a very choice gypsy-looking young widow of Chashkil. When the warriors reached their encampment with their booty, she was delivered over to the expectant Contreras.

3

Kankoat was badly wounded, but not to death. By a miracle, the bullet had passed right through him without breaking a bone or smashing his intestines. It was as great a miracle that he managed to crawl back to Harberton unaided. He told me afterwards that he had fainted several times and had done much of the journey on all fours because he was too weak to walk. The wound healed perfectly.

Teorati, who had now lost all three brothers at the hands of Halimink and Ahnikin, fled for his life through the enemy's country and made for the only sanctuary that remained for him: Harberton. The mountain men found his tracks and, guessing his objective, raced after him with the intention of silencing him for ever. Knowing the country better than he did, they almost succeeded in cutting him off by taking a short cut, but he eluded them and reached Harberton only a few minutes ahead of them.

Night had fallen and everyone was asleep. The terrified lad did not dare trust himself to the protection of the Yahgan Indians, who had their settlement a quarter of a mile from the little village, but ran straight on. The first building he reached was the home of the carpenter, a small, bushy-bearded, hard-working Spaniard named Dario Pereira, who never before that night had shown any sign of courage.

Teorati, with the mountain men a few hundred yards behind, battered on Pereira's door and awoke the little man. When the door was unbolted, Teorati, incoherent from exhaustion and fear, begged for protection. Though much alarmed, Pereira saw that it was a matter of life and death and instantly admitted the boy. Almost as he shot the bolt, the pursuers arrived. They banged on the door and demanded that Teorati should be given up to them, as he was very wicked and a great liar. Dario Pereira refused flatly and told them to go away. They became threatening, then, guessing maybe that the Spaniard was armed, went away without attempting to break into the house, leaving Teorati to tell his dreadful tale to his protector and later to the rest of us.

Contreras, the cattle-man, who had been the direct cause of all this bloodshed, knew that he could never work for us again. He took his young Ona wife from Lake Kami to the saw-mill at Ukukaia, where he secured employment. If married happiness came to him at all, it was short-lived. Soon after he had settled at Ukukaia, he had an argument over a matter of twenty Argentine *pesos* with a decent little fellow called Villareal. Contreras was a coward and a weakling. He would never have dared to tackle Villareal single-handed. But with the help of a friend of his own kidney, he cut Villareal about in such a brutal way that the poor man died whilst trying to reach his shanty.

Contreras was condemned, I believe, to three years' imprisonment at Ushuaia. Before the end of his term, he was liberated for good conduct. On his return to Ukukaia, his Ona wife, needless to say, had departed.

4

I was away from the district at the time of the massacre at Lake Hyewhin and did not hear of it until I put in an appearance at Harberton some days later. After the first moments of horror at this fresh crime of Halimink and Ahnikin, my thoughts became fixed on a single theme: those rifles. Kautempklh had one of them, but he would not be likely to use it; I felt he would rather trust to his bow and arrows. Not so Halimink and Ahnikin. I had to get their rifles away from them before any more mischief was done.

It was a tricky problem. I knew the hopelessness of going in search of the two men. With my inferior woodcraft, I should never have found them; and they were not likely to seek me out and give up the rifles of their own accord. Then, while I was thinking the matter over, Dame Fortune smiled on me.

There were always Indian children running around Harberton, even though their parents were elsewhere, and often a bunch of them were to be found hanging round the homestead in the hope of getting some tit-bit to eat. That morning there appeared at the house in search of delicacies two boys and a girl, all between the ages of nine and eleven. As soon as I set eyes on this trio, I saw in a flash a solution to my problem, for one of the boys was Ahnikin's little brother, Old Face, and his companions were Nana and his sister, children of Halimink.

Remembering how I had successfully kidnapped Garibaldi from Tininisk's encampment, I grabbed the three children and, to their immense surprise, put them on one of our little cutters and gave instructions for them to be taken to Picton Island, to be placed in the care of the trustworthy Modesto Pernas, who was in charge there.

With the first part of my stratagem accomplished, I let it be known among the natives at Harberton that the children would be returned to their relatives as soon as the rifles were delivered at the homestead. I added that the children would be well looked after, but that if the exchange was unduly delayed, they would be sent to Buenos Aires, from where it would not be easy to bring them back.

Knowing that this ultimatum would be duly passed on to Halimink and Ahnikin, I then went about the work that was to keep me at Harberton for a week or two. Though outwardly calm, I was inwardly in fear and trembling, for I knew those fellows would be furious at what I had done and, finding my hand against them on their return from an expedition in which they had lost their very best hunter, Yoknolpe, would be capable of any mad deed. My only safety lay in the possession of the three children. With these in my power, to do with them as I would, Halimink and Ahnikin might think twice before doing me any harm, in case I had given certain previous instructions to be carried out in the event of my sudden death.

For a while nothing happened. Then I had word that Halimink and Ahnikin, together with some of their people and a few women newly acquired from the northern group, had camped near Harberton. I continued with my usual daily round of tasks and did not hang about the homestead as if I was afraid. Halimink and Ahnikin avoided me for some days. Then one morning, when I was walking alone through the woods about a mile and a half to the north-east of our little village, they both casually appeared from among the trees, rifles in hand.

If they wanted to frighten me, they succeeded, for I was not at all sure of their intentions. I gave them no chance of guessing my real feelings, but—my usual procedure when alarmed—calmly sat down for a chat. In a quiet, assured tone, I pointed out to them that when their small reserve of ammunition gave out, they would find it more and more difficult to obtain fresh supplies; and that when the full story of their latest crime became public, they would be looked upon as dangerous by the white men who were coming to our part of Tierra del Fuego in ever-increasing numbers, as well as by their own people. I advised them, for their own good, to return the rifles without delay. After some more discussion, they finally agreed—Ahnikin with a very ill grace. I need not dwell on my feelings as I walked back to the homestead followed by the two disgruntled men, who came right to the house with me and there delivered up two of the three rifles that Contreras had bartered for a wife.

The three children were brought back from Picton. Happy and healthy—for Modesto in his lonely outpost had made real pets of them—they were passed back into the care of their relatives, and so the incident ended.

I felt that Halimink, that gay, conscience-less will-o'-the-wisp, bore me no grudge, but Ahnikin was of a different stamp. He who had often called me his father now had an inscrutable way of looking at me that I did not like at all.

CHAPTER FORTY

I

AFTER THE MASSACRE OF KIYOHNISHAH AND HIS PEOPLE, THERE WAS GREAT unrest amongst the Indians. It was impossible for the survivors of the northern and southern groups to work happily in the same neighbourhood, for each was expecting a further attack from the other. For those not acquainted with Tierra del Fuego as it was in those days, it may be difficult to appreciate the degree of nervous tension that, even in times of peace, went to make up the mental condition of an Indian, who from childhood had lived the part of hunter and hunted. The intranquillity of their minds was betrayed by the care with which they would examine anything that looked like a footprint; by the caution with which they hugged the forest shades and avoided crossing open spaces, where long shadows cast by a low sun might be seen from far away; by the anxiety with which they would notice a flock of birds rising in flight, or a guanaco running as though startled, and speculate on the cause. Much time would be spent lying motionless on some height, intently scanning leagues of forest and the blue distance, searching for the slight variation of tint that would betoken smoke rising from some encampment in the woods. If such should be spied, there would be serious discussion as to the identity of the wanderers and the reason for their presence there. It seemed second nature, too, that prompted them always to encamp in places affording a fair chance of escape or defence, in the event of a surprise attack.

I went continually from one party to another, although I knew they all disliked my doing so. How, they argued, could any friend of theirs be on good terms with their hated enemies? In fact, so strongly did they feel on this subject that, considering how impulsive they were and how little they seemed to count the consequences of their deeds, it is a wonder that one party or the other did not put an end to my wanderings.

At heart I liked the mountain men best, for they were my people, yet my sympathies were with the northerners. I always showed equal friendship to both, and would roll up in my guanaco skins and sleep peacefully in any of their encampments, with my treasured Winchester near my head. They all knew that I never thought of it as a weapon of defence. In any case, it would have been useless to me at close quarters.

I once spent two days and a night alone in the woods with Taäpelht, that renowned warrior who had ended the existence of the notorious Dancing Dan and seriously wounded at least two other white men, Don Ramón L. Cortéz, the Chief-of-Police, and Mr. McInch, the King of Rio Grande. Taäpelht seemed to radiate good nature. The night I passed in his company was cold and, not having intended to sleep out, I had failed to bring my robe. Taäpelht invited me to sleep close beside him. His robe, the only garment he wore, together with our proximity, kept me warm throughout the night.

Among the scores of Ona men that I knew, the only two I ever really feared were Minkiyolh, for his madness, and Ahnikin, for his badness.

Some little time after the incidents recorded in the previous chapter, I had another unpleasant encounter with Ahnikin. The wife of whom he had possessed himself after the butchery at Lake Hyewhin was, it will be remembered, the daughter of Kilehehen. Such of the northern men as had survived the massacre were now scattered over Ona-land, living in constant dread of further attacks by the mountain men and doing all they could to avoid meeting them. One of these survivors was Kilehehen, who, presumably because it gave him a sense of security, set up his encampment within a quarter of a mile of my Viamonte hut. There he lived with his wife, younger daughter and two small sons. He was a lean, unsmiling man, well past middle age and taller than his famous cousin, Kautempklh. The knowledge that Kilehehen took comfort from his nearness to us engendered a feeling of friendship on my part. He would often come of an evening and sit by my fire, with hardly a word, until I turned in. He never begged, but would not refuse a mug of coffee or a plate of stew, to which I felt that he as well as one or two other old fellows were entitled, seeing the contribution their women made to my larder.

One day Kilehehen appeared at my fire, evidently in serious trouble. He was accompanied by his worried wife and their young daughter, a girl of about thirteen, with a narrow, anxious face. Her looks were not improved by tear-stains and an apprehensive expression that may have been assumed partly for my benefit and partly for the sake of propriety.

The story Kilehehen had to tell me was that Ahnikin, having taken the elder sister, was about to demand the younger one as well. This news had filled them with apprehension, for they hated and feared their son-in-law, for which reason they lived so close to me.

The old man said: " My daughter is not a woman; she is a child. Her mother is old and needs her. Ahnikin is a bad man, but if we oppose him he will kill us."

I have, alas! often done foolish things on the impulse of the moment. I now said rashly:

" Let me know quickly when he is coming, and I will be your son and help you."

The following day one of the little boys came running to tell me that Ahnikin and some other mountain men were at hand. I knew that, sooner or later, Ahnikin and I must clash, so before hastening to Kilehehen's shelter, I slipped my revolver into the capacious pocket of my pilot coat. When one needs a revolver it is generally in a hurry, so I have always cut off the backs of the hammers of my revolvers and rounded them smooth, so that they will not catch on anything when being drawn. This is better than having to fire from the pocket. The flash from even a little revolver can be pretty hot. I once saw a coat smouldering in consequence.

The old couple were alone with their three children in the encampment. By the time Ahnikin arrived with his companions—three young fellows eager for adventure—we were ready to receive them, I being seated near the girl. Ahnikin carried a single-barrelled, muzzle-loading shot-gun; the others their bows and quivers. It was plain that they were not at all pleased to find me there, but I greeted them in my usual friendly way. After waiting a short while—doubtless hoping I would go—Ahnikin spoke to the parents.

" My wife," he said, " wants her sister to go and live with her, and I have come to fetch her."

He then spoke to the girl in no gentle terms, telling her to come with him. When, instead of obeying, she started to cry in earnest, he took a step forward, reached out his hand and was on the point of grasping her by the hair when I jumped to my feet.

" Leave her alone! " I said.

My hand was in the pocket of my pilot coat. He must have seen the bulge of the Webley ·455, which was pointing at the middle of his body, for he drew back and said angrily :

" What business is it of yours? What are you doing here in this, our country? "

Through the thin film of red paint dusted over his face, I could see that he was pale with rage and looked capable of anything. I answered him as gently as I could :

" Since my father died, I have been lonely; and since all Kilehehen's people have been killed, he is lonely, too. So now he is my father and I am his son; and my sister shall not leave home till she is grown up and wants to go."

Ahnikin stood for a moment, and I wondered what he was going to do Then, muttering something that I failed to catch, he turned and walked away, followed by his three companions.

During this episode Kilehehen's bow and arrows had been, as usual, close to his hand; but he had remained seated with drawn features, showing no sign of emotion. With three much younger men standing nearby, all with weapons and ready to use them, he had been wise enough not to make any sudden movement.

When the Ahnikin party was out of ear-shot, he made the following comforting remark :

" Karr imrh hansh pemrh. Ma matiash noöre." ("He is very angry. He will kill you by and by." [1])

2

Early that winter I crossed the mountains to Harberton, from where I proceeded on my second trip to Buenos Aires, in the hope of completing the business that had taken me there the first time—the legal transfer of the Harberton property into our ownership—which still remained unsettled. It was also my intention to make, if possible, a step towards securing as much land as I could in the Najmishk area, for the benefit of ourselves and the Ona inhabitants. Accustomed as I was to working at high tension, and always impatient of delay, I soon came to the conclusion that government employees held their posts with the sole intention of obstructing progress. Thwarted throughout the winter months, I could accomplish nothing, so in the early spring—wearied to a degree of city life—I took passage for Punta Arenas. The ship was one of the fortnightly Pacific liners, which, in those days, came from Liverpool, touched at various ports and passed through the Magellan Straits into the

---

[1] Literally : " Very angry is that one. You kill will by and by."

Pacific and up the Chilean coast; and my trip to Punta Arenas was consequently one of pure luxury.

It was one thing, however, to get to Punta Arenas, but quite another to get from there to southern Fireland. I found that there was no vessel going to the Beagle Channel for at least a month, so I crossed the Magellan Straits (here about as wide as the Straits of Dover) to the little town of Porvenir, capital of Chilean Tierra del Fuego. At Porvenir I bought a horse and rode off in the direction of Rio Grande, bound for far-away Harberton. The horse was not much good, but the kindly managers of the great farms of Useless Bay and San Sebastian lent me relays of fresh ones. They also made me welcome at their homes—so welcome, in fact, that it took me four days to reach Rio Grande, a distance by the track of about a hundred and seventy miles. From Rio Grande to Harberton, by the winding track *via* Najmishk, was some thirty miles less.

I got to the north side of the Rio Grande on a Saturday morning. For a man on horseback, this river is generally impassable and almost always dangerous, so I left my weary mount behind and crossed in the only boat, which was under the orders of Mr. McInch, by whom I was welcomed at the Primera Argentina farm settlement.

This uncrowned monarch of Rio Grande liked to exercise his authority and was always trying to get me under his thumb. I found it quite amusing to frustrate his efforts. I never had a row with him and never raised my voice, but once I told him that I had never believed in a blazing hell, because I did not think there was anyone bad enough to be sent there till I met him. His only reply was to call me a —— fool for not enjoying life while I had it. To be frank, I rather liked him. What a statement! But it is true. After knowing of far more of his crimes than I can publish, I could still accept his hospitality and shake hands with him.

On that Saturday morning in question, instead of letting me have another horse at once, he pressed me to stop over the week-end. He said that on Monday he would lend me a horse, which I could either leave with his last shepherd, or take as far as Najmishk, some thirty-six miles away. So eager was I to get back to my people and my work that I felt I could not face an idle Sunday and intimated to him that I was in a great hurry. He did not respond by offering me a horse forthwith and I was far too proud to beg for one, so after a friendly lunch and chat, I started off on foot for Najmishk with my skin robe and revolver, both of which had accompanied me to Buenos Aires.

By nightfall I had reached Rio Fuego, about twenty miles from Rio Grande. Finding the tide high, I determined to cross at daybreak. I slept near the river, but not supperless, for an early goose had already filled her nest with eggs. I roasted and ate a couple of them, then, rolled up like a cigar in my robe, slept well, in spite of a hard frost. At daybreak I waded the stream and went on my way.

I was crossing the wide, grassy valley a few miles to the south of Rio Fuego when I saw a line of Indians, all dressed in their robes, walking fast near the edge of the forest on my right, with the evident intention of intercepting me. As our paths converged, I was pleased to see amongst them some old friends from the north, including Pahchik, who had seconded Chashkil in his wrestling match with me, Ishtohn and my adopted father, Kilehehen. I walked up to them and stopped for a chat, from which it soon emerged that this was no casual meeting. These good fellows had come to warn me that Ahnikin, Halimink and a few followers were indignant at my desertion of their party, especially in the case of Kilehehen's daughter, and intended to kill me at the earliest opportunity.

In Ona-land, reports of what So-and-so was planning to do were generally spread by women going from camp to camp to visit their friends. As a rule these stories were exaggerated, but usually they had some foundation on fact. I listened, therefore, with close attention.

It seemed that, during the winter, Ahnikin and his people had killed many foxes. With the proceeds of the sale of the skins, they had bought two rifles from some miners working at Sloggett Bay and were now waiting to ambush me. Expecting that I would return to Harberton by sea and make my way from there back to Najmishk, they had stationed themselves near the track and intended to shoot me when I appeared from the south.

The northern men had at least one rifle and strongly advised that they should be allowed to accompany me to Harberton, so that the enemy would realize the number of my friends. Having thought the matter over, I came to the conclusion that, if I agreed to this suggestion, these people would know I was afraid to go on alone; and it would not be long before Ahnikin and company would also get the same impression. I had often been scared, but hoped none of them had ever suspected it. If I now advertised the fact that I dared not go through the woods by myself, I had better either quit the country at once, or move about for ever with an armed escort.

I told my northern friends that I did not need them and would proceed to Harberton alone. Before I left them, however, I wrote a short note to my brothers, telling them that if I were killed, found drowned, or disappeared on my way to Harberton, they should arm certain natives (whom I named) with rifles and put a reward on the heads of Ahnikin and Halimink, as I should like to meet those two in the next world as soon as possible. Naturally I did not tell Kilehehen and the others the contents of this letter, lest they should think it worth while to dispose of me themselves, in order to be sent by my brothers on such an attractive expedition. What I did tell them was that, if Ahnikin and Halimink were successful in an attempt on my life, they should hurry with all caution to Harberton and hand over the letter.

After enquiring where I was likely to meet the conspirators, I continued my tramp and spent that night at Viamonte. Dan Prewitt was no longer there. With my entire consent, he had accepted a better job elsewhere and his place had been taken by a man called Nicholas Buscovi*ć*, a placid Yugoslav who had worked for us under Modesto Pernas on Picton Island and knew how to build a timber fence. He was slow, but honest and, like Dan Prewitt before him, had the good sense—as far as I knew—to leave the Ona women alone. I found all was well at Viamonte. Buscović, " Uncle " Koiyot and the rest of the Najmishk folk were quite content, having spent an uneventful winter. They had all heard of Ahnikin's threats and expressed themselves very anxious that I should not go on alone. As Koiyot's people were supposed to be allies of the mountain men, their words carried far more weight than those of Kilehehen or Pahchik, who were Ahnikin's avowed enemies. For all that, I would not be deterred from my purpose.

After a couple of days at Viamonte, I started off in the afternoon for Harberton. It would have been impossible to get a horse over to Harberton at that time of year, so I went on foot, keeping a sharp look-out as I went. I knew approximately where Ahnikin's party were to be found and when, that same evening, I saw smoke across the Ewan River, I guessed it to be from their encampment. I spent the night where I was, and early next morning crossed the river. As I approached the camp, I noticed that it was so situated as to afford an excellent view of anyone approaching from the south, along my usual track. Northward their view was not so good and it was only the barking of the dogs that warned them that a visitor was near.

Ahnikin and Halimink appeared from behind their wind-screens.

With them came Puppup, Hinjiyolh, son of Tininisk, the lumbering Chalshoat, Kinimiyolh, son of Otrhshoölh, the boy Nana and several others. Puppup and Chalshoat bore me no grudge, but they could hardly break away from Halimink and Ahnikin. These last two now both held rifles in their hands; the rest their bows and quivers. This was not surprising, for when the dogs had rushed out barking, they must have thought the northerners were upon them. They were startled to find that it was only I who approached from the north.

I went up to the two leaders and said casually that I had heard they wished to kill me, so had come to talk to them about it. I said to Ahnikin:

" You were angry with me because I helped a poor old man who was alone, but if you were poor and alone, you would come to me and be sure of my help. Did I gain anything? Did I want the girl myself? You remember only the bad things, and forget the good things I have done for you. Have you forgotten that I helped and carried you to Harberton when your people thought you were dying, and then you said I was your father? Have you forgotten that when many Ona were taken to Ushuaia and were waiting to be exiled, one of them was your uncle, Yoknolpe? Have you forgotten that on hearing these tidings, I went to Ushuaia and told the Governor that your people were my people, so that he let Yoknolpe and two other mountain men go free? Many who were with them were taken to another country and have not come back. Have you also forgotten that when your uncle, Tininisk, was ill, I went to him with medicine and he recovered? Why do you forget these good things I have done for my people, the forest men, and only remember the things that vex you, and now stand here to talk to me with rifles in your hands? "

Ahnikin replied: " Your friends have been telling lies about us. We have not forgotten that you helped us before. We never wanted to kill you. They hate us, and are liars."

Halimink spoke in much the same tone. In spite of my having specifically referred to themselves as my people, they were evidently jealous of the northern men. I accepted their assurance that they did not wish to kill me and went on to tell them that, if they ever felt that way, they need not wait on the track, but should send a messenger to me. I would then come to their encampment, alone and without a gun.

After my harangue, I did not want to lose dignity by going into their shelters and sharing their food, so, saying that I was in a hurry to see my family at Harberton and would return when the goslings were hatched—which meant in about a month's time—I turned and walked away.

Here I will add that I have never felt more frightened in my life. I had been bluffing those fellows, and armed as they were, I knew they would find it hard, after the way they had boasted, to resist the temptation of shooting me in the back, whatever the consequences might be. I hoped that if they did so I should be killed outright. I had not forgotten what young Kautush had done to Kawhalshan in the last battle. I knew I must neither hurry nor look round, lest they should know what I was feeling. At the foot of the hill, about two hundred yards from them, I turned and waved a good-bye to the group, who were still watching, weapons in hand. Then I strode away towards Harberton.

That evening at dusk in the woods south of Lake Kami, I looked about for a place to sleep. When I had found it, I went some little distance from it and made a fire. When I had eaten and the fire was low, I smothered what remained of it and lay beside the place for some time, listening intently. Then, with the utmost caution, I slipped away in the pitch darkness to the spot I had chosen and slept there peacefully till the first gleam of dawn called me to the track again. I have played this trick, always needlessly, on other occasions when my nerves have troubled me.

So Ahnikin had still not killed me. Both before and after this incident he must often have longed to do so; and only the thought that even the people of his own group would be indignant, and that my brothers would arm his enemies and with them hunt for him until they got him, can have stayed his hand.

CHAPTER FORTY-ONE

Jelj, the Peace Ritual.

THE DISORDERED CONDITIONS PREVAILING AMONG THE REMNANT OF THE
Ona tribe still at liberty could not continue. My ambition now was to
unite these scattered groups into a law-abiding and mutually trustful community. With this object in view, I frequently left my Najmishk friends
and visited the mountain men in their forest home, or any band of the
dispersed northerners who might be in the vicinity. At every opportunity, I would point out the utter madness of hating and killing their
own people, almost their own brothers; and I told them that if this state
of things continued, there would soon be no Ona left.

Eventually the aggressors, the southern men, agreed to make the first
advance towards friendship. To this end, they proposed to revive a
traditional ceremony called *Jelj*. They asserted that this was a very
ancient way of ending bloody feuds and was performed only when all
were agreed that strife must end. It was a binding promise by all concerned not to fight again. Though greatly interested, I refrained from
showing childish curiosity, but, knowing that it would not lead to further
massacre, bided my time.

Messages were exchanged and wandering hunters were advised, so
that they could join the side to which they belonged. It was understood
that this peace ritual should take place on some open ground near my
shanty at the foot of Najmishk's wooded hills.

The northern party arrived on the eve of the appointed day and
camped just inside the forest, a hundred yards or so from the hut. In
spite of their losses, they were still numerous. The round-up had been
so thorough that it included two or three men that I had seldom seen
before. More familiar figures were Kautempklh, Kilehehen, Ishtohn,
Halah, Paloa and his cousin Kilkoat, Pahchik, Taäpelht, Koniyolh and
Hechelash the dwarf with his two diminutive brothers, A-yaäh and
Yoiyolh. This last named was now medicine-man of the northern group.
He was nicknamed Oklholh (Waterfall Duck) on account of his alertness.
Besides these there were Chorche, on whom I had practised jiu-jitsu,
Dante, the man who had wrestled with Dan Prewitt and whose Ona

name I have forgotten, Kostelen (Narrow Face), Dolal and Pechas. Dolal was a son-in-law of Talimeoat, the shag-hunter, and often came to help at Viamonte. Pechas was a famous wizard from further north and was a brother of Koniyolh. Hechelash and his brothers had no bitter enemies and Ishtohn was generally liked, but in times of trouble those four went unhesitatingly with the northern party. Ishtohn now carried the rifle that his father-in-law, Kautempklh, had snatched from the dead Yoknolpe. The northern party's only other fire-arm was in the hands of Kilkoat; the much-damaged weapon that had nearly cost Kankoat the Jester his life.

That evening a messenger from the mountain men came to tell us that they would be arriving on the morrow. From daybreak many keen eyes were on the watch for them, and at about ten o'clock in the morning they appeared : a long line of men, quite openly armed with their bows and quivers, followed by their womenfolk, children and dogs. They were all that were left of the Cape San Pablo and mountain groups. I saw among them Halimink and Ahnikin, still with their rifles, Kankoat, Puppup, Chalshoat, Talimeoat and Tininisk with their respective sons, Kaichin and Hinjiyolh, the three lads, Kautush, Tinis and Nana, and that extremely eccentric young man, Minkiyolh. Otrhshoölh, the medicine-man, had died, but his brothers, Shilchan (Soft Voice) and Aneki, were there with Otrhshoölh's son, Kinimiyolh, and Aneki's own two boys, Doihei and Metet, who have not hitherto been referred to, but will be met with again in a later chapter. All this party went straight to a wood about three-quarters of a mile to the east of us, where they pitched their camp.

The Najmishk party had not been quite exterminated in the massacre at the stranded whale. Besides " Uncle " Koiyot there were his nephews, Yoshyolpe and Ohrhaitush, the brothers Shijyolh and Shishkolh, their cousin Shaiyutlh (White Moss) and several others, one of them being Ishiaten, whose name meant Scratched Thighs. Although they had joined Ahnikin in the last attack on the northerners, when Kiyohnishah and others had been killed, the Najmishk men had not taken the unfair advantage of carrying fire-arms; and, as some of the northerners had called on me frequently at Viamonte, " Uncle " and his people were now almost on friendly terms with them. Nevertheless there was a vendetta that had to be wiped off the slate, so the Najmishk men now joined the mountain men in their encampment, where they doubtless put the finishing touches to their toilet.

The "Snake Dance." The ceremonial advance from the woods to the *Hain*, which is to be seen on the left. The leader (in the *goöchilh*) is Doihei, elder son of Aneki. Next in the line is Chorche, with K-Wamen, the recently initiated novice, beside him. The seventh from the left is Kankoat, the tenth is Metet, the younger son of Aneki, and the twelfth is Ahnikin.

Photo by the author.

Ona boys take part in the "Frog Dance."
Photo by the author.

Ona men shamming dead.
Photo by the author.

Koiyot, my adopted uncle, and Doihei show their hatred by making faces at the women, who are seated in a group nearly a quarter of a mile away. I am sorry that Pahchik, master of ceremonies at the time, is wearing a cloth cap instead of his *goöchilh*.

Photo by the author.

Ahnikin impersonates *Short*. On the left is Puppup. Halimink and Minkiyolh stand side by side, and on the right is Hatah, a good-looking young man who was one of Ahnikin's three companions in the incident described on page 392. The encampment is in the distant woods behind.

Photo by the author.

About three hours after their arrival, the southerners gathered outside the wood and sat down on the ground. On our side of the wide grassland, the northern men did the same, and for a considerable time the opposing parties were seated in silent thought, gazing across at each other. There was something grand and impressive in that long silence. I could not help thinking how memories of past grievances—now, I presumed, to be forgotten—must be filling the minds of all of them. Scarcely a man or woman there could not have told of some bereavement at the hands of the opposite group. Ageing warriors and women must have thought of massacres and killings long ago. For the younger ones, there were more recent wrongs to be remembered: the tragic deaths of Teëoöriolh and Jalhmolh (Slim Jim), both attributed, however, unjustly, to Houshken, the Joön of Hyewhin; the murder of Houshken and Ohtumn by Halimink and Ahnikin; the massacre near the stranded whale at Cape San Pablo, when Kiyohnishah and his companions had slaughtered, amongst others, Te-ilh, the strong man of Najmishk, and the two little sons of Shijyolh; and the final tragedy at Lake Hyewhin, when Kiyohnishah, Chashkil and others had died, Kawhalshan had been prodded to death by Kautush, Kautempklh had killed Yoknolpe, and Ahnikin had butchered the women. All these men and women now gathered for the Jelj had much to forget and forgive. They sat there for a long time in their two compact groups, as if contemplating some great plunge. Then, after perhaps three-quarters of an hour, as if suddenly making up their minds with one accord, the southern men rose to their feet and walked briskly across the open space, with their women and children behind them.

At a distance of about a hundred and fifty yards from us, the advancing party halted and ostentatiously stacked their bows and quivers. The two rifles had been left behind in their encampment. Then they came forward again and stopped a few yards in front of us, with the women and children some little distance to the rear of the men. We still did not rise to our feet.

It must have made a fine picture. Though many of these people possessed white man's clothing, every one now wore his primitive robes and paint. The men on both sides were painted with white and red spots or stripes in many patterns. Doubtless, for the initiated, these had some meaning. The women were also painted, but with less care. For the most part, they were smeared with deep red paint, in sign of mourning. On this occasion I saw no black paint.

The mountain men began to speak one at a time, quietly and with dignity. They were answered by the northerners in the same manner and, though some grew husky with emotion, they never interrupted one another or raised their voices unduly. This was the burden of their remarks:

"Where are the Shilknum [1] now? There are none left. We are the same people and to this country we belong. Why should we hate and kill one another till all are gone? We are not angry now. We do not wish to be angry any more. We want to forget."

Certainly their short phrases lacked the flow of easy eloquence one could listen to at any gathering of the Yahgans, who indulged in prolonged and fluent harangues.[2] These Ona, however, now managed to say all that was needful, avoiding anything that might raise the ire of the opposite party. Some of the northern women who had suffered bereavement more recently, remembering perhaps the women Ahnikin had shot, broke into a low wailing that rose, once or twice, to a continuous howl, till one of the older men told them sternly to be quiet.

These preliminary speeches went on until they were brought to an abrupt end by Shishkolh, who was impatient for action and could wait no longer. Just in the same way as he had been the initial challenger in the wrestling contest at Harberton, now he was again first in the field. He had been with the southerners in the Lake Hyewhin raid, and now stepped forward towards Kautempklh—who, having killed Yoknolpe, their finest hunter, was looked upon as the arch-enemy by the southern men—and, taking five arrows from beneath his robe, handed them to him. The barbed heads had been removed and replaced by pieces of thin hide, which had been bound round the ends of the arrows and tied tightly with sinew. This formed a kind of button, to prevent penetration deep enough to cause a mortal wound.

Having passed over the arrows, Shishkolh turned and walked off to a distance of nearly ninety yards, where he turned again to face the company, kicked off his moccasins, flung aside his robe with a dramatic gesture and stood naked and motionless.

[1] The Ona name for themselves.

[2] Darwin says in *A Naturalist's Voyage*, "The language of these people, according to our notions, scarcely deserves to be called articulate. Captain Cook has compared it to a man clearing his throat, but certainly, he adds, no European ever cleared his throat with so many hoarse, guttural and clicking sounds." As this can never be said of the Yahgan speech, both these observers must have referred to the Ona. When these people were much in earnest, they seemed to lay special emphasis on those harsh consonants, which came alone in quick succession without any vowel between to soften them; and at this meeting the speakers were earnest indeed.

Old Kautempklh had risen to his feet and now drew to the front of his group. Well out in the open, he dropped his robe. The land sloped away from where we were seated to the spot where Shishkolh had taken his stand, and he presented an excellent target. The marksman fitted an arrow into his bow. As he discharged it, Shishkolh began to run towards him. For all his advancing years, Kautempklh could still send his arrows in remarkably quick succession and with deadly force; and the other four arrows swiftly followed the first, while Shishkolh dodged them as he came. Some of the older men around me were critical. They said that Shishkolh not only jumped about too much instead of advancing faster, but was also incorrectly painted.

When all five arrows had missed their human target, Shishkolh went back for his robe, then rejoined his friends. His place was taken, one after the other, by all the southern men of fighting age, who had provided themselves likewise with five arrows and, generally selecting different opponents, followed each other through the same performance. Inexperienced lads such as Nana and Metet did not participate, nor did Tinis, whose withered arm prevented him from using a bow. When a man acting as target made a specially agile escape from the flying arrow, there were guttural ejaculations of approval from the audience; but if he failed to approach his adversary at a fair speed, or showed off by prancing about needlessly, there were expressions of disapproval, not from his enemies, but from his own people.

After the mountain men had all taken their turn, the northerners produced arrows and each allowed his particular enemy the customary five shots.

The quickness of sight and movement displayed by most of the men of both parties was astonishing. In spite of this, more than one had bleeding wounds, of which they took not the slightest notice.

The last of the northern men to offer himself as target was the little medicine-man, Yoiyolh, who proved that day that he had been well named Waterfall Duck. Having presented his five arrows to that famous killer, Halimink, he gave an amazing exhibition of dash and agility. He did not go the whole permissible distance, but turned to face Halimink when he was little more than sixty yards away; and though the flight of an arrow for that short distance was so swift that the eye could hardly follow it, he escaped without a scratch. Halimink fired the last arrow at a range of perhaps thirty yards, yet Yoiyolh evaded it. This display, which Yoiyolh had purposely reserved till the last, gave rise to favourable comment, which led to general chat and even laughter, all parties sitting down and exhibiting the best of humour.

For three days there was friendly intercourse between the northern and southern groups. Visits were exchanged. The women went fishing together. The lads met in friendly wrestling, very different from the rough tussles of the past. Even the infants were encouraged to wrestle, their struggles giving rise to great amusement among the onlookers.

I can safely claim to be the only white man ever to have witnessed *Jelj*, the peace ritual. Even amongst the Ona who took part in it, only the very oldest remembered a previous performance of this kind done in earnest. But it was traditional. Lads were prepared for it by being pelted with small pebbles, or a tree fungus called *terrh*, which was the shape and nearly the size of a golf ball and quite as hard when frozen. I have taken every opportunity available to read about the customs of primitive tribes in different parts of the world, but never have I come across anything quite like this ancient Ona ritual of peace-making.

The future was to show that the promises thus given were faithfully kept. Though deaths from individual quarrels did occur later, there were no more planned raids or fighting between the groups. The long, bloody feud was over at last.

CHAPTER FORTY-TWO

Ona Spirits of the Woods—Mehn, Yohsi *and* Hahshi. *I Hear of Other Monsters. I Enter the Ona Lodge as a Novice. The Origins of the Secret Society. Creatures of the Shades. The Conventions of the* Hain. *I See* Halpen, *the Woman from the Clouds, and* Hachai, *the Horned Man. Short Initiates the Novices. K-Wamen Learns the Great Secret. Duties of a* Klokten. *The Miraculous Healing of Halimink. Ritualistic Performances of Ona Men and Women. With the Advance of Civilization, the Secrets of the* Hain *are Laid Bare. Some Observations concerning Travellers' Tales.*

I

WITH THE END OF INTER-GROUP WARFARE IN ONA-LAND, THERE FOLLOWED for me a long, happy period in the company of my Indian friends. The old jealousies were forgotten and now I moved from one party to another without hurting the feelings of any of them. I was never quite certain of Ahnikin—his glance in my direction was as inscrutable as ever—but from the day of the *Jelj,* Halimink showed nothing but friendship towards me and ultimately became the most trusted of all the shepherds at Viamonte.

It was some time after the great peace ceremony that I was initiated into the secret society of the Ona men.

In earlier years at Ushuaia we knew that Yahgan lads underwent a term of trial and semi-starvation. The centre of these activities was a large wigwam called *Keena.* At times the Yahgans allowed their women to enter this *Keena* and there take part in certain theatrical performances.

The Ona had similar structures, totally different from anything they ever lived in. These places (*Hain*) were generally grass-grown and in disrepair, but occasionally towards autumn, when guanaco were fat and goslings plentiful, I noticed that some of them had been renovated and recently used. They were generally placed near clumps of trees, with a wide space separating them from some favourite camping-ground. In the *Hain,* boys from thirteen to seventeen years of age were instructed in the ways of life and, after a term of probation, were admitted into the society of men. The *Hain,* I gathered, was used also for mysterious functions at which no woman was ever permitted to be present. These meetings did not take place in times of turmoil.

I had known from early childhood that the Yahgans had great fear of magic and witchcraft and that their dread of the Ona was equalled—even exceeded—by their dread of those wild-men-of-the-woods, *Hanush* and *Cushpij*. With my increasing knowledge of Ona customs, there came the realization that they not only had a far vaster, more intimate and complicated field of superstition than the Yahgans, but also that the basis and origin of much of it must be kept secret.

As years passed, I classified Ona superstitions under four main headings:

First: Fear of magic and of the power of magicians, even on the part of those who, professing that art, must have known that they themselves were humbugs. They had great fear of the power of others.

Second: Folk-lore and legend, which led from before the Creation right on into modern history. These stories were told with meticulous care and long searching of memories. If the narrator was not quite certain of some detail he wished to emphasize, he would make enquiry of other wise men.

Third: Belief in two types of ghost (not the spirits of the dead), which haunted the more desolate parts of the country. These, like respectable, civilized ghosts, appeared only between dusk and dawn, and generally to men who were travelling alone.

Fourth: A more or less pretended belief in a fantastic family imbued with superhuman strength, which came out of rocks, trees, clouds, etc., and sometimes visited the men at their councils and, being short of temper, might, if roused, chase them and tear them to pieces.

With the first of these groups I have already dealt at some length. Folk-lore and legend have their place later in these pages. The third I shall deal with now, as a preliminary to the fourth.

Of the two types of Ona ghost, one was *Mehn*, who was generally of kindly disposition, and the other was *Yohsi*, an especially malignant pixy. The concept of *Mehn* cannot be precisely stated. Though I have never heard it used in the sense of life or thought, it might very well have meant either. It was both a chimera and an entity—or rather, numberless entities. It might be a man's shadow cast on the ground, or his reflection in a lake or mirror; or it might be an adumbration drifting through the forest as light as the thinnest wreath of smoke; like the faint shadow to be seen on a sunless day, or a chill that was almost visible. *Mehn* might give a man some premonition of danger or warn him of some impending calamity. Perhaps even a civilized man, especially one who has hunted alone, has felt *Mehn's* presence, yet not mentioned it afterwards to others, lest they should say that the poor fellow was crazy. When an Ona died, his *Mehn* departed as well. No one ever asked or wondered where it had gone, any more than they asked or wondered what had happened to his last breath. A man's *Mehn* might leave him and go into his shadow or into his reflection in water or glass, but it was not carried away; it returned to him and he lost nothing. With the introduction of cameras into Ona-land, the natives did not at first like to be photographed. Their objection was that some of their *Mehn* might thereby be taken away and, by being transferred to the paper, be forfeit for ever. *Mehn* was not confined to men alone; animals were influenced by it and every living creature had its own *Mehn*. For example, *Whash K-Mehn*, the foxes' spirit, might lead hunting dogs off the scent or warn the guanaco of a hunter's approach—though this would be more out of dislike for mankind than fondness for the guanaco.

The pixy *Yohsi* was cast in a less ethereal mould. He resembled a man and had females and little ones in his home. He was transparent, but not invisible, and might—or might not—leave some kind of mark when passing over the softest snow. He broke and collected dry twigs and pieces of wood for fires that he was unable to light. He appeared most frequently to the solitary hunter who was spending the night by his fire. When the hunter was asleep, *Yohsi* would come and stir the fire with his long middle finger. As the burnt logs subsided, the hunter would awake with a start, to find *Yohsi* sitting opposite him. *Yohsi* might drift or fade away on the instant, or he might remain a long time, causing great fear to his *vis-à-vis*. Instances have been known of solitary wanderers found dead and horribly mutilated, evidently by *Yohsi*, in the place where they had chosen to pass the night.

I was once travelling with a couple of Ona. We had come off the mountains late in the day and were camped in the scrub close to upper tree level, when the sharp snapping of twigs in the frosty air convinced my companions that *Yohsi* was about. They were certainly nervous, and when I was foolish enough to scoff at their superstition, one of them rebuked me, saying that, if I were alone and found *Yohsi* sitting on the other side of the fire, I should not be so brave.

For some unknown reason, the numbers of *Yohsi* had greatly diminished, even before the advent of the white man, and now they are found only in the most wretched and inaccessible parts of the country.

Those, then, were *Mehn* and *Yohsi*, the ghosts of Ona-land, both generally accepted supernatural beings whom the men professed to fear as much as did the women. Between these two ghosts and the other set of creatures of the shades, acting as a link, yet in a class by himself, was *Hahshi.*

Hahshi was a lonely, noisy imp, chocolate-brown in colour, like damp, rotten wood. He was said to come out of dead trees and generally to haunt the vicinity of long-burnt forests. He was thick-set, greedy, quite impervious to arrows and incredibly strong. He wandered through the woods at night, hooting at intervals, "Cooh-hooh! Cooh-hooh!" This was probably suggested by the cry of one of the many kinds of owl to be found in those parts. When such sounds were heard at night near an encampment and it was thought that *Hahshi*, having discovered the place, was approaching, there was very likely to be a general stampede.

This *Hahshi* was very mischievous. If he found the deserted encampment, he would pull about everything he could lay his hands on, dragging odds and ends of furniture and robes out of the different windbreaks and mixing them up hopelessly. He would pull down the shelters, spill the water-bags over the fire and, if he found guanaco skulls, break them with his teeth and eat the brains, of which he was very fond.

If *Hahshi's* retiring hoots failed to advise the refugees that he had gone, some courageous man would venture back to the camp to spy on his movements and at last bring news of his departure, whereupon the whole party would return to the task of sorting out the various goods and putting things in order again.

I have never seen *Hahshi*, but several times I have noticed that the cry of an owl has caused excited preparations for hasty flight, the men pretending they believed *Hahshi* to be near. By the women *Hahshi* was much feared, but the men regarded him, amongst themselves, as a huge joke. He gave them a chance to show every symptom of terror, yet, at the same time, to assume the heroic, protecting attitude that we men so dearly love. To add to the reality of his performance—and in case some women caught sight of him as he went about his naughty work in the deserted encampment—he would plaster himself with mud and wood-mould, with dead leaves and bits of bark adding dirtiness to his other unadmirable qualities.

It was not always the cry of a real owl that began the panic. A mischief-loving hunter, who had left the camp with the expressed intention of not returning for some days, could easily creep back at night to within a few hundred yards of the encampment and, by giving the orthodox "Cooh-hooh!" a few times, cause a buzz of excitement, purposely created and magnified by his men friends, without even going to the trouble of dressing up or painting himself for the part.

From *Hahshi*, who was neither a ghost nor a superhuman monster of the *Hain*, we come to that last set of creatures—the fantastic family falling under my fourth heading. These, with one exception, had a special hatred of women. Their history converges with, and is hard to separate from, some of the folk-lore. And they were the very life-blood of the Ona Lodge.

When, not long after my father's passing in 1898, I had followed the strayed cattle behind Flat Top with Ahnikin, Minkiyolh and Chauiyolh, the son of Te-ilh, I had an opportunity, during the ten or more days and nights I spent with them, to add to my knowledge of Ona mythology. They were all of different groups—Ahnikin from the mountains, Minkiyolh from Cape San Pablo and Chauiyolh from Najmishk, so it was reasonable to suppose that the legends I collected from them were common to Ona-land and not confined to one part of the country. It did not take me long to realize that, apart from a genuine fear of *Mehn* and *Yohsi* and illness caused by witchcraft, there were other weird, unearthly folk in whom they wished me to think they believed. They spoke in serious tones of strange monsters they claimed to have met in lonely places and how they had narrowly escaped being captured by them. They described a creature resembling a man, but with long, sharp horns; and two fierce sisters, one white and the other red. These three seemed to be the most dreaded of all, but there were many more besides. At night Ahnikin or one of the others would express fear that some of these might be haunting the forest around our encampment.

When they solemnly insisted that they had actually seen these sinister beings and been pursued by them, I thought what liars those young fellows must be. I knew that to show incredulity or, worse still, to ridicule their stories, was to put an end to them altogether; and feeling that some respect was due to those age-old tales, I listened with the greatest interest and every appearance of belief. It was not until later years that I received proof that these earnest reports of encounters with the horned man, the red and white sisters and other uncanny creatures had been imparted to me, not because Ahnikin, Minkiyolh and Chauiyolh believed in them as they did in witchcraft and the spirits of the woods, but because I was on a par with the Ona women; because I was among the uninitiated; because I did not belong to the Ona Lodge.

2

Though naturally full of curiosity, I did not want to force myself unasked into their secret society, so held aloof and bided my time. In the end my patience was rewarded. One evening, some while after peace had come to Ona-land, I was invited to join a large gathering of Indians. The meeting, which was attended by members of all the groups, took place near an old *Hain* in the woods, a short distance from the encampment where all the families had gathered.

When I took up my position in the party assembled round the fire, there was a debate in progress. The subject of it was my suitability for membership of the Lodge, and opinion was divided. A minority, headed by the conservative brothers, Shishkolh and Shijyolh, were against the proposal. Among those who spoke strongly in my favour were Halimink and that influential medicine-man, Tininisk. After enumerating various episodes in my past life—incidents that tended to raise me in the esteem of these primitive men—Tininisk concluded by saying that, though I looked like a white man, my heart, which he, as a *joön*, could see with his own eyes, was the heart of an Ona.

These words silenced the opposition and my entry as a novice into the *Hain* was proceeded with. Halimink began by telling me that I was now an Indian, a man and not a child; and that there was yet much for me to learn. My sponsor and guide, he said, would be Aneki, whose father, Heëshoölh, had been wise and had taught his sons, Aneki, Shilchan and the now dead Otrhshoölh, much ancient lore. Aneki would be seconded by his brother, Shilchan (Soft Voice). I must attend carefully to their words and obey the rules of the Lodge, which were strict. Should any man, Halimink warned me gravely, confide to a woman or an uninitiated lad anything of what went on in the *Hain*, both he and the person to whom he had spoken would be killed. There would be no one to defend the guilty man, for, in the event of such an unforgivable indiscretion, brother would kill brother, father would kill son.

When Halimink had finished his impressive lecture, he intimated that I should retire to the *Hain* with my sponsors. These guided me there with the utmost care, as though some invisible obstacle lay in the path, not only on the approach to the *Hain*, but also after we got inside that spacious wigwam. A fire burned in the centre of it. Along the walls were large supporting poles. One of these, which was about half-way from the entrance to the back of the building, had been blackened by burning. Aneki invited me to sit down beside this pole. The place had evidently been decided upon beforehand and was intended as my regular seat at all the meetings of the Lodge.

Others soon began to drift in after us, whilst Aneki expounded to me the rules of the *Hain*. From time to time his brother would throw in a word or two, but for the most part he remained silent. I gathered that his principal function was to watch and listen. It was evidently the correct thing for the tutor to have a witness—an interesting point of similarity between primitive man and ourselves. Also, if need arose—should, for instance, I prove an intractable pupil—Shilchan would be there to help Aneki to destroy me.

After a while Aneki asked me gently if I was afraid of fire. Knowing what was expected of me, I took a small, glowing ember in my fingers and, without haste, placed it on my arm, taking no notice of it, for I knew full well that several pairs of eyes were fixed on my face to see if I showed any sign of discomfort. After a moment, which appeared long to me, Aneki flicked it off, saying:

"K-pash kau." ("It is enough now.")

Conversation then became general and I was discussed from head to foot as to my fitness to impersonate one or other of the semi-human beings who visited the *Hain*. Standing over six feet, I qualified in height and build for a creature called *Short*.[1] This, however, would be too risky; the tracks of my bare feet would give me away. Not even the women could have failed to recognize them. The seriousness of the meeting soon began to give place to low chatter and guarded laughter. At short intervals, without troubling to leave their places, the men set up a most awful din, seeming to have lost all the self-control for which these stoics were remarkable. Shouts of anger and fear were intermingled with cries of excitement and pain. Between the outbursts could be heard weird noises that were supposed to be the voices of unearthly, though far from heavenly, visitors to our Lodge. One of these outbursts was so noisy and sustained that it brought the women out of the encampment. When there was a lull in the babel, I heard them calling out from a respectful distance at the back of the *Hain*. Above the others came the voice of Tininisk's wife, Leluwhachin, Ona-land's only sorceress. She asked if her elder brother (myself) had been killed. Tininisk answered that the men were protecting me from the two fierce sisters, *Halpen* and *Tanu*, and ordered the women to go back home.

[1] This is an Ona word, not its English equivalent.

To add conviction to this story, some of the men gave themselves quite nasty cuts on chests or arms with pieces of broken glass or sharp stones. They even inflicted a few lighter scratches on their faces and made their noses bleed profusely by jabbing pointed sticks deep into their nostrils. With these visible signs of struggle, they could then afterwards inform their wives that the evil sisters, one from the white clouds and the other from the red clay, had been enraged at finding a white man in their Lodge, and that the wounds had been inflicted by the long claws on the middle fingers (a peculiarity shared by *Halpen* and *Tanu* with *Yohsi*, the vengeful pixy of the woods), while the men had bravely defended me against them.

3

To gain some conception of the extreme gravity of this ludicrous show, we must go back to times far older than history. In the next chapter there are collected together some of the Ona legends and folk-lore that I culled over a period of many years, dating right back to the days when I first hunted with the Indians in the woods around Harberton. From this jumble of fable and ancient tales—told to me piecemeal, with no cohesion and much repetition—emerges the story of the Ona *Hain*.

In the days when all the forest was evergreen, before *Kerrhprrh* the parakeet painted the autumn leaves red with the colour from his breast, before the giants *Kwonyipe* and *Chashkilchesh* wandered through the woods with their heads above the tree-tops; in the days when *Krren* (the sun) and *Kreeh* (the moon) walked the earth as man and wife, and many of the great sleeping mountains were human beings: in those far-off days witchcraft was known only by the women of Ona-land. They kept their own particular Lodge, which no man dared approach. The girls, as they neared womanhood, were instructed in the magic arts, learning how to bring sickness and even death to all those who displeased them.

The men lived in abject fear and subjection. Certainly they had bows and arrows with which to supply the camp with meat, yet, they asked, what use were such weapons against witchcraft and sickness? This tyranny of the women grew from bad to worse until it occurred to the men that a dead witch was less dangerous than a live one. They conspired together to kill off all the women; and there ensued a great massacre, from which not one woman escaped in human form.

Even the young girls only just beginning their studies in witchcraft were killed with the rest, so the men now found themselves without wives. For these they must wait until the little girls grew into women. Meanwhile the great question arose : How could men keep the upper hand now they had got it? One day, when these girl children reached maturity, they might band together and regain their old ascendancy. To forestall this, the men inaugurated a secret society of their own and banished for ever the women's Lodge in which so many wicked plots had been hatched against them. No woman was allowed to come near the *Hain*, under penalty of death. To make quite certain that this decree was respected by their womenfolk, the men invented a new branch of Ona demonology : a collection of strange beings—drawn partly from their own imaginations and partly from folk-lore and ancient legends— who would take visible shape by being impersonated by members of the Lodge and thus scare the women away from the secret councils of the *Hain*. It was given out that these creatures hated women, but were well-disposed towards men, even supplying them with mysterious food during the often very protracted proceedings of the Lodge. Sometimes, how-ever, these beings were short-tempered and hasty. Their irritability was manifested to the women of the encampment by the shouts and uncanny cries arising from the *Hain*, and, it might be, the scratched faces and bleeding noses with which the men returned home when some especially exciting session was over.

Most direful of the supernatural visitors to the *Hain* were the horned man and two fierce sisters of whom Ahnikin and the other lads had spoken during our cattle-hunt behind Flat Top. The name of the horned man was *Halahachish* or, more usually, *Hachai*. He came out of the lichen-covered rocks and was as grey in appearance as his lurking-place. The white sister was *Halpen*. She came from the white cumulus clouds and shared a terrible reputation for cruelty with her sister, *Tanu*, who came from the red clay.

A fourth monster of the *Hain* was *Short*. He was a much more frequent participator in Lodge proceedings than the other three. Like *Hachai*, he came from the grey rocks. His only garment was a whitish piece of parchment-like skin over his face and head. This had holes in it for eyes and mouth and was drawn tight round the head and tied behind. There were many *Shorts*, and more than one could be seen at the same time. There was a great variation in colouring and pattern of the make-up. One arm and the opposite leg might be white or red, with spots or stripes (or both) of the other colour superimposed. The application to the body of grey down from young birds gave *Short* a certain resemblance to his lichen-covered haunts. Unlike *Hachai*, *Halpen* and *Tanu*, he was to be found far from the *Hain* and was sometimes seen by the women when they were out in the woods gathering firewood or berries. On such occasions they would hasten home with the exciting news, for *Short* was said to be very dangerous to women and inclined to kill them. When he appeared near the encampment, the women would bolt for their shelters, where, together with their children, they would lie face downward on the ground, covering their heads with any loose garments they could lay their hands on.

Besides those four, there were many other creatures of the *Hain*, some of whom had not appeared, possibly, for a generation. There was, for instance, *Kmantah*, who was dressed in beech bark and was said to come out of, and return to, his mother *Kualchink*, the deciduous beech tree. Another was *Kterrnen*. He was small, very young and reputed to be the son of *Short*. He was highly painted and covered with patches of down; and was the only one of all the creatures of the Lodge to be kindly disposed towards the women, who were even allowed to look up when he passed.

I wondered sometimes whether these strange appearances might be the remains of a dying religion, but came to the conclusion that this could not be so. There was no vestige of any legend to suggest that any of these creatures impersonated by the Indians had ever walked the earth in any form but fantasy.

The *Hain*, a large wigwam, was usually about a quarter of a mile from the village or camping-ground, and always faced away from it, to prevent the prying eyes of the women from seeing through its ever-open door. Whenever possible, it was built near a clump of trees, which helped to screen the interior of the *Hain* from other directions and served as a wing from behind which the actors could appear on the stage. The wigwam was always to the east of the village. Certain explorers have noticed these wigwams and have concluded that they were places of worship. It was not, however, any idea of religion or the cult of the rising sun that made them place the Lodge in that position, but merely because the prevailing winds came from the west. With the *Hain's* entrance facing east, there was more shelter from the weather. Another reason for having the meeting-place to the leeward of the village was the mystical nourishment with which the men were supposed to be supplied. The scent of roasting meat borne on the breeze to the village might have cast doubts on that story.

Aneki told me during that first discourse that, from the fire in the centre of the *Hain*, an imaginary chasm of untold depth, and with a flaming inferno at the bottom of it, ran out through the door and away eastward into the distance. Ages ago, when the *Hain* was new, this chasm had really existed and anyone trying to cross it had fallen in and been lost. Its presence now was only assumed, yet it was still not without its perils when a meeting was in session. Any man treading, however inadvertently, on the place where it was supposed to be would be thrown on the fire—though, added Aneki, he would not be held down there. This was a direct warning to me—and now I knew why my tutors had guided my footsteps so meticulously as we approached and entered the *Hain*.

This hypothetical chasm had another purpose. It divided the Lodge into two groups, according to parentage or place of birth. The men from the north sat to the south of the fissure, and the men from the south to the north. It also governed approach to the *Hain*. I, being from across the mountains to the south of Ona-land and having no connection, either by country or by blood, with the northerners, had to move out to the left when walking from the village, keeping the *Hain* on my right until I turned to go through the doorway. This I must on no account cross over, but must enter the wigwam with the wall close on my right and the fire on my left. There, half-way along, was *Kiayeshk*, which meant Black Shag and was the name of the pole darkened by burning. Beside *Kiayeshk* was to be my place at the councils, and I must not pass beyond it until the end of the proceedings, unless directly called upon to do so.

If a man had two places of origin, inasmuch as his parents came one from the north and the other from the south, there were no such restrictions imposed upon him. Aneki himself was one of these privileged members. His father, Heëshoölh, came from the south-east and his mother was a northern woman, so he could pass the Lodge on either side when approaching from the village and take his seat north or south of the fiery chasm.

At the end of the meetings all these restraints were lifted and we could leave the *Hain* in any way we liked. When not in use as a Lodge, the wigwam served as sleeping-quarters and living-house for bachelors, widowers such as Chalshoat, who had lost his wife as a result of an act of unpardonable carelessness with his bow and arrow, and *klokten* who had passed their entrance examination. The boys who did not know the secret had to sleep in the encampment.

4

During the afternoon following my initiation, it was decided to dress up the disabled Aush boy, Tinis, as that cruel female from the clouds, *Halpen*. The poor fellow was swathed in skin robes with the fur inwards. For this purpose everyone contributed his only garment, and the combined weight was so great that Tinis could hardly walk. He lost all semblance of a human being and was completely blinded by the clothes piled over his head. As this dressing up proceeded, great care was taken to avoid suffocation, and constant enquiries were made to know if he could breathe more or less freely. The outer robes, which hung right down to his feet, were then well whitened with chalk.

With these preparations complete, the unwieldy apparition was secretly conducted to a clump of trees, some eighty yards from the *Hain*. Here on top of the huge mass of skins was fastened a bundle in the shape of a large fish, with the likeness of a human face painted in front. When all was ready, the majority of the men returned to the *Hain*, leaving Tininisk and one or two others to take care of *Halpen*, and again set up that unearthly noise, beyond my powers to describe.

The women and children now appeared. They formed an excited group in front of the encampment, a few of the boldest venturing some way ahead of the others to get a better view. Poor Tinis could not see at all and it was difficult for him to move under the burden of so many skins, but Tininisk was there to help him. Well hidden from the women's line of vision behind *Halpen's* enormous bulk, the naked medicine-man steadied Tinis with his hands and directed him where to tread, as they left the shelter of the trees and made for the *Hain*. The shape of the head made it easy for Tininisk to manipulate it and so give the disguise a peculiarly menacing appearance that well supported *Halpen's* sinister repute. In fearsome silence *Halpen* was brought safely to the group of men waiting near the doorway of the *Hain*, which she then entered in their company.

This ceremony may sound childish and ridiculous to those who live in civilized surroundings, but, in that primitive atmosphere of excitement and superstition, *Halpen's* sluggish advance, with frequent pauses when the face was turned directly towards the women, was undoubtedly impressive.

The Ona said that *Halpen's* progress was not always so slow; she could move very quickly when so disposed. She had been known to

A lake on top of the cliffs of Gable Island, looking westward up the Beagle Channel.

The first shearing-sheds on Gable Island, with Mount Misery on Navarin Island in the hazy background.

Coastal view from Najmishk, with Ewan Cliffs in the distance and Cape Santa Inés (Shilan) beyond. Tijnolsh Hill is hidden by the Ewan Cliffs.

The huts in Ona-land.
On the extreme right is the original one-roomed hut, with its more commodious successor next to it. Both are put to shame by the new mansion, with its iron stove, glass window and boarded floor.

pounce on human beings and bear them off into the clouds, from which presently fell their bones, picked clean of flesh. Almost anyone who, like Tinis, was willing to carry a heavy load under trying conditions, could impersonate *Halpen* or her sister, *Tanu*. The only conspicuous difference between these sisters was that *Tanu* was red instead of white and had a far more genteel figure. That was the only time I saw *Halpen*. Her sister I never saw at all. In fact, her appearances were so rare that very few of the Ona I had met had seen her either.

Some of the creatures of the *Hain* called for greater dramatic ability than did *Halpen* or *Tanu*, and not many actors met with the complete approval of the Ona critics. Perhaps the most exacting role of all was *Hachai*, the horned man. On one of the numerous meetings of the Lodge that I subsequently attended, it was decided that *Hachai* should appear. The part was entrusted to one of the few men able to impersonate him well—Talimeoat, the bird-hunter. He was painted all over with white and red patterns, the general trend being towards white. Then a good deal of grey down was stuck on him, for *Hachai* was supposed to come out of the lichen-covered rocks. A small bow such as children used, less than a yard long and well padded so that it could not be recognized as such, was tied across his forehead. A mask of whitish colour, with red-rimmed holes for the eyes, covered his head and face, giving him the look of a short-nosed cow.

The women had, as usual, gathered in front of the encampment for the performance. *Hachai* came out of the bushes some distance beyond the *Hain* and, with threatening movements of his horns, made short rushes towards them, snorting as he did so. The women showed considerable alarm at this and some of the men ran over as though to protect them, should it be necessary. Notwithstanding the presence of these valiant defenders, the women fled to their homes, where they threw themselves on the ground in groups, face downwards, covering their heads with skins.

Hachai passed through the encampment accompanied by some of the men, whose business, no doubt, was to ensure that none of the women spied at close quarters. Then, having completed his tour, he backed away from the encampment towards the *Hain*. When he had withdrawn some distance, still snorting and rearing his head, the women were told that the danger was over and they hastened out into the open again, to get a last glimpse of the retreating monster before, with his face still turned towards them, he disappeared into the Lodge.

Here it is of interest to note that no horned animal of any kind is indigenous to Tierra del Fuego; yet a hunter of wild cattle would have admired Talimeoat's performance. His uncertain advances, his threatening tosses of the head, his snorting and sudden forward thrusts of one horn or the other—all were most realistic. The part he was playing came from a legendary myth and had doubtless been enacted by the Ona for countless generations.

That was the only occasion when *Hachai* visited the *Hain* while I was present. His fellow rock-dweller, *Short*, I saw many times. *Short* was the one indispensable participant in the mysteries of the Lodge. I remember one incident showing his pre-eminence and the importance attached to the secret of his identity. *Short* had appeared amongst the men and, masked, painted and covered with grey down, approached the encampment in their company. All the women fled to hide their heads. *Short*, as was his wont, darted to the encampment, seemingly in search of something. He would pick up some article, perhaps only a bit of stick, run a little way with it and, putting it down carefully, dart off after something else that took his fancy. Then he would lay hands on one of the shelters and shake it violently. The other men would hasten to undo the ties, in case he wished to pull the place down—as *Short* often did when he called at a village. All these antics were part of the conventional performance, but this *Short* suddenly acted in an unprecedented fashion. He snatched up a piece of rough firewood and, with an angry snort, threw it with great force at a woman cowering under her *oli*.

On our return to the *Hain*, I asked him why he had done it. He answered that the woman's head had not been well covered and that he had thought she was spying. The billet weighed several pounds and had given her a heavy blow, yet her husband had taken no action against *Short*. In other circumstances, such an attack on a man's wife would have led to a serious quarrel, in which the offender might well have lost his life. This episode is given added point by the fact that *Short* was played by the universally disliked Minkiyolh, that the husband was the formidable and much-respected Tininisk, and that the offending woman was no less a person than Leluwhachin. Notwithstanding this, Tininisk did not show, either then or later, the slightest resentment towards Minkiyolh for his action; and Ahnikin and Halimink, both also present, who would have welcomed any excuse to pick a quarrel with Minkiyolh, also held their hands.

The most important part played by *Short* in Lodge affairs was concerned with the *klokten* (novices). In the early stages of their instruction, before their initiation into the *Hain*, these lads implicitly believed in supernatural monsters, having, as children, often watched them from the encampment and joined in the stampede when *Halpen* or *Short* approached too near. Ahnikin, Minkiyolh and Chauiyolh had not been in this state of ignorance when they had told me tales behind Flat Top of the fierce sisters and the horned man, for their education had been completed some time previously. As a preliminary part of that education, *klokten* were sent off, either alone or in pairs, on one-day expeditions into the forest. In preparation for the event, some of the men would kill a guanaco leagues away from the encampment and leave the meat out of the reach of foxes, either hanging it in the branches of a tree or sinking it in a pond or slow-moving stream. The *klokten* would then be told where the meat was to be found. They were given instructions as to which pieces to bring back, the load possibly being equal to their own weight. They were also told which track to follow, and this, as a rule, was not the easiest or shortest way. They might be ordered to make long detours over certain hills or around lakes, both on the outward and return trips. To make certain that these commands were obeyed, one of the men would shadow them all the way, without allowing himself to be seen.

The real object of these expeditions was to reduce the *klokten* to such a condition of fear that it needed real courage to go on through the haunted woods. Before they departed, they were warned that they might meet *Short*. It was impressed upon them that it was useless to defend themselves with arrows, because *Short* was quite impervious to such things and would become so enraged by the attempt to injure him that he would kill anyone who tried it. They were advised instead to take refuge in trees if pursued by *Short*, who refused to climb them, however branchy they might be. These words of admonition were most necessary, for all the lads carried bows and arrows and were already skilful in their use. An impetuous action by a *klokten* might cost the man playing *Short* his life. The story was told that one terrified apprentice did discharge an arrow at *Short*, who fell mortally wounded. On returning to the Lodge, the *klokten* was killed in retaliation. But this unfortunate incident could not be used as a warning to the *klokten*, for its fatal termination did not coincide with *Short*'s supposed invulnerability.

With all this talk of *Short* fresh in their minds, *klokten* always started on their errands full of trepidation. Every yard of the way they were dogged by the fear of strange, ghostly beings in the vicinity. Their elders saw to it that *Short* duly made his appearance. Sometimes the lads might catch sight of the white-faced monster, evade him and bravely carry out the rest of their task without further adventure. On other occasions *Short* might rush out of a thicket in pursuit of them. Should they seek shelter in the branches of a tree, he would prance about below, flinging sticks and stones at them until he wearied of the sport and went away. Later, with his disguise put aside, he would listen with much amusement to the horrible adventures of his victims and their colourful descriptions of his appearance as they had looked down at him from a tree or fled in terror from him through the forest.

When the *klokten's* preliminary education had proceeded far enough, he was formally initiated into the Lodge. In this ceremony *Short* again figured prominently, for it was through meeting him face to face in the *Hain* and wrestling with him, that the *klokten* learnt the great secret : that *Short*, *Halpen*, *Hachai* and the rest were not supernatural beings, but merely characters in a masquerade.

I witnessed one of these initiations. The *klokten*, a boy called K-Wamen, was the son of Koniyolh, who was the renowned Taäpelht's nearest rival as a runner. *Short* was played by a man from Koniyolh's country in the north. He had been named Martin and became my chief shepherd at Viamonte. K-Wamen had already had some exciting escapes from *Short*, which, no doubt, he had recounted to his credulous mother and other women, thus confirming their beliefs. Now he was brought to the *Hain* by his father and informed that he was about to meet the dreaded *Short* at close quarters. Koniyolh told him that he need not be afraid and must be brave. There was a general air of expectancy. The men spoke in awed whispers that so impressed the candidate that, when the strange apparition appeared in the doorway, the boy was trembling with fear in every limb.

All *Short's* attention seemed concentrated on the boy, towards whom he advanced slowly by short jerks with long pauses in between. This approach was so menacing that the poor lad was hardly able to stand and would have undoubtedly bolted had not his father and friends blocked his retreat. With his hand on the boy's shoulder, Koniyolh spoke a few low words of encouragement. At last *Short* was close in front of the frightened novice. He went down on his knees and sniffed at him as an ill-mannered dog might have done, making swift darts towards him with his hands, which caused the boy to shrink backwards. None of these spirits could speak, but with sniffs and angry snorts, *Short* showed plainly that he disapproved strongly of the new candidate. By the most eloquent signs, he gave it to be understood that this lad had not been the well-conducted child his parents would have wished.

When *Short's* anger and disgust had grown almost to a frenzy, the terrified *klokten* was thrust into his embrace and urged by his father and friends to wrestle with the monster. This he did with all the strength of panic and the two of them struggled together, amidst the unrestrained laughter of the assembly, who encouraged the lad whole-heartedly, and were busy keeping the combatants out of the fire.

In these wrestling matches, *Short* always allowed the *klokten* to throw him in the end, so this fight ended in a victory for K-Wamen. But when he realized the identity of his tormentor, he attacked him again with such fury that he had to be dragged off, to the accompaniment of roars of laughter, in which *Short* joined heartily.

Whenever possible a relative of the novice was chosen for the part of *Short*, and the same man would have a large share in the education of the boy, who might not emerge from the state of *klokten* until two or three years after he had learnt the great secret.

At the initiation, there was no torture of the kind practised, we are told, among some tribes of North American Indians; but to prove his manhood a student might occasionally apply to his skin a burning ember that would leave a mark for years. It was said that one unfortunate candidate, who had been slow and unwilling to obey his instructor, had had the sinews cut behind his knees and, in consequence, had gone all his life on all fours. I am inclined to doubt this story, for instead of being a useful member, he would have become a burden to the tribe.

During his period of probation, the diet of a *klokten* was restricted almost entirely to lean meat. Luxuries such as marrow, brains, eyes or intestines were strictly forbidden. It was stated by the Indians that, whatever the opportunity and however great the temptation, no *klokten* would ever indulge himself, even if unobserved. In order to make a man of him, for some time after his initiation he was expected to go on long tramps, which might well have been called exploring expeditions, during which he must either kill for himself or subsist on tree fungus and roots. When on these lonely wanderings, he was not supposed to mix with other hunters. I saw an example of this. It happened some years before the Peace Ritual. One wretched evening in autumn, when I was walking late with two or three Ona, we approached a desirable clump of trees and decided to pass the night there. As we drew near, we observed a tinge of blue smoke through the mist. We advanced with the utmost caution, not knowing what kind of reception awaited us, but found only a tiny deserted fire. After carefully examining the ground, my companions decided that two *klokten* had been intending to spend the night there, but, on seeing us, had slipped away unobserved—the correct thing for them to do.

In his demeanour, the *klokten* was expected to be thoughtful and comparatively silent, listening attentively to words of wisdom from his elders. He must be obedient and industrious in carrying meat or fuel, must be serious and earnest in all his doings and must cease to play with the younger children. He must be reserved in his conduct towards women, acting frivolously neither with the wives, lest he excite the jealousy of their menfolk, nor with his female relatives, for fear men should say that he wished to marry his own sister—a most offensive implication.

The advice given to a *klokten* was generally sound, and reasons why it should be followed were always supplied. Here are a few examples:

A man should not be greedy, because it would make him corpulent and lazy and he would then cease to be a successful hunter, giving other men cause to say that his wife had to feed him on fish. On the other hand, a man's women should be fat, so that all would respect him, knowing him to be a successful hunter.

To avoid the dangers that might come from careless mixing with women of his own people, it was as well for a man to get wives from far away. This had the added advantage of making a wife more subservient to her husband's will, as she would have no relations to take her part when they quarrelled.

A man should give meat generously to old people, even if they were not his relations. It might then be that, when he himself was old and could not hunt, some young man would bring meat to him. In other words, "Cast thy bread upon the waters, for thou shalt find it after many days." This was the nearest approach to a religious precept that I ever heard while with these people.

Amongst the many creatures to visit the *Hain* was one *Ohlimink*, the medicine-man of that unholy band. If one of his human friends lay dying of a wound, in spite of all attempts by mortal *joön* to save his life, *Ohlimink* might be induced to come from the shades and, at the eleventh hour, miraculously cure the sufferer of his hurt.

Let me try to reproduce a performance of that immemorial drama.

While a meeting of the Lodge is in progress, Halimink is carried into the encampment, mortally wounded. The poor man is covered with blood and he gasps so painfully that it seems that every laboured breath will be his last. From other parts of the encampment and out of the *Hain*, a considerable number of men hasten to their dying friend. With them are those famed magicians, Tininisk and Yoiyolh, the Waterfall Duck. They all crowd round the unfortunate Halimink, who is lying on the ground, with only an occasional moan to show that he is still conscious. In the background hover the women, ready to bring water or do anything else that is required.

Brief throaty questions are asked of the men who brought in Halimink. They answer that the wound was inflicted by a lone hunter from another part of the country; that when the arrow was extracted, the barbed flint remained behind. At this, Tininisk and Yoiyolh set about the task of drawing forth the arrow-head. They chant. They draw their hands over his body. They suck at the wound. But all to no purpose. Finally, after exhausting efforts, they have to admit defeat and announce that the sufferer is nearing his end. The moans and grievous cries of the women give place to loud wailing, interspersed with prolonged howls in which all join. The case is hopeless and those nearest and dearest to Halimink start fiercely scraping their legs with rough stones and glass, till trickles of blood run down to their feet. They also scrape their arms in like manner. A bow and several arrows—property of the dying Indian —are broken and thrown on the fire to burn. Halimink is about to die.

It is at this solemn moment that some bright fellow suggests:

" Could we not summon *Ohlimink*? If he would come, might he save our brother? "

This last hope is eagerly seized upon. A rush is made for the *Hain*, with a sufficiency of men remaining behind to obstruct the women, should they, in their love and anxiety, unduly press in upon the sorely wounded man. From the *Hain* now come sounds of protracted squealing, broken at intervals by discordant shouts; and there is much movement between the *Hain* and the nearby forest.

At length the men appear. They are in a compact group and are walking rapidly towards the encampment, for every moment is precious. But who is that diminutive figure almost concealed in their midst? It cannot be little A-yaäh, who is even smaller than his brothers, Hechelash and Yoiyolh, for he is away hunting. No, this wondrous being is masked and grotesquely painted. He is *Ohlimink*, come from amongst that strange, dramatic, mythological group of creatures to which he belongs; come to save his wounded friend.

The women draw back as this excited party, beaming with success, approach; and even the doctors respectfully make room for their welcome colleague. With emphatic gutturals and vigorous signs, they explain to him the gravity and urgency of the case. *Ohlimink* has not the power of speech, but he makes visible efforts to understand what is said to him and, quickly grasping the situation, makes moaning sounds of assent and sympathy. He then concentrates all his mental powers on the gasping patient, making passes, such as an ordinary medicine-man would do, to gather the evil to the vicinity of the wound. Then, after mighty efforts of suction, he produces from his mask the offending arrow-head.

It is surprising, considering all he has gone through, how soon the wounded man, supported by *Ohlimink* and another and surrounded by his delighted companions, is able to retire, withal somewhat feebly, to the *Hain*. In this sanctuary, his cure is completed amidst animated discussion by the happy actors of their successful hoax. There may be some criticism from the older men who, of course, saw the act carried out very much better when they were young; but these observations are made tactfully and in all sincerity, and are therefore not resented.

The blood plastered over the patient to make the show more realistic was usually from the guanaco, with additional donations from willing helpers; and, of course, he would choose a bad bow and his worst arrows for destruction in the fire. For the part of *Ohlimink*, a medicine-man was not necessarily selected. The only essential qualification was that he must be small; and A-yaäh was an automatic choice. Instead of hunting, he had been making up ready to play his part in this serio-comic opera.

In cases of serious wounds or illness, the Ona doctors never called on *Ohlimink* for help, and certainly neither prayed to nor worshipped him— or any of his kind.

As women may be less foolish than they would like the other sex to imagine, I often suspected, while watching the antics of these grotesque and comic personifications, that those Ona women were not so deceived and terrified by their men's crude make-up as they pretended to be. When I once ventured to suggest to the men that the women only did it to please them, their reaction left me under no misapprehension as to their firm conviction of the women's blind credulity. To me it seemed impossible that the women were utterly deceived, yet the *klokten*, who had lived constantly with their mothers for the twelve or thirteen years prior to their initiation and would surely have heard any careless word had it been spoken, were undoubtedly terrified when they came face to face with *Short* for the first time. One thing is certain : that if any woman had been indiscreet enough to mention her doubts, even to another woman, and word of it had reached the ears of the men, the renegade would have been killed—and most likely others with her. Maybe the women suspected; if they did, they kept their suspicions to themselves.

5

There were certain ritualistic performances in which the monsters played no part at all. They took place outside the *Hain*, and in some of them the women participated. Sometimes the men and lads, their bodies, arms and legs encircled with clear horizontal stripes of white paint on a deep red background, would gather stealthily in a clump of trees near the village. They would stand side by side in a line, each with his arms round his neighbours' shoulders, as in a Rugby scrum. Care was taken that there should be a clear open space between the trees and the village, so that the women, who would be on the look-out, would have a good view of the line's snake-like progression from the tree-clump to the *Hain*. When all were in position and ready to emerge into the open, the line was set in motion by the man at the end. He would give a little jump sideways and forward. This action would be immediately copied by the man next to him, and so on right to the end. In a row of thirty men, there would be at least three waves or ripples running from the head to the tail, as the whole body slowly advanced sideways towards the *Hain*. From a distance, this gave the exact impression of a huge caterpillar's laborious motion. When the leaders had proceeded far enough to be out of sight of the village, they broke off one by one, until the lonely end of the tail gave its last wriggle and disappeared from view into the *Hain*.

The whole performance, if I remember rightly, was carried on in silence and greatly enjoyed by the actors. I have wondered if this dance —if such it could be called—was originated in honour of the snake. If it was, it must have been ages ago, when these people lived in a warmer clime, for there are no snakes in Tierra del Fuego.

The Snake Dance had form and a certain rhythm. A much more disjointed exhibition was the Frog Dance.[1] A crowd of men would daub themselves all over with ashes and earth and come out of the Lodge

---

[1] " Snake Dance " and " Frog Dance " are names of my own invention. The native names for them were not in daily use, and I cannot recall them.

en masse, squatting on their haunches and jumping along like a swarm of excited frogs, and making the most infernal hubbub. They never went far from the Lodge, and returned in the same disorderly manner. Boys, too young to become members of the Lodge, joined in this prank, which was greatly enjoyed by the participants.

Another hideous display would be given by two or three men. They would come out of the *Hain* and, squatting on the ground nearby, would start making ejaculations of disgust and pulling ugly faces to show their hatred and scorn of the women, who, unfortunately, were too far away to appreciate the efforts of their menfolk. The actors might stick bits of wood in their mouths, or even under their eyelids, to make themselves look even more dreadful.

One of the entertainments in which the women joined was to give them their revenge for the massacre said to have taken place ages before. The men assembled in the *Hain* and painted themselves with red stripes round their bodies and legs. They then whitened themselves considerably by dusting with chalk, under which the red stripes could still be distinguished. While this was going on, they would start a squeaky wailing, which may have been intended to advise the women that they were frightened and expected punishment. When ready, the men would come out of the Lodge and scatter as though blind, jumping along as if their feet were tied together and heading for the village, still keeping up their plaintive cries.

The women, usually discarding their capes, would come out in their *kohiyaten* and charge eagerly at the ridiculous band, who appeared quite unconscious of their approach. The women would rush up to them and, with evident enjoyment, push them vigorously. The men would fall like ninepins, making no effort to save themselves, and lie perfectly still in the exact position in which they had fallen. The conquering women, seeing their victims all motionless on the ground, would then return triumphant to the village. The old men who had been watching the proceedings from near the entrance to the Lodge would then call to the others that the coast was clear. The dead men would come to life, spring to their feet and run back to the Lodge as though frightened.

There was another diversion in which both men and women took part. The prelude was a low sound of complaint or mourning from the *Hain*. This gave the women ample time to prepare for the show by adding a little paint—stripes or spots of red or white—to their faces. They would come to a place some sixty yards on the village side of the

Lodge and plant themselves in a very compact row, each one embracing the woman in front of her. The strongest among them was selected as leader. I witnessed this performance twice, and on both occasions Leluwhachin was chosen for this position. She held a stout pole about eight feet in length. With one end of it on the ground and the other on her ample shoulder, and well supported by the women behind her, she took up her stand, waiting defiantly for the men to come out of the *Hain* and try to dislodge her.

The men, painted with red stripes as previously described, but without the light powdering of white chalk, now emerged from the *Hain*. Holding hands, they began to encircle the women, moving round them in a kind of dance. They drew closer and closer until the two ends linked up. Continuing to gyrate around the women, they jostled them with their shoulders as they passed, the object being to break up the group. The women's task was to stand their ground till the ring of men was broken. The men did not use violence. The women swayed from side to side, but Leluwhachin held firmly to her slanting pole. As they moved round, the men reached the pole in turn and tried to dislodge it as they stumbled over it. At length one of them missed his footing and lost his grip on his neighbour. The women won—as they always did—and the men hastened ignominiously to the shelter of the *Hain*. When they had all disappeared, the victorious women returned to the village in high glee.

A third form of primitive dance was called *Ewan*. It rarely took place and I had no opportunity of seeing it. The women—painted in spots and, for once, stark naked—came from the encampment, whilst the men, painted in stripes, advanced towards them from the Lodge. I do not know whether each party moved forward abreast or in single file, but conjecture that, when they passed each other, there would have been some disorder in such a large assembly. There was never any kind of drilling among the Ona, or anyone to give strict orders. There would, however, have been no jostling, as there was in the performance just described, no touching of one another and no sign of individual recognition. This last was a noticeable feature of all the ceremonial pranks in which men and women mixed or met each other. A good example was Minkiyolh's treatment of Leluwhachin. When he hit her with that billet of wood, he was punishing not the wife of Tininisk, the greatly esteemed *joön*, but one of the women, nameless and unacknowledged.

My own place in all these performances was in the background with the old men, who preferred to watch. If, during these times, some friendly wrestling was suggested, I, of course, joined in. I did not ever impersonate any of the monsters of the *Hain*. My function was to help dress and paint the actors and, though I kept strictly within the rules, my work in beautifying *Halpen* was praised by the experts.

6

When the white men began to settle in northern Ona-land, many of the natives were compelled to invade the hunting-grounds claimed by more southerly groups. These, in turn, were sometimes forced still farther back into the mountains. This led to even more jealousy and fighting than there had been before the white intruders came, with the result that large, friendly parties could not often meet. I heard of one small, isolated group who held a meeting of the Lodge and were severely criticized for having run the risk of betraying the whole secret to the women.

Unfortunately, whenever I was present during the various activities of the *Hain*, I was either without my camera or—if I had it with me—was well aware that the use of it would certainly have been disapproved of by my Ona friends. The few photographs I was able to obtain were all taken at the last session I ever attended. This was just before the First World War, which kept me away from Tierra del Fuego. I learnt later that the only two Germans we knew of in the district were singled out for destruction by the Lodge, should I fail to return. Pahchik, who had acted as Chashkil's second during our wrestling match, accepted personal responsibility for putting one of them—a harmless old blacksmith—out of the way. When I came back to Fireland, Pahchik, good fellow, told me that he would not have failed to keep his promise.

I am sorry now that, during my membership of the Lodge, I put work and the building up of the Viamonte farm so far ahead of everything else that I omitted to attend many meetings to which I was invited. The Ona had more leisure than I. At their gatherings in the *Hain*, time was no object. Whole days would be spent in futile talk, leading up to some seemingly childish performance. I did not sufficiently realize that these rites would shortly cease for ever. The advance of civilization soon laid bare the secrets of the Lodge, so jealously guarded for countless generations. They became common knowledge and the women were well aware of the hoax. Indians were induced, for a few dollars, to enact some of their plays before scientific audiences. I have seen photographs in which the performers had short hair and were painted in a fantastic way such as was never seen in the old days. Other photographs—purporting to be of primitive Ona savages—showed that many of the younger generation had forgotten—if ever they had known—the correct way to wear a guanaco skin.

The ceremonies of the Lodge had come into being and matured through the ages in the development of an exceedingly fine race of men. I have met white men who told strange stories of Tierra del Fuego, and, as far as I could judge, believed in what they told. One claimed to have found a mysterious spot in a forest, where there was a great stone on which human sacrifices had recently been made. Another spoke of a cave where young guanaco, fat birds and other luxuries were deposited as gifts to the gods, later to be devoured, no doubt, by some cunning medicine-man or native priest. I heard one lecturer solemnly telling his audience :

" They believe in a god called *Klokten*."

Imagine anyone giving a talk on the Navy, and announcing :

" They believe in a god called Midshipman."

According to other so-called explorers, the Ona also worshipped *Hyewhi*, which means a song or chant, and *Joön*, which has occurred too often in these pages to need translation here. One authority went so far as to prove, to his own satisfaction, that *Joön* is directly derived from the Hebrew Jehovah.

These stories demonstrate how a vivid imagination, combined with wishful thinking and the desire to impart interesting information, may influence a certain type of otherwise enlightened and educated men.

During the many hours I passed in the Lodge, listening to the exhortations of the older men, and during the years I spent almost exclusively in the company of the Ona Indians, I never heard a word that pointed to religion or worship of any kind; no expectation or hope of reward—no fear of punishment—in a future life. There was dread of death by witchcraft and a lesser dread of the ghosts of the woods, but not the ghosts of the departed dead. Respect there was for individual mountains such as Heuhupen, who, annoyed at being rudely pointed at, might wrap herself in clouds and bring on bad weather. Fear of death, the end of life, may have existed; possibly some unexpressed terror of the unknown; but there was no worship, no prayer, no god, no devil.

CHAPTER FORTY-THREE

The Story of Jack, the First White Novice of the Hain. *Story-Telling Round the Embers.* Kwonyipe *Makes the Sun and Moon Go Down.* Kwonyipe *Kills* Chashkilchesh, *the Giant. Ona Astrology.* Oklholh *Becomes the Waterfall Duck. Some Observations about Loggerhead Ducks.* Kwaweishen *Becomes the Crested Vulture.* Kiayeshk *is Changed into the Black Shag. How the Robin Got his Red Breast. The Horrible Fate of the Handsome Brother and Sister.* Shahmanink *Complains and is Turned into the Killer Whale. The Wizard's Head.* Kohlah, *the Only Object of Ona Reverence.* Kwonyipe *Makes the Guanaco Wild. The Story of the Four Winds.* Shai *Makes a Road. Legends of Animals not Found in Fireland. The Origins of the Ona and Aush.* Kamshoat *Jeers.*

I

I CANNOT SAY THAT I WAS THE ONLY WHITE MAN TO ENTER THE *HAIN.*
While I absented myself during the First World War, my brother Will
was invited to take my seat. I cannot even claim that I was the first and
only white novice, for that distinction was taken from me by a boy
called Jack. I never knew his other name. The rest of his sad story I
heard from the lips of the medicine-man, Otrhshoölh (White Eye), and
his brother, Aneki. It was endorsed by many of the older men, but the
testimony of Otrhshoölh and Aneki was sufficient, because Jack had lived
as their foster-brother for years, under the protection of their father,
Heëshoölh. I met this old man several times before he died, our original
meeting having been when he accompanied Kaushel on that first visit
of the Ona to Cambaceres in 1894.

It seems that some time in the 1870s—when Aneki was still a little
boy—a vessel was wrecked near Cape San Diego. The crew—among
them this boy Jack, who was anything from ten to fifteen years of age—
managed to get ashore and walked north-westward along the coast. The
natives of those parts, the Aush, did not interfere with them. Somewhere
near Cape San Pablo, Jack, who was suffering from burnt or frost-bitten
feet and a badly injured arm, could go no farther and was left behind.
The rest of the party continued on their journey north until, it is said,
they fell in with some Ona and were killed.

Jack would certainly have died where he lay, had he not been found
by Heëshoölh. It is almost incredible that an Indian should have done
such a thing, but Heëshoölh slung the helpless boy on his back and carried
him to the encampment. Jack, no doubt, had heard the usual stories of

torture and cannibalism, so, when an Ona daubed with paint and armed with bow and arrows bore him off into the woods and brought him into the presence of other equally fearsome warriors, he must have thought that his last hour had come. Nor could his terrors have been dispelled by the strong guttural remarks in the long and serious debate as to what should be done with him that probably followed.

Happily for Jack, Heëshoölh had taken a fancy to him and the outcome of the discussion was that his life was spared. He took up residence with Heëshoölh and his family and lived with them for a good many years. His foster-brothers told me that they well remembered his early days with them. He was a very good-natured boy and, after his feet had healed, was always willing to help either men or women at their work. He never regained full use of his arm and was unable to operate a bow successfully. He would, however, accompany the hunters and carry home a portion of meat. Otrhshoölh and his brother recalled how Jack would sometimes cross his fingers and, putting them to his tongue, whistle with tremendous force.

This English boy grew a good deal after joining the party and, although always quiet, learnt to speak the language well. He must have had an exceptional upbringing, for even when he reached the impressionable years, he was never attracted at all by women, except in a platonic way. In course of time, he was introduced as a novice to the Lodge.

With the passing of the years, Jack grew more and more sad with longing for his own people and for his native land. He knew that sailing vessels sometimes passed quite near to Cape San Diego, so, being well acquainted with the Aush, for Heëshoölh lived near the border-line, he often wandered far into that country, where seal was as much eaten as guanaco, and eventually, to the sorrow of his Ona friends, who were loth to lose him, went and settled there. He sewed guanaco skins together, making a big flag, which I imagine he must have painted. When an occasional vessel was sighted, he lit fires and hoisted his flag on a pole. He even shouted and whistled with fingers on his tongue, but no one took any notice of him.

At last word seems to have reached him of the Mission settlement at Ushuaia, and he started westward along the southern coast. The distance from Cape San Diego to Ushuaia as the crow flies is not much over a hundred miles, but in places there are precipices dropping down into the sea, with tangled thickets growing to the very edge of them. There are also a number of dangerous torrents to cross, so it was a rough walk for Jack to attempt.

He is known to have accomplished the first half of his journey, which was through the Aush country. The rest of his way lay through Yahga-land. He would doubtless have been dressed in guanaco skins and very likely carried a spear such as the Aush used for fish or seal, but as, by then, he would probably have grown a beard, no Yahgan would have taken him for a real Ona. It is said that near Moat Bay he ran into a party of eastern Yahgans. He could not speak their language and must have seemed to them a strange and suspicious figure.

Poor Jack! If he had only known, he could easily have avoided those frontier men by keeping a little farther inland for another twenty miles or so, then coming down at the place now called Harberton. The natives there had already felt the Mission influence and would have helped him on his way. But it is too late to talk now, for, after his long struggle, Jack found his death at the hands of the first Yahgans he met, when almost in sight of safety.

2

That was one of the many tales I heard around the fire. On autumn evenings, when the nights were growing long, we might be camping in the woods. After eating all the meat we wanted, we would lie by the embers of the fire, rolled up in our robes for the night. The light of a dying fire in the surrounding darkness seems to inspire the story-teller, and one of my companions—perhaps Tininisk, my hawk-nosed old friend—would start talking slowly, addressing his observations to the fire, which he would occasionally stir with a stick. All would listen, but no one would look at him especially or show any interest in what he was saying. Sometimes he would pause to think, and even ask if anyone remembered some forgotten name.

In this agreeable fashion, I learnt much of the legends and folk-lore of the Ona. As the years went by, I listened with growing interest, always careful not to prompt the narrator by questions that might in-fluence the telling. The untaught Ona did not recount these marvels in any kind of order, or with any artistic detail, but merely made a suc-cession of statements as they came to their minds. They seldom told one story after another, and such tales as I have to retell in this chapter were gathered over many years of listening, with apparent interest, to frequent repetitions of tales I had often heard before. I have refrained from adding any embroidery to these legends and present them as bare of romantic detail as they were when related to me by my Ona friends.

3

Before the great massacre of the women and the inauguration of the *Hain*, there lived on earth as husband and wife *Krren* (the sun) and *Kreeh* (the moon). Following the example of the other men, *Krren* attacked his wife, with the intention of killing her. She carries the marks of his blows on her face to this day, thus proving the truth of the story. Though badly knocked about, *Kreeh* managed to get away from her husband. With him in pursuit, she ran up a mountain called *Aklek Goöiyin* [1] and jumped from the peak. *Krren* relentlessly continued his chase and followed the tracks of the fleeing *Kreeh* round and round the horizon. Whenever he seemed on the point of catching her, she made herself small and disappeared for a time. With the sun thus always in the sky, there was continuous daylight, which did not suit the purpose of *Kwonyipe*.

Of all the Ona magicians, *Kwonyipe* was accounted the greatest. Not only was he great in magic; he was also a giant. When he walked in the forest, his head would appear above the tree-tops, and brushwood or thicket did not delay his advance. With his wife and little son, *Kwonyipe* lived very happily until, one day, he met a beautiful girl, with whom he fell in love. This maiden was so exceedingly wild and bashful that broad daylight was not the best time to woo her, and *Kwonyipe* soon saw that the chief obstacle to the consummation of his love affair was the perpetual presence of the sun, who still carried on his race with his wife around the horizon.

Kwonyipe decided that this could not be allowed to continue, so, choosing a time when *Krren* and *Kreeh* were approaching the south from the westward, he went out into the open and brought all his magic to bear. His efforts met with such success that they both sank for a short time below the horizon; and in the twilight of darkness that ensued, he brought his courtship of the lovely, shy creature to a satisfactory culmination.

With their orbits thrown out of dead level by the sorcery of *Kwonyipe*, the sun and moon continued to circle the earth. But slowly they dipped

---

[1] Red Clay Mountain. The Ona word for red clay was *Akel*, with the " A " long, as in " past ". In *Aklek* the " A " was short, as in " fat." I can advance no explanation of this difference.

farther to the south and climbed higher in the northern sky. The result of this continuing process was twofold: their periods below the southern horizon grew more and more prolonged; and in summer they rose nearer to the east and set nearer to the west. On account of this, said the Ona, the days were getting shorter and the nights longer as the years went by.

Kwonyipe appears to have lived very contentedly with his two wives. One day he met another giant as large as himself, but of different character, for *Chashkilchesh* had a sinister reputation for murdering children and carrying them off into the forest to eat.[1] *Kwonyipe* now saw that *Chashkilchesh* was carrying a heavy skin bag on his back. He knew that in that bag were many dead children, his enemy's favourite food, but feigned ignorance and demanded to be told what the bag contained. *Chashkilchesh* was annoyed at being thus questioned and retorted angrily. *Kwonyipe*, who was determined to put a stop to this horrible habit of *Chashkilchesh*, seized him and a tremendous struggle followed.

The scene of this fight and the manner of *Chashkilchesh's* death varied with the narrators. For each group, their hunting-grounds were the centre of the universe. The mountain men, from whom I first heard the story, said the contest took place in a shallow lake close to the east end of the great Lake Kami. They showed me the exact spot where, according to them, it happened. The giants fell together, but *Kwonyipe* was on top and managed to keep his adversary's head under the water until he was dead.

After this encounter, *Kwonyipe* went back to his two wives and little son. As they continued their wanderings they came upon two small orphan boys, who were either lost or had been deserted. Good-natured *Kwonyipe* adopted them. It is not known how long this family roamed the woods, but now they are in the sky. *Kwonyipe* is Antares, the large, rather red star in the Scorpion constellation. His wives rest at equal distance on either side of their lord. Farther along the curve is his little son and farther still the two orphan boys, hand in hand. *Chashkilchesh*, the cannibalistic giant, now haunts the southern sky in lonely grandeur as the star Canopus. How they all got there nobody knows.

The Ona were aware that Jupiter, Mars and Venus were *Kreeh-Kahn* (little moons) and not fixed in their places like other stars. They had not separate names for the planets, nor did they know how many there were. They called them all *Tehlus*, which was their general name for

---

[1] This legend is the only reference to cannibalism among the Ona.

stars. Nine or ten of the stars had been given individual names. It was an Ona belief that shooting stars flashed across the sky in search of wives. They were excited and alarmed at eclipses, whilst comets caused them anxiety.

They believed that men, women and children had been changed not only into stars, as was the fate of *Kwonyipe* and his family, but also into mountains, lakes, trees, rocks, animals, birds, fish, insects and yellow, red or white clay. I never heard, however, of any creature or thing being given human shape.

Some of these transformations took place at the time of the massacre of the women. There was, for instance, one very active young woman called *Oklholh*, who, fleeing from the men, jumped into a high waterfall. She was immediately changed into a duck—a brightly coloured and amazingly quick little diver, which now bears her name and is to be found only in waterfalls or mountain torrents. From that day forward, the waterfall into which she had leapt was known as Oklholh K-Warren, the last word meaning " roaring " or " waterfall."

Others to escape were a stout old lady and her daughters. The mother waddled down the beach, bravely sheltering the girls with her robes, which she spread over them as they ran. They all escaped into the sea and were changed into flapping loggerhead ducks, which cannot fly and are called *alahksh* in Ona. This is from the Yahgan *alacush*, one of the few words borrowed by the Ona from the canoe Indians.[1]

One young man who assisted in the slaughter of the women disgraced himself by abusing the dead bodies and was thereupon changed into the *korikek* (ibis), which, in consequence, has a raw and sore-looking patch on its throat.

Ona legend abounds in *Just So Stories*. There is, for instance, the fable of How the Crested Vulture got his Crest. *Kwaweishen* was a strong, ill-natured medicine-man. He came from a country in the far south and,

---

[1] A curious belief still held by some ornithologists is that the flying loggerhead duck (*tushca* in Yahgan) is a young flapping loggerhead (or steamer) duck. They say that the young bird, which can fly well and leaves the country for the winter, grows so heavy as it matures that it loses the power of flight. The Yahgans, who lived largely on these birds and knew their habits, were unaware of this strange freak of nature. There is other evidence to prove that the *tushca* and the *alacush* are distinct species. The *tushca* inhabits a large part of the country where the *alacush* is unknown ; the eggs of the *alacush* are double the size of the *tushca's* ; and in many other respects the birds are quite different from one another. It would be interesting to know in whose fertile imagination this idea was born. To me it is as marvellous as any of the legends retold in this chapter, so I hope people may be found who can believe them all.

as all the water down there was constantly frozen, he could get nothing to drink, so that the marrow in his bones had dried up. In Ona-land he attended a great wrestling match at which he fought with *Kiayeshk*. These two struggled fiercely. *Kwaweishen* was a rough and angry wrestler, and injured his opponent by trying to break his back. Nevertheless he did not escape unscathed, for *Kiayeshk* got him by the hair of his head and pulled him forward with such force that he raised the skin, giving him a permanent top-knot, while with his other hand he pressed *Kwaweishen's* throat so hard that the white patch remains there to this day. *Kwaweishen* was changed into the crested vulture and renamed *Karkaäi* on account of his croak, which he had acquired in the waterless land of his birth. *Kiayeshk* became the black shag or cormorant and still suffers from a stiff back. You can often see him standing upright on the rocks, stretching out his wings, yet making no attempt to fly, so it is evident that his back is still causing him pain.

Cheip was quite a small man, but he bravely challenged *Shija*, a strong, violent fellow more than twice his size, to a wrestling match. Little *Cheip* put up a grand fight, but in the end was grabbed—just as *Kwaweishen* had been—by the hair and throat. He struggled to free himself and, in doing so, gave his enemy a terrific blow on the nose, which caused it to bleed profusely. *Shija* retired from the fight and, never afterwards being able to wash the blood from his chest, became the Fuegian robin-redbreast or military starling. *Cheip* was the father of the sparrow, who is rather larger than his English relations. His top-knot and the white patch on his throat attest to the authenticity of the tale.

The story of the white owl and the bat is quite romantic. *O-Kerreechin* lived alone with his sister *Oklhtah*. They were a perfectly respectable couple, for they both knew what was right and correct between brother and sister, and were the best of friends. They were both tall and good-looking, and *O-Kerreechin*, being a most successful hunter, brought home abundance of good meat, as well as fox and guanaco skins. He was lightly built and very active, and his sister admired him so much that the other men who came to woo her seemed mis-shapen and ugly. She, in her turn, was greatly esteemed by her brother, for, besides her physical charms, she was industrious and clever at sewing skins.

Kwonyipe, the giant medicine-man, one day passed that way and, seeing the lovely *Oklhtah*, drew near and demanded her for his wife. The brother refused to let his sister go, saying that when she did leave him, it must be for a younger husband than *Kwonyipe* and not one who already had two wives. *Kwonyipe* was furious at this obstruction. When *O-Kerreechin* remained adamant, he said to him :

" You shall eat no more guanaco, but shall live on mice; and hide in the daytime because of your weak eyes. People shall hate you, for they will know when they hear you screech that blood and trouble are coming to them."

There and then *O-Kerreechin* was changed into a white owl and, with a shriek, flew away in search of a hollow tree in which to hide, as the wizard had predicted. On account of his cry, his name was altered to *Shee-et*. When he perches near an encampment at night and breaks the stillness of the woods with that horrid cry, death and violence are very near.

Poor *Oklhtah* was now left alone with the gigantic wizard. Furious at the fate he had brought upon her beloved brother, she fought him tooth and nail. At last *Kwonyipe*, failing to get his way with her, was seized again with rage and shouted :

" You shall be hated and feared by everyone, for you shall carry sickness wherever you go. Naked and black, hiding, like your brother, in some old and rotten tree, you, too, shall eat no more guanaco meat, but feed on worms and moths."

So *Oklhtah* the beautiful was transformed into a hideous bat. If in the evening she flutters in your face, sickness and death are not far off. So say the Ona, and as we have lain in our skin robes around a dying fire, the screech of a white owl has caused my fellow hunters to shudder with dread; and their anxiety when a few bats have flitted close to us has been a very real thing.

4

This enormous fellow *Kwonyipe* seems to have made quite a practice of metamorphosis before he was himself transferred to a celestial sphere of activity. There was, for example, his treatment of the hunter who was not content with guanaco meat. *Shahmanink* was always fortunate in his hunting, for he had three uncommonly good dogs. He belonged to the eastern part of Ona-land and may have been allied to the Aush, as he generally hunted on the borders of their country. *Shahmanink* was always grumbling. He said that the guanaco were small and thin, and the meat poor. *Kwonyipe* heard of these continual complaints and was so displeased by them that he changed him into the fierce creature known as the killer whale,[1] which ever afterwards, when in company with his fellows, fell upon and slew the mighty *Ohchin* (whale).

Shahmanink's three hunting dogs were also changed by *Kwonyipe* into savage fish, possibly swordfish, to help their master to hunt the whale. Sometimes they drove *Ohchin* on the beach, and then the Ona were pleased with *Shahmanink* and his dogs.

As for *Ohchin* the whale, she married *Sinu* the wind, which is not surprising, but it is one of mythology's unsolved mysteries that the result of this union of giants was *Sinu K-Tam* (Daughter of the Wind), the humming-bird.

There is another story, of a different kind, about *Ohchin*. In Yahga-land, on the beach near Lanushwaia (Woodpecker Creek), now known as Cambaceres, there may still be seen the mouldering, grass-grown bones of a huge whale. It was stranded there some generations before our time, and a large party of Yahgans congregated for the feast. The natives had a regular order in the dividing of a whale, the distribution being the privilege of the one who found it. Late arrivals did not get the portions they most desired, so there was always a good deal of discontent and grumbling.

In those days the cutting of the meat must have been done with sharp stones, a tedious job. The Yahgans were hard at work when a party of Aush appeared on the edge of the nearby forest. They ostentatiously piled their bows and arrows in a conspicuous place and walked down to the shambles, hoping to get a share in this grand supply of meat.

The Yahgans were not pleased to see them coming, as they wanted to keep it all for themselves, but they received the visitors with smiles of welcome and, offering them meat, suddenly set upon them with their spears. They killed all except *Kawhayulh*, an ancient, white-haired medicine-man. Though bristling with spears, this old fellow refused to

---

[1] Orca, I believe, is its generic name, though there are probably a number of varieties. The descriptions I have read do not always correspond with the creatures I have actually seen pursuing the whale. On Scott's tragic expedition, Ponting took some good photographs of this dangerous creature, and remarked on its habit of breaking or capsizing drift-ice on which seal were lying, in order to catch them in the water. I sat once in a whale-boat with a frightened crew that included two white men, both experienced whalers, while, silent and motionless, we watched two killer whales swim slowly past, less than a quarter of a mile away. They were longer than our boat, which was twenty-eight feet, and looked like huge porpoises, with the long, thin back fins that are said to account for the terrific gashes found in the bodies of dead whales ; and also for the cutting out of the whales' tongues, a most difficult operation that I am positive they perform, though I know not how. Neither Yahgans nor Ona had ever seen a stranded killer whale.

die and at last the Yahgans decided to cut his head off, which, considering the implements they had at their disposal, must have been a prolonged and painful operation.

According to the Indians' legend, the head, once severed from the body, gave a loud laugh and hopped away at a great rate, turning to laugh again before disappearing into the forest. It took a course eastward to Cape San Diego, then went west and north up the Atlantic coast and no one knows how far into Ona-land. Along that same track the head was followed by an epidemic, which had very likely started among the great crowd assembled at the feast. It was put down to the murder of the ancient wizard, whose head, its mission completed, returned, jeering and laughing, to the mountain ranges in the southern part of the country, where everyone who met it would soon be dead. I have known Ona discuss earnestly a white stone in the distance which they had not noticed before. When I was foolish enough to suggest lightly that it might be *Kawhayulh's* head, I was told not to be frivolous, as that was no laughing matter.

In Tierra del Fuego there exists a queer little insect which the Ona call *kohlah*. I doubt if a scientist would classify it as a beetle, for it has no movable shell with wings beneath, but a rough, solid case like a turtle's, whilst its head somewhat resembles that of a horse. It is much deeper than it is broad and is about an inch long. It is dark brown in colour and, with its bowed legs, most sluggish in movement. The *kohlah* is not plentiful and is generally found clinging like a sloth, with its back downwards, to thin branches in the dank evergreen forests. Feeling secure in its coat of mail, it makes not the slightest effort to escape, nor in any way to defend itself.

The most extraordinary thing about the *kohlah* is that, though the Ona have no pity for any living thing and would as soon tread on a nest of young birds as avoid doing so, they will pick up this helpless insect when it happens to be in a place where it might be trodden on and put it tenderly on a branch or in some other place of safety. When asked the reason for this attention, they always answered that long ago *Kohlah* had been a wise and most kindly *joön*, curing the sick and harming no one. I could never get any details about his life and believe that these few facts are all that is known of him. It is curious, however, that out of the vast creation of insect and animal life, the Ona should have selected this one creature for kindness amounting almost to reverence. As is demonstrated by Wilfred Grubb's adventure with the natives of Jujuy, certain

South American tribes, especially the Lengua of the Paraguayan Chaco, have in their legends a creature of much the same type, conspicuous for its supernatural powers; and surely the scarab of ancient Egypt was some relation to the little friend I have just described?

The scientists who belonged to the French expedition of 1882, mentioned in an earlier chapter, were greatly interested in the *kohlah*, which was known to the Yahgans as *owachijbana*, *owachij* being the name of a bright yellow fungus that grows on the *shushchi* (evergreen beech). The Yahgans, however, had no sentimental feelings that I know of for this or any other creature. The French scientists procured at least one specimen, which they put in a bottle deadly to all insects. To their surprise, *owachijbana*—or *kohlah*—seemed to thrive on it. I do not remember their putting it in alcohol, but suspect that, if they had done so, the creature would have simply got gloriously tight. Finally they placed it in a bottle with some leaves and paper; and the last we heard of it was that it seemed to prefer the paper as food and was doing well on it. Whether it arrived in France, and whether it still lived, we never heard.

Before dismissing *Kwonyipe*, I must tell the story of how it was his fault that the tame guanaco went wild. *Kwonyipe* had a lot of tame guanaco, which was the usual thing among the Ona in those days. On one occasion an ill-natured male attacked his little son and hurt him badly. The father, very angry, took a burning log from the fire and, rushing out, beat the offender without mercy. The guanaco was very sore at this rough treatment and retired into the thick forest to recover. There he met a fox, who said to him:

" How foolish you guanaco are! Do you think these men care for you? They only keep you to eat in the end. You can run faster than they, so why don't you take to the woods and live as I do—free? "

So the guanaco thought it over, then went about speaking to the other guanaco till, one day, they simultaneously took to the woods. And since then the Ona have always had to hunt for their meat.

The four great winds were once men and, as such, had difficulties amongst themselves, not knowing who was the strongest. They determined to settle their differences, once and for all, in a decisive wrestling match, as was the custom with the Ona when they wished to avoid the use of bows and arrows. A great crowd having assembled, the usual ring was formed. The challengers stepped out and took on one or another of their opponents indiscriminately—and with varying success.

Wintekhaiyin, the east wind, though persistent, was far too gentle. After being thrown several times by each of the others, he realized his case was hopeless. Accordingly he resumed his robe and joined the onlookers.

Orroknhaiyin,[1] the south wind, put up a much better show, as he was fierce and strong—a nasty, angry wrestler. But after a violent struggle and several falls, he had to give up and follow *Wintekhaiyin*, leaving the field to the other two.

Now came the real fight. *Hechuknhaiyin*, the north wind, was a tricky wrestler, powerful and bad-tempered. At last, however, he wore himself out against the tremendous strength of the untiring west wind, *Kenenikhaiyin*, and after a tempestuous bout was heavily thrown. On rising, being instantly challenged again, he drew back, thus acknowledging himself beaten.

This story describes, in a picturesque and remarkably clear manner, the characteristics of the four great winds, for after a warm morning in summer, when the others are sleeping or resting, *Wintekhaiyin* comes cautiously from his home in the east and blows with moderate strength till he wishes to rest, or sees the north wind threatening. Then he goes quietly home again. *Hechuknhaiyin*, still rough and ill-natured, often behaves badly until *Kenenikhaiyin* rushes down from the west, when he draws back, though most unwillingly, leaving the field to the champion. In the winter, *Orroknhaiyin*, the south wind, taking advantage of the fact that the others are resting, comes up fearlessly in full force to bring the snow.

5

In more recent times, there lived a very strong man called *Shai* who had studied magic and belonged to the Najmishk group. He was also a successful hunter, but, being enormously stout, knew that he was laughed at on that account by many of the others. Amongst the Ona from the western mountains was an exceedingly fast runner who, in his heart, scorned *Shai* because of his unwieldy build and clumsy gait. *Shai* knew this and one day—much to the amusement of all, including his

---

[1] The common ending *haiyin* does not mean wind, for that is *sinu*. *Haiyin* is the Ona verb "to like, etc." (See footnote to page 335.) A possible explanation is that the Ona much appreciated wind. In calm weather, approach to the guanaco was very difficult, even for them. Or it might be that *Wintekhaiyin* likes coming from the east, *Orroknhaiyin* from the south, and so on.

own people—offered to race this man from a spot near the Ewan Cliffs to Najmishk—a distance of over four miles through the woods running parallel with the coast.

The race was agreed upon. The day before it took place, *Shai* walked straight through the woods, which were generally low and tangled, pulling up trees by the roots and putting them on one side. By nightfall he had made an excellent track. A great crowd gathered next day at Najmishk to witness *Shai's* defeat and were surprised to see him come running out of his hidden gap in the woods, well ahead of his competitor, who had been running near him, but with all the usual obstacles to overcome.

This track has been mentioned before in these pages. It is called Shaiwaal (*Shai's* Road) in the Aush dialect and is still there, though a little overgrown in places. Probably the real cause of its existence was that, ages ago, a shingle ridge on which the trees did not thrive was thrown up by the ocean. About twelve miles to the west there is a lake called Shaipoöt, which means *Shai's* uncle. Shaikush, or *Shai's* wife, is a nearby hill; and on the little rising called Shai-w-num, *Shai's* son, the Estancia Viamonte, successor to my little hut, stands to-day. Te-ilh and his people, who had suffered so badly at the hands of the northern men during the massacre at the whale-feast, were supposed to be descendants of the mythical *Shai.*

6

Among the many stories that I heard from Tininisk by camp-fires in the woods was one about an old Indian who possessed a powerful magical object. It was something small but very strong and not at all like a man. He would leave it with a piece of meat where foxes were known to pass, and when the foxes approached to eat the meat, the thing would seize hold of them and cry out with a noise somewhat like a bell for its master to come and kill the fox. I wondered if long ago some castaway had invented a fox-trap, or more likely salvaged one from a wreck. Tininisk thought the story was older than that; and as I heard it from others who told me it had been handed down from ancient times, I am inclined to agree with him.

Tininisk also spoke of a large sailing-vessel, which was wrecked near Cape Santa Inés on the Atlantic coast about a hundred years ago. The timbers, though completely rotted away except for scraps attached to rust-eaten iron, may still be seen there. Some of the crew and a few women are said to have landed, while the bodies of a number of strange animals drifted ashore from the wreck and lay along the beach. Some of these animals were very large and fat, but the natives were afraid to eat them. There were, I suppose, no menageries travelling in those days, and the party may have been colonists voyaging with a stock of pigs, donkeys and other domestic animals.

I heard, too, from Tininisk of a strange creature named *Ohi*. It was half animal, half bird, with hind legs similar to a guanaco's and forelegs like wings, which it spread when running. It could not fly, but it ran faster than any dog. It laid huge eggs and its head resembled that of an upland goose. No doubt this was the rhea or Patagonian ostrich. This bird was not known in Tierra del Fuego, which suggests either that it had once lived there and been exterminated, or that the Ona had brought the story with them from Patagonia—and that they came from Patagonia is beyond doubt.

I am convinced that originally both Ona and Aush came from the Tehuelches of southern Patagonia, but that the Aush reached Tierra del Fuego long before the Ona. By the time the Ona arrived, their languages had become so different that only the border people could ever understand one another. There was certainly far more variation between Aush and Ona than there was between Ona and the tongue of the Tehuelches. At one time, I believe, the Aush occupied the whole of Ona-land, but were forced south and east by the second invaders, who took the pleasant, fertile country in the northern part of the island, while the Aush had to be content with the south-eastern point, where the climate was wet and the land consisted of stunted thickets or bogs. Another circumstance that confirms my theory is that in the country inhabited by the Ona there are place names that have no meaning in their language, but are really composite words having a suitable meaning in the Aush tongue. North of the Rio Grande, in the very heart of Ona-land, is a hill. It was known to the Ona as Shimkai, which was the Aush for "wooded hill." As far as I know, Shimkai has no significance at all in the Ona tongue.

Both these tribes must have lived in Tierra del Fuego for ages, for they had no legends of having come from abroad. Instead they believed that the country had always been their home, ever since the time when the mountains roamed the earth as men and women, before the days of *Kwonyipe* and *Chashkilchesh*. Unfortunately my time with the Aush was so limited, and my interest in the subject then so small, that I did not collect any of their legends and folk-lore. In customs, manners and appearance, they were very like the Ona. For food they relied more on seal and shell-fish, which were abundant round the coast, and less on the *apen* (tucu-tucu), which was comparatively scarce in their swampy country.

The Ona, as far as I know, had no legends about the puma, the skunk or the mountain deer, which are found in Patagonia as far south as the Magellan Straits. The only stories I heard that included any reference to other countries were those of *Kwaweishen*, who was changed into the crested vulture, and *Kamshoat*, who became *Kerrhprrh*, the parakeet.

Before I tell the story of *Kamshoat*, I must refer to a curious little habit of the Indians while walking through the forest. Almost from the beginning of our acquaintance, I had noticed that an Ona would sometimes speak to a bird as though in response to something the bird had said. Generally the man's remark raised a laugh amongst his companions, as was intended; but sometimes, instead of a witticism, the man would give an angry shout and fling a stick or stone at the offending bird, pretending that it had been deriding us poor human beings. I have often heard them upbraiding some little forest warbler for having warned guanaco of our approach, or for having expressed its amusement at our difficulties as we trudged laden across some nasty bit of country. Frequently a wag such as Kankoat would translate a bird's supposedly impudent observations, even venturing to make hints as to the personal peculiarities of certain of the hunters present—without, of course, naming his victims—much to the amusement of us all.

Among the forest birds to jeer at the hunter and advise the game of his presence were two diminutive species of woodpecker. These same birds, however, sometimes let the hunter know by their excited twittering of the presence of a fox in some thicket. I have known an Ona pause and, searching the bushes with his eyes, whisper the one word, " Whash " (" Fox "). When the creature was seen attempting to slip away, and the hunter was asked how he knew it had been there, he would say, but not figuratively :

" A little bird told me."

Foremost of the forest birds in the noise they made at the hunter's stealthy passage through the woods were the *Kerrhprrh*, the descendants of *Kamshoat*.

Long ago, when all the forest trees were evergreen and shed their leaves only when death came to them, young *Kamshoat* was undergoing his initiation into the secrets of the Lodge. He was no longer a *telken* (child) but a *klokten*. When the time came for him to make one of those journeys expected of novices, *Kamshoat* went off alone. He was away for so long that his people gave him up for dead and were greatly astonished when, one day, he appeared amongst them.

He seemed very little altered, but talked far too much for a *klokten*, who should be silent and thoughtful. He told the others of a wonderful country he had visited, far away to the north, where the forests, he maintained, were far more extensive than anything they had ever seen. *Kamshoat* went on to say that in that country the trees all lost their leaves in the autumn and died, but that in the spring the warm weather brought them to life again and the leaves came out as green as before. Naturally no one could believe such a story, for once a tree was dead it could not come to life again; so they made great fun of *Kamshoat*, laughing at his tales and calling him a liar.

At last he could stand it no longer. He left in a rage, but this time was not absent long. He returned in the form of a huge parakeet, with green feathers on his back and red ones on his chest, looking exactly like his descendants of to-day. It was autumn and *Kamshoat* flew through those evergreen forests from tree to tree, painting the leaves red with colour from his breast. These leaves soon fell to the ground and the people were anxious, for they feared that the trees had died. The tables had been turned; it was now *Kamshoat* who did the jeering. But in the spring, as he had told them, the trees came to life again and everyone was happy once more. *Kamshoat* was renamed *Kerrhprrh* because of his call.

It is worthy of note that, in spite of the wanderings of their ancestor and the high colouring of these birds—which, one would think, should belong to the tropics—they do not migrate and in winter can be seen looking very much out of place among the snow-laden branches. They are noisy birds. Flocks of them crowd together in the branches and make great fun of men as they walk through the forest, mocking at them for having called their father a liar.

CHAPTER FORTY-FOUR

Fuegian Animal and Bird Life. Talimeoat Finds Eggs. How Do Young Ducklings Reach Water? Yoshyolpe Catches an Owl. The Ona Snare Geese. The Cunning of the Fox. More about the Tucu-Tucu. I Beat the Ona at their Own Game and Supply Shishkolh with his Supper.

I

THIS BOOK WOULD NEVER BE FINISHED IF I WERE TO EMBARK ON A DETAILED account of the flora and fauna of Tierra del Fuego. I must confine myself to a few brief notes of my observation of animal and bird life during my continuous hunting trips with various Ona companions.

South of the Magellan Straits, the only indigenous quadruped, apart from such non-ruminant mammals as the fox and the otter, is the guanaco. Said to be the wild form from which the smaller and less graceful llama and alpaca are derived, the guanaco is found on the main island and Navarin Island. Both came from the same stock—the Navarin guanaco having probably crossed the channel on the ice during some very severe winter many centuries ago—but there were certain differences between them. The Navarin animals were larger and heavier boned, with a richer colour and longer hair. Their feet were more developed, the outer toes inclining to turn outwards to a greater degree. This last characteristic need not have taken many generations to develop, as the boggy nature of the Navarin hinterland would have quickly modified their feet, but the other divergencies proved that they had been separated from the species across the Beagle Channel for a very long time.

An extremely large breed of fox is native to the same two islands, and an even bigger animal, though of the same breed, is to be found on Hoste Island. There are no guanaco or foxes elsewhere in the Fuegian archipelago, and nowhere in Fireland are there indigenous wild dogs. The natives have their differing breeds of hunting dogs. The Ona liked fox flesh when it was fat, but it was the only meat I shared with them that I was never able to enjoy. The dogs joined with me in my dislike. If, when feeding mutton or guanaco meat to them, a piece of fox meat was inserted, the dogs would either drop it or, if they were eating too fast and had swallowed it, try to vomit it up. I have heard that this is not the case with fox-hounds in England, but perhaps they are not often fed with

446

good mutton, much less with guanaco meat, which, by the way, dogs seem to prefer to mutton.

Otters are fairly numerous. The large river otter and the smaller sea otter are both much valued for their fur. Of the rodent order, there are two kinds of *apen* (tucu-tucu), at least two kinds of mouse, and the huge water-rat known as the coypu (*sayapie*—pronounced say-a-pie— in Yahgan). The coypu, which is found on Gordon Island and in all the country west of Brecknock Peninsula on the main island, is non-carnivorous and makes very good eating. On Chiloé Island, off the coast of Chile, it is farmed nowadays for its fur, which is known as nutria. The coypu is strictly monogamous. The females, whose dugs are nearly half-way up their sides, are very jealous of one another and will fight to the death.

There are no snakes within five hundred miles of Tierra del Fuego. The nearest are in Chubut territory in Argentina. In Ona-land, but nowhere else on the principal island, there are small lizards, and, in the northern part, tiny frogs not more than an inch long.

In the profusion and diversity of its bird life, Fireland is rich indeed. There are over a hundred varieties: six of duck, five of widgeon and teal, four of geese, three of snipe, four of grebe, three of woodpecker, five of vulture, seven of hawk, two of eagle, seven of owl, ten of gull, four of shag (cormorant), three of sea hawk (skua), five of penguin, at least two of plover, and two of swan, the larger of which has a jet-black head and neck, and pure white body and wings. Besides these, there are numbers of forest, mountain and beach birds, such as woodcock, ibis, flamingo (in Ona-land), kingfisher, parakeet, curlew, oyster-catcher, thrush, sparrow, blackbird, starling, mollymauk, albatross, petrel, grouse, swift, swallow and wren. Rarer birds are pheasant, condor and humming-bird. Nearly all these birds migrate.

As well as the wonders of Nature, there was something else that gave me cause to marvel, again and again, as I walked the mountains and forests of Fireland—the woodcraft of the Ona Indians.

On one occasion I was with Talimeoat, the shag-hunter, and his son Kaichin, the young fellow who had astonished his Excellency the Governor at Ushuaia. The three of us were lying on a little ridge called Awul. Ahead of us stretched a valley leagues long and nearly half a mile wide, with a stream meandering down the centre. For the most part, the valley was covered with grasses, but here and there were large tufts of coarser grass and reeds. Beyond were the wooded hills.

We were, as usual, hunting for food, and our eyes searched intently the edges of the forest and the numberless clumps of trees that might have harboured guanaco. But, apart from a few birds in the sky, the country seemed asleep. After a while Talimeoat stirred. He pointed to a certain tuft nearly a quarter of a mile away and said to his son :

" There is a goose-nest in those reeds. Go and fetch the eggs."

Kaichin obeyed. As he drew near the reeds, out flew a goose ; and the boy came back to us with a number of eggs. I said to Talimeoat :

" How did you know that a goose was sitting in those reeds ? "

He answered with a patient smile, as if replying to the foolish enquiry of a child :

" A vulture told me."

When I questioned him further, he said :

" The *karkaäi* like eggs and I saw one flying many times over the reeds, hoping the goose would leave her nest, so that he could come and break the eggs."

But for once the vultures were human. Eggs are always good to eat and, though better when fresh, are not to be despised when half-hatched, for the less there is of egg, the more there is of bird.

On another excursion, Talimeoat and I were sitting on a little knoll on the northern slope of Tijnolsh Hill. We were about a quarter of a mile from the Ewan River. About the same distance behind us was the stunted forest crowning the summit of Tijnolsh. As we sat there, a good-sized widgeon (*haskerrh*) whirred suddenly over our heads and dropped into the river beside her mate. My companion said :

" Oush ta pe ihlh ? " (" Will there be eggs ? ")

He rose to his feet and, with frequent backward glances over the place where we had been seated to the spot where the duck had taken to the water, walked straight towards the woods whence she had flown. Six feet from the ground, in a hollow tree inside the edge of the woods, he found her clutch of eggs.

The nesting habits of the widgeon and other breeds of duck are curious. It is a mystery to me how the parent birds conduct their young ones safely to the water from nests often even farther from the ground than the one just mentioned. The fledglings, when very young indeed, are to be found swimming with their parents, and they never return to the nest once they have left it.

On moss-grown precipices where the sun never shines and the mist from waterfalls keeps everything dripping wet, there grows in Fireland

73

DESPARD.

74

ALICE.

a lovely scarlet flower in the centre of deep green leaves. Once I was lying at full length on the top of such a precipice, reaching over to gather some of these flowers, when I noticed on a tiny ledge three feet below me the deserted nest of a bird from which little Yoiyolh, the medicine-man, got his nickname: *oklholh*, the waterfall duck (*wayanbij* in Yahgan). Asking a trusted Indian to hold my feet firmly on the ground so that I should not overbalance, I examined the spot minutely. The state of the shells of the recently hatched eggs showed that the family had lately left their home. But how?

For tiny ducklings to fling themselves over a thirty-foot cliff into a foaming torrent, where fall after fall rushed amongst the rocks in a drop of well over a hundred feet, would have been suicidal; yet no mouse, cat or even woodpecker could have scaled or descended that precipice, for just below the nest the moss ended and the wet rock was worn and polished. Some fifty yards farther up stream was a still, deep basin, below which the falls commenced, but nothing on earth could have walked to it from the nest. Either the mother had gone to the trouble of hatching her brood in that ultra-secure spot, only for them to meet certain death as soon as they were hatched; or she had got them to the safe water by means other than their own weak little wings. The natives say they carry them; and so they must, but I have never seen them doing so. More than once the Ona called my attention to grebes teaching their young to dive. Two—perhaps three—little ones would lie flat on their mother's back, with their bills buried in her feathers, while she dived and surfaced again. This may be usual among diving birds in other parts of the world. If it is, I have never heard of it.

2

Most of us have watched a cat, its every movement charged with hope and longing as it stalks a bird; and we have noticed the evident disappointment in pussy's bearing when, just as he is about to make the final spring, the bird flies away. I once had the good fortune to see an Ona lad take on (if that were possible) the soul of a cat, which, combined with the cunning and patience of an Indian, proved more than a match for the unfortunate bird.

Yoshyolpe was by way of being a near relation of mine, for he was a nephew of " Uncle " Koiyot. He was about fourteen years of age and owed his good looks to his mother's people—the northerners—for the

Najmishk men were not renowned for facial beauty and I am sure his father, Koiyot's brother, had been no exception.

The boy and I were out together one day, when we saw a long-eared owl perched over thirty feet from the ground on one of those branchy trees that are easy to climb. We were not hungry and I did not wish to expend a bullet, but Yoshyolpe badly wanted to get that bird. I watched to see what he would do. He found a rod some six feet long and tied to the thin end of it a piece of dried sinew. This was thin and nearly as stiff as a guitar string, so that the good-sized loop that he made in it remained open like a lasso.

Leaving me twenty yards away to watch the proceedings, Yoshyolpe approached the tree. As he drew near, the owl seemed very much inclined to fly off, then changed its mind. Having removed his robe and moccasins, the boy began to climb the tree as cautiously as a cat creeping up on a sparrow. The owl gazed down in wonder, not unmixed with fear, and for minutes at a time the boy would remain perfectly motionless. Then, when a look of boredom had come over the bird's face and a film over its eyes, the human cat would climb a few feet more, or perhaps only inches, until another startled look on the part of the owl caused the hunter to pause again.

At last Yoshyolpe got within reach of the bird with his stick. He slowly advanced it until it was well above his victim, then as slowly lowered the loop. The owl could not understand the piece of sinew dangling over its head and gave two or three vigorous pecks at it, then, finding it harmless, seemed to become engrossed once more in its own reflections. Without any haste, the loop was gently slipped over its head—and the next moment a jerk of the stick brought the owl from its perch to dangle at the end of Yoshyolpe's fishing-rod, helplessly flapping its mighty wings.

A method somewhat similar to Yoshyolpe's was used by Ona and Yahgan alike for snaring wild geese. They would choose a spot where there was short, sweet grass near water. There they would plant sticks near together to form fences going in all directions, with narrow openings here and there. The geese would soon realize that these fences were not at all dangerous and, being too lazy to hop over them, would soon get into the habit of passing through the gateways. When the natives happened to camp in the vicinity, they would set sticks with nooses of sinew tied to them in these gateways. When a goose was caught, either by the head or a leg, the others, alarmed by its struggles, might fly away, but sometimes, seeing no attack from outside, they would gather round their friend, taking solicitous though startled interest in its predicament, and some of them be caught themselves by other nooses.

A great many wild geese nested on Gable Island. About shearing-time and later, one could catch the goslings not yet able to fly. This entailed no little running, for besides the great length of sea-coast, there were eight lakes on the island, and once the goslings got to the water, they were safe from pursuit.

Most of the wild birds, from wrens to geese, when their nest of young ones is approached by a dog or a fox, will pretend to have a broken wing and flop along on the ground to tempt their enemy to pursue them, instead of searching for their young. Dogs can always be deceived in this way, but the fox is a cunning animal. He will ignore the parent bird and start at once to hunt about for the nest.

With the advent of sheep and the consequent destruction of the foxes, the number of geese in Tierra del Fuego increased enormously in later years. On some farms they ate or spoiled over twenty per cent. of the grass intended for sheep. When they gather in autumn for migration, which always seems to start at night, the flocks are so vast that, if one does not know the cause, one is alarmed at the noise of their wings as they fly off for the winter. They return in early spring; the older birds in pairs, but last year's goslings in large flocks, for they do not find their partners till their second migration.

I think these birds are strictly monogamous and may go so far as to remain faithful to their first loves. When I was a lad at Cambaceres, the geese were far less plentiful and very much wilder than they are to-day, but there was one happy couple that used to feed near a little pool within sight of my shanty. One day I shot the goose, and the gander flew away. For years afterwards a single gander haunted the place. He always looked so lonely that I felt really sorry for having robbed him of his mate.

3

Along the northern fringes of the great forest, there is a district many leagues in width where most of the hills are covered with stunted *Nothofagus pumilio*, the dwarf deciduous beech (*kicharrn* in Ona). In autumn the foliage of this tree takes on the most vivid and variegated colours. In some clumps are to be found every conceivable shade of red and yellow, whilst some of the branches still prolong the hopeless struggle to retain their summer green. For seven months of the year in Tierra del Fuego, the dwarf beech remains bare of leaves, so that enough sunlight reaches the ground to allow a good growth of wholesome grass—and here the tucu-tucu are to be found in considerable numbers.

These little burrowing creatures, to which I have already referred, are very like guinea-pigs, but much the colour of mice. They have insignificant tails in proportion to their stout bodies and are decidedly nocturnal in their habits. The name tucu-tucu is very like the somewhat metallic sound they make underground, especially towards evening. It resembles a smart double tap with a tiny hammer. This is immediately repeated, then there is an interval of about a minute, after which the sound comes again if the animal is undisturbed. They burrow fairly deep, but come up near the surface for their sleeping-quarters. This is their undoing, for once the land is stocked with sheep or cattle, the nests—unless they happen to be beneath a rock or under the roots of strong bushes or trees—are trodden in and destroyed, together with their occupants.

Through these low forests are innumerable glades that are covered with water in wet weather and in winter become sheets of ice. On moonlight nights in winter, the Indian boys would go out, some with bows and arrows, others with sticks, and watch for tucu-tucu, which showed up clearly in the moonlight as they crossed and recrossed the ice. The boys had great sport, running down their victims and knocking them over with sticks or shooting them with arrows. Sometimes a tiny boy would come back carrying his first kill with a pride he was unable to conceal. His elders would examine the creature with exclamations of delight at its fatness, thus increasing the young hunter's conceit and their own amusement at his efforts to hide it.

As food the tucu-tucu were a delicious change from guanaco meat, but their tiny bones were so brittle that one had to be careful when eating, lest the splinters got into one's tongue or gums.

In the northern part of the island, where the country was dry for burrowing, only the swampy patches and stony ridges were free from these little pests. The land was so honeycombed that a horse could not gallop, but simply had to plunge through it. I believe they are strictly vegetarian and probably eat many roots from underground, thus causing the plants to die.

It is not the habit of the tucu-tucu to penetrate far into densely wooded country, yet in Tierra del Fuego there must have been some adventurers amongst them, for little isolated colonies were to be found in places which, though suitable for burrowing, were surrounded by leagues of thick forest.

One morning Shishkolh and I were crossing a piece of open land some miles in extent. We came upon a newly dug mound, looking very like hundreds of others, which showed that a tucu-tucu had been at work recently. Shishkolh examined it and decided that the tenant was not at home. With a bit of fencing wire he carried for the purpose, he started prodding the ground. Several yards from the mound he found what he was searching for—the sleeping-place just below the surface. He drew out his knife and cut all round the sides of a turf something over a foot square, disturbing the ground in no other way.

That evening we returned across the same flat, following, as far as I could see, no track at all. I had forgotten the morning's incident and was surprised when Shishkolh broke into a run, sprang into the air and came down with both feet on the turf he had cut that morning. This he removed and disclosed a nest with an outsized tucu-tucu dying in it. I looked around and could see no bush or any sign that marked the place where he had cut that turf. The nearest tree that might have served as a landmark was over a mile away.

4

Whilst on the subject of the Ona's acute faculties of observation, I must recount—for I still feel a thrill of pride when I think of it—how once I outdid one of them at his own game.

My companion was again Shishkolh. We were badly in need of meat at Najmishk, so Shishkolh and I went off to hunt guanaco in the high woods of Tamshk. Owing to much hunting in that vicinity, the animals had grown scarce and were exceedingly wild. We sighted several that day, but they were on the look-out and wary. As the day was perfectly calm and the guanaco's hearing is wonderfully acute, the rustling of the tall seeding grasses of autumn made approach difficult, and I managed to bungle the only fair chance I had of getting a shot.

For a hunter to begin the day with a heavy meal would not be approved of, I think, even in civilized countries; and as, among the Ona, carrying food away from an already hungry encampment was not only contemptible, but also an acknowledgement of defeat before starting, that night found us as hungry as hunters traditionally are. Since daybreak we had eaten nothing but a few dandelion roots and some most unsatisfactory tree-fungus.

It was autumn and we had been walking quite twelve hours when we lit our sad fire, at which we had nothing to cook after a long day's hunting.   Shishkolh admitted failure and it was left to the helpless white man to supply the supper.   Just before we had stopped for the night, I had noticed a greenish stain on the bark of a great hollow tree.   I went back, tapped the tree and listened intently.   From inside came a low purring sound that indicated the presence of a nest of *kerrhprrh* (parakeets).   The young of these birds are fully grown before they take to the air.   The parents bring food to them in the nests, carrying it, I believe, in their crops.

The hole in this tree by which the parent birds came and went was small and in a very awkward place to get at, but we found a long stick and, having made a barb at the end of it as on a spear, managed to transfix and fish out eight protesting young birds, almost fully grown.   If there had been a member of the R.S.P.C.A. with us, I wonder if he would have remonstrated as these unhappy victims were dragged screeching from their nest, and if, in consequence, he would have refused to join us in our evening meal.

The birds were delicious.   We ate only six, keeping two for the next morning.   Thus fortified, we had an excellent hunt the following day. A fresh westerly breeze made stalking possible, and we reached Najmishk that night with a good load of meat.   I listened modestly while, amidst laughter, Shishkolh told the story of the parakeets, generously giving me full credit for providing our appetizing supper.

CHAPTER FORTY-FIVE

Improvements at Najmishk.   I Go to Buenos Aires and Try to Establish our Rights to the Land.   I Meet Mr. Ronaldo Tidblom and Find a New Friend.   The Government Surveyor Admits Defeat and I Take Over his Task.   Encouraged by Success I Accept More Surveying Work, from which I Gain Nothing but Experience in the Ways of Smart Young Men from the City.   Father Juan Zenoni Visits Viamonte and Baptizes the Ona Children.

I

THINGS HAD GREATLY CHANGED AT NAJMISHK SINCE I HAD COME TO SETTLE there over five years earlier. We no longer lived on guanaco meat with only an occasional mare for a change. With the land fenced and streams bridged, the Viamonte farm now carried from twelve to fifteen thousand sheep, giving permanent employment to never less than thirty Ona. Sometimes we had as many as sixty working as shepherds, shearers or fencers, and all receiving, when engaged on contract jobs, the same wages per piece as white men.

Building improvements had been slow, on account of the shortage of materials. The dwarf beech, especially in that coastal neighbourhood, was so stunted, gnarled and faulty that it could not be used satisfactorily, even for a log-hut; and as, right from the beginning, I had been obliged to exercise the utmost economy and prove to the rest of the family that we were not heading for ruin, I had avoided the expense of transporting timber and had contented myself for the first two years with the original shanty. We had then managed to get enough materials to Najmishk for a somewhat larger hut alongside the first; and it was not until over three years later that I felt entitled to spend money on having timber and corrugated iron for a third and more imposing building brought by steamer from Harberton to Rio Grande. The erection of this was entrusted to Dario Pereira, who came from Harberton for that purpose. He will be remembered as the little Spanish carpenter who had given sanctuary to Teorati, the Ona boy, when he had fled from the massacre in which his two remaining brothers had lost their lives. Pereira's face, except for two tiny dark eyes and the point of his nose, was entirely buried in a mat of beard, moustache and eyebrows, which merged into each other and gave him a fierce expression that his character belied. He was a hard worker and made a good job of the new mansion, which put its two humble neighbours to shame and was looked on locally as the last word in luxury and comfort. It was twenty feet long by twelve feet wide and was divided into two rooms, one of which served as a store and deposit, and the other as kitchen, living-room and sleeping-quarters. It boasted a board floor, an iron stove, a table, stools, two bunks, one above the other against the wall, and a glass window.

Nicholas Buscović, the Yugoslav, was no longer with me. He had noticed how very scarce women were in that country peopled by men and had left with the intention of building a house near Rio Grande and bringing to it from Punta Arenas a number of young women, who would help him with the sale of liquor and other delights of civilization. When Dario Pereira had finished his building work, he took Buscović's place until, after a short time, he was succeeded by Zapata, an Argentine cattleman of mixed origin.

Though all was going well with the farm and livestock, the general position was not so reassuring. The transfer of the Harberton property had been legally concluded and we had been supplied with identification papers as Argentine citizens by birth,[1] but our rights in the new land at Najmishk still remained in abeyance. To work on virgin land, making tracks through thickets, bridges over streams and swamps, fences and houses of a kind, with the knowledge that at any time you may be ordered off without recompense, is indeed an unhappy situation. In winter, when work was slack, I made several trips to Buenos Aires, but found it impossible to advance our interests. I spent days waiting in ante-rooms with no more to show for my patience than useless interviews with the underlings of officialdom, who seemed to exist for the sole purpose of putting off visitors such as myself.

At last I had the good fortune to be introduced to Mr. Ronaldo Tidblom, a business man and land agent. He had a strong, broad face and figure, yet if, the first time I met him, I could have melted away gracefully, I would certainly have done so, for this fine man had some twist in his eyes that made it impossible for me to look straight at either of them. Nobody need ever tell me again that first impressions are reliable, for I shall not agree. I soon developed an almost brotherly affection for this new friend, a regard that has never diminished since that day in Buenos Aires when, fixing my gaze on anything but my *vis-à-vis*, I plunged straight into business.

---

[1] I became Esteban instead of Stephen, Will became Guillermo, and Despard's first name was altered from Thomas to Tomas.

It appeared that a law had recently been made, forbidding the sale of blocks of land exceeding four square leagues to any one person or company. This, in reality, was shutting the stable door after the horse had been stolen, because vast tracts of the best land in the most accessible places had already been disposed of to various persons and companies. In addition to purchasing, one was permitted to acquire a further four square leagues on a rental basis.

With the efficient Mr. Tidblom acting as our representative, my brothers and I put in for the limit; and in order to obtain as large a combined area as possible, Mr. Tidblom and Percy Reynolds also filed applications. Percy was now my brother-in-law. He had married Bertha and bought a farm in Paraguay. Though they were still living there, they were anxious to get back to Tierra del Fuego, having found the climate of Paraguay uncomfortably hot. If these claims of ours were approved by the Government, we should obtain eight square leagues, or about fifty thousand acres, each. For the first five years, the whole of the land would be rented to us, but at the end of that period we would have an option to purchase four square leagues each, provided we fulfilled certain very reasonable conditions. The remainder of the land we would continue to hold as lessees.

There was one essential preliminary : before the Government could make any promises about this land or take any steps towards its disposal, it had to be measured. After much delay, by which time I was back in Tierra del Fuego, an accredited surveyor was sent from Buenos Aires. The cost of the survey would be charged by the Government to the future purchaser of the land, whoever he might be.

I went with a troop of horses to meet the surveyor at Rio Grande. He was a Herr Carlos Sewart, an aged German who had been in the Franco-Prussian war. He arrived at Rio Grande with a bedstead, a tent, two theodolites and what seemed to me enough luggage for an army. I managed to transport this old man and his numerous possessions to Najmishk.

After we had worked together for a few days, it became plain to me that Herr Sewart was too infirm ever to finish the job he had undertaken. When, for the second time, he fell with his horse and rolled in the shallow water of a swamp, he completely broke down. Choking with tears and anger, he said it was impossible to carry on work in that horrible country and that he would return to Buenos Aires.

My hobby had always been arithmetic. Near my camping grounds in the forest, I had left behind me a trail of numberless chips of wood covered with hieroglyphics which, had they found them, might have puzzled a senior wrangler, or defeated an Egyptologist's attempts to decipher them. I now felt desperate at the thought of further delay and told Sewart that I would make the survey for him if he would explain to me the mysteries of his book of logarithms.

He said that such a thing was out of the question; that a man must have a University degree in order to make the intricate calculations that were necessary. Notwithstanding this, I insisted and, not wishing to be burdened right through the summer with the ancient gentleman and his belongings, which included demijohns of wine in a country where water was so abundant, drew a true, though gloomy, picture of the difficulties of forest and bog to be encountered if we pursued our trip together. I contrasted this existence with the life he could lead in his tent, pitched beside the sheltering wooded hill called Najmishk, with the faithful Kaichin, son of Talimeoat, whom I proposed to leave as servant, and a demijohn of wine which I promised would never be allowed to go dry. Here he could verify my work in every detail and draw the beautiful maps at which he was such an expert.

He protested at first, but at last gave way. The next day, armed with one of his precious theodolites and book, I started off on a test measurement of two square leagues. It was impossible to follow the straight lines, on account of lakes and other obstacles, so I had to work my way round these and pick up the line beyond. After three or four days, I returned with my report to Herr Sewart. Measuring along the coast, he estimated that I had made an error of only thirteen metres in all, so decided that he could safely let me carry on with the work.

I had a most interesting summer, roving the country with an exclusively bachelor party of young Ona, who were the best possible companions. Our work was never monotonous, varied, as it was, by hunting. The evenings, when I was not immersed in problems connected with the day's survey, we spent in wrestling. At night round our camp-fire, we were kept interested by the weird and fascinating Ona legends, or local gossip brought by some sociable visitor, alternating with such of our well-known English stories as I deemed best suited to my listeners' mentalities.

Sewart had arrived in early spring and for a time we had an abundance of eggs—goose, swan and duck. The sunshine and strong, dry winds of spring caused our noses to peel most conspicuously. The Ona lads did not put this down to wind and weather; as we were living largely on wild birds' eggs, it seemed quite natural to them that our faces should resemble the film that lies underneath the eggshell.

The survey took four months. When it was finished, I was able to prove to Sewart's satisfaction that a very considerable mistake had been made in a previous survey to the north of us, on which we had had to base our work. With these proofs at his disposal, he went off to Buenos Aires with, figuratively speaking, a feather in his cap. Before leaving, he took a ride over the land, in order to be in a position to report on it; and, after presenting me with the more worn of his two theodolites and the precious book of logarithms, bade me good-bye, and embarked at Rio Grande.

The expenses of that survey fell on us. Two or three years later, we had to pay them over again, when we were charged by the Government with the fee they had paid Sewart—well over a thousand pounds.

After the departure of Herr Sewart, though still without title deeds to the land or any recognized rights to it, we felt that it should not lie idle, so we brought over from Harberton a further four thousand breeding ewes, our first experiment having proved a success. We were soon able to drive across in the opposite direction a thousand wethers for sale at Ushuaia.

Apart from the pleasure of that prolonged picnic with the Ona and the satisfaction of getting a good job done, I had gained something that summer. Armed with theodolite and logarithm tables, I now felt myself to be an expert surveyor and looked around for new fields of endeavour.

The Lawrence family, as will be recalled, had obtained land at Punta Remolino, about half-way between Harberton and Ushuaia—a total of four square leagues, or twenty-five thousand acres. They were in much the same position as ourselves. The acquisition of the title deeds had been delayed because the land surveyor sent by the Government had failed to reach, much less to follow, their northern boundary, because of the precipitous nature of the country.

I seized the opportunity of killing two birds with one stone : indulging in my passion for wandering among the mountains and, at the same time, doing a service to our old friends. The country was truly rugged, but from some places a marvellous view could be obtained; and although I and my Ona companions did not accomplish all I could have wished, my report, presented by the licensed surveyor, was accepted by the Office of Lands in Buenos Aires, and finally the title deeds were obtained.

This having been satisfactorily accomplished, another attractive little job called my attention. I thought that at last I might make some money out of the work I enjoyed so much. I agreed with a land surveyor in Buenos Aires that I would survey and stake some land with which he was concerned, then pass on to him the necessary data, which he would go over and present in correct form to the Office of Lands. We were to halve the proceeds.

The land in question was another four-league block, this time on Moat Bay. It had to be divided into two lots of equal area and connected with a stake many leagues away, the exact position of which was known to the Government. The work had to be done on foot, as, except along the beach, it was impossible to use horses. The weather was cold and stormy, the woods wet and the rivers swollen, yet with four young Ona I finished the work in a fortnight and sent the results to my friend in Buenos Aires. He kept all the money himself.

I had paid my helpers well for their arduous toil, so was rather out of pocket. I made up my mind that in future I would avoid making arrangements with smart young men from the city.

2

My habit of paying the natives, when possible, in money had been criticized by Father Juan Zenoni of the Silesian Mission, north of Rio Grande. His reason for objecting was that it made the Mission natives discontented and put it in the power of mine to purchase liquor, etc., if so inclined. I will not say that drunkenness was unknown, but up till 1916 it was very exceptional among those we regarded as our people—well over two hundred in number. In fact, I never saw one of them really drunk in my life.

In 1907 I received a visit at Viamonte from this same Father Juan Zenoni. He was a fair-skinned Italian, well into middle age, lean and of medium height—a jovial, kindly man with a real affection for the natives and an earnest desire for their welfare. He was accompanied by a lay brother called Dalmazzo, who was somewhat older than himself. Brother Dalmazzo had grey eyes and greying brown hair. He was a toiler who could plod steadily through a good day's work with hardly a pause, ready to take on almost any kind of labour that needed to be done. He was a rough carpenter—or perhaps " wood butcher " would better describe him—and gardener, too. In truth, he was a slave, driven by an urge to serve the Church and, incidentally, to make things as comfortable as possible for his leader.

Seeing a gathering of over a hundred and twenty Ona at Viamonte, with a goodly number of infants, Padre Juan said to me tactfully :

" I would very much like to baptize these little ones and make Christians of them, if you and the natives have no objection."

" I also would like to make Christians of them," I replied, " and I don't think baptism can possibly do them any harm."

At the priest's request, I called the Indians together, to inform them that what the padre proposed to do was good. At that time my knowledge of their language, though ample for ordinary conversation—talk of our daily needs, of hunting and current events—did not go much farther; but even if I had been able to speak the tongue perfectly, it would not have been possible for me to expound to these people the meaning of baptism, as we think we understand it.

" We white people," I told my listeners, " have all been through the same ceremony when we were small. The main object is to help our spirits when we die to reach a happy land, but this can only be attained if, after the ceremony proposed by the priest, we try our utmost to lead good lives."

This attempt to explain may seem sketchy and crude, but it was the best I could do.

Some of the Indians had visited the mission at Rio Grande before, and knew Padre Juan. At least one, Ishtohn, had been baptized (with the name of Felipe) and had survived, so now the Ona brought their little ones to Padre Juan. He had come supplied with the necessary paraphernalia on a pack horse. At my suggestion, he set up his stand at one end of a sheltered grassy opening in the forest, about half an acre in extent. Here all the party gathered.

This ideal spot was encircled by a luxuriant growth of fragrant wild currant bushes, backed by dwarf beech. A more suitable setting could not have been found anywhere, whether the congregation were Catholic, Protestant, Mohammedan, Buddhist or Parsee. The green surroundings, untouched by the destructive hand of man, with, overhead, a blue sky flecked with drifting white clouds; the solemn, black-robed priest and that strange congregation, painted and clad in skins, listening and watching with awed attention, for they could never separate religion from magic : all formed a picture long to be remembered.

Padre Juan had, at that time, a few words of Ona that were exceedingly difficult for anyone to understand, though later he acquired a fair smattering of the tongue. The ceremony was conducted in Latin, which was as incomprehensible to me as it was to the Ona. Dalmazzo, with the rapt face and solemn mien befitting this sacred occasion, made the required responses and, I suppose, became godfather to a host of young Ona, varying in age from a few days to several years.

Padre Juan was delighted with the success of his visit, which he afterwards repeated from time to time.

CHAPTER FORTY-SIX

The Wreck of the Glen Cairn. *Halimink Saves the Lives of the Ship's Company and Wants to Steal Me a Wife. I Entertain a Large Party at Viamonte. A Memory of Paraguay. Captain Nichol's Drinking Match with Mr. McInch. The Rest of the Ship's Company Leave for England, but the Steward and his Wife Remain Behind. I Conduct Them to Harberton. An Interesting Outcome of a Broadcast from the B.B.C.*

I

TOWARDS THE END OF JULY, 1907, I RECEIVED UNEXPECTED VISITORS TO my shanty in Ona-land. For nearly a fortnight a strong north-easterly wind had been blowing with rain and thaw, and though at last it was dying down, a very heavy sea was still rolling in from the Atlantic, and the mist and rain continued. These breaks in the winter weather melt the Fuegian ice and snow. They come as a blessing to the sheep farmer by enabling his hungry animals to get at the long-buried grass, but nevertheless they are most unpleasant.

Shortly after one midday, the excited barking of our dogs at Viamonte warned us that strangers were approaching. Presently out of the mist appeared the tall figure of our friend Chalshoat, wrapped in his skins. He was followed by two haggard-looking white men. As they drew nearer, I noticed that one of these was a most striking figure. Over six feet tall, he looked as hard as nails. His square jaw and direct gaze made me feel that, though saturated and weary, he was a long way from exhaustion. His companion was just about done up.

I guessed at once that these were shipwrecked sailors, and the grip of the big man's horny hand showed me that, even if he were an officer, he was not above heaving on the rough ropes of a sailing-vessel. The manner of his speech revealed him to be Irish and later I learned that he came from Donegal Bay, a rugged coast where stout seamen are raised. He produced papers that showed him to be the second mate of a large barque, the *Glen Cairn*. Unless my memory plays me false, his name was Nielson.

He told me that the *Glen Cairn* had got off her course on account of the long spell of thick weather and had struck a reef near Policarpo Cove, to the west of Cape San Diego. The vessel had come clear of the rocks, but had been leaking badly. The captain had steered a north-westerly course, keeping in sight of the coast, until, near Cape San Pablo, the vessel had foundered. Three of the boats had been launched, but one had capsized and two of the seamen had been drowned. The remainder, twenty-three men, two women and the captain's fifteen-months-old son, had landed safely and had been cared for by an Ona party under the leadership of our old friend, Halimink. I gathered afterwards from the captain and others that their successful abandoning of the sinking ship had been due, in great measure, to the courage and prowess of the second mate.

The condition of Nielson's companion was serious enough to make him a hospital case and Nielson himself was very footsore from the unusual exercise of continuous walking, so they were both glad to get into some dry clothes and, after a feed, to turn in in our bunks.

My next step was to write a letter asking for a relief vessel to be sent to Rio Grande, to pick up the shipwrecked crew. This message I entrusted to an Ona, who would take it to Mr. McInch at Rio Grande, whence it could be relayed overland to the Chilean settlement at Porvenir and thence across the Straits of Magellan to Punta Arenas. If all went well, the vessel should arrive at Rio Grande within ten days.

Chalshoat, for reasons best known to himself, had come by such an erratic trail from Cape San Pablo that the journey had taken three days, and the mate had expressed the opinion that the captain, thinking something had happened to them, might try to reach Ushuaia. The boats had been smashed by the rising tide soon after they had landed, so that if the attempt were made, it would be overland. The captain had as his guide some old South Atlantic or South Pacific directory which, when it had been issued long before, had been right in telling shipwrecked mariners to make for the Anglican Mission at Ushuaia. I knew that if this party, equipped as they were, followed this plan in the depth of winter, very few, if any, would survive.

I determined, therefore, to go at once to their help, but because of the fog, it took a long time to find our horses and dusk had settled on the land before, with three young Ona, a troop of tame horses and as many saddles as we could muster, I was ready to set off. It was now raining steadily and the night was soon to grow as black as pitch, yet that indefatigable second mate, aroused from his sleep by our preparations for departure, wanted to accompany the rescue party. Some man!

He was prevailed upon to remain behind and the four of us started

Oxen dragging logs down the track to the saw-mill.

Our carts arriving at Viamonte from Rio Grande.

The Viamonte saw-mill with Dolal in the doorway.

Bertram cutting grass for fodder at Viamonte.

The Estancia Viamonte in summer-time.

The same in winter.

out. At first we found the going along the beach was easy. Farther on, the cliffs forced us inland, where our progress became slower because of the dense, low forest streaming with water, and the slippery hillsides. We crossed the valley where San Martin and his companions had met their deaths twelve years before at the hands of Capelo and his band, which had included Chalshoat, Halimink and other Indians who were now sheltering this shipwrecked crew of the *Glen Cairn*. Whilst crossing a deep stream, one of our horses broke through the ice and it cost us hard work to drag him out. Towards daybreak the rain ceased and soon after sunrise we arrived at an encampment in the woods where the stranded party received us with shouts of joy.

Captain Nichol, though somewhat past his prime, was still a powerful man, with a broad, genial face and mighty shoulders. He must have weighed quite eighteen stone. His wife was a " bonnie wee woman " from Scotland. The second lady of the company was Mrs. Perry, the wife of the ship's steward. When the first happy greetings had been exchanged and it had been decided to start back for Najmishk early the following morning, Captain Nichol told me his story.

After leaving the *Glen Cairn* in their two boats, they had sometimes seen the cliffs and wooded hills through the mist, and had followed the coast north-westward. For all that, they might have been in mid-ocean; the formidable rows of breakers all along the shore had made landing impossible. This coast is very shallow and has reefs far out, so that in many places the sea breaks over a mile from the cliffs. At last one spot had attracted their attention, for there the water had seemed deeper; yet it is doubtful whether they would have tried it had they not been heartened by seeing on the shore a smoke which they had rightly taken for a signal. They had noticed, too, that just off the smoke there had been a spot where the waves, though dangerously steep, had not been actually breaking, so they had made up their minds to take the risk and attempt a landing.

The captain, knowing the ability of the second mate, had relinquished the helm to him. The other boat had been in charge of the first mate, who, after some exciting moments when both boats had been in the greatest danger of being capsized or swamped, had followed the leader into a deep, but comparatively quiet lagoon. They had rowed across it to where Halimink had been awaiting them by the fire he had kindled. He had even had the thoughtfulness to don civilized clothes for the occasion, so as not to frighten the visitors by appearing in his guanaco-skin robes.

He had waded into the water as the boats had grounded and had carried the Nichols' baby ashore, all the while smiling and making friendly gestures.

When all had landed safely with the few things they had brought with them, several other Ona, dressed in their robes, had begun to appear from behind rocks and trees where Halimink, fearing they might alarm the shipwrecked people and prevent their approaching· the shore, had advised them to hide.

Numerous lurid stories of Fuegian cannibalism, told by self-styled explorers who had been more influenced by the desire to feature as heroes of sensational adventures than by any love of veracity, had reached Mrs. Nichol; and seeing the numbers of their Ona escort increasing and the costume and paint that had made them appear far more fearsome than Halimink, had felt great alarm for the fate of their tender infant. Nevertheless she had soon been reassured by Halimink's beaming countenance and his pantomime indications that he and his people intended the visitors nothing but kindness.

A few of the Ona had already learnt some Spanish (Halimink was one of them), but none knew English, and as their guests were unacquainted with either Spanish or Ona, the two parties had been unable to converse with one another. The "eloquent language of signs" is not always correctly interpreted and has given rise to many fantastic stories. Halimink had insisted on making some curious hieroglyphics with a pencil in Captain Nichol's pocket-book, which he had then handed back with gestures that the captain had taken to mean that he was expected to sign his name below Halimink's scribble. Halimink had not, in fact, been collecting autographs, nor had he been trying to trick the captain into signing an I.O.U. It had merely been his way of indicating that the captain should write me a letter giving details of the wreck, which he had then intended sending me by a swift runner. The suspicious master had misunderstood his intention and refused to have anything to do with it, so other steps had had to be taken. The second mate, whose energies had not abated in spite of his ordeal on the wreck, had offered to go in search of assistance with an Indian guide, and had duly set off with Chalshoat and a seaman companion.

The captain assured me that their safe landing had been entirely due to Halimink's smoke signal. By attracting them to the only spot where they could land and then taking them under his wing, he had undoubtedly saved their lives; and this action of his, without thought of reward, wiped out, let us hope, the dark blots on his chequered past.

2

When Mrs. Nichol learnt that, after coming through such dangers and anxieties with her husband and child, there was now practically an open, easy road from Halimink's windbreak in the leafless forest of Fireland to her beloved Scottish homeland, she was warmly grateful to those painted natives, amongst whom she and her family had rested in security since they had landed. And when she heard that we were preparing to start as early as possible the following morning, she simply radiated happiness.

I found that Halimink had something on his mind. He seized the first favourable opportunity to call me aside for a serious talk.

"The white woman is young," he said, "and very friendly to us Indians. She is good-natured and always smiles at us. You help the men to get away to their own country, and I will kidnap the woman and keep her in the woods till you return. Why should you live alone?"

I would have risen greatly in the esteem of this good fellow had I been game enough to play my part in his most attractive scheme. As it was, I regretfully declined.

On the following morning, the visitors, after first bidding good-bye to their new Ona friends, made the quiet woods echo by giving them three hearty cheers. Mrs. Nichol, Mrs. Perry and some of the men rode most of the way to Najmishk, always at a walking pace. The baby was entrusted to me. For the first ten miles, Captain Nichol refused a horse so that some of the older seamen could take it in turns to ride. About six miles from Najmishk an Ona met us with two or three saddled horses and only then would this stout ship's-master accept a mount. A mile farther on, a short time before sunset, I conducted the party across the Ewan River and past the cliffs just north of its mouth.

There was now no possibility of their getting lost while I rode on ahead. The tide was low and a hard sand beach made walking easy, so I advised them to follow the coast till they should come to a large fire, where someone would be waiting to show them the way to our "mansion." Then I galloped on with the intention of telling Zapata to get out our two paraffin-tin pots and prepare a good stew of mutton and rice, besides roasting two or three sheep on spits. A native, however, had warned my assistant of our approach and, upon dismounting, I found that he was already well on with the job.

When the party following arrived at the fire on the beach, Nielson, the stalwart second mate, was there with some Indians to welcome them. One or two of them were so tired after their unaccustomed walk that they could get no farther without assistance and had to be helped up the hill to Viamonte. We gave the two women and the baby the living-room, while some of the rest slept in the store-room. Our little medicine-man, Yoiyolh, who had earned the title of Waterfall Duck, had built himself a most extraordinary wigwam. At my suggestion, he willingly vacated this to make room for most of the crew.

We spent two or three very happy days at Najmishk before con-tinuing our journey to Rio Grande. In the evenings, rather than crowd in Yoiyolh's wigwam, we gathered round great fires in the wood, where the sailors intermixed happily with the silent Indians, whose sombre faces did not hide the contagious gaiety they caught from that joyous crew. The sailors frequently sang their songs or shanties, and a cadet played excellent music on a mouth-organ rescued from the wreck. After months of listening at night to the chanting of the medicine-men or the wailing of some bereaved squaw, both the singing of the men and the cadet's musical efforts sounded heavenly to me.

No one can call me musical, yet four times music has sunk deep into my memory. Once was in Paraguay, when I was on a trip with my brother-in-law, Percy Reynolds, and a Guarani guide. We were on horseback and had been following a little-used footpath through forest country during an intensely hot morning. In the afternoon there came a thunderstorm, followed by a steady downpour that lasted some twenty-four hours. The track grew worse and worse on account of the water, and we were soon soaked to the skin. We passed two or three hovels on the way, but our guide knew a place where, for certain reasons of his own, he wished to pass the night. We were much delayed and it was dark when we reached this haven. When we realized what kind of a place it was, Percy and I wished we had halted hours earlier. We found a leaky, thatched roof supported by three *adobe* walls. The front was open and the place had, in very truth, a mud floor. There were already at least twenty persons sheltering there.

The guide hailed someone he knew and, as a matter of form, asked permission to dismount and spend the night there. This, as always, was generously granted and we joined the gathering. They were wrapped in their soaking *ponchos* and standing round the embers of a fire or sitting on blocks of wood or cows' skulls. The fire was nearly out and no one seemed to have energy enough to cut firewood and make a good blaze.

Among the party were three prisoners, with a like number of police guards to take care of them. The six seemed very friendly with one another and, but for the handcuffs, one could not have told which was which.

Another man had a guitar and had managed somehow to keep the strings dry. In response to the appeals of his friends, he produced it and, after the usual tuning, started to play. Except for the dying embers and the glowing ends of thick home-made cigars, there was utter blackness around. The *guitarrero* would strum a few notes and then sing a few more, which always ended in a wailing note one could almost call a howl. I did not understand a word of Guarani, but the lilt of the tune suited the circumstances and the surroundings perfectly.

That weird tune is one of my four memories. The second is of those evenings at Najmishk, when the seamen sang their songs and the cadet played his mouth-organ, while the Ona in their robes squatted in the background. The third is of the *Romance* by Sibelius played on a drawing-room piano by the girl who was destined to be my wife, with the notes drifting out across an English lawn. The last is of a long line of soldiers singing *Tipperary* as they marched up to the front against a sunset sky. These four instances are indelibly imprinted on my mind and, though I have heard the wonderful voices of Caruso and other grand singers, their memory does not haunt me so.

3

Mr. Perry, the steward of the *Glen Cairn*, and his wife were most anxious to remain in Tierra del Fuego and told me so, saying they had nothing to go home for except to look for a job. They were willing to turn their hands to anything and, though Mrs. Perry was a tiny little woman—fortunately, as it proved—they both seemed strong and wiry. I agreed to take them to Harberton as soon as the road was passable. There they would be assured of employment, either cooking, baking, washing clothes, gardening, or perhaps all four.

So Mr. and Mrs. Perry remained behind at Najmishk when the rest of the *Glen Cairn* party set off for Rio Grande, under the guidance of myself and three or four Indians. We were all mounted and two days later we arrived at our destination. Most of the sailors enjoyed their ride immensely, but I lost count of the tumbles they had, for though the animals they rode were tame and used to carrying packs, they had never carried sailors before, and some of them objected.

Mr. McInch placed ample accommodation at the disposal of his guests while they waited for the arrival of the steamer from Punta Arenas. He received Captain Nichol and his family in his private house, and there was considerable speculation between the farm hands and the *Glen Cairn's* officers and men as to which of the two was the better man. Captain Nichol, his sailors believed, was able to drink any ordinary man under the table and walk off steadily and straight; but I had seen McInch drinking and knew how he prided himself on being the world's champion, able and willing to take on and beat all comers. I did not remain to see this clash of giants and only heard McInch's account of the contest afterwards. He claimed to have won, though he had the grace to acknowledge that it had been one of the most strenuous efforts of his life. McInch drank enormously, yet he was never drunk. The poor fellow, in spite of his strength, could not last long. When he died in Punta Arenas, he could not have been much more than forty-five years old.

The morning after the drinking bout, having left my friends comfortably housed, I sent off my Indians with our troop of saddled horses and was just starting out to overtake them when I saw, at the gateway of the settlement, the crew of the *Glen Cairn* lined up on either side of the track. Upright on top of one of the huge gate-posts was Nielson, whose heroic figure might have inspired some sculptor who had heard his story to make a splendid statue of him. The first mate was standing on the other gate-post. He was a typical salt, somewhat past his prime, and had seemed rather reserved until that moment. As my pony and I passed between the two rows of happy men, they gave us both three cheers, boisterously led by the first mate, who seemed suddenly to have become the jolliest of that jolly crew. The pony was frightened at being subjected to such unusual attention, so he lost no time in passing the crowd and getting away from all the noise—and I did nothing to check him. If, however, those men had been wealthy and had sent me a gold watch in acknowledgement of the little I had done, it would not have given me more pleasure than that send-off.

4

At Najmishk I turned over my little shack to the Perrys and retired to a shelter close by, until such time as conditions improved enough for me to escort them to Harberton. But in spite of the abundance of meat, flour and even sugar, the lack of the luxuries to which they had been accustomed was soon pointed out to me. This required me to move from Najmishk sooner than I had intended, so on the 20th August, hoping that the hard frosts that had followed the thaw would have dried up the streams and hardened the snow on the moors, we left Viamonte for Harberton. We were accompanied by my stalwart "Uncle" Koiyot and Kankoat's second son, David, now a sturdy boy of twelve with his father's sense of humour.

"Uncle" and I each had a fair load, for we took a small tent, a certain amount of bedding, some odds and ends that the Perrys had rescued from the wreck, and about a week's provisions. The boy David carried a couple of billy cans, spoons, mugs, sugar and coffee. Perry was willing to take a load, but I knew that, however strong he might be in his own element, he would find this unaccustomed exercise very trying, so I told him not to do so, but to stand by to help his wife.

It was a frosty morning when our little party started off on foot towards the mountains, which shone clear and enticing in the distance. Alas for my hopes! Instead of continued frost, that evening there came a fog and drizzle. I had my rifle and, on the second evening out, went on ahead of the party. Coming on a guanaco in the fog, I shot him at pointblank range, and we camped there for the night. On reaching the tall forest, I shot several parakeets. Though the rifle's ·44 calibre bullets blew the birds to pieces, Mrs. Perry thoroughly enjoyed them when roasted. In spite of these luxuries, which were specially reserved for her, on our fifth day out she finally broke down. By that time her husband was in no condition to help her, either mentally or physically. At last she consented to ride on top of my pack and from then on—perched either there or on "Uncle's" bundle—had a good ride for the rest of the journey, whilst poor Perry, footsore and disillusioned, limped painfully behind. I do not think the woman weighed seven stone, and when Koiyot had carried her a mile or two through slushy snow with frozen bog beneath and I called out to him that it was my turn now, he answered cheerfully :

"This is not a woman. She is only a little bird."

We reached Harberton that same evening.

5

There is a postscript to the story of the wreck of the *Glen Cairn*. Some thirty years later, whilst I was on a visit to London, I was asked to broadcast for the B.B.C. A few days after having done so, I received many letters from different persons, some of whom had been succoured by my father in the 1870s and 1880s, and remembered his family. Amongst my mail was one letter that pleased me greatly. It was from Mrs. Nichol, who was then a widow, with children born since the wreck—and grandchildren, too. She told me that the baby I had carried on my back had now a good position in the Glasgow Police Force, with a family of his own. The good lady wrote that she would be glad to see me again, and later, when I happened to be near Ardrossan, I called on her and thoroughly enjoyed my visit. To my surprise, she asked after several of the Indians by name. When I told her of Halimink's kindly solicitude for my happiness in Tierra del Fuego so long ago, and how attractive I had found his proposal to kidnap her and hide her in the woods till all the men had left for their native land, she was greatly amused.

PART V

THE ESTANCIA VIAMONTE
1907–1910

CHAPTER FORTY-SEVEN

Our Rights to the Najmishk Land are Established and Arrangements are Made for a New Settlement. Members of the Family Move from Harberton to Viamonte. The Faithful Halimink Almost Goes Too Far. Our New Saw-Mill Arrives from England and is Installed. Work on the Estancia Viamonte Proceeds. The Meteor.

I

MY PREDICTION THAT THE HARBERTON HOMESTEAD WOULD BECOME TOO small for our growing family was to prove correct. By 1907, Despard and Tina had two children. Their first-born, Mary Christina, was known as Tinita, whilst her baby brother, Walter Despard, had acquired the nickname Boofy. Will and his wife Minnie also had a girl and a boy —Clara Mary (Clarita), the elder of the two, and Thomas Lawrence (Laurenzo). This party was increased towards the end of 1907 by the arrival of Bertha and Percy Reynolds from Paraguay. They had received a good offer for the farm and, as the climate of that country was proving too much for them, had sold the property and come to join us in Tierra del Fuego. They brought with them their little son, Percito, whose English names were Percival William.

For some time I had been planning a grand new settlement. It was to have a shearing-shed and all modern conveniences, and was to provide a new home for some of the folk from Harberton. The proposed site was some four leagues nearer to Rio Grande than was Viamonte. Everything depended, of course, on the establishment of our legal right to the land. Pending this, we had already placed an order in England for a steam saw-mill and building materials, all of which were to be dispatched with all speed on the receipt of a cabled word from Buenos Aires. It had been decided at a family conference at Harberton that Will was to stop behind, the efficient yet benevolent lord of our old domain. His wife and children, Mother and Yekadahby were also to remain at Harberton. The participants in the new enterprise were to be Despard and Percy with their families, my sister Alice and myself. In addition we should have with us Miss María Jorgelina Reynolds, known as Manina, the elder sister of Tina and Percy. She had been injured as a child and walked painfully with a stick. She was to live with Despard and his family for years—a cheerful Yekadahby to the children. For the new venture, as distinct from the Harberton concern, we formed a private limited company, trading as the Bridges & Reynolds Farming Co., Ltd.

When I arrived at Harberton with Mr. and Mrs. Perry, I found waiting for me there some recent correspondence from our friend, Ronaldo Tidblom. He gave us to hope that, though some dangerously wealthy and important people had become interested in the land we were occupying at Najmishk, we still had a chance. Things, he said, were moving towards a climax.

After two days at Harberton, " Uncle ", young David and I hurried back to Viamonte, where there was much to be done and only Zapata, the caretaker, in charge. I had not been back at Viamonte a month when A-yaäh, the little man who had impersonated *Ohlimink*, the familiar wizard of the *Hain*, arrived from Harberton, bringing glad tidings. The Government had signed a contract with Ronaldo Tidblom, leasing us eight square leagues of land each for five years. At the end of that time, if we fulfilled the conditions stipulated, we could each purchase half of the block at a price previously agreed upon. We would also be given the preference, as first settlers, over the remaining four square leagues, should the Government continue leasing out the land.

As soon as I received this good news, I went to work with a few chosen Ona. In a patch of forest three leagues from our future settlement, we felled a thousand logs ready for the saw-mill. This had to be done with all speed, before the warmth of spring caused the sap to flow, thus greatly reducing the quality of the timber. Next we started to make a road up which to bring the semi-portable steam-engine, which we hoped might arrive before the frost came out of the ground. By then it was October and there was still enough ice in the valleys to support the engine.

Despard arrived from Harberton with two Chilote[1] workmen and at once started to improve my humble abode at Najmishk, which was given the name of Old Viamonte to distinguish it from the new settlement, which would be called, when it was completed, the Estancia Viamonte. It was proposed that the others should not wait until the new building was ready for occupation, but should move to Old Viamonte as soon as Despard and his helpers had finished their preparations. In less than three weeks we returned together to Harberton to fetch the rest of the party.

The cavalcade that set out from the homestead on a perfect summer

---

[1] From the island of Chiloé, off the Chilean coast. Short, sturdy and capable of real affection, the Chilotes are a product of the union between Spanish soldiers of the invasion and native women of the Chonos, the Mapuches and the unconquerable Araucanos.

morning was such as that track of mine had never seen before. There were four ladies—Tina, Bertha, Alice and Miss Reynolds—three small children, and Despard, Percy and myself. In charge of our string of pack-horses were half-a-dozen Ona, one of them Chorche, the hefty young chap on whom I had played that wrestling trick at the first Najmishk shearing. There had been delays in starting on such an unusual trip, and the weather, as it turned out, was too fine to last—or perhaps, as the Ona suggested, the mountains were annoyed at having their peace disturbed by so many foreigners. Whatever the reason, on the second day out we had such a downpour of rain that the stream we had to follow down the northern slope of the range flooded its banks; and, with the rain pouring on us, we were obliged to pitch our camp in a bleak, desolate spot where there was no food for the horses. It was rough on the children, too— especially Boofy, the youngest of the party, who attained the first anniversary of his birth on that wild day.

Before leaving Harberton, I had offered Tina the services of a sturdy young Ona mother, who would have willingly and proudly carried little Boofy over, keeping him warm against her own body inside her robes, nourishing him splendidly on the journey and delivering him at the other end—plus, no doubt, some ornamental smudges of red paint. I had so often seen the bright-eyed youngsters peering out at the world over their mothers' shoulders, or snuggling down in their comfortable nest behind their parents' ample manes; and I was sure that the elastic tread of a moccasin-shod Indian would be far better for the child than the movement of a horse struggling over such an irregular track. Needless to say, my sage advice on the management of infants had gone unheeded and Tina had been, or pretended to be, outraged at my suggestion. Of course I was right, for the little one suffered from his hardships on the trip and took some days to regain his usual health and good humour.

My greatest anxiety was for Miss Reynolds. She was heavy and so helpless, but fortunately brave. For most of the trip she was able to ride on horseback, but when the road was very bad, she had to dismount. Then Chorche and I shared the honour of carrying her.

Upon reaching Najmishk, the ladies took over my little home, while I went on and settled down to work at the site of the new settlement. Despard and Percy got busy preparing the ground for our saw-mill, generally managing to get back to Old Viamonte at night. During their absences, Halimink, who still retained the rifle he had purchased, so it was said, to rid the world of *this* interloper, was left to protect the ladies. The good fellow was proudly eager to do something to prove his devotion, and when Despard realized the childlike heroism—perhaps I should call it the knightly chivalry—of Halimink, he was much amused and rather encouraged it, little dreaming what the consequences might be.

Halimink had his shelter among some giant currant bushes about eighty yards from the shanty. One day he appeared, rifle in hand, to inform the ladies that two men were approaching from the south on horseback. That they were mounted should have allayed his suspicions, for in a country where there were only one or two tracks that a horse could traverse, bad men would be more likely to go on foot. The men appeared along the valley, but, while they were still some distance away, one of them remained with the pack-horse, leaving his companion to come on alone.

This man was dressed in cowboy garb, even to the big revolver, and had a Mexican saddle, so the ladies were sure he was all right. Halimink, however, found something sinister in his appearance. He suddenly cocked his rifle and brought it to his shoulder, saying in Spanish:

" Quien sabe—hombre malo. Mejor yo mata." (" Who knows— a bad man. Better I kill.")

One of my sisters—or it may have been Tina—stopped him before he could pull the trigger, and Mr. Charles Wellington Furlong (later Colonel) of the U.S.A., a writer and explorer, who had followed the track from Harberton, rode up to the shanty without the least idea of the narrow escape he had had. Halimink the faithful was an excellent shot.

2

At last a steamer arrived at Rio Grande with our cargo. We took up some sixteen oxen with three carts we had recently purchased, to receive the goods. The rise and fall of the tide at Rio Grande is about thirty feet in the perpendicular, and in those days there was no jetty there. Steamers were put aground at high water, then, when the tide went out, the cargo was landed on the loose shingle alongside the vessel, which got off again when the tide rose.

The all-important steam saw-mill, which weighed about five tons, was lowered over the side and stood on its wheels beside the vessel. The beach was so steep that I decided to tie in seven of our best yoke of oxen, to drag it up through the heavy shingle. I was proud of these animals. We had brought them from Harberton and they were the finest team in the country, accustomed to dragging heavy timber through the woods.

They were perfectly tame, but in the midst of a crowd of strangers and the noise and stench of the steamer—all so different from the quiet forests—it was no easy task to get them to approach the saw-mill; and when finally we managed to attach four yoke to the chains, they broke away and fairly stampeded with it, covering nearly a quarter of a mile, with the saw-mill racing behind them, before we could overtake them. Five days later the saw was carving out boards thirty-five miles from the port.

Whilst the long summer days lasted, all of us worked sixteen hours a day. Sometimes it was nearer twenty. The thousand logs, which lay scattered as they had fallen, had to be carted from the forest to the saw-mill, where some of my best Ona proudly worked with Despard at the bench, ripping the logs into board and scantling of the required dimensions. Other chosen men were occupied carting the sawn timber to the site of our new homestead and stacking it to dry. With young Kautush as boss carter, others were going to and fro between Viamonte and Rio Grande, collecting the building materials that had come from England with the saw-mill: a heap of corrugated iron, fencing wire, drums of nails of all sizes, screws, ropes, paints and tools galore, as well as provisions for our growing colony. Now that we were sure of the land, we were ready to spend money on it.

With Despard working like a Trojan at the saw-mill, I—always with the Ona—was fencing, road-making, bridge-making, delivering timber in the rough to the saw-mill, and looking after the stock. The sheep, which now passed into five figures, could not be neglected. They had to be gathered from a wide extent of wooded land for the purpose of lamb marking.[1] Then came the shearing. Percy, at the new site, was as busy as any of us. Besides giving out provisions to all and sundry, he had to keep tally of everything: timber arriving from the saw-mill and goods sent back there, or out to the shepherds; materials collected by the carters from Rio Grande, and still more supplies from England. In addition to all this, Percy dealt with the pile of correspondence that such an enterprise entails and kept the daily wage-sheet.

The ladies did not all remain long at Old Viamonte. Soon Tina and Bertha with their children had moved to the saw-mill. When enough timber had been prepared, the centre of activity shifted to the new settlement; and by March, 1908, the whole party were at the new Viamonte. None of the buildings were habitable yet, so the families lived in tents in

---

[1] A registered mark on the ears, tails cut off and castration.

the shelter of a copse. I slept in a corrugated-iron structure, open on one side. About a hundred yards away was the Ona encampment.

3

That was the month of the meteor. Some time after 11 p.m. one night, I was just falling off to sleep when a strong light commenced to grow till it was almost dazzling. I had never seen this kind of lightning before and, much perturbed, hastened outside. There, right overhead, at least seventy degrees across the sky, stretched a light like the tail of a huge comet. Its brightest end was some sixty degrees above our E.S.E. horizon and the body of the tail was immediately above us.

The sleepers in the tents were aroused and the Ona had sprung from their rest to run to where we stood. The natives were greatly excited. Some of them claimed to have actually seen the moon on fire rush across the sky and go out in a blaze of light. A dreadful thing had happened up aloft, they said. They would never see the moon again, and other troubles would follow.

Several minutes after we had been disturbed by the light, we heard a strange sound that terminated in a muffled boom. I wish I had taken the exact time when the light was at its brightest, so as to get an idea of the height above the earth at which our heavenly visitor had disintegrated. It may have been another two minutes before the light completely died away and left the stars again in possession of their domain. I have never heard or read of the detonation of a meteor being heard by those who saw it, but there was no mistake about this one.

The phenomenon was neither heard nor seen at Rio Grande, twenty miles to the north-west, or at Harberton, which was more than double that distance to the southward. By that late hour, most of the people were doubtless asleep in their houses and had not been awakened, as we had been, by the disturbance.

I told the natives that what we had seen was just an out-sized shooting star and explained again, as I had done before, all I had learnt about these wanderers and the grand protection our atmosphere is against their doing us harm. Somewhat reassured, they went back to their encampment, while the rest of us retired again to our interrupted repose.

It is worth adding here that I was with the Ona in 1910, when Halley's comet made its last appearance. I stood with the natives before dawn, watching the vast expanse of tail rising, so it seemed, from the ocean. It was followed by the nucleus, which faded slowly as the daylight strengthened. The awe of my companions was no greater than my own.

Sheep-gathering at Viamonte.

Sheep in the woods.

One of the many sheltered glades on Viamonte farm.

Double-fleeced sheep. They escaped the
last shearing.

Sheep crossing the Ewan River.

In the centre are the champion shearers, the brothers Metet and Doihei. The man in the *goöchilh*
who stands next to Metet is Yoshyolpe, the nephew of my adopted uncle, Koiyot. On the extreme
right is Ishtohn, who still clings to the fancy robe to be seen in photo No. 35.

Photo by Will's daughter, Mrs. Goodall.

CHAPTER FORTY-EIGHT

The Estancia Viamonte. The Ona Learn the Value of Money. Martin's Two Letters. Gathering Sheep. A Dog that Thought for Himself. The Intelligence of the Mule. Señor Lopez Sanchez Uses the Track. A Horse Attempts to Commit Suicide.

I

WORK AT ESTANCIA VIAMONTE WENT ON APACE—AND THERE WAS NEED for haste. The *casa grande* had to be made habitable before the gypsy life being led by the families was made less desirable by winter frosts and snow. Despard did not merely work—he slaved. With all the experience gained in building up Harberton, Cambaceres, a settlement on Gable Island and another on Picton, he knew exactly what to do. He was as good a blacksmith as he was a carpenter; could weld a broken cart-axle, or put a link in a chain so neatly that it was hard to distinguish it from the others. Our old friend Dario Pereira had returned to Spain, so now Despard had the assistance of a carpenter from Punta Arenas and three or four useful Chilotes. Between them, working with scarcely a pause throughout the long day, they managed to get enough of the house done for the families to be snugly installed before the cold weather came. It was as well that they did, for during the month of July, 1908, the temperature never rose as high as four degrees centigrade below zero.

The *casa grande* was seventy-five feet long and forty-eight feet from front to back—by far the biggest building Despard had yet tackled. It was partially two-storeyed. Half of the ground floor took the form of a verandah, with glass along the whole front of the building and half-way to the back at the ends. Here—if one had the time—one could sit and enjoy the winter sunshine without being exposed to the winter cold. The upstairs bedrooms had sky-lights in the gabled roof.

Before the new homestead was started, we had already fixed up temporary shelters of corrugated iron for the storage of provisions and other stores; and long before it was really finished in all its luxury, there were other buildings under way. We erected an ample cook-house, stables, a shearing-shed and store, and about fifteen comfortable cottages for the Ona whenever they cared to occupy them. Another building was put up in due course for use by our workers, both Indian and Chilote, as a

481

club. When the settlement was well established, Padre Juan Zenoni asked permission to come and live there, in order to run a school and church, enterprises for the carrying out of which he also solicited our help. After the family had debated the matter, a simple agreement was drawn up, in which we promised to fence in some acres of land, build a bungalow for the priest and his assistant, and a schoolroom that could be used as a church. In addition we undertook to supply the mission with firewood and certain rations, also agreeing that Padre Juan could keep a limited number of horses and yoke-oxen on our farm. In return, Padre Juan guaranteed that if at any time we considered his teaching or presence harmful, either to the farm or to the natives, he would, without argument or protest, pack up and leave at once. This simple contract was signed by both parties and held good for years, during which Padre Juan kept regular school for the children and the more ambitious of the young men, who went to his evening classes and learnt to read and write. Long after, when more settlers arrived in the country, the mission obtained a small government concession farther south.

In the early days at the new Viamonte, we had two additions to our pay-roll. The first was a Basque. His name was Gastelumendi and he had married a Yahgan wife. Being well acquainted with him, we felt we could trust him to act as assistant store-keeper. His little house was close to the store, from which he gave out provisions. Under the supervision of Percy or Despard, he also helped with the book-keeping. The second was Pedro Barrientos, a man from southern Chile who had worked long at Harberton. Though I had tried hard to do so, I had found it impossible to be in two places at once, so I asked Will if he could spare this rather tall, lightly built artist with an axe. I use the word "artist" intentionally, for to see Barrientos squaring a log with a six-pound axe-head on a three-foot handle and leaving it as smooth almost as if it had been planed was to know that there was artistry in axe work. Such a man was valuable to Will, yet he generously sent him across to Viamonte. Barrientos could read after a fashion and could write laboriously a pencilled letter that anyone used to that kind of missive could decipher. Most important of all, he was popular with the Ona and consequently proved a great acquisition.

The Ona were not suited to the humdrum work around the new homestead, but fortunately there was plenty for them to do without condemning them to that. When their hands had hardened, many of them became—if not artists—good workmen with the axe, which they always preferred to shovel work. They liked to get on with the job and would work hard at fencing, taking a pride in the amount they had been able to do. Some of the younger men, being strong and fearless, were, after a few years, even training colts by contract, and many worked at contract fencing, doing very well indeed with less and less supervision. Some of the older men found a way of making all the money they required to supply their modest needs by hunting the young guanaco for their skins in late spring and early summer. When taken before they are a fortnight old, these little animals [1] have very soft fur, which fetches a good price with the furriers. The men found they could put in a month at this congenial occupation, then, after helping us at the sheep-gathering and shearing, go off in the late summer, when the guanaco were fat, to hunt in the mountains and initiate their youths into the mysteries of the *Hain*.

From the very beginning, I saw the need for them to learn the use and value of money, especially after one poor fellow had presented himself at the store with an important, official-looking, but utterly worthless piece of paper that he had received from some unscrupulous white man in exchange for a valuable fox-skin robe. Of course they knew nothing about keeping accounts and so were sure to suspect that they were being cheated unless they were paid every evening in cash for their day's work. We paid those who worked well more than the lazy ones and something was discounted from those who habitually turned up unduly late. Whenever possible we gave them contract work, either cutting firewood by measurement, building up log fences, or digging drains. Some of them excelled at contract shearing.

In this way, they earned very good money, for we paid them exactly the same as white men were receiving throughout the country for similar work. The Indians found that, by working hard, they could make enough money to keep them in everything they needed through the winter.

All the stock work of the farm, which, a few years later, carried a standing flock of over 80,000 sheep, with the yearly increase bringing the total up to 120,000, was done entirely by Ona. Halimink, Talimeoat, Ishtohn and many other old friends were permanently employed as shepherds. If they wished to take a short holiday, they would duly advise us, perhaps suggesting one of their own countrymen to fill their post till their wander-lust had been satisfied for the time being.

Our leading shepherd was now Martin, the man who had imperson-

---

[1] The Ona name for the little guanaco is *toül*, both vowels being clearly and separately sounded. Throughout Patagonia they are known as *chulengos*.

ated *Short* at the initiation of K-Wamen into the *Hain*.   There is a story about him that is worth recounting here.   When still a lad, Martin had been caught with a party of Ona companions driving off a flock of sheep from the Primera Argentina farm.   All but two of these offenders had been sent to the mission.   The exceptions—two likely young fellows, one of them Martin—had been transferred to a farm on the north shore of the Magellan Straits.   A certain Mr. Kemp had been the kindly and able manager of the place and, under his tuition, those lads had grown into excellent shepherds, gaining renown even among the Scottish shepherds whom that company always employed on account of their good work with sheep and dogs.

After some years, Martin returned to La Primera Argentina.   Now grown into a man of medium height, he liked to be clean and well dressed, so was rather a dandy and only returned to his native state on the occasion of Lodge meetings.   Generally there was a thin smile on his face, as though he were amused at the useless chatter of the others.   He spoke seldom himself and was too silent and taciturn to be called good-natured. He understood Spanish and English, speaking the latter with a strong Scots accent, but liked best to use his native Ona tongue.   He never attempted to show off his Spanish or English, which he used only when addressing some curt order to his dog.

Back on the Rio Grande farm, Martin got a job as shepherd and was given a shanty about fifteen miles south-east of the head station.   Our bullock carts, on their way from Viamonte to the port with wool, passed within a mile of this shanty;   and Martin had the bright idea that his winter supplies could be brought back from Rio Grande on the returning empty carts and so save him the trouble of going for them with pack-horses.   Mr. McInch agreed to this arrangement and, knowing that Martin could neither read nor write, humorously suggested that he should send a letter by one of our carters, listing the things he needed for the winter.   This Martin solemnly promised to do.

Time passed till one day a carter—as illiterate as Martin himself— presented Mr. McInch with a sheet of paper covered with continuous wavy lines, not unlike a very hastily scribbled note.   The manager studied the missive with the utmost gravity, then, without betraying the slightest amusement, went to the store, where a number of men were working.   There he commenced to recite, as if reading from Martin's letter, a list of articles that, as he knew from experience, Martin would be sure to require.

Martin's reputation was made. Soon everyone knew that he really could write long letters that his boss had no difficulty in deciphering.

Some while later Martin asked to be paid off and applied to me for a job. As I disliked taking men from my neighbours, I enquired of Mr. McInch whether he objected. Answering in his usual expressive language, which no publisher would care to print, he told me that the fellow wanted a wife and that as he was not going to have women hanging about his shepherds' shanties, he would be very glad to get rid of him. So that was that.

In a country half covered with forest or thicket, we had found shepherding a job well suited to the Ona. They had, nevertheless, a great deal to learn about handling sheep and training sheep-dogs, so knowing that Martin was well qualified to teach them, we welcomed him and gave him a permanent post. In due course he found happiness in the arms of the daughter of Puppup by the wife whose husband Puppup had murdered long ago.

A month or two later, I was working with Martin and some other Ona at a brushwood fence some twenty miles from home. While we were so engaged, something called me back to the Estancia Viamonte and I departed hurriedly, leaving Martin in charge. I was absent longer than I had expected, and one day a messenger arrived from the encampment with a pack-horse. He handed me a closely scribbled sheet from Martin. I scrutinized the paper, then, forgetting all about the previous letter episode, handed it back with the indiscreet remark :

" This is not writing at all. I cannot read a word of it. What does Martin want? "

The messenger folded the letter and put it away with as much care as if it had been a bank-note. Taking up the cudgels in defence of his fellow countryman, he said scornfully :

" How is it that his other boss could read his letters perfectly and that you are unable to do so? Martin writes very well."

In a milder tone he then enumerated certain tools, nails of different sizes, and provisions such as sugar, coffee, flour and rice; but he forgot needles and thread—and, alas! tobacco, which, above all else, Martin yearned for. When the messenger returned with his pack-horse to the encampment and the stores were unpacked, Martin said with much annoyance :

" Where are the tobacco, needles and thread that I mentioned in my letter? "

"I gave your letter to Lanushwaiwa," answered the envoy, "but he said it was not writing, and he could not read it."

Flabbergasted, Martin realized how they had all been deceived in me! The story spread and soon, in the same way as he had gained his reputation, I lost mine.

Later on, talking the matter over with Martin, I found that he would take a sheet of paper, think earnestly of the things he wanted to say, and scribble away, believing that his thoughts were thus transcribed on the paper and that an intelligent eye and brain would translate them into words. As he had arrived at so satisfactory a conclusion, I did not attempt to prove that Mr. McInch had made a fool of him, but humbly accepted my defeat.

2

The combined farms at Viamonte covered just over 254,000 acres, which were completely fenced in. This area was divided by natural boundaries such as streams and lakes, but these were not secure in winter, when the animals could cross the ice and stray for miles; so, little by little, division fences had to be made. Even then one of the fields had an area of fourteen square leagues—nearly 90,000 acres. It was half covered with wooded hills and intersected by valleys with numberless narrow streams running through them. These streams, except where there were fords, or bridges had been made, were very nasty traps for sheep. In attempting to jump over them, the weaker animals fell in and, as the banks were overhanging, could not scramble out again.

When 20,000 woollies were scattered over such an area and left undisturbed for a time, it was some task to round them up. An army of thirty or more men, with horses and dogs, would spend the night at the far corner of this vast field. They would kill and eat a couple of sheep and be ready to begin at daybreak. An early start was essential, because, as the sun grew hot, sheep were inclined to linger in the shade of the thickets. It was as well, therefore, to move them as far as possible before noon, then, when the afternoon grew cooler, keep right on till nightfall. When the drive began, the men would have to scatter right across the whole territory, then slowly beat through it. Moving down so wide an expanse, their horizon would be generally limited by forest and they would not be able to keep one another in sight; yet none must get too far ahead of the others, or the sheep would be turned back. The Ona were splendid for gathering the flocks in those large fields, seeming by instinct to know where their companions were; but even so, in the wooded parts many sheep would remain, and the thickets had to be combed time after time.

Before long there were over a hundred sheep-dogs belonging to the Ona shepherds employed on the farm. Some of these dogs were outstanding in sagacity and skill. One, whose name was Ben, thought out for himself a most useful branch of the business, in which, as it came natural to him, he soon greatly excelled. Ben belonged to me, but as I had other dogs, he seemed to think he was not wanted and began to keep so far from the flock that frequently neither sheep nor shepherd knew where he was.

At the big gatherings, Ben would work absolutely on his own. He would often turn up after all the rest had arrived at their halting place, bringing with him a bunch of sheep that we had left behind in the country we imagined had been thoroughly combed. When driving a little flock, if Ben found some shepherd on the way, he would turn over the bunch to him and then go tearing back over the land we had been clearing, as if he had urgent business to attend to there. Perhaps he would not be seen again till late in the evening, then, when we were seated around our camp-fire, preparing our supper or even turning in, he might appear with another bunch from the cleared land behind. When his charges had joined the bleating flocks, either in an enclosure or guarded in some suitable spot, Ben would come to the encampment tired out and lie down for the night with my other dogs, as near to me as he could squeeze.

Dogs under orders were generally more useful, yet I never saw another dog who could plan his work as Ben did and carry it through on his own. Every evening on these drives, more than one shepherd would tell how Ben had appeared with some bunch of sheep, had delivered them over almost ostentatiously and immediately raced off in search of more. Except on these occasions, no one ever saw the dog at all. Probably he found it irksome to be told what to do when he knew so well what was wanted.

In one place there was a swampy flat over half a league wide, with several streams winding through it. We had made a track across this, with numbers of log bridges over the worst places, and were taking a large number of sheep through it. These should have been held up and taken across in small bunches. Alternatively someone should have gone ahead to turn the leaders to the left after they had crossed the last bridge and landed on the hills beyond, which were largely covered with forest. As things were, something had delayed both me and my leading Ona shepherd, Martin, so that when we arrived at the entrance to the first bridge, a line of sheep over a mile long was already streaming across the valley. Except by using the bridges, it was impossible to cross on horseback, and the reeds were so long in swampy places that Martin feared even his best dog, Gaucho, could not get past that bunch and wheel them before they took to the woods. If we had attempted to hurry them at all, they would have crowded the narrow bridges and many would have fallen into the streams, so Martin and I had to stand helplessly by, watching the leading sheep pouring over the farther bridge and scattering up the hill beyond towards their beloved forest.

Then suddenly something happened; the sheep were turning to the left along the track we wanted them to follow, and the foremost were fleeing from the woods that crowned the hill as though the Devil himself had rushed out upon them.

"There goes Ben!" my companion exclaimed.

I had to use my field-glasses before I could pick him out. He worked like the hero he was till the leading shepherds were able to get across with their dogs and take over the job, then he again disappeared into the woods. When he turned up at the encampment at supper-time, he was complimented and patted. I hope and believe that he understood the reason why.

3

Dogs, we all know, are wonderfully intelligent, but I have one tale to show that sometimes one may appeal successfully to the thinking powers even of a mule.

One winter I had occasion to go from Viamonte to Punta Arenas. At that time of year no steamer touched at Rio Grande, so I determined to cross overland to Porvenir and take ship from there across the Straits. Unfortunately mid-winter was long past, the ice in river and stream was breaking up and the track was at its worst, so I chose a single trusty mule, shod with spikes, and started off.

The Rio Grande at its mouth was full of broken ice. When the tide from the ocean commences to rise, there is no current there; so I crossed in a small, two-oared ferry-boat, with the mule swimming astern. Farther on I would have to cross the Rio Chico, which I hoped might be frozen higher up. I found it in flood and full of drifting ice.

I had heard that a light bridge of board, hanging from fencing wire, had been constructed at a point where the river flowed between rocks and was under fifty feet wide. Sheep could cross it in single file, but I had been given to understand that it was out of the question to attempt a crossing with a horse. Nevertheless, I determined to examine it for myself. I rode along on the hill some distance from the river and finally saw the bridge. Putting my mule at a trot, I went straight towards it as though intending to cross at once.

The animal, as I expected he would, gave a snort of apprehension and stopped dead when he saw what lay before him. Had I applied whip and spur, I might have killed that mule without getting him on the bridge. Instead I gently slipped off and fastened the strong halter—which was attached to the head-stall—to the bridge. This structure was not over eighteen inches wide across the bottom and had a couple of boards at either side to keep sheep from falling into the river. The fencing wire supporting it was suspended from four posts, two on each side of the river, and the bridge swung about considerably.

Leaving the mule tied there, where he could not help but see me, I crossed to the other bank, strolled about for a few minutes, then returned, unsaddled him and carried the saddle over. I repeated the crossing several times, soothing the animal each time I came back to him. At last my strategy produced the desired effect. From the other side of the river, I saw the mule prick up his ears and display interest. I went back and gently took in all possible slack on the halter, whilst carefully keeping a turn on the strut to which I had secured it. Finally the mule, suspecting my intention, gave a mighty heave backwards. Strut and halter held, so, abandoning resistance, he followed me across the bridge, trembling with anxiety and crouching low, apparently in the hope that this would make him lighter.

I would never have tried to get a horse across that bridge. Even had I been foolish enough to make such an attempt, I would certainly not have wasted time walking backwards and forwards over it myself to convince him it was safe. I much prefer a horse to a mule, one reason for my preference being that the mule thinks and understands too much to make him a willing and obedient slave to man.

4

I once had a little mare resembling a well-grown Exmoor pony. She was one of that bunch of wild horses we had caught on Picton Island [1]

[1] These were known locally as the *Agua Fresca* breed and were greatly valued in the days when tracks were bad. A consignment of them had been sent by the Chilean government to Punta Arenas. Years later, when I was going over the Royal stud at Madrid, it occurred to me that the *Agua Fresca* were descendants of the Moorish ponies, which they greatly resembled. Their ancestors had doubtless been brought over to South America by the Spaniards.

and, at that time, had never had a colt.   I bought her from the old home-stead for fifteen Argentine *pesos*—just over a pound sterling—and when, years later, I was offered the fantastic price of five hundred *pesos* for her, I refused to let her go.   After we had acquired her, she became a mother, and before departing this life produced a fine string of young ones, though I do not believe that any of her offspring could possibly have been her equal.

This little mare figured in an incident that happened soon after I had completed the track from Harberton to Najmishk.   Señor Lopez Sanchez, who had succeeded Señor Pessoli as Chief-of-Police of the Rio Grande district, was anxious to come through this track and go on horseback to Ushuaia for the first time.   I agreed to meet him near a point known as Cape Maria, some fifteen miles south of the Rio Grande settlement. I kept the appointment on the mare.   When the police party came galloping up, I must have.looked to them like an overgrown Sancho Panza on his donkey.   They themselves were all splendidly mounted on well-grown, well-fed animals.   Among their spare horses was a fine-looking beast, intended for the Governor at Ushuaia.

Lopez Sanchez cast a critical glance at my little mount and said with a smile :

" That animal will never carry you across the mountains at the rate we need to go.   You are welcome to one of ours."

I declined with thanks, thinking my own thoughts.

In those days I always wore moccasins and had the habit, when travelling on a tame horse, of dismounting without checking him as he trotted or ambled along.   This I did by throwing my right leg over his neck and landing beside him face forward, as city men jump off a moving bus.   I would then run beside him, perhaps for a mile, with one hand on the saddle or holding a stirrup.   To remount I would take advantage of the jerk every cavalryman knows a horse will give and would vault on the horse's back without altering his pace.   This gave each of us a rest in turn.

I adopted this procedure on that trip with the police.   As we got deeper into the wooded hills with rather marshy valleys between, those heavier animals from the open prairie found it impossible to keep pace with my little mare, and it was clear that their riders had revised their opinion of her.   On the morning of the third day we came to the edge of the slide or *tumbadero* described in an earlier chapter.   There had been a fair rainfall the night before, but the mare knew the procedure well and, gathering her hind legs under her, shot down the slope in splendid style with me, bursting with conceit, on her back.

It took the others a long time to induce their horses to start and, when they did come down, it was in the most undignified positions. They emerged liberally plastered with mud. By this time the horse that was being taken over specially for the Governor had grown thoroughly disgusted with the whole business; and, as we approached the moor called Spion Kop and the track became very steep, he determined to commit suicide. His first attempt failed, for though he flung himself off the track without any warning, he landed on a patch of winter snow and slid down it onto slippery moss. He was then led over the divide and freed when going down the south side, where the path ran along a ridge, with a small gorge and stream on the left and the boggy moor on the right. But this fine animal was evidently still set on ending it all. Suddenly leaving the plainly marked track, he plunged over the edge of the gorge into the stream, some twenty feet below.

The water broke his fall and he landed safely on his feet. Nearby was a track made by guanaco in their habitual crossings of the little gully. I took the saddle off my mare and coaxed her down this track into the pool at the bottom, hoping to convince the big horse that life was worth living, in spite of the rough road we had to travel. I threw a lasso over his neck and, drawing him to one side, put a head-stall on him. The other end of the lasso I threw up to the police, then—just to show the horse how it should be done—I gave the mare a pat so that she rushed at the bank and scrambled up to the top. It cost her an effort and I felt that the big fellow would never do it.

The Chief-of-Police said with reason :

" Better shoot him and let us go on."

However, I thought there was just a chance of saving the animal. Having tied two lassos together, I sent the men farther down stream to haul away when told, and drove the beast over the edge of the next fall, which must have been over thirty feet high. The rocks under the rushing water were polished smooth and the animal shot over them and out of sight, diving into the pool below. From this he waded down stream and landed safely. He had lost one front tooth and cut his mouth a little, but reached Ushuaia without further accident.

I have seen only two horses deliberately attempt to escape from their troubles in this way. Angry colts will sometimes throw themselves violently down without caring what happens to them, but it is done in blind rage, not with premeditation.   I have never seen a cow or a mule go to its death intentionally.   On the other hand, sheep not uncommonly commit suicide.   Several times I have observed a sheep stand on a cliff and, after gazing round, as though for a last look at the land it had decided to quit, spring out into space to certain death.

CHAPTER FORTY-NINE

Pedro Barrientos Settles his Accounts.   The Story of Arevalo.

I

ONE YEAR, AS WINTER WAS APPROACHING, WHEN THE SWALLOWS HAD ALL flown north and the geese were leaving the country, the families at Viamonte were all preparing to follow their example and spend a few months elsewhere. Alice was reluctant to leave me alone, but I felt she would enjoy a holiday in the wide, interesting world, so insisted that she should accompany the others. I was, in fact, sorely tempted to go as well; it would be much pleasanter than spending the winter alone in that big house. It would seem all the bigger and emptier after they had gone, and far more lonely than any makeshift encampment in the snowy woods. Besides, there was nothing much to be done during the months to follow. The sheep were on their winter pastures, with reliable Ona shepherds looking after them. The store was well stocked with all the necessities of life—and even some of the luxuries: tobacco, cigarettes, gramophones, records, concertinas and alarm-clocks. We had never allowed any kind of intoxicating drink to be sold in the settlement. The nearest place where it could be obtained was a *boliche* or saloon, twenty-five miles away beyond the Rio Grande, which happily had no bridge across it at that time and was very dangerous to ford.

In the winter months there would be no moving of stock, and no travellers were likely to pass near Viamonte. There was not much to worry about, especially as the Ona feuds were now a thing of the past. Yet there remained one vital problem to be solved: whom could we leave in charge of our precious farm? If we employed an outsider, however good he might be, he would be severely handicapped by his lack of knowledge of the country and the people; nor would the people know him. Will was fully occupied at Harberton, and in winter the snow-covered mountain formed an almost impassable barrier. We discussed this important question and reached a conclusion that was unanimous: who better than Pedro Barrientos? semi-illiterate, but honest, resolute and dependable. With this decision made, we passed the Estancia Viamonte into his care. We agreed with Percy that Gastelumendi, the Basque, should look after the store, but was to take his orders from Barrientos while we were away. Arrangements were made with Mr. McInch at La Primera Argentina that Barrientos should be advanced any reasonable sum he might require, but there was to be no supervision from outside.

Pedro Barrientos, as I have mentioned, came from southern Chile. Like most South Americans, Chileans are a people of very mixed race. It is said that the gentlemen and officers of the Spanish invasion, as soon as the state of the country allowed, brought their wives and families from Europe to live with them. The soldiers and poorer settlers, however, were unable to afford this indulgence, so chose their wives from among the natives they had conquered, or, as in the case of the Chilean Araucanos, from among those whom they had failed to subdue. To-day in Chile there are descendants of all the European nations, but while some of the old families are of the purest Spanish blood, the mass of the people, including some high officials, are strongly mixed with aboriginal stock, which, in some instances, hides all trace of their European ancestry. In the pedigree of these half-breed families are many native fathers, with the result that Indian names are not uncommon. Barrientos, though he had a Spanish name, was a good specimen of this intermixture.

Not wishing to offend him, I offered him no rise in salary on our departure. I simply asked him, as a friend might do, to take care of the place while we were away.

I was absent from Tierra del Fuego for nearly four months. I toured Europe. I reached Norway through Italy, Switzerland and Germany, then returned *via* France and Spain to Lisbon, where I took ship for South America. I was the first of the family to get back to Tierra del Fuego. In Rio Grande I met Kautush, our boss carter from Viamonte—that same Kautush who, as a lad, had prodded his enemy to death with a blunt arrow. When I asked him how things were going at Viamonte, he answered :

" The weather has been fine, few sheep have died, but Barrientos is very thin."

" Is he ill? " I enquired.

" I do not think so," said Kautush, " but he never sleeps. He works all day and walks about all night. He seems afraid that someone will steal the houses and longs very much for you to come back."

I arrived at Viamonte. Barrientos, though he seemed to have aged somewhat, did not look as bad as I had been led to believe. After going over the place with him and hearing what I thought had been his major difficulties during my absence, I told him how pleased I was with his stewardship and that we wished him to accept a bonus of fifty pounds. He answered decidedly:

" No, *Patrón*. I am quite satisfied with my salary and am very proud that you trusted me and left me in charge while you were away. If I accepted that money, it would spoil it all."

I replied: "That is a very small part of what we owe you, Barrientos. I will gladly make it one hundred and still be in your debt."

He answered again: " No, *Patrón*, that would make matters worse. I don't want anything."

When I saw that he really preferred not to accept the gift, I did not press it on him any more. We sat there talking for a while and it was late when he rose to go to his little house nearby.

" Tell me, *Patrón*," he said as he took his leave, " have you taken over the management now? Am I in the same position as before you went away? "

I saw that something was troubling him.

" You are," I told him, " except that I owe you a big debt of gratitude and you will not let me pay even a part of it."

He said no more, but I noticed a grim look on his face as he turned on his heel and went out. It was not till the next morning, when I went on my rounds, that I understood the meaning of that look. One of the first men I met asked me if I had seen the Basque that morning. Feeling something was wrong, I hurried to the store.

Gastelumendi had never been a handsome man, but now his lips would have been noticeable on a West African negro. With both eyes discoloured and his nose like an over-ripe pear, he was almost unrecognizable. I cannot repeat here the language he used as he mumbled his version of the brutal attack that " savage " Barrientos had made on him and the revenge he would take through the law. He asked to be paid off at once, as he would not stop a day longer among such barbarians.

I met Barrientos shortly afterwards and said as sternly as I could to a man I liked so well:

" Why did you beat up that wretched little fellow so savagely, Barrientos? "

" While you were away, *Patrón*," he answered, " *el Basco* continually held me up to ridicule before the men, never losing a chance to prove, when there were witnesses, that I was an utterly incompetent and ignorant fool. He referred to me—and addressed me—with exaggerated politeness as ' Señor Don Pedro Barrientos ' or ' el Señor Administrador '. He showed clearly that it was he who was the educated man who would have been left in charge but for the favouritism of the *patrón*.

" I knew," Barrientos went on, " that I could not manage without him. I could not keep the accounts and dole out rations, so I just had to push my hands deep into my pockets and keep them there, when they were itching to knock him to pieces. When you told me last night, however, that you were now in charge and that I was just one of your workmen as before, I felt the time had come for me to settle up with him."

What could I say? In spite of his having made such a ferocious onslaught on so miserable an object as the Basque, Barrientos was a sportsman. I believe he expected to be discharged, in which case his refusal to take the money I had offered him was all the more astonishing. But the idea of dismissing him was very far from my mind. When, later on, Despard and Tina engaged a lovely little nurse from Portugal to look after the children, Barrientos soon fell in love with her and asked her to be his wife. Knowing a good man when she met one, she accepted.

2

There is another study in loyalty to be recorded before my story is done.

One afternoon in spring a man on foot turned up at the Estancia Viamonte. He was darker than an Ona and had that inscrutable yet watchful look one often sees on the faces of men who have been hunted. He came up to me without hesitating and, though he spoke most respectfully, there was in his mien the almost insolent dignity of those men from the wide, free lands of the northern Argentine. His manner seemed to imply:

" You have the money, boss, but as a man I am your equal, if not your superior."

When I looked at him I felt there might be something in that notion, for he stood almost six feet tall and, in spite of his powerful frame, was lithe and active. For the breadth of his shoulders, his head was small and, if his face reminded me of some bird of prey, his movements were more like those of a leopard pacing up and down behind the bars of his cage. In a sheath thrust diagonally through the front of his sash was a huge knife almost as big as a sword, with the hilt of it close to his right hand.

WILL.
Taken at Viamonte by his daughter.

Miles of swampy moor near the track to Najmishk. Here we carried the sedan-chair to avoid steeper gradients near the streams.

He told me his name was Arevalo, and that he had walked over from Ushuaia.

"You will be hungry," I said. "You had better go to the cook-house and tell the cook I sent you."

"I saw the cook-house door open and went in," he replied. "The cook fed me well and sent me on to you."

I felt sure that he was an escaped or discharged convict looking for a job, always with the idea of getting north to the land of his childhood or the scenes of his former exploits.

"What can I do for you?" I asked.

"I am, sir, a discharged convict from Ushuaia, but not one of those miserable thieves and cheats who are being sent there nowadays. My only crime was that I killed a man in self-defence, and he was as well armed as I."

Now I remembered having heard of this man long ago. He was said to be a really hard case. He had escaped from Staten Island before the general rising of the convicts there and, for a long time, had been given up for dead. I felt he must have had some terrible experiences and so I encouraged him to tell me his story. I invited him to sit down with me on a heap of firewood that lay near. I began by asking him if he had been to Staten Island as well as Ushuaia.

He then told me how he had escaped from the prison and found his way to the south-west part of the island, where he had lived on seal for many months, hoping that some passing vessel might pick him up. When his matches had been exhausted, he had tried to keep a fire banked up, but at last it had gone out and he had been reduced to continuously wet garments and to eating his seal flesh raw. The coast was so steep and rugged that sometimes he had taken to the water and swum, rather than try to scramble along the shore. At last a vessel had passed close enough to see him and, the weather having been calm, a boat had been sent to take him off.

"I tried," Arevalo continued, "to make the captain believe I was a shipwrecked sailor, but how could I, who knew nothing about the sea, deceive him? When we passed an Argentine vessel, he treacherously gave me up to them—and shortly afterwards I found myself in the penal settlement at Ushuaia. Among the prisoners there I discovered some of my old jail-mates from Staten Island. They told me how they had revolted after I had made my escape."

On one of the great feast days of this patriotic Republic, Arevalo, with many other prisoners who had behaved well, had been given his freedom. For some time he had worked at Ushuaia, but had soon begun to long for his native land in the province of Corrientes, near the Argentine–Paraguayan frontier. Hearing of our track through the mountains, which was now in frequent use, he had come by it to Viamonte, in the hope of working his way back, little by little, to his distant home some two thousand miles away.

Arevalo slept that night at Viamonte. When we met next day I offered him a temporary job, warning him seriously as to his conduct towards the Ona. As tactfully as possible, I suggested that he should carry his great knife behind, where it would look less fearsomely aggressive.

" The bravest man," I said, " is he who draws his weapon last. If ever you feel angry, fold your arms tightly across your chest and hold on—like this."

He agreed with my remarks and, thanking me for them—with a flicker of a smile in which there may have been a little scorn at my simplicity—at once changed the place of his knife, remarking as he did so that in his province it was customary to carry the bush-knife in front. I took this opportunity to say that, whatever his past might have been, he had certainly paid for it; and I assured him that the thought of it would never cross my mind again. I strongly recommended to him that if he should ever feel a grievance against me, or anyone else on the farm, he was not to nurse it, but to come to me and talk it over.

Arevalo worked for us for over a year. He proved himself to be a loyal and willing fellow. As soon as I won his confidence he told me, bit by bit, the lurid story of his life. I am afraid that his killing of a man " in self-defence " was not by any means the only thing he had done to earn a life sentence on Staten Island. At first I had feared that he might disregard my advice and make trouble with the Indians, but I never heard any complaints from them about him. Some of his fellow-workers, however, regarded him with apprehension. When excited, he would tell them stories of crimes in which he had participated, with a wealth of vivid and hair-raising detail that shocked his listeners. He and I worked together, sometimes in the water, building timber bridges across streams, and I had an opportunity to notice that his fine athletic body was covered with scars. These he attributed either to knife wounds incurred in fights of long ago, or to the rough treatment he had received when a prisoner.

As civilization advanced, there had been strikes among the workers on

some of the farms to the north.   These naturally took place at shearing-
time, when they were most harmful to the employers.

One day, while I was working on a job near the homestead—as
roughly clad and toil-stained as any of the men with me—two well-
dressed strangers approached.   I guessed at once that they were professional agitators and had come on no friendly errand.   I watched them
out of the corner of my eye as they went up to two of my helpers, who
seemed amused at their opening remarks and pointed in my direction.
The visitors then walked across to me and, after being unnecessarily
apologetic for not having recognized me as the *patrón*, asked for permission to turn their horses loose in the field and remain on the place till
the following day.   This request, of course, was never refused to a
passer-by.   These men, however, sought an additional favour—and one
they found a little difficult to put into words.   Ultimately one of them
said :

" We want to give a lecture to the men and would be grateful if we
could hold a meeting in the club."

" The club," I answered, " has been built for the men.   If I wished to
use it myself, I should feel obliged to ask their permission, so I cannot give
it to visitors.   The men will probably consent to your using it if you ask
them."

There were, at that time, about eighty men in the settlement, among
them some forty Ona, most of whom understood a great deal of Spanish.
The same evening, when work was over, they crowded into the club to
hear what the visitors had to say.   One of these two orators waxed
eloquent over the crimes of the money-grabbing, capitalistic employers
and pointed out the sum each bale of wool was worth in England—without dwelling, of course, on the expense of running the farm and getting
the produce to the distant market.   He finished his discourse by saying
that their employers were robbing them.

This was too much for Arevalo.   Quite forgetting my advice, he
suddenly went berserk, rushed at the speaker and with blood-curdling
curses called on him to come outside and be disembowelled.   Then,
drawing his enormous knife, he struck him across the face with the flat
of it.   Never did a meeting end more abruptly.   The lecturers took to
their heels and fled for their lives.

I never mentioned this incident to Arevalo, being far too pleased to
want to rebuke him for his little outburst, yet it seemed to have preyed on
his mind, for shortly afterwards he asked for his money, saying he must

go to his home in the far north. He probably realized how very near he had been to qualifying for a second life sentence. Later I heard that he had reached Santa Cruz, a coastal town in Patagonia, where he had stopped for some time, until one day, when drunk, he had become violent and had been shot dead by a police officer.

Poor wild, faithful Arevalo.

CHAPTER FIFTY

The Champion Shearers. Metet, Son of Aneki, Beats All Comers. The End of Ahnikin. Minkiyolh Goes on his Last Hunting Trip.

I

ANEKI, WHO HAD BEEN MY MENTOR AT THE TIME OF MY INCEPTION INTO the *Hain*, had two sons, Doihei and Metet. Doihei, the elder, was nearly six feet tall and of sturdy build, exceedingly strong and a splendid worker. We put him in charge of the circular-saw bench, at first cutting up fire-wood, but later sawing boards for buildings. With what pride he watched the saw rushing through the timber! As Viamonte grew larger, a second saw-mill was bought and installed there; and we introduced machine-shears driven by the same engine as the saw.

Shearing was our harvest, a time of great activity, when all energy was devoted to getting on with the job as speedily and as well as possible, in order to get the sheep back to their pastures and to start the wool on its way to the distant market. The fact that, besides their ample, well-prepared meals in the cook-house, the shearers—both Chilote and Ona—received approximately a pound for every hundred sheep shorn, was enough to encourage them to do all they could. For those grown-up children, the Ona, an even greater incentive than money was pride in their speed and good work. Racing, with no regard for quality of workmanship, was frowned upon. A careless shearer will cut the sheep or leave too much wool on it. I was especially insistent that apprentices should shear clean and with no cuts. Had they been allowed to start badly, they would never have made good shearers.

The shearing-shed, with its steam-engine and whistle to summon the eager workers, and the long floor on which they vied with each other in skill and speed, was a scene of striking bustle as compared with the normally quiet routine of the Viamonte homestead. For the full length of the inside walls of the shed ran the two shearing-boards, one on each side. Each of these boards was about seven feet wide and on it the shearers worked side by side. Opening onto it were a series of small enclosures fitted with self-closing doors. Each shearer had his own en-closure, which held about a dozen unshorn sheep and was refilled by a shepherd from larger enclosures running down the middle of the shed as soon as the last of the bunch had been removed by the shearer and placed on the shearing-board. The machine-shears were driven by an overhead shaft. A sheep did not have to be tied for shearing, nor firmly held; either restriction made it inclined to struggle.

In the main wall of the building, opposite each enclosure, was a window and below it a door giving access to a chute that led down into a corresponding enclosure outside the building. The shorn sheep were put by the shearer on the chute, down which they slid into the outside enclosure, where they were counted every two or three hours by the man in charge. A sheep badly cut or carelessly shorn was not credited to the shearer, and if either fault occurred frequently, he was liable to be reprimanded or fired. To facilitate the work of counting and crediting, every shearer and every door and enclosure bore a number. The fleeces were collected from the shearing-board by boys, who ran off with them to the sorting-table, where they were rolled up and put into the wool-press, from which they emerged in bales, each bound with iron hoops and weighing between four and six hundredweight.

There were twenty-four shearers in the shed, most of them Ona. Doihei, after his first year, was one of the best of them, and certainly the fastest. When in the evening the count was written up on a board, he would be ten or even twenty sheep ahead of the rest, and his animals were beautifully shorn. The sheep were nearly all of Romney Marsh breed, large creatures with smooth skins, much easier to shear than the smaller, but wrinkled, Merinos.

Metet was a good deal younger than his brother. He must have been less than eighteen when he started as a shearer. Somewhat taller than Doihei and of lighter build, he seldom spoke and habitually wore a slightly amused smile on his face, as though he were quite sure of himself and in no hurry. He always looked as if he were not trying. He would come to the shearing floor a little late, when the others already had two or three sheep to their credit, look out of his window for a moment or two, leisurely take off his coat, and at last settle down to work. In his second season, he shot well ahead of his wonderful brother. He worked so efficiently and with such little effort that one day when we were shearing ewes I said to him, knowing that he would not sacrifice quality for speed:

"Why don't you try to-morrow and see how many ewes you can do?"

Putting his hand to the small of his back, Metet answered solemnly:

"I am not at all strong, and when I work hard my back aches."

Ewes, when living in the open country, generally have bare bellies and little wool on their lower legs. They are, therefore, easier to shear than dry sheep—that is, rams, wethers and young females that have not yet reached the lambing stage. A good, experienced shearer can average a hundred and twenty dry sheep a day, and probably as many as a hundred and fifty ewes. The next day, in a little under eight hours of actual work, Metet reached a total of three hundred and twenty-nine well-shorn ewes. The rush seemed infectious, for Doihei reached the three hundred mark and two or three others sheared as many as two hundred and fifty.

Thirty-five miles away from Viamonte, on the north side of the Rio Grande, was another of the truly magnificent farms belonging to the Menendez Behety family. It was known as La Segunda Argentina and was under separate management from La Primera Argentina on the south side of the river. I believe that La Segunda Argentina then accounted at shearing-time for nearly two hundred thousand sheep. Among some thirty-six shearers in their employment was a Yugoslav who was famous throughout the country for his fast shearing. Young Metet's renown spread and, when the Segunda Argentina shearing was finished, a party of men, including the Yugoslav, came down to Viamonte on horseback to see if there was any truth in the story. They were all prepared to back their champion and very big wagers were spoken of.

Before anything concrete was arranged, however, the Yugoslav, having watched with much interest our Ona at work, asked for permission to use the machine beside Metet and work there for a little while. And it was work indeed! The Yugoslav's teeth gritted audibly as the shears flew through the wool. Metet well knew what it was all about and lost no time, yet that self-confident smile never left his face. Twenty well-shorn sheep shot down each of those little slides in less than thirty minutes, then the visitor joined his friends again, while Metet went on with his day's work. The white champion said openly:

" It is quite useless. I was working all out, and I am certain that Indian wasn't really trying."

For over twenty years those brothers came to every shearing and, though closely followed by Doihei, never once was Metet beaten, nor did the quality of his work deteriorate. They were both quiet, inoffensive fellows and often, to supplement their earnings, took on a job of contract fencing, Doihei always being the leader and spokesman for the pair. One day in 1935, far off in the forest, they quarrelled. I do not think there was a woman in the case, but I am afraid they had both been drinking, and those Indians become very nasty when intoxicated. They wounded each other with their revolvers and Dohei died from the effects. Metet, I have heard, was shot later by a low-class white man.

2

Many years before the pitiful ending of those two magnificent brothers, there was another shooting affray in which were involved the only two Ona of whom I was ever afraid—one, as I have said, for his badness, the other for his madness.

The woods had assumed their gorgeous autumn colours, and after each still, calm day, the frost took hold of the land at sunset. On one of those peaceful nights, Ahnikin was sitting by the fire with his two wives, for he had acquired both Kilehehen's daughters by that time, when a shot rang out in the darkness. Ahnikin fell forward towards the burning embers and the startled women fled into the woods. Nothing more occurred and all was silent, so eventually they returned and found their husband lying unconscious with his left arm roasting on the fire. The bullet had passed through his shoulder blade, coming out through his left breast, and I do not know how it had missed his heart. Needless to say, his arm remained useless for the rest of his life. He never quite recovered from the bullet wound and died about two years later.

No one saw the shot fired, but the culprit was undoubtedly Minki-yolh. He thought it wise to leave the Ona country and hastened to the Catholic Mission beyond Rio Grande with his two wives, Yomsh and Ohmchen (Comb), who had been named by my sisters Small. As polygamy was not encouraged there, Small was taken into the care of the nuns. During his stay at the Mission, Minkiyolh passed himself off as an important chief. He styled himself Captain Minkiyolh Kaushel, but from Rio Grande to the Beagle Channel he had long been known as *el Loco* (the Madman).

After Ahnikin's death, Minkinyolh returned to Viamonte and tried to rejoin his people, but they had not forgotten his past and at a meeting of the Ona men it was decided that he was a crazy wizard and a danger to the community. One day he went hunting with two others, whose names I need not mention. After a time they returned without him, saying that he had gone on to hunt alone in that great forest that fringes the Lake Kami. No one was surprised to hear this, and apparently Minkiyolh is still hunting there, for he has not been seen or heard of since.

CHAPTER FIFTY-ONE

The Sedan-Chair.

AFTER SOME TRYING YEARS IN THE PARAGUAYAN CHACO, MARY BROUGHT her daughter Bertha to spend a summer at Harberton. In the early winter I walked across from Viamonte to enjoy a few days with them in the old home, and then went with Mary and my little niece to Punta Arenas. It was a small vessel and a rough trip, but Mary was splendid. They did not return to Paraguay, but took ship for England. Having seen them off on their long voyage, I started on my shorter but more strenuous one across the Straits and over the snowy hills to Viamonte.

Mary never came back to South America. She made a home with Bertha in Edinburgh, where her second daughter, Mary, was born. They were occasionally visited by Wilfred, when his Mission work took him to the Old Country. In spite of his life of adventurous discomfort in the " Green Hell," I can truthfully write that the woman, as usual, had the harder part to play; and she faced it bravely to the end of her days.

By the beginning of 1910 there were twelve of us at Viamonte. We had been joined by Yekadahby, who had spent the winter in England with others of the family and had returned with them to Viamonte; and we had also been joined by Professor Reynolds, who, on the loss of his wife in Buenos Aires, had retired to our fireside at Viamonte. White-bearded and bald, Professor Reynolds had been one of the three leading professors in the Republic and a final examiner for the Naval and Military Universities.

Alice and I were often away from the homestead and were great chums. From time to time we went across together to Harberton, where we were always sure of a warm welcome. Will had to spend much time among the islands, or on the western lands, where most of our sheep grazed. He had built two cottages in suitable places, so that it was easy in summer-time for his young wife and two children to go with him by boat or cutter and make a home near where his work called him.

With the advancing years, it was not right to expose Mother to unnecessary hardship, of which she had had a full share already, so that

506	UTTERMOST PART OF THE EARTH

even an occasional holiday away from the old homestead was out of the question. We felt that if we could get her over to Viamonte, where there was ample room for all in the big house, there would be more life and movement to interest her than in the quiet home at Harberton.

Mother went for a daily walk of anything up to two miles, but she could not be expected to tramp all the way to Viamonte. There was, therefore, only one way open to her—by sea. Mother had never recovered from the scares she had had long ago, when Father had driven his whale-boat gunwale down wherever duty had seemed to call; and when I now put the suggestion to her, she said she would never go on a steamer again until she embarked on her last trip. She always hoped that she might be buried in an English country churchyard.

So the matter rested until one day at Harberton I said, more in jest than in earnest, that in order to reach Viamonte, Mother need not go on a steamer at all. We would make a tiny room with a small stove and easy chair and she could sit in comfort whilst a party of stalwart Ona carried her little house over the mountains.

Will brought his inventive genius to bear on the subject and his efforts resulted in a contraption which I called the sedan-chair. He made a strong, light platform about five feet long by three feet wide, with little notches to hold firmly the legs of a specially constructed deck-chair, which could be adjusted to all angles, either for sitting or reclining. The platform was swung from a wooden arch shaped like an inverted " U " with its ends turned out. Ropes from each corner of the platform went to a swivel in the centre of this arch. The protruding ends of the arch ran through holes in the carrying poles and were well stayed. With the poles on the bearers' shoulders, the platform swung two feet above the ground, and the whole thing was so constructed that, should one of the bearers drop a foot, the floor would still remain level and suffer an overall drop of only three inches. A tent, any side of which could be opened according to the weather, fitted the sedan-chair closely. Finally there were four sticks like those used for skiing, each about five feet long, with a handle resembling a small crutch at the end to support the carrying poles, so that, when the bearers rested for a few minutes, there would be no need to lay the floor of the chair on uneven ground or soaking bog.

Alice and I arrived at Harberton, where the sedan-chair was duly examined and admired. With us had come from Viamonte seven chosen Ona—among them Halimink, Kankoat, Shaiyutlh (White Moss), Shilchan (Soft Voice), who was the brother of Aneki, and Shishkolh. Halimink's son Nana and another lad came with us to bring back the pack-horses. I do not think I slept at all on the night before we started back for Viamonte. I was haunted by the thought of some wet trips I had made, when snow-storms, which might come on at any time in summer and lasted sometimes for two or three days, had been followed by a thaw so sudden that every mountain stream had been changed into a torrent capable of sweeping a horse off its feet.

But the saying that " most of our troubles are those that never come " proved correct this time. On a perfect summer day we set out for the north. I had determined that this should be a picnic for us all, so we were well supplied with luxuries, the outstanding being condensed milk for coffee in the mornings and cocoa at night, with sugar *ad lib.* and other good things.

I had promised my Ona companions double the usual wage while Mother was with us, with the understanding that if any of them fell, giving the precious chair a jolt, he would forfeit a day's pay. All were agreeable, thinking it a great joke, and, of course, no one was fined. I could hardly have expected those fellows to carry my aged mother, who, though eleven inches shorter than myself, weighed almost as much, with any real pleasure, unless I took a full share of the work myself, so we had two teams of four men to take it in turns as bearers. Alice, who when travelling usually wore moccasins, walked beside the chair to steady its swing with one hand; and Will started off with us with the intention of accompanying us part of the way.

The horse track would have necessitated continual crossing of mountain streams, with consequent going up and down of steep banks, and was, therefore, quite unsuitable for the conveyance of our chair. So we determined to follow the sheep track across the swampy moors, arranging with the pack-horse party where we would meet and pitch camp for the night. It was our intention to camp near Spion Kop on the first night —on no account hurrying or tiring our cherished burden—and, while the weather held fine, enter the shelter of the forest beyond. We knew that there were several places where Mother would have to leave the sedan-chair and walk.

We crossed the Varela river, climbed the hills and after the first few miles of bog came to K-Wheipenohrrh (Naked Ridge or Nose). Before us now lay a lovely picture of winding streams fringed with grass or bushes, and mountain valleys full of bright yellow bog, with clumps of dark evergreen beech trees clinging to the side where the rocks were not so steep. In the background were rock and patches of snow. A short distance away two small streams joined and, in the form of a diminutive waterfall, broke through a narrow gash in the second range.

At this point in our journey, Will, feeling satisfied that his contraption was everything we had hoped, left us and started on a steady run back home. After a convenient rest, we set off again. In order to shorten our journey across a bog ahead, we deemed it best to cross a stream. It ran down a little gully over thirty feet deep, with moss-grown sides of slippery rock and a steep and slimy bank. There was no question of zig-zagging up, so, after crossing the stream, the ascent had to be tackled straight. Mother had, of course, left the chair. If I could have carried her pick-a-back, I might have scrambled up on all fours, grasping roots or stones with my hands, but this kind of manoeuvre had not entered into our agreement, so I had to take her in my arms. On my feet were moccasins, fine for slithering down hills, but with no grip for an upward struggle like the present. My seven companions clustered round me with the utmost goodwill, some pushing and others pulling, and thus Mother was wafted up to the top of the ridge with little effort on my part, as a queen bee is borne aloft by a swarm of willing workers.

Here the chair was requisitioned again. Two miles farther on, where there was a good clump of tall trees, we found our pack-horses waiting. We camped there for the night and enjoyed, before retiring to rest, the unusual treat of hot, sweet cocoa. I remember that cocoa, for ere we reached Viamonte I was to bring down four guanaco at long range with the same number of Winchester bullets. Searching for the reason for this exceptional marksmanship, Shishkolh discovered that it lay in the evening potions of " Kho-kho."

On the second day of our journey we left the valley and ascended a ridge a few feet wide, with a waterfall on our right and scrub and moor stretching away to our left. On we plodded up a long incline that slowly changed from a dry, moss-covered ridge to wet clay and stone from which the winter snow had but recently melted.

Some twelve miles from Harberton, we came to the highest point we had to pass—just over two thousand feet above sea-level. The sky was somewhat overcast, giving a wonderful visibility never attained in bright sunshine. The gloomy sky and the perfect stillness of that barren upland suited our mood, so here we halted.

To the eastward a fine mass of rock rose another eight hundred feet above us. To the north, and still more to the west, higher snow-clad peaks shut off the distant scene. But southward was a marvellous panorama. Mother left her chair and I gave her an arm. We walked with Alice along a stony ridge until we paused and stood near to one another, gazing in silence at the view.

The great moors with their numberless lakes and yellow moss or reeds were broken in many places by outcrops of rock such as No Top, Flat Top and Harberton Mountain, all wooded to a certain height. Beyond these the moors gave place to hilly forest-land and then we could see the irregular shores of the Beagle Channel, with groups of islands scattered around the coasts.

How welcome had been the shelter of those islands, and how beautiful they must have seemed to Mother, when, nearly forty years before, she had stood on the deck of the little Mission vessel, *Allen Gardiner*, with Father beside her and her baby Mary in her arms, and sailed into those land-locked waters.

To the south-eastward, over twenty-five miles away, we could plainly see Picton Island, with the sheltered nook called Banner Cove where in 1871 Mother had seen, for the first time, a Yahgan family in their native state, paddling alongside the vessel in their bark canoe; the same Banner Cove where, twenty years earlier still, Captain Allen Gardiner and his gallant band had waited in vain for the relief vessel, which had arrived too late to save a single one of them.

Beyond Picton lay New Island and, opposite us across the Beagle Channel, Navarin. This last, with its forests and lakes, high moorlands and snow-clad peaks, would have cut off further view had it not been for one wide wooded valley with a great lake in the bottom, which ages ago may have divided the island in two. Through this valley we could see a large expanse of the southern ocean and, blue in the distance, the lonely Wollaston group, of which the southernmost rock is Cape Horn.

In this wild, beautiful land that lay before us, so cold, calm and desolate, Mother had spent the greater part of her life. She had held " Mothers' Meetings " with the Yahgan women; had taught hundreds of them to knit and to perform other household tasks; and had comforted many a dying native or crying child. In addition she had raised her six children, five of whom had been born there, far from the comforts and help demanded by civilized people. She had nursed and solaced a very sick man and had mourned his death like a true wife, carrying on his work and redoubling—if that were possible—her own efforts for their children's good.

Now she knew that she was looking for the last time over that southern world we all loved so well, and the warm pressure of her arm on mine told me that she was thinking of that other arm on which she had leaned so securely during those happy, useful years long past.

It was hard to turn our backs on that picture, but at length I was obliged to break into her reverie. It was growing cold, rain was threatening and our destination still a long way off. We returned to our bearers, crossed a great snow-drift, descended a steep shale slide and, after a mile of bog, reached the edge of the forest.

The entrance to our six-foot track looked like a tunnel. As we advanced along it, bound for Mother's new home some four days' walk away and the wide, wide world beyond, we felt that we had reached the end of a long and strenuous chapter whose earlier anxieties and dangers were more than offset by so many happy memories.

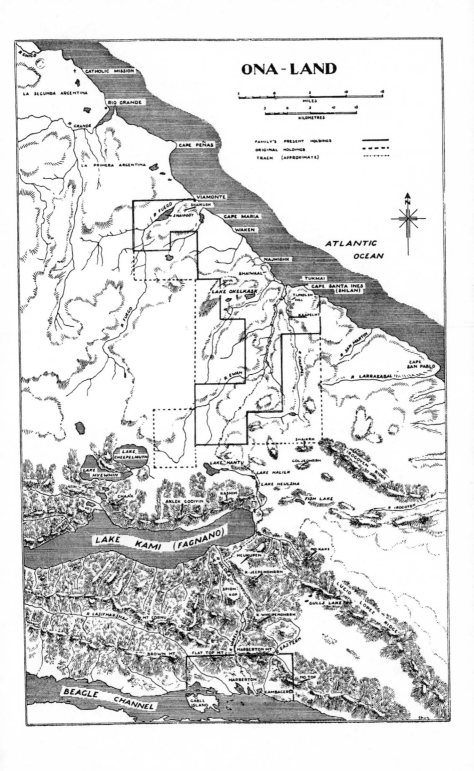

ONA - LAND

MILES

KILOMETRES

FAMILY'S PRESENT HOLDINGS
ORIGINAL HOLDINGS
TRACK (APPROXIMATE)

R. CHICO

CATHOLIC MISSION

LA SEGUNDA ARGENTINA

RIO GRANDE

R. GRANDE

CAPE PEÑAS

LA PRIMERA ARGENTINA

VIAMONTE

SHAIKUSH

R. FUEGO

SNAIPOOT

CAPE MARIA

WAKEN

NAJMISHK

SHAIWAAL

ATLANTIC
OCEAN

TUKMAI

CAPE SANTA INES
(SHILAN)

LAKE OKELKASK

TIJNOLSH
HILL

KAAPELMT

R. FUEGO

R. SAN MARTIN

R. FUEGO

CAPE
SAN PABLO

R. LARRAZABAL

R. EWAN

R. CHELEL

SHAIKM

COLJEOMRRH

IROCOVEN
RIDGE

LAKE,
CHEEPELMUTH

LAKE MANTU

LAKE MALILK

FISH LAKE

R. IROCOVEN

LAKE
NYEWHIN

LAKE HEULJMA

CHAAK

AKLEK GOOIYIN

KASHIM

LAKE KAMI (FAGNANO)

MO KAKE

HEUHUPEN

R. JEEPENOHRRH

SPION
KOP

LUCIO
LOPEZ

GULLS LAKE

RIDGE

R. LASIFMARSHAI

MT COBNU

R. WHEIPENOHRRH

MT
TOP

BROWN MT

FLAT TOP MT

HARBERTON MT

EASTERN

BEAGLE CHANNEL

HARBERTON

MO TOP

KAMBACERD

GABLL
ISLAND

EPILOGUE
1947

I

MY STORY BEGAN WITH THE ARRIVAL OF MY MOTHER IN SOUTHERN FIRELAND, and it would be fitting if it could end with her final departure from there. But the incidents of real life are not so neatly knit together as those of fiction, and I am left with a number of loose ends that must be dealt with before this book can be brought to a tidy conclusion.

Here, then, in as brief a manner as I can devise, is the subsequent history of my family and our Indian friends.

Mother was to have her wish. After two and a half happy years at Viamonte, she said farewell to Fireland and, with Yekadahby, made her last voyage to England. Nine years later Yekadahby passed away and eighteen months afterwards, on the 28th December, 1922, Mother followed her. They were laid to rest side by side in the beautiful little village churchyard of Shipbourne, near Tonbridge in Kent. My sister Alice was with dear Mother when she died.

In November, 1910, the year in which Mother came to live with us at Viamonte, Will suffered a sad bereavement. In spite of a doctor who had been summoned to Harberton for the event, his beloved wife Minnie died in childbirth. The child, a boy, survived and was named William Pakenham. After our brother's grievous loss, Alice renounced for ever her free life with me and became foster-mother to Will's three children.

In 1913 Professor Reynolds died in his easy chair by the fire in the Viamonte homestead. He was greatly missed.

Later in the same year Despard decided to leave Tierra del Fuego in order to educate his children in the Old Country. He booked passages for himself and his family in the little local steamer on her last trip of the season from Rio Grande to Punta Arenas. The weather was bitterly cold, which caused Tina, Miss Reynolds and the children to be grateful for the shelter of the family coach.

We had bought this in 1911. It was the custom of most of the Viamonte contingent to emulate the wise birds and follow the sun northwards as winter approached. They would leave in April or May and return in September. On occasions when this migration took them as far as England, they were able to enjoy three summers in succession. As this escape from the Fuegian winters was generally left until after even the upland geese had flown, some form of comfortable conveyance for the women and children from Viamonte to Rio Grande had been called for. At that time in England, motor-cars had been replacing horse-drawn coaches, and we had been able to purchase in London a magnificent landau with a gorgeous coat of arms on it. We had got it for ten guineas, less than a tenth of what it had cost by the time it had reached Rio Grande.

In addition to our four largest horses in orthodox harness, we were accustomed to attach a dozen or more others to the coach with lassos. Over half of these had horsemen on their backs.

I was to accompany Despard and his family as far as Rio Grande. It was blowing hard when we left Viamonte, with powdered snow being driven almost horizontally by the wind. As, with Despard on the box and myself and Indian riders to help control the horses, the coach was dragged at a gallop through shingle and snow, I could not help contrasting our progress with that of earlier days, when, with splendid, well-groomed horses, and coachman and footmen in livery, the coach had paraded grandly along the English roads.

The occupants of the coach had a bumpy time, but the children, at any rate, much relished the excitement. Through the windows they watched the efforts of the riders, each trying to take his full share of the load—and those stolid-looking Ona, though they would not have let it be suspected for worlds, enjoyed themselves quite as much as the children.

After the first ten miles, we stopped on a windswept plain to give the horses a breather and tighten our saddle-girths. My sister-in-law, mindful of this midway halt, had brought two large thermos-flasks full of sweet coffee, which she now passed out to us steaming hot in mugs. This was the first time we had used thermos-flasks and, as we gratefully swallowed the coffee, I heard the Ona talking.

" How hot it is," said one.

" The woman had no fire in the coach," said another.

" I saw no smoke," added a third.

It was left to a fourth to solve the mystery to the satisfaction of everyone.

" It is white man's magic," he decided.

MOTHER.
After her long Odyssey, she spent ten happy years in her native land before being laid to her
final rest there.

JANNETTE,
to whom this work is dedicated, snapped near Viamonte with her husband.

2

Despard took a long lease of a beautiful home in Kent. The following year saw the outbreak of the First World War. He had strained his heart in Fireland, which was not surprising, so was not accepted for the Army. Nevertheless he worked with his usual fierce energy and was soon active head of the Priority Department, dealing with applications for permits to carry out civilian building and engineering work.

Before finally leaving South America to join the Army in England, I went on a trip into the southern Andes. A company—Messrs. Hobbs & Co.—had been formed for £100,000 to open up a large tract of land behind the Gulf of Peñas, and the Bridges & Reynolds Farming Co., Ltd., were proposing to buy shares in it. It was a most interesting excursion and the outcome of it was that our company took up twenty per cent. of the shares. There were a number of other shareholders, but none of them were committed for so large an amount as ourselves. A manager—an admirable gentleman named Charley Wood—was placed in charge of the farm.

A soldier is liable to do impetuous things. In 1917, when disguised in the King's uniform, I acquired a wife. Her name was Jannette McLeod Jardine and she came from a delightful home in Scotland. She must have thought that, as I had come right across the world to defend my aged mother, there must be some good in me, so we were married on the 30th January, 1917. I was given fourteen days' leave for the honeymoon, but, alas! after five of them, I was recalled and hurried off to France.

Thirteen days before the Armistice our daughter Stephanie was born. When I was demobilized in January, 1919, I took a short lease of a house four miles from Despard's home; and happy indeed I was with my precious little wife and Stephanie. We had three acres of land and a car. But life was too easy. That thrice-accursed—or thrice-blessed—wanderlust was on me and I could not rest in such peaceful surroundings. The only work I felt fitted for was breaking new trails; reclaiming unused land; and the thought of the thousands of leagues in distant parts of the world, unpeopled and producing nothing, continually troubled me.

Viamonte was getting on very well without me, so I looked towards the Dominions and finally determined on South Africa. On a large-scale map in Government House, I saw a district where the Devuli and Sabi Rivers joined. It was marked in red letters, " Unsuitable For White Settlement." When I had made sure that this condemnation was not due to the dreaded tsetse fly, of course I had to go there. On my first trip there, I was accompanied by John Yeoman, a sturdy son of one of my mother's sisters, who had been demobilized in the same month as myself.

We inspected the neighbourhood and decided on it for our future home. I named it Devuli Ranch. Leaving Yeoman in Africa, I returned to England, arriving there on Christmas Eve, 1919, and receiving a welcome that I, the truant, certainly did not deserve.

Having come to a satisfactory agreement with the Chartered Company of Southern Rhodesia in London and cabled Yeoman to carry on at the spot we had decided upon for our ranch, I prepared to return there. What a splendid wife I had found! Instead of divorcing me for desertion, as well she might have done, she understood my feelings and decided to make the best of a very bad job by going with me back to the Devuli Ranch. In her sister, Louise—later Mrs. Mortimer E. Webb—we found another devoted Yekadahby and left baby Stephanie in her care, while that unfortunate lady who had, in a moment of patriotic enthusiasm, consented to be my wife was borne overseas, to live in a rude, two-roomed mud hut without windows or doors.

Jannette later gave me a very good reason why she should, for a time, at any rate, go back to our Kentish home. I saw my brave little woman onto the Union Castle ship and, after watching the vessel away, went back to the ranch. Immediately after her departure, with a promise from me that I would be with her before the advent of our second child, John Yeoman and I were joined by a friend of the family, Donald M. Somerville, who had been studying law at Cambridge when the war had disturbed the even tenor of his career. He was now anxious to start a new life in a new land.

My return to England was hastened by an urgent summons from Despard. The Andes enterprise was in trouble. There had been cattle-lifting, neglect—and worse. Charley Wood, the manager, had been stabbed to death. His successor had been dishonest and had ended by committing suicide. The next man was afraid to ride over the farm and, for the lack of transport, wool had lain out through the winter and rotted. The assets were quite unsaleable. The original £100,000 had disappeared and now Hobbs & Co. had run into debt for a like amount.

This was serious enough, but I was to have an even more unpleasant surprise: the shareholders in Hobbs & Co. were collectively and individually responsible for the debts of the company. In my innocence,

I had thought it was a limited company. We had thrown all our surplus capital into the Devuli Ranch and, being the largest shareholders in Hobbs & Co., would be the ones selected by the creditors if they chose to foreclose. The position was indeed grave—and was not made easier by the most regrettable death of John Yeoman, whom I had left in charge at Devuli. He took a fever and died in three days.

At that time Donald Somerville had had practically no experience of that kind of work, so there was no alternative but for Despard to take over in Africa, while I went to the Andes and tried to get the shipwreck off the rocks. I departed for South America with the boastful claim, " It'll go or burst." I cannot go into all the details here; suffice it to say that I had a lot of fun up there and now the place is on its feet.

Despard went alone to Rhodesia and took up the reins. When he had made a comfortable home there, he was joined by Tina, Miss Manina Reynolds and the three children, for by that time Tina had given him another daughter, Violet Bertha. The years have gone by and now all the children are married; Tinita to Donald Somerville, Violet to Ian de la Rue, and Boofy—Walter Despard Bridges—after coming safely through War No. 2, to Josephine née Aldridge. The Somervilles and the de la Rues have each one child, a daughter and a son respectively, while Boofy and Josephine have a little boy, Peter, and a baby girl, Stephanie, who was born on the 7th May, 1947, and is, at the time I write these closing lines, the youngest great-grandchild of Thomas and Mary Bridges.

Boofy has taken up mining, Somerville successfully runs the Devuli Ranch—now ranches—and Violet and her husband have a place of their own. Despard, Tina and Miss Reynolds have all passed away and are buried in Southern Rhodesia. That branch of the family still hold their interests in Tierra del Fuego, while the rest of us, in like proportion, retain ours in Africa. We have received many tempting offers for Harberton, Cambaceres, Gable Island and the rest of the land originally granted to my father by the Argentine Government. Had these offers been trebled, our answer would have been the same: " It is not for sale." It remains to this day in the possession of the family. Ronaldo Tidblom was in the process of making over to us his interest in the Viamonte land when he died; the transfer was completed by his widow. We later lost the half that we had held on lease from the Government, which left us with only 125,000 acres. Perhaps that seems a lot, but it should be remembered that barely 50,000 sheep can be carried on it—and it is a long, long way to the world market.

3

On the death of Minnie, Will had moved to Viamonte, continuing to keep a watchful eye on Harberton. His daughter and two sons spent most of their young lives at Viamonte, as did Percito Reynolds and his two young brothers, Robert and Harold. All the children, however, had several years schooling in England. When the five boys could, under Percy's guidance, take over the Viamonte farm, Will went back to Harberton and has lived there ever since. To lighten his load, he has now with him there a young ex-pilot officer named John Douglas Henderson, with his young wife and baby. Henderson worked with me for five years in the Andes before he went into the R.A.F. He is a sterling fellow; otherwise he would not have stopped with me for so long—and I would certainly not have sent him to Will.

Will could never have been happy away from Fireland—nor could Alice. She has seldom deserted it for twelve consecutive months.

Bertha's eldest son, Percito, a born naturalist, left Viamonte to join up at the beginning of War No. 2. He was told that he could not pass the Army or Air Force test without undergoing an operation for hernia. This he willingly accepted, but things were more serious than the doctors had supposed and a second operation became necessary. This was successful and, delighted to think that he would no longer be a crock, Percito was on the point of leaving hospital when something went wrong—embolism, they called it—and he died suddenly when at tea.

Two years later Percy Reynolds had a heart attack and followed his son. Bertha has remained at Viamonte ever since. She gave the Old Country a Spitfire in memory of her son, who had wished to be an aviator. With her at Viamonte are her two surviving sons, one daughter-in-law, two grandchildren and my youngest sister, who is known to English-speaking people in those parts as Auntie Alice.

Jannette and I have three children. Our daughter, Stephanie, married John Rawle, an Englishman, in Montevideo, where they now live. Stephanie has given us three grandchildren—Anne, John and little Jacqueline, who was born in 1945. Our elder son, Ian, after going through Uppingham, took his entrance examination to Cambridge, but when he saw that war was imminent, he enlisted before hostilities began. As a captain in the Royal Artillery, he saw his full share of active service right through to the end and is now demobilized and very happily married. After his eight years' break, he is to enter Cambridge. Our younger son, David, is still only nineteen. He was at a preparatory school in Berkshire until just before the war, when we brought him away and put him in an excellent school in this country. At holiday times he had to do some real travelling to join us in the Southern Andes, in Tierra del Fuego or in Montevideo. Now he is studying in Buenos Aires for the University examinations.

My sister Mary died in Scotland in 1922, eleven months before Mother. She was followed in 1930 by Wilfred Grubb. They left behind them a monument of good works and self-sacrifice difficult to equal. Their daughters, the Misses Bertha and Mary Grubb, are still living in the Old Country.

4

While the First World War kept me occupied in Europe, Will automatically took the part of counsellor and judge among the Ona. Most of these now had horses of their own and no longer found it necessary—except in mountain country—to take the long walks to which they had formerly been accustomed. Nor did they need to keep their nerves at high tension for fear of being arrowed as they passed some bush. The result of this, to my sorrow, was that the keen huntsmanship once needed to approach the guanaco and kill it with an arrow was no longer required. For all that, they had not lost their vigour, and a fine, healthy group of children were coming on apace. It looked, in fact, as though the country might, in a few generations, be peopled by the descendants of the ancient lords of the soil, now a law-abiding and happy community.

Will has never given me a precise account of the questions he was called upon to settle during my absence, but one amusing little story came to me through Bertha. One evening one of the most civilized of the Ona came to Will for advice. He was accompanied by his wife and daughter and was followed at a respectful distance by two men, Kaukokiyolh and Tek, who were rivals for the maiden's hand. Kaukokiyolh was barely twenty years old, over six feet tall and of pleasant disposition. He liked to be well clad and well mounted, and to bet a little on horseracing. Though gay and smiling by nature, he was now grave and solemn.

Tek was some five inches shorter than Kaukokiyolh and nearly ten years his senior. Besides owning a number of horses, he was reputed to have some money hidden away. He was not such a dandy as Kaukokiyolh and a few straggling bristles did not increase the attractions of his heavy jowl and upper lip. He was a fast shearer and sometimes, at the end of the shearing, inspired by the size of his remuneration, would go on a spree to Punta Arenas, where, in addition to enjoying his tot, he was to be seen driving madly about in a hired car with some gaily dressed and painted white lady.

The matter now to be settled was indeed serious. The girl's father pulled himself together and, facing Will, told his story, with occasional shrill interruptions from his wife. The girl stood demurely by with crossed hands, and the two suitors drew near to listen in silence to what the old man and my brother had to say. It seemed that, to further his cause, the wily Tek had made the old couple the present of a bag of sugar, and, in consequence, they had tried to thrust their daughter into his arms. She, however—foolish, wayward girl—had favoured Kauko-kiyolh and had obstinately refused to have anything to do with Tek, and as the deciding of such matters by bow and arrow—or even by wrestling —was out of the question, they had come to Will to settle it for them.

Will's usually grave visage took on, if that were possible, a still more thoughtful expression and, after due consideration, he gave his verdict. He said that the suitors, both excellent fellows, were, in his opinion, equally eligible, so the girl should be allowed to choose her life's companion.

" But," protested the mother, " we cannot return the sugar, for we have eaten it. How can we give our daughter to Kaukokiyolh, who has given us nothing? "

The oracle concentrated on this new problem. After sufficient time had elapsed, it spoke again :

" Even that can be arranged. Kaukokiyolh must buy two bags of sugar and give them to you. One of these you must pass on to Tek in exchange for the bag he gave you. The other you will keep, so that you will like Kaukokiyolh as much as you now like Tek."

The elder man looked even more surly than usual, whilst Kaukokiyolh made a truly heroic effort to appear impassive. No voice, however, was raised against Will's judgement, and the girl got the man of her choice.

Anyone searching the records of our farm will find that, some twenty-five years ago, two bags of sugar were charged to Will's account.

5

There were others besides Tek who acquired a troop of horses and amassed secret little hoards of cash. One of these was " Uncle " Koiyot.

He was a good workman and, like Halimink, Ishtohn and others, was kept regularly employed at Viamonte. In summer-time he joined in the shearing and wool-pressing, then, when work slackened towards winter, would settle down at the back of the farm, where he was always sure of a welcome and a home when he might want it. In late spring, when the young guanaco are born, the skins of these little animals are quite valuable and their flesh is good meat. It was " Uncle's " custom to get a supply of skins during the short season when they were at their best, and with them Olenke would make very good sleeveless waistcoats, which they sold at a fair price to the ever-encroaching white man. These untanned, or rawhide, garments are far warmer and stronger than anything tanned could be, though they need a lot of careful softening to begin with, which must be repeated if they become saturated with water.

Koiyot and his wife had very few needs. He showed considerable business capacity and augmented his income from the skin clothing by selling an occasional horse. It was said that his fortune was well over 3,000 Argentine *pesos* (say £250), so " Uncle " seemed to have learned something from his adopted nephew after all.

When I visited Tierra del Fuego in 1920, my wife accompanied me and I was able to introduce her to some of my Ona friends. She and I were walking one morning in the woods near the settlement when we were joined, after the casual fashion of the Ona, by Koiyot. We walked on some way side by side with hardly a word. When we reached a comfortable spot, we sat down on the ground and Koiyot told me slowly, with long pauses, of how he had lost Olenke. Between his short, guttural sentences, I translated the sad little story for Jannette, who was very touched by it.

" After you had left us," said Koiyot, " when the trees were red, we were encamped in the woods near Lake Hyewhin, where there is little snow and there are plenty of guanaco in winter. My wife was making skin coats for sale, when that wizard Minkiyolh passed that way, and soon afterwards she felt that he had done her harm. Worse and worse she grew throughout the winter, and in the spring, when the geese came back to nest, she died. So now I am living alone with my little son."

6

My hopes that Tierra del Fuego would be the happy home of worthy descendants of their proud, splendid forebears, who had so freely roamed the woods, were not to be realized. With the inrush of civilization into such a small country, the Indian way of life could not prevail against it. Those of the Indians who avoided hard work as much as possible fast degenerated into "poor whites." Even then, the Ona might have survived as a people had it not been for two epidemics of measles that swept through Ona-land—as another had swept years before through Yahga-land—and destroyed over seventy per cent. of the remnants of the tribe. The first plague was in 1924 and was brought to Rio Grande by some white family. When Will, who passed much time at Viamonte, realized what it was, he advised the Ona to scatter for their lives and hide in the forests as of yore, cutting off all communication with others of their kind. The few who followed this sage advice escaped the first outbreak, only to be caught by the second, which visited the country five years later, in 1929.

It is worthy to remark that the eight or nine half-breeds in our district, though living exactly the same lives as their Indian kindred, all survived both epidemics and completely recovered their usual health. Doubtless they had inherited from their fathers the power to withstand the devastating fever.

When I went back to pass a winter at Viamonte in 1932, there were pitifully few Ona faces to welcome me : the brothers, Doihei and Metet, who were later to die in such tragic circumstances; Nana, the eldest son of Halimink; Tinis with the withered arm, who, as a boy had impersonated *Halpen*, the white sister, and is to-day the only surviving male Aush; Hinjiyolh, the son of Tininisk; Kankoat's two boys, Nelson and David; Garibaldi, the half-breed whom I had kidnapped from Tininisk; Yoshyolpe, Koiyot's nephew; Koiyot's young son, who was a replica of his unhandsome father; and Ishtohn, who was getting dimmer in the eyes and was delighted when I gave him a pair of my spectacles, which he found helped him greatly. There were also some fifteen young men who had been boys in my time, one of them Yohn (guanaco), a younger son of Otrhshoölh,[1] and nearly a dozen half-breeds. There were even fewer women, among them Honte, who was Garibaldi's mother and the last surviving Aush woman; and Matilde, the grand-daughter of Tininisk and Leluwhachin.

All the rest—Halimink, Kankoat the Jester, "Uncle" Koiyot, the gentle Puppup, Aneki, Taäpelht, Tininisk, Leluwhachin—had died of measles. Talimeoat, it was said, had perished with Kaichin and his

---

[1] Yohn was murdered by Nelson in 1945 when they were both drunk. Nelson is now in prison at Rio Gallegos.

second son as the result of a spell cast upon them by that powerful *joön* from the north, Pechas, the brother of Koniyolh.

On that visit I took with me Jannette and our younger son, David, who was then aged four. We had a little house of our own and could give our Ona friends a snug meal in our kitchen and have a little chat with them. Their one question to me was:

" Why have you been away so long? "

Twelve years later, in February, 1944, I visited the home of Matilde. She had married Garibaldi and was living with him in a six-roomed house less than a quarter of a mile from Lake Fagnano (Kami). They had sheep, milch cows and a good kitchen garden, and also indulged in the luxury of flowers. In a little hut of her own nearby resided Honte. The old lady had not forgotten how I had abducted her son and exchanged him for young Nelson nearly fifty years before, and still thought it a good joke.

Matilde, at my request, rang up Viamonte on their telephone, so that I could tell my wife not to expect me back till the next day, as I was spending the night with my old friends. Telephones have been installed in Tierra del Fuego wherever there are sheep in numbers. Almost all the shepherds' shanties north of the range have them. In 1910 or thereabouts we made a line from Viamonte to Rio Grande. Harberton is connected to Ushuaia. It is not yet possible to telephone from Rio Grande to Ushuaia; radio is used instead. I hope that, before long, there will be radio communication between Harberton and Viamonte.

It was queer to hear Ona spoken on the telephone.

7

And what of Fireland to-day? Of the seven to nine thousand natives —Yahgan, Ona, Aush and Alacaloof—who inhabited the country when this story began, there are now (1947) less than a hundred and fifty pure-blooded Indians and possibly a slightly larger number of half-breeds. The white population at the last census was 9,560, made up as follows:

Argentine Tierra del Fuego
Northern territory (including Rio Grande) . . . . 2,700 [1]
Southern territory (including Ushuaia) 2,960
5,660

Chilean Tierra del Fuego
Northern territory (including Porvenir) 3,800
Southern territory (including islands) 100
3,900

[1] This is the off-season census. From November to April, shearing and slaughtering increase this figure by 800.

The three chief centres are Ushuaia, the capital of Argentine Tierra del Fuego, Rio Grande and Porvenir, the Chilean capital, with its adjacent village of Gente Grande (Big People), so named because of the exceptional size of the Ona originally found there. By far the most important of these three towns commercially is Porvenir. The figures for population are :

Ushuaia	2,860
Porvenir	2,300
Rio Grande (north side)	1,800
Rio Grande (south side)	80

There is a road linking Porvenir with Rio Grande. This can be used by motor-traffic during the summer, provided there has been no unusual fall of rain. Soon after leaving Porvenir, the motorist will see the ruined and deserted skeletons of several huge land-dredgers, built there during the frantic gold-rush of nearly half a century ago. He will also see, on both sides of the Chilean–Argentine boundary, some flourishing farmsteads, some of which could be called—not villages, for that conveys the idea of rural settlements, cottages and rusticity—but towns. After passing the finest of these, once known as La Segunda Argentina and now called Estancia María Behety,[1] the motorist will reach Rio Grande. On the north side of the river mouth is the place of the same name, a growing town that is kept alive largely by the salaries gained by shearers and butchers in the busy summer-time. Some of these have their families there. Police and government officials abound and there are a number of stores and establishments of the *Café y Billar* kind. The well-paid government road-makers, who have been employed for years on the construction of a road from Rio Grande to Ushuaia, also find this a convenient place in which to relax from their labours and spend their wages.

It is a flat, wind-swept part of the country, with not a tree within twelve miles; and the other attractions of the town are such that the motorist can say good-bye to Rio Grande without a tear, and drive back six miles along the north bank of the river to a point where he can cross by an imposing bridge that we, the old settlers, led by the Menendez family, erected by our combined efforts some twenty-five years ago. The motorist will, when he has crossed the bridge, turn his car back towards the river mouth and drive along the south side of the river until he reaches,

[1] La Primera Argentina, on the south side of the river, is now the Estancia José Menendez.

opposite the main town, the meat-freezer established by us at the time the bridge was built. The freezer has attracted a little town of workers; and there is also to be found there a landing-ground for aircraft. This is the terminus for the passenger planes from Buenos Aires *via* Rio Gallegos. There are at least two planes a week. The most important flies from Buenos Aires to Rio Gallegos on Sunday. On Monday it flies to Rio Grande, takes off an hour after landing, to return to Rio Gallegos. Tuesday sees it back in Buenos Aires.

The road built by the Argentine authorities can be used by horses for six or seven months of the year. Motor-vehicles can use it for almost as long a period, but only as far from Rio Grande as Lake Fagnano, and then not in rainy weather. Government aircraft of smaller size than the passenger planes connect Rio Grande with Ushuaia and, as the officials are most obliging, the motorist will do well to leave his car at Rio Grande and, if there is room in the government plane, complete his journey to Ushuaia by air.

When the weather is bad and the mountains behind Ushuaia thick with storm-clouds, the aircraft will follow the coast over Viamonte as far as, and even farther than, Cape San Pablo. Several modest farmsteads may be sighted some distance from the coast. Near Cape San Pablo there is a bay where, in fair weather, goods can be landed and wool shipped. Here there is a settlement called the Estancia San Pablo, which, after Rio Grande and Viamonte, is the most important along this south-east coast. The government aircraft does not come down here, for once away from Rio Grande, it has no official landing-ground until it reaches Ushuaia.[1] It flies over San Pablo and turns south. Below are innumerable lakes scattered through the yellow *shana* bog or amid the green forest.[2] In twenty minutes the plane alters course and heads westward, over Harberton, with its creeks and inlets, over Gable Island, with its settlement, its cliffs and lakes, over the hamlets dotted close to the coast on both sides of the Beagle Channel; and lands at length at Ushuaia.

On the south side of Ushuaia harbour, where Stirling House and the other Mission buildings were erected by my father and his loyal little band of helpers nearly eighty years ago, now stand the barracks for the Naval and Naval-Air Arm personnel, together with some twenty houses,

[1] There is a primitive landing-ground at Viamonte. Two of my nephews, the Reynolds brothers, bought a small plane and have managed to take off from it and land again.

[2] I remember once counting, from one mountain peak, over forty lakes at the back of No Top.

among them the residences of the Governor and the Vice-Governor. There are two good landing-strips for aircraft.

On the north side of the harbour—Alacushwaia—where the first sub-prefecture was set up in 1884, there are now the prison, the maritime sub-prefecture, various buildings in which are housed the Land Office, the Agricultural Office and the Naval and Civil Accountancy Department. There are also the headquarters of the police, a meteorological station and three radio stations, one public, the second for the police and the third for the Naval-Air Arm. General stores and saloons amount to six and further entertainment is provided by a cinema. A Roman Catholic church stands on this side of the harbour. The last representative of the South American Missionary Society was John Lawrence, my father's faithful companion in those brave early years, who ended his days at Punta Remolino.

Of the 2,860 population of Ushuaia, over 1,400 are Naval and Naval-Air personnel, prisoners, warders, police or government labourers. The resident population is 1,450, yet if the seat of government were removed from there, the population would dwindle to a mere twenty or thirty persons. I understand from my nephew, Guillermo, Will's younger son, who has supplied me with these particulars of present-day Fireland, that the prison at Ushuaia is in the process of being given up completely.

Guillermo Bridges, born at Harberton, has the honour of being the only British Vice-Consul in the country.

8

In the northern part of Chile's Fuegian territory is the largest extent of good grazing land in the entire archipelago. Here, though she has spent much less on the land than her wealthier neighbour, three large companies and many smaller farmers have established themselves. This land carries an aggregate of something over 800,000 sheep. In 1946 oil was struck in that district, the only promising discovery of the kind to be made, as far as I know, in the whole country. If Chilean hopes are fulfilled, there are great doings looming on the near horizon.

The northern part of Argentine Fireland carries about 700,000 sheep, of which nearly two thirds belong to the Menendez family and the Braun family, with whom they are closely interwoven. Of the late Don José Menendez, there are at least a hundred descendants alive at the present time.

Divided fairly equally between the two countries in southern Fireland there are maybe 1,200 head of cattle. Of these a considerable number are yoke-oxen, which provide almost the only traction power in that area. In the north, yoke-oxen are still used, but not so extensively. On the longer tracks, motor-lorries have taken their place.

In all the Argentine country south of a line drawn due east from Lake Fagnano, the only land on which the most optimistic can hope to raise a few animals or produce any vegetables is a narrow strip near the coast, in places that are not too precipitous and where there is sufficient soil. This pleasant, picturesque country, though fully stocked, carries only a handful of cattle and less than 22,000 sheep, nearly half of which are at Harberton. Chile is in much the same plight as Argentina with her southern lands. With the exception of a farm of some 7,000 sheep at the head of Yendagaia Bay, the country is sparsely peopled by a few small farmers, who, by making use of all the stretches of grassland that can support sheep, manage to eke out a living with the help of garden produce and, it may be, a little game and fish.

Along the coast to the west of the boundary line, which is twelve miles westward of Ushuaia, and on all the islands south of the Beagle Channel, I doubt if there are to-day—apart from those on the Yendagaia farm—more than 10,000 sheep and a few hundred head of cattle. On Horn Island, almost all the rest of the Wollaston group, the outer coast of Hoste Island and on the western islands of the archipelago, only a few otter hunters still roam about, just managing to keep themselves alive.

That is the Fireland of 1947.

APPENDICES

MANY TRAVELLERS HAVE WRITTEN TALES ABOUT THE ONA. SOME OF these have been founded on fact, but it would fill a great volume which no one would read to refute all the mis-statements that have been made. Of all these writers I will cite but three.

The first of these was my friend, the late Carlos R. Gallardo, who wrote a book called *Los Onas*. Gallardo was once sent on an important government mission to Ushuaia and spent, I think, two days at Harberton, when there happened to be a large number of Ona there. He took a few photographs and heard many stories from Will and myself. He never went more than half a mile from the homestead, and that was the only time he came in contact with the Ona in their native state.

Later, when I was on a visit to Buenos Aires, I met him frequently and was delighted to have such an interested listener to my stories. When I knew that he intended to write a book, I gave him what information I could, but asked him on no account to mention my name in connection with it, for I did not want my friends the Ona to realize in years to come that I had been telling tales about them. I feel obliged to refer to this because some of the experiences that appear in this book of mine have already been related by Gallardo as if they had been his own.

There are some minor mistakes in *Los Onas* and many of the illustrations are not at all like any Ona I have seen. The paint in some cases has, in my opinion, been put on after the pictures were taken. The picture of Yoknolpe that appears opposite page 273 is reproduced from *Los Onas*. I knew this proud hunter well and never saw him with his face painted in that manner.

Teorati, brother of the ill-fated Kiyohnishah and the only one of the family to survive the massacre near Lake Hyewhin, lived for a considerable time in Buenos Aires. Mr. Gallardo obtained some information from this lad, who had been given the name of Pedro, and many of the photographs of Ona in action were taken in a garden of that city.

In spite of the above remarks, I should like to have congratulated Mr. Gallardo on his praiseworthy and conscientious effort, considering the poor opportunities he had, to perpetuate some knowledge of the customs of this disappearing race.

In a neatly bound volume called *Los Shelknum*, Father J. M. Beauvoir of the Silesian Mission has ventured to criticize certain statements made by my father. In Chapter VI (page 216), he writes:

" Another blow was received by the Protestant Mission in Ushuaia when the Argentine Government in 1885 made that port the seat of the Governor's residence. This caused the Protestant Mission so much disturbance that a few years later they were obliged to move again in search of tranquillity and the Mission was established at Tekenika. . . ."

It is true that a branch of the Mission was established at that place, but I never heard it attributed to the above cause till Padre Beauvoir gave me that mischievous piece of information. The branch Mission was first set up on Bayly Island, one of the Wollaston Group, and Mr. Leonard H. Burleigh was put in charge. The spot was badly chosen and after two or three years, the branch Mission was moved to Tekenika Sound on Hoste Island. But the main Mission remained at Ushuaia. Mr. Aspinall, who was later ordained and eventually became Canon of Ipswich, stayed at Ushuaia for years as superintendent. Mr. Lawrence was with him there until the end of the century, fifteen years after the Argentine flag was first hoisted by my father.

Padre Beauvoir went to considerable pains to collect some thousands of words from the Ona. Of these, half are quite unknown to me; nearly a quarter I believe may be fairly correct; and the remaining quarter are so far from correct that I am convinced that the author, though he, with commendable diligence, collected and tried to write the words as he had heard them from the Ona, neither understood nor spoke the language himself. On page 171 of his book he gives us two hundred and twenty words which he claims to be Aush. I have never encountered any of them.

Here are two of the many examples of incorrect translation in Padre Beauvoir's list of Ona words. The Ona word for " deaf" is *ahlahkin*. For this, the priest gives us *yoisohn*, which should be spelt *yohishoön* and means, " Me (he) hears not." For " lazy," instead of *goötn* we have *kareiksowén*, which means " working not " and is more correctly spelt *karheikeshoön*.

My father had asserted that neither the Yahgan nor the Ona had any idea of a god or expectation of a future life. Beauvoir, after attacking this assertion with considerable bitterness, goes on to prove, to his own satisfaction, that the word *Jhown* (which I spell *Joön*) is derived directly from the Hebrew Jehovah. He further adds that *Jhowkon Klal* means " The Son of the Great One," i.e., " The Son of God." In a smaller dictionary compiled by the Padre we find *Jon-listón* [1] as meaning " God the Father " and *Jow-Jon Klal* [2] as meaning " The Son of God the Father."

Advancing these groundless assumptions as proven facts, the Padre challenges my father, who departed this life some sixteen years before the book was written, asking him " if he still persists in the statements, as erroneous as they were unjust, which he made regarding the Ona, insulting them so cruelly, while showing at the same time his utter ignorance on the subject."

When I read Father Beauvoir's remarks, I asked myself, " What would Father have said? " He would have read the passage to the end, then, as he closed the book, would have laughed and said, " Poor fellow! " I cannot adopt so philosophic an attitude and feel it my duty to the memory of my father to rebut these charges.

Beauvoir, who gives us to understand that he lived many years with the untouched Ona, tells us something of their customs and habits. Much of the information passed on to us in *Los Shelknum* is already clearly enough presented in Mr. Gallardo's book to preclude the need for repetition. As for a great deal of the rest, he has, on his own admission, gleaned his facts from a source that is, to say the least, questionable.

One cannot wonder that travellers, hurrying through a country to write an article or book about the natives, should gather what material they can from Indians who haunt the white settlements and have learned to speak the traveller's own tongue. Padre Beauvoir acknowledges indebtedness to such an informant. He gives as his authority for a number of facts included in his historical work " Captain Minkiyolh Kaushel " —that same Minkiyolh who had attacked me with a hatchet; who had gone off into the woods with his young brother and come back alone; who, holding a newspaper upside down, had read messages of affection and admiration addressed to him personally by the President of the Republic; who had become a laughing-stock, as well as a menace, to his

---

[1] In *listón* one can detect a resemblance to Ishtohn (Thick Thighs), with *tohn* used in the sense of " big " or " great."
[2] The correct Ona version is *Joön Tohn K-Lal*—" Wizard Great His Son."

Will crossing from Ushuaia to Lake Fagnano on the new government road.

Bertha on her favourite horse, a typical Chilean Criollo. In the background is Lake Hantu.

The modern settlement on Gable Island. Harberton Mountain on the left, No Top Hill on the right and, between them, the Twins.

Ushuaia town, north of the harbour, taken about 1920.

own people; and who had been known from Rio Grande to the Beagle Channel as *el Loco*.

Here I beg leave to quote from a third writer, who in the summer of 1924–25 spent over three months in the country. He was Samuel Kirkland Lothrop and was sent with Mr. J. Lenzer Wild by the New York Museum of American Indians, Heye Foundation. In his book, *The Indians of Tierra del Fuego*, he writes at some length on my father's great work among the Yahgan tribe. After calling his writings " a mine of ethnological information," and describing his dictionary as " probably the most extensive study of primitive linguistics ever carried out," Lothrop goes on to say:

" In recent years the Bridges children, especially Messrs. Lucas and William Bridges, have sponsored practically all information about the Ona tribe which has found its way into print, indeed (without detracting from the merits of other writers) it may be said that the importance of most published data on the Ona varies according to whether or not the information was obtained from this generous and hospitable family."

II. THE CASE OF THE WANDERING DICTIONARY

On the 10th November, 1945, the following article was published in the Buenos Aires *Standard*, which is printed in English. It is reproduced by kind permission of the Editor.

THE CASE OF THE WANDERING DICTIONARY
By
Miss Rosemary H. Moeller

Not many weeks ago, a brief, official letter from the H.Q. of the Military Government of Germany chronicled what, to all appearances, was the final act of a fantastic Odyssey that began nearly half a century back on a windswept sheep station on the shores of the Beagle Channel— the Odyssey of a dictionary.

No ordinary dictionary this, but the life-work of a man who combined the toughness of a frontier pioneer with the brilliant mind and tireless patience of a great scientist—a priceless manuscript written to preserve for the human race a language that has now almost vanished from the face of the earth. Once stolen, twice submerged in the flood-tide of world war, the original manuscript in which the late Rev. Thomas Bridges made an exhaustive translation into English of 32,000 words of the Yamana language, came to light last July, for the third time in forty-six years, in the kitchen cupboard of a German farmhouse.

In his flat in the Kavanagh building a few days ago, Mr. E. Lucas Bridges took time off from the writing of his own memoirs to recount the strange story of his father's famous work.

Thomas Bridges' acquaintance with the aboriginal tribes of Tierra del Fuego began on Keppel Island in the Falklands, ninety-one years ago. Thither he, a boy of 13, had gone with his foster-father, the Rev. George P. Despard, who had undertaken to found a mission station on the island as a base for work in the Tierra del Fuego Archipelago. Several Indians had been brought to the island to form a preliminary link between the mission and the tribes, and from them the boy received his first lessons in the Yahgan, or Yamana, speech.

The two names of the tribe and its language are explained, many years later, in his own words:

" I gave these natives the name Yahgan because it was convenient. The Murray Narrows, near which our mission [in Tierra del Fuego] was established, called by the natives Yahga, may be considered the centre of their land and the language as spoken there was that which I learned, and its purest form, being the mean between its varieties spoken southward, eastward and westward. For these reasons, Yahgan seemed a suitable name, and is now known everywhere."

But the natives called themselves Yamana, for the following fascinating reason:

" Ignorant races have no special name for themselves, though they invariably have for the tribes around them; in default of such names they are content to use for their own tribe terms meaning man, persons, people. Thus a Yahgan, wanting to know whether one of his tribe was aboard, would ask: ' Undagarata yamana?' i.e., ' Is there a man or a person on board?' He did not consider the English or other persons in the same sense as he did his own people. . . . This word 'yamana' plainly points to the idea of man being the highest form of life. The word means living, alive."

The young missionary was fascinated by the extraordinary richness of this aboriginal tongue and the grammatical beauty of its construction. In an article published in " The Standard " on September 6, 1886, he wrote:

" Incredible though it may appear, the language of one of the poorest tribes of men, without any literature, without poetry, song, history or science, may yet through the nature of its structure and its necessities have a list of words and a style of structure surpassing that of other tribes far above them in the arts and comforts of life."

On another occasion he wrote:

"Owing to the eminently social life of the people who spend so large a part of their lives in talking and, both men and women, in giving lengthy harangues called by them 'Teehamunan,' they perfectly keep up the knowledge of their language and early learn to speak it well. . . . The wigwam life of ease and sociability is eminently favourable to talk."

Mention of the project that was to be completed over thirty years later is found in one of the letters he wrote on Keppel Island in 1864:

"Although I am improving in my knowledge of their language, yet, owing to the multitude of other business, my progress is slow and I am yet far from perfectly knowing it. To thoroughly acquire it, reduce it to writing and to form a dictionary and grammar is my longing desire, and I shall be very happy when I shall be able to tell them, to my satisfaction and their conviction, of the love of Jesus."

But, rich as it was in sounds and numbers of words, the language when he acquired it proved "a very poor means of educating them [the natives] for a higher life, as it is sadly wanting in definite terms for ideas which the natives had never entertained."

When Mr. Despard returned to England in January, 1862, the young Thomas Bridges, then barely eighteen years of age, was left in charge of the Keppel Island station. Some years later, after a visit to England from which he returned with a young wife, he was himself ordained a priest of the Church of England by the late Bishop Stirling,[1] prior to setting out to found a permanent mission headquarters in Tierra del Fuego itself.

It was not the first such attempt, an earlier expedition having ended in massacre in 1859. But the Bridges family were destined to succeed where others had failed, and in the course of time Mr. Bridges so won the confidence of the Cape Horn Indians that he became their unofficial chieftain and law-giver in a land that the white man's law had scarcely reached. The orderly and happy home at Harberton within the Beagle Channel, where five of their six children were born and grew up, became a noted outpost of civilization.[2]

Although in 1887 Mr. Bridges resigned his direct connection with the

[1] This took place in Valparaiso. He had already been ordained deacon by the Bishop of London.

[2] There is a slight inaccuracy here. Certainly all of us except Mary were born in Tierra del Fuego, but at Ushuaia, not Harberton.

South American Missionary Society, the family remained in Tierra del Fuego, where the Argentine Government gave him a grant of land in recognition of his pioneer work in the Beagle Channel. He never lost his deep interest in the life and problems of the Indian tribes, and his study of their language ended only with his death.

To render all the sounds of the Yamana speech in writing, he had recourse to the Ellis system of phonetics, adapting it and adding to it, and also devising a phonetic alphabet of his own to express sounds that the system lacked. It was no easy task. In his own words :

"It is utterly impossible at first to get hold correctly of the pronunciation of a new language from the lips of a savage. He cannot, before he is taught, pronounce words of his own tongue slowly and distinctly. Often have I, until I was ashamed, made the Indians pronounce words so repeatedly that they have called me deaf, being unable to satisfy my mind as to whether I had it correctly, and after all being compelled to write it down when dissatisfied with my pronunciation, and consequently with my spelling of the word."

The original manuscript, containing about 23,000 words, was completed, according to one of his letters, in 1879. But opportunity for publication did not at once present itself, partly owing to the isolation in which the writer lived, and partly to his self-invented phonetic system which did not exist in type. At the same time he continued to work on it, adding, revising and improving, until at the time of his death it contained 32,000 words. He was working on the final revision of the grammar during his voyage to Buenos Aires in the brig *Phantom* shortly before his death.

The result of his labours was an absolutely irreplaceable document, for the Yamana Indians were dying out. In Darwin's time they had numbered about three thousand, but, hardy as they were in the face of their rigorous climate, they succumbed like flies to the diseases brought by civilization. In Darwin's time there were about three thousand of them. In 1884 their number was down to rather less than one thousand, and in that same year an epidemic of measles brought by the first expedition from Buenos Aires swept the territory, exterminating whole villages and reducing the tribe to about four hundred.

By 1908 there were 170 left, and the end of November, 1932, saw only 43 survivors, including some half-breeds, hangers-on of the settlements, whose speech had lost its purity and become interlarded with Spanish terms. Thus the opportunity which Mr. Bridges enjoyed was one that would never occur again.

That fact was instantly recognized by a certain Dr. Frederick A. Cook, who was later to achieve notoriety as the self-styled " discoverer " of the North Pole, and who visited Harberton on New Year's Day, 1898, when the *Belgica* carrying the Belgian Antarctic Expedition of 1897–99 put in there on her way south.   Dr. Cook declared that a society in the United States interested in all aboriginal American languages would overcome the difficulty of the phonetic system, and would be glad to publish the work. Mr. Bridges would not then consent to his taking the manuscript; the expedition was on the way south and he feared that it might be lost in the Antarctic.   He promised, however, that Dr. Cook should have it if he called for it on his return journey.

He himself did not live to see that return, for he died in Buenos Aires that same year.   But Dr. Cook called for the dictionary the following year as he had said, leaving the *Belgica* in Punta Arenas and coming down on a small vessel expressly to obtain the manuscript, which the Bridges family, remembering their father's promise, entrusted to him.

From that day to this, no member of the family has set eyes on it.

Letters came at first from Dr. Cook, telling of the difficulties he had encountered on account of the alphabet used.   But these communications grew less and less frequent, and eventually ceased altogether, the letter sent to him by the family in Tierra del Fuego remaining unanswered.

Twelve years later a party of Scandinavian scientists called at the remote sheep station, as many scientific expeditions did on the way to the Antarctic, and from them Mr. Bridges' children learned that the precious dictionary was being printed at the Observatoire Royal in Brussels as the work of Dr. Frederick A. Cook, and that it had, in fact, already been advertised under the latter's name.

Outraged at this bare-faced piracy, Mr. Lucas Bridges took the first opportunity to go to Brussels and visit the curator of the Observatoire, M. Lequent.   He found that, as the Norwegians had said, matters were already well under way.   The Belgian Parliament had voted the sum of 22,000 francs towards the cost of publication, and Dr. Cook had agreed with the authorities of the Observatoire on a proposed cover for the work. It was to read :

YAMANA–ENGLISH DICTIONARY

By

FREDERICK A. COOK,

Dr. of Anthropology.

At the foot of the cover, it was stated in small print that the Rev. Thomas Bridges had been " instrumental in collecting the words."

M. Lequent was not, however, ignorant of the work's real authorship, which was already known in the scientific world and which he had himself pointed out to Dr. Cook. He recognized the justice of the family's claim, and, after some discussion, it was settled that, while the manuscript was to remain for the time being at the Observatoire and the work of the publishing was to continue, there should be a reversal of the order of the names on the cover, which was to read :

YAMANA–ENGLISH DICTIONARY

By

The Rev. Thomas Bridges,

while at the foot it was to be stated in small type that Dr. Frederick A. Cook had brought the work to the notice of the Observatoire Royal. To this Mr. Lucas Bridges agreed in the name of his family. The curator was enthusiastic in his praises of the work, declaring that it was incredible that it should have been completed in the life-time of one man, and told Mr. Bridges that copies of it were to be sent to the major universities and libraries all over the world. The difficulty of publication was, however, still to be surmounted, for it was necessary to transpose the alphabet used into a universal phonetic system—a labour of years. He expected, however, that it could be off the presses before the end of 1914. With that prospect in view, Mr. Bridges took his leave. But before the end of 1914, the first world war came down on Europe, engulfing Brussels and the Observatoire Royal. The precious dictionary was lost again.

Mr. Bridges took up the search after the Armistice, but his letters to the Observatoire brought no satisfaction. It seemed that this time the manuscript had really gone, and after a while the family gave up the task as hopeless.

And then, in September, 1929, fifteen years after its last disappearance, the document turned up again. A member of the Bridges family in England received, out of the blue, a letter signed by a Dr. Ferdinand Hestermann, Professor of the University of Munster, announcing that both dictionary and grammar were in his hands, that he was enormously interested in the work and its author and desired to know more of both.

This time it was Miss Alice Bridges who made an expedition to the Continent in pursuit of her father's book.

In her haste, she went to Hamburg by plane, met the professor, and embarked with him on yet another plan for its publication—a plan that this time bore fruit. The money voted by the Belgian Government had disappeared, but the Bridges family decided to finance the undertaking themselves as a memorial to their father.

At this point another character appeared in the story. Mr. W. S. Barclay, one-time secretary of the British Trade Exhibition that visited Buenos Aires in 1931, and for many years a staunch friend of the Bridges family, whom he had visited in their southern home thirty years before, was asked by them to supervise the business of publication and to write an introductory preface. This he did, and it was due to him that the book appeared in its present form, retaining the human interest of its story. The final translation of Thomas Bridges' phonetic alphabet into the Anthropos system, well known to students, was carried out by Dr. Hestermann, and the dictionary was eventually printed at Mödling, Austria, in 1933, in a limited edition of three hundred copies which were distributed to universities and libraries all over the world.

This should have been the end of the story, but it was not. The original document in Thomas Bridges' handwriting remained in Europe —indeed it had not been even seen by any member of the family—and when Professor Hestermann asked leave to continue studying it, they consented. However, they decided that its ownership ought to devolve eventually on the British Museum, and when Mr. Lucas Bridges offered it to that body in 1939 it was accepted.

But, before it could be brought from Germany, war broke out again, and Dr. Hestermann and the document vanished together.

This time its recovery seemed altogether improbable. Dr. Hestermann had last been heard of in Hamburg, and as time went on and the raids on that city grew heavier, Thomas Bridges' children resigned themselves regretfully to its loss.

But one man maintained an obstinate faith in its survival. Mr. Barclay—now seventy years of age—refused to believe that the lucky star that had brought the manuscript unharmed through so many vicissitudes should have abandoned it to perish in the blast of an English block-buster. He set out to move Heaven and earth in a fixed resolve to trace it. For a long time he met only with failure. The International Red Cross informed him, after a year, that though they had ascertained that Dr. Hestermann had the document in his possession at the outbreak of war, they had not been able to establish contact with him.

Negative as this clue was, Mr. Barclay pursued the quest. As Belgium was freed from the enemy he wrote to the British Minister in Brussels, who referred him to the Arts, Monuments and Archives Department, set up by the Allies to restore property looted by the enemy to its rightful owners. He called on the Adviser to the Civil Affairs Directorate, Col. Sir Leonard Woolley, and wrote to the director of the Control Commission for Germany, urging the advisability of tracing Dr. Hestermann, if still alive.

Within a week he had a reply from the Military Government Main Headquarters, 21st Army Group.

" Dear Sir,—The MS of the Yamana Dictionary of the Rev. Thomas Bridges has now been discovered, as the result of a search put in train from your letters to Sir Leonard Woolley and the Control Commission. It is held in safe custody by the Military Government Authorities.

"I may add that Dr. Hestermann was discovered by a Military Government Officer and led by him to the kitchen cupboard of a farm-house where the manuscript was kept. Dr. Hestermann was apparently only too glad to hand it over into safe keeping."

The story roused such interest that an account of it was broadcast from Berlin, and Mr. Barclay immediately telegraphed Mr. Lucas Bridges in Buenos Aires: " Manuscript of your father's dictionary found in Germany. Now in safe keeping. Will write fully."

But even now, the wandering dictionary has not come home to roost. The fraud perpetrated by Dr. Cook thirty-five years ago has left a tangle that has yet to be unravelled, for the letter from the Military Government suggests that Liège University has some obscure claim to it. Not till it is delivered in Bloomsbury will those connected with it be able to rest content that the elusive treasure is safe at last.

We can now add a postscript to Miss Moeller's article. On the 9th January, 1946, I received the following cable in Buenos Aires:
" Manuscript your father's dictionary arrived British Museum to-day January ninth. Will be reported on by Eric Miller curator Manuscript Department to Museum Trustees on February ninth and after acceptance we will celebrate as arranged. Barclay."

A month later, in that historic building which houses the Codex Sinaiticus and so many of the world's most treasured manuscripts, my father's dictionary found a final resting place. It was proudly displayed in an illuminated case in an otherwise empty room, and a number of

Ishtohn, the Ona, ageing fast.
1939.

Clement Waiyellen, the Yahgan, aged over seventy.
1945.
Photo by my niece, Mrs. Goodall.

The Yahgan Phonetic Alphabet.

The letter written	printed	is always sounded as	The letter written	printed	is always sounded as	The letter written	printed	is always sounded as
A a	A a	a in at	O o	O o	oa in oat	Đ đ	Đ đ	th in thise
A ɐ	A ɐ	a - alms	S s	S s	ur - fur	S s	S s	s in so
O o	O o	a - all	*Consonants.*			Z z	Z z	s - is
O o	O o	o - olive	C c	C c	c in cot	Ʃ ʃ	Σ ʃ	sh - show
U u	W u	oo - foot	G g	G g	g " go	Z z	Z z	s - pleasure
U u	Ч u	oo - food	T t	T t	t " to	L l	L l	l - low
I i	I i	i - ill	D d	D d	d " do	L l	L l	ll - welsh
E ɛ	E ɛ	ee - eel	P p	P p	p " put	M m	M m	M - me
E e	E e	e - ell	B b	B b	b " but	N n	N n	n - no
A ɑ	A ɑ	ai - aim	F f	F f	f - foe	N n	N n	hn - ahman
I i	I i	i - isle	V v	V v	v - vase	Ŋ ŋ	Ŋ ŋ	ng - wing
O o	O o	oi - oil	C ç	C ç	ch - chin	R r	R r	r - row
U u	U u	u - us	J j	J j	j - jade	R r	R r	hr - welsh
Ꝩ ꝩ	8 ꝩ	ow - owl	T t	T t	th - thin	K k	K k	ch - german

Beside the above letters there are these three vowel marks,
´ = h, ` = y, ⌄ - = w only found over vowels, hence their names.
These marks are often found united over vowels, thus
ūă - uhwa sij. ashes; ūâ - wuhya sij. a door; & ūă =
wuhwa sij tinder of birds' down. The effect of these marks
always precedes the vowels over which they are found.

97

My father's alphabet, founded on Ellis's Phonetic System.

those who knew its history came to inspect it and to celebrate the triumphant ending of its adventurous career. Afterwards the party, with Mr. Barclay as host, assembled for lunch in honour of the occasion, the only toast being, "The Yamana–English Dictionary and its author, the Reverend Thomas Bridges."

Would that I had been present to propose another toast to the man who refused to take "No" for an answer or to listen to the word "impossible"; that quiet, diffident, dogged, ultra-English Englishman, Mr. William S. Barclay, without whose inspired confidence and tenacity no further search would have been made for the lost heirloom.

It was he who gave a brief summary of the progress of the dictionary since its commencement almost one hundred years ago on a windswept hill on Keppel Island, where in order to study the language my father, himself only a boy, had shared a little wooden hut with a few Yahgan youths, to listen to and later join in their chatter. Barclay will have told how the work grew in many a smoky wigwam in Tierra del Fuego and through long nights in our kitchen at Ushuaia, where Father, as scholar, with some chosen native as professor, would brew and consume strong coffee in the small hours of the morning, in an attempt to cheat Nature of the sleep she claimed from them. Later, on prolonged trips by sailing vessel and during winters in Tierra del Fuego, the work was corrected and arranged in its present form.

After Barclay's story, Lieut.-Col. Robert Whyte, D.S.O., M.C., a life-long friend of ours, took up the tale. He was the only one present who had been personally acquainted with my father, so a light verbal sketch of the man he had known was followed by a few amusing anecdotes.

Mr. A. F. Tschiffely, recently arrived from the Argentine, gave an interesting talk. He was followed by others till, at about four-thirty, the guests departed.

I am sorry that many who had helped in the work so happily concluded were unable to attend the meeting, and especially that Sir Leonard Woolley, the famous Egyptologist, who came second only to Barclay in his efforts to recover the lost manuscript, was absent, having left for Syria to carry on his excavations there.

There is one other who would have been warmly welcomed by all. Dr. Ferdinand Hestermann, who had studied the dictionary and guarded it with such devotion for over thirty years, could not, for obvious reasons, be present to occupy his rightful position as guest of honour.

III. GENEALOGICAL TREE

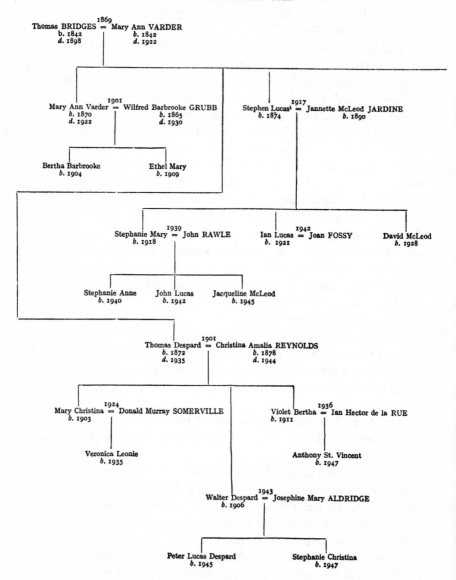

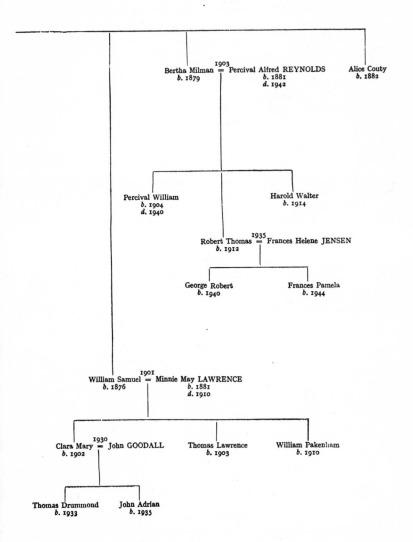

INDEX

Notes: The native men and women who figure in the story are listed separately after the main index.

The letter " P " indicates Photograph(s). A numbered list of illustrations will be found on Page 17.

Acualisnan Channel: 133.
Afluruwaia (Puerto Toro): See Puerto Toro.
Aguirre, Serafín: 129–30, 146, 168, 180.
Ainawaia Valley: 110.
Aklek Goöiyin (Red Clay Mountain): 433.
Alacaloof: 61, 131–3.
Alacush (Flapping Loggerhead Duck): See under Birds.
Alacushwaia (Bay of Flapping Loggerhead Ducks): 123, 524.
Alisimoonoala (Outer Coast People): 83.
Allen Gardiner
  Schooner: 23, 41, 68.
  Steamer: 131.
  Yawl: 68–9.
Alvarez, Dr.: 125.
Andes: 139, 156, 513–5.
Anson, Admiral George: 25, 59.
Archaeology: See under Tierra del Fuego.
Arevalo: 496–500.
Argentina: 122, 140, 340.
Armstrong, Mr.: 128–9.
Arrows
  Alacaloof: 61.
  Ona: See under Ona.
  Yahgan: See under Yahgan.
Aslaksen, Olaf: 189–93.
Aspinall, Edward: 141, 150, 527.
Astronomical Beliefs: See under Ona.
Asuncion: 341.
Aush (Eastern Ona): 61, 108, 110, 151, 194, 431–2, 438, 443.
Awul: 447.

Badcock, John: 40.
Bahia Aguirre: See Spaniard Harbour.
Bahia Blanca: 235.
Balmaceda, Lavino: 207–8.
Banner Cove: 23, 37, 38, 39, 53, 104, 107, 509.

Barberry, Sweet: 71, 145, 376.
  Holly-leafed: 376.
Barclay, William S.: 535–7.
Barrientos, Pedro: 482, 493–6.
Bartlett, William: 51, 52, 158.
Bats: 436–7.
Bayly Island: 527.
B.B.C.: 471.
Beagle Channel: 23, 29, 48, 61, 100, 117, 118, 122, 124, 509. *P. 2, 3, 69.*
Beagle, H.M.S.: 29–33, 83.
Beauvoir, Father J. M.: 527–8.
Beech: See under Trees.
Behety, José Menendez: 251.
Belgica, S.S.: 226–9, 239, 533.
Berries, Edible: 71–3.
Bertram: 186, 199, 201. *P. 78.*
Bird, Junius: 74.
BIRDS: 53, 96, 355, 447.
  Albatross: 447.
  Blackbird: 447.
  Condor: 447.
  Cormorant (Shag): 87, 98, 217, 332–3, 334–5, 369, 447.
  Curlew: 447.
  Duck: 64, 96, 333–4, 447.
  Flapping Loggerhead (*Alacush*): 97, 435.
  Flying Loggerhead (*Tushca*): 64, 435.
  Steamer: See Flapping Loggerhead.
  Waterfall (*Oklholh*): 435, 449.
  Eagle: 254, 447.
  Finch: 96, 355.
  Flamingo: 447.
  Goose: 53, 96, 355, 447, 451.
  Grebe: 375, 447, 449.
  Grouse: 447.
  Gull: 254, 447.
  Hawk: 447.
  Heron: 64.
  Humming-Bird (*Sinu K-Tam*): 232 (footnote), 438, 447.

541